UNCHAINED VOICES

AN ANTHOLOGY OF BLACK AUTHORS IN THE ENGLISH-SPEAKING WORLD OF THE 18TH CENTURY

VINCENT CARRETTA
Editor

UNCHAINED VOICES

UNCHAINED VOICES

AN ANTHOLOGY OF BLACK AUTHORS IN THE ENGLISH-SPEAKING WORLD OF THE EIGHTEENTH CENTURY

Vincent Carretta

EDITOR

The University Press of Kentucky

Scholarly publisher for the Commonwealth,
serving Bellarmine College, Berea College, Centre
College of Kentucky, Eastern Kentucky University,
The Filson Club, Georgetown College, Kentucky
Historical Society, Kentucky State University,
Morehead State University, Murray State University,
Northern Kentucky University, Transylvania University,
University of Kentucky, University of Louisville,
and Western Kentucky University.

Editorial and Sales Offices: The University Press of Kentucky
663 South Limestone Street, Lexington, Kentucky 40508-4008

96 97 98 99 00 5 4 3 2 1

Library of Congress Cataloging-in-Publication Data

Unchained voices : an anthology of Black authors in the English-speaking world of the eighteenth century / Vincent Carretta, editor.
p. cm.
Includes bibliographical references and index.
ISBN 0-8131-1976-6 (cloth : alk. paper). —ISBN 0-8131-0884-5 (pbk. : alk. paper)
1. English literature—Black authors. 2. Blacks—English-speaking countries—History—18th century—Sources. 3. Blacks—English-speaking countries—Literary collections. 4. Blacks—Great Britain—History—18th century—Sources. 5. English literature—English speaking countries. 6. Afro-Americans—History—18th century—Sources. 7. Blacks—Great Britain—Literary collections. 8. American literature—Afro-American authors. 9. Afro-Americans—Literary collections. 10. English literature—18th century.
I. Carretta, Vincent.
PR9085.U55 1996
820.8'0896'09033—dc20 96-1019

This book is printed on acid-free recycled paper meeting
the requirements of the American National Standard
for Permanence of Paper for Printed Library Materials.

Manufactured in the United States of America

For

Pat, Nat, Maude,

and the Guys on the Porch

Contents

Acknowledgments

My greatest debts are to the staffs and collections of the following institutions: in the United Kingdom: the British Library; the British Museum; the Public Record Offices (PRO) in Kew and London; Dr. Williams's Library in London; the Library of the Society of Friends House, London; the Greater London Record Office; the City of Westminster Archives Centre; the Guildhall Library of the City of London; the Islington Local History Collection; the Goldsmiths' Library of the University of London Library; the Cambridgeshire County Record Office; and the University of Glasgow Library; in the United States: the McKeldin Library of the University of Maryland; the John Carter Brown Library; the Folger Shakespeare Library; the Van Pelt Library of the University of Pennsylvania; the Morris Library of the University of Delaware; the Connecticut College Library; the Boston Public Library; the American Antiquarian Society, and the Library of Congress.

Generous support from the University of Maryland, in the forms of a sabbatical leave and an award from the Committee on Africa and the Americas, enabled me to conduct research on both sides of the Atlantic. For help in the preparation for publication of some of the texts I thank Carol L. Warrington and her staff at the Computer Science Center at the University of Maryland.

The complete text of Equiano's *Interesting Narrative* appears in the Penguin edition of *Olaudah Equiano's The Interesting Narrative and Other Writings* (New York: Penguin USA, 1995). I thank Penguin USA and the University Press of Kentucky for giving me permission to reproduce approximately two thirds of the Penguin text, some of its notes, and part of its Introduction in *Unchained Voices.*

I am also very grateful to Seymour Drescher and William L. Andrews, readers for the University Press of Kentucky, for their comments and suggestions.

Introduction

This anthology reproduces the major works published during the eighteenth century by authors of African birth or descent who wrote or dictated their stories in English, and who spent some part of their lives in Britain or its colonies. All were subjects of the British monarch before the American Revolution, and many chose to remain so during and after that event, continuing to identify themselves as Afro-Britons rather than embracing the new political identity of African-Americans subject to the government of the United States. Non-aboriginal Americans born in the Americas were called Creoles during the eighteenth century. Thus all African or Creole Black authors (Phillis Wheatley and Briton Hammon, for examples) publishing in North America before the official separation of the thirteen colonies from Britain in 1783 were Afro-British writers, though several, including Wheatley, Belinda, Johnson Green, Benjamin Banneker, and Venture Smith, accepted, with varying degrees of enthusiasm, the new status of being African-Americans. Although the sixteen authors included here do not easily fit into a coherent group united by any organizing principle other than their African heritage, one theme can be identified in virtually all of their works: liberation from either physical or spiritual captivity and often from both. The range of representations of the theme of liberation reflects the various geographical, social, and temporal settings in which the different eighteenth-century Afro-British and African-American authors produced their writings.

The shared theme of liberation in these works will not surprise readers familiar with the nineteenth-century North American model of slavery, Africa, slave (or escape) narratives by former slaves, and the abolition movement. But such readers may be surprised by the diversity of the authors, subjects, and forms of the writings produced by Blacks during the eighteenth century. The nineteenth-century model includes tobacco or cotton plantations worked by Creole Black slaves owned by Creole American Whites; and Africa is carved up by imperialist European powers. In this model, slaves are all native-born in America and essentially undifferentiated from one another except by occupation. Slave-owners and traders are all White (though in reality, some free Blacks owned Black slaves in the United States), and the whole economic institution of slavery is defended by assertions of the racial inferiority of the enslaved.

The eighteenth century presents a more varied picture. Throughout the period, slaves were imported directly to the colonies from Africa, especially to the sugar-growing plantations of the West Indies, where the very high mortality rate meant that the native slave population was not self-sustaining. By 1750, the majority of slaves in British North America, on the other hand, were native born, with the population growing by natural increase. Mainly because of disease, before the widespread use of quinine, Europeans were restricted to factories (trading posts) on the coast of Africa, and were dependent on Africans for the maintenance of the slave trade. Without the complicity of their fellow Africans, very few Black slaves could have been exported to the Americas. Much was made of the differing suitability of the various African peoples for enslavement: some African nations were seen as too warlike, for example. Because many slaves, and most in the West Indies, knew from their own African experience that being Black was not equivalent to being enslaved, the fairly frequent West Indian slave revolts were almost always led by non-Creole Black Africans, for whom freedom was a memory of the recent past rather than a dream of the distant future. The sense of freedom lost is expressed by several of the authors in this anthology, of whom six were natives of Africa, and a seventh was born on the passage from Africa to the West Indies. In the nineteenth-century model, however, slaves have been at least somewhat acculturated to slavery, having been born into it and knowing no other way of life.

For most of the eighteenth century, certainly the first half, slavery was perceived primarily as an economic concern, not a moral problem, and the initial basis of African slavery was predominantly financial rather than racial. When, in the 1740s, George Whitefield (whose religious teachings were to become so influential for several of the Black writers collected here) considered possessing slaves in Georgia he saw the subject not in a moral context but as an economic necessity. The use of slaves on the rice-growing farm that supported Whitefield's Orphan House in Bethesda, Georgia, made the Countess of Huntingdon, patron of several of the writers in this anthology, a slave owner as well when she inherited Whitefield's Georgia holdings at his death in 1770. Like most evangelicals during the period, Huntingdon did not see slavery and Christianity as incompatible. Nowhere in the New Testament is slavery explicitly prohibited, and to those who believed that the afterlife was far more important than temporal existence, what mattered most was that pagan Africans be exposed to the truth of Christianity and be humanely treated in whatever social condition they were placed. Thus slavery could even be seen as a kind of fortunate fall, whereby the discomfort of the slaves' present life was overcompensated by the chance given them of achieving eternal salvation. This notion of a fortunate fall is promoted by the African Jacobus Elisa Joannes Capitein in his Latin dissertation that justifies slavery as having biblical precedent in the past and serving evangelical ends in the present and future.[1] The fortunate fall into slavery is also the subject of Phillis Wheatley's short poem "On being Brought from Africa to America."

The actions as well as the words of some of the writers represented in this anthology demonstrate their acceptance of the institution of slavery at some points in their lives. Briton Hammon, a free Black, was willing to take employment on a slave-trading ship; Francis Williams and John Marrant owned slaves; and Olaudah Equiano, as a free man, was a slave-driver in the 1770s. Supporters of slavery developed the dominant nineteenth-century racist defence of the institution primarily in the last quarter of the century, when the slave trade came under sustained religious, moral, and economic attack. Prior to 1770, slavery was usually accepted as one of the long-familiar statuses of the social and economic structure that formed the hierarchy of society. All recorded history, including the Bible, recognized the existence of slavery, and while some people called for the amelioration of the conditions of the enslaved, very few people imagined that slavery could, or perhaps even should, be eradicated. An idealized vision of a perfect society, like that found in Thomas More's *Utopia* (1516), could include slavery. Even though Europeans brought a particularly virulent form of slavery—large-scale, hereditary, and race-restricted—they did not introduce the concept of slavery itself to the Americas, where small-scale, domestic slavery already existed. We should remember that from the perspective of history we are living in an unusually slave-free time. Slavery ended in Brazil barely one hundred years ago; and slavery was outlawed in Saudi Arabia only in 1970. But the evil has not yet been completely eradicated: anti-slavery societies still exist because of the estimated two hundred thousand slaves (mainly women and children) remaining in the world.

During the eighteenth century, slavery was not strictly defined by White ownership of Black workers. Throughout the century, writers remarked on the existence of White slaves, especially in eastern Europe, and the word *slave* itself comes from the word *Slav*. Slavery was not abolished in Muscovy (Russia) until 1723, when it was superseded by serfdom. The enslavement of Christian Europeans by Moslem African Whites on the Barbary Coast or by Moslem Turks in Asia was a major concern during the period, getting more treatment in print before 1770 than the condition of Black African slaves. As the performance and publication of Susanna Haswell Rowson's play *Slaves in Algiers; Or, A Struggle for Freedom* (Philadelphia, 1794) indicate, the subject remained topical throughout the century. Indeed, Britain was not able to force North African Moslems to abolish the enslavement of Christians until 1816, nearly a decade after it had abolished its own trade in Black Africans. In his *Interesting Narrative* (London, 1789), Equiano comments on the brutal treatment of White galley slaves in Italy. Various forms of coerced labor existed in Britain itself, some of which were introduced into the American colonies. Scots miners, although they were not chattels (personal possessions of an owner), belonged, like feudal serfs, to the mine in which they worked. This labor system did not legally end until the middle of the eighteenth century. Coerced labor of Whites in Britain and its colonies included indentured servants (and even apprentices), who signed away their freedom for a specified amount of time in exchange for room and board and a guaranteed job (or job-training), in effect becoming voluntary slaves. And, after the Transportation Act of 1718, at least fifty thousand convicts were transported from Britain, at the government's expense, to the colonies to be sold as servants to work out their sentences.[2]

Nor did Britons believe that to be Black necessarily meant that one was suited for slavery. Social status could supersede race as a defining category, as it does in the fictional accounts of Oronokoo by Aphra Behn and Thomas Southerne, or in the historical cases of Ayuba Suleiman Diallo or Prince William Ansah Sessarakoo that found their way into print in the 1730s and 1740s. One of the cruel ironies of the "democratic" revolution in the thirteen colonies was that it also "democratized" slavery, making all people of African descent equally eligible for enslavement. Throughout the eighteenth century the more hierarchical Britons recognized slavery as an inappropriate status for at least some Africans.

The implicit acceptance of the institution of slavery is seen in what are perhaps the earliest Afro-British publications, Briton Hammon's *A Narrative of the Most Uncommon Sufferings and Surprizing Deliverance of Briton Hammon, a Negro Man* (Boston, 1760) and (apparently no relation) Jupiter Hammon's *An Evening Thought. Salvation, by Christ, with Penitential Cries: Composed by Jupiter Hammon, a Negro Belonging to Mr. Lloyd* (New York, 1760). Neither Hammon seems to have been known to any of the succeeding Afro-British authors, probably because their works were published solely in the provinces of the British Empire and never reprinted in London. But the Hammons used the two primary forms employed by almost every one of the later writers: the autobiographical prose narrative with varying degrees of religious implications, and the religious poem. Had not Briton and Jupiter Hammon each identified himself in his title as "a Negro," nothing in either of these first two works would have enabled us with certainty to recognize them as Afro-Britons.

Both works are about captivity, liberation, and restoration. Briton is sold to the Governor of Spanish Cuba by the Caribbean Indians who have captured him. He is rescued by the captain of an English ship who refuses to "deliver up any *Englishman* under *English* Colours" (emphasis in original) to the pursuing Spaniards from whom Briton has escaped. Eventually, through the providence of God, he is reunited with his "Master" (probably employer rather than owner), and together they return to Massachusetts. Briton emphasizes his physical captivity; Jupiter focuses exclusively on his spiritual captivity by sin and his faith in liberation by Christ. Neither Hammon may have felt overly offended or oppressed by the reality of slavery because they were fortunate to live in colonies where the conditions of slavery were generally relatively mild (as compared, for example, with those in the West Indies) and in a period when the separate colonies had a great deal of latitude in the creation of internal legislation. From the perspective of Afro-Britons, one of the harshest ironies of the last half of the eighteenth century was the White colonists' fierce defense of local legislative control as the bulwark of freedom from political slavery imposed by the Mother Country. In effect, however, such local control meant that the colonies could pass far more repressive laws regulating slavery and free Blacks than were in force in England itself, where racial intermarriage was legal and relatively unremarkable, as the lives of James Albert Ukawsaw Gronniosaw, Ottobah Cugoano, and Equiano demonstrate. And in Britain, being Black did not automatically disqualify one from voting, as the case of Ignatius Sancho demonstrates.

The irony of fighting for the freedom to enslave was highlighted in 1772. In June of that year, the Lord Chief Justice of the King's Bench, Lord Mansfield, declared in the Somerset case that a slave-owner could not legally force his slave to return from England to the West Indies. Mansfield's ruling was immediately recognized to confirm that a slave was free as soon as he or she set foot on English soil.[3] Following the precedent Mansfield set, the Scots court declared slavery illegal in 1778. The legality of slavery in England, disputed since the Cartwright case of 1569, which concerned the status of a Russian slave, and long ignored *de facto* (in practice), was now definitively rejected *de jure* (by law) as well. Advertisements for sales of slaves, notices of run-away slaves, and attempts to enforce Colonial slave laws in Britain—all already rare in England—disappeared after the Mansfield ruling.[4] Although the great jurist Sir William Blackstone qualified his statement in later editions in light of the Mansfield judgment, the first edition of his *Commentaries on the Laws of England* (London, 1765) declared "that a slave or negro, the instant he lands in England, becomes a freeman."[5] And the magistrate Sir John Fielding was already complaining in 1768 that slaves brought to London from the West Indies "no sooner arrive here, than they put themselves on a Footing with other Servants, become intoxicated with Liberty, grow refractory, and either by Persuasion of others, or from their own Inclinations, begin to expect Wages according to their own Opinion of their Merits" (*Extracts from Such of the Laws, as Particularly Relate to the Peace and Good Order of this Metropolis* [London, 1768]).

As Fielding's comment indicates, even before the ruling of June 1772, England was seen by Afro-Britons as the promised land of social and economic liberation. The Mansfield decision was popularly received as a virtual emancipation proclamation for the approximately fourteen to twenty thousand Blacks living in Britain, about 0.2 percent of the national population, but perhaps as much as 2 percent of London's population.[6] By comparison, the Declaration of Independence, signed four years later in Philadelphia, offered nothing to the nearly five hundred thousand Blacks in North America, or 20 percent of the total population. (The five hundred thousand Blacks in the British West Indies, more than 90 percent of the population, were unaffected by either the Mansfield ruling or the Declaration of Independence.)

Moreover, the Mansfield decision arguably played a measurable role in the development of Afro-British writing. At the end of 1772, Gronniosaw's *A Narrative of the Most Remarkable Particulars in the Life of . . . an African Prince, as Related by Himself* was published in Bath, capitalizing on the attention brought to the existence and status of Afro-Britons by the Mansfield decision. Phillis Wheatley, unable to find a publisher in Boston, published her *Poems on Various Subjects, Religious and Moral* in London in 1773. Wheatley shared Gronniosaw's patron, the Methodist Countess of Huntingdon, and acknowledged Gronniosaw's work in a letter to the Countess.[7] England was obviously a far more receptive environment than North America for Afro-British writers, and publication there almost guaranteed distribution if not reprinting throughout the British Empire. Thus, although Jupiter Hammon's previous work was very probably unknown to Wheatley, hers became the subject of one of his poems. Significantly, Hammon chose to respond in his *Address to Miss Phillis Wheatly, Ethiopian Poetess* (Hartford, 1778) to her "On Being Brought from Africa to America," a poem about her paradoxical deliverance from the spiritual slavery of Africa to her physically enslaved but spiritually liberated condition in America. The Mansfield decision could also affect the lives of Afro-Britons quite directly. Wheatley, who came to England as a slave, returned to Boston a slave but with the promise of freedom. No doubt knowing that she could not be legally forced to return, she probably maneuvered her master into agreeing before witnesses that he would emancipate her if she returned with him. The attention Mansfield brought to the subject of British slavery may also be at least partially responsible for the publication of Francis Williams's "Ode" in Edward Long's *History of Jamaica* (London, 1774). As a defender of slavery, particularly in the West Indies, Long translated and reproduced Williams's poem in hopes of disproving arguments that Afro-Britons were capable of creating literature, even when given the benefit of education. But Long's attempt to discredit Williams, and by extension all Black writers, backfired almost completely. Without Long's attack, we would know virtually nothing of Williams and have no certain example of his work.

The contrast between the legal statuses of Afro-Britons in the Mother Country and the colonies was underscored by the hypocrisy of the White North American colonists demanding liberty for themselves while enslaving others. This hypocrisy prompted criticism by Granville Sharp and Samuel Johnson. The White Americans' position gave their English opponents an easy opportunity to demonstrate moral and political superiority. Thus, in a letter written in 1776 (though not published until 1784) to an American correspondent, Thomas Day observes,

> Slavery . . . is a crime so monstrous against the human species that all those who practise it deserve to be extirpated from the earth. . . .
>
> If men would be consistent, they must admit all the consequences of their own principles; and you and your countrymen are reduced to the dilemma of either acknowledging the rights of your Negroes, or of surrendering your own.—If there be certain natural and universal rights, as the declarations of your Congress [including the Declaration of Independence] so repeatedly affirm, I wonder how the unfortunate Africans have incurred their forfeiture.—Is it the antiquity, or the virtues, or the great qualities of the English Americans, which constitutes the difference, and entitles them to rights from which they totally exclude more than a fourth part of the species?—Or do you choose to make use of that argument, which the great Montesquieu has thrown out as the severest ridicule, that they are black, and you white; that you have lank, long hair, while theirs is short and woolly?

Given Afro-Britons' association of England with potential liberation, King George III, represented in the Declaration of Independence as a tyrant to colonial American Whites, was often seen by their slaves as a potential savior. Hence, in her *Poems* Wheatley includes a panegyric addressed "To the King's Most Excellent Majesty. 1768." Not surprisingly then, given the opportunity, most of the eighteenth-century Blacks whose voices we can recover, either directly or through intermediaries, chose a British rather than an American identity, taking advantage of the British promises of emancipation for refugee slaves of the colonial rebels (but not for refugees from Loyalist masters). For every Johnson Green, or the more famous Crispus Attucks, who identified with the Rebel cause, many more Blacks chose the other side: for example, the freeman John Marrant; George Liele, the slave of a Loyalist; and David George and Boston King, slaves of rebels. Of the half-million Blacks in the thirteen colonies, the overwhelming majority of whom were slaves, approximately five thousand served the colonists' cause while tens of thousands, perhaps as many as one hundred thousand, were lost to the British, though many of those remained as slaves under Loyalist masters. After the war, Britain and not the new United States continued to serve as the promised land of freedom for present and former slaves in the British Empire, such as Equiano, who had spent about five years of his life as a slave in the West Indies, as well as about a month in Virginia. Not surprisingly, in his posthumously published *Letters* (London, 1782), Sancho never questioned the validity of the British cause in the war he supported against the Americans led by the man he mockingly called "Washintub."[8] In 1789, Equiano referred to "England, where my heart had always been," and in 1793, writing from the Sierra Leone settlement in Africa, George, who had been born and raised in South Carolina, considered England to be "home."

Not all eighteenth-century Black writers, of course, chose to retain a British identity. As Wheatley's poem "To His Excellency General Washington" (1775) demonstrates, some free Blacks chose the new African-American identity now available. And in the aftermath of the Revolution, the period known as the "first emancipation," when the anti-slavery movement grew, especially in the North, the petition of the ex-slave Belinda to the Massachusetts legislature and Banneker's letter to Thomas Jefferson indicate the optimism among African-Americans concerning universal freedom and justice. The choice of identities was possible because both British and American identities were recent political constructions invented in the eighteenth century, rather than the traditional ethnic or religious categories, which they subsumed. Thus one could be (after the Union of 1707) a Scots-Briton, a Welsh-Briton, and (in the nineteenth century) an Irish-Briton, as well as an English-Briton. Or an Afro-Briton.[9]

Calling attention to one's loyalty to Britain was conventional in the works by almost all the Afro-British writers. As Briton Hammon had first identified himself, Gronniosaw and Marrant represent themselves as loyal British subjects by speaking of their military service in the British army and navy; Sancho does so by commenting on the conduct of the war against the North American colonists; and Williams and Wheatley write poems praising, respectively, the Governor of Jamaica and the King of Great Britain. The military careers of most of the Afro-British men are understandable, given that the British army and navy were open to all talents in ways that most occupations were not. Competence mattered more than color, as Equiano's own service record demonstrates.

Another way of displaying British values was through the endorsement of Christianity expressed by almost all the Afro-British writers, many of whom were Methodist members of the Church of England, embracing the predestinarian Calvinism preached by George Whitefield and the clergymen associated with his aristocratic patron, the Countess of Huntingdon.[10] As the satiric representation of a Black member of the congregation in William Hogarth's print *Credulity, Superstition and Fanaticism* (London, 1762) indicates, Marrant and Equiano were not the only Afro-Britons influenced by Whitefield's doctrine and preaching. Sancho's dismissive image of "a methodist preacher" as "flat, dull, and tedious" was almost certainly ironic: he attended a Methodist chapel.[11] The beliefs that salvation was freely granted by God rather than earned by humans and that particular people were predestined to be saved may have appealed to so many Afro-Britons for several reasons. The evangelical Methodists took religion to the people, rather than waiting for the people to come to church, and they saw all levels of society, including slaves, as having a potential share in salvation. When physical liberation from enslavement in the present seemed impossible, spiritual freedom and equality in the afterlife offered some solace. And a faith that depends on predestination for salvation rather than on spiritual rewards for good works may have been especially attractive to those whose ability to perform good works was severely limited by their social condition.

Undoubtedly underlying the emphasis on religion in the narratives of Black writers was the long-standing belief that conversion to Christianity merited emancipation from slavery, a belief so strong that it led to colonial statutes denying its validity. By 1706 the British colonies of the Carolinas, New Jersey, and New York all had declared conversion and baptism irrelevant to a slave's status. But faith in the effects of conversion abided, especially in England itself, where no positive (formulated and passed by Parliament) laws specifically addressed the issue of slavery. Sir John Fielding complained in 1768 about the continuing belief in the equation of Christianity and freedom and its disruptive social effects:

> There are already a great Number of black Men and Women who have made themselves so troublesome and dangerous to the Families who brought them over [to England from the American colonies] as to get themselves discharged; they enter into Societies, and make it their Business to corrupt and dissatisfy the Mind of every fresh black Servant that comes to *England*; first, by getting them christened or married, which they inform them makes them free (tho' it has been adjudged by our most able Lawyers, that neither of these Circumstances alter the Master's Property in a Slave). (*Extracts from Such of the Laws*)[12]

Even after the 1772 Mansfield ruling, as the Cugoano's case demonstrates, Blacks continued to see baptism as a rite of passage to freedom in England. The slaves' association of Christianity and emancipation was reinforced by the leading role played in the anti-slave-trade movement by the Society of Friends, or Quakers, and evangelical Anglicans like Equiano's friend James Ramsay.

Most of the writers represented in this collection were also beneficiaries and/or agents of the evangelical Christian movement, led by Methodist and Baptist missionaries, that pervaded the eighteenth-century British Empire. The earliest Protestant missionary sent from England to Africa, however, was a non-Methodist Anglican. Philip Quaque and two other Fante boys were brought from present-day Ghana to England in 1754 to be trained to become missionaries to their native countrymen. Baptized in 1759 and ordained a priest by the Church of England in 1765, Quaque and his English wife, Catherine Blunt, left for his homeland in 1766, where he served as "Missionary, School Master, and Cathechist to the Negroes on the Gold Coast in Africa" until his death there in 1816. The opportunity to preach gave Jupiter Hammon, Marrant, Liele, George, and King influence and power rarely experienced by Blacks in the period. With the power to preach could come the threat to the status quo occasionally perceived by those in power. Belief in the equality of souls might be taken to imply belief in the equality of bodies and civil rights. Hence, though eventually acquitted, the Black Baptist missionary Liele was arrested in Jamaica on a charge of preaching sedition in the wake of slave uprisings in the Caribbean during the 1790s. As the texts by Liele and Marrant in this anthology show, members of the White ruling class were not certain whether spreading Christianity encouraged submission or insubordination among the converted slaves.

For most of the Black writers, Protestant Christianity with its emphasis on direct knowledge of the Bible was the primary motive for literacy. Virtually all the Afro-British publications in prose took the form of spiritual autobiographies that trace the transition from pagan beliefs to the Christianity shared with the authors' British readers. In each case, men and women escape from some type of physical captivity, whether it be slavery or the capture by Indians suffered by the free Black Marrant in *A Narrative of the Lord's Wonderful Dealings with John Marrant, a Black* (London, 1785). Although not constructed as a conversion narrative, Sancho's posthumously published letters repeatedly attest to his faith in Christianity. Even Green's *Life and Confession* (Worcester, 1786), sensationalist though it is as a cautionary tale, is a spiritual autobiography. The pointedly nonconversion *Narrative* of Smith may reflect in its form Smith's disillusion at the end of the century with the failed promises of the "first emancipation" and the bitter irony of his being a subject of the United States of America, mentioned on his title page. Smith is pointedly only a "resident" of the country, which, as the anonymous voice in the preface to his story reminds us, has denied him the citizenship and thus the opportunities that might have allowed him to rival the achievements of Benjamin Franklin or George Washington. Smith's text is the only example of a work written or dictated by a Black during the period that is entitled a "narrative" but is not a story of conversion, and his reference to the "christian land" in which he lives is clearly ironic.

Equiano asserts his identity as a Briton more fully than any of his predecessors. African by birth,[13] he is British by acculturation and choice. He can, of course, never be *English*, in the ethnic sense in which that word was used during the period, as his White wife is *English*. He adopts, however, the cultural, political, religious, and social values that enable him to be accepted as *British*. Yet he always retains his perspective as an African who has been deracinated and thus has the advantage of knowing his adopted British culture from both the inside and the outside, a perspective that W.E.B. Du Bois calls the double consciousness of the Black person in a predominantly White society. This double consciousness is reflected in the use of dual identities by Olaudah Equiano/Gustavus Vassa and Ottobah Cugoano/John Stewart, as well as in the comment by Sancho, a voting British citizen, in a letter to his friend Rush (7 September 1779), that he saw himself as "only a lodger [in England]—and hardly that."

The legal status of the people like Equiano, Cugoano, and Sancho who were British yet not English was brought to public attention by the Mansfield judgment. Their political status became a subject for public argument in light of the ideological conflict during the American Revolution, and their status as human beings was disputed during the crusade in the 1790s to end British involvement in the slave trade with Africa.

Although the sustained political struggle to end the slave trade (and later slavery itself) in the British Empire did not begin until 1787, slavery was a topic of public discussion throughout the century, though many of these discussions did not directly treat the subject of abolishing the trade in slaves, let alone the abolition of the institution of slavery itself. It should be noted that *abolition* in the eighteenth-century British context almost always refers to abolition of the trade in slaves from Africa to the remaining British colonies in the West Indies, not to the abolition of the institution of slavery itself, though many of the slave-trade abolitionists no doubt saw slavery as the ultimate target.

Typical of the abolitionist's public position was that expressed by Equiano's friend, the Reverend James Ramsay, writing in 1786 of his *An Essay on the Treatment and Conversion of African Slaves in the Sugar Colonies* (London, 1784), which can justly be called the opening salvo in the war over the slave trade: "Though I sincerely hope, that *some* plan will be devised for the future gradual abolition of slavery; and though I am convinced that this may, without any prejudice to the planter, or injury to commerce, be brought about by some such progressive method as is pointed out in the Essay; yet this was not the first, or immediate object of that book." Such circumspection reappears in Equiano's *Narrative*, where he concentrates on the evils of the slave trade, though in some of his letters to the newspapers his opinion of slavery is more directly and forcefully stated. Even by the end of the century, when we speak of the British abolitionist movement we are almost always referring to the movement to abolish the trade, not the institution. Some advocates of the abolition of the trade no doubt saw that as the first step toward total emancipation of the slaves in the British Empire, but they were usually careful not to diminish the size of their potential audience by appearing too radical, Cugoano being the most notable exception.

The Americans' victory in the civil war that we now call the American Revolution led to a great and very visible increase after 1783 in the numbers of free Blacks accompanying their Loyalist former masters as they left the former thirteen colonies for Canada and London, along with the many slaves who had emancipated themselves by joining the British forces in the war. The sight of unemployed and impoverished Blacks in London prompted the formation in 1786 of the Committee for the Relief of the Black Poor, which promoted the project for resettlement in Sierra Leone, in which Equiano played a major role. According to a report in the newspaper *The Public Advertiser* (6 January 1787), sympathy for the Black Poor was so widespread that White beggars disguised themselves as Blacks to increase their incomes. The aftermath of the defeat by the colonists was a time for national reassessment in Britain, a time well suited for the potentially spiritually regenerating moral crusade initiated by the publication in 1784 of Ramsay's *Essay*, the first attack on slavery by a former West Indian slave owner. At the same time, the loss of the thirteen colonies both weakened the political base of slavery in Parliament and concentrated attention on the slave trade, without which West Indian slavery apparently could not survive. The Committee for Effecting the Abolition of the Slave Trade, most of whose members were Quakers, was created in London in 1787 and began distributing anti-slave-trade pamphlets throughout the country at the peak of the African trade, when approximately eighty thousand Africans, more than half of them in British ships, were being brought annually to the Americas in the late 1780s. The Committee, allied with other dissenting sects as well as with the evangelical Methodists of the Anglican Church, formed the base for the wider movement that exploited the extraparliamentary methods of political pressure and petitioning that had been developed during the 1760s. Between 1788 and 1792, hundreds of petitions from around the country were presented to Parliament in support of the abolition of the African slave trade.

The most overt challenge to slavery by an Afro-Briton was made in 1787 by Equiano's friend and sometime collaborator, Cugoano (who also went by the name John Stewart or Stuart), in *Thoughts and Sentiments on the Evil and Wicked Traffic of the Slavery and Commerce of the Human Species, Humbly Submitted to the Inhabitants of Great-Britain, by Ottobah Cugoano, a Native of Africa* (London). The title of his book, which may have been revised for publication by Equiano, clearly alludes to *An Essay on the Slavery and Commerce of the Human Species, Particularly the African* (London, 1786), written by another friend of Equiano, Thomas Clarkson. The body of Cugoano's work, full of acknowledged and unacknowledged debts to the writings of others, like his title, demonstrates that he sees the struggle against the trade as a kind of group project. Similarly, Equiano's *Narrative* often relies on the evidence, examples, and arguments of others (usually acknowledged).

Against this background, Equiano published his *Interesting Narrative*, the first full account of the slave trade and slavery published by a former African slave. Equiano's work, which went through nine British editions between 1789 and 1794, is the longest and most significant publication by an Afro-Briton in the century. Appearing amid the mass national petitioning movement that began in 1788 against the African slave trade,[14] the *Narrative*, as published in 1789, was structured as a petition against the trade, beginning with an address to the members of both Houses of Parliament and virtually ending with a petition to Queen Charlotte. Like Sancho's *Letters* (1782) and the abbreviated version of Cugoano's *Thoughts and Sentiments* (1791), the *Narrative* was sold by subscription, that is, by convincing buyers to commit themselves to purchasing copies of the book prior to its publication, usually requiring at least partial payment in advance to cover living and production costs. Equiano's list of subscribers, which includes the Prince of Wales, acts as an additional catalogue of petitioners. Each succeeding edition includes further numbers of subscribers. Publication by subscription, with its attendant lists, was a form of self-promotion. An increasing number of people clearly wanted to be publicly associated with the *Narrative* and its author, whose credibility and stature were enhanced by the presence of the names of royalty, members of the aristocracy, and other socially and politically prominent figures. The lists also served to link Equiano with the larger movement against the slave trade by including names of others who had already attacked in print or from the pulpit the invidious practice.

By 1789 a recognized tradition of Afro-British authors had been established, with new writers aware of the works of their predecessors. Jupiter Hammon and Sancho acknowledge and praise the poetry of Wheatley, and Cugoano refers explicitly to the works of Gronniosaw and Marrant. The subscription lists for Equiano's *Narrative* connect the author and his work explicitly and implicitly with the Afro-British writers of the preceding fifteen years, whose works had already been reprinted: Cugoano's name appears; Sancho appears via his son William; Gronniosaw and Wheatley by association with the Countess of Huntingdon; and Marrant by association with his editor, Reverend William Aldridge. Less directly, the presence of the name of his patron's successor, the Duke of Montagu, recalls the poem by Williams.

Although Wheatley, Williams, and Sancho rarely address the issues of the abolition of the slave trade or of slavery itself, all to some extent became involved in the arguments of the 1780s and later about the literary and intellectual capacities of Africans. Having obvious pretensions to literary achievement while remaining apparently politically disinterested, and safely dead and thus not able, as were Cugoano and Equiano, to engage in the controversy, Wheatley, Williams, and Sancho were at the center of the late-eighteenth-century debate over the innate intelligence and even humanity of the African. Thomas Jefferson's comments in *Notes on the State of Virginia* (London, 1787) exemplify the kind of attacks defenders of the slave trade made on the achievements of Afro-Britons: "Religion indeed has produced a Phyllis Whately [*sic*]; but it could not produce a poet. . . ." "[Ignatius Sancho] has approached nearer to merit in composition. . . . [T]hough we admit him to the first place among those of his own colour who have presented themselves to the public judgment, yet when we compare him with the writers of the race among whom he lived, and particularly with the epistolary class, in which he has taken his own stand, we are compelled to enroll him at the bottom of the column."[15]

Many White abolitionists defended the accomplishments of the Afro-British authors and used them as evidence of their shared humanity. For example, in his *Letter to the Treasurer of the Society Instituted for the Purpose of Effecting the Aboli-*

tion of the Slave Trade (London, 1788), the Reverend Robert Boucher Nikkols [Nichols], one of Equiano's subscribers, writes,

> The stupidity of negroes is . . . urged by the friends of slavery as a plea for using them as brutes; for they represent the negroes as little removed above the monkey, or the oran-outang, with regard to intellects. But I am very certain, nothing has been written by the late defenders of slavery, that discovers [displays] half the literary merit or ability of two negroe writers. Phillis Wheatley wrote correct English poetry within a few years after her arrival in Boston from Africa; and there is a Latin ode of considerable length written in classic language by Francis Williams. . . . I never heard of poems by a monkey, or of Latin odes by an oran-outang.

One need not have been an abolitionist to admit the merit of some Black writers, as John Gabriel Stedman does in his *Narrative of a Five Years Expedition against the Revolted Negroes of Surinam* (London, 1796):

> That these people are neither divested of a good ear, nor poetical genius, has been frequently proved, when they had the advantages of a good education. Amongst others, *Phillis Wheatley*, who was a slave at *Boston* in New England, learned the Latin language, and wrote thirty-eight elegant pieces of poetry on different subjects, which were published in 1773. . . .
>
> *Ignatius Sancho*, a negro, many years servant to the Duke of Montagu, whose sentimental letters, so generally known, would not disgrace the pen of an European, may also be mentioned on this occasion.

Equiano's placing himself centrally in the context of eighteenth-century writings against the slave trade by Whites as well as Afro-Britons again serves to assert his British identity. Reading his *Narrative* in light of other abolitionist publications, one gets the impression that what James Field Stanfield later says of accounts of slave-trade voyages can be applied as well to the writings of Equiano and his immediate contemporaries and predecessors:

> The principles of the Slave trade . . . are *alike*, in all the cases I have met with, whether from actual knowledge, or well-attested information. Publications therefore of this kind must grow tiresome, and be necessarily marked with an unfavourable degree of sameness; unfavourable, I mean, with regard to the patience of cold, dispassionate readers: for, taken in another point of view, it seems to give additional strength to the cause. Is it not a strong presumptive proof of the veracity of the circumstances that have been offered, that a number of men, unknown to each other, from different parts of the kingdom, dating their facts so long asunder, bringing their scenes of destruction from different places and vessels, without an invitation, without interest to serve, without any other purpose than that of supporting the cause of humanity, should concur, in such a wonderful degree. (*The Guinea Voyage, a Poem* [Edinburgh, 1807])

Spiritual autobiography, captivity narrative, travel book, adventure tale, narrative of slavery, economic treatise, and *apologia* (justification and vindication of one's life), among other things, Equiano's *Narrative* marks the culmination of the Afro-British tradition of the eighteenth century.

In response to the growing public interest in the controversy over the African slave trade, in February 1788, by the order of King George III, the Privy Council Committee for Trade and Plantations began an investigation of British commercial relations with Africa and the nature of the slave trade. The Committee, as well as the House of Commons from 1789 to 1792, heard evidence for and against the trade. From 1789 on, William Wilberforce led attempts in the House of Commons to pass an abolition bill, only to see it either fail by narrow margins or be blocked in the House of Lords in 1792, after the Commons had voted in that year to end the Trade in 1796. The outbreak of the French Revolution and the subsequent Terror during the period from 1789 to 1794 made Britons reluctant to pursue any major social reforms lest they lead to revolutionary results, and the slave revolts in the West Indies during the 1790s seemed to justify conservative fears. The British government's attempt to suppress dissident voices probably accounts for Equiano's apparent public silence after 1794, when his former landlord and friend Thomas Hardy, Secretary of the London Corresponding Society, was tried and acquitted on a charge of treason. Among the papers the government seized at Hardy's arrest was a letter to him from Equiano. Later in the decade, the threat posed by Napoleonic France to national survival eclipsed all other issues until 1804, when the agitation for abolition, relatively quiescent since 1796, revived.

The texts from the 1790s in this anthology appeared during a relative lull in the anti-slave-trade agitation and only implicitly comment on the trade. But the three Afro-British texts demonstrate that people of African descent could succeed as free British subjects and good Christians, even after the dehumanizing experiences of slavery. All three recount the escape of North American slaves who sought refuge with the British during the American Revolution and found freedom in new homelands. The letters and biography of Liele tell the story of a slave evacuated from Savannah, Georgia, by the retreating British and brought to Jamaica, and the autobiographies by George and King tell of former slaves who settled in Sierra Leone after having been evacuated from the American South to Nova Scotia. The written lives of Liele, George, and King anticipate more directly than those of any of their Afro-British predecessors the narrative story lines of African-American fugitive slave narratives of the nineteenth century, exemplified by the *Narrative of the Life of Frederick Douglass, an American Slave. Written by Himself* (Boston, 1845).

None of the Afro-British writers included in this anthology, with the exceptions of George and Liele, lived to see the legal abolition in 1807 of the British slave trade, but all arguably played a part in that partial success on the way to the abolition of nonindigenous slavery itself in the British Empire in 1838.

NOTES

1. Capitein (1717-1747), one of the most celebrated and learned Blacks in the eighteenth century, had been brought from present-day Ghana, where the Dutch had a slave-trading factory at Elmina, to Holland, where he studied theology from 1726 to 1742, when he was ordained. He was returned to Elmina as a missionary, but he soon grew disillusioned with his fellow Christians and gave up his ministry to pursue an unsuccessful career in trade.

2. Before 1718, convicts like Benjamin Banneker's English grandmother, Molly Welsh, who arrived in Maryland around 1683, frequently received pardons on the condition that they would either pay for their own passage to America, or go at the expense of merchants who then sold them as indentured servants in the Colonies.

3. On the meaning of the Mansfield decision and its implications, see William R. Cotter, "The Somerset Case and the Abolition of Slavery in England," *History* 79 (1994), 31-56.

4. In addition to Cotter, see Seymour Drescher, *Capitalism and Antislavery: British Mobilization in Comparative Perspective* (London: Macmillan Press, 1986), 25-49.

5. The development of the legal assault on British slavery is told in David Brion Davis, *The Problem of Slavery in the Age of Revolution 1770-1823* (Ithaca: Cornell University Press, 1975), 469-522.

6. The most reliable general history of Afro-Britons is Peter Fryer, *Staying Power: The History of Black People in Britain* (London: Pluto Press, 1984).

7. I believe that Wheatley refers to Gronniosaw as the "African so worthy to be honored with your Ladiship's approbation & Friendship . . . him whom you call your Brother," in an undated letter Wheatley sent to the Countess while she was in England in 1773.

8. In a letter sent on 5 November 1777 to Mrs. C[ocksedge].

9. On the construction of the *British* identity, see Linda Colley, *Britons: Forging the Nation 1707-1837* (New Haven: Yale University Press, 1992).

10. Whitefield (1714-1770) preached the doctrine of John Calvin (1509-1564), who taught that very few Christians were the elect, predestined, or elected, by the grace of God to be saved. Everyone else was a reprobate, doomed to eternal damnation, despite faith or acts of charity. Grace could only be freely given by God and could not be earned by the good works of professed believers. Whitefield's position was consistent with Article 17, the most Calvinistic of the Thirty-Nine Articles of the Church of England that loosely constituted the Church's Creed.

But other Articles allowed for a more liberal, or Arminian, interpretation of the requirements for salvation. Named after Jacobus Arminius (Jakob Hermandszoon) (1560-1609), one of Calvin's earliest theological opponents, this doctrine held that all who believed and repented of their sins could be saved. Being omniscient, God of course knew who would be saved, but had not arbitrarily predetermined and restricted their number. John Wesley (1703-1791), along with his brother Charles (1707-1788) and Whitefield, a co-founder of Methodism, subscribed to the Arminian doctrine and published *The Arminian Magazine* (renamed *The Methodist Magazine* after John Wesley's death). The most significant Wesleyan, or Arminian, Methodist in this anthology is Boston King.

Arminians and Calvinists agreed in their emphasis on personal salvation gained in the process of recognizing that one was a sinner undeserving of redemption, who, by submitting oneself completely to God, might be granted grace, whereby one experienced the joy of the new birth through the revelation of one's personal salvation.

11. Sancho's presumably ironic comment appears in his letter of 9 October 1779 to John Meheux, 1st Clerk in the Board of Control. In his letter of 20 October 1769 to Mr. Kisby, Sancho says, "I am for my sins turned Methodist"; in his 15 September 1770 letter to

Mr. Simon, he declares himself "half a Methodist" after hearing the evangelical Erasmus Middleton (1739-1805) preach (Middleton, with five other students, had been expelled from Oxford in 1768 for praying and preaching in public); and by 1 November 1773 (letter to Mrs. H—), he was regularly attending services conducted by William Dodd (1729-1777) at the Charlotte Chapel in Pimlico.

12. For a wider discussion of what actions were believed to entitle slaves to freedom in England, see Seymour Drescher, "Manumission in a Society without Slave Law: Eighteenth Century England," *Slavery and Abolition* 10 (1989), 85-101.

13. Although I accept Equiano's assertion of his African identity as true, in part because I want it to be, I recognize that this identity was challenged in his lifetime. That his baptismal record and naval record from his Arctic expedition list him as a native of South Carolina, and that he rarely used the name Olaudah Equiano in public or private writings outside *The Interesting Narrative* before, during, or after its publication, could serve as evidence to argue he invented an African identity for rhetorical and/or marketing ends. For the challenge and his other writings, see my edition of *Olaudah Equiano's Interesting Narrative and Other Writings* (Penguin, 1995).

14. On the national petitioning movement, see Drescher, *Capitalism and Antislavery*, 50-66.

15. Unlike the pamphlet literature, the Slave-Trade debates in Parliament from 1788 to 1807 were notably free of race-based arguments. On the development of such arguments in Britain during the last half of the eighteenth century, see Philip D. Curtin, *The Image of Africa: British Ideas and Action, 1780-1850* (London: Macmillan, 1965) and Anthony J. Barker, *The African Link: British Attitudes to the Negro in the Era of the Atlantic Slave Trade, 1550-1807* (London: Frank Cass, 1978).

A Note on the Texts and Editorial Policy

I have intentionally not included literary analyses of the works in this anthology in order to avoid, as much as possible, the appearance of trying to direct the ways they are read and interpreted. My goal has been to give an accurate introductory historical context for a collection of reliably edited and annotated primary texts, many of which have been hitherto unavailable. In the notes, documents in the Public Records Office (PRO) are cited by their class codes and piece numbers. The following class codes are used: ADM (Admiralty); PC (Privy Council Office); PRIS (King's Bench Prison); PROB (Prerogative Court of Canterbury); and T (Treasury).

Except where indicated, I have chosen first editions as copy-texts. Spelling (including the various spellings of proper names) and punctuation have not been modernized unless the original usage would confuse or mislead a twentieth-century reader. The eighteenth-century long "s" has been replaced throughout. Obvious errors in printing, such as dropped or inverted letters, have been silently corrected.

The copy-text of Olaudah Equiano's *Interesting Narrative* is that of the ninth edition (London, 1794) in the Marylandia and Rare Books Collection of the University of Maryland at College Park. I chose this edition because it incorporates Equiano's final substantive changes in his autobiography, whose production and distribution he oversaw through all its British editions. I am very grateful to Timothy D. Pyatt, Curator of the Collection, for his aid in making the text available for publication. I am equally grateful to Dr. Sidney E. Berger, Head of Special Collections at the University of California at Riverside for enabling me to reproduce the frontispiece of the 1794 edition.

A Note on Money

Before the British monetary system was decimalized in 1971, British money was counted in pounds sterling (£), shillings (s.), and pence, or pennies (d.), and farthings. One pound sterling = 20 shillings; 5 shillings = 1 crown; 1 shilling = 12 pennies; 1 farthing = 1/4d. One guinea (so-called because the gold from which it was made came from the Guinea Coast of Africa) = 21 shillings.

The colonies each issued their own local paper currency, and a colonial pound was worth less than a pound sterling, with the conversion rates for the currencies of the various colonies fluctuating throughout the century. Because of restrictions on the export of coins from England, the colonies relied on foreign coins, particularly Spanish, for local transactions. The basic Spanish denomination for silver coinage was the real ("royal"), with the peso (piece of eight reals), or pieces of eight, known in British America as the dollar. Hence, 2 reals, or bits, became known as a quarter. Spanish reals were preferred as specie because their face value was equivalent to their intrinsic silver value. The Spanish pistareen, on the other hand, had a face value of 2 reals, but an intrinsic value of only 1/5 of a Spanish dollar. The Spanish doubloon was an 8 escudo gold coin worth, in 1759 pounds sterling, 3£ 6s. od. At the same time, a Spanish dollar was worth, in local currency, 0£ 7s. 6d. in Philadelphia, and 0£ 8s. od. in New York. Conversion charts showing the value of foreign money in colonial currency and pounds sterling were frequently published throughout the eighteenth century. Also in circulation were coins, like the copper ones Equiano was forced to accept, which had neither face nor intrinsic value.

To arrive at a rough modern equivalent of eighteenth-century money multiply by about 80. In mid-eighteenth-century urban England a family of four could live modestly on £40 sterling a year, and a gentleman could support his standard of living on £300 sterling a year. A maid might be paid (in addition to room and board, cast-off clothes, and vails, or gratuities) around 6 guineas per year; a manservant, around 10£ per year; and an able seaman, after deductions, earned 14£ 12s. 6d. a year, in addition to room and board. The price of a four-pound loaf of bread ranged from 5.1 to 6.6 d. between 1750 and 1794, when Olaudah Equiano was charging 5s. for a copy of his *Interesting Narrative.* Samuel Johnson left his Black servant, Francis Barber, an annuity of 70£ sterling a year; the Duchess of Montagu left Ignatius Sancho a sum of 70£ sterling and 30£ sterling a year; Sancho's widow received more than 500£ sterling from the sales of his *Letters*; and Equiano's daughter inherited 950£ sterling from her father's estate.

Notes on the Illustrations

~

FRONTISPIECE

Francis Williams

Anonymous oil painting, circa 1740

The painting shows the poet in his library in Spanish Town, Jamaica. Since the painting, apparently executed in naive colonial style, belonged to descendants of Edward Long, Williams's hostile biographer, it may have been satiric in intent. Reproduced by courtesy of the Board of Trustees of the Victoria & Albert Museum, London

1.

Phillis Wheatley

Frontispiece to *Poems on Various Subjects, Religious and Moral* (London, 1773)

The frontispiece was added at the suggestion of the Countess of Huntingdon. The painter and engraver are unknown, though the painter may have been Scipio Moorhead, the subject of Wheatley's poem "To S.M. a Young *African* Painter, on Seeing his Works." Reproduced by courtesy of the Library of Congress

2.

Ignatius Sancho

Frontispiece to *Letters of the Late Ignatius Sancho* (London, 1782)

Engraved by Francesco Bartolozzi, after a painting (1768) by Thomas Gainsborough. Reproduced by courtesy of the Library of Congress

3.

Olaudah Equiano, or Gustavus Vassa

Frontispiece to the 9th edition of *The Interesting Narrative of the Life of Olaudah Equiano, or Gustavus Vassa, The African. Written by Himself* (London, 1794; 1st ed. 1789)

Engraved by Daniel Orme, after a painting by William Denton. The illustration of the frontispiece of *The Interesting Narrative* is reprinted here with the permission of the Special collections Department, Rivera Library, University of California, Riverside.

4.

Benjamin Banneker

Anonymous portrait on the cover of his *Almanac for the Year of our Lord 1795* (Baltimore, 1794), reproduced by permission from the Collection of the Maryland Historical Society, Baltimore

Briton Hammon[1]

NARRATIVE of the UNCOMMON SUFFERINGS AND Surprizing DELIVERANCE OF BRITON HAMMON, *A Negro Man,—Servant to GENERAL WINSLOW, of* Marshfield, *in NEW-ENGLAND;*[2] *Who returned to* Boston, *after having been absent almost Thirteen Years. CONTAINING An Account of the many Hardships he underwent from the Time he left his Master's House, in the Year 1747, to the Time of his Return to* Boston.—*How he was Cast away in the Capes of* Florida;—*the horrid Cruelty and inhuman Barbarity of the* Indians *in murdering the whole Ship's Crew;—the Manner of his being carry'd by them into Captivity. Also, An Account of his being Confined Four Years and Seven Months in a close Dungeon,—And the remarkable Manner in which he met with his* good old Master *in* London; *who returned to* New-England, *a Passenger, in the same Ship. BOSTON,* Printed and Sold by [John] GREEN & [Joseph] RUSSELL, in Queen-Street, 1760.

TO THE READER,

AS my Capacities and Condition of Life are very low, it cannot be expected that I should make those Remarks on the Sufferings I have met with, or the kind Providence of a good GOD for my Preservation, as one in a higher Station; but shall leave that to the Reader as he goes along, and so I shall only relate Matters of Fact as they occur to my Mind—

On Monday, 25th Day of *December*, 1747, with the leave of my Master,[3] I went from *Marshfield*, with an Intention to go a Voyage to Sea, and the next Day, the 26th, got to *Plymouth*, where I immediately ship'd myself on board of a Sloop,[4] Capt. *John Howland*, Master,[5] bound to *Jamaica* and the *Bay*[6]—We sailed from *Plymouth* in a short Time, and after a pleasant Passage of about 30 Days, arrived at *Jamaica*; we was detain'd at *Jamaica* only 5 Days, from whence we sailed for the *Bay*, where we arrived safe in 10 Days. We loaded our Vessel with Logwood,[7] and sailed from the *Bay* the 25th Day of May following, and the 15th Day of *June*, we were cast away on *Cape Florida*,[8] about 5 Leagues from the Shore; being now destitute of every Help, we knew not what to do or what Course to take in this our sad Condition:—The Captain was advised, intreated, and beg'd on, by every

Person on board, to heave over but only 20 Ton of the *Wood*, and we should get clear, which if he had done, might have sav'd his Vessel and Cargo, and not only so, but his own Life, as well as the Lives of the Mate and Nine Hands, as I shall presently relate.

After being upon this Reef two Days, the Captain order'd the Boat to be hoisted out, and then ask'd who were willing to tarry on board? The whole Crew was for going on Shore at this Time, but as the Boat would not carry 12 persons at once, and to prevent any Uneasiness, the Captain, a Passenger, and one Hand tarry'd on board, while the Mate, with Seven Hands besides myself, were order'd to go on Shore in the Boat, which as soon as we had reached, one half were to be Landed, and the other four to return to the Sloop, to fetch the Captain and the others on Shore. The Captain order'd us to take with us our Arms, Ammunition, Provisions and Necessaries for Cooking, as also a Sail to make a Tent of, to shelter us from the Weather; after having left the Sloop we stood towards the Shore, and being within Two Leagues of the same, we espy'd a Number of Canoes, which we at first took to be Rocks, but soon found our Mistake, for we perceiv'd they moved towards us; we presently saw an English Colour hoisted in one of the Canoes, at the Sight of which we were not a little rejoiced, but on our advancing yet nearer, we found them, to our very great Surprize, to be *Indians* of which there were Sixty; being now so near them we could not possibly make our Escape; they soon came up with and boarded us, took away all our Arms, Ammunition, and Provision. The whole Number of Canoes (being about Twenty,) then made for the Sloop, except Two which they left to guard us, who order'd us to follow on with them; the Eighteen which made for the Sloop, went so much faster than we that they got on board above Three Hours before we came along side, and had kill'd Captain *Howland*, the Passenger and the other hand; we came to the Larboard side of the Sloop, and they order'd us round to the Starboard,[9] and as we were passing round the Bow, we saw the whole Number of *Indians*, advancing forward and loading their Guns, upon which the Mate said, "*my Lads we are all dead Men*," and before we had got round, they discharged their Small Arms upon us, and kill'd Three of our hands, viz.[10] *Reuben Young* of *Cape-Cod*, Mate; *Joseph Little* and *Lemuel Doty* of *Plymouth*, upon which I immediately jump'd overboard, chusing rather to be drowned, than to be kill'd by those barbarous and inhuman Savages. In three or four Minutes after, I heard another Volley which dispatched the other five, viz. *John Nowland*, and *Nathaniel Rich*, both belonging to *Plymouth*, and *Elkanah Collymore*, and *James Webb*, Strangers, and *Moses Newmock*, Molatto.[11] As soon as they had kill'd the whole of the People, one of the Canoes padled after me, and soon came up with me, hawled me into the Canoe, and beat me most terribly with a Cutlass, after that they ty'd me down, then this Canoe stood for the Sloop again and as soon as she came along side, the *Indians* on board the Sloop betook themselves to their Canoes, then set the Vessel on Fire, making a prodigious shouting and hallowing like so many Devils. As soon as the Vessel was burnt down to the Water's edge, the *Indians* stood for the Shore, together with our Boat, on board of which they put 5 hands. After we came to the Shore, they led me to their Hutts, where I expected nothing but immediate Death, and as they spoke broken English, were often telling me, while coming from the Sloop to the Shore, that they intended to roast me alive. But the Providence of God order'd it other ways, for He appeared for my Help, *in this Mount of Difficulty*, and they were better to me then my Fears, and soon unbound me, but set a Guard over me every Night. They kept me with them about five Weeks, during which Time they us'd me pretty well, and gave me boil'd Corn, which was what they often eat themselves. The Way I made my Escape from these Villains was this; A Spanish Schooner[12] arriving there from *St. Augustine*,[13] the Master of which, whose Name was *Romond*, asked the *Indians* to let me go on board his Vessel, which they granted, and the Captain[14] knowing me very well, weigh'd Anchor and carry'd me off to the *Havanna*,[15] and after being there four Days the *Indians* came after me, and insisted on having me again, as I was their Prisoner;—They made Application to the Governor,[16] and demanded me again from him; in answer to which the Governor told them, that as they had put the whole Crew to Death, they should not have me again, and so paid them Ten Dollars for me, adding, that he would not have them kill any Person hereafter, but take as many of them as they could, of those that should be cast away, and bring them to him for which he would pay them Ten Dollars a-head. At the *Havanna* I lived with the Governor in the Castle about a Twelve-month, where I was walking thro' the Street, I met with a Press-Gang who immediately prest me,[17] and put me into Goal,[18] and with a Number of others I was confin'd till next Morning, when we were all brought out, and ask'd who would go on board the King's Ships, four of which having been lately built, were bound to *Old-Spain*, and on my refusing to serve on board, they put me in a close Dungeon, where I was confin'd *Four Years and seven months*; during which time I often made application to the Governor, by Persons who came to see the Prisoners, but they never acquainted him with it, nor did he know all this Time what became of me, which was the means of my being confin'd there so long. But kind Providence so order'd it, that after I had been in this Place so long as the Time mention'd above the Captain of a Merchantman, belonging to *Boston*, having sprung a Leak was obliged to put into the *Havanna* to rest, and while he was at Dinner at Mrs. *Betty Howard's*, she told the Captain of my deplorable Condition, and said she would be glad, if he could by some means or other relieve me; The Captain told Mrs. *Howard* he would use his best Endeavours for my Relief and Enlargement.

Accordingly, after Dinner, [the Captain] came to the Prison, and ask'd the Keeper if he might see me; upon his Request I was brought out of the Dungeon, and after the Captain had Interrogated me, told me, he would intercede with the Governor for my Relief out of that miserable Place, which he did, and the next Day the Governor sent an order to release me; I lived with the Governor about a Year after I was delivered from the Dungeon, in which Time I endeavour'd three Times to make my Escape, the last of which proved effectual; the first Time I got on board of Captain *Marsh*, an *English* Twenty Gun Ship, with a Number of others, and lay on board conceal'd that Night; and the next Day the Ship being under sail, I thought myself safe, and so made my Appearance upon Deck, but as soon as we were discovered the Captain ordered the Boat out, and sent us all on Shore — I intreated the Captain to let me, in particular, tarry on board, begging, and crying to him, to commiserate my unhappy Condition, and added, that I had been confin'd almost five Years in a close Dungeon, but the Captain would not hearken to any Intreaties, for fear of having the Governor's Displeasure, and so I was obliged to go on Shore.

After being on Shore another Twelvemonth, I endeavour'd to make my Escape the second Time, by trying to get on board of a Sloop bound to *Jamaica*, and as I was going from the City to the Sloop, was unhappily taken by the Guard, and ordered back to the Castle, and there confined.—However, in a short Time I was set at Liberty, and order'd with a Number of others to carry the[19] Bishop from the Castle, thro' the Country, to confirm the old People, baptize Children, &c. for which he receives large Sums of Money.—I was employ'd in this Service about Seven Months, during which Time I lived very well, and then returned to the Castle again, where I had my Liberty to walk about the City, and do Work for my self;—The *Beaver*, an *English* Man of War then lay in the Harbour, and having been informed by some of the Ship's Crew that she was to sail in a few Days, I had nothing now to do, but to seek an Opportunity how I should make my Escape.[20]

Accordingly one Sunday Night the Lieutenant of the Ship with a Number of the Barge Crew were in a Tavern, and Mrs. *Howard* who had before been a Friend to me, interceded with the Lieutenant to carry me on board: the Lieutenant said he would with all his Heart, and immediately I went on board in the Barge. The next Day the *Spaniards* came along side the *Beaver*, and demanded me again, with a Number of others who had made their Escape from them, and got on board the Ship, but just before I did; but the Captain, who was a true *Englishman*, refus'd them, and said he could not answer it, to deliver up any *Englishman* under *English* Colours.—In a few Days we set Sail for *Jamaica*, where we arrived safe, after a short and pleasant Passage.

After being at *Jamaica* a short Time we sail'd for *London*, as convoy to a Fleet of Merchantmen, who all arrived safe in the *Downs*, I was turned over to another Ship, the *Arcenceil*,[21] and there remained about a Month. From this Ship I went on board the *Sandwich* of 90 Guns; on board the *Sandwich*, I tarry'd 6 Weeks, and then was order'd on board the *Hercules*, Capt. *John Porter*,[22] a 74 Gun Ship, we sail'd on a Cruize, and met with a *French* 84 Gun Ship, and had a very smart Engagement,[23] in which about 70 of our Hands were Kill'd and Wounded, the Captain lost his Leg in the Engagement, and I was Wounded in the Head by a small Shot. We should have taken this Ship, if they had not cut away the most of our Rigging; however, in about three Hours after, a 64 Gun Ship, came up with and took her—I was discharged from the *Hercules* the 12th Day of *May* 1759 (having been on board of that Ship 3 Months) on account of my being disabled in the Arm, and render'd incapable of Service, after being honourably paid the Wages due to me. I was put into the *Greenwich* Hospital where I stay'd and soon recovered.—I then ship'd myself a Cook on board Captain *Martyn*, an arm'd Ship in the King's Service. I was on board this Ship almost Two Months, and after being paid my Wages, was discharg'd in the Month of *October*.—After my discharge from Captain *Martyn*, I was taken sick in *London* of a Fever, and was confin'd about 6 Weeks, where I expended all my Money, and left in very poor Circumstances; and unhappy for me I knew nothing of my *good Master's* being in *London* at this my very difficult Time. After I got well of my sickness, I ship'd myself on board of a large Ship bound to *Guinea*,[24] and being in a publick House one Evening,[25] I overheard a Number of Persons talking about Rigging a Vessel bound to *New-England*, I ask'd them to what Part of *New-England* this Vessel was bound? They told me, to *Boston*; and having ask'd them who was Commander? they told me, Capt. *Watt*; in a few Minutes after this the Mate of the Ship came in, and I ask'd him if Captain Watt did not want a Cook, who told me he did, and that the Captain would be in, in a few Minutes; and in about half an Hour the Captain came in, and then I ship'd myself at once, after begging off from the Ship bound to *Guinea*; I work'd on board Captain *Watt's* Ship almost Three Months, before she sail'd, and one Day being at Work in the Hold, I overheard some Persons on board mention the Name of *Winslow*, at the Name of which I was very inquisitive, and having ask'd what *Winslow* they were talking about? They told me it was *General Winslow*; and that he was one of the Passengers, I ask'd them what *General Winslow*? For I never knew *my good Master*, by that Title before; but after enquiring more particularly I found it must be *Master*, and in a few Days Time the Truth was joyfully verify'd by a happy Sight of his Person, which so overcome me, that I could not speak to him for some Time—*My good Master* was exceeding glad to see me, telling me that I was like one arose from the Dead, for he thought I had been Dead a great many Years, having heard nothing of me for almost Thirteen Years.

I think I have not deviated from Truth, in any particular of this my Narrative, and tho' I have omitted a great many Things, yet what is wrote may suffice to convince the Reader, that I have been most grievously afflicted, and yet thro' the Divine Goodness, as miraculously preserved, and delivered out of many Dangers; of which I desire to retain a *grateful Remembrance*, as long as I live in the World.

And now, That in the Providence of that GOD, who delivered his Servant David out of the Paw of the Lion and out of the Paw of the Bear,[26] *I am freed from a* long *and* dreadful Captivity, among worse Savages than they; *And am return'd to my* own Native Land, to Shew how Great Things the Lord hath done for Me; *I would call upon all Men, and Say*, O Magnifie the Lord with Me, and let us Exalt his Name together!—O that Men would Praise the Lord for His Goodness, and for his Wonderful Works to the Children of Men!

NOTES

1. All that is known of Briton Hammon is found in his *Narrative*, which was advertised in the 7, 14, 21, and 28 July issues of *The Boston Evening-Post*, a weekly newspaper.

2. John Winslow (1703-1774), appointed Major-General in 1754 by colonial Massachusetts Governor William Shirley.

3. Master: apparently used here in the sense of *employer* rather than owner. Hammon seems to have been a free man. The first definition of *master* in Samuel Johnson's *Dictio-*

nary of the English Language (London, 1755) is "One who has servants; opposed to man or servant." Although slave owners often leased their own slaves out to work for others, for an owner to have permitted a slave to work more than a thousand miles away would have been an extraordinary act of faith.

4. Sloop: a single-masted vessel.

5. It was common practice at the time to identify the captain of a vessel immediately after the name of the vessel. Note that Howland is the *master* (captain of a merchant vessel) of the sloop, not the owner of Hammon.

6. The Bay: either the Bay of Honduras (Yucatan) or of Campeachy.

Compare Adam Alexander (1692?-1765), *An Historical and Chronological Deduction of the Origin of Commerce. . . .* (London, 1764): "It was in . . . 1662 that the *English*, from their Colonies on the North Continent of *America*, first began to cut down the *Logwood* Trees, growing in infinite Quantities on the uninhabited Coasts of the Province of *Jucatan*, and more especially in the *Bay of Campeachy*, where they made a Settlement for that End, as it was not near to any *Spanish* Settlement or Inhabitants. . . . By the Year 1669, that *English* Settlement was considerably increased; and much *Logwood* was carried thence both to *New-England* and *Jamaica*" (2:119). In 1672 the Spanish began to attack the English cutters and vessels, and the dispute remained unresolved throughout the eighteenth century.

7. Logwood: the source of a commercial dye.

8. Florida was a Spanish colony.

9. Larboard and Starboard: the left-hand (port) and right-hand sides, respectively, of a vessel as one looks forward.

10. Viz.: videlicet, that is, namely.

11. Molatto: mulatto, the offspring of one White and one Black parent.

12. Schooner: a two-masted vessel.

13. St. Augustine, Florida: the oldest European city in the present-day United States.

14. [Hammon's note.] The Way I came to know this Gentleman was, by his being taken last War by an *English* Privateer, and brought into *Jamaica*, while I was there. [A privateer was a privately owned, manned, and armed ship authorized by a government to conduct military operations in wartime.]

15. The capital of the Spanish colony of Cuba.

16. Francisco Antonio Cagigal de la Vega (1695-1777).

17. Press-Gang: a group of men authorized by the government to impress (press), or draft, men off the streets for naval service.

18. Gaol: jail.

19. [Hammon's note.] He is carried (by Way of Respect) in a large Two-arm Chair; the Chair is lin'd with crimson Velvet, and supported by eight Persons. [The Bishop was Pedro Augustín Morell de Santa Cruz (1694-1768).]

20. The *Beaver*, formerly a French privateer named *Trudaine*, captured in 1757, was an 18–gun sloop. Its captain was Edward Gascoigne. According to its muster book (PRO ADM 36/5071), "Britain Hammell," ordinary seaman, joined the vessel in Cuba in December 1758 and was discharged at Chatham, England, on 10 May 1759 to serve on the *Hercules*, though his name does not appear on any of the ship's muster lists through December 1759.

21. A 50–gun ship, captured from the French in 1756.

22. Jervis Henry Porter (d. 1763).

23. [Hammon's note.] A particular Account of this Engagement, has been Publish'd in the *Boston* News-Papers. [Because the French ship escaped from the encounter on 10 October 1759, her identity has been disputed. She may have been either the *Florissant* or the *Soverain*, both of which were in Admiral de la Clue Sabran's fleet.]

24. Ship bound to Guinea: a ship going to Africa to buy slaves.

25. Publick house: a tavern.

26. See 1 Samuel 17:34-37.

Jupiter Hammon[1]

(17 October 1711-ca.1800)

~

AN Evening THOUGHT. SALVATION BY CHRIST, *WITH PENETENTIAL CRIES: Composed by Jupiter Hammon, a Negro Belonging to Mr. Lloyd, of Queen's-Village, on Long-Island, the 25th of December, 1760.*

SALVATION comes by Jesus Christ alone,
  The only Son of God;
Redemption now to every one,
  That love his holy Word.
Dear Jesus we would fly to Thee,
  And leave off every Sin,
Thy tender Mercy well agree;
  Salvation from our King.
Salvation comes now from the Lord,
  Our victorious King;
His holy Name be well ador'd,
  Salvation surely bring.
Dear Jesus give thy Spirit now,
  Thy Grace to every Nation,
That han't the Lord to whom we bow,
  The Author of Salvation.
Dear Jesus unto Thee we cry,
  Give us thy Preparation;
Turn not away thy tender Eye;
  We seek thy true Salvation.
Salvation comes from God we know,
  The true and only One;
It's well agreed and certain true,
  He gave his only Son.
Lord hear our penetential Cry:
  Salvation from above;
It is the Lord that doth supply,
  With his Redeeming Love.
Dear Jesus by thy precious Blood,
  The World Redemption have:
Salvation comes now from the Lord,
  He being thy captive Slave.

Dear Jesus let the Nations cry,
    And all the People say,
Salvation comes from Christ on high,
    Haste on Tribunal Day.
We cry as Sinners to the Lord,
    Salvation to obtain;
It is firmly fixt his holy Word,
    Ye shall not cry in vain.
Dear Jesus unto Thee we cry,
    And make our Lamentation:
O let our Prayers ascend on high;
    We felt thy Salvation.
Lord turn our dark benighted Souls;
    Give us a true Motion,
And let the Hearts of all the World,
    Make Christ their Salvation.
Ten Thousand Angels cry to Thee,
    Yea louder than the Ocean.
Thou art the Lord, we plainly see;
    Thou art the true Salvation.
Now is the Day, excepted Time;
    The Day of Salvation;
Increase your Faith, do not repine:
    Awake ye every Nation.
Lord unto whom now shall we go,
    Or seek a safe Abode;
Thou hast the Word Salvation too
    The only Son of God.
Ho! every one that hunger hath,
    Or pineth after me,
Salvation be thy leading Staff,
    To set the Sinner free.
Dear Jesus unto Thee we fly;
    Depart, depart from Sin,
Salvation doth at length supply,
    The Glory of our King.
Come ye Blessed of the Lord,
    Salvation gently given;
O turn your Hearts, accept the Word,
    Your Souls are fit for Heaven.
Dear Jesus we now turn to Thee,
    Salvation to obtain;
Our Hearts and Souls do meet again,
    To magnify thy Name.
Come holy Spirit, Heavenly Dove,
    The Object of our Care;
Salvation doth increase our Love;

Our Hearts hath felt thy fear.
Now Glory be to God on High,
Salvation high and low;
And thus the Soul on Christ rely,
To Heaven surely go.
Come Blessed Jesus, Heavenly Dove,
Accept Repentance here;
Salvation give, with tender Love;
Let us with Angels share.

~

Hartford, August 4, 1778

AN ADDRESS to Miss PHILLIS WHEATLY, Ethiopian Poetess, in Boston, who came from Africa at eight years of age, and soon became acquainted with the Gospel of Jesus Christ.

Miss WHEATLY; pray give leave to express as follows:

1.

O Come you pious youth! adore
The wisdom of thy God, — Eccles[iastes]. xii.
In bringing thee from distant shore,
To learn his holy word.

2.

Thou mightst been left behind,
Amidst a dark abode; — Psal[ms]. cxxxv, 2, 3.
God's tender mercy still combin'd,
Thou hast the holy word.

3.

Fair wisdom's ways are paths of peace,
And they that walk therein, — Psal. i. 1, 2;
Shall reap the joys that never cease, — Prov[erbs]. iii, 7.
And Christ shall be their king.

4.

God's tender mercy brought thee here,
Tost o'er the raging main; — Psal. ciii, 1, 3, 4.
In Christian faith thou hast a share,
Worth all the gold of Spain.

5.

While thousands tossed by the sea,
And others settled down, — Death.

God's tender mercy set thee free
From dangers still unknown.

6.

That thou a pattern still might be,
To youth of Boston town,
The blessed Jesus set thee free,
From every sinful wound.

2 Cor[inthians]. v, 10.

7.

The blessed Jesus, who came down,
Unvail'd [sic] his sacred face,
To cleanse the soul of every wound,
And give repenting grace.

Rom[ans]. v, 21.

8.

That we poor sinners may obtain
The pardon of our sin;
Dear blessed Jesus now constrain,
And bring us flocking in.

Psal. xxxiv, 6, 7, 8.

9.

Come you, Phillis, now aspire,
And seek the living God,
So step by step thou mayst go higher,
Till perfect in the word.

Matth[ew]. vii, 7, 8.

10.

While thousands mov'd to distant shore,
And others left behind,
The blessed Jesus still adore,
Implant this in thy mind.

Psal. lxxxix, 1.

11.

Thou hast left the heathen shore,
Thro' mercy of the Lord,
Among the heathen live no more,
Come magnify thy God.

Psal. xxxiv, 1, 2, 3.

12.

I pray the living God may be,
The shepherd of thy soul;
His tender mercies still are free,
His mysteries to unfold.

Psal. lxxx, 1, 2, 3.

13.

Thou, Phillis, when thou hunger hast,
Or pantest for thy God;

Psal. xiii, 1, 2, 3.

Jesus Christ is thy relief,
Thou hast the holy word.

14.
The bounteous mercies of the Lord,
Are hid beyond the sky, — Psal. xvi, 10, 11.
And holy souls that love his word,
Shall taste them when they die.

15.
These bounteous mercies are from God,
The merits of his Son; — Psal. xxxiv, 15.
The humble soul that loves his word,
He chooses for his own.

16.
Come, dear Phillis, be advis'd,
To drink Samaria's flood: — John iv, 13, 14.
There nothing is that shall suffice,
But Christ's redeeming blood.

17.
While thousands muse with earthly toys,
And range about the street, — Matth. vi, 33.
Dear Phillis, seek for heaven's joys,
Where we do hope to meet.

18.
When God shall send his summons down,
And number saints together, — Psal. cxvi, 15.
Blest angels chant, (triumphant sound)
Come live with me for ever.

19.
The humble soul shall fly to God,
And leave the things of time, — Matth. v, 3, 8.
Start forth as 'twere at the first word,
To taste things more divine.

20.
Behold! the soul shall waft away,
Whene'er we come to die, — 1 Cor. xv, 51, 52, 53.
And leave its cottage made of clay,
In twinkling of an eye.

21.
Now glory be to the Most High,
United praises given, — Psal. cl, 6.

By all on earth, incessantly,
And all the host of heav'n.

Composed by JUPITER HAMMON, a Negro Man belonging to Mr. Joseph Lloyd, of Queen's Village on Long-Island, now in Hartford.

The above lines are published by the Author, and a number of his friends, who desire to join with him in their best regards to Miss Wheatly.

NOTES

1. No evidence exists to suggest any relationship between Briton and Jupiter Hammon. Jupiter Hammon's exact birthdate is recorded in one of the ledgers of his owner, Henry Lloyd (d. 1763). Throughout his life, Hammon belonged to members of the Lloyd family, wealthy merchants on Long Island, New York, whom he served as clerk and bookkeeper. He was also an occasional preacher. When the British captured Long Island in 1776, Joseph, one of the few non-Loyalist members of the Lloyd family, fled to Hartford, Connecticut, taking Hammon with him.

Hammon published two other poems, besides those reproduced here: "A Poem for Children with Thoughts on Death," in *A Winter Piece* (Hartford, 1782), and "A Dialogue, Entitled, 'The Kind Master and Dutiful Servant,'" in *An Evening's Improvement* (Hartford, n.d.). In addition to his poems and sermons, Hammon published *An Essay on the Ten Virgins* (Hartford, 1779), no copy of which is known to exist, and *An Address to the Negroes in the State of New York* (New York and reprinted in Philadelphia, 1787), advising his fellow slaves to bear their own condition patiently while trying to persuade their masters to manumit their children.

JAMES ALBERT UKAWSAW GRONNIOSAW

(ca.1710-1772+)

A NARRATIVE OF THE Most Remarkable Particulars *In the LIFE of* James Albert Ukawsaw Gronniosaw, *AN AFRICAN PRINCE, As related by HIMSELF.* Bath: Printed by W. Gye in Westgate-Street; and Sold by T. Mills, Bookseller, in King's-Mead-Square. Price Six-Pence. [1772.][1]

I will bring the Blind by a Way that they know not, I will lead them in Paths that they have not known: I will make darkness light before them and crooked things straight. these things will I do unto them and not forsake them. Isaiah. xlii. 16.[2]

TO THE RIGHT HONOURABLE The *Countess* of HUNTINGDON,[3] THIS NARRATIVE of my *LIFE,* And of GOD'S wonderful Dealings with me, is, *(Through Her LADYSHIP's Permission) Most humbly dedicated, By her LADYSHIP's Most obliged And obedient Servant,* JAMES ALBERT.

THE PREFACE

To the READER.

THIS *Account of the Life and spiritual Experience of* JAMES ALBERT *was taken from his own Mouth, and committed to Paper by the elegant Pen of a young* LADY *of the Town of* LEOMINSTER,[4] *for her own private Satisfaction, and without any Intention at first that it should be made public. But she has now been prevail'd on to commit it to the Press, both with a view to serve* ALBERT *and his distressed Family, who have the sole Profits arising from the Sale of it; and likewise*[5] *as it is apprehended, this little History contains Matter well worthy the Notice and Attention of every Christian Reader.*

Perhaps we have here in some Degree a Solution of that Question that has perplex'd the Minds of so many serious Persons, viz. In what Manner will God deal with those benighted Parts of the World where the Gospel of Jesus Christ hath never reached? Now it appears from the Experience of this remarkable Person, that God does not save without the Knowledge of the Truth; but, with respect to those whom he hath fore-known, though born under every outward[6] *Disadvantage, and in Regions of the grossest Darkness and Ignorance, he most amazingly acts upon and influences their Minds, and in the Course of wisely and most wonderfully appointed Providences, he brings them to the Means of spiritual Information, gradually opens to their View the Light of his Truth, and gives them full Possession and Enjoyment of the inestimable Blessings*[7] *of his Gospel. Who can doubt but that*[8] *the Suggestion so forcibly press'd upon the Mind of* ALBERT *(when a Boy) that there was a Being superior to the Sun, Moon, and Stars (the Objects of African Idolatry) came from the Father of Lights, and was, with Respect to him, the First-Fruit of the Display of Gospel-Glory? His long and perilous Journey to the Coast of Guinea,*[9] *where he was sold for a Slave, and so brought into a Christian Land; shall we consider this as the alone Effect of a curious and inquisitive Disposition? Shall we in accounting for it refer to nothing higher than mere Chance and accidental Circumstances? Whatever Infidels and Deists*[10] *may think; I trust the Christian Reader will easily discern an All-wise and Omnipotent Appointment and Direction in these Movements. He belong'd to the Redeemer of lost Sinners; he was the Purchase of his Cross; and therefore the Lord undertook to bring him by a Way he knew not, out of Darkness into his marvellous Light, that he might lead him to a saving Heart-Acquaintance and Union with the triune God in Christ reconciling the World unto himself; and not imputing their Trespasses. As his Call was very extraordinary, so there are certain Particulars exceedingly remarkable in his Experience. God has put a singular honor upon him in the Exercise of his Faith and Patience, which in the most distressing and pitiable Trials and Calamities have been found to the Praise and Glory of God. How deeply it must affect a tender Heart, not only to be reduc'd to the last Extremity himself, but to have his Wife and Children perishing for Want before his Eyes! Yet his Faith did not fail him; he put his Trust in the Lord and he was delivered. And at this Instant, though born in an exalted Station of Life, and now under the Pressure of various afflicting Providences, I am persuaded (for I know the Man) he would rather embrace the Dung-hill, having Christ in his Heart, than give up his spiritual Possessions and Enjoyment, to fill the Throne of Princes. It perhaps may not be amiss to observe that* JAMES ALBERT *left his native Country, (as near as I can guess from certain Circumstances) when he was about* 15 *Years old. He now appears to be turn'd of Sixty; has a good natural Understanding; is well acquainted with the Scriptures,*[11] *and the Things of God, has an amiable and tender Disposition, and his Character can be well attested not only at Kidderminster,*[12] *the Place of his Residence but likewise by many creditable Persons in London and other Places. Reader, recommending this Narrative to your perusal, and him who is the Subject of it to your charitable Regard,*[13]

I am your faithful and obedient Servant,
For Christ's Sake,
W. SHIRLEY.[14]

AN ACCOUNT OF *James Albert*, &c.

I Was born in the city of BOURNOU;[15] my mother was the eldest daughter of the reigning King there,[16] of which BOURNOU is the chief city. I was the youngest of six children, and particularly loved by my mother, and my grand-father almost doated on me.

I had, from my infancy, a curious turn of mind; was more grave and reserved in my disposition than either of my brothers and sisters. I often teazed them with questions they could not answer: for which reason they disliked me, as they supposed that I was either foolish, or insane. 'Twas certain that I was, at times, very unhappy in myself: it being strongly impressed on my mind that there was some GREAT MAN of power which resided above the sun, moon, and stars, the objects of our worship. My dear indulgent mother would bear more with me than any of my friends beside.—I often raised my hand[17] to heaven, and asked her who lived there? was much dissatisfied when she told me the sun, moon and stars, being persuaded, in my own mind, that there must be some SUPERIOR POWER.—I was frequently lost in wonder at the works of the Creation: was afraid, uneasy and restless, but could not tell for what. I wanted to be informed of things that no person could tell me; and was always dissatisfied.—These wonderful impressions begun in my childhood, and followed me continually 'till I left my parents, which affords me matter of admiration and thankfulness.

To this moment I grew more and more uneasy every day, in so much that one saturday, (which is the day on which we keep our sabbath) I laboured under anxieties and fears that cannot be expressed; and, what is more extraordinary, I could not give a reason for it.—I rose, as our custom is, about three o'clock, (as we are oblig'd to be at our place of worship an hour before the[18] sun rise) we say nothing in our worship, but continue on our knees with our hands held up, observing a strict silence 'till the sun is at a certain height, which I suppose to be about 10 or 11 o'clock in England: when, at a certain sign made by the priest, we get up (our duty being over), and disperse to our different houses.—Our place of meeting is under a large palm tree; we divide ourselves into many congregations; as it is impossible for the same tree to cover the inhabitants of the whole City, though they are extremely large, high and majestic; the beauty and usefulness of them are not to be described; they supply the inhabitants of the country with meat, drink and clothes;[19] the body of the palm tree is very large; at a certain season of the year they tap it, and bring vessels to receive the wine, of which they draw great quantities, the quality of which is very delicious: the leaves of this tree are of a silky nature; they are large and soft; when they are dried and pulled to pieces it has much the same appearance as the English flax, and the inhabitants of BOURNOU manufacture it for cloathing &c. This tree likewise produces a plant or substance which has the appearance of a cabbage, and very like it, in taste almost the same: it grows between the branches. Also the palm tree produces a nut, something like a cocoa, which contains a kernel, in which is a large quantity of milk, very pleasant to the taste: the shell is of a hard substance, and of a very beautiful appearance, and serves for basons, bowls, &c.

I hope this digression will be forgiven.—I was going to observe that after the duty of our Sabbath was over (on the day in which I was more distressed and afflicted than ever) we were all on our way home as usual, when a remarkable black cloud arose and covered the sun; then followed very heavy rain and thunder more dreadful than ever I had heard: the heav'ns roared, and the earth trembled at it: I was highly affected and cast down; in so much that I wept sadly; and could not follow my relations and friends home.—I was obliged to stop and felt as if my legs were tied, they seemed to shake under me: so I stood still, being in great fear of the MAN of POWER that I was persuaded in myself, lived above. One of my young companions (who entertained a particular friendship for me and I for him) came back to see for me: he asked me why I stood still in such very hard rain? I only said to him that my legs were weak, and I could not come faster: he was much affected to see me cry, and took me by the hand, and said he would lead me home, which he did. My mother was greatly alarmed at my tarrying out in such terrible weather; she asked me many questions, such as what I did so for, and if I was well? My dear mother, says I, pray tell me who is the great MAN of POWER that makes the thunder? She said, there was no power but the sun, moon and stars; that they made all our country.—I then enquired how all our people came? She answered me, from one another; and so carried me to many generations back.—Then says I, who made the *First Man*? and who made the first Cow, and the first Lyon, and where does the fly come from, as no one can make him? My mother seemed in great trouble; she was apprehensive that my senses were impaired, or that I was foolish. My father came in, and seeing her in grief asked the cause, but when she related our conversation to him, he was exceedingly angry with me, and told me he would punish me severely if ever I was so troublesome again; so that I resolved never to say any thing more to him. But I grew very unhappy in myself; my relations and acquaintance endeavoured by all the means they could think on, to divert me, by taking me to ride on goats, (which is much the custom of our country) and to shoot with a bow and arrow; but I experienced no satisfaction at all in any of these things; nor could I be easy by any means whatever: my parents were very unhappy to see me so dejected and melancholy.

About this time there came a merchant from the *Gold Coast* (the third city in GUINEA) he traded with the inhabitants of our country in ivory &c. he took great notice of my unhappy situation, and enquired into the cause; he expressed vast concern for me, and said, if my parents would part with me for a little while, and let him take me home with him, it would be of more service to me than any thing they could do for me.—He told me that if I would go with him I should see houses with wings to them walk upon the water, and should also see the white folks; and that he had many sons of my age,[20] which should be my companions; and he added to all this that he would bring me safe back again soon.—I was highly pleased with the account of this strange place, and was very desirous of going.—I seemed sensible of a secret impulse upon my mind which I could not resist that seemed to tell me I must go. When my dear mother saw that[21] I was willing to leave them, she spoke to my father and grandfather and the rest of my relations, who all agreed that I should accompany the merchant to the Gold Coast. I was the more willing as my brothers and sisters despised me, and looked on me with contempt on the account of my unhappy disposition; and even my servants slighted me, and disregarded all I said to them. I had one sister who was always exceeding fond of me, and I loved her entirely; her name was LOGWY, she was quite white, and fair, with fine light hair though my father and mother were black.—I was truly concerned to leave my beloved sister, and she cry'd most sadly to part with me, wringing her hands, and discovered[22] every sign of grief that can be imagined. Indeed if I could have known when I left my friends and country that I should never return to them again my misery on that occasion would have been inexpressible. All my relations were sorry to part with me; my dear mother came with me on a camel more than three hundred miles, the first of our journey lay chiefly through woods: at night we secured ourselves from the wild beasts by making fires all around us; we and our camels kept within the circle, or we must have been tore to pieces by the Lyons, and other wild creatures that roared terribly as soon as night came on, and continued to do so 'till morning.—There can be little said in favour of the country through which we passed; only a valley of marble that we came through which is unspeakably beautiful.—On each side of this valley are exceedingly high and almost inaccessible mountains—Some of these pieces of marble are of prodigious length and breadth, but of different sizes and colour, and shaped in a variety of forms, in a wonderful manner.—it is most of it veined with gold mixed with striking and beautiful colours; so that when the sun darts upon it, it is as pleasing a sight as can be imagined.—The merchant that brought me from BOURNOU, was in partnership with another gentleman who accompanied us; he was very unwilling that he should take me from home, as, he said, he foresaw many difficulties that would attend my going with them.—He endeavoured to prevail on the merchant to throw me into a very deep pit that was in the valley, but he refused to listen to him, and said, he was resolved to take care of me: but the other was greatly dissatisfied; and when we came to a river, which we were obliged to pass through, he purpos'd throwing me in and drowning me; but the Merchant would not consent to it, so that I was preserved.

We travelled 'till about four o'clock every day, and then began to make preparations for night, by cutting down large quantities of wood, to make fires to preserve us from the wild beasts.—I had a very unhappy and discontented journey, being in continual fear that the people I was with would murder me. I often reflected with extreme regret on the kind friends I had left, and the idea of my dear mother frequently drew tears from my eyes.—I cannot recollect how long we were in[23] going from BOURNOU to the GOLD COAST; but as there is no shipping nearer BOURNOU than that City, it was tedious in travelling so far by land, being upwards of a thousand miles.—I was heartily rejoiced when we arrived at the end of our journey: I now vainly imagin'd that all my troubles and inquietudes would terminate here; but could I have looked into futurity, I should have perceiv'd that I had much more to suffer than I had before experienc'd, and that they had as yet barely commenced.

I was now more than a thousand miles from home, without a friend or means to procure one. Soon after I came to the merchant's house, I heard the drums beat remarkably loud, and the trumpets blow—the persons accustom'd to this employ, are oblig'd to go upon[24] a very high structure, appointed for that purpose, that the sound may be heard at a great distance: They are higher than the steeples in England. I was mightily pleas'd with sounds so entirely new to me, and was very inquisitive to know the cause of this rejoicing, and ask'd many questions concerning it: I was answer'd that it was meant as a compliment to me, because I was Grandson to the King of BOURNOU.

This account gave me a secret pleasure; but I was not suffer'd[25] long to enjoy this satisfaction, for in the evening of the same day, two of the merchant's sons (boys about my own age) came running to me, and told me, that the next day I was to die, for the King intended to behead me.—I reply'd that I was sure it could not be true, for that[26] I came there to play with them, and to see houses walk upon the water with wings to them, and the white folks; but I was soon inform'd that their King imagined I was sent by my father as a spy, and would make such discoveries at my return home, as would enable them to make war with the greater advantage to ourselves; and for these reasons he had resolved that I should never return to my native country.—When I heard this I suffered misery that cannot be described.—I wished a thousand times that I had never left my friends and country. But still the ALMIGHTY was pleased to work miracles for me.

The morning I was to die, I was washed and all my gold ornaments made bright and shining, and then carried to the palace, where the King was to behead me himself (as is the custom of the place).—He was seated upon a throne at the top of an exceeding large yard, or court, which you must go through to enter the palace, it is as wide and spacious as a large field in England.—I had a lane of life-guards[27] to go through.—I guessed it to be about three hundred paces.

I was conducted by my friend, the merchant, about half way up; then he durst proceed no further: I went up to the KING alone—I went with an undaunted courage, and it pleased GOD to melt the heart of the King, who sat with his scymitar in his hand ready to behead me; yet, being himself so affected, he dropped it out of his hand, and took me upon his knee and wept over me. I put my right hand round his neck, and pressed him to my heart.—He sat me down and blessed me; and added that he would not kill me, that I should not go home, but be sold for a slave, so then I was conducted back again to the merchant's house.

The next day he took me on board a French brig;[28] but the Captain did not chuse to buy me: he said I was too small; so the merchant took me home with him again.

The partner, whom I have spoken of as my enemy, was very angry to see me return, and again proposed putting an end to my life; for he represented to the other, that I should bring them into troubles and difficulties, and that I was so little that no person would buy me.

The merchant's resolution began to waver, and I was indeed afraid that I should be put to death: but however he said he would try me once more.

A few days after a Dutch ship came into the harbour, and they carried me on board, in hopes that the Captain would purchase me.—As they went, I heard them agree, that if they could not sell me *then*, they would throw me overboard.—I was in extreme agonies when I heard this; and as soon as ever I saw the Dutch Captain, I ran to him, and put my arms round him, and said, "father, save me," (for I knew that if he did not buy me, I should be treated very ill, or, possibly, murdered). And though he did not understand my language, yet it pleased the ALMIGHTY to influence him in my behalf, and he bought me *for two yards of check*,[29] which is of more value *there*, than in England.

When I left my dear mother I had a large quantity of gold about me, as is the custom of our country, it was made into rings, and they were linked one into another, and formed into a kind of chain, and so put round my neck, and arms and legs, and a large piece hanging at one ear, almost in the shape of a pear. I found all this troublesome, and was glad when my new Master took it from me—I was now washed, and clothed in the Dutch or English manner.—My master grew very fond of me, and I loved him exceedingly. I watched every look, was always ready when he wanted me, and endeavoured to convince him, by every action, that my only pleasure was to serve him well.—I have since thought that he must have been a serious man. His actions corresponded very well with such a character.—He used to read prayers in public to the ship's crew every Sabbath day; and when I first saw him read, I was never so surprised in my life, as when I saw the book talk to my master; for I thought it did, as I observed him to look upon it, and move his lips.—I wished it would do so with me. As soon as my master had done reading I follow'd him to the place where he put the book, being mightily delighted with it, and when nobody saw me, I open'd it, and put my ear down close upon it, in great hope[30] that it wou'd say something to me; but I was very sorry and greatly disappointed, when I found it would not speak,[31] this thought immediately presented itself to me, that every body and every thing despis'd me because I was black.

I was exceedingly sea-sick at first; but when I became more accustom'd to the sea, it wore off.—My master's ship was bound for Barbadoes. When we came there, he thought fit to speak of me to several gentlemen of his acquaintance, and one of them expressed a particular desire to see me.—He had a great mind to buy me; but the Captain could not immediately be prevail'd on to part with me; but however, as the gentleman seem'd very solicitous, he at length let me go, and I was sold for fifty dollars (*four and six-penny pieces in English.*) My new master's name was Vanhorn, a young Gentleman; his home was in New-England, in the City of New-York; to which place he took me with him. He dress'd me in his livery,[32] and was very good to me. My chief business was to wait at table, and tea, and clean knives, and I had a very easy place; but the servants us'd to curse and swear surprizingly; which I learnt faster than any thing, 'twas almost the first English I could speak. If any of them affronted me, I was sure to call upon God to damn them immediately; but I was broke of it all at once, occasioned by the correction of an old black servant that liv'd in the family—One day I had just clean'd the knives for dinner, when one of the maids took one to cut bread and butter with; I was very angry with her, and called[33] upon God to damn her; when this old black man told me I must not say so. I asked him why? He replied that there was a wicked man call'd the Devil, that[34] liv'd in hell, and would take all who said these words, and put them in the fire, and burn them.—This terrified me greatly, and I was entirely broke of swearing.—Soon after this, as I was placing the china for tea, my mistress came into the room just as the maid had been cleaning it; the girl had unfortunately sprinkled the wainscot with the mop; at which my mistress was angry; the girl very foolishly answer'd her again, which made her worse, and she call'd upon God to damn her.—I was vastly concern'd to hear this, as she was a fine young lady, and was very good to me, insomuch that I could not help speaking to her, "Madam, says I, you must not say so," Why, says she? Because there is a black man call'd the Devil that lives in hell, and he will put you into the fire and burn you, and I shall be very sorry for that. Who told you this, replied my lady? Old Ned, says I. Very well, was all her answer; but she told my master of it, and he order'd that old Ned should be tyed up and whipp'd, and was[35] never suffer'd to come into the kitchen with the rest of the servants afterwards.—My mistress was not angry with me, but rather diverted with my simplicity, and by way of talk, She repeated what I had said, to many of her acquaintances that visited her; among the rest, Mr. Freelandhouse,[36] a very gracious, good Minister, heard it, and he took a great deal of notice of me, and desired my master to part with me to him. He would not hear of it at first, but, being greatly persuaded, he let me go, and Mr. Freelandhouse gave £50.[37] for me.—He took me home with him, and made me kneel down, and put my two hands together, and pray'd for me, and every night and morning he did the same.—I could not make out what it was for,[38] nor the meaning of it, nor what they spoke to when they talk'd—I thought it comical, but I lik'd it very well.—After I had been a little while with my new master I grew more familiar, and ask'd him the meaning of prayer: (I could hardly speak English to be understood) he took great pains with me, and made me understand that he pray'd to God, who liv'd in Heaven; that He was my Father and BEST Friend.—I told him that this must be a mistake; that *my* father lived at BOURNOU, and[39] I wanted very much to see him, and likewise my dear mother, and sister, and I wish'd he would be so good as to send me home to them; and I added, all that I could think of to induce him to convey me back. I appeared in great trouble, and my good master was so affected, that the tears ran down his face. He told me that God was a GREAT and GOOD SPIRIT, that He created all the world, and every person and thing in it, in Ethiopia, Africa, and America, and every where. I was delighted when I heard this: There, says I, I always thought so when I liv'd at home! Now if I had wings like an Eagle, I would fly to tell my dear mother that God is greater than the sun, moon, and stars; and that they were made by Him.

I was exceedingly pleas'd with this information of my master's, because it corresponded so well with my own opinion; I thought now if I could but get home, I should be wiser than all my country-folks, my grandfather, or father, or mother, or any of them—But though I was somewhat enlighten'd by this information of my master's, yet, I had no other knowledge of God but that He was a GOOD SPIRIT, and created every body, and every thing—I never was sensible in myself nor had any one ever told me, that He would punish the wicked, and love the just. I was only glad that I had been told there was a God because I had always thought so.

My dear kind master grew very fond of me, as was his Lady; she put me to School, but I was uneasy at that, and did not like to go; but my master and mistress requested me to learn in the gentlest terms, and persuaded me to attend my school without any anger at all; that, at last, I began to like it better, and learnt to read pretty well. My schoolmaster was a good man, his name was Vanosdore, and very indulgent to me.—I was in this state, when one sunday, I heard my master preach from these words out of the Revelations, chap. i. v. 7. "*Behold, He cometh in the clouds and every eye shall see him and they that pierc'd Him.*" These words affected me excessively: I was in great agonies because I thought my master directed them to me only; and, I fancied, that he observ'd me with unusual earnestness—I was farther confirm'd in this belief, as I look'd round the church, and could see no one person besides myself in such grief and distress as I was; I began to think that my master hated me, and was very desirous to go home, to my own country; for I thought that if God did come (as he said) He would be sure to be most angry with *me*, as I did not know what He was, nor had ever heard of him before.

I went home in great trouble, but said nothing to any body.—I was somewhat afraid of my master; I thought he disliked me.—The next text I heard him preach from was, Heb. xii. 14. "*follow peace with all men, and holiness, without which no man shall see the LORD.*" He preached the law so severely, that it made me tremble.—He said that GOD would judge the whole world, ETHIOPIA, ASIA, and[40] AFRICA, and every where.—I was now excessively perplexed, and undetermined what to do; as I had now reason to believe that my situation would be equally bad to go, as to stay.—I kept these thoughts to myself, and said nothing to any person whatever.

I should have complained to my good mistress of this great trouble of mind; but she had been a little strange to me for several days before this happened, occasioned by a story told of me by one of the maids. The servants were all jealous, and envied me the regard, and favour, shewn me by my master and mistress; and the Devil being always ready, and diligent in wickedness, had influenced this girl, to make a lye on me.—This happened about hay-harvest, and one day when I was unloading the waggon, to put the hay into the barn, she watched an opportunity, in my absence, to take the fork out of the stick,[41] and hide it: when I came again to my work, and could not find it, I was a good deal vexed, but I concluded it was dropt somewhere among the hay; so I went and bought another with my own money: when the girl saw that I had another, she was so malicious that she told my mistress that I was very unfaithful, and not the person she took me for; and that she knew, I had, without my master's permission, order'd many things in his name, that he must pay for; and as a proof of my carelessness, produc'd the fork she had taken out of the stick, and said, she found it out of doors—My lady, not knowing the truth of these things, was a little shy to me, till she mention'd it, and then I soon cleared myself, and convinc'd her these accusations were false.

I continued in a most unhappy state for many days. My good mistress insisted on knowing what was the matter. When I made known my situation, she gave me John Bunyan on the holy war, to read;[42] I found his experience similar to my own, which gave me reason to suppose he must be a bad man; as I was convinc'd of my own corrupt nature, and the misery of my own heart: and[43] as he acknowledg'd that he was likewise in the same condition, I experienc'd no relief at all in reading his work, but rather the reverse.—I took the book to my lady, and inform'd her I did not like it at all, it[44] was concerning a wicked man as bad as myself; and I[45] did not chuse to read it, and I desir'd her to give me another, wrote by a better man that was holy and[46] without sin.—She assur'd me that John Bunyan was a good man, but she could not convince me; I thought him too much like myself to be upright, as his experience seemed to answer with my own.

I am very sensible that nothing but the great power and unspeakable mercies of the Lord could relieve my soul from the heavy burden it laboured under at that time.—A few days after my master gave me Baxter's *Call to the unconverted*:[47] This was no relief to me neither; on the contrary, it occasioned as much distress as the other had done before, *as it* invited all to come to *Christ*; and I found myself so wicked and miserable, that I could not come—This consideration threw me into agonies that cannot be described; insomuch, that I even attempted to put an end to my life—I took one of the large case-knives, and went into the stable with an intent to destroy myself; and as I endeavoured with all my strength to force the knife into my side, it bent double. I was instantly struck with horror at the thought[48] of my own rashness, and my conscience told me that had I succeeded in this attempt I should probably have gone to hell.

I could find no relief, nor the least shadow of comfort; the extreme distress of my mind so affected my health that I continued very[49] ill for three Days and Nights; and would admit of no means to be taken for my recovery, though my lady was very kind, and sent many things to me; but I rejected every means of relief and wished to die—I would not go into my own bed, but lay in the stable upon straw—I felt all the horrors of a troubled conscience, so hard to be born, and saw all the vengeance of God ready to overtake me—I was sensible that there was no way for me to be saved unless I came to *Christ*, and I could not come to Him: I thought it was impossible that He should receive such a sinner as me.

The last night that I continued in this place, in the midst of my distress, these words were brought home upon my mind, "*Behold the Lamb of God*."[50] I was something comforted at this, and began to grow easier and wished for day that I might find these words in my bible—I rose very early the following morning, and went to my school-master, Mr. Vanosdore, and communicated the situation of my mind to him: he was greatly rejoiced to find me enquiring the way to Zion,[51] and blessed the Lord who had worked so wonderfully for me, a poor heathen.—I was more familiar with this good gentleman than with my master, or any other person; and found myself more at liberty to talk to him: he encouraged me greatly, and prayed with me frequently, and I was always benefited by his discourse.

About a quarter of a mile from my Master's house stood a large remarkably fine Oak-tree, in the midst of a wood; I often used to be employed there in cutting down trees, (a work I was very fond of) and I seldom failed going to this place every day; sometimes twice a day if I could be spared. It was the greatest pleasure I ever experienced to set[52] under this Oak, for there I used to pour out my complaints to[53] the LORD: and when I had any particular grievance, I used to go there, and talk to the tree, and tell my sorrows, as if it were to a friend.

Here I often lamented my own wicked heart, and undone state; and found more comfort and consolation than I ever was sensible of before.—Whenever I was treated with ridicule or[54] contempt, I used to come here and find peace. I now began to relish the book my Master gave me, Baxter's *Call to the unconverted*, and took great delight in it. I was always[55] glad to be employ'd in cutting wood, 'twas a great part of my business, and I follow'd it with delight, as I was then quite alone, and my heart lifted up to GOD, and I was enabled to pray continually; and blessed for ever be his Holy Name, he faithfully answer'd my prayers. I can never be thankful enough to Almighty GOD for the many comfortable opportunities I experienced there.

It is possible the circumstance I am going to relate will not gain credit with many; but this I know, that the joy and comfort it conveyed to me, cannot be expressed and only conceived by those who have experienced the like.

I was one day in a most delightful frame of mind; my heart so overflowed with love and gratitude to the Author of all my comforts.—I was so drawn out of myself, and so fill'd and awed by the Presence of God that I saw (or thought I saw) light inexpressible dart down from heaven upon me, and shone around me for the space of a minute.—I continued on my knees, and joy unspeakable took possession of my soul.—The peace and serenity which filled my mind after this was wonderful, and cannot be told.—I would not have changed situations, or been any one but myself for the world. I blessed God for my poverty, that I had no worldly riches or grandeur to draw my heart from Him. I wish'd at that time, if it had been possible for me, to have continued on that spot for ever. I felt an unwillingness in myself to have any thing more to do with the world, or to mix with society again. I seemed to possess a full assurance that my sins were forgiven me. I went home all my way rejoicing, and this text of scripture came full upon my mind. "*And I will make an everlasting covenant with them, that I will not turn away from them, to do them good; but I will put my fear in their hearts that they shall not depart from me.*"[56] The first opportunity that presented itself, I went to my old school-master, and made known to him the happy state of my soul who joined with me in praise to God for his mercy to me the vilest of sinners.—I was now perfectly easy, and had hardly a wish to make beyond what I possess'd, when my temporal comforts were all blasted by the death of my dear and worthy Master[57] Mr. Freelandhouse, who was taken from this world rather suddenly: he had but a short illness, and died of a fever. I held his hand in mine, when he departed; he told me he had given me my freedom, I was at liberty to go where I would.—He added, that he had always pray'd for me and hop'd I should be kept unto the end. My master left me by his will ten pounds, and my freedom.

I found that if he had lived, 'twas his intention to take me with him to Holland, as he had often mention'd me to some friends of his there that were desirous to see me; but I chose to continue with my Mistress who was as good to me as if she had been my mother.

The loss of Mr. Freelandhouse distress'd me greatly, but I was render'd still more unhappy by the clouded and perplex'd situation of my mind; the great enemy of my soul being ready to torment me, would present my own misery to me in such striking light, and distress me with doubts, fears, and such a deep sense of my own unworthiness, that after all the comfort and encouragement I had received, I was often tempted to believe I should be a Cast-away[58] at last.—The more I saw of the Beauty and Glory of God, the more I was humbled under a sense of my own vileness. I often repair'd to my old place of prayer, and I seldom came away without consolation. One day this Scripture was apply'd to my mind, "*And ye are compleat in Him which is the Head of all principalities and powers.*"[59]—The Lord was pleas'd to comfort me by the application of many gracious promises at times when I was ready to sink under my trouble. "*Wherefore He is able also to save them to the uttermost that come unto God by Him seeing He ever liveth to make intercession for them.*"[60] Heb[rews]. x. ver.[61] 14. "*For by one offering He hath perfected forever them that are sanctified.*"

My kind indulgent Mistress lived but two years after my Master. Her death was a great affliction to me. She left five sons, all gracious young men, and Ministers of the Gospel.—I continued with them all, one after another, till they died; they liv'd but four years after their parents, when it pleased God to take them to Himself. I was now quite destitute, without a friend in the world,[62] but I who had so often experienced the Goodness of GOD, trusted in Him to do what He pleased with me.—In this helpless condition I went into the wood to prayer as usual; and tho' the snow was a considerable height, I was not sensible of cold, or any other inconveniency.—At times indeed when I saw the world frowning round me, I was tempted to think that the LORD had forsaken me. I found great relief from the contemplation of these words in Isaiah xlix. v.[63] 16. "*Behold I have graven thee on the palms of my hands; thy walls are continually before me.*" And very many comfortable promises were sweetly applied to me. The lxxxix.[64] Psalm and 34th verse, *My covenant will I not break, nor alter the thing that is gone out of my lips.* Hebrews, chap. xvi.[65] v. 17. 18. Phillipians, chap. i. v. 6;[66] and several more.

As I had now lost all my dear and valued friends, every place in the world was alike to me. I had for a great while entertain'd a desire to come to ENGLAND.—I imagined that all the Inhabitants of this Island were *Holy*; because all those who had visited my Master from thence were good, (Mr. Whitefield[67] was his particular friend) and the authors of the books that had been given me were all English. But above all the places in the world, I wish'd to see Kidderminster, for I could not but think that on the spot where Mr. Baxter had liv'd, and preach'd, the people must be all *Righteous*.

The situation of my affairs requir'd that I should tarry a little longer in NEW-YORK, as I was something in debt, and was embarrass'd how to pay it.—About this time a young Gentleman that was a particular acquaintance of one of my young Master's, pretended to be a friend to me, and promis'd to pay my debts, which was three pounds; and he assur'd me he would never expect the money again.—But, in less than a month, he came and demanded it; and when I assur'd him I had nothing to pay, he threatened to sell me.—Though I knew he had no right to do that, yet as I had no friend in the world to go to, it alarm'd me greatly.—At length he purpos'd[68] my going a Privateering,[69] that I might by these means be enabled to pay him, to which I agreed.—Our Captain's name was — —. I went in Character of Cook[70] to him.—Near St. Domingo[71] we came up to five French ships, Merchant-men.—We had a very smart engagement that continued from eight in the morning till three in the afternoon; when victory declar'd on our side.—Soon after this we were met by three English ships which join'd us, and that encourag'd us to attack a fleet of 36 Ships.—We boarded the three first and then follow'd the others; and had the same success with twelve; but the rest escap'd us.—There was a great deal of blood shed, and I was near death several times, but the LORD preserv'd me.

I met with many enemies, and much persecution, among the sailors; one of them was very unkind to me, and studied ways to vex and teaze me.—I can't[72] help mentioning one circumstance that hurt me more than all the rest, which was, that he snatched a book out of my hand that I was very fond of, and used frequently to amuse myself with, and threw it into the sea.—But what is remarkable he was the first that was killed in our engagement.—I don't pretend to say that this happen'd because he was not my friend; but I thought 'twas a very awful Providence to see how the enemies of the LORD are cut off.

Our Captain was a cruel hard-hearted man. I was excessively sorry for the prisoners we took in general; but the pitiable case of one young Gentleman grieved me to the heart.—He appeared very amiable; was strikingly handsome. Our Captain took four thousand pounds from him; but that did not satisfy him, as he imagin'd he was possess'd of more, and had somewhere conceal'd it, so that the Captain threatened him with death, at which he appear'd in the deepest distress, and took the buckles out of his shoes, and untied his hair, which was very fine and long; and in which several valuable rings were fasten'd. He came into the Cabbin to me, and in the most obliging terms imaginable ask'd for something to eat and drink; which when I gave him, he was so thankful and pretty in his manner that my heart bled for him; and I heartily wish'd that I could have spoken in any language in which the ship's crew would[73] not have understood me; that I might have let him know his danger; for I heard the Captain say he was resolv'd upon his death; and he put his barbarous design in execution, for he took him on shore with one of the sailors, and there they shot him.

This circumstance affected me exceedingly, I could not put him out of my mind a long while.—When we returned to NEW-YORK the Captain divided the prize-money among us, that we had taken. When I was call'd upon[74] to receive my part, I waited upon Mr. ——, (the Gentleman that[75] paid my debt and was the occasion of my going abroad) to know if he chose to go[76] with me to receive my money or if I should bring him what I owed.—He chose to go with me; and when the Captain laid my money on the table ('twas an hundred and thirty-five pounds) I desir'd Mr. —— to take what I was indebted to him; and he swept it all into his handkerchief, and would[77] never be prevail'd on to return a farthing of money,[78] nor any thing at all beside.—And he likewise secur'd a hogshead[79] of sugar which was my property from the same ship. The Captain was very angry with him for this piece of cruelty to me, as was every other person that heard it.—But I have reason to believe (as he was one of the Principal Merchants in the city) that he transacted business for him and on that account did not chuse to quarrel with him.

At this time a very worthy Gentleman, a Wine Merchant, his name Dunscum,[80] took me under his protection, and would have recovered my money for me if I had chose it; but I told him to let it alone; that I wou'd rather be quiet.—I believed that it would not prosper with him, and so it happen'd, for by a series of losses and misfortunes he became poor, and was soon after drowned, as he was[81] on a party of pleasure.—The vessel was driven out to sea, and struck against a rock by which means every soul perished.

I was very distress'd when I heard it, and felt greatly for his family who were reduc'd to very low circumstances.—I never knew how to set a proper value on money. If I had but a little meat and drink to supply the present necessaries of life, I never wish'd for more; and when I had any, I always gave it if ever I saw an object in distress. If it was not for my dear Wife and Children I should pay as little regard to money now as I did at that time.—I continu'd some time with Mr. Dunscum as his servant; he was very kind to me.—But I had a vast inclination to visit ENGLAND, and wish'd continually that it would please Providence to make a clear way for me to see this Island. I entertain'd a notion that if I could get to ENGLAND I should never more experience either cruelty or ingratitude, so that I was very desirous to get among Christians. I knew Mr. Whitefield very well.—I had heard him preach often at NEW-YORK. In this disposition I listed[82] in the twenty eighth Regiment of Foot,[83] who were design'd for Martinico, in the late war.—We went in Admiral Pocock's fleet,[84] from New-York to Barbadoes; from thence to Martinico.—When that was taken, we proceded to the Havannah, and took that place likewise.—There I got discharged.

I was then worth about thirty pounds; but I never regarded money in the least, nor would I tarry to receive[85] my prize-money least I should lose my chance of going to England.—I went with the Spanish prisoners to Spain; and came to Old-England with the English prisoners.—I cannot describe my joy when we arrived within sight of Portsmouth. But I was astonished when we landed to hear the inhabitants of that place curse and swear, and otherwise profane. I expected to find nothing but goodness, gentleness and meekness in this Christian Land, I then suffer'd great perplexities of mind.

I enquir'd if any serious Christian people resided there, the woman I made this enquiry of, answer'd me in the affirmative; and added that she was one of them.—I was heartily glad to hear her say so. I thought I could give her my whole heart: she kept a Public-House. I deposited with her all the money that I had not an immediate occasion for; as I thought it would be safer with her.—It was 25 guineas but 6 of them I desired her to lay out to the best advantage, to buy me some shirts, hat[86] and some other necessaries. I made her a present of a very handsome large looking glass that I brought with me from Martinico, in order to recompence her for the trouble I had given her. I must do this woman the justice to acknowledge that she did lay out some little for my use, but the 19 guineas and part of the 6,[87] with my watch, she would not return, but denied that I ever gave it her.

I soon perceived that I was got among bad people, who defrauded me of my money and watch; and that all my promis'd happiness was blasted. I had no friend but GOD and I pray'd to Him earnestly. I could scarcely believe it possible that the place where so many eminent Christians had lived and preached could abound with so much wickedness and deceit. I thought it worse than *Sodom*[88] (considering the great advantages they have) I cryed like a child and that almost continually: at length GOD heard my prayers, and rais'd me a friend indeed.

This publican had a brother who lived on Portsmouth-common, his wife was a very serious good woman.—When she heard of the treatment I had met with, she came and enquired into my real situation and was greatly troubled at the ill usage I had received, and took me home to her own house.—I now began to rejoice, and my prayer was turned into praise. She made use of all the arguments in her power to prevail on her who had wronged me, to return my watch and money, but it was to no purpose, as she had given me no receipt and I had nothing to show for it, I could not demand it.—My good friend was excessively angry with her and obliged her to give me back four guineas, which she said she gave me out of charity: Though in fact it was my own, and much more. She would have employed some rougher means to oblige her to give up my money, but I would not suffer[89] her. let it go says I "My GOD is in heaven." Still I did not mind my loss in the least; all that grieved me was, that I had been disappointed in finding some Christian friends, with whom I hoped to enjoy a little sweet and comfortable society.

I thought the best method that I could take now, was to go to London, and find out Mr. Whitefield, who was the only living soul I knew in England, and get him to direct me to some way or other[90] to procure a living without being troublesome to any Person.—I took leave of my christian friend at Portsmouth, and went in the stage to London.—A creditable tradesman in the City, who went up with me in the stage, offer'd to show me the way to Mr. Whitefield's Tabernacle.[91] Knowing that I was a perfect stranger, I thought it very kind, and accepted his offer; but he obliged me to give him half-a-crown for going with me, and likewise insisted on my giving him five shillings more for conducting me to Dr. Gifford's Meeting.[92]

I began now to entertain a very different idea of the inhabitants of England, than what I had figur'd to myself before I came amongst[93] them.—Mr. Whitefield received me very friendly, was heartily glad to see me, and directed me to a proper place to board and lodge in Petticoat-Lane, till he could think of some way to settle me in, and paid for my lodging, and all my expences. The morning after I came to my new lodging, as I was at breakfast with the gentlewoman of the house, I heard the noise of some looms over our heads: I enquir'd what it was; she told me that a person was weaving silk.—I expressed a great desire to see it, and asked if I might: She told me she would go up with me; she[94] was sure I should be very welcome. She was as good as her word, and as soon as we enter'd the room, the person that was weaving look'd about, and smiled upon us, and I loved her from that moment.—She ask'd me many questions, and I in return talk'd a great deal to her. I found that she was a member of Mr. Allen's Meeting,[95] and I begun to entertain a good opinion of her, though I was almost afraid to indulge this inclination, least she should prove like all the rest that I had met with at Portsmouth, &c. and which had almost given me a dislike to all white women.—But after a short acquaintance I had the happiness to find she was very different, and quite sincere, and I was not without hope that she entertain'd some esteem for me. We often went together to hear Dr. Gifford, and as I had always a propensity to relieve every object in distress as far as I was able, I used to give to all that complain'd to me; sometimes half a guinea at a time, as I did not understand the real value of it.—This good woman took great pains to correct and advise me in that and many other respects.

After I had been in London about six weeks I was recommended to the notice of some of my late Master Mr. Freelandhouse's acquaintance, who had heard him speak frequently of me. I was much persuaded by them to go to Holland.—My Master lived there before he bought me, and used to speak of me so respectfully among his friends there, that it raised in them a curiosity to see me; particularly the Gentlemen engaged in the Ministry, who expressed a desire to hear my experience and examine me. I found that it was my good old Master's design that I should have gone if he had lived; for which reason I resolved upon going to Holland, and informed my dear friend Mr. Whitefield of my intention; he was much averse to my going at first, but after I gave him my reasons appeared very well satisfied. I likewise informed my Betty (the good woman that I have mentioned above) of my determination to go to Holland and I told her that I believed she was to be my Wife: and if it was the LORD's Will I desired it, but not else.—She made me very little answer, but has since told me, she did not think it at that time.

I embarked at Tower-warf at four o'clock in the morning, and arriv'd at Amsterdam the next day by three o'clock in the afternoon. I had several letters of recommendation to my old master's friends who receiv'd me very graciously. Indeed, one of the chief Ministers was particularly good to me; he kept me at his house[96] a long while, and took great pleasure in asking me questions, which I answer'd with delight, being always ready to say, "*Come unto me all ye that fear GOD, and I will tell what he hath done for my Soul.*"[97] I cannot but admire the footsteps of Providence; astonish'd that I should be so wonderfully preserved! Though the Grandson of a King, I have wanted bread, and should have been glad with the hardest crust I ever saw. I who, at home, was surrounded and guarded by slaves, so that no indifferent person might approach me, and clothed with gold, have been inhumanly threatened with death; and frequently wanted clothing to defend me from the inclemency of the weather; yet I never murmured, nor was I ever discontented.—I am willing, and even desirous of being counted as nothing, a stranger in the world, and a pilgrim here; for "*I know that my* REDEEMER *liveth,*"[98] and I'm thankful for every trial and trouble that I've met with, as I am not without hope that they have all been sanctified to me.

The Calvinist Ministers desired to hear my Experience from myself, which proposal I was very well pleased with: So I stood before 38[99] Ministers every Thursday for seven weeks together, and they were all very well satisfied, and persuaded I was what I pretended to be.—They wrote down my experience as I spoke it; and the LORD ALMIGHTY was with me at that time in a remarkable manner, and gave me words and enabled me to answer them; so great was his mercy to take me in hand a poor blind heathen.

At this time a very rich Merchant at[100] AMSTERDAM offered to take me into his family in the capacity of his Butler, and I very willingly accepted it.—He was a gracious worthy Gentleman and very good to me.—He treated me more like a friend than a servant.—I tarried there a twelvemonth but was not thoroughly contented, I wanted to see my wife; (that is now) and for that reason I wished to return to ENGLAND, I wrote to her once in my absence, but she did not answer my letter; and I must acknowledge if she had, it would have given me a less opinion of her.[101]—My Master and Mistress persuaded me much not to leave them and likewise their two Sons who entertained a good opinion of me; and if I had found my Betty married on my arrival in ENGLAND, I should have returned to them again immediately.

My Lady purposed my marrying her maid; she was an agreeable young woman, had saved a great deal of money, but I could not fancy her, though she was willing to accept of me, but I told her my inclinations were engaged in ENGLAND, and I could think of no other Person.—On my return home, I found my Betty disengaged.—She had refused several offers in my absence, and told her sister that, she thought, if ever she married I was to be her husband.

Soon after I came home, I waited on Doctor Gifford, who took me into his family and was exceedingly good to me. The character of this pious worthy Gentleman is well known; my praise can be of no use or signification at all.—I hope I shall ever gratefully remember the many favours I have received from him.—Soon after I came to Doctor Gifford I expressed a desire to be admitted into their Church, and set[102] down with them; they told me I must first be baptized; so I gave in my experience before the Church, with which they were very well satisfied, and

I was baptized by Doctor Gifford with some others. I then made known my intentions[103] of being married; but I found there were many objections against it because the person I had fixed on was poor. She was a widow, her husband had left her in debt, and with a child, so that they persuaded me against it out of real regard to me.—But I had promised and was resolved to have her; as I knew her to be a gracious woman, her poverty was no objection to me, as they had nothing else to say against her. When my friends found they could not alter my opinion respecting her, they wrote to Mr. Allen, the Minister she attended, to persuade her to leave me; but he replied he would not interfere at all, that we might do as we would. I was resolved that[104] all my wife's little debt should be paid before we were married; so that I sold almost every thing I had, and[105] with all the money I could raise cleared all that she owed, and I never did any thing with a better will in all my Life, because I firmly believed that we should be very happy together, and so it prov'd, for she was given me from the LORD. And I have found her a blessed partner, and we have never repented, tho' we have gone through many great troubles and difficulties.

My wife got a very good living by[106] weaving, and could do extremely well; but just at that time there was great disturbance among the weavers; so that I was afraid to let my wife work, least they should insist on my being one of the rioters[107] which I could not think of, and, possibly, if I had refused to do so, they would have knock'd me on the head.—So that by these means my wife could get no employ, neither had I work enough to maintain my family. We had not yet been married a year before all these misfortunes overtook us.

Just at this time a gentleman, that seemed much concerned for us, advised us to go into *Essex* with him and promised to get me employed.—I accepted his kind proposal, and he spoke to a friend of his, a Quaker, a gentleman of large fortune, who resided a little way out of the town of *Colchester*, his name was *Handbarar*; he ordered his steward to set me to work.

There were several employed in the same way with myself. I was very thankful and contented though my wages were but small.—I was allowed but eight-pence a day, and found myself;[108] but after I had been in this situation a fortnight, my Master, being told that a Black was at work for him, had an inclination to see me. He was pleased to talk with me for some time, and at last enquired what wages I had; when I told him he declared, it was too little, and immediately ordered his Steward to let me have eighteen pence a day, which he constantly gave me after; and I then did extremely well.

I did not bring my wife with me: I came first alone, and it was my design, if things answered according to our wishes, to send for her—I was now thinking to desire her to come to me, when I receiv'd a letter to inform me she[109] was just brought to bed and in want of many necessaries.—This news was a great trial to me and a fresh affliction: but my GOD, *faithful and abundant in mercy*,[110] forsook me not in this trouble.—As I could not read *English*, I was obliged to apply to some person to read the letter I received, relative to my wife.[111] I was directed by the good Providence of GOD, to a worthy young gentleman, a Quaker, and friend of my Master.—I desired he would take the trouble to read my letter for me, which he readily comply'd with and was greatly moved and affected at the contents; insomuch that he said he would undertake to make a gathering[112] for me, which he did and was the first to contribute to it himself. The money was sent that evening to LONDON by a person who happen'd to be going there; nor was this ALL the goodness I experienced from these kind friends, for, as soon as my wife came about and was fit to travel, they sent for her to me, and were at the whole expence of her coming; so evidently has the love and mercy of GOD appeared through every trouble that ever I experienced. We went on very comfortably all the summer.—We lived in a little cottage near Mr. *Handbarrar's* House; but when the winter came on I was discharged, as he had no further occasion for me. And now the prospect began to darken upon us again. We thought it most adviseable to move our habitation a little nearer to the Town, as the house we lived in was very cold, and wet, and ready to tumble down.

The boundless goodness of GOD to me has been so very great, that with the most humble gratitude I desire to prostrate myself before Him; for I have been wonderfully supported in every affliction.—My GOD never left me. I perceived light *still* thro' the thickest darkness.

My dear wife and I were now both unemployed, we could get nothing to do. The winter prov'd remarkably severe, and we were reduc'd to the greatest distress imaginable.—I was always very shy at asking for any thing; I could never beg; neither did I chuse to make known our wants to any person, for fear of offending, as we were entire strangers; but our last bit of bread was gone, and I was obliged to think of something to do for our support.—I did not mind for myself at all; but to see my dear wife and children in want, pierc'd me to the heart.—I now blamed myself for bringing her from London, as doubtless had we continued there we might have found friends to have kept us from starving. The snow was at this season remarkably deep; so that we could see no prospect of being relieved: In this melancholy situation, not knowing what step to pursue, I resolved to make my case known to a Gentleman's Gardiner, that lived near us, and entreat him to employ me: but when I came to him my courage failed me, and I was ashamed to make known our real situation.—I endeavoured all I could to prevail on him to set me to work, but to no purpose: he assur'd me it was not in his power: but just when I was about to leave him, he asked me if I would accept of some Carrots? I took them with great thankfulness, and carried them home: he gave me four, they were very large and fine.—We had nothing to make a fire with, so consequently we could not boil them: But was glad to have them to eat *raw*. Our youngest child was then an infant; so that my wife was obliged to chew it, and fed her in that manner for several days.—We allowed ourselves but one every day, least they should not last 'till we could get some other supply. I was unwilling to eat at all myself; nor would I take any the last day that we continued in this situation, as I could not bear the thought that my dear[113] wife and children would be in want of every[114] means of support. We lived in this manner 'till our carrots were gone: then my Wife began to lament because of our poor babies: but I comforted her all

I could; still hoping and believing, that *my* GOD would not let us die: but that it would please Him to relieve us, which *He* did almost by a Miracle.

We went to bed, as usual, before it was quite dark, (as we had neither fire nor candle) but we had not been there long before some person knocked at the door & enquir'd if *James Albert* lived there? I answer'd in the affirmative, and rose immediately; as soon as I open'd the door I found it was the servant of an eminent Attorney who resided at *Colchester*.—He asked how it was with me? if I was almost starv'd? I burst out a crying, and told him that I was indeed. He said that his master suppos'd so, and that he wanted to speak with me, and I must return with him. This Gentleman's name was *Danniel*, he was a sincere good christian. He used to stand and talk with me frequently when I work'd on the road for Mr. *Handbarrar*, and would have employed me himself, if I had wanted work.—When I came to his house he told me that he had thought a great deal about me of late, and was apprehensive that I must be in want, and could not be satisfied till he had sent to enquire after me. I made known my distress to him, at which he was greatly affected; and generously gave me a guinea; and promis'd to be kind to me in future. I could not help exclaiming, *O the boundless mercies of my God*! I pray'd unto Him, and He has heard me; I trusted in Him, and He has preserv'd me: where shall I begin to praise Him, or how shall I love Him enough?

I went immediately and bought some bread and cheese and coal and carried it home. My dear wife was rejoiced to see me return with something to eat. She instantly got up and dressed our Babies, while I made a fire, and the first Nobility in the land never made a better meal.—We did not forget to thank the LORD for all his goodness to us.—Soon after this, as the spring came on, Mr. Peter *Daniel* employed me in helping to pull down a house, and rebuilding it. I had then very good work, and full employ: he sent for my wife, and children to *Colchester*, and provided us a house where we lived very comfortably.—I hope I shall always gratefully acknowledge his kindness to myself and family. I worked at this house for more than a year, till it was finished; and after that I was employed by several successively, and was never so happy as when I had something to do; but perceiving the winter coming on, and work rather slack, I was apprehensive that we should again be in want or become troublesome to our friends.

I had at this time an offer made me of going to *Norwich* and having constant employ.—My wife seemed pleased with this proposal, as she supposed that she might get work there in the weaving-manufactory, being the business she was brought up to, and more likely to succeed there than any[115] other place; and we thought as we had an opportunity of moving to a Town where we could[116] both be employ'd, it was most adviseable to do so; and that probably we might settle there for our lives.—When this step was resolv'd on, I went first alone to see how it would answer; which I very much repented after, for it was not in my power immediately to send my wife any supply, as I fell into the hands of a Master[117] that was neither kind nor considerate; and she was reduced to great distress, so that she was oblig'd to sell the few goods that we had, and when I sent for her was[118] under the disagreeable necessity of parting with our bed.

When she came to *Norwich*, I hired a room ready furnished.—I experienced a great deal of difference in the carriage of my Master from what I had been accustomed to from some of my other Masters. He was very irregular in his payments to me.—My wife hired a loom and wove all the leisure time she had and we began to do very well, till we were overtaken by fresh misfortunes. Our three poor children fell ill of the small pox; this was a great trial to us; but still I was persuaded in myself we should not be forsaken.—And[119] I did all in my power to keep my dear partner's spirits from sinking. Her[120] whole attention was now taken up with the children as[121] she could mind nothing else, and all I could get was but little to support a family in such a situation, beside paying for the hire of our room, which I was obliged to omit doing for several weeks: but the woman to whom we were indebted would not excuse us, tho' I promised she should have the first money we could get after my children came about, but she would not be satisfied and had the cruelty to threaten us that if we did not pay her immediately she would turn us all into the street.

The apprehension of this plunged me in[122] the deepest distress, considering the situation of my poor babies: if they had been in health I should have been less sensible of this misfortune. But My GOD, *still faithful to his promise*, raised me up a friend. Mr. Henry Gurdney,[123] a Quaker, a gracious gentleman heard of our distress, he sent a servant of his own to the woman we hired our room of, paid our rent, and bought all the goods, with my wife's loom, and gave it us all.

Some other gentlemen, hearing of his design, were pleased to assist him in these generous acts, for which we never can be thankful enough; after this my children soon came about; we began[124] to do pretty well again; my dear wife work'd hard and constant when she could get work, but it was upon a disagreeable footing as[125] her employ was so uncertain, sometimes she could get nothing to do and at other times when the weavers at *Norwich* had orders from LONDON they were so excessively hurried, that the people they employ'd were oblig'd to work on the *Sabbath-day*; but this my wife would never do, and it was matter of uneasiness to us that we could not get our living in a regular manner, though we were both diligent, industrious, and willing to work. I was far from being happy in my Master, he did not use me well. I could scarcely ever get my money from him; but I continued patient 'till it pleased GOD to alter my situation.

My worthy friend Mr. Gurdney advised me to follow the employment of chopping chaff, and bought me an instrument for that purpose. There were but few persons in the town that made this their business beside myself; so that I did very well indeed and became quite easy and happy.—But we did not continue long in this comfortable state: Many of the inferior people were envious and ill-natur'd and set up the same employ and work'd under price on purpose to get my business from me, and they succeeded so well that I could hardly get anything to do, and became again unfortunate: Nor did this misfortune come alone, for just at this time we lost one of our little girls who died of a fever; this circumstance occasion'd us new troubles, for the Baptist Minister refused to bury her because we were not their members. The Parson of the parish denied us[126] because she had never been baptized.[127] I applied to the Quakers, but met with no success; this was one of the greatest trials I had ever met with, as we did not know what to do with our poor baby.—At length I resolv'd to dig a grave in the garden behind the house, and bury her there; when the Parson of the parish sent to tell me he would bury the child, but did not chuse to read the burial service over her. I told him that I did not mind[128] whether he would or no, as the child could not hear it.

We met with a great deal of ill treatment after this, and found it very difficult to live.—We could scarcely get work to do, and were obliged to pawn our cloaths. We were ready to sink under our troubles.—When I proposed to my wife to go to *Kidderminster* and try if we could do there. I had always an inclination for that place, and now more than ever as I had heard *Mr. Fawcet*[129] mentioned in the most respectful manner, as a pious worthy Gentleman, and I had seen his name in a favourite book of mine, Baxter's[130] *Saints everlasting rest*; and as the manufactory of[131] *Kidderminster* seemed to promise my wife some employment, she readily came into my way of thinking.

I left her once more, and set out for *Kidderminster*, in order to judge if the situation would suit us.—As soon as I came there, I waited on *Mr. Fawcet*, who was pleased to receive me very kindly and recommended me to *Mr. Watson* who employed me in twisting silk and worsted together. I continued here about a fortnight, and when I thought that it would answer our expectation, I returned to *Norwich* to fetch my wife; she was then near her time,[132] and too much indisposed. So we were obliged to tarry until she was brought to bed, and as soon as she could conveniently travel we came to *Kidderminster*, but we brought nothing with us as we were obliged to sell all we had to pay our debts and the expences of my wife's illness, &c.

Such is our situation at present.—My wife, by hard labor at the loom, does every thing that can be expected from her towards the maintenance of our family; and GOD is pleased to incline his People at times to yield us their charitable assistance; being myself through age and infirmity able to contribute but little to their support.[133] As Pilgrims, and very poor Pilgrims, we are travelling through many difficulties towards our HEAVENLY HOME, and waiting patiently for his gracious call, when the LORD shall deliver us out of the evils of this present world[134] and bring us to the EVERLASTING GLORIES of the world to come.—To HIM be PRAISE for EVER and EVER, AMEN.

FINIS.

NOTES

1. Because several of the earliest editions of the *Narrative* were published undated, the date and identity of the first edition of this work have been uncertain. The following advertisement, which appeared in the 21 and 27 December 1772 issues of *Boddely's Bath Journal*, may establish both: "*This Day is Published, Price Six-Pence*, A NARRATIVE of the most Remarkable PARTICULARS in the LIFE of JAMES ALBERT UKAWSAU [sic]

GRONIOSAU [sic], an African Prince, as related by Himself; with a Recommendatory PREFACE by the Rev. Mr. SHIRLEY. N.B. [Nota bene, that is, note well.] The whole Profits arising from the Sale are for the sole Benefit of JAMES ALBERT and his distress'd Family. Bath: Printed by W[illiam]. Gye, in Westgate-street; and sold by T[homas]. Mills, Bookseller in King's-mead-square." The Gye and Mills 1772 edition is my copy text.

The edition of Gronniosaw's *Narrative* published by Samuel Hazard of King's-Mead-Square in Bath has been proposed as the first edition, with a suggested date of 1770, but Hazard did not acquire Mills's business at that address until the beginning of 1774 (*Bath Chronicle*, 6 January 1774). The "second edition" of the *Narrative*, "printed and sold by S. Hazard," is advertised in Sir Richard Hill (1733-1808), *Several Seats in Parliament, to Be Had Gratis; or, the Only Method of Securing the Best Election. Being the Substance of a Letter to a Gentleman in Shrewsbury* (Bath: Printed and Sold by S. Hazard. Sold also by T. Mills, Bristol, [1774]).

The timing of the publication of the Gye and Mills 1772 edition may have been designed to take advantage of both the increased interest in the plight and status of Afro-Britons in light of the recent Mansfield decision and of the heightened concern with charity associated with the Christmas season.

Gronniosaw's *Narrative* was published at least twelve times before the end of the eighteenth century, including twice in Rhode Island (1774, 1781), twice in Ireland (1786, 1790), and once as a serial publication in New York (*American Moral and Sentimental Magazine*, 3 July through 25 September 1797).

2. Slightly modified from Isaiah 42:16; incorrectly cited in Hazard (1774) as Isaiah 43:16.

3. Selina Hastings, Countess of Huntingdon (1707-1791), the most socially prominent Methodist leader and patron of Afro-Britons, including Gronniosaw, Wheatley, Marrant, and Equiano. In 1748 she chose the Calvinist George Whitefield (1714-1770) as one of her chaplains and promoted his brand of Methodism, especially through the missionary associations she called her Connexion, conceived as mediating between the Church of England and the Dissenting sects. Forced by the Church in 1779 to register her chapels as Dissenting meeting houses, the Countess and her Connexion left the Church of England in 1782.

4. The "young Lady" is identified in *The Black Prince; Being a Narrative of the Most Remarkable Occurrences and Strange Vicissitudes, Exhibited in the Life and Experience of James Albert Ukawsaw Gronniosaw, an African Prince, as Was Related by Himself* (Salem, N.Y., 1809) as Hannah More (1745-1833), a conservative writer, reformer, and abolitionist who subscribed to Olaudah Equiano's *Interesting Narrative.*

5. Both with . . . and likewise: lacking in Hazard (1774).

6. Outward: lacking in Hazard (1774).

7. Blessings: "blessing" in Hazard (1774).

8. Who can doubt but that: "Who can doubt that" in Hazard (1774).

9. Coast of Guinea: a phrase used in the eighteenth century to include all the lands along the Gulf of Guinea, roughly from present-day Guinea in the north to at least Nigeria in the south and extending many miles inland all along the coast. Guinea was further divided into the territories of its principal peoples: upper Guinea (Mande); Gold Coast, extending east and west from present-day Ghana (Akan); Yoruba/Aja territory, present-day western Nigeria; and eastern Nigeria (Ibo/Ibibio).

10. Deists: those who believed that, although God created the world, He does not actively intervene in it and that the created world offers sufficient evidence for human reason to understand the nature of God. Thus, knowledge of the Bible is not necessary for belief in the true God.

11. Scriptures: "scripture" in Hazard (1774).

12. Kidderminster: a town southwest of Birmingham.

13. And him . . . Regard: lacking in Hazard (1774).

14. Walter Shirley (1725-1786), clergyman, writer, collector and publisher of hymns, and cousin of the Countess of Huntingdon.

15. Bournou: Bornu, formerly in the southernmost area, around Lake Chad, of the Kanem-Bornu Empire, which at its height in the fifteenth century stretched from present-day Sudan to northern Nigeria. By the beginning of the eighteenth century, Bornu had come to dominate Kanem as a trading empire, one of whose principal goods were slaves taken by the dominant Moslems from among their pagan fellow Blacks, who, like Gronniosaw's people, were animists. Most of these slaves from near Lake Chad were sent north and east to be sold in other Islamic countries.

16. King there: "King of ZAARA" in Hazard (1774).

17. Hand: "hands" in Hazard (1774).

18. The: lacking in Hazard (1774).

19. [Gronniosaw's note.] It is a generally received opinion, in *England*, that the natives of *Africa* go entirely unclothed; but this supposition is very unjust: they have a kind of dress so as to appear decent, though it is very slight and thin.

20. Sons of my age: Hazard (1774) reads "sons nearly of my age."

21. That: lacking in Hazard (1774).

22. Discovered: displayed.

23. In: lacking in Hazard (1774).

24. Upon: "on" in Hazard (1774).

25. Suffered: permitted.

26. That: lacking in Hazard (1774).

27. Life-guards: the king's personal guard.

28. Brig: a two-masted vessel.

29. Check: checkered cloth.

30. Hope: Hopes in Hazard (1774).

31. For variations on this incident of the talking book, see the selections in this anthology from Marrant, Cugoano, and Equiano.

32. Livery: the costume or uniform worn by a domestic male servant.

33. And called: Hazard (1774) reads "and immediately called.'

34. That: "who" in Hazard (1774).

35. And was: "and he was" in Hazard (1774).

36. Theodorus Jacobus Frelinghuysen (1691-ca.1748), Reformed Dutch clergyman in the Colony of New Jersey, married to Eva Terhune Frelinghuysen (1708-ca.1750). His success as a preacher made him an influential figure in the transatlantic evangelical religious revival, called The Great Awakening, during the second quarter of the eighteenth century, winning him the praises of the American theologian Jonathan Edwards (1703-1758) and the Methodist missionary George Whitefield.

Peter Van Arsdalen—probably Gronniosaw's "schoolmaster" "Vanosdore"—was one of Frelinghuysen's "helpers" in his ministry. The misspellings of "Frelinghuysen" as "Freelandhouse" and "Van Arsdalen" as "Vanosdore" are very plausible phonetic attempts by an English speaker to inscribe from memory names he may never have seen written down.

37. £50.: Hazard (1774) reads "fifty pounds."

38. What . . . for: "what he did this for" in Hazard (1774).

39. And I: "and that I" in Hazard (1774).

40. And: lacking in Hazard (1774).

41. Stick: the wooden handle to which the fork was attached.

42. *The Holy War* (1682) was written by the Puritan John Bunyan (1628-1688).

43. And: lacking in Hazard (1774).

44. All, it: Hazard (1774) reads "all, as it."

45. Myself; and I: "myself, I" in Hazard (1774).

46. And: lacking in Hazard (1774).

47. *A Call to the Unconverted to Turn and Live* (1658) was written by Richard Baxter (1615-1691).
48. Thought: "thoughts" in Hazard (1774).
49. Very: lacking in Hazard (1774).
50. John 1:29.
51. Zion: Jerusalem as a theological symbol of messianic salvation.
52. Set: "sit" in Hazard (1774).
53. To: "before" in Hazard (1774).
54. Or: "and" in Hazard (1774).
55. Always: lacking in Hazard (1774).
56. Jeremiah 32:40.
57. My . . . Master: lacking in Hazard (1774).
58. A Cast-away: "cast away" in Hazard (1774).
59. Colossians 2:10, slightly modified.
60. Hebrews 7:25. Hazard (1774) incorrectly reads "also able."
61. Ver.: lacking in Hazard (1774).
62. World: lacking in Hazard (1774).
63. V.: lacking in Hazard (1774).
64. Hazard (1774) incorrectly reads "69th."
65. The Book of Hebrews has only 13 chapters. Compare, however, Hebrews 6:17-18.
66. Chap., v., chap., v.,: lacking in Hazard (1774).
67. George Whitefield made several trips to North America, including a visit to Frelinghuysen's church.
68. Purpos'd: "proposed" in Hazard (1774).
69. Privateering: to sail in a privately owned, manned, and armed vessel under government contract to act as a warship, authorized to seize and sell the enemy's commercial and military vessels. In practice, the line between a privateer and a pirate was often barely discernible. The value of the prizes, or ships and goods seized, called prize-money, was divided among the officers and crew of the privateer.
70. Of Cook: "of a cook" in Hazard (1774).
71. St. Domingo: the island of Hispaniola, the location of the present-day Haiti and the Dominican Republic.
72. Can't: "can not" in Hazard (1774). As with "don't" in the next sentence, the use of contractions throughout the first edition better expresses the sense of an orally related tale than the more formal diction of the 1774 edition.
73. Would: "could" in Hazard (1774).
74. Upon: "up" in Hazard (1774).
75. That: "who" in Hazard (1774).
76. Chose to go: "would go" in Hazard (1774).
77. "Could" in Hazard (1774).
78. Of money: "of the money" in Hazard (1774).
79. Hogshead: a large cask.
80. Name Dunscum: "name was Dunscum" in Hazard (1774).
81. As he was: lacking in Hazard (1774).
82. Listed: "enlisted" in Hazard (1774).
83. "28th" in Hazard (1774). I have found no plausible variation on Gronniosaw's name(s) in the musters of the Twenty-eighth Regiment of Foot recorded at Staten Island before the unit set out for Martinique, but the records are probably not complete and do not include any musters from the time the unit spent in the Caribbean.
84. Admiral George Pocock (1706-1792) commanded the fleet that captured the French colony of Martinique and the Spanish colony of Cuba in the late summer of 1762.
85. To receive: "for" in Hazard (1774).
86. Shirts, hat: "shirts, a hat" in Hazard (1774).

87. 6: "6 guineas" in Hazard (1774).

88. Sodom: a city near the Dead Sea in Israel, destroyed, along with Gomorrah, by God because of the vices practiced by its inhabitants. The destruction of Sodom and Gomorrah became a proverbial example of God's wrath and judgment. See Genesis 18 and 19.

89. Suffer: allow.

90. To some way or other: "how" in Hazard (1774).

91. Tabernacle: Whitefield's Tabernacle opened in Moorfields in mid-April 1741. It was a temporary wooden structure built by his friends so that he might have a place to preach upon his return from almost two years in North America. It was replaced on the same site by a brick building that opened 10 June 1753.

The Moorfields Tabernacle is sometimes confused with the Chapel in Tottenham Court Road, built by Whitefield in 1756 about a half-mile north of the present-day British Museum. From the Tabernacle and the Chapel, which could seat eight thousand after 1760, Whitefield published and distributed new writings by himself and others. He also reprinted Puritan classics.

92. Gifford: perhaps Andrew Gifford (1700-1784), the eminent Baptist minister and antiquarian who became assistant librarian to the new British Library in 1757 in addition to his ministry.

93. Amongst: "among" in Hazard (1774).

94. Me; she: "me, and she" in Hazard (1774).

95. Allen: John Allen, the strict Calvinist pastor of a Baptist church in Petticoat Lane, Spitalfields, from January 1764 to May 1767.

96. His house: "his own house" in Hazard (1774).

97. Slightly modified from Psalms 66:16.

98. Job 19:25.

99. "Thirty-eight" in Hazard (1774).

100. At: "in" in Hazard (1774).

101. For an unmarried woman to write to a man to whom she was not formally betrothed was considered immodest.

102. "Sit" in Hazard (1774).

103. "Intention" in Hazard (1774).

104. That: lacking in Hazard (1774).

105. And: lacking in Hazard (1774).

106. "At" in Hazard (1774).

107. Spitalfields silk weavers, whose employment was highly vulnerable to market fluctuations, rioted frequently during the eighteenth century, especially during the depression of the mid-sixties that followed the Seven Years' War. For example, they broke their machines in October 1763, and in May 1765 they attacked the London home of the Duke of Bedford, who had negotiated the Peace of Paris that ended the war. Parliament enacted laws in 1765 and 1773 restricting French silk imports and regulating the wages of weavers.

108. Found myself: provided for my own care.

109. Me she: "me that she" in Hazard (1774).

110. Compare 1 Peter 1:3: "Blessed *be* the God and Father of our Lord Jesus Christ, which according to his abundant mercy hath begotten us again unto a lively hope by the resurrection of Jesus Christ from the dead."

111. Perhaps his prior reading was in Dutch.

112. Gathering: charitable collection.

113. Dear: lacking in Hazard (1774).

114. Every: "the" in Hazard (1774).

115. Than any: "than in any" in Hazard (1774).

116. Could: "might" in Hazard (1774).

117. Master: an employer, not an owner.

118. Her was: "her, she was" in Hazard (1774).

119. And: lacking in Hazard (1774).

120. Sinking. Her: "sinking; as her" in Hazard (1774).

121. Children as: "children, she" in Hazard (1774).

122. "Into" in Hazard (1774).

123. Perhaps Henry Gurney (1721-1777), who, along with his brother John (1718-1779), succeeded their father, John (1688-1740), in his worsted manufacturing and banking interests.

124. About; we began: "about, and we began" in Hazard (1774).

125. As: lacking in Hazard (1774).

126. Us: lacking in Hazard (1774).

127. Unlike the Baptists, the Anglican Church practiced infant baptism.

128. Mind: "care" in Hazard (1774).

129. Benjamin Fawcett (1715-1780) was a dissenting minister who invited the Countess of Huntingdon to establish the chapel she opened in Kidderminster in 1774. He abridged and published a number of Baxter's works, including *The Saints' Everlasting Rest*, first published in 1650, and reproduced by Fawcett as early as 1744 and several more times by 1772. His interest in Blacks is indicated by his *A Compassionate Address to the Christian Negroes in Virginia* (Salop and London, 1756). Fawcett's *The Religious Weaver; or, Pious Meditations on the Trade of Weaving* (Shrewsbury and London, 1773) appeared after the publication of the first edition of Gronniosaw's *Narrative.*

130. Mine, Baxter's: "mine, called Baxter's" in Hazard (1774).

131. "At" in Hazard (1774).

132. Near her time: about to give birth.

133. Since the provision of poor relief was dependent upon having a "settlement," a parish obligated by law to support its indigent, the Gronniosaw family, like any other aliens (White as well as Black), was offically rootless in England and thus ineligible for government help.

134. Compare Galatians 1:4: "Who [our Lord Jesus Christ] gave himself for our sins, that he might deliver us from this present evil world, according to the will of God and our Father."

Phillis Wheatley

(1753?-5 December 1784)

~

AN ELEGIAC POEM, ON THE DEATH OF THAT CELEBRATED DIVINE, AND EMINENT SERVANT OF JESUS CHRIST, THE LATE REVEREND AND PIOUS GEORGE WHITEFIELD, CHAPLAIN TO THE RIGHT HONOURABLE THE COUNTESS OF HUNTINGTON, &c. &c. (Boston: Sold by Ezekiel Russell, in Queen-Street, and John Boyles, in Marlboro-Street, 1770).[1]

Who made his exit from this transitory state, to dwell in the celestial Realms of Bliss, on Lord's-Day, 30th of September, 1770, when he was seiz'd with a fit of the asthma, at Newbury-Port, near Boston, in New-England. In which is a Condolatory Address to his truly noble benefactress the worthy and pious Lady Huntingdon, and the Orphan-children in Georgia; who, with many thousands, are left, by the death of this great man, to lament the loss of a Father, Friend, and Benefactor.

By Phillis, a Servant Girl of 17 Years of Age, belonging to Mr. J. Wheatley, of Boston, and has been but 9 years in this country from Africa.

Hail happy Saint on thy immortal throne!
To thee complaints of grievance are unknown;
We hear no more the music of thy tongue,
Thy wonted auditories cease to throng.
Thy lessons in unequal'd accents flow'd!
While emulation in each bosom glow'd;
Thou didst, in strains of eloquence refin'd,
Inflame the soul, and captivate the mind.
Unhappy we, the setting Sun deplore!
Which once was splendid, but it shines no more;
He leaves this earth for Heaven's unmeasur'd height:
And worlds unknown, receive him from our sight;
There WHITEFIELD wings, with rapid course his way,
And sails to Zion, through vast seas of day.

When his AMERICANS were burden'd sore,
When streets were crimson'd with their guiltless gore!

Phillis Wheatley, Negro Servant to Mr. John Wheatley, of Boston.
Published according to Act of Parliament, Sept. 1, 1773 by Archd. Bell,
Bookseller No. 8 near the Saracens Head Aldgate.

Unrival'd friendship in his breast now strove:
The fruit thereof was charity and love
Towards *America* — couldst thou do more
Than leave thy native home, the *British* shore,
To cross the great Atlantic's wat'ry road,
To see *America*'s distress'd abode?[2]
Thy prayers, great Saint, and thy incessant cries,
Have pierc'd the bosom of thy native skies!
Thou moon hast seen, and ye bright stars of light
Have witness been of his requests by night!
He pray'd that grace in every heart might dwell:
He long'd to see *America* excell;
He charg'd its youth to let the grace divine
Arise, and in their future actions shine;
He offer'd THAT he did himself receive,
A greater gift not GOD himself can give:
He urg'd the need of HIM to every one;
It was no less than GOD's co-equal SON!
Take HIM ye wretched for your only good;
Take HIM ye starving souls to be your food.
Ye thirsty, come to this life-giving stream:
Ye Preachers, take him for your joyful theme;
Take HIM, "my dear AMERICANS," he said,
Be your complaints in his kind bosom laid;
Take HIM ye *Africans*, he longs for you;
Impartial SAVIOUR, is his title due;
If you will chuse to walk in grace's road,
You shall be sons, and kings, and priests to GOD.

Great COUNTESS! we *Americans* revere
Thy name, and thus condole thy grief sincere:
We mourn with thee, that TOMB obscurely plac'd,
In which thy Chaplain undisturb'd doth rest.
New-England sure, doth feel the ORPHAN'S smart;
Reveals the true sensations of his heart:
Since this fair Sun, withdraws his golden rays,
No more to brighten these distressful days!
His lonely *Tabernacle*,[3] sees no more
A WHITEFIELD landing on the *British* shore:
Then let us view him in yon azure skies:
Let every mind with this lov'd object rise.
No more can he exert his lab'ring breath,
Seiz'd by the cruel messenger of death.
What can his dear AMERICA return?
But drop a tear upon his happy urn,
Thou tomb, shalt safe retain thy sacred trust,
Till life divine re-animate his dust.

~

From *POEMS ON VARIOUS SUBJECTS, RELIGIOUS AND MORAL. BY* PHILLIS WHEATLEY, *NEGRO SERVANT to Mr. JOHN WHEATLEY, of BOSTON, in NEW ENGLAND.* London: Printed for A[rchibald]. BELL, Bookseller, Aldgate; and sold by Messrs. COX and BERRY, King-Street, *BOSTON.* 1773.

To the King's Most Excellent Majesty. 1768.[4]

YOUR subjects hope, dread Sire—
The crown upon your brows may flourish long,
And that your arm may in your God be strong!
O may your sceptre num'rous nations sway,
And all with love and readiness obey!

But how shall we the *British* king reward!
Rule thou in peace, our father, and our lord!
Midst the remembrance of thy favours past,
The meanest peasants most admire the last.*
May *George*, belov'd by all the nations round,
Live with heav'ns choicest constant blessings crown'd!
Great God, direct, and guard him from on high,
And from his head let ev'ry evil fly!
And may each clime with equal gladness see
A monarch's smile can set his subjects free!

*The Repeal of the Stamp Act.[5]

~

On Being Brought from Africa to America.

'TWAS mercy brought me from my *Pagan* land,
Taught my benighted soul to understand
That there's a God, that there's a *Saviour* too:
Once I redemption neither sought nor knew.
Some view our sable race with scornful eye,
"Their colour is a diabolic die."
Remember, *Christians, Negroes,* black as *Cain,*[6]
May be refin'd, and join th'angelic train.[7]

~

An Hymn to the Morning.

ATTEND my lays, ye ever honour'd nine,[8]
Assist my labours, and my strains refine;
In smoothest numbers pour the notes along,
For bright *Aurora*[9] now demands my song.

Aurora hail, and all the thousand dies,
Which deck thy progress through the vaulted skies:
The morn awakes, and wide extends her rays,
On ev'ry leaf the gentle zephyr plays;
Harmonious lays the feather'd race resume,
Dart the bright eye, and shake the painted plume.

Ye shady groves, your verdant gloom display
To shield your poet from the burning day:
Calliope awake the sacred lyre,[10]
While thy fair sisters fan the pleasing fire:
The bow'rs, the gales, the variegated skies
In all their pleasures in my bosom rise.

See in the east th'illustrious king of day!
His rising radiance drives the shades away—
But Oh! I feel his fervid beams too strong,
And scarce begun, concludes th'abortive song.

~

An Hymn to the Evening.

SOON as the sun forsook the eastern main
The pealing thunder shook the heav'nly plain;
Majestic grandeur! From the zephyr's wing,
Exhales the incense of the blooming spring.
Soft purl the streams, the birds renew their notes,
And through the air their mingled music floats.

Through all the heav'ns what beauteous dies are spread!
But the west glories in the deepest red:
So may our breasts with ev'ry virtue glow,
The living temples of our God below!

Fill'd with the praise of him who gives the light,
And draws the sable curtains of the night,
Let placid slumbers sooth each weary mind,
At morn to wake more heav'nly, more refined;
So shall the labours of the day begin
More pure, more guarded from the snares of sin.

Night's leaden sceptre seals my drousy eyes,
Then cease, my song, till fair *Aurora* rise.

~

On Imagination.

THY various works, imperial queen, we see,
How bright their forms! how deck'd with pomp by thee!
Thy wond'rous acts in beauteous order stand,
And all attest how potent is thine hand.

From *Helicon's*[11] refulgent heights attend,
Ye sacred choir, and my attempts befriend:
To tell her glories with a faithful tongue,
Ye blooming graces, triumph in my song.

Now here, now there, the roving *Fancy* flies,
Till some lov'd object strikes her wand'ring eyes,
Whose silken fetters[12] all the senses bind,
And soft captivity involves the mind.

Imagination! who can sing thy force?
Or who describe the swiftness of thy course?
Soaring through air to find the bright abode,
Th'empyreal palace of the thund'ring God,
We on thy pinions can surpass the wind,
And leave the rolling universe behind:
From star to star the mental optics rove,
Measure the skies, and range the realms above.
There in one view we grasp the mighty whole,
Or with new worlds amaze th'unbounded soul.

Though *Winter* frowns to *Fancy's* raptur'd eyes
The fields may flourish, and gay scenes arise;
The frozen deeps may break their iron bands,
And bid their waters murmur o'er the sands.
Fair *Flora*[13] may resume her fragrant reign,
And with her flow'ry riches deck the plain;
Sylvanus[14] may diffuse his honours round,
And all the forest may with leaves be crown'd:
Show'rs may descend, and dews their gems disclose,
And nectar sparkle on the blooming rose.

Such is thy pow'r, nor are thine orders vain,
O thou the leader of the mental train:
In full perfection all thy works are wrought,
And thine the sceptre o'er the realms of thought.
Before thy throne the subject-passions bow,
Of subject-passions sov'reign ruler Thou,
At thy command joy rushes on the heart,
And through the glowing veins the spirits dart.

Fancy might now her silken pinions try,
To rise from earth, and sweep th'expanse on high;
From *Tithon's* bed[15] now mighty *Aurora* rise,
Her cheeks all glowing with celestial dies,
While a pure stream of light o'erflows the skies.
The monarch of the day I might behold,
And all the mountains tipt with radiant gold,
But I reluctant leave the pleasing views,
Which *Fancy* dresses to delight the *Muse*;
Winter austere forbids me to aspire,
And northern tempests damp the rising fire;
They chill the tides of *Fancy's* flowing sea,
Cease then, my song, cease the unequal lay.

~

To the Right Honourable William, Earl of Dartmouth, His Majesty's Principal Secretary of State for North-America, &c.[16]

HAIL, happy day, when, smiling like the morn,
Fair *Freedom* rose *New-England* to adorn:
The northern clime beneath her genial ray,
Dartmouth, congratulates thy blissful sway:
Elate with hope her race no longer mourns,
Each soul expands, each grateful bosom burns,
While in thine hand with pleasure we behold
The silken reigns, and *Freedom's* charms unfold.
Long lost to realms beneath the northern skies
She shines supreme, while hated *faction* dies:
Soon as appear'd the *Goddess* long desir'd,
Sick at the view, she languish'd and expir'd;
Thus from the splendors of the morning light
The owl in sadness seeks the caves of night.

No more, *America*, in mournful strain
Of wrongs, and grievance unredress'd complain,
No longer shalt thou dread the iron chain,
Which wanton *Tyranny* with lawless hand
Had made, and with it meant t'enslave the land.

Should you, my lord, while you peruse my song,
Wonder from whence my love of *Freedom* sprung,
Whence flow these wishes for the common good,
By feeling hearts alone best understood,
I, young in life, by seeming cruel fate

Was snatch'd from *Afric's* fancy'd happy seat:
What pangs excruciating must molest,
What sorrows labour in my parent's breast?
Steel'd was that soul and by no misery mov'd
That from a father seiz'd his babe belov'd:
Such, such my case. And can I then but pray
Others may never feel tyrannic sway?

For favours past, great Sir, our thanks are due,
And thee we ask thy favours to renew,
Since in thy pow'r, as in thy will before,
To sooth the griefs, which thou did'st once deplore.
May heav'nly grace the sacred sanction give
To all thy works, and thou forever live
Not only on the wings of fleeting *Fame*,
Though praise immortal crowns the patriot's name,
But to conduct to heav'ns refulgent fane,
May fiery coursers sweep th'ethereal plain,
And bear thee upwards to that blest abode,
Where, like the prophet,[17] thou shalt find thy God.

~

To S.M. a Young African Painter, on Seeing his Works.[18]

TO show the lab'ring bosom's deep intent,
And thought in living characters to paint,
When first thy pencil did those beauties give,
And breathing figures learnt from thee to live,
How did those prospects give my soul delight,
A new creation rushing on my sight?
Still, wond'rous youth! each noble path pursue,
On deathless glories fix thine ardent view:
Still may the painter's and the poet's fire
To aid thy pencil, and thy verse conspire!
And may the charms of each seraphic theme
Conduct thy footsteps to immortal fame!
High to the blissful wonders of the skies
Elate thy soul, and raise thy wishful eyes.
Thrice happy, when exalted to survey
That splendid city, crown'd with endless day,
Whose twice six gates on radiant hinges ring:
Celestial *Salem*[19] blooms in endless spring.

Calm and serene thy moments glide along,
And may the muse inspire each future song!

Still, with the sweets of contemplation bless'd,
May peace with balmy wings your soul invest!
But when these shades of time are chas'd away,
And darkness ends in everlasting day,
On what seraphic pinions shall we move,
And view the landscapes in the realms above?
There shall thy tongue in heav'nly murmurs flow,
And there my muse with heav'nly transport glow:
No more to tell of *Damon's* tender sighs,[20]
Or rising radiance of *Aurora's* eyes,
For nobler themes demand a nobler strain,
And purer language on th'ethereal plain.
Cease, gentle muse! the solemn gloom of night
Now seals the fair creation from my sight.

~

"To His Excellency General Washington"[21]

Celestial choir! enthron'd in realms of light,
Columbia's[22] scenes of glorious toils I write.
While freedom's cause her anxious breast alarms,
She flashes dreadful in refulgent arms,
See mother earth her offspring's fate bemoan,
And nations gaze at scenes before unknown!
See the bright beams of heaven's revolving light
Involved in sorrows and veil of night!

The goddess comes, she moves divinely fair,
Olive and laurel bind her golden hair:
Wherever shines this native of the skies,
Unnumber'd charms and recent graces rise.

Muse! bow propitious while my pen relates
How pour her armies through a thousand gates;
As when Eolus[23] heaven's fair face deforms,
Enwrapp'd in tempest, and a night of storms;
Astonish'd ocean feels the wild uproar,
The refluent[24] surges beat the sounding shore;
Or thick as leaves in Autumn's golden reign,
Such, and so many, moves the warrior's train.
In bright array they seek the work of war,
Where high unfurl'd the ensign waves in air.
Shall I to Washington their praise recite?
Enough thou know'st them in the fields of fight.
Thee, first in place and honours,—we demand

The grace and glory of thy martial band.
Fam'd for thy valour, for thy virtues more,
Hear every tongue thy guardian aid implore!

One century scarce perform'd its destined round,
When Gallic powers Columbia's fury found;[25]
And so may you, whoever dares disgrace
The land of freedom's heaven-defended race!
Fix'd are the eyes of nations on the scales,
For in their hopes Columbia's arm prevails.
Anon Britannia droops the pensive head,
While round increase the rising hills of dead.
Ah! cruel blindness to Columbia's state!
Lament thy thirst of boundless power too late.

Proceed, great chief, with virtue on thy side,
Thy ev'ry action let the goddess guide.
A crown, a mansion, and a throne that shine,
With gold unfading, WASHINGTON! be thine.

NOTES

1. Republished, with slight variations, in Wheatley's *Poems on Various Subjects, Religious and Moral* (London, 1773). Her poem on Whitefield (1714-1770), which she sent to Selina Hastings (1707-1791), Countess of Huntingdon, gained Wheatley the attention and support of the Methodist minister's patron. Although Wheatley never met the Countess in person, Huntingdon and the Earl of Dartmouth helped the young poet arrange for the publication of her book in London. Boston publishers had declined the opportunity, doubting that an Afro-British slave who had been brought to America at the age of eight was capable of writing poetry that contained classical allusions. Wheatley was brought to London in 1773 by Nathaniel Wheatley, son of her master, John Wheatley. Phillis carried with her a letter from her master and the signed "attestation" by a group of Boston dignitaries who had examined her, certifying the authenticity of her poetry. These documents preface the published *Poems.*

Wheatley's unpublished correspondence in 1773-1774 reveals that she was aware of the Countess's role in the publication of Gronniosaw's *Narrative* and that while in London she met "Greenville" [Granville] Sharp (1735-1813), the already famous abolitionist writer and activist, who took her to see the lions at the Tower of London. Sharp had brought the Somerset case before the King's Bench; this resulted in the Mansfield decision, which denied slave owners the legal authority to force slaves back to the Colonies once they had reached England. Sharp may have persuaded Wheatley to agree to return to Boston only on the condition that she be manumitted there, "at the desire of my friends in England."

Soon after Phillis's return to Boston, her now former mistress, Susannah Wheatley, died. When John Wheatley died in March 1778, his daughter Mary had already married, and Nathaniel was living abroad. Left to support herself, Phillis married John Peters, a free Black Bostonian, in April 1778. He could not support her and their three children, all of whom died in infancy. For reasons unknown, John was not with his wife when she died in poverty on 5 December 1784. *The Independent Chronicle*, a weekly Boston newspaper, reported her death the following week.

Wheatley's *Poems*, published in London in September 1773, after she had returned to America, was generally favorably reviewed during 1773 in the following English periodicals: *The Monthly Review, The Critical Review, The London Magazine, The Town and Country Magazine,* and *The Universal Catalogue.* Wheatley's poems quickly became part of the Afro-British literary tradition in the eighteenth century and were cited by the disputants in the slave-trade debate. As a part of that debate, the second, "Corrected," London edition of Wheatley's *Poems* appeared in 1787. Her *Poems* was also published in Philadelphia in 1786, 1787, and 1789, and in Albany in 1793. It appeared as an addendum to Equiano's *Narrative* (Halifax) in 1814. American publishers never accepted Wheatley's proposals for a second volume of poems.

2. Whitefield died on his seventh evangelizing trip to North America.

3. Tabernacle: the name of Whitefield's headquarters in London.

4. The King was George III (1738-1820).

5. Passed in 1765 by Parliament at the behest of the ministry of George Grenville (1712-1770), the Stamp Act was successfully resisted in America and was consequently repealed in the following spring. The widespread belief in the colonies that George III was their ally against the Act was wishful thinking. The King had, of course, signed the Act and had expressed doubts about the wisdom of repealing it.

6. Black as *Cain*: a reference to the contemporaneous assertion that the "mark" that Cain was doomed in Genesis 4: 15 to wear as a result of killing his brother, Abel, was the black complexion of Africans.

7. Compare the comments on slavery and Christianity that Wheatley makes to the Reverend Samson Occom (1732-1792), a converted Mohegan Indian from Connecticut, in a letter dated 11 February 1774, four months after she had gained her freedom. The letter was published in the *Connecticut Gazette; and the Universal Intelligencer* (11 March 1774) and in a dozen other New England newspapers thereafter:

> Rev'd and honor'd Sir,
>
> I have this Day received your obliging kind Epistle, and am greatly satisfied with your Reasons respecting the Negroes, and think highly reasonable what you offer in Vindication of their natural Rights: Those that invade them cannot be insensible that the divine Light is chasing away the thick Darkness which broods over the land of Africa; and the Chaos which has reign'd so long, is converting into beautiful Order, and [r]eveals more and more clearly, the glorious Dispensation of civil and religious Liberty, which are so inseparably united, that there is little or no Enjoyment of one without the other: Otherwise, perhaps, the Israelites had been less solicitous for their Freedom from Egyptian slavery; I do not say they would have been contented without it, by no means, for in every human Breast, God has implanted a Principle, which we call Love of Freedom; it is impatient of Oppression, and pants for Deliverance; and by the Leave of our modern Egyptians I will assert, that the same Principle lives in us. God grant Deliverance in his own Way and Time, and get him honour upon all those whose Avarice impels them to countenance and help forward the Calamities of their fellow Creatures. This I desire not for their Hurt, but to convince them of the strange Absurdity of their Conduct whose Words and Actions are so diametrically opposite. How well the cry for Liberty, and the reverse Disposition for the exercise of oppressive Powers over others agree,—I humbly think it does not require the penetration of a Philosopher to determine.

8. Nine: the nine daughters of Zeus and Mnemosyne—Calliope, Clio, Erato, Euterpe, Melpomene, Polyhymnia, Terpsichore, Thalia, and Urania—each of whom presided over an art or science.

9. Aurora: in Roman mythology, the goddess of the dawn.

10. *Calliope*: the Muse of epic poetry.

11. Helicon: in Greek mythology, the mountaintop home of the Muses.

12. Silken fetters: compare "The silken fetters of delicious ease" in Mark Akenside (1721-1770), *Pleasures of the Imagination* (1744, rev. ed. 1757), 2:562.

13. *Flora*: Roman goddess of flowers.

14. *Sylvanus*: Roman god of fields, forests, and herding.

15. *Tithon's* bed: in Roman mythology, Tithonus was the mortal lover of Aurora.

16. William Legge (1731-1801), second Earl of Dartmouth, was the Secretary of State from August 1772 through November 1775 and a friend of the Countess of Huntingdon. As president of the Board of Trade and Plantations from 20 July 1765 until 16 August 1766 in the ministry of Charles Watson-Wentworth (1730-1782), second Marquess of Rockingham, Dartmouth, like George III in Wheatley's poem on the king, was seen as one of the heroes who had saved America from the alleged political and economic "slavery" threatened by the Stamp Act.

17. 2 Kings 2:1-18 is the story of the prophet Elijah's being carried to heaven in a chariot of fire.

18. S.M. has been identified as the Reverend John Moorhead's slave, Scipio Moorhead, perhaps the artist who designed the frontispiece for Wheatley's *Poems*.

19. Celestial *Salem*: the heavenly Jerusalem of the afterlife.

20. *Damon*: a type of the idealized pastoral poet found, for example, in the eighth "Eclogue" (39 B.C.) of Virgil (70-19 B.C.) and in the first "Pastoral" (1709) of Alexander Pope (1688-1744).

21. Sent by Wheatley to George Washington (1732-1799) in a letter dated 26 October 1775, the poem was published, apparently without the permission of either Wheatley or Washington, in the *Virginia Gazette* on 20 March 1776, and by Thomas Paine (1737-1809) in the April 1776 issue of *The Pennsylvania Magazine*.

In the letter of 26 October 1775, which accompanied the poem, Wheatley writes,

SIR,

I have taken the freedom to address your Excellency in the enclosed poem, and entreat your acceptance, though I am not insensible of its inaccuracies. Your being appointed by the Grand Continental Congress to be Generalissimo of the armies of North America, together with the fame of your virtues, excite sensations not easy to suppress. Your generosity, therefore, I presume, will pardon the attempt. Wishing your Excellency all possible success in the great cause you are so generously engaged in, I am,

Your Excellency's most obedient humble servant,
PHILLIS WHEATLEY

Providence, Oct. 26, 1775.
His Excellency General Washington.

Washington acknowledged receipt of the poem in a letter to Wheatley:

Miss Phillis, Your favor of the 26th of October did not reach my hands, till the middle of December. Time enough, you will say, to have given an answer ere this. Granted. But a variety of important occurrences, continually interposing to distract the mind and withdraw the attention, I hope will apologize for the delay, and plead my excuse for the seeming but not real neglect. I thank you most sincerely for your polite notice of me, in the elegant lines you enclosed; and however undeserving I may be of such encomium and panegyric, the style and manner exhibit a striking proof of your poetical talents; in honour of which, and as a tribute justly due to you, I would have published the poem, had I not been apprehensive, that, while I only meant to give the world this new instance of your genius, I might

> have incurred the imputation of vanity. This, and nothing else, determined me not to give it place in the public prints.
>
> If you should ever come to Cambridge, or near headquarters, I shall be happy to see a person so favored by the Muses, and to whom nature has been so liberal and beneficent in her dispensations. I am, with great respect, your obedient humble servant.

On 10 February 1776, Washington wrote to Colonel Joseph Reed (1741-1785), his former secretary and the person who sent the letter and poem to the press:

> I recollect nothing else worth giving you trouble of, unless you can be amused by reading a letter and poem addressed to me by Miss Phillis Wheatley. In searching over a parcel of papers the other day, in order to destroy such as were useless, I brought it to light again. At first, with a view of doing justice to her poetical genius, I had a great mind to publish the poem; but not knowing whether it might not be considered rather as a mark of my own vanity, than a compliment to her, I laid it aside, till I came across it again in the manner just mentioned.

22. Columbia: an allegorical representation of America.
23. Eolus: the god of the wind.
24. Refluent: ebbing and flowing.
25. This couplet presumably refers to the defeat of France by British regular and colonial militia forces, including George Washington, in the French and Indian War (1756-1763), just over a century after the first permanent English settlements were established in North America.

Francis Williams

(ca. 1700-ca. 1770)

~

From Edward Long (1735-1813), *THE HISTORY OF* JAMAICA. *OR, GENERAL SURVEY OF THE ANCIENT AND MODERN STATE OF THAT ISLAND: WITH Reflections on its Situation, Settlements, Inhabitants, Climate, Products, Commerce, Laws, and Government.* IN THREE VOLUMES. (London: Printed for T. Lowndes, in Fleet-Street, 1774), 2: 475-485.[1]

"To That most upright and valiant Man, GEORGE HALDANE, Esq; Governor of the Island of *Jamaica*; Upon whom All military and moral Endowments are accumulated."

An ODE.

AT length revolving fates th' expected year
Advance, and joy the live-long day shall cheer,
Beneath the fost'ring law's auspicious dawn
New harvests rise to glad th' enliven'd lawn.
With the bright prospect blest, the swains repair
In social bands, and give a loose to care.
Rash councils now, with each malignant plan,
Each faction, that in evil hour began,
At your approach are in confusion fled,
Nor, while you rule, shall rear their dastard head.
Alike the master and the slave shall see
Their neck reliev'd, the yoke unbound by thee.
Ere now our guiltless isle, her wretched fate
Had wept, and groan'd beneath th' oppressive weight
Of cruel woes; save thy victorious hand,
Long fam'd in war, from Gallia's[2] hostile land;
And wreaths of fresh renown, with generous zeal,
Had freely turn'd, to prop our sinking weal.
Form'd as thou art, to serve *Britannia's* crown,
While *Scotia*[3] claims thee for her darling son;
Oh! blest of heroes, ablest to sustain
A falling people, and relax their chain.
Long as this isle shall grace the Western deep,

From age to age, thy fame shall never sleep.
Thee, her dread victor *Guadaloupe* shall own,
Crusht by thy arm, her slaughter'd chiefs bemoan;
View their proud tents all level'd in the dust,
And, while she grieves, confess the cause was just.
The golden *Iris*[4] the sad scene will share,
Will mourn her banners scatter'd in the air;
Lament her vanquisht troops with many a sigh,
Nor less to see her towns in ruin lie.
Fav'rite of *Mars*![5] believe, th'attempt were vain,
It is not mine to try the arduous strain.
What! shall an *AEthiop* touch the martial string,
Of battles, leaders, atchievements sing?
Ah no! *Minerva*,[6] with th'indignant *Nine*,[7]
Restrain him, and forbid the bold design.
To a *Buchanan* does the theme belong;[8]
A theme, that well deserves *Buchanan's* song.
'Tis he, should swell the din of war's alarms,
Record thee great in council, as in arms;
Recite each conquest by thy valour won,
And equal thee to great *Peleides'* son.[9]
That bard, his country's ornament and pride,
Who e'en with *Maro* might the bays divide:[10]
Far worthier he, thy glories to rehearse,
And paint thy deeds in his immortal verse.
We live, alas! where the bright god of day,
Full from the zenith whirls his torrid ray:
Beneath the rage of his consuming fires,
All fancy melts, all eloquence expires.
Yet may you deign accept this humble song,
Tho' wrapt in gloom, and from a falt'ring tongue;
Tho' dark the stream on which the tribute flows,
Not from the *skin*, but from the *heart* it rose.
To all of human kind, benignant heaven
(Since nought forbids) one common soul has given.
This rule was 'stablish'd by th'Eternal Mind;
Nor virtue's self, nor prudence are confin'd
To *colour*; none imbues the honest heart;
To science none belongs, and none to art.
Oh! *Muse*, of blackest tint, why shrinks thy breast,
Why fears t'approach the *Caesar* of the *West*!
Dispel thy doubts, with confidence ascend
The regal dome, and hail him for thy friend:
Nor blush, altho' in garb funereal drest,
Thy body's white, tho' clad in sable vest.
Manners unsullied, and the radiant glow
Of genius, burning with desire to *know*;

And learned speech, with modest accent worn,
Shall best the sooty *African* adorn.
An heart with wisdom fraught, a patriot flame,
A love of virtue; these shall lift his name
Conspicuous, far beyond his kindred race,
Distinguish'd from them by the foremost place.
In this prolific isle I drew my birth,
And *Britain* nurs'd, illustrious through the earth;
This, my lov'd isle, which never more shall grieve,
Whilst you our common friend, our father live.
Then this my pray'r—"May earth and heaven survey
A people ever blest, beneath your sway!"

NOTES

1. Long has translated Williams's Latin verse into English. I have separated the poem from its context so that the reader may approach the verse uninfluenced by Long's biased commentary on the author and his work:

Francis Williams.

I have forborne till now to introduce upon the stage a personage, who made a conspicuous figure in this island, and even attracted the notice of many in England. With the impartiality that becomes me, I shall endeavour to do him all possible justice; and shall leave it to the reader's opinion, whether what they shall discover of his genius and intellect will be sufficient to overthrow the arguments, I have before alledged, to prove an inferiority of the Negroes to the race of white men. It will by this time be discovered, that I allude to *Francis Williams*, a native of this island, and son to John and Dorothy Williams, free Negroes. Francis was the youngest of three sons, and, being a boy of unusual lively parts, was pitched upon to be the subject of an experiment, which, it is said, the Duke of Montague [the same Duke who acted as Ignatius Sancho's patron] was curious to make, in order to discover, whether, by proper cultivation, and a regular course of tuition at school and the university, a Negroe might not be found as capable of literature as a white person. In short, he was sent to England, where he underwent a regular discipline of classic instruction at a grammar school, after which he was fixed at the university of Cambridge, where he studied under the ablest preceptors, and made some progress in the mathematics. During his abode in England, after finishing his education, it is said (I know not with what truth) that he composed the well-known ballad of "Welcome, welcome, brother debtor, &." But I have likewise heard the same attributed to a different author [the ballad has been attributed to Wetenhall Wilkes (d. 1751)]. Upon his return to Jamaica, the duke would fain have tried his genius likewise in politics, and intended obtaining for him a privy seal, or appointment to be one of the governor's council; but this scheme was dropped, upon the objections offered by Mr. Trelawny, the governor at that time [Edward Trelawney (1699-1754), Governor of Jamaica, 1738-1752]. Williams therefore set up a school in Spanish Town, which he continued for several years, where he taught reading, writing, Latin, and the elements of the mathematics; whilst he acted in this profession, he selected a Negroe pupil, whom he trained with particular care, intending to make him his successor in the school; but of this youth it may be said, to use the expression of Festus to Paul, that "much learning made him mad" [Acts 26:24]. The abstruse problems of mathematical institution turned his brain; and he still remains, I believe, an unfortunate example, to shew that every African head is not adapted by nature to such profound contemplations. The chief pride of this disciple consists in imitating the garb and deportment of his tutor. A tye perriwig, a sword, and ruffled shirt, seem in his opinion to comprehend the very marrow and quintescence of all erudition, and philosophic dignity. Probably he imagines it a more easy way of acquiring, among the Negroes, the reputation of a great scholar, by these superficial marks, which catch their eye, than by talking of Euclid, whom they know nothing about.

Considering the difference which climate may occasion, and which Montesquieu has learnedly examined, the noble duke would have made the experiment more fairly on a native African; perhaps too the Northern air imparted a tone and vigour to his organs, of which they never would have been susceptible in a hot climate; the author I have mentioned will not allow, that in hot climates there is any force or vigor [sic] of mind necessary for human action, "there is (says he) no curiosity, no noble enterprize, no generous sentiment" [Long quotes Charles de Secondat, Baron de La Brède et de Montesquieu (1689-1755), *The Spirit of the Laws* (1748; Thomas Nugent's London ed., 1750), bk. 14, sec. 2].

The climate of Jamaica is temperate, and even cool, compared with many parts of Guiney; and the Creole Blacks have undeniably more acuteness and better understandings than the natives of Guiney. Mr. Hume, who had heard of Williams, says of him, "In Jamaica indeed they talk of one Negroe as a man of parts and learning; but 'tis likely he is admired for very slender accomplishments, like a parrot who speaks a few words plainly" [Long quotes David Hume (1711-1776), "Of National Characters," in *Essays and Treatises on Several Subjects* (London and Edinburgh, 1764), 234n]. And Mr. Estwick, pursuing the same idea, observes, "Although a Negroe is found in Jamaica, or elsewhere, ever so sensible and acute; yet, if he is incapable of moral sensations, or perceives them only as beasts do simple ideas, without the power of combination, in order to use; it is a mark that distinguishes him from the man who feels, and is capable of these moral sensations, who knows their application, and the purposes of them, as sufficiently, as he himself is distinguished from the highest species of brute" [Samuel Estwick (ca. 1736-1795), *Considerations on the Negroe Cause Commonly So Called, Addressed to the Right Honourable Lord Mansfield, Lord Chief Justice of the Court of King's Bench, &c. By a West Indian* (London, 1772; 2nd. ed. 1773), 79n, only in second and subsequent eds.] I do not know, if the specimen I shall exhibit of his abilities will, or will not, be thought to militate against these positions. In regard to the general character of the man, he was haughty, opinionated, looked down with sovereign contempt on his fellow Blacks, entertained the highest opinion of his own knowledge, treated his parents with much disdain, and behaved towards his children and his slaves with a severity bordering upon cruelty; he was fond of having great deference paid to him, and exacted it in the utmost degree from the Negroes about him; he affected a singularity of dress, and particularly grave cast of countenance, to impress an idea of his wisdom and learning; and, to second this view, he wore in common a huge wig, which made a very venerable figure. The moral part of his character may be collected from these touches, as well as the measure of his wisdom, on which, as well as some other attributes to which he laid claim, he had not the modesty to be silent, whenever he met with occasion to expatiate upon them. Of this piece of vanity, there is a very strong example in the following poem, which he presented to Mr. Haldane, upon his assuming the government of the island; he was fond of this species of composition in Latin, and usually addressed one to every new governor. He defined himself "a *white* man acting under a *black* skin." He endeavoured to prove logically, that a Negroe was superior in quality to a Mulatto, or other cast. His proposition was, that "as a simple white or a simple black complexion was respectively perfect: but a Mulatto, being a heterogeneous medley of both, was imperfect, *ergo* inferior."

His opinion of Negroes may be inferred from a proverbial saying, that was frequently in his mouth; "Shew me a *Negroe*, and I will shew you *a thief*." He died, not long since, at the age of seventy, or thereabouts.

[Here follows Williams's Latin verse and Long's translation.]

There is, in this performance, a strain of superlative panegyric, which is scarcely allowable even to a poet. *Buchanan* is compared with *Virgil*, and Mr. *Haldane* [Governor of Jamaica, 1758-1762] made equal to *Achilles*; nay, exalted still higher, for he is hailed the *Caesar* or emperor of *America.* The author has taken care, whilst he is dealing about his adulation, not to forget himself. His speech is represented erudite and modest; his heart is filled with wisdom; his morals are immaculate; and he abounds with patriotism and virtue.

To consider the merits of this specimen impartially, we must endeavour to forget, in the first place, that the writer was a *Negroe*; for if we regard it as an extraordinary production, merely because it came from a *Negroe*, we admit at once that *inequality* of genius which has been before supposed, and admire it only as a rare phaenomenon. . . .

We are to estimate it as having flowed from the polished pen of one, who received an academic education, under every advantage that able preceptors, and munificent patrons, could furnish; we must likewise believe it to be, what it actually was, a piece highly laboured; designed, modeled, and perfected, to the utmost stretch of his invention, imagination, and skill.

Should we, or should we not, have looked for something better from one, upon whom [all learning has been bestowed]? or, is it at all superior, in classic purity and numbers, in sentiment and propriety, in poetic images and harmony, to any composition we might expect from a middling scholar at the seminaries of Westminster or Eaton [sic]? It is true, *poeta nascitur, non fit* [poets are born, not made]: but the principal forte and excellence of this man lay in versification; however, as I mean not to prejudge the cause, I shall leave it to the fair verdict of a jury of critics. The Spaniards have a proverbial saying, "*Aunque Negros somos gente*"; "though we are Blacks, we are men." The truth of which no one will dispute; but if we allow the system of created beings to be perfect and consistent, and that this perfection arises from an exact scale of gradation, from the lowest to the highest, combining and connecting every part into a regular and beautiful harmony, reasoning them from the visible plan and operation of infinite wisdom in respect to the human race, as well as every other series in the scale, we must, I think, conclude, that,

The general *order*, since the whole began,
Is kept in *nature*, and is kept in *man*.
Order is heaven's first law; and, this confest,
Some are, and *must be, greater* than the rest.

[Alexander Pope (1688-1744), *An Essay on Man* (London, 1733-1734), 1:171-172, 4:49-50.]

2. Gallia: France.
3. Scotia: Scotland, Haldane's native land.
4. Iris: the goddess of the rainbow.
5. Mars: the chief Italian god after Jupiter and the Roman name for the Greek god of war, Ares.
6. Minerva: the Roman name for the Greek war-goddess Athena, who was also the goddess of wisdom.
7. The nine Muses, or Greek female deities of the arts and sciences.
8. George Buchanan (1506-1582), author of a Latin *History of Scotland* (1582).
9. Peleides' son: Achilles, hero of Homer's *Iliad.*
10. Maro: Virgil (70-19 B.C.), author of the *Aeneid*, virtually completed by the time of his death, which celebrates the exploits of Aeneas and, indirectly, the achievements of Caesar Augustus (63 B.C.-A.D. 14).

Ignatius Sancho

(1729-1780)[1]

~

From *LETTERS OF THE LATE IGNATIUS SANCHO, AN AFRICAN. IN TWO VOLUMES. TO WHICH ARE PREFIXED, MEMOIRS OF HIS LIFE.* (London: J. Nichols, 1782).

THE Editor of these Letters thinks proper to obviate an objection, which she finds has already been suggested, that they were originally written with a view to publication. She declares, therefore, that no such idea was ever expressed by Mr. Sancho; and that not a single letter is here printed from any duplicate preserved by himself, but all have been collected from the various friends to whom they were addressed. Her motives for laying them before the publick were, the desire of shewing that an untutored African may possess abilities equal to an European; and the still superior motive, of wishing to serve his worthy family. And she is happy in thus publicly acknowledging she has not found the world inattentive to the voices of obscure merit.[2]

Letter XII. To Mr. B[rowne, Steward to Sir Charles Bunbury].

London, July 18, 1772.

I thank you for your kindness to my poor black brethren—I flatter myself you will find them not ungrateful—they act commonly from their feelings:—I have observed a dog will love those who use him kindly—and surely, if so, negroes—in their state of ignorance and bondage will not act less generously, if I may judge them by myself—I should suppose kindness would do any thing with them;—my soul melts at kindness—but the contrary—I own with shame—makes me almost a savage.

Letter XIII. To Mr. S[oubis]e.[3] Richmond, Oct. 11, 1772.

. . . Happy, happy lad! what a fortune is thine!—Look round upon the miserable state of almost all of our unfortunate colour—superadded to ignorance,—see slavery, and the contempt of those very wretches who roll in affluence from our labours superadded to this woeful catalogue—hear the ill-bred and heart-racking

Ignatius Sancho.

abuse of the foolish vulgar.—You, S—e, tread as cautiously as the strictest rectitude can guide ye—yet must you suffer from this—but armed with truth—honesty—and conscious integrity—you will be sure of the plaudit and countenance of the good;—if, therefore, thy repentance is sincere—I congratulate thee as sincerely upon it—it is thy birth-day to real happiness.

Letter XXIV. To Mr. B[rowne]. August 12, 1775.

Dear Sir,

If I knew a better man than yourself—you would not have had this application—which is in behalf of a merry—chirping—white tooth'd—clean—tight—and light little fellow;—with a wooly pate—and face as dark as your humble;—Guiney-born, and French-bred—the sulky gloom of Africa dispelled by Gallic vivacity—and that softened again with English sedateness—a rare fellow!—rides well—and can look upon a couple of horses—dresses hair in the present taste—shaves light—and understands something of a table and side-board;—his present master will authenticate him a decent character—he leaves him at his own (Blacky's) request:—he has served him three years—and, like Teague,[4] would be glad of a good master—if any good master would be glad of him.—as I believe you associate chiefly with good-hearted folks—it is possible your interest may be of service to him.—I like the rogue's looks, or a similarity of colour should not have induced me to recommend him.—Excuse this little scrawl from your friend, &c. IGN. SANCHO.

Letter XXXV. To Mr. Sterne.[5] [21] July 1766.

REVEREND SIR,

It would be an insult on your humanity (or perhaps look like it) to apologize for the liberty I am taking.—I am one of those people whom the vulgar and illiberal call "*Negurs*."—The first part of my life was rather unlucky, as I was placed in a family who judged ignorance the best and only security for obedience.—A little reading and writing I got by unwearied application.—The latter part of my life has been—thro' God's blessing, truly fortunate, having spent it in the service of one of the best families in the kingdom.—My chief pleasure has been books.—Philanthropy I adore.—How very much, good Sir, am I (amongst millions) indebted to you for the character of your amiable uncle Toby!—I declare, I would walk ten miles in the dog-days, to shake hands with the honest corporal.—Your Sermons have touch'd me to the heart, and I hope have amended it, which brings me to the point.—In your tenth discourse, page seventy-eight, in the second volume—is this very affecting passage—"Consider how great a part of our species—in all ages down to this—have been trod under the feet of cruel and capricious tyrants, who would neither hear their cries, nor pity their distresses.—Consider slavery—what it is—how bitter a draught—and how many millions are made to drink it!"[6]—Of all my favorite authors, not one has drawn a tear in favor of my miserable black brethren—excepting yourself, and the humane author of Sir George Ellison.[7]—I think you will forgive me;—I am sure you will applaud me for beseeching you to give one half-hour's attention to slavery, as it is at this day practised in our West Indies.—That subject, handled in your striking manner, would ease the yoke (perhaps) of many—but if only of one—Gracious God!—what a feast to a benevolent heart!—and, sure I am, you are an epicurean in acts of charity.—You, who are universally read, and as universally admired—you could not fail—Dear Sir, think in me you behold the uplifted hands of thousands of my brother Moors.[8]—Grief (you pathetically observe) is eloquent;—figure to yourself their attitudes;—hear their supplicating addresses!—alas!—you cannot refuse.—Humanity must comply—in which hope I beg permission to subscribe myself,

Reverend Sir, &c.
IGN. SANCHO.

For *The General Advertiser.*

The outline of a plan for establishing a most respectable body of Seamen, to the number of 20,000, to be ever ready for the manning a fleet upon twelve days' notice.

The proposer is humbly of opinion, that his plan is capable of many wholesome improvements, which he thinks would prove no unprofitable study, even to the Lords of the Admiralty.

Ist, Let the number of seamen, now upon actual service, be each man inrolled upon His Majesty's books, at the rate of 5£ *per annum* for life; let them also receive the same quarterly, or half-yearly, upon personal application.

IIdly, Let books be opened for them in all His Majesty's different yards and sea-ports, and there their dwelling, age, time they have served, &c. to be fairly entered: each man to bring a certificate from his ship, signed by the captain, or some one he shall please to depute.

IIIdly, As an encouragement to His Majesty's service, and population at the same time, let there be instituted in each of the ship yards, or ports, &c. of these Kingdoms, a kind of asylum, or house of refuge, for the sons of these honest tars, to be received therein at the age of six years; there to be taught navigation, or, after the common school learning, to be bound to such parts of ship-building as they by nature are most inclined to; such as chuse sea service, to be disposed on board His Majesty's ships at fifteen years old, and to be enrolled upon the pension-books after ten years' faithful service, unless better provided for.

Might not there be some plan hit on to employ the daughters, as well as sons, of poor sailors? Do not our Fisheries (if they should ever happen to be attended to) open many doors of useful employment for both sexes?

To defray the above, I would advise the following methods:

First, The pension of 5£ *per* man for 20,000 amounts only to 100,000£; let this be taken from the Irish list;[9] it will surely be better employed than in the present mode for Pensioners of noble blood.

Secondly, Let the book and office-keepers at the different yards, ports, &c. be collected from under-officers who have served with reputation; it will be a decent retreat for them in the evening of life, and only a grateful reward for past service.

May some able hand, guided by a benevolent heart, point out and strongly recommend something of this sort, that the honoured name of England may be rescued from the scandalous censure of man-stealing, and from the ingratitude also of letting their preservers perish in the time of peace!

I am, Sir, yours, &c.
AFRICANUS.

Letter XLVII. To Mr. [John] M[eheux, Clerk in the Board of Control]. August 25, 1777.

JACK-ASSES.

My gall has been plentifully stirred—by the barbarity of a set of gentry, who *every morning* offend my feelings—in their cruel parade through Charles Street to and from market—they vend potatoes in the day—and thieve in the night season.—A tall lazy villain was bestriding his poor beast (although loaded with two panniers of potatoes at the same time), and another of his companions was good-naturedly employed in whipping the poor sinking animal—that the gentleman-rider might enjoy the two-fold pleasure of blasphemy and cruelty—This is a too common evil—and, for the honor of rationality, calls loudly for redress.—I do believe it might be in some measure amended—either by a hint in the papers, of the utility of impressing such vagrants for the king's service—or by laying a heavy tax upon the poor Jack-asses—I prefer the former, both for thy sake and mine;—and, as I am convinced we feel instinctively the injuries of our *fellow creatures*, do insist upon your exercising your talents in behalf of the honest sufferers.—I ever had a kind of sympathetic (call it what you please) for that animal—*and do I not love you*?—Before Sterne had wrote them into respect,[10] I had a friendship for them—and many a civil greeting have I given them at casual meetings—What has ever (with me) stamped a kind of uncommon value and dignity upon the long-ear'd kind of the species, is, that our Blessed Saviour, in his day of worldly triumph, chose to use that in preference to the rest of his own blessed creation—"meek and lowly, riding upon an ass."[11] I am convinced that the general inhumanity of mankind proceeds—first, from the cursed false principle of common education—and, secondly, from a total indifference (if not disbelief) of the Christian faith,—A heart and mind impressed with a firm belief of the Christian tenets, must of course exercise itself in a constant uniform general philanthropy—Such a being carries his heaven in his breast—and such be thou! Therefore write me a bitter Philippick against the misusers of Jack-asses—it shall honor a column in the Morning Post—and I will bray—bray my thanks to you—thou shalt figure away the champion of poor friendless asses here—and hereafter shalt not be ashamed in the great day of retribution.

Mrs. Sancho would send you some tamarinds.[12]—I know not her reasons;—as I hate contentions, I contradicted not—but shrewdly suspect she thinks you want cooling.—Do you hear, Sir? send me some more good news about your head.—Your letters will not be the less welcome for talking about J— M—, but pray do not let vanity so master your judgment, to fancy yourself upon a footing with George for well-looking—If you were indeed a proof sheet, you was marred in the taking off—for George (ask the girls) is certainly the fairest impression.

I had an order from Mr. H[enderson][13] on Thursday night to see him do Falstaff—I put some money to it, and took Mary and Betsy with me—It was Betty's first affair—and she enjoyed it in truth—H[enderson]'s Falstaff is entirely original—and I think as great as his Shylock:—he kept the house in a continual roar of laughter:—in some things he falls short of Quin[14]—in many I think him equal.—When I saw Quin play, he was at the height of his art, with thirty years judgment to guide him. H[enderson], in seven years more, will be all that better—and confessedly the first man on the English stage, or I am much mistaken.

I am reading a little pamphlet, which I much like: it favours an opinion which I have long indulged—which is the improbability of eternal Damnation—a thought which almost petrifies one—and, in my opinion, derogatory to the fullness, glory, and benefit of the blessed expiation of the Son of the Most High God—who died for the sins of all—all—Jew, Turk, Infidel, and Heretic;—fair—sallow—brown—tawny—black—and you and I—and every son and daughter of Adam.—You must find eyes to read this book—head and heart, with a quickness of conception, thou enjoyest—with many—many advantages—which have the love—and envy almost of yours,

I. SANCHO

Respects in folio to Mrs. H—.

Letter XLVIII. to Mr. R[ush, Valet to Sir Charles Bunbury]. August 27, 1777.

. . . I know a man who delights to make every one he can happy—that same man treated some honest girls with expences for a Vauxhall evening.—If you should happen to know him.—you may tell him from me—that last night—three great girls—a boy—and a fat old fellow—were as happy and pleas'd as a fine evening—fine place—and good music—could make them. Heaven and Earth!—how happy, how delighted, were the girls!—Oh! the pleasures of novelty to youth!—We went by water—had a coach home—were gazed at—followed, &c. &c.—but not much abused.

Letter LV. To Mr. [William] S[tevenson, a painter in Norwich]. December 20, 1777.

. . . But let me return to my senses;—for God's sake! what has a poor starving Negroe, with six children, to do with kings and heroes, and armies and politics?—aye, or poets and painters?—or artists—of any sort?

. . . When it shall please the Almighty that things shall take a better turn in America—when the conviction of their madness shall make them court peace—and the same conviction of our cruelty and injustice induce us to settle all points in equity—when that time arrives, my friend, America will be the grand patron of genius—trade and arts will flourish—and if it shall please God to spare us till that period—we will either go and try our fortunes there—or stay in Old England and talk about it.

Letter LVII. To Mr. F[isher].[15] Charles Street, January 27, 1778.

Full heartily and most cordially do I thank thee—good Mr. F—, for your kindness in sending the books[16]—that upon the unchristian and most diabolical usage of my brother Negroes—the illegality—the horrid wickedness of the traffic—the cruel carnage and depopulation of the human species—is painted in such strong colours—that I should think would (if duly attended to) flash conviction—and produce remorse in every enlightened and candid reader.—The perusal affected me more than I can express;—indeed I felt a double or mixt sensation—for while my heart was torn for the sufferings—which, for aught I know—some of my nearest kin might have undergone—my bosom, at the same time glowed with gratitude—and praise toward the humane—the Christian—the friendly and learned Author of that most valuable book.—Blest be your sect![17]—and Heaven's peace be ever upon them!—I who, thank God! am no bigot—but honour virtue—and the practice of the great moral duties equally in the turban—or the lawn-sleeves[18]—who think Heaven big enough for all the race of man—and hope to see and mix amongst the whole family of Adam in bliss hereafter—I with these notions (which, perhaps, some may style absurd) look upon the friendly Author—as a being far superior to any great name upon your continent.—I could wish that every member of each house of parliament had one of these books.—And if his Majesty perused one through before breakfast—though it might spoil his appetite—yet the consciousness of having it in his power to facilitate the great work—would give an additional sweetness to his tea.—Phyllis's poems do credit to nature—and put art—merely as art—to the blush.[19]—It reflects nothing either to the glory or generosity of her master—if she is still his slave—except he glories in the *low vanity* of having in his wanton power a mind animated by Heaven—a genius superior to himself.—The list of splendid—titled—learned names, in confirmation of her being the real authoress—alas! shows how very poor the acquisition of wealth and knowledge is—without generosity—feeling—and humanity.—These good great folks—all know—and perhaps admired—nay, praised Genius in bondage—and then, like the Priests and the Levites in sacred writ, passed by—not one good Samaritan amongst them.[20]—I shall be ever glad to see you—and am, with many thanks,

Your most humble servant,
IGNATIUS SANCHO.

Letter LXV. To Mr. M[eheux]. June 10, 1778.

"'Tis with our judgements as our watches—none
Go just alike—yet each believes his own." POPE[21]

So, my wise critic—blessings on thee—and thanks for thy sagacious discovery!—Sterne, it seems, stole his grand outline of character from Fielding[22]—and whom did Fielding plunder? thou criticizing jack ape!—As to S—, perhaps you may be right—not absolutely right—nor quite so very *altogether* wrong—but that's not my affair.—Fielding and Sterne both copied nature—their palettes stored with proper colours of the brightest dye—these masters were both great originals—their outline correct—bold — and free—Human Nature was their subject—and though their colouring was widely different, yet *here* and there some features in each might bear a little resemblance—some faint likeness to each other—as, for example—in your own words—Toby and Allworthy[23]—The external draperies of the two are as wide as the poles—their hearts—perhaps—twins of the same blessed form and principles;—but, for the rest of the Dramatis Personae, you must strain hard, my friend, before you can twist them into likeness sufficient to warrant the censure of copying.—Parson Adams is yet more distant[24]—his chief feature is absence of thought—The world affords me many such instances—but in the course of my reading I have not met with his likeness, except in mere goodness of heart—in that perhaps Jack M— may equal him — but then he is so confounded jingle-headed!—Read boy, read—give Tom Jones a second *fair* reading!—Fielding's wit is obvious—his humour poignant—dialogue just—and truly dramatic—colouring quite nature—and keeping chaste.—Sterne equals him in every thing, and in one thing excels him and all mankind—which is the distribution of his lights, which he has so artfully varied throughout his work, that the oftener they are examined the more beautiful they appear.—They were two great masters, who painted for posterity—and, I prophesy, will charm to the end of the English speech.—If Sterne has had any one great master in his eye—it was Swift, his countryman[25]—the first wit of this or any other nation.—But there is this grand difference between them—Swift excels in grave-faced irony—whilst Sterne lashes his whips with jolly laughter.—I could wish you to compare (after due attentive reading) Swift and Sterne—Milton and Young—Thomson and Akenside[26]—and then give your free opinion to yours ever,

I. SANCHO

I want a handful or two of good fresh peach leaves—contrive to send me them when opportunity serves—and word, at the first leisure period, how Miss *Anne Sister-like*—*George Grateful-look*—Mrs. &c. &c.—and how your worship's hip does.—You had set up my bristles in such guise—in attacking poor Sterne—that I had quite forgot to give you a flogging for your punning grocery epistle—But omittance is no quittance.—Swift and Sterne were different in this—Sterne was truly a noble philanthropist—Swift was rather cynical. What Swift would fret and fume at—such as the petty accidental *sourings* and *bitters* in life's cup—you plainly may see, Sterne would laugh at—and parry off by a larger humanity, and regular good will to man. I know you will laugh at me—do—I am content:—if I am an enthusiast in any thing, it is in favor of my Sterne.

Vol. 2. Letter I. To Mr. [Jack] W[ingrav]e. 1778.

Your good father insists on my scribbling a sheet of absurdities, and gives me a notable reason for it, that is, "Jack will be pleased with it."—Now be it known to you—I have a respect both for father and son—yea for the whole family, who are every soul (that I have the honor or pleasure to know any thing of) tinctured—and leavened with all the obsolete goodness of old times—so that a man runs some hazard in being seen in the W—e's society of being biassed to Christianity. I never see your poor father but his eyes betray his feelings for the hopeful youth in India—A tear of joy dancing upon the lids is a plaudit not to be equalled this side death!—See the effects of right-doing, my worthy friend—Continue in the track of rectitude—and despise poor paltry Europeans—titled—Nabobs[27]—Read your Bible—As day follows night, God's blessing follows virtue—honor and riches bring up the rear—and the end is peace.—Courage, my boy—I have done preaching.—Old folks love to seem wise—and if you are silly enough to correspond with gray hairs, take the consequence.—I have had the pleasure of reading most of your letters, through the kindness of your father.—Youth is naturally prone to vanity—Such is the weakness of Human Nature, that pride has a fortress in the best of hearts—I know no person that possesses a better than Johnny W—e:—but although flattery is poison to youth, yet truth obliges me to confess that your correspondence betrays no symptom of vanity—but teems with truths of an honest affection, which merits praise—and commands esteem.

In some one of your letters which I do not recollect—you speak (with honest indignation) of the treachery and chicanery of the Natives.[28]—My good friend, you should remember from whom they learnt those vices:—The first Christian visitors found them a simple, harmless people—but the cursed avidity for wealth urged these first visitors (and all the succeeding ones) to such acts of deception—and even wanton cruelty—that the poor ignorant Natives soon learnt to turn the knavish—and diabolical arts which they too soon imbibed—upon their teachers.

I am sorry to observe that the practice of your country (which as a resident I love—and for its freedom, and for the many blessings I enjoy in it, shall ever have my warmest wishes—prayers—and blessings); I say it is with reluctance, that I must observe your country's conduct has been uniformly wicked in the East—West-Indies—and even on the coast of Guinea.—The grand object of English navigators—indeed of all Christian navigators—is money—money—money—for which I do not pretend to blame them—Commerce was meant by the goodness of the Deity to diffuse the various goods of the earth into every part—to unite mankind in the blessed chains of brotherly love—society—and mutual dependence:—the enlightened Christian should diffuse the riches of the Gospel of peace—with the commodities of his respective land—Commerce attended with strict honesty—and with Religion for its companion, would be a blessing to every shore it touched at.—In Africa, the poor wretched natives—blessed with the most fertile and luxuriant soil—are rendered so much the more miserable for what Providence meant as a blessing:—the Christians' abominable Traffic for slaves—and the horrid cruelty and treachery of the petty Kings—encouraged by their Christian customers—who carry them strong liquors—to enflame their national madness—and powder and bad fire-arms—to furnish them with the hellish means of killing and kidnapping.—But enough—it is a subject that sours my blood—and I am sure will not please the friendly bent of your social affections.—I mentioned these only to guard my friend against being too hasty in condemning the knavery of a people who, bad as they may be—possibly—were made worse by their Christian visitors.—Make human nature thy study, wherever thou residest—whatever the religion—or the complexion—study their hearts.—Simplicity, kindness, and charity be thy guide!—with these even Savages will respect you—and God will bless you.

Your father—who sees every improvement of his boy with delight—observes that your handwriting is much for the better—In truth, I think it as well as any modest man can wish:—If my long epistles do not frighten you—and I live till the return of next spring—perhaps I shall be enabled to judge how much you are improved since your last favour:—write me a deal about the natives—the soil and produce—the domestic and interior manners of the people—customs—prejudices—fashions—and follies.—Alas! we have plenty of the two last here—and, what is worse, we have politics—and a detestable Brothers' war[29]—where the right hand is hacking and hewing the left—whilst Angels weep at our madness—and Devils rejoice at the ruinous prospect.

Mr. R[ush] and the ladies are well.—Johnny R[ush] has favoured me with a long letter—He is now grown familiar with danger—and can bear the whistling of bullets—the cries and groans of the human species—the roll of drums— clangor of trumpets—shouts of combatants—and thunder of cannon—all these he can bear with soldier-like fortitude—with now and then a secret wish for the society of his London friends—in the sweet blessed security of peace and friendship.

This, young man, is my second letter—I have wrote till I am stupid, I perceive—I ought to have found it out two pages back.—Mrs. Sancho joins me in good wishes—I join her in the same—in which double sense believe me,

Yours, &c. &c.
I. SANCHO

Very short.
Postscript.

It is with sincere pleasure I hear you have a lucrative establishment—which will enable you to appear and act with decency—your good sense will naturally lead you to proper economy—as distant from frigid parsimony, as from a heedless extravagancy—but as you may possibly have some time to spare upon your hands for necessary recreation—give me leave to obtrude my poor advice.—I have heard it more than once observed of fortunate adventurers—they have come home enriched in purse—but wretchedly barren in intellects—The mind, my dear Jack, wants food—as well as the stomach—Why then should not one wish to increase in knowledge as well as money?—Young says—"Books are fair Virtue's advocates and friends"—now my advice is—to preserve about 20£ a year for two or three seasons—by which means you may gradually form a useful, elegant, little library—suppose now the first year you send the order—and the money, to your father—for the following books—which I recommend from my own superficial knowledge as useful.—A man should know a little of Geography—History, nothing more useful, or pleasant.

Robertson's *Charles the Fifth*, 4 vols.
Goldsmith's *History of Greece*, 2 vols.
Ditto, *of Rome*, 2 vols.
Ditto, *of England*, 4 vols.[30]

Two small volumes of Sermons useful—and very sensible—by one Mr. Williams, a dissenting minister[31]—which are as well as fifty—for I love not a multiplicity of doctrines—a few plain tenets, easy, simple, and directed to the heart, are better than volumes of controversial nonsense.—Spectators—Guardians—and Tatlers[32]—you have of course.—Young's Night-Thoughts—Milton—and Thomson's Seasons were my summer companions—for near twenty years—they mended my heart—they improved my veneration to the Deity—and increased my love to my neighbours.

You have to thank God for strong natural parts—a feeling humane heart—You write with sense and judicious discernment—improve yourself, my dear Jack, that, if it should please God to return you to your friends with the fortune of a man in upper rank, the embellishments of your mind may be ever considered as greatly superior to your riches—and only inferior to the goodness of your heart. I give you the above as a sketch—your father and other of your friends will improve upon it in the course of time—I do indeed judge that the above is enough at first—in conformity with the old adage—"A few Books and a few Friends, and those well chosen."

Adieu, Yours,
I. SANCHO.

Letter XIV. To Mr. I[reland]. Jan. 1, 1779.

. . . . I address myself to you therefore, because my heart tells me—you will be a successful advocate for the blunders of a true Blackamoor.

Letter XVI. To Mr. F—. Jan. 1779.

. . . . As to the letters in question; you know, Sir, they are not now mine, but the property of the parties they are addressed to.—If you have had their permission—and think that the simple effusions of a poor Negro's heart are worth mixing with better things—you have my free consent to do as you please with them—though in truth there wants no increase of books in the epistolary way, nor indeed in any way—except we could add to the truly valuable names of Robertson—Beattie—and Mickle—new Youngs—Richardsons—and Sternes.[33]—Accept my best thanks for the very kind opinion you are so obliging to entertain of me—which is too pleasing (I fear) to add much to the humility of,

Dear Sir,

Yours, &c.

I. SANCHO.

Letter XXIX. To Mr. I[reland]. August 3, 1779.

. . . . Mr. Sharpe's [sic] strictures upon Slavery . . . I think of consequence to every one of humane feelings.[34]

Letter XXX. To Mr. M[eheux]. August 14, 1779.

. . . . I will that ye observe the above simile to be a good one . . . as pat to the purpose as dram-drinking to a bawd—or oaths to a serjeant of the guards—or—or—dullness to a Black-a-moor . . . .

Letter XXXIII. To Mr. S[tevenson]. August 31, 1779.

. . . . I meant this—not as an epistle of cold thanks—but the warm ebullitions of African sensibility.

Letter XXXVI. To Mr. M[eheux]. Sept. 4, 1779

The *Lamb*[35] just now kindly delivered to the *Bear*[36] the *Monkey's*[37] letter.—I am glad at heart that the forced exercise did thy hip no hurt—But that N[ancy] of thine—I do not like such faces—if she is half what she looks, she is too good for any place but heaven—where the hallelujahs are for ever chanting by such cherub-faced sluts as she—Thank God! she is neither daughter nor sister of mine—I should live in perpetual fear.—But why do I plague myself about her?

She has a protector in you—and foul befall the being (for no man would attempt it) that wishes to injure her!—Mrs. D— I could like so well, that I wish to know but very little of her;—strange, but true—and when you have been disappointed in your schemes of domestic happiness, and deceived in your too hasty-formed judgements, to the age of fifty, as oft as your friend, you will fully enter into my meaning.

She looks open—honest—intelligently sensible—good-natured—easy—polite and kind—knowledge enough of the world to render her company desirable—and age just sufficient to form her opinions, and fix her principles;—add to all this an agreeable face, good teeth, and a certain *Je ne sai quoi*[38] (forgive the spelling, and do not betray me):—but I say again and again—when one has formed a great opinion of either male or female—'tis best, for that opinion's sake, to look no further—there, rogue!

I shall take no notice of the tricking fraudulent behaviour of the driver of the stage—*as how* he wanted to palm a bad shilling upon us—and *as how* they stopped us in the town, and most generously insulted us—and *as how* they took up a fat old man—his wife *fat* too—and child—and after keeping us half an hour in sweet converse of the—of the *blasting* kind—how that the fat woman waxed wroth with her plump master, for his being serene—and how that he caught choler at her friction, tongue-wise—how he ventured his head out of the coach-door, and swore liberally—whilst his —, in direct line with poor S[tevenso]n's nose, entertained him with *sound* and sweetest of exhalations.—I shall say nothing of being two hours almost on our journey—neither do I remark that S[tevenso]n turned sick before we left G[reenwich], nor that the child p— upon his legs:—in short, it was near nine before we got into Charles Street.

Sir, the pleasures of the day made us more than amends—for the nonsense that followed.—Receipt in full.

I. SANCHO

My best respects to Mr. Y—; and my love, yea, cordial love to Nancy—Tell her—No—if I live to see her again, I will tell her myself.

Observe, we were seven in the coach—The breath of the old lady, in her heat of passion, was not rose-scented;—add to that, the warmth naturally arising from crowd—and anger—you will not wonder at S—t—'s being sick.—And he S—wanted to be in town rather sooner.—My compliments to George.—Mr. L— is so kind to promise to call for this scrawl—thank him for me, as well as for thyself.—Adieu.—Mrs. S[ancho] pretty well, the two Fanny's and Kitty but indifferent.

Letter XLI. To Mr. M[eheux]. October 5, 1779.

. . . . such beings I say as the one I am now scribbling to—should make elections of wide different beings—than Blackamoors for their friends:—the reason is obvious—from Othello to Sancho the big—we are either foolish—or mulish—all—all without a single exception.—Tell me, I pray you—and tell me truly—were there any Blackamoors in the Ark.—Pooh! why there now—I see you puzzled—well—well—be that as the learned shall hereafter decide.—I will defend and maintain my opinion—simply—I will do more—wager a crown upon it—nay, double that—and if my simple testimony faileth—Mrs. Sancho and the children five-deep will back me—that Noah, during his pilgrimage in the blessed ark—never with wife and six children set down to a feast upon a bit of finer—goodlier—fatter—sweeter—saltier—well-fed pork; we eat like hogs.

Letter XLVIII. To [John] S[pink], Esq. [Banker]. Charles Street, Nov. 21, 1779.

. . . . as I write first, and think afterwards, my epistles, are commonly in the Irish fashion.[39]

Letter LI. To D— B—e, ESQ. Dec. 17, 1779.

GOOD SIR,

A stranger to your person (not to your virtues) addresses you—will you pardon the interested intrusion? I am told you delight in doing good.—Mr. W[ingrav]e (who honors me with his friendships, by whose persuasion I presume to trouble you) declares—you are no respecter of country or colours—and encourages me further—by saying, that I am so happy (by the good offices of his too partial friendship) to have the interest and good wishes of Mr. B—e.

Could my wish be possibly effected to have the honor of a General-post-office settled in my house, it would certainly be a great good—as (I am informed) it would emancipate me from the fear of serving the parish offices—for which I am utterly unqualified through infirmities—as well as complexion.—Figure to yourself, my dear Sir, a man of a convexity of belly exceeding Falstaff—and a black face into the bargain—waddling in the van of poor thieves and pennyless prostitutes[40]—with all the supercilious mock dignity of little office—what a banquet for wicked jest and wanton wit—as needs must, when, &c. &c.—Add to this, my good Sir, the chances of being summoned out at midnight in the severity of easterly winds and frosty weather—subject as I unfortunately am to gout six months in twelve—the consequence of which must be death:—death! now I had much rather live—and not die—live indebted to the kindness of a few great and good—in which glorious class, you, dear Sir, have the pre-eminence—in the idea of

Your most respectful and obliged humble servant,

IGN. SANCHO [Sancho's request to operate a post office was denied.]

Letter LX. To Mr. [Jack] W[ingrav]e. Charles Street, Jan. 5, 1780.

Dear W—e,

Were I as rich in worldly commodity—as in hearty will, I would thank you most princely for your very welcome and agreeable letter;—but, were it so, I should not proportion my gratitude to your wants:—for, blessed be the God of thy hope! thou wantest nothing—more than—what's in thy possession—or in thy power to possess:—I would neither give thee *Money*—nor *Territory*—*Women*—nor *Horses*—nor *Camels*—nor the height of Asiatic pride—*Elephants*;—I would give thee *Books*—

"Books, fair Virtue's advocates and friends;"

but you have books plenty—more than you have time to digest:—after much writing—which is fatiguing enough—and under the lassitude occasioned by fatigue—and not sin—the cool recess—the loved book—the sweet pleasures of imagination poetically worked up into delightful enthusiasm—richer than all your fruits—your spices—your dancing girls—and the whole detail of eastern, effeminate foppery—flimsy splendour—and glittering magnificence—so thou thinkest—and I rejoice with thee and for thee: shall I say what my heart suggests? No, you will feel it praise—and call it flattery—shall I say, Your worthy parent read your filial letter to me—and embalmed the grateful tribute of a virtuous son with his precious tears.—Will you believe?—he was for some minutes speechless through joy:—imagine you see us—our heads close together—comparing notes;—imagine you hear the honest plaudits of love and friendship—sounding in thy ears;—'tis glory to be proud on such occasions—'tis the pride of merit—and as you allow me to counsel you with freedom—I do strongly advise you to love praise—to court praise—to win it by every honest, laudable exertion—and be oft—very often jealous of it: examine the source it proceeds from—and encourage and cherish it accordingly;—fear not—mankind are not too lavish of it—censure is dealt out by wholesale, while praise is very sparingly distributed—nine times in ten mankind may err in their blame—but in its praises the world is seldom, if ever, mistaken.—Mark—I praise thee *sincerely*, for the *whole* and every *part* of thy *conduct*, in regard to my two sable brethren.[41] I was an ass, or else I might have judged, from the national antipathy and prejudice through custom even of the Gentoos[42] towards their woolly-headed brethren, and the well-known dignity of my Lords the Whites, of the impropriety of my request.—I therefore not only acquit thee honourably—but condemn myself for giving thee the trouble to explain a right conduct.—I fear you will hardly make out this scrawl, although it is written with a pen of thy father's—a present, mended from a parcel of old quills by his foreman, or brother C—d.—Your honest brother Joseph came post with your letters—good-will shining in his face—joy in his innocent eyes:—

he promises to be as much a W—e as his Indian brother:—you flatter my vanity in supposing my friendship of any utility to Joe.;—he has in his good father Moses and the Prophets—which you have had—and availed yourself well of the blessing—and I trust Joe will do the same—besides having precept and example from a worthy and loving brother.—Poor M—, your favourite—I scarce knew her—she was as pure within, as amiable without—she enriches the circle of the blest—and you have a friend in heaven.

I hope you sometimes—aye often—consult with Dr. Young's *Night Thoughts*—carry him in your pockets—court him—quote him—delight in him—make him your own—and laugh at the wit, and wisdom, and fashion of the world:—that book well studied will make you know the value of death—and open your eyes to the snares of life;—its precepts will exalt the festive hour—brighten and bless the gloom of solitude—comfort thy heart, and smooth thy pillow in sickness—and gild with lustre thy prosperity—disarm death itself of its terrors—and sweetly soften the hour of dissolution.—I recommend all young people, who do me the honor to ask my opinion—I recommend, if their stomachs are strong enough for such intellectual food—Dr. Young's *Night Thoughts*—the *Paradise Lost*—and *the Seasons*;—which, with Nelson's *Feasts and Fasts*[43]—a Bible and Prayerbook—used for twenty years to make my traveling library—and I do think it a very rich one. I never trouble my very distant friends with articles of news—the public prints do it so much better—and then they may answer for their untruths—for among the multitude of our public prints, it is hard to say which lyes most.

Your enclosed trust was directly delivered to the fair hands it was addressed to;—I have the authority to say, it gave great pleasure to both the ladies and your friend Mr. R—, who wears the same cordial friendly heart in his breast as when you first knew him.—Your friend Mr. John R[ush] is still at New York with the guards—where he is very deservedly honored, loved, and esteemed:—he corresponds with his old acquaintance, and does me the honor to remember me amongst his friends:—our toast in P[rivy] Gardens is often the three Johns: R[ush], W[ingrav]e, and O[sborne, Mrs. Sancho's brother], an honest—therefore a noble triumvirate.

I feel old age insensibly stealing on me—and, alas! am obliged to borrow the aid of spectacles, for any kind of small print:—Time keeps pacing on, and we delude ourselves with the hope of reaching first this stage, and then the next;—till that ravenous rogue Death puts a final end to our folly.

All this is true—and yet I please and flatter myself with the hope of living to see you in your native country—with every comfort possessed—crowned with the honest man's best ambition— a fair character:—may your worthy, your respectable parents, relations, and friends, enjoy that pleasure! and that you may realize every fond hope of all who love you, is the wish of

Your sincere friend,
IGNATIUS SANCHO

Postscript.

This letter is of a decent length—I expect a return with interest.—Mrs. Sancho joins me in good wishes, love, and compliments.

Letter LXII. To Mr. S[tevenson]. Charles Street, Jan. 17, 1780.

. . . . I do request you to thank Mr. W— for me, and tell him he has the prayers—not of a raving mad whig—nor fawning deceitful tory—but of a coal-black, jolly African, who wishes health and peace to every religion and country throughout the ample range of God's creation!

Letter LXIV. To Mrs. H—. Charles Street, March 23, 1780.

. . . . We are all patriots, all politicians, all state quacks, and all fools: the ladies are turned orators, and declaim in public, expose their persons, and their erudition, to every jackanapes who can throw down half a crown:[44] as to the men, they are past saving . . . .

Letter LXV. For *The GENERAL ADVERTISER*. April 29, 1780 [1778].

FRIEND EDITOR,

"In the multitude of Counsellors there is wisdom,"[45] sayeth the preacher—and at this present crisis of national jeopardy, it seemeth to me befitting for every honest man to offer his mite of advice towards public benefit and edification.—The vast bounties offered for able-bodied men sheweth the zeal and liberality of our wise lawgivers—yet indicateth a scarcity of men. Now, they seem to me to have overlooked one resource (which appears obvious); a resource which would greatly benefit the people at large (by being more usefully employed), and which are happily half-trained already for the service of their country—by being—*powder proof*—light, active, young fellows:—I dare say you have anticipated my scheme, which is to form ten companies at least, out of the very numerous body of hairdressers—they are, for the most part, clean, clever, young men—and, as observed above, the utility would be immense:—the ladies, by once more getting the management of their heads into their own hands, might possibly regain their native reason and oeconomy—and the gentlemen might be induced, by mere necessity, to comb and care for their own heads—those (I mean) who have heads to care for.—If the above scheme should happily take place, among the many advantages, too numerous to particularize, which would of course result from it—one, not of the least magnitude, would be a prodigious saving in the great momentous article of time;—people of the *ton* of both sexes (to speak within probability) usually losing between two or three hours daily on that important business.—My plan, Mr. Editor, I have the comfort to think, is replete with good—it tends to serve my king and country in the first instance—and to cleanse, settle, and emancipate from the cruel bondage of French as well as native friseurs,[46] the heads of my fellow-subjects.

Yours, &c.
AFRICANUS.

Letter LXVI. To Mrs. H—. Charles Street, May, 20, 1780.

DEAR MADAM,

Your goodness is never tired with action—how many, very many times, have I to thank you, for your friendly interesting yourself in our behalf!—You will say, thanks are irksome to a generous mind—so I have done—but must first ask pardon for a sin of omission. I never sent you word, that your good son, as friendly as polite, paid me the note directly—and would not suffer it to run its sight;[47] they that know Sir Jacob will not wonder, for he is a Christian—which means, in my idea, a gentleman not of the modern sort.—Trade is at so low an ebb, the greatest are glad to see ready money.—In truth, we are a ruined people—let hirelings affect to write and talk as big as they please—and, what is worse, religion and morality are vanished with our prosperity—every good principle seems to be leaving us:—as our means lessen, luxury and every sort of expensive pleasure increases.—The blessed Sabbath-day is used by the trader for country excursions—tavern dinners—rural walks—and then whipping and galloping through dust and over turnpikes, drunk home.—The poorer sort do any thing—but go to church—they take their dust in the field, and conclude the sacred evening with riots, drunkenness, and empty pockets:—the beau in upper life hires his whisky and beast for twelve shillings; his girl dressed *en militaire* for half-a-guinea,[48] and spends his whole week's earnings to look and be thought *quite the thing*.—And for upper tiptop high life—cards and music are called in to dissipate the chagrin of a tiresome, tedious Sunday's evening.—The example spreads downwards from them to their domestics;—the laced valet and the livery beau either debauch the maids, or keep their girls—thus profusion and cursed dissipation fill the prisons, and feed the gallows.—The clergy—hush! I will not meddle with them—God forbid I should! they are pretty much the same in all places;—but this I will affirm, wherever a preacher is in earnest in his duty, and can *preach*, he will not want for crouded congregations.—As to our politics—now don't laugh at me—for every one has a right to be a politician; so have I; and though only a poor, thick-lipped son of Afric! may be as notable a Negro state-botcher as * * * * *, and so on for five hundred—I do not mean B—e, S—lle, B—e, nor D—n—g, mind that—no, nor N—th, G—m—e, J—k—n, nor W—dd—ne,[49] names that will shine in history when the marble monuments of their earthly flatterers shall be mouldering into dust.—I have wrote absolute nonsense—I mean the monuments of N—h, G—m—e, &c. and not of their flatterers—but it is right I should give you an apology for this foolish letter.—Know then, my dear Madam, I have been seriously and literally fast asleep for these two months;—true, upon the word of a poor sufferer, a kind of lethargy—I can sleep standing, walking, and feel so intolerably heavy and oppressed with it, that sometimes I am ready to tumble when walking in the street.—I am exceeding sorry to hear Mr. H— is so poorly—and hope, through God's mercy, the waters will have the wished effect;—for my own part, I feel myself ten years older this year than the last.—Time tries us all—but, blessed be God! in the end we shall be an over-match for Time, and leave him, scythe and all, in the lurch—when we shall enjoy a blessed Eternity.—In this view, and under the same hope, we are as great—yea, as respectable and consequential—as Statesmen! Bishops! Chancellors! Popes! Heroes! Kings! Actors of every denomination—who must all drop the mask when the fated minute arrives—and, alas! some of the very high be obliged to give place to Mr. and Mrs. H—. May you and yours enjoy every felicity here! every blessing hereafter! with thy much obliged friends!

THE SANCHOS.

Letter LXVII. To J— S—, Esq. Charles Street, June 6, 1780.[50]

DEAR AND MOST RESPECTED SIR,

In the midst of the most cruel and ridiculous confusion—I am now set down to give you a very imperfect sketch of the maddest people—that the maddest times were ever plagued with.—The public prints have informed you (without doubt) of last Friday's transactions;—the insanity of Lord G[eorge] G[ordon] and the worse than Negro barbarity of the populace;—the burnings and devastations of each night—you will also see in the prints:—this day, by consent, was set apart for the further consideration of the wished-for repeal;—the people (who had their proper cue from his lordship) assembled by ten o'clock in the morning.—Lord N[orth], who had been up in Council at home till four in the morning, got to the house before eleven, just a quarter of an hour before the associators reached Palace-yard:—but, I should tell you, in council there was a deputation from all parties;—The S[helburne][51] party were for prosecuting Ld G[ordon], and leaving him at large;—The A[ttorne]y G[enera]l laughed at the idea, and declared it was doing just nothing;—The M[inorit]y were for his expulsion, and so dropping him gently into insignificancy;—that was thought wrong, as he would still be industrious in mischief;—The R—m[52] party, I should suppose, you will think counselled best, which is, this day to expel him the house—commit him to the Tower—and then prosecute him at leisure—by which means he will lose the opportunity of getting a seat in the next parliament—and have decent leisure to repent him of the heavy evils he has occasioned.—There is at this present moment at least a hundred thousand poor, miserable, ragged rabble, from twelve to sixty years of age, with blue cockades in their hats[53]—besides half as many women and children—all parading the streets—the bridge—the park—ready for any and every mischief.—Gracious God! what's the matter now? I was obliged to leave off—the shouts of the mob—the horrid clashing of swords—and the clutter of a multitude in swiftest motion—drew me to the door—when every one in the street was employed in shutting up shop.—It is now just five o'clock—the ballad-singers are exhausting their musical talents—with the downfall of Popery, S[andwic]h, and N[ort]h.—Lord S[andwic]h narrowly escaped with life about an hour since;[54]—the mob seized his chariot going to the house, broke his glasses, and, in struggling to get his lordship out, they somehow have cut his face;—the guards flew to his assistance—the light-horse scowered the road, got his chariot, escorted him from the coffee-house, where he had fled for protection, to his carriage, and guarded him bleeding very fast home. This—this—is liberty! genuine British liberty!—This instant about two thousand liberty boys are swearing and swaggering by with large sticks—thus armed in hopes of meeting with the Irish chairmen[55] and labourers—all the guards are out—and all the horse;—the poor fellows are just worn out for want of rest, having been on duty ever since Friday.—Thank heaven, it rains; may it increase, so as to send these deluded wretches safe to their homes, their families, and wives! About two this afternoon, a large party took it into their heads to visit the King and Queen, and entered the Park for that purpose—but found the guard too numerous to be forced, and after some useless attempts gave it up.—It is reported, the house will either be prorogued, or parliament dissolved, this evening—as it is in vain to think of attending any business while this anarchy lasts.

I cannot but felicitate you, my good friend, upon the happy distance you are placed from our scene of confusion.—May foul Discord and her cursed train never nearer approach your blessed abode! Tell Mrs. S—, her good heart would ache, did she see the anxiety, the woe, in the faces of mothers, wives, and sweethearts, each equally anxious for the object of their wishes, the beloved of their hearts. Mrs. Sancho and self both cordially join in love and gratitude, and every good wish—crowned with the peace of God, which passeth all understanding, &c.

I am, dear Sir
Yours ever by inclination,
IGN. SANCHO

Postscript.

The Sardinian ambassador offered 500 guineas to the rabble, to save a painting of our Saviour from the flames, and 1000 guineas not to destroy an exceeding fine organ:[56] the gentry told him, they would burn him if they could get at him, and destroyed the picture and organ directly.—I am not sorry I was born in Afric.—I shall tire you, I fear—and, if I cannot get a frank,[57] make you pay dear for bad news.—There is about a thousand mad men, armed with clubs, bludgeons, and crows, just now set off for Newgate,[58] to liberate, they say, their honest comrades.—I wish they do not some of them lose their lives of liberty before morning. It is thought by many who discern deeply, that there is more at the bottom of this business than merely the repeal of an act—which has as yet produced no bad consequences, and perhaps never might.—I am forced to own that I am for an universal toleration. Let us convert by our example, and conquer by our meekness and brotherly love!

Eight o'clock. Lord G[eorge] G[ordon] has this moment announced to my Lords the mob—that the act shall be repealed this evening:—upon this, they gave a hundred cheers—took the horses from his hackney-coach—and rolled him full jollily away:—they are huzzaing now ready to crack their throats.

Huzzah.

I am forced to conclude for want of room—The remainder in our next.

Letter LXVIII. To J— S—. Esq. Charles Street, June 9, 1780.

MY DEAR SIR,

Government is sunk in lethargic stupor—anarchy reigns—when I look back to the glorious time of a George II and a Pitt's administration,[59] my heart sinks at the bitter contrast. We may now say of England, as was heretofore said of Great Babylon—"the beauty of the excellency of the Chaldees—is no more;"[60]—The Fleet Prison, the Marshalsea, King's-Bench, both Compters, Clerken-well, and Tothill Fields, with Newgate, are all flung open;—Newgate partly burned, and 300 felons from thence only let loose upon the world.—Lord M[ansfield]'s house in town suffered martyrdom, and his sweet box at Caen Wood escaped almost miraculously,[61] for the mob had just arrived, and were beginning with it—when a strong detachment from the guards and light-horse came most critically to its rescue—the library, and, what is of more consequence, papers and deeds of vast value, were all cruelly consumed in the flames.—L[or]d N[orth]'s house was attacked; but they had previous notice, and were ready for them. The Bank, the Treasury, and thirty of the chief noblemen's houses, are doomed to suffer by the insurgents.—There were six of the rioters killed at L[or]d M[ansfield]'s, and, what is remarkable, a daring chap, escaped from Newgate, and condemned to die this day, was the most active in mischief at L[or]d M[ansfield]'s, and was the first person shot by the soldiers: so he found death a few hours sooner than if he had not been released.—The ministry have tried lenity, and have experienced its inutility; and martial law is this night to be declared.—If any body of people above ten in number are seen together, and refuse to disperse, they are to be fired at without any further ceremony—so we expect terrible work before morning;—the insurgents visited the Tower, but it would not do—they had better luck in the Artillery-ground, where they found and took to their use 500 stand of arms; a great error in city politics not to have secured them first.—It is wonderful to hear the execrable sense that is industriously circulated amongst the credulous mob—who are told his M[ajest]y regularly goes to mass at L[or]d P[et]re's chapel[62]—and they believe it, and that he pays out of his privy purse Peter-pence to Rome.[63] Such is the temper of the times—from too relaxed a government;—and a King and Queen on the throne who possess every virtue. May God in his mercy grant that the present scourge may operate to our repentance and amendment! that it may produce the fruits of better thinking, better doing, and in the end make us a wise, virtuous, and happy people!—I am, dear Sir, truly Mrs. S—'s and your most grateful and obliged friend and servant,

I. SANCHO

The remainder in our next.

Half past nine o'clock. King's-Bench prison is now in flames, and the prisoners at large; two fires in Holborn now burning.

Letter LXIX. June 9, 1780.

DEAR SIR,

Happily for us the tumult begins to subside—last night much was threatened, but nothing done—except in the early part of the evening, when about fourscore or an hundred of the reformers got decently knocked on the head;—they were half killed by Mr. Langdale's spirits[64]—so fell an easy conquest to the bayonet and butt-end.—There is about fifty taken prisoners—and not a blue cockade to be seen:—the streets once more wear the face of peace—and men seem once more to resume their accustomed employments;—the greatest losses have fallen upon the great distiller near Holborn-bridge, and Lord M[ansfield];—the former, alas! has lost his whole fortune;—the latter, the greatest and best collection of manuscript writings, with one of the finest libraries in the kingdom.—Shall we call it a judgment?—or what shall we call it? The thunder of their vengeance has fallen upon gin and law—the two most inflammatory things in the Christian world.—We have a Coxheath and Warley of our own;[65] Hyde Park has a grand encampment, with artillery, Park, &c. &c. St. James's Park has ditto—upon a smaller scale. The Parks, and our West end of the town, exhibit the features of French government. This minute, thank God! this moment Lord G[eorge] G[ordon] is taken. Sir F. Molineux[66] has him safe at the horse-guards. Bravo! he is now going in state in an old hackney-coach, escorted by a regiment of militia and troop of light horse to his apartments in the Tower.

"Off with his head—so much—for Buckingham."[67]

We have taken this day numbers of the poor wretches, in so much we know not where to place them. Blessed be the Lord! we trust this affair is pretty well concluded. . . .

Letter LXX. To J— S—, Esq. June 13, 1780.

. . . . Sickness! cruel sickness! triumphs through every part of the constitution:—the state is sick—the church (God preserve it!) is sick—the law, navy, army, all sick—the people at large are sick with taxes—the Ministry with Opposition, and Opposition with disappointment.—Since my last, the temerity of the mob has gradually subsided;—numbers of the unfortunate rogues have been taken:—yesterday about thirty were killed in and about Smithfield, and two soldiers were killed in the affray.—There is no certainty yet as to the number of houses burnt and gutted, for every day adds to the account—which is a proof how industrious they were in their short reign. Few evils but are productive of some good in the end:—the suspicious turbulence of the times unites the royal brothers;[68]—the two Dukes, dropping all past resentments, made a filial tender of their services:—His Majesty, God bless him! as readily received it—and on Thursday last the brothers met—They are now a triple cord— God grant a blessing to the union! There is a report current this day, that the mob of York city have rose, and let 3000 French prisoners out of York-castle—but it meets with very little credit, I do not believe they have any thing like the number of French in those parts, as I am informed the prisoners are sent more to the western inland counties,—but every hour has its fresh cargo of lies. The camp in St. James's Park is daily increasing—that and Hyde Park will be continued all summer.—The K[in]g is much among them, walking the lines, and examining the posts—He looks exceeding grave. Crowns, alas! have more thorns than roses. . . .

America seems to be quite lost or forgot amongst us . . . .

Letter LXXIX. To Mrs. C[ocksedge, later Lady Bunbury]. Charles Street, Sept. 7, 1780.

. . . .—The shew of hands was greatly in favour of Mr. Charles Fox and Sir George Rodney; they will carry it all to nothing, is the opinion of the knowing.—Lord L[incoln] met with a coarse reception, at which he was a little displeased. . . . the glorious Fox was the father and school of oratory himself—the Friend! the Patron! the Example!—There now.—I attended the hustings from ten to half past two—gave my free vote to the Honorable Charles James Fox and to Sir George Rodney;[69] hobbled home full of pain and hunger . . . .

NOTES

1. Ignatius Sancho's 159 letters were published posthumously. Sancho is the only eighteenth-century Afro-Briton to be accorded an entry in the *Dictionary of National Biography*, but we have little more biographical information about him than was available to his contemporaries, and that is found in "The life of Ignatius Sancho," by Joseph Jekyll (1754-1837), which prefaces the *Letters*:

> The extraordinary Negro, whose Life I am about to write, was born A.D. 1729, on board a ship in the Slave-trade, a few days after it had quitted the coast of Guinea for the Spanish West-Indies; and at Cathagena [in the Spanish colony of New Granada, present-day Colombia] he received from the hand of the Bishop, Baptism, and the name of Ignatius [in honor of the sixteenth-century Spanish founder of the Jesuits, Saint Ignatius of Loyola].
>
> A disease of the new climate put an early period to his mother's existence; and his father defeated the miseries of slavery by an act of suicide.
>
> At little more than two years old, his master brought him to England, and gave him to three maiden sisters, resident at Greenwich; whose prejudices had unhappily taught them, that African ignorance was the only security for his obedience, and that to enlarge the mind of their slave would go near to emancipate his person. The petulance of their disposition surnamed him Sancho, from a fancied resemblance to the 'Squire of Don Quixote [Sancho Panza, the comic servant in *Don Quixote* (1605, 1615), by Miguel de Cervantes Saavedra (1547-1616)].
>
> But a patron was at hand, whom Ignatius Sancho had merit enough to conciliate at a very early age.
>
> The late Duke of Montagu [John, second Duke of Montagu (1688?-1749), who had met Job Ben Solomon, and who was the patron of Francis Williams as well] lived on Blackheath: he accidentally saw the little Negro, and admired in him a native frankness of manner as yet unbroken by servitude, and unrefined by education.—He brought him frequently home to the Duchess, indulged his turn for reading with presents of books, and strongly recommended to his mistresses the duty of cultivating a genius of such apparent fertility.
>
> His mistresses, however, were inflexible, and even threatened on angry occasions to return Ignatius Sancho to his African slavery. The love of freedom had increased with years, and began to beat high in his bosom.—Indignation, and the dread of constant reproach arising from the detection of an amour, infinitely criminal in the eyes of three maiden ladies, finally determined him to abandon the family.
>
> His noble patron was recently dead.—Ignatius flew to the Duchess for protection, who dismissed him with reproof.—He retired from her presence in a state of despondency and stupefaction.
>
> Enamoured still of that liberty, the scope of whose enjoyment was now limited to his last five shillings, and resolute to maintain it with life, he procured an old pistol for purposes which his father's example had suggested as familiar, and had sanctified as hereditary.
>
> In this frame of mind the futility of remonstrance was obvious. The Duchess secretly admired his character; and at length consented to admit him into her household, where he remained as butler [a position which usually earned about 15£ per year at the time] till her death [in 1751], when he found himself, by her Grace's bequest and his own oeconomy, possessed of seventy pounds in money, and an annuity of thirty.
>
> Freedom, riches, and leisure, naturally led a disposition of African texture into indulgences; and that which dissipated the mind of Ignatius completely drained the purse. In his attachment to women, he displayed a profuseness which not unusually characterizes the excess of the passion.—Cards had formerly seduced him; but an unsuccessful contest at cribbage with a Jew, who won his clothes, had determined him to abjure the propensity, which appears to be innate among his countrymen.—A French writer relates, that in the

kingdoms of Ardrah, Whydah, and Benin, a Negro will stake at play his fortune, his children, and his liberty. Ignatius loved the theatre to such a point of enthusiasm, that his last shilling went to Drury-Lane, on Mr. [David] Garrick's representation of Richard [III].—He had been even induced to consider the stage as a resource in the hour of adversity, and his complexion suggested an offer to the manager [Garrick (1717-1779) became the manager of Drury Lane Theater in 1747] of attempting [Shakespeare's] Othello and Oroonoko [the title role in the 1695 play by Thomas Southerne (1659-1746) based on the 1688 romance/novel by Aphra Behn (1640-1689)]; but a defective and incorrigible articulation rendered it abortive.

He turned his mind once more to service, and was retained a few months by the Chaplain at Montagu-house. That roof had been ever auspicious to him; and the present Duke [George Brudenell (1712-1790), became, in 1766, the 1st Duke of Montagu of the new creation, having changed his name to Montagu in 1749; he married Mary, daughter of the 2nd Duke] soon placed him about his person, where habitual regularity of life led him to think of a matrimonial connexion, and he formed one accordingly with a very deserving young woman of West-Indian origin. [Charles Ignatius Sancho (Sancho's full name) married Ann Osborne on 17 December 1758 in St. Margaret's Church, Westminster, the same church in which Olaudah Equiano would be baptized two months later. Ann died at the age of 84 and was buried on 25 November 1817.]

Towards the close of the year 1773, repeated attacks of the gout, and a constitutional corpulence, rendered him incapable of further attendance in the Duke's family.

At this crisis, the munificence which had protected him through various vicissitudes did not fail to exert itself; with the result of his own frugality, it enabled him and his wife to settle themselves in a shop of grocery [at No. 20 Charles Street, Westminster], where mutual and rigid industry decently maintained a numerous family of [six] children, and where a life of domestic virtue engaged private patronage and merited public imitation.

In December 1780, a series of complicated disorders destroyed him. [He died on 14 December and was buried at Westminster Broadway. *The Gentleman's Magazine* recorded his death: "In Charles-str. Westminster, Mr. Ignatius Sancho, grocer and oilman; a character immortalized by the epistolary correspondence of Sterne." In *A Dictionary of the English Language* (London, 1755), Samuel Johnson defines an *oilman* as "One who trades in oils and pickles."]

Of a Negro, a Butler, and a Grocer, there are but slender anecdotes to animate the page of the biographer; but it has been held necessary to give some sketch of the very singular man, whose letters, with all their imperfections, on their head, are now offered to the public.

The display those writings exhibit of epistolary talent, of rapid and just conception, of wild patriotism, and of universal philanthropy, may well apologize for the protection of the Great, and the friendship of the Literary.

The late Duchesses of Queensbury [Catherine Hyde, third Duchess of Queensberry, 1700-1777] and Northumberland [Lady Elizabeth Seymour, second Duchess of Northumberland, 1716-1776] pressed forward to serve the author of them. The former intrusted to his reformation a very unworthy favourite of his own complexion [Julius Soubise].—Garrick and [Laurence] Sterne were well acquainted with Ignatius Sancho.

A commerce with the Muses was supported amid the trivial and momentary interruptions of a shop; the Poets were studied, and even imitated with some success;—two pieces were constructed for the stage;—the Theory of music was discussed, published, and dedicated to the Princess Royal;—and Painting was so much within the circle of Ignatius Sancho's judgment and criticism, that [John Hamilton] Mortimer [1741-1779] came often to consult him.

Such was the man whose species philosophers and anatomists have endeavoured to degrade as a deterioration of the human. . . .

To the harsh definition of the naturalist, oppressions political and legislative have been added; and such are hourly aggravated towards this unhappy race of men by vulgar prejudice and popular insult. To combat these on commercial principles, has been the labour of . . . Bennezet [*sic*, Anthony Benezet (1713-1784), Quaker abolitionist writer]—such an effort here would be an impertinent digression.

Of those who have speculatively visited and described the slave-coast, there are not wanting some who extol the mental abilities of the natives. . . . [Francis] Moore and [Willem, or William] Bosman speak highly of their mechanical powers and indefatigable industry. . . .

He who could penetrate the interior of Africa, might not improbably discover negro arts and polity, which could bear little analogy to the ignorance and grossness of slaves in the sugar-islands, expatriated in infancy, and brutalized under the whip and the task-master.

And he who surveys the extent of intellect to which Ignatius Sancho had attained by self-education, will perhaps conclude, that the perfection of the reasoning faculties does not depend on a peculiar conformation of the skull or the colour of a common integument [skin]. (i-ix)

The noted painter Thomas Gainsborough (1727-1788) completed Sancho's portrait at Bath in one hour and forty minutes. That portrait was the model for the frontispiece engraved by Francesco Bartolozzi (1727-1815) for Sancho's *Letters.* The sculptor Joseph Nollekens (1737-1823) and the painter Richard Cosway (1742?-1821) were also among Sancho's famous friends. Sancho commissioned Nollekens to cast for him a bust of Sterne; Cosway was Ottobah Cugoano's employer during the mid-1780s, a subscriber to Cugoano's 1791 publication, and, like Cugoano (and Sancho's son William), one of Olaudah Equiano's original subscribers. Samuel Johnson (1709-1784), according to Jekyll's handwritten note on the flyleaf of his copy of the fifth edition of the *Letters* (London, 1803), had promised to write the introductory life of Sancho but neglected to fulfill the task. Sancho's fame in his own lifetime was primarily due to the appearance of his correspondence with Sterne in *Letters of the Late Rev. Mr. Laurence Sterne to his Most Intimate Friends etc., and Published by his Daughter, Mrs. Medalle,* 3 vols. (London, 1775). A manuscript letter from the aspiring author George Cumberland (1754-1848) to his brother Richard, vicar of Driffield in Gloucester County, attests to Sancho's reputation as a literary critic:

Now we are upon this subject [George's publications] I must tell you (because it pleases my vanity so to do) that a Black Man, Ignatius Sancho, has lately put me into unbounded conceit with myself—he is said to be a great Judge of literary performances (G-d send it may be true.) and has praised my Tale of Cambambo and Journal wh. I read to him, so highly, that I shall like him as long as I live, nothing less than publishing I fear will satisfy him—but what would not one do to oblige so good a kind of Man?—In the mean time as he is a grocer I think it would be proper to buy all my Tea & Sugar of him, and make him heir to all the emoluments arising from the consumption of those articles in my houshold.—It is true they are *not* very great at present—but *when* I have *gained a fortune* by *my writings,* they must be very considerable! (ADD. Ms. 36492, ff. 204 recto and verso.)

Sancho's *Letters* was reviewed rather dismissively in *The Gentleman's Magazine* 52 (September 1782), 437-439: "with all their philanthropy, for which we give the author his due credit, few of them are little more than common-place effusions, such as many other Negroes, we suppose, could, with the same advantages, have written" (438). The review in *The European Magazine and London Review* 2 (September 1782), 199-202, is more favorable:

THE volumes here presented to the public, will be read with avidity and pleasure by those who desire to promote the common elevation of the human race. To those who wish

> to degrade the species, and to set limits to the kindness of the Deity, these letters will be no welcome repast; for they will shew them the error of that ill opinion. . . . These letters may bear to be examined with severe criticism. They have the ease of epistles written in the openness of nature, and in the playful familiarity of friendship. They breathe unaffected piety—and have the ardour of genuine patriotism. At the same time it must not be expected that these letters are to be taken as models of this species of writing. They have more warmth than elegance of diction, and more feeling than correctness. (199)

Both reviews make much of Sancho's correspondence with Sterne, printing lengthy excerpts.

Subsequent editions of Sancho's *Letters* were published in 1783 (London); 1784 (London); 1784 (Dublin); 1802 (London); and 1803, the "Fifth Edition" (London). Published by Sancho's son William, the "Fifth Edition" has been reliably edited by Paul Edwards and Polly Rewt, *The Letters of Ignatius Sancho* (Edinburgh: University of Edinburgh Press, 1994).

2. The editor, to whom several of the letters are addressed, was probably Frances Crew (or Crewe), who married on 5 March 1782 John Phillips, surgeon of the household of the Prince of Wales, the future King George IV (1762-1830).

According to Alexander Chalmers (1759-1834), *The General Biographical Dictionary* (London, 1812-1817), "The first edition was patronized by a subscription [of 1,216 names] not known since the days of the *Spectator*. . . . From the profits of the first edition, and a sum paid by the booksellers for liberty to print a second edition [1783], Mrs. Sancho . . . received more than 500£."

The favorable notices Sancho's *Letters* received in the published reviews were seconded by William Whitehead (1715-1785), Poet Laureate since 1757, in an August 1782 letter to George Simon Harcourt, second Earl Harcourt (1736-1809):

> I should likewise, naturally, from the word *grocer*, digress to Ignatius Sancho's letters, to which, I perceive, your Lordship is not a subscriber, tho' a Mr. Mason is; whether the Revd. Precentor or not, he only can determine. Lady Jersey is, & the books are here, & there is a long list likewise of many of your acquaintance. I shall read them immediately, for he seems a worthy creature from what I have seen by dipping, but I have not time to say anything more about him. (Edward William Harcourt, ed., *The Harcourt Papers* [Oxford: James Parker and Co., 1880], 7:356)

3. Brought to England from St. Kitt's as a slave at the age of ten, Julius Soubise (1754-1798) gained the favor of Sancho's friend, the Duchess of Queensberry, who had Soubise taught fencing and riding and whose generosity enabled him to live a life of womanizing and fashion. An amateur violinist, singer, and actor, he soon became the subject of satiric engravings as a macaroni or fop, ran up debts, ignored Sancho's advice to reform, and finally caused his patroness to send him to Calcutta as a riding instructor to repair his fortunes and recover his reputation after he raped one of the Duchess's maids. He departed on 15 July 1777, just before a report of the rape was published in *The Morning Post* on 22 July. Two days after his departure, the Duchess died. Soubise never returned. His success in India was abruptly ended by his death on 25 August 1798 from injuries sustained in a fall from a horse.

His only known publication is "A Love letter" to "the Honourable Miss G—, a celebrated toast, with a fortune of 30,000£," in Anonymous, *Nocturnal Revels, or the History of King's Place* (London, 1779), 2:210-232:

> Dear Miss,
>
> I have often beheld you in public with rapture; indeed it is impossible to view you without such emotions as must animate every man of sentiment. In a word, Madam, you have

seized my heart, and I dare tell you, I am your *Negro Slave.* You startle at this expression, Madam; but I love to be sincere. I am of that swarthy race of ADAM, whom some despise on account of their complexion; but I begin to find from experience, that even this trial of our patience may last but for a time, as Providence has given such knowledge to Man, as to remedy all the evils of this life. There is not a disorder under the sun which may not, by the skill and industry of the learned, be removed: so do I find, that similar applications in the researches of medicine, have brought to bear such discoveries, as to remove the tawny hue of any complexion, if applied with skill and perseverance. In this pursuit, my dear Miss, I am resolutely engaged, and hope, in a few weeks, I may be able to throw myself at your feet, in as agreeable a form as you can desire; in the mean time, believe me with the greatest sincerity,

Your's most devotedly,
My Lovely Angel,
Soubise

Besides Sancho's *Letters*, the other main sources of information about Soubise are two works by his friend Henry Angelo (1756-1835): *Reminiscences* (London, 1828) and *Angelo's Pic Nic* (London, 1834).

4. Teague: a stock contemptuous name for an Irishman.

5. Laurence Sterne (1713-1768): the clergyman author of the extremely popular comic novel *The Life and Opinions of Tristram Shandy, Gentleman* (London, 1759-1767), *A Sentimental Journey through France and Italy* (London, 1768), and *The Sermons of Mr. Yorick* (London, 1760-1769). Sancho flatteringly imitates the distinctive prose style of Sterne, especially in his use of dashes, and after Sancho solicited subscriptions from the Duke and Duchess of Montagu for the ninth volume of *Tristram Shandy*, Sterne addressed him on 16 May 1767 as "my good Sancho." By 30 June 1767, he is "My honest friend Sancho."

Sterne's initial response to Sancho, whom he had never met, is dated 27 July 1766 and was written as Sterne was working on the ninth, the last, volume of *Tristram Shandy*:

There is a strange coincidence, Sancho, in the little events (as well as in the great ones) of this world: for I had been writing a tender tale of the sorrows of a friendless poor negro-girl, and my eyes had scarce done smarting with it, when your Letter of recommendation in behalf of so many of her brethren and sisters, came to me—but why *her brethren*?—or your's, Sancho! any more than mine? It is by the finest tints, and most insensible gradations, that nature descends from the fairest face about St. James's [fashionable people strolled in St. James's Park, adjoining the Royal Palace of St. James], to the sootiest complexion in africa: at which tint of these, is it, that the ties of blood are to cease? and how many shades must we descend lower still in the scale, 'ere Mercy is to vanish with them?—but 'tis no uncommon thing, my good Sancho, for one half of the world to use the other half of it like brutes, & then endeavour to make 'em so. for my own part, I never look *Westward* (when I am in a pensive mood at least) but I think of the burdens which our Brothers and Sisters are *there* carrying—& could I ease their shoulders from one ounce of 'em, I declare I would set out this hour upon a pilgrimage to Mecca for their sakes—. . . .

If I can weave the Tale I have wrote into the Work I'm abt—tis at the service of the afflicted—and a much greater matter; for in serious truth, it casts a sad Shade upon the World, That so great a part of it, are and have been so long bound in chains of darkness & in Chains of Misery.

The "poor negro-girl" appears in chapter 6 of volume 9 of *Tristram Shandy*:

When Tom, an' please your honour, got to the shop, there was nobody in it, but a poor negro girl, with a bunch of white feathers slightly tied to the end of a long cane, flapping away flies—not killing them.—'Tis a pretty picture! said my uncle Toby—she had suffered persecution, Trim, and had learnt mercy—

—She was good, an' please your honour, from nature as well as from hardships; and there are circumstances in the story of that poor friendless slut [a hard-working girl, not an immoral one] that would melt a heart of stone, said Trim; and some dismal winter's evening, when your honour is in the humour [mood], they shall be told you with the rest of Tom's story, for it makes a part of it—

Then do not forget, Trim, said my uncle Toby.

A Negro has a soul? an' please your honour, said the Corporal (doubtingly).

I am not much versed, Corporal, quoth my uncle Toby, in things of that kind; but I suppose, God would not leave him without one, any more than thee or me—

—It would be putting one sadly over the head of another, quoth the Corporal.

It would be so; said my uncle Toby. Why then, an' please your honour, is a black wench to be used worse than a white one?

I can give no reason, said my uncle Toby—

—Only, cried the Corporal, shaking his head, because she has no one to stand up for her—

—'Tis that very thing, Trim, quoth my uncle Toby,—which recommends her to protection—and her brethren with her; 'tis the fortune of war which has put the whip into our hands *now*—where it may be hereafter, heaven knows!—but be it where it will, the brave, Trim! will not use it unkindly.

—God forbid, said the Corporal.

Amen, responded my uncle Toby, laying his hand upon his heart.

6. Sancho quotes from Sterne's "Job's Account of the Shortness and Troubles of Life, Considered," in Sterne's *The Sermons of Mr. Yorick* (London, 1760), 2:98. Sancho misidentifies the page as 78.

7. Sarah Scott (1723-1795), *The History of Sir George Ellison* (London, 1766).

8. Moors: a general name for all Africans.

9. The Irish pension list was one of the more notorious abuses of the power England had over Ireland, using income from Ireland to fund dependents of the Crown.

10. Sancho refers to an episode in *A Sentimental Journey*.

11. See Zechariah 9:9 and Matthew 21:5.

12. Tamarinds: the tamarind tree had long seed pods, in which the seeds were embedded in a pulp called tamarinds, used during the period as a laxative.

13. John Henderson (1747-1785).

14. James Quin (1693-1766).

15. Probably Jabez Fisher of Philadelphia.

16. Perhaps a reference to recent antislavery works like *A Short Account of that Part of Africa, Inhabited by the Negroes. . . . and the Manner by which the Slave Trade is Carried on. . . .* (Philadelphia, 1762), by Benezet, or to those by Sharp, mentioned in note 33.

17. Your sect: like Benezet, Mr. F- was probably a Quaker, or member of the Society of Friends, who were among the first to come out against slavery and the slave trade.

18. Turban . . . lawn-sleeves: the dress, respectively, of the Moslem and Anglican clergy.

19. Phyllis's poems: Phillis Wheatley, *Poems on Various Subjects, Religious and Moral* (London, 1773).

20. See Luke 10:30-37.

21. Quoted from Alexander Pope (1688-1744), *An Essay on Criticism* (London, 1711), 9-10.

22. Henry Fielding (1707-1754), author of comic dramas and the novels *Joseph Andrews* (London, 1742), *Tom Jones* (London, 1749), and *Amelia* (London, 1751).

23. Allworthy: the good but flawed country gentleman in *Tom Jones*, who eventually learns to distinguish the good from the bad characters and makes Tom his heir.

24. Parson Adams: the comic hero of Fielding's *Joseph Andrews.*
25. Jonathan Swift (1667-1745), author of *Gulliver's Travels* (London, 1726).
26. John Milton (1608-1674), author of *Paradise Lost* (London, 1667).

Edward Young (1683-1765), author of *The Complaint; or Night Thoughts on Life, Death and Immortality* (London, 1742-1745).

James Thomson (1700-1748), author of *The Seasons* (London, 1726-1730).

Mark Akenside (1721-1770), author of *Pleasures of the Imagination* (London, 1744).

27. Nabob: someone who has returned to Britain with a fortune made in India.
28. [Note in original.] Extracts from two letters from Mr. W—e to his Father, dated Bombay, 1776 and 1777.

1776. I have introduced myself to Mr. G—, who behaved very friendly in giving me some advice, which was very necessary, as the inhabitants, who are chiefly Blacks, are a set of canting, deceitful people, and of whom one must have great caution.

1777. I am now thoroughly convinced, that the account which Mr. G— gave me of the natives of this country is just and true, that they are a set of deceitful people, and have not such a word as Gratitude in their language, neither do they know what it is—and as to their dealings in trade, they are like unto Jews.

29. The American Revolution, from the English perspective, was a civil war.
30. William Robertson (1721-1793), author of *The History of the Reign of Charles V* (London, 1769).

Oliver Goldsmith (1730?-1774), author of a *Grecian History* (London, 1774), a *Roman History* (London, 1769), and a *History of England in a Series of Letters from a Nobleman to his Son* (London, 1764).

31. Probably David Williams (1738-1816), *Sermons, Chiefly upon Religious Hypocrisy...* (London, 1774).
32. Joseph Addison (1672-1719) contributed to the collections of essays primarily written and published by Richard Steele (1672-1729): *The Tatler* (1709-1711), and *The Spectator* (1711-1712), and *The Guardian* (1713).
33. James Beattie (1735-1803), author of the *Essay on the Nature and Immutability of Truth* (1770) and *The Minstrel* (London, 1771, 1774), a poem.

William Julius Mickle (1734-1788), author of many poems and translator of *The Lusiad*, a Portuguese epic by Camoens.

Samuel Richardson (1689-1761), author of the novels *Pamela* (London, 1740), *Clarissa* (London, 1747-1748), and *The History of Sir Charles Grandison* (London, 1754).

34. Sharpe: Granville Sharp (1753-1813), a leader of the movement to abolish slavery, and author of many abolitionist works, including *A Representation of the Injustice and Dangerous Tendency of Tolerating Slavery; or of Admitting the Least Claim of Private Property in the Persons of Men, in England* (London, 1769) and *The Just Limitation of Slavery in the Laws of God, Compared with the Unbounded Claims of the African Traders and British American Slaveholders* (London, 1776). Sharp brought a number of cases of fugitive slaves before the courts, including the Somerset case, which led to the Mansfield judgment in June 1772.
35. [Note in original.] Mr. M—'s Sister.
36. [Note in original.] Meaning himself.
37. [Note in original.] Mr. M—, to whom he often gave that title.
38. French for "I know not what."
39. Sterne was born in Ireland.
40. Sancho imagines himself performing the parish duty of a night watchman rounding up petty criminals
41. [Note in original.] Mr. W—e having wrote word, that if any European in India associated with those of that complexion, it would be considered as a degradation, and would be an obstacle to his future preferment: he laments in very strong terms the cruelty of such an opinion, hopes not to forfeit Mr. Sancho's good opinion from being compelled

to comply with the custom of the country, with repeated assurances of serving them, if in his power; though he must remain unknown to them.

42. Gentoos: Hindus (from the Portuguese for "pagans").

43. The often reprinted *Companion for the Festivals and Fasts of the Church of England* (1704), by the Anglican divine Robert Nelson (1656-1715).

44. Jackanapes: coxcomb, impertinent fellow. Half a crown: the traditional price for the services of the most inexpensive streetwalker.

45. Compare Proverbs 24:6: "For by wise counsel thou shalt make thy war: and in multitude of counsellors *there is* safety."

46. Friseurs: French hairdressers.

47. To run its sight: to come due, to reach the date by which it must be paid.

48. En militaire: at this stage in the war with the North American colonies, fashionable young women dressed in the military uniforms of British soldiers.

49. Sancho's list of politicians includes both opponents and members of the governing ministry of Lord North. Probable identifications include the following:

B—e: Edmund Burke (1729-1797), a leading Parliamentary opponent of the North ministry (1770-1782), especially its American policy. Listed as a subscriber to Sancho's *Letters.*

S—lle: perhaps Sir George Savile (1726-1784), a consistent Parliamentary opponent of the ministry. In 1778 he introduced the bill for the relief of Roman Catholics against which the Gordon Riots of 1780 were directed.

B—e: Isaac Barré (1726-1802), another vigorous Parliamentary opponent of the ministry.

D—n—g: John Dunning (1731-1783), a strong opponent of the ministry and most famous for his resolution in Parliament on 6 April 1780 that the influence of the Crown had increased, was increasing, and ought to be diminished.

N—th: Frederick North (1732-1792), First Lord of the Treasury and thus head of the governing ministry, 10 February 1770-27 March 1782. Listed as a subscriber to Sancho's *Letters.*

G—m—e: George Sackville (1716-1785), assumed the surname Germain(e) in 1770, appointed by North in December 1775 as Secretary of State for the Colonies. His rigidity alienated him from the British military leaders against the rebels, and he quickly became the primary target of opponents of the ministry's American policy as well as a political embarrassment to the government because he refused to resign without a peerage, which George III finally promised him in February 1782.

J—k—n: Charles Jenkinson (1729-1808), Secretary at War, 1778-1782, and very influential within the ministry and in its dealings with the King.

W—dd—ne: Alexander Wedderburn(e) (1733-1805), joined the North ministry as Solicitor General in 1771, in 1778 became Attorney General and shortly thereafter Chancellor to the Queen, Privy Councillor, and Lord Chief Justice of the Court of Common Pleas.

50. Letters XVII-XX to John Spink, a banker at Bury St. Edmunds, relate Sancho's rare eyewitness account of the Gordon Riots, the worst riots in English history, with probably far more than the government's estimate of about 300 people killed, an inestimable amount of property damaged and demolished, and 192 people convicted, with 25 executed. What began as a relatively peaceful demonstration on 2 June 1780 by fifty thousand people petitioning Parliament to repeal a recently enacted law granting Roman Catholics minor relief from legal restrictions, quickly degenerated into a mob. They released prisoners, destroyed prisons, and ransacked and demolished the homes of the wealthy, the powerful, and those they considered sympathetic to the Roman Catholics, as well as Roman Catholic chapels in Moorfields and Spitalfields. As President of the Protestant Association for the Repeal of the Relieving Act of 1778, Lord George Gordon (1751-1793) was widely held responsible for instigating the almost two weeks of disturbances. What prompted the delayed

reaction to the Act of 1778 was the proposal of similar legislation for Scotland in 1779. The Royal Proclamation against the rioters, issued on 7 June by King George III (1738-1820), brought in twenty thousands troops to restore order. Arrested and sent to the Tower of London on 9 June 1780, Gordon was held for eight months before being tried in the King's Bench on 5 February 1781 and acquitted on a charge of treason.

51. William Petty (1737-1805), first Marquis of Lansdowne and second Earl of Shelburne, a leading spokesman in the House of Lords for reform. As prime minister from July 1782 to February 1783, Shelburne conducted the final peace negotiations with the former thirteen colonies in British North America.

52. The Rockingham party: Charles Watson-Wentworth (1730-1782), second Marquess of Rockingham, and his political allies, including Edmund Burke, who formed the most organized Parliamentary opposition to the North ministry. Rockingham led the ministry (13 July 1765 to 2 August 1766) that repealed the Stamp Act.

53. Blue cockades: worn by Protestants to distinguish them from supporters of the Roman Catholic Relief Act.

54. John Montagu (1718-1792), fourth Earl of Sandwich, First Lord of the Admiralty, 12 January 1771 to 30 March 1782.

55. Irish immigrants frequently took jobs as chairmen, carriers of people in sedan chairs, an occupation that required great strength.

56. The mob destroyed the Roman Catholic chapel of the Sardinian Ambassador.

57. Frank: before the development of the modern postal service a letter writer had to pay a carrier for a *frank*, or stamp. Otherwise, the recipient paid for postage due. Members of the Houses of Parliament were privileged to send and receive mail unfranked and free of charge.

58. Crows: crowbars. Newgate: rebuilt betweenn 1770 and 1778, Newgate prison was destroyed during the Gordon Riots, with hundreds of prisoners released by the mob. After it was again rebuilt between 1780 and 1783, one of its most famous inmates was Lord Gordon, who was imprisoned on a charge unrelated to the riots and died therein of jail fever in 1793.

59. Sancho refers to the British victories over France and Spain (Britain's current enemies) in the Seven Years' War of 1756 to 1763, during the ministry of William Pitt "the Elder" (1708-1778), at the end of the reign of George II (1683-1760).

60. Isaiah 13:19.

61. William Murray (1705-1793), Baron Mansfield (1756), and Earl Mansfield (1792), Lord Chief Justice of the King's Bench.

62. Father Edmund Petre was the confessor of James II, whose apparent attempts to reestablish Roman Catholicism in England led to his overthrow in the Glorious Revolution of 1688-1689. Robert Petre (1742-1801), 9th Baron Petre, was a leading Roman Catholic peer.

63. Peter's Pence: the annual penny tribute paid to the pope at the feast of St. Peter. Henry VIII abolished this custom in England in 1534.

64. Langdale, a Roman Catholic who owned one of the largest distilleries in London, lost more than £100,000 when the mob set fire to his distillery. Many rioters were poisoned by drinking the unrectified gin released into the streets by the heat of the flames.

65. After the French formed a military alliance with the American colonists against the British in 1778, military camps were set up in Cavenham, Coxheath, and Warley.

66. The features of French government: unlike Britain, France had a professional police force, a concept that struck most Britons as a threat to individual liberty.

Sir Francis Molyneux (ca. 1736-1812), Baronet.

67. The most famous, or notorious, line that dramatist and poet laureate Colley Cibber (1671-1757) added to his 1700 adaptation of William Shakespeare's *Richard III* (4.4.189).

68. William Henry (1743-1805), Duke of Gloucester, and Henry Frederick (1745-1790), Duke of Cumberland, were alienated from their brother George III because he disapproved of the marriages they had made.

69. As recipients of the two highest vote totals, George Brydges Rodney (1719-1792), with 5,298 votes, and Charles James Fox (1749-1806), with 4,878 votes, defeated the ministerial candidate, Thomas Pelham Clinton (1752-1795), styled twelfth Earl of Lincoln, who received 4,157 votes. Admiral Rodney was serving in the West Indies during the election. Fox was one of the leading voices in Parliament who opposed the policies of the North ministry in the war with the North American Colonies.

In his 9 September 1780 letter to John Spink, Sancho says that he "had the honour of [Fox's] thanks personally." Fox was one of the subscribers to Sancho's *Letters.* Sancho is the only identifiable Afro-British voter in the eighteenth century, but as Thomas Rowlandson's print *Every Man Has His Hobby Horse,* published during the 1784 election, illustrates, he was probably not the only Afro-Briton whose vote Fox received. Sancho's votes for Fox and Rodney are recorded in *Copy of the Poll for the Election of Two Citizens to Serve in the Present Parliament for the City and Liberty of Westminster* (London, 1780), 234. In 1774, Sancho had voted for the winning candidates: Hugh, commonly called Earl, Percy, running as an opposition candidate; and the same ministerial candidate Sancho would vote against in 1780, Thomas Pelham Clinton (*A Correct Copy of the Poll, for Electing Two Representatives in Parliament, for the City and Liberty of Westminster* [London, 1774], 15.) The bipartisan nature of the subscribers to Sancho's *Letters* reflects his own bipartisan voting record.

John Marrant

(15 June 1755-15 April 1791)

A NARRATIVE OF THE LORD's wonderful DEALINGS WITH JOHN MARRANT, A BLACK, *(Now going to Preach the GOSPEL in Nova-Scotia) Born in NEW-YORK, in NORTH-AMERICA.* Taken down from his own Relation, ARRANGED, CORRECTED, and PUBLISHED By the Rev. Mr. *ALDRIDGE.* The Fourth Edition, Enlarged by Mr. MARRANT, and Printed (with Permission) for His Sole Benefit, WITH NOTES EXPLANATORY (*London*: PRINTED FOR THE AUTHOR, By R. HAWES, No. 40, Dorset-Street Spitalfields, [1785]).[1]

THY PEOPLE SHALL BE WILLING IN THE DAY
OF THY POWER, Psalm. cx. 3.

DECLARE HIS WONDERS AMONG ALL THE PEOPLE,
Psalm. xcvi. 3.

PREFACE

READER,

THE following Narrative is as plain and artless, as it is surprising and extraordinary. Plausible reasonings may amuse and delight, but facts, and facts like these, strike, are felt, and go home to the heart. Were the power, grace and providence of God ever more eminently displayed, than in the conversion, success, and deliverances of John Marrant? *He and his companion enter the meeting at* Charles-Town[2] *together; but the one is taken, and the other is left. He is struck to the ground, shaken over the mouth of hell, snatched as a brand from the burning; he is pardoned and justified; he is washed in the atoning blood, and made happy in his God. You soon have another view of him, drinking into* [*sic*] *his master's cup; he is tried and perplext, opposed and despised; the neighbours hoot at him as he goes along; his mother, sisters, and brother, hate and persecute him; he is friendless and forsaken of all. These uneasy circumstances call forth the corruptions of his nature, and create a momentary debate, whether the pursuit of ease and pleasure was not to be preferred to the practice of religion, which he now found so sharp and severe? The stripling is supported and strengthened. He is persuaded to forsake his family and kindred altogether. He crosses the fence, which marked the boundary between the wilderness and the cultivated country; and prefers the habitations of brutal residence, to the less hospitable dwellings of enmity to God and godliness. He wanders, but Christ is his guide and protector. Who can view him among the* Indian *tribes without wonder? He arrives among the* Cherokees, *where gross ignorance wore its rudest forms, and savage despotism exercised its most terrifying empire. Here the child just turned fourteen, without sling or stone, engages, and with the arrow of prayer pointed with faith, wounded* Goliah, *and conquers the King.*[3]

The untutor'd monarch feels the truth, and worships the God of the Christians; the seeds of the Gospel are disseminated among the Indians *by a youthful hand, and Jesus is received and obeyed.*

The subsequent incidents related in this Narrative are great and affecting; but I must not anticipate the reader's pleasure and profit.

The novelty or magnitude of the facts contained in the following pages, may dispose some readers to question the truth of them. My answer to such is,—1. I believe it is clear to great numbers, and to some competent judges, that God is with the subject of them; but if he knowingly permitted an untruth to go abroad in the name of God, whilst it is confessed the Lord is with him, would it not follow, that the Almighty gave his sanction to a falsehood?—2. I have observed him to pay a conscientious regard to his word.—3. He appeared to me to feel most sensibly, when he related those parts of his Narrative, which describe his happiest moments with God, or the most remarkable interpositions of Divine Providence for him; and I have no reason to believe it was counterfeited.

I have always preserved Mr. Marrant's *ideas, tho' I could not his language; no more alterations, however, have been made, than were thought necessary.*

I now commit the whole to God.—That he may make it generally useful is the prayer of thy ready servant, for Christ's sake,

W. ALDRIDGE.[4]
London,
July 19th, 1785.

A

NARRATIVE, &c.

I, JOHN MARRANT, born June 15th, 1755, in New-York, in North-America, wish these gracious dealings of the Lord with me to be published, in hopes they may be useful to others, to encourage the fearful, to confirm the wavering, and to refresh the hearts of true believers. My father died when I was little more than four years of age, and before I was five my mother removed from New-York to St. Augustine, about seven hundred miles from that city.[5] Here I was sent to school, and taught to read and spell; after we had resided here about eighteen months, it was found necessary to remove to Georgia, where we remained; and I was kept to school until I had attained my eleventh year. The Lord spoke to me in my early days, by these removes, if I could have understood him, and said, "Here we have no continuing city."[6] We left Georgia, and went to Charles-Town, where it was intended I should be put apprentice to some trade. Some time after I had been in Charles-Town, as I was walking one day, I passed by a school, and heard music and dancing, which took my fancy very much, and I felt a strong inclination to learn the music. I went home, and informed my sister, that I had rather learn to play upon music than go to a trade. She told me she could do nothing in it, until she had acquainted my mother with my desire. Accordingly she wrote a letter concerning it to my mother, which, when she read, the contents were disapproved of by her, and she came to Charles-Town to prevent it. She persuaded me much against it, but her persuasions were fruitless. Disobedience either to God or man, being one of the fruits of sin,[7] grew out from me in early buds. Finding I was set upon it, and resolved to learn nothing else, she agreed to it, and went with me to speak to the man, and to settle upon the best terms with him she could. He insisted upon twenty pounds currency,[8] which was paid, and I was engaged to stay with him eighteen months, and my mother to find me every thing during that term. The first day I went to him he put the violin into my hand, which pleased me much, and, applying close, I learned very fast, not only to play, but to dance also; so that in six months I was able to play for the whole school. In the evenings after the scholars were dismissed, I used to resort to the bottom of our garden, where it was customary for some musicians to assemble to blow the French-horn. Here my improvement was so rapid, that in a twelve-month's time I became master both of the violin and of the French-horn, and was much respected by the Gentlemen and Ladies whose children attended the school, as also by my master. This opened to me a large door of vanity and vice, for I was invited to all the balls and assemblies that were held in the town, and met with the general applause of the inhabitants. I was a stranger to want, being supplied with as much money as I had any occasion for; which my sister observing, said, "You have now no need of a trade." I was now in my thirteenth year, devoted to pleasure, and drinking in iniquity like water; a slave to every vice suited to my nature and to my years. The time I had engaged to serve my master being expired, he persuaded me to stay with him, and offered me anything, or any money, not to leave him.[9] His intreaties proving ineffectual, I quitted his service, and visited my mother in the country; with her I staid two months, living without God or hope in the world, fishing and hunting on the sabbath-day. Unstable as water, I returned to town, and wished to go to some trade. My sister's husband being informed of my inclination, provided me with a master, who was a carpenter in that town, on condition that I should serve him one year and a half on trial, and afterwards be bound,[10] if he approved of me. Accordingly I went, but every evening I was sent for to play on music, somewhere or another; and I often continued out very late, sometimes all night, so as to render me incapable of attending my master's business the next day, yet in this manner I served him a year and four months, and was much approved of by him. He wrote a letter to my mother to come and have me bound, and whilst my mother was weighing the matter in her own mind, the gracious purposes of God, respecting a perishing sinner, were now to be disclosed. One evening I was sent for in a very particular manner to go and play for some Gentlemen, which I agreed to do, and was on my way to fulfill my promise; and passing by a large meeting house I saw many lights in it, and crowds of people going in. I enquired what it meant, and was answered by my companion, that a crazy man was hallooing there; this raised my curiosity to go in, that I might hear what he was hallooing about. He persuaded me not to go in, but in vain. He then said, "If you will do one thing I will go in with you." I asked him what that was? He replied, "Blow the French horn among them." I liked the proposal well enough, but expressed my fears of being beaten for disturbing them; but upon his promising to stand by and defend me, I agreed. So we went, and with much difficulty got within the doors. I was pushing the people to make room, to get the horn off my shoulder to blow it, just as Mr. Whitefield was naming his text,[11] and looking round, and, as I thought, directly upon me, and pointing with his finger, he uttered these words, "PREPARE TO MEET THY GOD, O ISRAEL."[12] The Lord accompanied the word with such power, that I was struck to the ground, and lay both speechless and senseless near half an hour. When I was come a little too, I found two men attending me, and a woman throwing water in my face, and holding a smelling-bottle to my nose; and when something more recovered, every word I heard from the minister was like a parcel of swords thrust into me, and what added to my distress, I thought I saw the devil on every side of me.[13] I was constrained in the bitterness of my spirit to halloo out in the midst of the congregation, which disturbing them, they took me away; but finding I could neither walk or stand, they carried me as far as the vestry, and there I remained till the service was over. When the people were dismissed Mr. Whitefield came into the vestry, and being told of my condition he came immediately, and the first word he said to me was, "JESUS CHRIST HAS GOT THEE AT LAST." He asked where I lived, intending to come and see me the next day; but recollecting he was to leave the town the next morning, he said he could not come himself, but would send another minister; he desired them to get me home, and then taking his leave of me, I saw him no more. When I reached my sister's house, being carried by two men, she was very uneasy to see me in so distressed a condition. She got me to bed, and sent for a doctor, who came immediately, and after looking at me, he went home, and sent me a bottle of mixture, and desired her to give me a spoonful every two hours; but I could not take anything the doctor sent, nor indeed keep in bed; this distressed my sister very much, and she cried out, "The lad will surely die." She sent for two other doctors, but no medicine they prescribed could I take. No, no; it may be asked, a wounded spirit who can cure? as well as who can bear? In this distress of soul I continued for three days without any food, only a little water now and then.[14] On the fourth day, the minister[15] Mr. Whitefield had desired to visit me came to see me, and being directed upstairs, when he entered the room, I thought he made my distress much worse. He wanted to take hold of my hand, but I durst not give it to him. He insisted upon taking hold of it, and I then got away from him on the other side of the bed; but being very weak I fell down, and before I could recover he came to me and took me by the hand, and lifted me up, and after a few words desired to go to prayer. So he fell upon his knees, and pulled me down also; after he had spent some time in prayer he rose up, and asked me how I did now; I answered much worse; he then said, "Come, we will have the old thing over again," and so we kneeled down a second time, and after he had prayed earnestly we got up, and he said again, "How do you do now?" I replied worse and worse, and asked him if he intended to kill me? "No, no," said he, "you are worth a thousand dead men, let us try the old thing over again," and so falling upon our knees, he continued in prayer a considerable time, and near the close of his prayer, the Lord was pleased to set my soul at perfect liberty, and being filled with joy I began to praise the Lord immediately; my sorrows were turned into peace, and joy, and love. The minister said, "How is it now?" I answered, all is well, all happy. He then took his leave of me; but called every day for several days afterwards, and the last time he said, "Hold fast that thou hast already obtained, 'till Jesus Christ come."[16] I now read the Scriptures very much. My master sent often to know how I did, and at last came himself, and finding me well, asked me if I would not come to work again? I answered no. He asked me the reason, but receiving no answer he went away. I continued with my sister about three weeks, during which time she often asked me to play upon the violin for her, which I refused; then she said I was crazy and mad, and so reported it among the neighbours, which opened the mouths of all around against me. I then resolved to go to my mother, which was eighty-four miles from Charles-Town. I was two days on my journey home, and enjoyed much communion with God on the road, and had occasion to mark the gracious interpositions of his kind Providence as I passed along. The third day I arrived at my mother's house, and was well received. At supper they sat down to eat without asking the Lord's blessing, which caused me to burst out into tears. My mother asked me what was the matter? I answered, I wept because they sat down to supper without asking the Lord's blessing. She bid me, with much surprise, to ask a blessing. I remained with her fourteen days without interruption; the Lord pitied me, being a young soldier.[17] Soon, however, Satan began to stir up my two sisters and brother, who were then at home with my mother; they called me every name but that which was good. The more they persecuted me, the stronger I grew in grace. At length my mother turned against me also, and the neighbours joined her, and there was not a friend to assist me, or that I could speak to; this made me earnest with God. In these circumstances, being the youngest but one of our family, and young in Christian experience, I was tempted so far as to threaten my life; but reading my Bible one day, and finding that if I did destroy myself I could not come where God was, I betook myself to the fields, and some days staid out from morning to night to avoid the persecutors. I staid one time two days without any food, but seemed to have clearer views into the spiritual things of God.

Not long after this I was sharply tried, and reasoned the matter within myself, whether I should turn to my old courses of sin and vice, or serve and cleave to the Lord; after prayer to God, I was fully persuaded in my mind, that if I turned to my old ways I should perish eternally. Upon this I went home, and finding them all as hardened, or worse than before, and every body saying I was crazy; but a little sister I had, about nine years of age, used to cry when she saw them persecute me, and continuing so about five weeks and three days, I thought it was better for me to die than to live among such people. I rose one morning very early, to get a little quietness and retirement, I went into the woods, and staid till eight o'clock in the morning; upon my return I found them all at breakfast; I passed by them, and went up-stairs without any interruption; I went upon my knees to the Lord, and returned him thanks; then I took up a small pocket Bible and one of Dr. Watts's hymnbooks,[18] and passing by them went out without one word spoken by any of us. After spending some time in the fields, I was persuaded to go from home altogether. Accordingly I went over the fence, about half a mile from our house, which divided the inhabited and cultivated parts of the country from the wilderness. I continued travelling in the desart all day without the least inclination of returning back. About evening I began to be surrounded with wolves; I took refuge from them on a tree, and remained there all night. About eight o'clock next morning I descended from the tree, and returned God thanks for the mercies of the night. I went on all this day without anything to eat or drink.

The third day, taking my Bible out of my pocket, I read and walked for some time, and then being wearied and almost spent, I sat down, and after resting awhile I rose to go forward; but had not gone above a hundred yards when something tripped me up, and I fell down; I prayed to the Lord upon the ground that he would command the wild beasts to devour me, that I might be with him in glory. I made this request to God the third and part of the fourth day.

The fourth day in the morning, descending from my usual lodging, a tree, and having nothing all this time to eat, and but a little water to drink, I was so feeble that I tumbled half way down the tree, not being able to support myself, and lay upon my back on the ground about an hour and a half, praying and crying; after which, getting a little strength, and trying to stand upright to walk, I found myself not able; then I went upon my hands and knees, and so crawled till I reached a tree that was tumbled down, in order to get across it, and there I prayed with my body leaning upon it above an hour, that the Lord would take me to himself. Such nearness to God I then enjoyed, that I willingly resigned myself into his hands. After some time I thought I was strengthened, so I got across the tree without my feet or hands touching the ground; but struggling I fell over on the other side, and then thought the Lord will now answer my prayer, and take me home. But the time was not come. After laying there a little, I rose, and looking about, saw at some distance bunches of grass, called deer-grass; I felt a strong desire to get at it; though I rose, yet it was only on my hands and knees, being so feeble, and in this manner I reached the grass. I was about three-quarters of an hour going in this form twenty yards. When I reached it I was unable to pull it up, so I bit it off like a horse, and prayed the Lord to bless it to me, and I thought it the best meal I ever had in my life, and I think so still, it was so sweet.[19] I returned my God hearty thanks for it, and then lay down about an hour. Feeling myself very thirsty, I prayed the Lord to provide me with some water. Finding I was something strengthened, I got up, and stood on my feet, and staggered from one tree to another, if they were near each other, otherwise the journey was too long for me. I continued moving so for some time, and at length passing between two trees, I happened to fall upon some bushes, among which were a few large hollow leaves, which had caught and contained the dews of the night, and lying low among the bushes, were not exhaled by the solar rays; this water in the leaves fell upon me as I tumbled down and was lost, I was now tempted to think the Lord had given me water from Heaven, and I had wasted it, I then prayed the Lord to forgive me.[20] What poor unbelieving creatures we are! though we are assured the Lord will supply all our needs. I was presently directed to a puddle of water very muddy, which some wild pigs had just left; I kneeled down, and asked the Lord to bless it to me, so I drank both mud and water mixed together, and being satisfied I returned the Lord thanks, and went on my way rejoicing. This day was much chequered with wants and supplies, with dangers and deliverances. I continued travelling on for nine days, feeding upon grass, and not knowing whither I was going; but the Lord Jesus Christ was very present, and that comforted me through the whole.

The next morning, having quitted my customary lodging, and returned thanks to the Lord for my preservation through the night, reading and travelling on, I passed between two bears, about twenty yards distance from each other. Both sat and looked at me, but I felt very little fear; and after I had passed them, they both went the same way from me without growling, or the least apparent uneasiness. I went and returned God thanks for my escape, who had tamed the wild beasts of the forest, and made them friendly to me: I rose from my knees and walked on, singing hymns of praise to God, about five o'clock in the afternoon, and about fifty-five miles from home, right through the wilderness. As I was going on, and musing upon the goodness of the Lord, an Indian hunter, who stood at some distance, saw me; he hid himself behind a tree; but as I passed along he bolted out, and put his hands on my breast, which surprized me a few moments. He then asked me where I was going? I answered I did not know, but where the Lord was pleased to guide me. Having heard me praising God before I came up to him, he enquired who I was talking to? I told him I was talking to my Lord Jesus; he seemed surprized, and asked me where he was? for he did not see him there. I told him he could not be seen with bodily eyes. After a little more talk, he insisted upon taking me home; but I refused, and added, that I would die rather than return home. He then asked me if I knew how far I was from home? I answered, I did not know; you are fifty-five miles and a half, says he, from home. He farther asked me how I did to live? I said I was supported by the Lord. He asked me how I slept? I answered, the Lord provided me with a bed every night; he further enquired what preserved me from being devoured by the wild beasts? I replied, the Lord Jesus Christ kept me from them. He stood astonished, and said, you say the Lord Jesus Christ do this, and do that, and do every thing for you, he must be a very fine man, where is he? I replied, he is here present. To this he made me no answer, only said, I know you, and your mother and sister; and upon a little further conversation I found he did know them, having been used in winter to sell skins in our Town. This alarmed me, and I wept for fear he should take me home by force; but when he saw me so affected, he said he would not take me home if I would go with him. I objected against that, for fear he would rob me of my comfort and communion with God: But at last, being much pressed, I consented to go. Our employment for ten weeks and three days was killing deer, and taking off their skins by day, which we afterwards hung on the trees to dry till they were sent for; the means of defence and security against our nocturnal enemies always took up the evenings: We collected a number of large bushes, and placed them nearly in a circular form, which uniting at the extremity, afforded us both a verdant covering, and a sufficient shelter from the night dews. What moss we could gather was strewed upon the ground, and this composed our bed. A fire was kindled in the front of our temporary lodging-room, and fed with fresh fuel all night, as we slept and watched by turns; and this was our defense from the dreadful animals, whose shining eyes and tremendous roar we often saw and heard during the night.

By constant conversation with the hunter, I acquired a fuller knowledge of the Indian tongue: This, together with the sweet communion I enjoyed with God, I have considered as a preparation for the great trial I was soon after to pass through.

The hunting season being now at an end, we left the woods, and directed our course towards a large Indian town, belonging to the Cherokee nation; and having reached it, I said to the hunter, they will not suffer me to enter in. He replied, as I was with him, nobody would interrupt me.

There was an Indian fortification all round the town, and a guard placed at each entrance. The hunter passed one of these without molestation, but I was stopped by the guard and examined. They asked me where I came from, and what was my business there? My companion of the woods attempted to speak for me, but was not permitted; he was taken away, and I saw him no more. I was now surrounded by about fifty men, and carried to one of their principal chiefs and Judge to be examined by him. When I came before him, he asked me what was my business there? I told him I came there with a hunter, whom I met with in the woods. He replied, "Did I not know that whoever came there without giving a better account of themselves than I did, was to be put to death?" I said I did not know it. Observing that I answered him so readily in his own language, he asked me where I learnt it? To this I returned no answer, but burst out into a flood of tears, and calling upon my Lord Jesus. At this he stood astonished, and expressed a concern for me, and said I was young. He asked me who my Lord Jesus was?—To this I gave him no answer, but continued praying and weeping. Addressing himself to the officer who stood by him, he said he was sorry; but it was the law, and it must not be broken. I was then ordered to be taken away, and put into a place of confinement. They led me from their court into a low dark place, and thrust me into it, very dreary and dismal; they made fast the door, and set a watch. The judge sent for the executioner, and gave him his warrant for my execution in the afternoon of the next day. The executioner came, and gave me notice of it, which made me very happy, as the near prospect of death made me hope for a speedy deliverance from the body: And truly this dungeon became my chapel, for the Lord Jesus did not leave me in this great trouble, but was very present, so that I continued blessing him, and singing his praises all night without ceasing.[21] The watch hearing the noise, informed the executioner that somebody had been in the dungeon with me all night; upon which he came in to see and to examine, with a great torch lighted in his hand, who it was I had with me; but finding nobody, he turned round, and asked me who it was? I told him it was the Lord Jesus Christ; but he made no answer, turned away, went out, and fastened the door. At the hour appointed for my execution I was taken out, and led to the destined spot, amidst a vast number of people. I praised the Lord all the way we went, and when we arrived at the place I understood the kind of death I was to suffer, yet, blessed be God, none of those things moved me.

When the executioner shewed me a basket of turpentine wood, stuck full of small pieces, like skewers; he told me I was to be stripped naked, and laid down on one side by the basket, and these sharp pegs were to be stuck into me, and then set on fire, and when they had burnt to my body,[22] I was to be turned on the other side, and served in the same manner, and then to be taken by four men and thrown into the flame, which was to finish the execution; I burst into tears, and asked what I had done to deserve so cruel a death? To this he gave me no answer. I cried out, Lord, if it be thy will that it should be so, thy will be done: I then asked the executioner to let me go to prayer; he asked me to whom? I answered, to the Lord my God; he seemed surprized, and asked me where he was? I told him he was present; upon which he gave me leave. I desired them all to do as I did, so I fell down upon my knees, and mentioned to the Lord his delivering of the three children in the fiery furnace,[23] and of Daniel in the lion's den,[24] and had close communion with God. I prayed in English a considerable time, and about the middle of my prayer, the Lord impressed a strong desire upon my mind to turn into their language, and pray in their tongue. I did so, and with remarkable liberty, which wonderfully affected the people. One circumstance was very singular, and strikingly displays the power and grace of God. I believe the executioner was savingly converted to God. He rose from his knees, and embracing me round the middle was unable to speak for about five minutes; the first words he expressed, when he had utterance, were, "No man shall hurt thee till thou hast been to the king."[25]

I was taken away immediately, and as we passed along, and I was reflecting upon the deliverance which the Lord had wrought out for me, and hearing the praises which the executioner was singing to the Lord, I must own I was utterly at a loss to find words to praise him. I broke out in these words, what can't the Lord Jesus do! and what power is like unto his! I will thank thee for what is passed, and trust thee for what is to come. I will sing thy praise with my feeble tongue whilst life and breath shall last, and when I fail to sound thy praises here, I hope to sing them round thy throne above: And thus, with unspeakable joy, I sung two verses of Dr. Watts's hymns:

My God, the spring of all my joys,
The life of my delights;
The glory of my brightest days,
And comfort of my nights.
In darkest shades, if thou appear,
My dawning is begun;
Thou art my soul's bright morning star,
And thou my rising sun.[26]

Passing by the judge's door, he stopped us, and asked the executioner why he brought me back? The man fell upon his knees, and begged he would permit me to be carried before the king, which being granted, I went on, guarded by two hundred men with bows and arrows. After many windings I entered the king's outward chamber, and after waiting some time he came to the door, and his first question was, how came I there? I answered, I came with a hunter whom I met with in the woods, and who persuaded me to come there. He then asked me how old I was? I told him not fifteen. He asked me how I was supported before I met with this man? I answered, by the Lord Jesus Christ, which seemed to confound him. He turned round, and asked me if he lived where I came from? I answered, yes, and here also. He looked about the room, and said he did not see him; but I told him I felt him. The executioner fell upon his knees, and intreated the king in my behalf, and told him what he had felt of the same Lord. At this instant the king's eldest daughter came into the chamber, a person about nineteen years of age, and stood at my right hand. I had a Bible in my hand, which she took out of it, and having opened it, she kissed it, and seemed much delighted with it. When she had put it into my hand again, the king asked me what it was? And I told him the name of my God was recorded there; and after several questions, he bid me read it, which I did, particularly the fifty-third chapter of Isaiah,[27] in the most solemn manner I was able; and also the twenty-sixth chapter of Matthew's Gospel;[28] and when I pronounced the name of Jesus, the particular effect it had upon me was observed by the king. When I had finished reading, he asked me why I read those names[29] with so much reverence? I told him, because the Being to whom those names belonged made heaven and earth, and I and he; this he denied. I then pointed to the sun, and asked him who made the sun, and moon, and stars, and preserved them in their regular order; He said there was a man in their town that did it. I laboured as much as I could to convince him to the contrary. His daughter took the book out of my hand a second time; she opened it, and kissed it again; her father bid her give it to me, which she did; but said, with much sorrow, the book would not speak to her.[30] The executioner then fell upon his knees again, and begged the king to let me go to prayer, which being granted, we all went upon our knees, and now the Lord displayed his glorious power. In the midst of the prayer some of them cried out, particularly the king's daughter, and the man who ordered me to be executed, and several others seemed under deep conviction of sin: This made the king very angry; he called me a witch, and commanded me to be thrust into the prison, and to be executed the next morning. This was enough to make me think, as old Jacob once did, "All these things are against me;"[31] for I was dragged away, and thrust into the dungeon with much indignation; but God, who never forsakes his people, was with me. Though I was weak in body, yet was I strong in the spirit:[32] The executioner went to the king, and assured him, that if he put me to death, his daughter would never be well. They used the skill of all their doctors that afternoon and night; but physical prescriptions were useless. In the morning the executioner came to me, and, without opening the prison door, called to me, and hearing me answer, said, "Fear not, thy God who delivered thee yesterday, will deliver thee to-day." This comforted me very much, especially to find he could trust the Lord. Soon after I was fetched out; I thought it was to be executed; but they led me away to the king's chamber with much bodily weakness, having been without food two days. When I came into the king's presence, he said to me, with much anger, if I did not make his daughter and that man well, I should be laid down and chopped into pieces before him. I was not afraid, but the Lord tried my faith sharply. The king's daughter and the other person were brought out into the outer chamber, and we went to prayer; but the heavens were locked up to my petitions. I besought the Lord again, but received no answer: I cried again, and he was intreated. He said, "Be it to thee as thou wilt;"[33] the Lord appeared most lovely and glorious; the king himself was awakened, and the others set at liberty. A great change took place among the people; the king's house became God's house; the soldiers were ordered away, and the poor condemned prisoner had perfect liberty, and was treated like a prince. Now the Lord made all my enemies to become my great friends. I remained nine weeks in the king's palace, praising God day and night: I was never out but three days all the time. I had assumed the habit of the country, and was dressed much like the king, and nothing was too good for me. The king would take off his golden ornaments, his chain and bracelets, like a child, if I objected to them, and lay them aside. Here I learnt to speak their tongue in the highest stile.

I began now to feel an inclination growing upon me to go farther on, but none to return home. The king being acquainted with this, expressed his fears of my being used ill by the next Indian nation, and to prevent it, sent fifty men, and a recommendation to the king, with me. The next nation was called the Creek Indians, at sixty miles distance. Here I was received with kindness, owing to the king's influence, from whom I had parted; here I staid five weeks. I next visited the Catawar[34] Indians, at about fifty-five miles distance from the others: Lastly, I went among the Housaw[35] Indians, eighty miles distant from the last mentioned; here I staid seven weeks. These nations were then at peace with each other, and I passed among them without danger, being recommended from one to the other. When they recollect, that the white people drove them from the American shores, they are full of resentment. These nations have often united, and murdered all the white people in the back settlements which they could lay hold of, men, women, and children. I had not much reason to believe any of these three nations were savingly wrought upon, and therefore I returned to the Cherokee nation, which took me up eight weeks. I continued with my old friends seven weeks and two days.

I now and then found, that my affections to my family and country were not dead; they were sometimes very sensibly felt, and at last strengthened into an invincible desire of returning home. The king was much against it; but feeling the same strong bias towards my country, after we had asked Divine direction, the king consented, and accompanied me sixty miles with one hundred and forty men. I went to prayer three times before we could part, and then he sent forty men with me a hundred miles farther; I went to prayer, and then took my leave of them, and passed on my way. I had seventy miles now to go to the back settlements of the white people. I was surrounded very soon with wolves again, which made my old lodging both necessary and welcome. However it was not long, for in two days I reached the settlements, and on the third I found a house: It was about dinner-time, and as I was coming to the door the family saw me, were frightened, and ran away. I sat down to dinner alone, and eat[36] very heartily, and, after returning God thanks, I went to see what was become of the family. I found means to lay hold of a girl that stood peeping at me from behind a barn. She fainted away, and it was upwards of an hour before she recovered; it was nine o'clock before I could get them all to venture in, they were so terrified.

My dress was purely in the Indian stile; the skins of wild beasts composed my garments; my head was set out in the savage manner, with a long pendant down my back, a sash round my middle, without breeches, and a tomohawk by my side. In about two days they became sociable. Having visited three or four other families, at the distance of sixteen or twenty miles, I got them altogether to prayer on the Sabbath days, to the number of seventeen persons. I staid with them six weeks, and they expressed much sorrow when I left them. I was now one hundred and twelve miles from home. On the road I sometimes met with a house, then I was hospitably entertained; and when I met with none, a tree lent me the use of its friendly shelter and protection from the prowling beasts of the woods during the night. The God of mercy and grace supported me thus for eight days, and on the ninth I reached my uncle's house.

The following particulars, relating to the manner in which I was made known to my family, are less interesting; and yet, perhaps, some readers would not forgive their omission: I shall, however, be as brief as I can. I asked my uncle for a lodging, which he refused. I enquired how far the town was off; three quarters of a mile, said he. Do you know Mrs. Marrant and family, and how the children do? was my next question. He said he did, they were all well, but one was lately lost; at this I turned my head and wept. He did not know me, and upon refusing again to lodge me, I departed. When I reached the town it was dark, and passing by a house where one of my old school-fellows lived, I knocked at the door; he came out, and asked me what I wanted? I desired a lodging, which was granted: I went in, but was not known. I asked him if he knew Mrs. Marrant, and how the family were?

He said, he had just left them, they were all well; but a young lad, with whom he went to school, who after he had quitted school, went to Charles-Town to learn some trade; but came home crazy, rambled in the woods, and was torn in pieces by the wild beasts.[37] How do you know, said I, that he was killed by wild beasts? I, and his brother, and uncle, and others, said he, went three days into the woods in search of him, and found his carcase torn, and brought it home and buried it.[38] This affected me very much, and I wept; observing it, he said what is the matter? I made no answer. At supper they sat down without craving a blessing, for which I reproved them; this so affected the man, that I believe it ended in a sound conversion. Here is a wild man, says he, come out of the woods to be a witness for God, and to reprove our ingratitude and stupefaction! After supper I went to prayer, and then to bed. Rising a little before daylight, and praising the Lord, as my custom was, the family were surprised, and got up: I staid with them till nine o'clock, and then went to my mother's house in the next street. The singularity of my dress drew everybody's eyes upon me, yet none knew me. I knocked at my mother's door, my sister opened it, and was startled at my appearance. Having expressed a desire to see Mrs. Marrant, I was answered, she was not very well, and that my business with her could be done by the person at the door, who also attempted to shut me out, which I prevented. My mother being called, I went in, and sat down, a mob of people being round the door. My mother asked, "what is your business;" only to see you, said I. She said she was much obliged to me, but did not know me. I asked, how are your children? how are your two sons? She replied, her daughters were in good health, of her two sons, one was well, and with her, but the other, — unable to contain, she burst into a flood of tears, and retired. I was overcome, and wept much; but nobody knew me.[39] This was an affecting scene! Presently my brother came in: He enquired, who I was, and what I was? My sister did not know; but being uneasy at my presence, they contrived to get me out of the house, which, being over-heard by me, I resolved not to stir. My youngest sister, eleven years of age, came in from school, with a book under her arm. I was then sitting in the parlour, and as she passed by the parlour door, she peep'd in and seeing a strange person there, she recollected me; she goes into the kitchen, and tells the servants, her brother was come; but her report finding no credit, she came and peep'd again, that she might be certain it was me; and then passing into the next room, through the parlour where I was sitting, she made a running curtsy, and says to my eldest sister, who was there, it is my brother John! She called her a foolish girl, and threatened to beat her: Then she came again and peep'd at me, and being certain she was not mistaken, she went back, and insisted that it was me: Being then beat by my sister she went crying up-stairs to my mother, and told her; but neither would my mother believe her.[40] At last they said to her, if it be your brother, go and kiss him, and ask him how he does? She ran and clasped me round the neck, and, looking me in the face, said, "Are not you my brother John?" I answered yes, and wept. I was then made known to all the family, to my friends, and acquaintances, who received me, and were glad, and rejoiced: Thus the dead was brought to life again; thus the lost was found.[41] I shall now close the Narrative, with only remarking a few incidents in my life, until my connection with my Right Honourable Patroness, the Countess of HUNTINGDON.[42]

I remained with my relations till the commencement of the American troubles.[43] I used to go and hear the Word of God, if any Gospel ministers came into the country, though at a considerable distance,[44] and thereby got acquainted with a few poor people, who feared God in Wills' Town, and Borough Town, Dorchester Town, and other places thereabouts; and in those places we used to meet and associate together for Christian Conversation, and at their request I frequently went to prayer with them, and at times enjoyed much of the Lord's presence among them.

About this time I went with my brother, who was a house-carpenter, to repair a plantation belonging to Mr. Jenkins, of Cumbee, about seventy miles from Charles-Town, where after I had done work in the evening, I used to spend my time in reading God's Word, singing Watts's hymns and in Prayer, the little negro children would often come round the door with their pretty wishful looks, and finding my heart much drawn out in Love to their souls, I one evening called several of them in, and asked them if they could say the Lord's Prayer, &c. finding they were very ignorant, I told them, if they would come every evening I would teach them, which they did, and learned very fast, some of them in about four weeks could say the Lord's Prayer, and [a] good part of the Catechism, after teaching, I used to go to prayer with them before we parted; this continued without interruption for three or four months, in which time, by the children acquainting their parents with it, I soon had my society increased to about thirty persons; and the Lord was pleased often to refresh us with a sense of his love and presence amongst us; one of the negro boys made a very great proficiency in that time, and could exercise in extemporary prayer much to my satisfaction. We are well advised in Ecclesiasticus, chap. ii. *v.* 1. *My Son, if thou come to serve the Lord, prepare thy heart for temptation*: Nor was it long before they were made to pledge our dear Lord in the bitter cup of suffering; for now the old Lion began to roar,[45] their mistress became acquainted with our proceedings, and was full of rage at it, and determined to put a stop to it. She had two of the children brought before her to examine, and made them say the Lord's prayer to her, she then asked who taught them? and they told her the free Carpenter. She also enquired, how many he had instructed, and at what time he taught them; and they told her, it was in the Evening after they had done work. She then stirred up her husband against us, who before had several times come in while I was instructing the children, and did not appear displeased with it: she told him it was the ready way to have all his negroes ruin'd, and made him promise to examine further into the matter, and break up our meeting; which he then very soon did, for a short space; for he, together with his overseer and negro-driver, and some of his neighbours, beset the place wherein we met, while we were at prayers; and as the poor creatures came out they caught them, and tied them together with cords, till the next morning, when all they caught, men, women, and children were strip'd naked and tied, their feet to a stake, their hands to the arm of a tree, and so savagely flogg'd that the blood ran from their backs and sides to the floor, to make them promise they would leave off praying, &c. though several of them fainted away with the pain and loss of blood, and lay upon the ground as dead for a considerable time after they were untied. I did not hear that she obtained her end of any of them. She endeavoured to perswade her husband to flog me also, but he told her he did not dare to do it because I was free, and would take the law of him, and make him pay for it; which she told him, she had rather he should run the hazard of, than let me go without the benefit of a good flogging, and was afterwards very angry with him because he was afraid to gratify her. He told me afterwards that I had spoiled all his Negroes, but could not help acknowledging, that they did their tasks sooner than the others who were not instructed, and thereby had time after their tasks were done, to keep their own fields in better order than the others, who used to employ the Sabbath for that purpose, as is the common practice among the Negroes. He then said, I should make them so wise that he should not be able to keep them in subjection. I asked him whether he did not think they had Souls to be saved? He answered, yes. I asked him whether he thought they were in the way to save their Souls whilst they were ignorant of that God who made and preserved them. He made me no answer to that. I then told him that the blood of those poor negroes which he had spilt that morning would be required by God at his hands. He then left me. Soon after, meeting with his wife, I told her the same; but she laughed at it, and was only sorry that she had not been able to get me flog'd with them. Finding I could not any longer live peaceably there, I encouraged the poor creatures to call upon God as well as they could, and returned home; where I afterwards heard that their Mistress continued to persecute them for meeting together as often as she discover'd them, and her husband for not being more severe against them; they were then obliged to meet at midnight in different corners of the woods that were about the plantation, and were sure to be flog'd if ever she caught them, they nevertheless continued their meetings though in such imminent danger, and by what I have since heard, I believe it continues to this day, by which it appears that the work was of God; therefore neither the devil nor his servants could overthrow it; and to our faithful Covenant God be all the Glory.

In about two months after I left them, it pleased God to lay his hand upon their Mistress, and she was seized with a very violent fever, which no medicine that they could procure would remove, and in a very few days after she was taken ill, she died in a very dreadful manner, in great anger with her husband, for not preventing their meetings, which she had heard they continued, notwithstanding all her endeavours to stop it. After she was dead, her husband gave them liberty to meet together as before, and used sometimes to attend with them; and I have since heard that it was made very useful to him.

About this time I was an eye-witness of the remarkable conversion of a child seven and a half years old, named Mary Scott, which I shall here mention, in hopes the Lord may make it useful and profitable to my young readers. Her parents lived in the house adjoining to my sister's. One day as I was returning from my work, and passing by the school where she was instructed, I saw the children coming out, and stop'd and looked among them for her, to take her home in my hand; but not seeing her among those that were coming out, I supposed she was gone before, and went on towards home; when passing by the church-yard, which was in my way, I saw her very busy walking from one tomb to another, and went to her, and asked her what she was doing there? She told me, that in the lesson she had set herself at school that morning, in the Twentieth of the Revelations, she read, "I saw the Dead, small and great, stand before God," &c. and she had been measuring the graves, with a tape she then held in her hand, to see if there were any so small as herself among them, and that she had found six that were shorter. I then said, and what of that? She answered, "I will die, Sir." I told her I knew she would, but hoped she would live till she was grown a woman; but she continued to express her desire to depart, and be with Christ, rather than to live till she was grown up. I then took her by the hand and brought her home with me. After this, she was observed to be always very solid and thoughtful, and that passage appeared always to be fresh upon her mind. I used frequently to be with her when in town, and at her request we often read and prayed together, and she appeared much affected. She never afterwards was seen out at play with other children; but spent her leisure time in reading God's word and prayer. In about four months after this she was taken ill, and kept her room about three weeks; when first taken, she told me, she should never come down stairs alive. I frequently visited her during her illness, and made light of what she said about her dying so soon; but in the last week of her illness she said to me in a very solemn manner, "Sir, I shall die before Saturday-night." The Physicians attended her, but she took very few if any medicines, and appeared quite calm and resigned to God's will. On Friday morning, which was the day she died, I visited her, and told her that I hoped she would not die so soon as she said, but she told me that she should certainly die before six o'clock that Evening. About five o'clock I visited her again. She was then sitting in a chair, and reading in her Bible, to all appearance pretty well recovered. After setting with her about a quarter of an hour, she got up, and desired me to go down, and send her mother up with a clean shift for her, which I did; and after a little time, when I went up again, I found her lying on the bed, with her eyes fixed up to heaven; when turning herself and seeing me, she said, "Mr. Marrant, don't you see that pretty town, and those fine people, how they shine like gold?—O how I long to be with my Lord and his redeemed Children in Glory!" and then turning to her parents and two sisters, (who were all present, having by her desire been called to her) she shook hands with them, and bade them farewell; desiring them not to lament for her when she was dead, for she was going to that fine place where God would wipe away all tears from her eyes, and she should sing Hallelujahs to God and the Lamb for ever and ever,[46] and where she hoped afterwards to meet them; and then turning again to me, she said,—"Farewell, and God bless you," and then fell asleep in the arms of Jesus. This afterwards proved the conversion of her mother.

In those troublesome times, I was pressed on board the Scorpion, sloop of war,[47] as their musician, as they were told I could play on music.—I continued in his majesty's service six years and eleven months; and with shame confess, that a lamentable stupor crept over all my spiritual vivacity, life and vigour; I got cold and dead. What need, reader, have we to be continually mindful of our Lord's exhortation, "*What I say unto you, I say unto all, Watch.*"[48] My gracious God, my dear Father in his dear Son, roused me every now and then by dangers and deliverances.—I was at the siege of Charles-Town,[49] and passed through many dangers. When the town was taken, my old royal benefactor and convert, the king of the Cherokee Indians, riding into the town with General Clinton, saw me, and knew me: He alighted off his horse,[50] and came to me; said he was glad to see me; that his daughter was very happy, and sometimes longed to get out of the body.

Some time after this I was cruising about in the American seas, and cannot help mentioning a singular deliverance I had from the most imminent danger, and the use the Lord made of it to me. We were overtaken by a violent storm; I was washed overboard, and thrown on again; dashed into the sea a second time, and tossed upon deck again. I now fastened a rope round my middle, as a security against being thrown into the sea again; but, alas! forgot to fasten it to any part of the ship; being carried away the third time by the fury of the waves, when in the sea, I found the rope both useless and an encumbrance. I was in the sea the third time about eight minutes, and several sharks came round me;[51] one of an enormous size, that could easily have taken me into his mouth at once, passed and rubbed against my side. I then cried more earnestly to the Lord than I had done for some time, and he who heard Jonah's prayer, did not shut out mine, for I was thrown aboard again;[52] these were the means the Lord used to revive me, and I began now to set out afresh.

I was in the engagement with the Dutch off the Dogger Bank, on board the Princess Amelia, of eighty-four guns.[53] We had a great number killed and wounded; the deck was running with blood; six men were killed, and three wounded, stationed at the same gun with me; my head and face were covered with the blood and brains of the slain: I was wounded, but did not fall, till a quarter of an hour before the engagement ended, and was happy in my soul[54] during the whole of it. After being in the hospital three months and 16 days, I was sent to the West-Indies, on board a ship of war, and, after cruising in those seas we returned home as a convoy. Being taken ill of my old wounds I was put into the hospital at Plymouth, and had not been there long when the physician gave it as his opinion, that I should not be capable of serving the king again; I was therefore discharged, and came to London, where I lived with a respectable and pious merchant near three years,[55] who was unwilling to part with me. During this time I saw my call to the ministry fuller and clearer; had a feeling concern for the salvation of my countrymen: I carried them constantly in the arms of prayer and faith to the throne of grace, and had continual sorrow in my heart for my brethren, for my kinsmen, according to the flesh.[56]—I wrote a letter to my brother, who returned me an answer, in which he prayed some ministers would come and preach to them, and desired me to show it to the minister whom I attended. I used to exercise my gifts on a Monday evening in prayer and exhortation, in Spa-fields chapel,[57] and was approved of, and sent down to Bath; where I was ordained,[58] in Lady Huntingdon's

Chapel.[59] Her Ladyship having seen the letter from my brother in Nova Scotia,[60] thought Providence called me there: To which place I am now bound, and expect to sail in a few days.[61]

I have now only to intreat the earnest prayers of all my kind Christian friends, that I may be carried safe there; kept humble, made faithful, and successful; that strangers may hear of and run to Christ; that Indian tribes may stretch out their hands to God; that the black nations may be made white in the blood of the Lamb; that vast multitudes, of hard tongues, and of a strange speech, may learn the language of Canaan, and sing the song of Moses, and of the Lamb; and, anticipating the glorious prospect, may we all with fervent hearts, and willing tongues, sing Hallelujah; the kingdoms of the world are become the kingdoms of our God, and of his Christ. Amen and Amen.[62]

Nor can I take my leave of my very dear London Friends without intreating GOD to bless them with every blessing of the upper and nether Springs:[63]—May the good will of Him that dwelt in the bush[64] ever preserve and lead them! is the fervent prayer of their affectionate and grateful Servant in the Gospel,

J. MARRANT.
London, No. 69,
MILE-END ROAD
Aug. 18. 1785.[65]

PSALM CVII. Dr. WATTS.

1 GIVE Thanks to God; He reigns above;
Kind are his Thoughts, his Name is Love;
His Mercy Ages past have known,
And Ages long to come shall own.

2 Let the Redeemed of the LORD
The Wonders of his Grace record;
Isr'el, the Nation whom he chose,
And rescu'd from their mighty Foes.

3 When GOD's Almighty Arm had broke
Their Fetters and th'Egyptian Yoke,
They trac'd the Desert, wand'ring round
A wild and solitary Ground!

4 There they could find no leading Road,
Nor City with a fix'd Abode;
Nor Food, nor Fountain to assuage
Their burning Thirst, or Hunger's Rage.

5 In their Distress to GOD they cry'd;
GOD was their Saviour and their Guide;

He led their March, far wand'ring round,
'Twas the right Path to Canaan's Ground.

6 Thus when our first Release we gain
From Sin's old Yoke, and Satan's Chain,
We have this desert World to pass,
A dang'rous and a tiresome Place.

7 He feeds and clothes us all the Way,
He guides our Footsteps lest we stray;
He guards us with a pow'rful Hand,
And brings us to the heav'nly Land.

8 O let the Saints with Joy record
The Truth and Goodness of the LORD!
How great his Works! how kind his Ways!
Let ev'ry Tongue pronounce his Praise.

FINIS.

NOTES

1. Of the perhaps as many as ten printings of the *Narrative* that were published in 1785, I have chosen as my copy-text the undated fourth edition, "Printed for the Author, By R[obert]. Hawes," because, dated at the end "Aug. 18, 1785," it was the last edition published in London before Marrant went to Canada.

The review of Marrant's *Narrative* in *The Monthly Review; or, Literary Journal* (November 1785), 399, concentrates on his conversion to Methodism, which it mocks.

2. Charles-Town: Charleston, South Carolina.

3. The story of David and Goliath is found in 1 Samuel 17.

4. William Aldridge (1737-1797), Methodist clergyman and subscriber to Olaudah Equiano's *Interesting Narrative.* He disassociated himself from the Countess of Huntingdon's Connexion (see the Gronniosaw selection in this anthology), though he remained her friend, in 1776, when the Countess rejected the request of his congregation at her Mulberry Gardens Chapel that he be made its permanent minister. Her action was probably prompted at least as much by her doctrinal refusal to accept the means by which Congregational churches chose their ministers as by any anger at a threat to her personal authority and power. Aldridge became the minister at the Calvinistic Methodist Jewry Street Chapel, where he delivered and published a funeral sermon on her death in 1791.

5. St. Augustine: the oldest European city in the present-day United States, about one thousand miles south of New York in what was then the Spanish colony of Florida. Marrant's dates indicate that he left Florida for the British colony of Georgia upon the outbreak of war between the mother countries at the beginning of 1762.

6. Compare Hebrews 13:14: "For here we have no continuing city, but we seek one to come."

7. Compare Proverbs 10:16: "The labour of the righteous *tendeth* to life: the fruit of the wicked to sin."

8. Currency: colonial paper money, as opposed to pounds sterling.

9. Marrant, a free Black, is not using *master* and *slave* to refer to an owner-chattel relationship. His master is his trainer/employer, and Marrant is a slave to sin. His mother has paid the master £20 to employ and teach the young Marrant as an apprentice for eighteen months.

One of the details of his life Marrant does not mention is his ownership of the slave Millia (or Mellia) Marrant, "a Squat Wench," age thirty, and her two children, Amelia, six, and Ben, four. Identified as "Formerly the property of John Marrant near Santee Carolina left him at the siege of Chas Town," Millia, along with each "Child of Millia Marrant," escaped from slavery at the siege of Charleston and fled with the British to New York City at the end of the war (Carleton Papers in Records of British Army Headquarters in America, 1775-1783: PRO 30/55/100, ff. 52-53). Freed slaves often took or were given the surnames of their former owners. For another example, in the same "Book of Negroes," we find "Harry Washington," forty-three, a "Stout fellow," "Formerly the property of General Washington" (ff. 90-91).

10. Again, *master* is not being used in the sense of *owner*: an employer has agreed to hire Marrant on a trial basis for a probationary period of sixteen months, and if at the end of that period he is satisfied with the promise Marrant shows, he will agree to have Marrant bound to him by a mutually advantageous contract as an apprentice, typically for seven years.

11. George Whitefield (1714-1770), along with John Wesley (1703-1791), was a founder of Methodism within the Church of England. Noted for his fervid and energetic style of delivery, he preached in the North American colonies during seven trips there from England, on the last of which, begun in September 1769, he died.

12. Amos 4:12.

13. Compare Hebrews 4:12: "For the word of God *is* quick, and powerful, and sharper than any two-edged sword, piercing even to the dividing asunder of soul and spirit, and of the joints and marrow, and *is* a discerner of the thoughts and intents of the heart"; and Ephesians 6:17: "And take the helmet of salvation, and the sword of the spirit, which is the word of God."

14. Compare the account of the conversion of Saul in Acts 9:1-20.

15. [Marrant's note.] Mr. HART, a Baptist Minister at Charles-Town.

16. Compare Revelation 2:25: "But that which ye have *already* hold fast till I come"; and 3:11: "Behold, I come quickly: hold that fast which thou hast, that no man take thy crown."

17. Soldier: in a metaphorical sense, a soldier of Christ.

18. Isaac Watts (1674-1748). His hymns and psalms were published in *Horae Lyricae* (1706), *Hymns and Spiritual Songs* (1707-1709), and *Psalms of David Imitated* (1719). Copies of the Bible and Watts's hymns were the most popular books during the eighteenth century.

19. Compare Proverbs 27:7: "The full soul loatheth an honey-comb; but to the hungry soul every bitter thing is sweet."

20. Compare Exodus 15:22-27.

21. Compare 1 Thessalonians 5:17: "Pray without ceasing."

22. [Marrant's note.] These Pegs were to be kindled at the opposite end from the Body.

23. See Daniel 3:1-30.

24. See Daniel 6:1-29.

25. [Marrant's note.] The Office of Executioner there, in many respects resembles that of a High Sheriff in this country.

26. The three volumes of *Hymns and Spiritual Songs* by Isaac Watts were frequently published in Great Britain and North America during the eighteenth century. Marrant slightly alters Watts's Hymn 54.

27. Isaiah 53: the story of the suffering servant of the Lord was interpreted by Christians as an anticipation of the later sufferings of Christ.

28. Matthew 26 includes the Last Supper, the betrayal of Jesus by Judas in the Garden of Gethsemane, Jesus's arrival before the Jewish court, and Peter's denial.

29. [Marrant's note.] Or what those parts were which seemed to affect me so much, not knowing what I read, as he did not understand the English language.

30. Versions of the incident of the speaking book can be found in the selections from Gronniosaw, Cugoano, and Equiano in this anthology.

31. Genesis 42:36.

32. Compare 2 Corinthians 12:10: "Therefore I take pleasure in infirmities, in reproaches, in necessities, in persecutions, in distresses for Christ's sake: for when I am weak, then am I strong."

Between "in spirit" and "The executioner," earlier editions read "The Lord works, and who shall let [obstruct] it?"

33. Compare Matthew 26:39: "And he went a little farther, and fell on his face, and prayed, saying, O my Father, if it be possible, let this cup pass from me: nevertheless not as I will, but as thou *wilt*."

34. Catawar: Choctaw.

35. Housaw: Chickasaw.

36. Eat: ate.

37. Compare the story in Genesis 37, 39-47 of Joseph and his reunion with his family.

38. At this point, earlier editions add, "and are now in mourning for him."

39. [Marrant's note.] I had been absent from them near twenty-three months.

40. Earlier editions read: "My youngest sister, eleven years of age, came in from school, and knew me the moment she saw me: She goes into the kitchen, and tells the woman her brother was come; but her news finding no credit there she returns, passes through the room where I sat, made a running curtsey, and says to my eldest sister in the next room, it is my brother! She was then called a foolish girl, and threatened; the child cried, and insisted upon it. She went crying up-stairs to my mother, and told her; but neither would my mother believe her."

41. Compare the story in Luke 15:11-32 of the return of the Prodigal Son.

42. Marrant was ordained at the Countess of Huntingdon's Chapel in Bath on 15 May 1785. Rebuffed in 1779 in her attempt to establish her Connexion as a mediator between the Church of England and Dissent, the Countess was compelled to register her chapels as Disenting meetinghouses. Unlike the Wesleyan Methodists, who did not separate from the Church of England until the end of the century, the Huntingdon Connexion split off in 1782.

43. The American Revolution.

44. At this point, some earlier editions, which include neither the rest of this paragraph nor the next three paragraphs, read "and yet, reader, my soul was got into a declining state. Don't forget our Lord's exhortation, "What I say unto you, I say unto all, WATCH [Mark 13:37]." "The Fourth Edition . . . Printed and Sold by Gilbert and Plummer," dated at the end "July 18, 1785," adds the passage "and yet, reader . . . WATCH" at the end of "I remained with my relations . . . . the Lord's presence among them," but lacks the following two paragraphs found here in the later "Fourth Edition," published by R. Hawes.

45. Compare 1 Peter 5:8: "Be sober, be vigilant; because your adversary the devil, as a roaring lion, walketh about, seeking whom he may devour."

46. The "Lamb" is Christ in the New Jerusalem described in Revelation 21-22, where "the Lord God Almighty and the Lamb are the temple of it" (21:22).

47. In time of war, vessels of the Royal Navy were authorized to forcibly recruit, or press, qualified men into naval service. The 14-gun *Scorpion*, which was the renamed *Aetna* (itself renamed from *Borryan*, but not the same vessel on which Olaudah Equiano served) was sold in North America on 27 December 1780. Commanded by John Tollemache, the

Scorpion was stationed in the the Carolina coastal waters from 12 November 1775 until 2 October 1776.

Marrant may have fabricated his career "in his Majesty's service": I have not found his name on any of the muster lists recorded before, during, and after the *Scorpion* was stationed off the Carolina coast (PRO ADM 36/8377, ADM 36/8378); nor have I found his name on any of the muster lists of the *Princess Amelia* between January 1779 and September 1782 (PRO ADM 36/9165, ADM 36/9985).

48. This sentence is lacking here in earlier editions.

49. After a siege lasting from 11 February until 12 May 1780, Charleston, defended by General Benjamin Lincoln (1733-1810), fell to the British under the command of General Henry Clinton (1738?-1795). For the siege and fall of Charleston, see also the narratives of David George and Boston King in this anthology.

50. [Marrant's note.] Though it is unusual for Indians to have a horse, yet the king accompanied the general on the present successful occasion riding on horse-back.—If the king wished to serve me, there was no opportunity; the town being taken on Friday afternoon, Saturday an express arrived from the commander in chief at New-York, for a large detachment, or the town would fall into the hands of the Americans, which hurried us away on Sunday morning.

51. Earlier editions read "the sharks came round me in great numbers."

52. See Jonah 2.

53. [Marrant's note.] This action was on the 5th of August, 1781.

[The Dogger Bank, a sandbank in the North Sea, about sixty miles off the northeast coast of England, was the site of the inconclusive engagement between Sir Hyde Parker (the elder) and the Dutch, with whom Britain had been at war since 20 December 1780.]

54. Happy: lucky. Earlier editions lack "in my soul."

55. [Marrant's note, lacking in this edition but included in others, like the Gilbert and Plummer "Fourth Edition," with "Notes Explanatory."] About three years; it might be a few weeks over or under. [The other editions lack the word "near" in the phrase "near three years."]

[The identity of the "respectable and pious merchant" is given in the affidavit that concludes the Gilbert and Plummer "Fourth Edition":

London, August, 16, 1785.

Mr John Marrant liv'd with us about 3 years, which he did with honesty and sobriety — he feared God, and had a desire to save his soul before he ever came to live with us; — he shewed himself to be such while he lived with us, by attending the means of Grace diligently, and by being tender hearted to the poor, by giving them money and victuals if he had left himself none. He left us with no misunderstanding whatever, about April last.

This is nothing but the truth.

(Signed)
Cotton-Merchant,
no. 38, Dowgate-Hill.
John Marsden,
H. Marsden.]

56. Compare Romans 9:2-3: "That I have great heaviness and continual sorrow in my heart. For I could wish that myself were accursed from Christ for my brethren, my kinsmen according to the flesh."

57. Spa-fields chapel: the building, seating some 2,500 people, adjoining the Countess of Huntingdon's residence in St. James's parish in Clerkenwell. It opened on Palm Sunday, 28 March 1779.

58. Thomas Wills (1740-1802) and William Romaine (1714-1795) reportedly ordained Marrant on 15 May 1785 at the Huntingdonian chapel in Bath. The roles of Wills and Romaine in the religious career of Marrant are mentioned in Samuel Whitchurch, *The Negro Convert, A Poem; Being the Substance of the Experience of Mr. John Marrant, A Negro, As Related by Himself, Previous to His Ordination, at the Countess of Huntingdon's Chapel in Bath, on Sunday the 15th of May, 1785, Together with a Concise Account of the Most Remarkable Events in His Very Singular Life* (Bath, 1785?). Romaine was a Calvinist Anglican who, though not officially a member of the Huntingdon Connexion, was very sympathetic to the Countess's beliefs and goals. He was a very popular preacher and prolific author of works on religious subjects, including some that were notably anti-Semitic. His popularity led Equiano to attend his sermons at St. Anne's Church, Blackfriars.

Wills, one of the Countess of Huntingdon's closest advisors and married to her niece, was appointed resident preacher at the Spa-Fields Chapel in January 1782. But the Countess dismissed him on 8 July 1788, after he charged that she, under the influence of Rev. John Bradford (1750-1805), had embraced antinomianism (the belief that the elect need not concern themselves about the morality of their own actions). Wills recovered his admiration for the Countess and her goals, preaching a funeral sermon on the occasion of her death in 1791. Perhaps because Wills, after his dismissal from the Connexion, became the resident minister at the newly completed Islington Chapel in 1793, two years after Marrant's death, that chapel has mistakenly been assumed to have been Huntingdonian when Marrant had been one of its preachers.

No mention of Marrant is made in *Memoirs of the Life of the Rev. Thomas Wills .... Carefully Compiled from the Journals in His Own Hand-Writing, and Other Authentic Documents. By a Friend. Published under the Full Patronage of Mrs. Wills* (London, 1804). The *Memoirs* suggests that Wills remained in London between 20 August 1784 and 14 June 1785. Wills was one of Equiano's original subscribers.

59. Earlier editions read "I used to exercise my gifts on a Monday evening in prayer and exhortation, and was approved of, and ordained at Bath."

60. The "Sixth Edition" of Marrant's *Narrative*, published in London in 1788 by Gilbert and Plummer, before the Marsdens' affidavit, includes the following notice: "SINCE Mr. MARRANT's arrival at Nova-Scotia, several letters have been received from him by different persons, and some by Mr. ALDRIDGE, the Editor of this Narrative; from which it appears, that Mr. MARRANT has travelled through that province preaching the Gospel, and not without success; that he has undergone much fatigue, and passed through many dangers; that he has visited the Indians in their Wigwams, who, he relates, were disposed to hear and receive the Gospel.—This is the substance of the letters transmitted by him to the Editor above-mentioned."

61. John Marrant's brother was one of the 3,500 Black Loyalists evacuated by the British to Nova Scotia after the American Revolution. John Marrant left England on 18 August 1785 to preach the Methodist predestinarian doctrine associated with Whitefield and the Huntingdon Connexion to the native Micmacs and doctrinally more moderate Black and White Wesleyan Methodists in Nova Scotia. He was so effective that he earned the opposition of several White ministers who lost parishioners to the all-Black chapels he introduced.

Despite his success as a preacher, however, Marrant was virtually penniless without the aid he futilely implored from the Countess of Huntingdon. After suffering from smallpox for six months, Marrant moved to Boston, where he became chaplain to the first lodge of African Masons, founded by Prince Hall in 1784. On 15 August 1788, he returned briefly to Nova Scotia to marry the Black Loyalist Elizabeth Herries in Birchtown. He published *A Sermon Preached on the 24th Day of June 1789, Being the Festival of St. John the Baptist, at the Request of the Right Worshipful the Grand Master Prince Hall, and the Rest of the Brethren of the African lodge of the Honorable Society of Free and Accepted Masons in Boston. By the Reverend Brother Marrant, Chaplain* (Boston, 1789) and returned to England after 7 March

1790, never having heard from the Countess. He continued his ministry in the neighborhood of Whitechapel, London, as well as at the Independent chapel (sometimes mistakenly thought to have been, at that time, a Huntingdonian chapel) on Church Street in Islington, then a suburb of London (see note 58). His last publication was *A Journal of the Rev. John Marrant, from August the 18th, 1785 to the 16th of March 1790. To which Are Added, Two Sermons; One Preached on Ragged Island on Sabbath Day, the 27th Day of October 1787; the Other at Boston, in New England, on Thursday, the 24th of June, 1787.* (London, 1790). Marrant died in Islington and was buried in the graveyard adjoining the chapel. His memorial inscription read, "Rev. John Marrant, April 15, 1791, aged thirty-five."

62. For some of the allusions in this paragraph, see Revelation 7:14; 11:15; 15:3; and 17:15. The following paragraph and the hymn by Watts appear only in the "Fourth Edition" published by R. Hawes.

63. See Joshua 15:19.

64. See Exodus 3.

65. Both earlier and later editions bear the dateline "London, Prescot-street, No. 60, July 18, 1785."

Johnson Green

(7 February 1757-17 August 1786)

The Life and Confession of JOHNSON GREEN, Who is to be Executed this Day, August 17TH, 1786, for the Atrocious Crime of BURGLARY; Together with his LAST and DYING WORDS.[1]

I *JOHNSON GREEN*, having brought myself to a shameful and ignominious death, by my wicked conduct, and, as I am a dying man I leave to the world the following History of my Birth, Education, and vicious Practices, hoping that all people will take warning by my evil example, and shun vice and follow virtue.

I was born at Bridgwater, in the County of Plymouth, in the Commonwealth of Massachusetts, was twenty-nine years of age the seventh day of February last. My father was a negro, and a servant to the Hon. Timothy Edson, Esq., late of Bridgwater, deceased. My mother was an Irish woman named Sarah Johnson, she was a widow, and her maiden name was Green. I have been called Joseph-Johnson Green.[2] When I was five years of age my mother bound me as an Apprentice to Mr. Seth Howard of said Bridgwater, to be instructed in Agriculture. I was used very tenderly, and instructed in the principles of the Christian Religion. Whilst I was an apprentice my mother gave me much good advice, cautioned me against keeping company with those that used bad language and other vicious practices. She advised me not to go to sea nor into the army, foretold what has come to pass since the commencement of the late war,[3] and said it would not come to pass in her day. She died about sixteen years ago, and if I had followed her good advice I might have escaped an ignominious death.

When I was eighteen years of age (contrary to my mother's advice) I enlisted into the American service, and remained in the same for the duration of the war. I would just observe to the world, that my being addicted to drunkenness, the keeping of bad company, and a correspondence I have had with lewd women, has been the cause of my being brought to this wretched situation.

In March, 1781, I was married at Eastown, to one Sarah Phillips, a mustee,[4] who was brought up by Mr. Olney, of Providence. She has had two children since I was married to her, and I have treated her exceeding ill.

When I began to steal I was about 12 years old, at which time I stole four cakes of gingerbread and six biscuits, out of a horse cart, and afterwards I stole sundry small articles, and was not detected.

When I was about fourteen, I stole one dozen of lemons and one cake of chocolate, was detected, and received reproof. Soon after I stole some hens, and my conduct was so bad that my master sold me[5] to one of his cousins, who used me well.

I continued the practice of stealing, and just before I went into the army I took my master's key, unlocked his chest, and stole two shillings; he discovered what I had done, gave me correction, but not so severely as I deserved.

Sometime after I was engaged in the American service, at a certain tavern in Sherburne I stole fifteen shillings, one case bottle[6] of rum, one dozen of biscuit, and a pillow case with some sugar.

In April, 1781, I stole at the Highlands, near West-Point, a pair of silver shoe buckles, was detected, and received one hundred lashes.

In October, the same year, when I was at West-Point, and we were extremely pinched for the want of provisions, three of us broke open a settler's markee,[7] stole three cheeses, one small firkin[8] of butter, and some chocolate. I only was detected, and punished by receiving one hundred stripes.[9]

Sometime in the winter of 1783, at Easton, I broke into a grist mill, belonging to Mr. Timothy Randall, and stole about a bushel of corn, and at sundry times the same year I broke into a cellar belonging to Mr. Ebenezer Howard, of the same place, and stole some meat and tobacco; and I also broke into a cellar and a corn house belonging to Mr. Abiel Kinsley, of the same place, and stole some meat and corn; and at East-Bridgewater, the same year, I broke open a grist mill, and stole near a bushel of meal; and at the same time I stole three or four dozen herrings out of a corn house. I also went to a corn house belonging to Mr. Nathaniel Whitman, of Bridgwater, and stole two cheeses out of it.

August 1st, 1784, I broke open a house in Providence, and stole goods to the value of forty dollars. Soon after I broke open a shop near Patuxet Falls, stole one pair of cards, two cod fish, and sundry other articles.

In 1784 I also committed the following crimes, viz. I broke into a cellar about a mile from Patuxet Bridge, stole about thirty weight of salt pork, one case bottle, and several other articles. About the same time I stole out of a washing tub in Patuxet a pair of trowsers, three pair of stockings, and a shirt; and at Seaconk I stole two shirts and some stockings through an open window. I stole at a barn between Seaconk and Attleborough, a woolen blanket, and through an open window near the same place I stole two sheets, one gown, and one shirt. At Mr. Amos Sheperdson's, in Attleborough, I stole out of a wash-tub, one shirt, two shifts,[10] one short gown, and one pair of stockings.

At Norton, I broke into a cellar belonging to Col. George Leonard, and stole a quarter of mutton. The same night I broke into another cellar near that place, and stole between twenty and thirty weight of salt pork.

About the same time, I broke into a tavern near the same place, and stole near two dollars in money, and one case-bottle of rum.

Between Providence and Attleborough, I broke open two cellars, and stole some meat.

I broke into a house in Johnston, and stole betwixt twenty and thirty wt. of salt pork and beef, and one broom.

Some of the things I stole this year, I sold at the market in Providence.

April 23d, 1785, I was imprisoned at Nantucket, for striking a truckman[11] and some other persons, at a time when I was intoxicated with liquor: The next day I was released upon my paying a fine and the cost of prosecution.

I broke open a house in Stoughton, stole several aprons, some handkerchiefs, and some other apparel.

I stole about two yards and an half of tow cloth[12] from Col. David Lathrop, of Bridgewater; and the same night I stole a shirt from a clothier, in the same town; and I also stole one apron, one pocket-handkerchief, one pair of stockings, and one shift from Thomas Howard of East-Bridgewater, upon the same night.

The next week I stole a piece of tow-cloth in Halifax, and at the same time I broke into a house, and stole about twenty pounds of salt beef, and three pounds of wool.

October 15th, 1785, I broke open a shop in Walpole, and stole seven pair of shoes.

Nov. 1785, I broke open a store in Natick and stole a quantity of goods from the owner, viz. Mr. Morris.

At Capt. Bent's tavern, in Stoughtonham, I went down chimney, by a rope, opened a window and fastened it up with my jack-knife; immediately after, a man came to the house for a gallon of rum; he called to the landlord, and his daughter (as I took her to be) arose and waited upon him. She discovered the open window, with the jack-knife, and said it did not belong to the house; it was concluded that it belonged to some boys who were gone to a husking,[13] and had called there that evening.—It was my design to have made my escape out at the window, when I opened it, in case I should be discovered by any person in the house: But when the man came up to the house, I fearing I might be discovered, drawed myself up chimney and stood on the cross-bar until he was gone and all the people were asleep; I then descended again, and stole near three dollars out of the bar; than ascended the chimney and escaped without being discovered.

The same month I hid a quantity of goods which I had stole (part of them being the goods I had stolen at Natick) in a barn belonging to Mr. Nathaniel Foster, in Middleborough, and I engaged to come and work for the said Foster: It happened that I was taken up on suspicion that I had stolen a horse (which I had taken and rode about four miles) and committed to gaol in the county of Plymouth, but as no sufficient evidence appeared, I was set at liberty. In the mean time the said Foster found the goods and advertised them. I sent my wife to him, she owned and received the goods, and I escaped undiscovered, by her telling him that I came to his house in the evening preceding the day I had promised to work for him; that as it was late in the night, and the weather rainy, I did not choose to disturb him and his family, by calling them up; that I was obliged to leave the goods and return home, and being taken up on the suspicion aforesaid, I could not take care of the goods, &c.

April 1st, 1786, I broke into a house, in Medford and stole two pair of stockings, one scarf, one gown, and one pair of buckles.

The same month I broke into the house of one Mr. Blake, innholder, opposite the barracks in Rutland, and stole a bottle of bitters, and three or four dollars in money.

Soon after I broke into Mr. Chickery's house, in Holden, and stole about thirty dollars worth of clothing. The next day I lodged in the woods, and at evening Mr. Chickery took me up after I had got into the high-way, searched my pack, and found his things. On his attempting to seize me, I ran off, and made my escape.—I left my pack, and the money I had stolen from Mr. Blake.

Not long after, I went to Mr. Jotham Howe's in Shrewsbury, and opened a window, and stole a blanket.

I then went to another house, broke in, and stole a fine apron out of a desk. The same night I went to a barn belonging to Mr. Baldwin, in said Shrewsbury, and lodged in it the next day, and at evening I broke into his house, and stole about three shillings and three pence in money, and about nine dollars worth of clothing, for which crime I am now under sentence of death.

The same night I broke open the house of Mr. Farror, in said Shrewsbury, and stole in money and goods, to the value of near six dollars.

I also broke into the house of Mr. Ross Wyman, of the same town, and upon the same night, and stole from him near two dollars.

Moreover, I stole a pair of thread stockings at a house just beyond said Wyman's, and hid myself in the woods, where I lay all the next day, and at evening I set off towards Boston, and was taken up by a guard that was placed by a bridge in the end of Westborough. I was taken before General Ward, confessed the crimes alledged, was committed to gaol, and in April last, I received sentence of death, for the crime aforementioned.

Upon the evening of the first day of June, I cleared myself of all my chains, and made an escape from the gaol: And not withstanding all the admonitions, counsels and warnings that I had received from the good ministers and other pious persons who had visited me under my confinement, I returned again to my vicious practices, "like the dog to his vomit, and the sow that is washed, to her wallowing in the mire;"[14] for the very same evening I stole a cheese out of a press[15] in Hold: And the next Saturday I broke into the house of Mr. James Caldwell, in Barre, and stole near twenty five dollars worth of clothing.

I tarried in Barre about twelve days, and then set off for Natick, and on the way I broke into a cellar, in Shrewsbury, and stole some bread and cheese.—Whilst I tarried in Barre, I lived in the woods all the time—when I had got to Natick, I stole two pair of stockings and two pocket handkerchiefs, that were hanging out near a house.

From Natick I went to Sherburne, and broke open a store belonging to Mr. Samuel Sanger, and stole between four and five dozen of buttons.

From thence I went to Mr. John Sanger's house, in the same town, broke it open, and stole a case bottle of rum, one bottle of cherry rum, six cakes of gingerbread, and as many biscuits: I searched for money, but found none.

At another tavern in the same town, I took out a pane of glass, and opened the window, but I was discovered by the landlord, made my escape, and went back to Natick, and tarried there two days.

From Natick I went to Stoughtonham, and at Capt. Bent's (the place where I went down the chimney) the cellar being open, I went through it, and in the bar-room I stole fifteen shillings in money, one case bottle of rum, and one half dozen of biscuits.

Afterwards I went to Easton, and on the way I broke open a house, and stole some cheese, and two pair of shoes, and two pair of shoe buckles. At Easton I tarried two days, and then made my escape from two men who attempted to take me up on suspicion that I had broken gaol. From thence I went to Attleborough, and through a window I stole two cheeses, and at a tavern near the same place, I stole six shillings and eight pence, one case bottle of rum, a sailor's jacket, and one pair of silver knee buckles.

I then set off for Providence, and by the way I opened a window, and stole one cotton jacket, one jack-knife; and at another house on the same way, I stole through a window, one fine apron, one pocket handkerchief, and one pillow case.

I came to Providence the 26th day of June, and not long after, I broke open a cellar, and stole one bottle of beer, some salt fish, and ten pounds of butter.

A few nights after, I went to Col. Manton's, in Johnston, and the cellar being open, I went into it, and stole twenty pounds of butter, near as much salt pork, one milk pail, one cheese cloth, and one frock.

A few nights after, I went to Justice Belknap's, in the same place, and broke into his cellar, and stole about thirty pounds of salt pork, one neat's[16] tongue, one pair of nippers, one box of awls, and one bag.—It remarkably happened on the 13th ultimo[17] (the day that had been appointed for my execution) that I was committed to gaol in Providence, on suspicion of having stolen the things last mentioned, and on the 18th ult. I was brought back and confined in this gaol again.—Many more thefts and other vicious practices have I been guilty of, the particulars of which might tire the patience of the reader.

Some of the things I have stolen I have used myself—some of them I have sold—some have been taken from me—some I have hid where I could not find them again—and others I have given to lewd women, who induced me to steal for their maintenance. I have lived a hard life, by being obliged to keep in the woods; have suffered much by hunger, nakedness, cold, and the fears of being detected and brought to justice—have often been accused of stealing when I was not guilty, and others have been accused of crimes when I was the offender. I never murdered any person, nor robbed any body on the highway. I have had great dealings with women, which to their and my shame be it spoken, I often too easily obtained my will of them. I hope they will repent, as I do, of such wicked and infamous conduct. I have had a correspondence[18] with many women, exclusive of my wife, among whom were several abandoned[19] Whites, and a large number of Blacks; four of the whites were married women, three of the blacks have laid children to me besides my wife, who has been much distressed by my behaviour.

Thus I have given a history of my birth, education and atrocious conduct, and as the time is very nigh in which I must suffer an ignominious death, I earnestly intreat that all people would take warning by my wicked example; that they would shun the paths of destruction by guarding against every temptation; that they would shun vice, follow virtue, and become (through the assistance of the ALMIGHTY) victorious over the enemies of immortal felicity, who are exerting themselves to delude and lead nations to destruction.

As I am sensible of the heinousness of my crimes, and am sorry for my wicked conduct, in violating the laws of the great Governour of the Universe, whose Divine Majesty I have offended; I earnestly pray that he would forgive my sins, blot out my multiplied transgressions, and receive my immortal spirit into the Paradise of never ending bliss.

I ask forgiveness of my wife, and of all persons whom I have injured. I return my sincere thanks to the Ministers of the Gospel, and others, who have visited me under my confinement, for their counsels and admonitions, and for the good care they have taken of me: God reward them for their kindness, and conduct us all through this troublesome world to the regions of immortal felicity in the kingdom of Heaven.—AMEN.

his
JOHNSON + GREEN.
mark.

Worcester Gaol, August 16, 1786.

The following POEM was written at the request of JOHNSON GREEN, by a prisoner in Worcester Gaol, and is at said GREEN'S *special request, added to his Life and Confession, as a PART of his DYING WORDS.*

LET all the people on the globe
Be on their guard, and see
That they do shun the vicious road
That's trodden been by me.
If I had shun'd the paths of vice;
Had minded to behave
According to the good advice
That my kind mother gave,
Unto my friends I might have been
A blessing in my days,
And shun'd the evils that I've seen
In my pernicious ways.
My wicked conduct has been such,
It's brought me to distress;
As often times I've suffer'd much
By my own wickedness.

My lewdness, drunkenness, and theft
    Has often times—(behold)
Caus'd me to wander, and be left
    To suffer with the cold.
Hid in the woods, in deep distress,
    My pinching wants were such,
With hunger, and with nakedness
    I oft did suffer much.
I've liv'd a thief; it's a hard life;
    To drink was much inclin'd;
My conduct has distress'd my wife,
    A wife both good and kind.
Though many friends which came to see
    Me, in these latter times,
Did oft with candour,[20] caution me
    To leave my vicious crimes;
Yet when I had got out of gaol,
    Their labour prov'd in vain;
For then, alas! I did not fail
    To take to them again.
If I had not conducted so;
    Had minded to refrain;
Then I shou'd not have had to go
    Back to the gaol again.
Thus in the Devil's service, I
    Have spent my youthful days,
And now, alas! I soon must die,
    For these my wicked ways.
Repent, ye thieves, whilst ye have breath,
    Amongst you let be wrought
A reformation, lest to death,
    You, like myself, be brought.
Let other vicious persons see
    That they from vice abstain;
Lest they undo themselves, like me,
    Who in it did remain.
I hope my sad and dismal fate
    Will solemn warning be
To people all, both small and great,
    Of high and low degree.
By breaking of the righteous laws,
    I to the world relate,
That I thereby have been the cause
    Of my unhappy fate.
As I repent, I humbly pray
    That God would now remit
My sins, which in my vicious way
    I really did commit.

May the old TEMPTER soon be bound
    And shut up in his den,
And peace and honesty abound
    Among the sons of men.
May the great GOD grant this request,
    And bring us to that shore
Where peace and everlasting rest
    Abides for ever more.

his
JOHNSON —+— GREEN.
mark.

Printed and Sold at the Printing-Office in Worcester.

NOTES

1. Green's *Life and Confession* was "Printed and Sold at the Printing-Office at Worcester" by Isaiah Thomas (1749-1831) on 17 August 1786 as a single-sheet broadside, illustrated with an engraving of a hanging.

2. Green's use of his mother's surnames implies that his parents were not married and that his birth was therefore illegitimate.

3. Late war: the American Revolution, 1775-1783.

4. Mustee: the offspring of a White and a Quadroon (a person one-fourth Black and three-fourths White).

5. Sold me: exchanged the time remaining in the apprenticeship for money.

6. Case bottle: a bottle, often square, designed to fit in a case.

7. Markee: marquee, a large tent.

8. Firkin: a small cask.

9. Stripes: lashes of the whip.

10. Shifts: smocks or chemises.

11. Truckman: someone whose business was conducted by trade or barter.

12. Tow-cloth: cloth made of untwisted natural fibers.

13. Husking: a festive gathering of neighbors to remove the husks from the harvested corn.

14. Compare Proverbs 26:11: "As a dog returneth to his vomit, *so* a fool returneth to his folly"; 2 Peter 2:22: "The dog *is* turned to his own vomit again; and the sow that was washed to her wallowing in the mire."

15. Press: a large cupboard.

16. Neat: an ox or any similar animal, including a bullock, cow, or heifer.

17. Ultimo: of last month, abbreviated ult. or ulto.

18. Correspondence: sexual intercourse.

19. Abandoned: abandoned to sin; immoral; utterly bad.

20. Candour: fair-mindedness; generosity.

Belinda

~

"Petition of an African slave, to the legislature of Massachusetts." From *The American Museum, or Repository of Ancient and Modern Fugitive Pieces, Prose and Poetical.* For June, 1787. Volume 1. Number 6. (Philadelphia: Mathew Carey, 1787.

To the honourable the senate and house of representatives, in general court assembled:

The petition of Belinda, an African,

Humbly shews,

THAT seventy years have rolled away, since she, on the banks of the Rio de Valta,[1] received her existence. The mountains, covered with spicy forests—vallies, loaded with the richest fruits spontaneously produced—joined to that happy temperature of air, which excludes excess, would have yielded her the most complete felicity, had not her mind received early impressions of the cruelty of men, whose faces were like the moon, and whose bows and arrows were like the thunder and the lightning of the clouds. The idea of these, the most dreadful of all enemies, filled her infant slumbers with horror, and her noon-tide moments with cruel apprehensions! But her affrighted imagination, in its most alarming extension, never represented distresses equal to what she has since really experienced: for before she had twelve years enjoyed the fragrance of her native groves, and ere she had realized that Europeans placed their happiness in the yellow dust,[2] which she carelessly marked with her infant foot-steps—even when she, in a sacred grove, with each hand in that of a tender parent, was paying her devotion to the great Orisa, who made all things, an armed band of white men, driving many of her countrymen in chains, rushed into the hallowed shades! Could the tears, the sighs, the supplications, bursting from the tortured parental affection, have blunted the keen edge of avarice, she might have been rescued from agony, which many of her country's children have felt, but which none have ever described. In vain she lifted her supplicating voice to an insulted father, and her guiltless hands to a dishonoured deity! She was ravished from the bosom of her country, from the arms of her friends, while the advanced age of her parents rendering them unfit for servitude, cruelly separated them from her for ever.

Scenes which her imagination had never conceived of, a floating world, the sporting monsters of the deep, and the familiar meeting of billows and clouds, strove, but in vain, to divert her attention from three hundred Africans in chains, suffering the most excruciating torment; and some of them rejoicing that the pangs of death came like a balm to their wounds.

Once more her eyes were blessed with a continent: but alas! how unlike the land where she received her being! Here all things appeared unpropitious. She learned to catch the ideas, marked by the sounds of language, only to know that her doom was slavery, from which death alone was to emancipate her. What did it avail her, that the walls of her lord were hung with splendor, and that the dust trodden under foot in her native country, crouded his gates with sordid worshippers! The laws rendered her incapable of receiving property: and though she was a free moral agent, accountable for her own actions, yet never had she a moment at her own disposal! Fifty years her faithful hands have been compelled to ignoble servitude for the benefit of an Isaac Royall,[3] until, as if nations must be agitated, and the world convulsed, for the preservation of that freedom, which the Almighty Father intended for all the human race, the present war commenced. The terrors of men, armed in the cause of freedom, compelled her master to fly, and to breathe away his life in a land, where lawless dominion sits enthroned, pouring blood and vengeance on all who dare to be free.

The face of your petitioner is now marked with the furrows of time, and her frame feebly bending under the oppression of years, while she, by the laws of the land, is denied the enjoyment of one morsel of that immense wealth, a part whereof hath been accumulated by her own industry, and the whole augmented by her servitude.

Wherefore, casting herself at the feet of your honours, as to a body of men, formed for the extirpation of vassalage, for the reward of virtue, and the just returns of honest industry—she prays that such allowance may be made her, out of the estate of colonel Royall, as will prevent her, and her more infirm daughter, from misery in the greatest extreme, and scatter comfort over the short and downward path of their lives: and she will ever pray.

BELINDA.

Boston, February, 1782. (538-540).[4]

NOTES

1. The Volta River flows through present-day Ghana, known in the eighteenth century as the Gold Coast.

2. Yellow dust: gold. Belinda remembers the type of African paradise—fruitful, temperate, and where minerals precious to Europeans have no real value—often described in abolitionist literature.

3. Isaac Royall (1719?-1781) was one of the wealthiest and most prominent Loyalists in Massachusetts. He and his brother Jacob, both born in the West Indian colony of Antigua, were slave dealers as well as major slave owners in Massachusetts. Isaac Royall fled from Medford, Massachusetts, to Boston just days before the battle of Lexington in April 1775. After the battle, he sought refuge in England, where he died. Like many colonial soldiers, he

had two military ranks, one in the colonial service, in which he was Brigadier-General of the Artillery Company of Boston, and the other in the Royal Army, in which he was a colonel. Significantly, in Belinda's petition he is later called Colonel Royall, to emphasize his Loyalist position. After he fled, his property was declared forfeited and confiscated by the state, which did not sell the Royall estate until 1805.

4. *The American Museum* frequently published antislavery pieces. For example, the essay that immediately follows Belinda's petition is entitled "Address to the Heart, on the Subject of African Slavery." In 1787 the magazine printed Belinda's original petition of 1783 because she had repetitioned the legislature in spring 1787 for the resumption of payment of the pension of £15 per year she had been awarded out of the rents and profits from her former master's expropriated estate but which had ceased to be paid her after the first year. In November 1787, Belinda was granted her pension for another year, in response to "The Memorial of Belinda, an African, formerly a Servant to the late Isaac Royal Esq an Absentee." We do not not what became of Belinda, her daughter, or the pension.

QUOBNA OTTOBAH CUGOANO

(CA.1757-1791+)

~

THOUGHTS AND SENTIMENTS ON THE EVIL AND WICKED TRAFFIC OF THE SLAVERY AND COMMERCE OF THE HUMAN SPECIES, HUMBLY SUBMITTED TO The INHABITANTS of GREAT-BRITAIN, *BY OTTOBAH CUGOANO, A NATIVE of* AFRICA (London, 1787).

One law, and one manner shall be for you, and for the stranger that sojourneth with you; and therefore, all things whatsoever ye would that men should do to you, do ye even so to them.
Numb[ers] xv.16.—Matthew vii.12.[1]

As several learned gentlemen of distinguished abilities, as well as eminent for their great humanity, liberality and candour, have written various essays against that infamous traffic of African Slave Trade, carried on with the West-India planters and merchants, to the great shame and disgrace of all Christian nations wherever it is admitted in any of their territories, or place or situation amongst them; it cannot be amiss that I should thankfully acknowledge these truly worthy and humane gentlemen with the warmest sense of gratitude, for their beneficent and laudable endeavours towards a total suppression of that infamous and iniquitous traffic of stealing, kid-napping, buying, selling, and cruelly enslaving men!

Those who have endeavoured to restore to their fellow-creatures the common rights of nature, of which especially the unfortunate Black People have been so unjustly deprived, cannot fail in meeting with the applause of all good men, and the approbation of that which will for ever redound to their honor; they have the warrant of that which is divine: *Open thy mouth, judge righteously, plead the cause of the poor and needy; for the liberal deviseth liberal things, and by liberal things shall stand.*[2] And they can say with the pious Job, *Did not I weep for him that was in trouble; was not my soul grieved for the poor?*[3]

The kind exertions of many benevolent and humane gentlemen, against the iniquitous traffic of slavery and oppression, has been attended with much good to many, and must redound with great honor to themselves, to humanity and their country; their laudable endeavours have been productive of the most beneficent effects in preventing that savage barbarity from taking place in free countries at home. In this, as well as in many other respects, there is one class of people (whose virtues of probity and humanity are well known) who are worthy of universal approbation and imitation, because, like men of honor and humanity, they have jointly agreed to carry on no slavery and savage barbarity among them; and, since the last war, some mitigation of slavery has been obtained in some respective districts of America, though not in proportion to their own vaunted claims of freedom; but it is to be hoped, that they will yet go on to make a further and greater reformation.[4] However, notwithstanding all that has been done and written against it, that brutish barbarity, and unparalleled injustice, is still carried on to a very great extent in the colonies, and with an avidity as insidious, cruel and oppressive, as ever. The longer that men continue in the practice of evil and wickedness, they grow the more abandoned; for nothing in history can equal the barbarity and cruelty of the tortures and murders committed under various pretences in modern slavery, except the annals of the Inquisition and the bloody edicts of Popish massacres.[5]

It is therefore manifest, that something else ought yet to be done; and what is required, is evidently the incumbent duty of all men of enlightened understanding, and of every man that has any claim or affinity to the name of Christian, that the base treatment which the African Slaves undergo ought to be abolished; and it is moreover evident, that the whole, or any part of that iniquitous traffic of slavery, can nowhere, or in any degree, be admitted, but among those who must eventually resign their own claim to any degree of sensibility and humanity, for that of barbarians and ruffians.

But it would be needless to arrange an history of all the base treatment which the African Slaves are subjected to, in order to shew the exceeding wickedness and evil of that insidious traffic, as the whole may easily appear in every part, and at every view, to be wholly and totally inimical to every idea of justice, equity, reason and humanity. What I intend to advance against that evil, criminal and wicked traffic of enslaving men, are only some Thoughts and Sentiments which occur to me, as being obvious from the Scriptures of Divine Truth, or such arguments as are chiefly deduced from thence, with other such observations as I have been able to collect. Some of these observations may lead into a larger field of consideration, than that of the African Slave Trade alone; but those causes from wherever they originate, and become the production of slavery, the evil effects produced by it, must shew that its origin and source is of a wicked and criminal nature.

No necessity, or any situation of men, however poor, pitiful and wretched they may be, can warrant them to rob others, or oblige them to become thieves, because they are poor, miserable and wretched: But the robbers of men, the kidnappers, ensnarers and slave-holders, who take away the common rights and privileges of others to support and enrich themselves, are universally those pitiful and detestable wretches; for the ensnarings of others, and taking away their liberty by slavery and oppression, is the worst kind of robbery, as most opposite to every precept and injunction of the Divine Law, and contrary to that command which enjoins that *all men should love their neighbours as themselves*, and *that they should do unto others, as they would that men should do to them.*[6] As to any other laws that slave-holders may make among themselves, as respecting slaves, they can be of no better kind, nor give them any better character, than what is implied in the common report—that there may be some honesty among thieves. This may seem a harsh comparison, but the parallel is so coincident that, I must say, I can find no other way of expressing my Thoughts and Sentiments, without making use of some harsh words and comparisons against the carriers on of such abandoned wickedness. But, in this little undertaking, I must humbly hope the impartial reader will excuse such defects as may arise from want of better education; and as to the resentment of those who can lay their cruel lash upon the backs of thousands, for a thousand times less crimes than writing against their enormous wickedness and brutal avarice, is what I may be sure to meet with.

However, it cannot but be very discouraging to a man of my complexion in such an attempt as this, to meet with the evil aspersions of some men, who say "That an African is not entitled to any competent degree of knowledge, or capable of imbibing any sentiments of probity; and that nature designed him for some inferior link in the chain,[7] fitted only to be a slave."[8] But when I meet with those who make no scruple to deal with the human species, as with the beasts of the earth, I must think them not only brutish, but wicked and base; and that their aspersions are insidious and false: And if such men can boast of greater degrees of knowledge, than any African is entitled to, I shall let them enjoy all the advantages of it unenvied, as I fear it consists only in greater share of infidelity, and that of a blacker kind than only skin deep. And if their complexion be not what I may suppose, it is at least the nearest in resemblance to an infernal hue. A good man will neither speak nor do as a bad man will; but if a man is bad, it makes no difference whether he be a black or a white devil.

By some of such complexion, as whether black or white it matters not, I was early snatched away from my native country, with about eighteen or twenty more boys and girls, as we were playing in a field. We lived but a few days journey from the coast where we were kid-napped, and as we were decoyed and drove along, we were soon conducted to a factory,[9] and from thence, in the fashionable way of traffic, consigned to Grenada. Perhaps it may not be amiss to give a few remarks, as some account of myself, in this transposition of captivity.

I was born in the city of Agimaque, on the coast of Fantyn; my father was a companion to the chief in that part of the country of Fantee, and when the old king died I was left in his house with his family; soon after I was sent for by his nephew, Ambro Accasa, who succeeded the old king in the chiefdom of that part of Fantee known by the name of Agimaque and Assinee.[10] I lived with his children, enjoying peace and tranquillity, about twenty moons, which, according to their way of reckoning time, is two years. I was sent for to visit an uncle, who lived at a considerable distance from Agimaque. The first day after we set out we arrived at Assinee, and the third day at my uncle's habitation, where I lived about three months, and was then thinking of returning to my father and young companion at Agimaque; but by this time I had got well acquainted with some of the children of my uncle's hundreds of relations, and we were some days too venturesome in going into the woods to gather fruit and catch birds, and such amusements as pleased us. One day I refused to go with the rest, being rather apprehensive that something might happen to us; till one of my play-fellows said to me, because you belong to the great men, you are afraid to venture your carcase, or else of the *bounsam*, which is the devil. This enraged me so much, that I set a resolution to join the rest, and we went into the woods as usual; but we had not been above two hours before our troubles began, when several great ruffians came upon us suddenly, and said we had committed a fault against their lord, and we must go and answer for it ourselves before him.

Some of us attempted in vain to run away, but pistols and cutlasses were soon introduced, threatening, that if we offered to stir we should all lie dead on the spot. One of them pretended to be more friendly than the rest, and said, that he would speak to their lord to get us clear, and desired that we should follow him; we were then immediately divided into different parties, and drove after him. We were soon led out of the way which we knew, and towards the evening, as we came in sight of a town, they told us that this great man of theirs lived there, but pretended it was too late to go and see him that night. Next morning there came three other men, whose language differed from ours, and spoke to some of those who watched us all the night, but he that pretended to be our friend with the great man, and some others, were gone away. We asked our keepers what these men had been saying to them, and they answered, that they had been asking them, and us together, to go and feast with them that day, and that we must put off seeing the great man till after; little thinking that our doom was so nigh, or that these villains meant to feast on us as their prey. We went with them again about half a day's journey, and came to a great multitude of people, having different music playing; and all the day after we got there, we were very merry with the music, dancing and singing. Towards the evening, we were again persuaded that we could not get back to where the great man lived till next day; and when bedtime came, we were separated into different houses with different people. When the next morning came, I asked for the men that brought me there, and for the rest of my companions; and I was told that they were gone to the sea side to bring home some rum, guns and powder, and that some of my companions were gone with them, and that some were gone to the fields to do something or other. This gave me strong suspicion that there was some treachery in the case, and I began to think that my hopes of returning home again were all over. I soon became very uneasy, not knowing what to do, and refused to eat or drink for whole days together, till the man of the house told me that he would do all in his power to get me back to my uncle; then I eat[11] a little fruit with him, and had some thoughts that I should be sought after, as I would be then missing at home about five or six days. I enquired every day if the men had come back, and for the rest of my companions, but could get no answer of any satisfaction. I was kept about six days at this man's house, and in the evening there was another man came and talked with him a good while, and I heard the one say to the other he must go, and the other said the sooner the better;

that man came out and told me that he knew my relations at Agimaque, and that we must set out to-morrow morning, and he would convey me there. Accordingly we set out next day, and travelled till dark, when we came to a place where we had some supper and slept. He carried a large bag with some gold dust, which he said he had to buy some goods at the sea side to take with him to Agimaque. Next day we travelled on, and in the evening came to a town, where I saw several white people, which made me afraid that they would eat me, according to our notion as children in the inland parts of the country. This made me rest very uneasy all the night, and next morning I had some victuals brought, desiring me to eat and make haste, as my guide and kid-napper told me that he had to go to the castle with some company that were going there, as he had told me before, to get some goods. After I was ordered out, the horrors I soon saw and felt, cannot be well described; I saw many of my miserable countrymen chained two and two, some hand-cuffed, and some with their hands tied behind. We were conducted along by a guard, and when we arrived at the castle, I asked my guide what I was brought there for, he told me to learn the ways of the *browsow*, that is the white faced people. I saw him take a gun, a piece of cloth, and some lead for me, and then he told me that he must now leave me there, and went off. This made me cry bitterly, but I was soon conducted to a prison, for three days, where I heard the groans and cries of many, and saw some of my fellow-captives. But when a vessel arrived to conduct us away to the ship, it was a most horrible scene; there was nothing to be heard but rattling of chains, smacking of whips, and the groans and cries of our fellow-men. Some would not stir from the ground, when they were lashed and beat in the most horrible manner. I have forgot the name of this infernal fort; but we were taken in the ship that came for us, to another that was ready to sail from Cape Coast. When we were put into the ship, we saw several black merchants coming on board, but we were all drove into our holes, and not suffered to speak to any of them. In this situation we continued several days in sight of our native land; but I could find no good person to give any information of my situation to Accasa at Agimaque. And when we found ourselves at last taken away, death was more preferable than life, and a plan was concerted amongst us, that we might burn and blow up the ship, and to perish all together in the flames; but we were betrayed by one of our own countrywomen, who slept with some of the head men of the ship, for it was common for the dirty filthy sailors to take the African women and lie upon their bodies; but the men were chained and pent up in holes. It was the women and boys which were to burn the ship, with the approbation and groans of the rest; though that was prevented, the discovery was likewise a cruel bloody scene.

But it would be needless to give a description of all the horrible scenes which we saw, and the base treatment which we met with in this dreadful captive situation, as the similar cases of thousands, which suffer by this infernal traffic, are well known. Let it suffice to say, that I was thus lost to my dear indulgent parents and relations, and they to me. All my help was cries and tears, and these could not avail; nor suffered long, till one succeeding woe, and dread, swelled up another.

Brought from a state of innocence and freedom, and, in a barbarous and cruel manner, conveyed to a state of horror and slavery: This abandoned situation may be easier conceived than described. From the time that I was kid-napped and conducted to a factory, and from thence in the brutish, base, but fashionable way of traffic, consigned to Grenada, the grievous thoughts which I then felt, still pant in my heart; though my fears and tears have long since subsided. And yet it is still grievous to think that thousands more have suffered in similar and greater distress, under the hands of barbarous robbers, and merciless task-masters; and that many even now are suffering in all the extreme bitterness of grief and woe, that no language can describe. The cries of some, and the sight of their misery, may be seen and heard afar; but the deep sounding groans of thousands, and the great sadness of their misery and woe, under the heavy load of oppressions and calamities inflicted upon them, are such as can only be distinctly known to the ears of Jehovah Sabaoth.[12]

This Lord of Hosts, in his great Providence, and in great mercy to me, made a way for my deliverance from Grenada.—Being in this dreadful captivity and horrible slavery, without any hope of deliverance, for about eight or nine months, beholding the most dreadful scenes of misery and cruelty, and seeing my miserable companions often cruelly lashed, and as it were cut to pieces, for the most trifling faults; this made me often tremble and weep, but I escaped better than many of them. For eating a piece of sugarcane, some were cruelly lashed, or struck over the face to knock their teeth out. Some of the stouter ones,[13] I suppose often reproved, and grown hardened and stupid with many cruel beatings and lashings, or perhaps faint and pressed with hunger and hard labour, were often committing trespasses of this kind, and when detected, they met with exemplary punishment. Some told me they had their teeth pulled out to deter others, and to prevent them from eating any cane in future. Thus seeing my miserable companions and countrymen in this pitiful, distressed and horrible situation, with all the brutish baseness and barbarity attending it, could not but fill my little mind with horror and indignation. But I must own, to the shame of my own countrymen, that I was first kid-napped and betrayed by some of my own complexion, who were the first cause of my exile and slavery; but if there were no buyers there would be no sellers. So far as I can remember, some of the Africans in my country keep slaves, which they take in war, or for debt; but those which they keep are well fed, and good care taken of them, and treated well; and, as to their cloathing, they differ according to the custom of the country. But I may safely say, that all the poverty and misery that any of the inhabitants of Africa meet with among themselves, is far inferior to those inhospitable regions of misery which they meet with in the West-Indies, where their hard-hearted overseers have neither regard to the laws of God, nor the life of their fellow-men.

Thanks be to God, I was delivered from Grenada, and that horrid brutal slavery.—A gentleman coming to England,[14] took me for his servant, and brought me away, where I soon found my situation become more agreeable. After coming to England, and seeing others write and read, I had a strong desire to learn, and getting what assistance I could, I applied myself to learn reading and writing, which soon became my recreation, pleasure, and delight; and when my master perceived that I could write some, he sent me to a proper school for that purpose to learn. Since, I have endeavoured to improve my mind in reading, and have sought to get all the intelligence I could, in my situation of life, towards the state of my brethren and countrymen in complexion, and of the miserable situation of those who are barbarously sold into captivity, and unlawfully held in slavery.

But, among other observations, one great duty I owe to Almighty God, (the thankful acknowledgement I would not omit for any consideration) that, although I have been brought away from my native country, in that torrent of robbery and wickedness, thanks be to God for his good providence towards me; I have both obtained liberty, and acquired the great advantages of some little learning, in being able to read and write, and, what is still infinitely of greater advantage, I trust, to know something of HIM *who is that God whose providence rules over all, and who is the only Potent One that rules in the nations over the children of men. It is unto Him, who is the Prince of the Kings of the earth ,that I would give all thanks.* And, in some manner, I may say with Joseph, as he did with respect to the evil intention of his brethren, when they sold him into Egypt, that whatever evil intentions and bad motives those insidious robbers had in carrying me away from my native country and friends, I trust, was what the Lord intended for my good. In this respect, I am highly indebted to many of the good people of England for learning and principles unknown to the people of my native country. But, above all, what I have obtained from the Lord God of Hosts, the God of the Christians! in that divine revelation of the only true God, and the Saviour of men, what a treasure of wisdom and blessings are involved? How wonderful is the divine goodness displayed in those invaluable books the Old and New Testaments, that inestimable compilation of books, the Bible? And, O what a treasure to have, and one of the greatest advantages to be able to read therein, and a divine blessing to understand![15]

But, to return to my subject, I begin with the Cursory Remarker.[16] This man stiles himself a friend to the West-India colonies and their inhabitants, like Demetrius, the silversmith, a man of some considerable abilities, seeing their craft in danger, a craft, however, not so innocent and justifiable as the making of shrines for Diana, though that was base and wicked enough to enslave the minds of men with superstition and idolatry;[17] but his craft, and the gain of those craftsmen, consists in the enslaving both soul and body to the cruel idolatry, and most abominable service and slavery, to the idol of cursed avarice: And as he finds some discoveries of their wicked traffic held up in a light where truth and facts are so clearly seen, as none but the most desperate villain would dare to obstruct or oppose, he therefore sallies forth with all the desperation of an Utopian assailant, to tell lies by a virulent contradiction of facts, and with false aspersions endeavour to calumniate the worthy and judicious essayist of that discovery, a man, whose character is irreproachable. By thus artfully supposing, if he could bring the reputation of the author, who has discovered so much of their iniquitous traffic, into dispute, his work would fall and be less regarded. However, this virulent craftsman has done no great merit to his cause and the credit of that infamous craft; at the appearance of truth, his understanding has got the better of his avarice and infidelity, so far, as to draw the following concession: "I shall not be so far misunderstood, by the candid and judicious part of mankind, as to be ranked among the advocates of slavery, as I most sincerely join Mr. Ramsay, and every other man of sensibility, in hoping the blessings of freedom will, in due time, be equally diffused over the whole globe."[18]

By this, it would seem that he was a little ashamed of his craftsmen, and would not like to be ranked or appear amongst them. But as long as there are any hopes of gain to be made by that insidious craft, he can join with them well enough, and endeavour to justify them in that most abandoned traffic of buying, selling, and enslaving men. He finds fault with a plan for punishing robbers, thieves and vagabonds, who distress their neighbours by their thrift, robbery and plunder, without regarding any laws human or divine, except the rules of their own fraternity, and in that case, according to the proverb, there may be some honor among thieves; but these are the only people in the world that ought to suffer some punishment, imprisonment or slavery; their external complexion, whether black or white, should be no excuse for them to do evil. Being aware of this, perhaps he was afraid that some of his friends, the great and opulent banditti of slaveholders in the western part of the world, might be found guilty of more atrocious and complicated crimes, than even those of the highwaymen, the robberies and the petty larcenies committed in England. Therefore, to make the best of this sad dilemma, he brings in a ludicrous invective comparison that it would be "an event which would undoubtedly furnish a new and pleasant compartment to that well known and most delectable print, call'd, *The world turn'd up side down*, in which the cook is roasted by the pig, the man saddled by the horse," &[19] If he means that the complicated banditries of pirates, thieves, robbers, oppressors and enslavers of men, are those cooks and men that would be roasted and saddled, it certainly would be no unpleasant sight to see them well roasted, saddled and bridled too; and no matter by whom, whether he terms them pigs, horses or asses. But there is not much likelihood of this silly monkeyish comparison as yet being verified, in bringing the opulent pirates and thieves to condign punishment, so that he could very well bring it in to turn it off with a grin. However, to make use of his words, it would be a most delectable sight, when thieves and robbers get the upper side of the world, to see them turned down; and I should not interrupt his mirth, to see him laugh at his own invective monkeyish comparison as long as he pleases.

But again, when he draws a comparison of the many hardships that the poor in Great-Britain and Ireland labour under, as well as many of those in other countries; that their various distresses are worse than the West India slaves—It may be true, in part, that some of them suffer greater hardships than many of the slaves; but, bad as it is, the poorest in England would not change their situation for that of slaves. And there may be some masters, under various circumstances, worse off than their servants; but they would not change their own situation for theirs: Nor as little would a rich man wish to change his situation of affluence, for that of a beggar: and so, likewise, no freeman, however poor and distressing his situation may be, would resign his liberty for that of a slave, in the situation of a horse or a dog. The case of the poor, whatever their hardships may be, in free countries, is widely different from that of the West-India slaves. For the slaves, like animals, are bought and sold, and dealt with as their capricious owners may think fit, even in torturing and tearing them to pieces, and wearing them out with hard labour, hunger and oppression; and should the death of a slave ensue by some other more violent way than that which is commonly the death of thousands, and tens of thousands in the end, the haughty tyrant, in that case, has only to pay a small fine for the murder and death of his slave. The brute creation in general may fare better than man, and some dogs may refuse the crumbs that the distressed poor would be glad of; but the nature and situation of man is far superior to that of beasts; and, in like manner, whatever circumstances poor freemen may be in, their situation is much superior, beyond any proportion, to that of the hardships and cruelty of modern slavery. But where can the situation of any freeman be so bad as that of a slave; or, could such be found, or even worse, as he would have it, what would the comparison amount to? Would it plead for his craft of slavery and oppression? Or, rather, would it not cry aloud for some redress, and what every well regulated society of men ought to hear and consider, that none should suffer want or be oppressed among them? And this seems to be pointed out by the circumstances which he describes; that it is the great duty, and ought to be the highest ambition of all governors, to order and establish such policy, and in such a wise manner, that every thing should be so managed, as to be conducive to the moral, temporal and eternal welfare of every individual from the lowest degree to the highest; and the consequence of this would be, the harmony, happiness and good prosperity of the whole community (1-18).

"Some pretend that the Africans, in general, are a set of poor, ignorant, dispersed, unsociable people; and that they think it no crime to sell one another, and even their own wives and children; therefore they bring them away to a situation where many of them may arrive to a better state than ever they could obtain in their own native country."[20] This specious pretence is without any shadow of justice and truth, and, if the argument was even true, it could afford no just and warrantable matter for any society of men to hold slaves. But the argument is false; there can be no ignorance, dispersion, or unsociableness so found among them, which can be made better by bringing them away to a state of a degree equal to that of a cow or a horse.

But let their ignorance in some things (in which the Europeans have greatly the advantage of them) be what it will, it is not the intention of those who bring them away to make them better by it; nor is the design of slave-holders of any other intention, but that they may serve them as a kind of engines and beasts of burden; that their own ease and profit may be advanced, by a set of poor helpless men and women, whom they despise and rank with brutes, and keep them in perpetual slavery, both themselves and children, and merciful death is the only release from their toil. By the benevolence of some, a few may get their liberty, and by their own industry and ingenuity, may acquire some learning, mechanical trades, or useful business; and some may be brought away by different gentlemen to free countries, where they get their liberty, but no thanks to slave-holders for it. But amongst those who get their liberty, like all other ignorant men, are generally more corrupt in their morals, than they possibly could have been amongst their own people in Africa; for, being mostly amongst the wicked and apostate Christians, they sooner learn their oaths and blasphemies, and their evil ways, than any thing else. Some few, indeed, may eventually arrive at some knowledge of the Christian religion, and the great advantages of it. Such was the case of Ukawsaw Groniosaw, an African prince, who lived in England.[21] He was a long time in a state of great poverty and distress, and must have died at one time for want, if a good and charitable attorney had not supported him. He was long after in a very poor state, but he would not have given his faith in the Christian religion, in exchange for all the kingdoms of Africa, if they could have been given to him, in place of his poverty, for it. And such was A. Morrant in America.[22] When a boy, he could stroll away into a desart, and prefer the society of wild beasts to the absurd Christianity of his mother's house. He was conducted to the king of the Cherokees, who, in a miraculous manner, was induced by him to embrace the Christian faith. This Morrant was in the British service last war, and his royal convert, the king of the Cherokee Indians, accompanied General Clinton at the siege of Charles-Town (21-23).

And now, as to the Africans being dispersed and unsociable, if it was so, that could be no warrant for the Europeans to enslave them; and even though they may have many different feuds and bad practices among them, the continent of Africa is of vast extent, and the numerous inhabitants are divided into several kingdoms and principalities, which are governed by their respective kings and princes, and those are absolutely maintained by their free subjects. Very few nations make slaves of any of those under their government; but such as are taken prisoners of war from their neighbours, are generally kept in that state, until they can exchange and dispose of them otherwise; and towards the west coast they are generally procured for the European market, and sold. They have a great aversion to murder, or even in taking away the lives of those which they judge guilty of crimes; and, therefore, they prefer disposing of them otherwise better than killing them.[23] This gives their merchants and procurers of slaves a power to travel a great way into the interior parts of the country to buy such as are wanted to be disposed of. These slave-procurers are a set of as great villains as any in the world. They often steal and kidnap many more than they buy at first, if they can meet with them by the way; and they have only their certain boundaries to go to, and sell them from one to another; so that if they are sought after and detected, the thieves are seldom found, and the others only plead that they bought them so and so. These kid-nappers and slave-procurers, called merchants, are a species of African villains, which are greatly corrupted, and even vitiated by their intercourse with the Europeans; but, wicked and barbarous as they certainly are, I can hardly think, if they knew what horrible barbarity they were sending their fellow-creatures to, that they would do it. But the artful Europeans have so deceived them, that they are bought by their inventions of merchandize, and beguiled into it by their artifice; for the Europeans, at their factories, in some various manner, have always kept some as servants to them, and with gaudy cloaths, in a gay manner, as decoy ducks to deceive others, and to tell them that they want many more to go over the sea, and be as they are. So in that respect, wherein it may be said that they will sell one another, they are only ensnared and enlisted to be servants, kept like some of those which they see at the factories, which, for some gewgaws,[24] as presents given to themselves and friends, they are thereby enticed to go; and something after the same manner that East-India soldiers are procured in Britain; and the inhabitants here, just as much sell themselves, and one another, as they do; and the kidnappers here, and the slave-procurers in Africa, are much alike. But many other barbarous methods are made use of by the vile instigators, procurers and ensnarers of men; and some of the wicked and profligate princes and chiefs of Africa accept of presents, from the Europeans, to procure a certain number of slaves; and thereby they are wickedly instigated to go to war with one another on purpose to get them, which produces many terrible depredations; and sometimes when those engagements are entered into, and they find themselves defeated of their purpose, it has happened that some of their own people have fallen a sacrifice to their avarice and cruelty. And it may be said of the Europeans, that they have made use of every insidious method to procure slaves whenever they can, and in whatever manner they can lay hold of them, and that their forts and factories are the avowed dens of thieves for robbers, plunderers and depredators.

But again, as to the Africans selling their own wives and children, nothing can be more opposite to every thing they hold dear and valuable; and nothing can distress them more, than to part with any of their relations and friends. Such are the tender feelings of parents for their children, that, for the loss of a child, they seldom can be rendered happy, even with the intercourse and enjoyment of their friends, for years. For any man to think that it should be otherwise, when he may see a thousand instances of a natural instinct, even in the brute creation, where they have a sympathetic feeling for their offspring; it must be great want of consideration not to think, that much more than meerly what is natural to animals, should in a higher degree be implanted in the breast of every part of the rational creation of man. And what man of feeling can help lamenting the loss of parents, friends, liberty, and perhaps property and other valuable and dear connections. Those people annually brought away from Guinea, are born as free, and are brought up with as great a predilection for their own country, freedom and liberty, as the sons and daughters of fair Britain. Their free subjects are trained up to a kind of military service, not so much by the desire of the chief, as by their own voluntary inclination. It is looked upon as the greatest respect they can shew to their king, to stand up for his and their own defence in time of need. Their different chieftains, which bear a reliance on the great chief, or king, exercise a kind of government something like that feudal institution which prevailed some time in Scotland. In this respect, though the common people are free, they often suffer by the villainy of their different chieftains, and by the wars and feuds which happen among them. Nevertheless their freedom and rights are as dear to them, as those privileges are to other people. And it may be said that freedom, and the liberty of enjoying their own privileges, burns with as much zeal and fervour in the breast of an AEthiopian,[25] as in the breast of any inhabitant on the globe.

But the supporters and favourers of slavery make other things a pretence and an excuse in their own defence; such as, that they find that it was admitted under the Divine institution by Moses, as well as the long continued practice of different nations for ages; and that the Africans are peculiarly marked out by some signal prediction in nature and complexion for that purpose.

This seems to be the greatest bulwark of defence which the advocates and favourers of slavery can advance, and what is generally talked of in their favour by those who do not understand it. I shall consider it in that view, whereby it will appear, that they deceive themselves and mislead others. Men are never more liable to be drawn into error, than when truth is made use of in a guileful manner to seduce them. Those who do not believe the scriptures to be a Divine revelation, cannot, consistently with themselves, make the law of Moses, or any mark or prediction they can find respecting any particular set of men, as found in the sacred writings, any reason that one class of men should enslave another. In that respect, all that they have to enquire into should be whether it be right, or wrong, that any part of the human species should enslave another; and when that is the case, the Africans, though not so learned, are just as wise as the Europeans; and when the matter is left to human wisdom, they are both liable to err. But what the light of nature, and the dictates of reason, when rightly considered, teach, is, that no man ought to enslave another; and some, who have been rightly guided thereby, have made noble defences for the universal natural rights and privileges of all men. But in this case, when the learned take neither revelation nor reason for their guide, they fall into as great, and worse errors, than the unlearned; for they only make use of that system of Divine wisdom, which should guide them into truth, when they can find or pick out any thing that will suit their purpose, or that they can pervert to such—the very means of leading themselves and others into error. And, in consequence thereof, the pretences that some men make use of for holding of slaves, must be evidently the grossest perversion of reason, as well as an inconsistent and diabolical use of the sacred writings. For it must be a strange perversion of reason, and a wrong use or disbelief of the sacred writings, when any thing found there is so perverted by them, and set up as a precedent and rule for men to commit wickedness. They had better have no reason, and no belief in the scriptures, and make no use of them at all, than only to believe, and make use of that which leads them into the most abominable evil and wickedness of dealing unjustly with their fellow men.

But this will appear evident to all men that believe the scriptures, that every reason necessary is given that they should be believed; and, in this case, that they afford us this information: "That all mankind did spring from one original, and that there are no different species among men. For God who made the world, hath made of one blood all the nations of men that dwell on all the face of the earth."[26] Wherefore we may justly infer, as there are no inferior species, but all of one blood and of one nature, that there does not an inferiority subsist, or depend, on their colour, features or form, whereby some men make a pretence to enslave others; and consequently, as they have all one creator, one original, made of one blood, and all brethren descended from one father, it never could be lawful and just for any nation, or people, to oppress and enslave another.

And again, as all the present inhabitants of the world sprang from the family of Noah, and were then all of one complexion, there is no doubt, but the difference which we now find, took its rise very rapidly after they became dispersed and settled on the different parts of the globe. There seems to be a tendency to this, in many instances, among children of the same parents, having different colour of hair and features from one another. And God alone who established the course of nature, can bring about and establish what variety he pleases; and it is not in the power of man to make one hair white or black. But among the variety which it hath pleased God to establish and caused to take place, we may meet with some analogy in nature, that as the bodies of men are tempered with a different degree to enable them to endure the respective climates of their habitations, so their colours vary, in some degree, in a regular gradation from the equator towards either of the poles. However, there are other incidental causes arising from time and place, which constitute the most distinguishing variety of colour, form, appearance and features, as peculiar to the inhabitants of one tract of country, and differing in something from those in another, even in the same latitudes, as well as from those in different climates. Long custom and the different way of living among the several inhabitants of the different parts of the earth, has a very great effect in distinguishing them by a difference of features and complexion. These effects are easy to be seen; as to the causes, it is sufficient for us to know, that all is the work of an Almighty hand. Therefore, as we find the distribution of the human species inhabiting the barren, as well as the most fruitful parts of the earth, and the cold as well as the most hot, differing from one another in complexion according to their situation; it may be reasonably, as well as religiously, inferred, that He who placed them in their various situations, hath extended equally his care and protection to all; and from thence, that it becometh unlawful to counteract his benignity, by reducing others of different complexions to undeserved bondage (25-32).

Many of the Canaanites who fled away in the Time of Joshua, became mingled with the different nations, and some historians think that some of them came to England, and settled about Cornwall, as far back as that time; so that, for any thing that can be known to the contrary, there may be some of the descendants of that wicked generation still subsisting among the slave-holders in the West-Indies. For if the curse of God ever rested upon them, or upon any other men, the only visible mark thereof was always upon those who committed the most outrageous acts of violence and oppression. But colour and complexion has nothing to do with that mark; every wicked man, and the enslavers of others, bear the stamp of their own iniquity, and that mark which was set upon Cain. (35-36)

But again, in answer to another part of the pretence which the favourers of slavery make use of in their defence, that slavery was an ancient custom, and that it became the prevalent and universal practice of many different barbarous nations for ages: This must be granted; but not because it was right, or any thing like right and equity. A lawful servitude was always necessary, and became contingent with the very nature of human society. But when the laws of civilization were broken through, and when the rights and properties of others were invaded, that brought the oppressed into a kind of compulsive servitude, though often not compelled to it by those whom they were obliged to serve. This arose from the different depredations and robberies which were committed upon one another; the helpless were obliged to seek protection from such as could support them, and to give unto them their service, in order to preserve themselves from want, and to deliver them from the injury either of men or beasts. For while civil society continued in a rude state, even among the establishers of kingdoms, when they became powerful and proud, as they wanted to enlarge their territories, they drove and expelled others from their peaceable habitations, who were not so powerful as themselves. This made those who were robbed of their substance, and drove from the place of their abode, make their escape to such as could and would help them; but when such a relief could not be found, they were obliged to submit to the yoke of their oppressors, who, in many cases, would not yield them any protection upon any terms. Wherefore, when their lives were in danger otherwise, and they could not find any help, they were obliged to sell themselves for bond servants to such as would buy them, when they could not get a service that was better. But as soon as buyers could be found, robbers began their traffic to ensnare others, and such as fell into their hands were carried captive by them, and were obliged to submit to their being sold by them into the hands of other robbers, for there are few buyers of men, who intend thereby to make them free, and such as they buy are generally subjected to hard labour and bondage. Therefore at all times, while a man is a slave, he is still in captivity, and under the jurisdiction of robbers; and every man who keeps a slave, is a robber, whenever he compels him to his service without giving him a just reward. The barely supplying his slave with some necessary things, to keep him in life, is no reward at all, that is only for his own sake and benefit; and the very nature of compulsion and taking away the liberty of others, as well as their property, is robbery; and that kind of service which subjects men to a state of slavery, must at all times, and in every circumstance, be a barbarous, inhuman and unjust dealing with our fellow men. A voluntary service and slavery are quite different things; but in ancient times, in whatever degree slavery was admitted, and whatever hardships they were, in general, subjected to, it was not nearly so bad as the modern barbarous and cruel West-India slavery.

Now, in respect to that kind of servitude which was admitted into the law of Moses, that was not contrary to the natural liberties of men, but a state of equity and justice, according as the nature and circumstances of the times required.

There was no more harm in entering into a covenant with another man as a bond-servant,[27] than there is for two men to enter into partnership the one with the other; and sometimes the nature of the case may be, and their business require it, that the one may find money and live at a distance and ease, and the other manage the business for him: So a bond-servant was generally the steward in a man's house, and sometimes his heir. There was no harm in buying a man who was in a state of captivity and bondage by others, and keeping him in servitude till such time as his purchase was redeemed by his labour and service. And there could be no harm in paying a man's debts, and keeping him in servitude until such time as an equitable agreement of composition was paid by him. And so, in general, whether they had been bought or sold in order to pay their just debts when they became poor, or were bought from such as held them in an unlawful captivity, the state of bondage which they and their children fell under, among the Israelites, was into that of a vassalage state, which rather might be termed a deliverance from debt and captivity, than a state of slavery. In that vassalage state which they were reduced to, they had a tax of some service to pay, which might only be reckoned equivalent to a poor man in England paying rent for his cottage. In this fair land of liberty, there are many thousands of the inhabitants who have no right to so much land as an inch of ground to set their foot upon, so as to take up their residence upon it, without paying a lawful and reasonable vassalage of rent for it—and yet the whole community is free from slavery. And so, likewise, those who were reduced to a state of servitude, or vassalage, in the land of Israel, were not negotiable like chattels and goods; nor could they be disposed of like cattle and beasts of burden, or ever transferred or disposed of without their own consent; and perhaps not one man in all the land of Israel would buy another man, unless that man was willing to serve him. And when any man had gotten such a servant, as he had entered into a covenant of agreement with, as a bond-servant, if the man liked his master and his service, he could not oblige him to go away; and it sometimes happened, that they refused to go out free when the year of jubilee came.[28] But even that state of servitude which the Canaanites were reduced to, among those who survived the general overthrow of their country, was nothing worse, in many respects, than that of poor labouring people in any free country. Their being made hewers of wood and drawers of water, were laborious employments; but they were paid for it in such a manner as the nature of their service required, and were supplied with abundance of such necessaries of life as they and their families had need of, and they were at liberty, if they chose, to go away, there was no restriction laid on them. They were not hunted after, and a reward offered for their heads, as it is the case in the West-Indies for any that can find a strayed slave; and he who can bring such a head warm reeking with his blood, as a token that he had murdered him—inhuman and shocking to think!—he is paid for it; and, cruel and dreadful as it is, that law is still in force in some of the British colonies (38-42).

Nothing but heavenly wisdom, and heavenly grace, can teach men to understand. The most deplorable of all things is, that the dreadful situation of our universal depraved state, which all mankind lyeth under, is such, that those who are not redeemed in time, must for ever continue to be the subjects of eternal bondage and misery. Blessed be God! he hath appointed and set up a deliverance, and the Saviour of Men is an Almighty Redeemer. When God, the Almighty Redeemer and Saviour of his people, brought his Israel out of Egypt and temporal bondage, it was intended and designed thereby, to set up an emblematical representation of their deliverance from the power and captivity of sin, and from the dominion of that evil and malignant spirit, who had with exquisite subtilty and guile at first seduced the original progenitors of mankind. And when they were brought to the promised land, and had gotten deliverance, and subdued their enemies under them, they were to reign over them; and their laws respecting bond-servants, and other things of that nature, were to denote, that they were to keep under and in subjection the whole body of their evil affections and lusts. This is so declared by the Apostle, that the law is spiritual, and intended for spiritual uses. The general state of slavery which took place in the world, among other enormous crimes of wicked men might have served for an emblem and similitude of our spiritual bondage and slavery to sin; but, unless it had been admitted into the spiritual and divine law, it could not have stood and become an emblem that there was any spiritual restoration and deliverance afforded to us. By that which is evil in captivity and slavery among men, we are thereby so represented to be under a like subjection to sin; but by what is instituted in the law by Moses, in that respect we are thereby represented as Israel to have dominion over sin, and to rule over and keep in subjection all our spiritual enemies. And, therefore, any thing which had a seeming appearance in favour of slavery, so far as it was admitted into the law, was to shew that it was not natural and innocent, like that of different colours among men, but as necessary to be made an emblem of what was intended by it, and, consequently, as it stands enjoined among other typical representations, was to shew that every thing of any evil appearance of it was to be removed, and to end with the other typical and ceremonial injunctions, when the time of that dispensation was over. This must appear evident to all Christian believers; and since therefore all these things are fulfilled in the establishment of Christianity, there is now nothing remaining in the law for a rule of practice to men, but the ever abiding obligations, and ever binding injunctions of moral rectitude, justice, equity and righteousness. All the other things in the Divine law, are for spiritual uses and similitudes, for giving instruction to the wise, and understanding to the upright in heart, that the man of God may be perfect, thoroughly furnished unto all good works (49-50).

None but men of the most brutish and depraved nature, led on by the invidious influence of infernal wickedness, could have made their settlements in the different parts of the world discovered by them, and have treated the various Indian nations, in the manner that the barbarous inhuman Europeans have done; and their establishing and carrying on that most dishonest, unjust and diabolical traffic of buying and selling, and of enslaving men, is such a monstrous, audacious and unparalleled wickedness, that the very idea of it is shocking, and the whole nature of it is horrible and infernal. It may be said with confidence as a certain general fact, that all their foreign settlements and colonies were founded on murders and devastations, and that they have continued their depredations in cruel slavery and oppression to this day: for where such predominant wickedness as the African slave-trade, and the West Indian slavery, is admitted, tolerated and supported by them, and carried on in their colonies, the nations and people who are the supporters and encouragers thereof must be not only guilty themselves of that shameful and abandoned evil and wickedness, so very disgraceful to human nature, but even partakers in those crimes of the most vile combinations of various pirates, kid-nappers, robbers and thieves, the ruffians and stealers of men, that ever made their appearance in the world[29] (77-78).

The history of those dreadfully perfidious methods of forming settlements, and acquiring riches and territory, would make humanity tremble, and even recoil, at the enjoyment of such acquisitions and become reverted into rage and indignation at such horrible injustice and barbarous cruelty, "It is said by the Peruvians, that their Incas, or Monarchs, had uniformly extended their power with attention to the good of their subjects, that they might diffuse the blessings of civilization, and the knowledge of the arts which they possessed, among the people that embraced their protection; and during a succession of twelve monarchs, not one had deviated from this beneficent character."[30] Their sensibility of such nobleness of character would give them the most poignant dislike to their new terrible invaders that had desolated and laid waste their country. The character of their monarchs would seem to vie with as great virtues as any King in Europe can boast of. Had the Peruvians been visited by men of honesty, knowledge, and enlightened understanding, to teach them, by patient instruction and the blessing of God, they might have been induced to embrace the doctrines and faith of Christianity, and to abandon their errors of superstition and idolatry. Had Christians, that deserve the name thereof, been sent among them, the many useful things that they would have taught them, together with their own pious example, would have captivated their hearts; and the knowledge of the truth would have made it a very desirous thing for the Americans to have those who taught them to settle among them. Had that been the case the Americans, in various parts, would have been as eager to have the Europeans come there as they would have been to go, so that the Europeans might have found settlements enough, in a friendly alliance with the inhabitants, without destroying and enslaving them. And had that been the case it might be supposed, that Europe and America, long before now, would both, with a growing luxuriancy, have been flourishing with affluence and peace, and their long extended and fruitful branches, loaden with benefits to each other, reaching over the ocean, might have been more extensive, and greater advantages been expected, for the good of both than what has yet appeared. But, alas! at that time there [were] no Christians to send, (and very few now), these were obliged to hide themselves in the obscure places of the earth; that was, according to Sir Isaac Newton,[31] to mix in obscurity among the meanest of the people, having no power and authority; and it seems at that time there was no power among Christians on earth to have sent such as would have been useful to the Americans; and if there had they would have sent after the depredators, and rescued the innocent.

But as I said before, it is surely to the great shame and scandal of Christianity among all the Heathen nations, that those robbers, plunderers, destroyers and enslavers of men should call themselves Christians, and exercise their power under any Christian government and authority. I would have my African countrymen to know and understand, that the destroyers and enslavers of men can be no Christians; for Christianity is the system of benignity and love, and all its votaries are devoted to honesty, justice, humanity, meekness, peace and good-will to all men. But whatever title or claim some may assume to call themselves by it, without possessing any of its virtues, can only manifest them to be the more abominable liars, and the greatest enemies unto it, and as belonging to the synagogue of Satan, and not the adherers to Christ. For the enslavers and oppressors of men, among those that have obtained the name of Christians, they are still acting as its greatest enemies, and contrary to all its genuine principles; they should therefore be called by its opposite, the Antichrist. Such are fitly belonging to that most dissolute sorceress of all religion in the world: "With whom the kings of the earth have lived deliciously; and the inhabitants of the earth have been made drunk with the wine of her abominations; and the merchants of the earth are waxed rich through the abundance of her delicacies, by their traffic in various things, and in slaves and souls of men!"[32] It was not enough for the malignant destroyer of the world to set up his hydra-headed kingdom of evil and wickedness among the kingdom of men; but also to cause an image to be made unto him, by something imported in the only true religion that ever was given to men; and that image of iniquity is described as arising up out of the earth, having two horns like a lamb, which, by its votaries and adherents, has been long established and supported. One of its umbrageous horns of apostacy and delusion is founded, in a more particular respect, on a grand perversion of the Old Testament dispensations, which has extended itself over all the Mahometan nations in the East;[33] and the other horn of apostacy, bearing an allusion and professional respect to that of the new, has extended itself over all the Christian nations in the West. That grand umbrageous shadow and image of evil and wickedness, has spread its malignant influence over all the nations of the earth, and has, by its power of delusion, given countenance and support to all the power of evil and wickedness done among men; and all the adherents and supporters of that delusion, and all the carriers on of wickedness, are fitly called Antichrist. But all the nations have drunk of the wine of that iniquity, and become drunk with the wine of the wrath of her fornication, whose name, by every mark and feature, is the Antichrist; and every dealer in slaves, and those that hold them in slavery, whatever else they may call themselves, or whatever else they may profess. And likewise, those nations whose governments support that evil and wicked traffic of slavery, however remote the situation where it is carried on may be, are, in that respect, as much Antichristian as any thing in the world can be. No man will ever rob another unless he be a villain: nor will any nation or people ever enslave and oppress others, unless themselves be base and wicked men, and who act and do contrary and against every duty in Christianity.

The learned and ingenious author of Britannia Libera, as chiefly alluding to Great-Britain alone, gives some account of that great evil and wickedness carried on by the Christian nations, respecting the direful effects of the great devastations committed in foreign parts, whereby it would appear that the ancient and native inhabitants have been drenched in blood and oppression by their merciless visitors (which have formed colonies and settlements among them) the avaricious depredators, plunderers and destroyers of nations. As some estimate of it, "to destroy eleven million, and distress many more in America, to starve and oppress twelve million in Asia, and the great number destroyed, is not the way to promote the dignity, strength and safety of empire, but to draw down the Divine vengeance on the offenders, for depriving so many of their fellow-creatures of life, or the common blessings of the earth: whereas by observing the humane principles of preservation with felicitation, the proper principles of all rulers, their empire might have received all reasonable benefit, with the encrease of future glory."[34] But should it be asked, what advantages Great-Britain has gained by all its extensive territories abroad, the devastations committed, and the abominable slavery and oppression carried on in its colonies? It may be answered according to the old proverb,

It seldom is the grand-child's lot,
To share of wealth unjustly got.

This seems to be verified too much in their present situation: for however wide they have extended their territories abroad, they have sunk into a world of debt at home, which must ever remain an impending burden upon the inhabitants. And it is not likely, by any plan as yet adopted, to be ever paid, or any part of it, without a long continued heavy annual load of taxes. Perhaps, great as it is some other plan, more equitable for the good of the whole community, if it was wanted to be done, and without any additional taxes, might be so made use of to pay it all off in twenty or thirty years time, and in such manner as whatever emergencies might happen, as never to need to borrow any money at interest. The national debt casts a sluggish deadness over the whole realm, greatly stops ingenuity and improvements, promotes idleness and wickedness, clogs all the wheels of commerce, and drains the money out of the nation. If a foreigner buys stock, in the course of years that the interest amounts to the principal, he gets it all back; and in an equitable time the same sum ever after, and in course must take that money to foreign parts. And those who hold stock at home, are a kind of idle drones, as a burden to the rest of the community: whereas if there were no funds, those who have money would be obliged to occupy it in some improvements themselves, or lend it to other manufacturers or merchants, and by that means useful employments, ingenuity and commerce would flourish. But all stock-jobbing, lotteries, and useless business, has a tendency to slavery and oppression; for as the greater any idle part of the community is, there must be the greater labour and hardships resting upon the industrious part who support the rest; as all men are allotted in some degree to eat their bread with the sweat of their brow; *but it is evil with any people when the rich grind the face of the poor.*[35] Lotteries must be nearly as bad a way of getting money for the good of a nation, as it is for an individual when he is poor, and obliged to pawn his goods to increase his poverty, already poor. On the reverse, if a nation was to keep a bank to lend money to merchants and others, that nation might flourish, and its support to those in need might be attended with advantage to the whole; but that nation which is obliged to borrow money from others, must be in a poor and wretched situation, and the inhabitants, who have to bear the load of its taxes, must be greatly burdened, and perhaps many of those employed in its service (as soldiers and others) poorly paid. It was otherwise with *the people of Israel of old*; it was the promise and blessing of God to them, *That they should lend unto many nations, but should not borrow.*[36]

But when a nation or people do wickedly, and commit cruelties and devastations upon others, and enslave them, it cannot be expected that they should be attended with the blessings of God, neither to eschew evil. They often become infatuated to do evil unawares; and those employed under their service sometimes lead them into debt, error and wickedness, in order to enrich themselves by their plunder, in committing the most barbarous cruelties, under pretences of war, wherein they were the first aggressors, and which is generally the case in all unnatural and destructive disputes of war. In this business money is wanted, the national debt becomes increased, and new loans and other sums must be added to the funds. The plunderers abroad send home their cash as fast as they can, and by one means and another the sums wanted to borrow, are soon made up. At last when the wars subside, or other business calls them home, laden with the spoils of the East or elsewhere, they have then the grand part of their business to negotiate, in buying up bank stock, and lodging their plunder and ill-got wealth in the British or other funds. Thus the nation is loaded with more debt, and with an annual addition of more interest to pay, to the further advantage of those who often occasioned it by their villainy; who, if they had their deserts, like the Popish inquisitors, are almost the only people in the world who deserve to be hung on the rack.

But so it happens in general, that men of activity and affluence, by whatever way they are possessed of riches, or have acquired a greatness of such property, they are always preferred to take the lead in matters of government, so that the greatest depredators, warriors, contracting companies of merchants, and rich slaveholders, always endeavour to push themselves on to get power and interest in their favour; that whatever crimes any of them commit they are seldom brought to a just punishment. Unless that something of this kind had been the case, 'tis impossible to conceive how such an enormous evil as the slave-trade could have been established and carried on under any Christian government: and from hence that motly system of government, which hath so sprung up and established itself, may be accounted for, and as being an evident and universal depravity of one of the finest constitutions in the world; and it may be feared if these unconstitutional laws, reaching from Great-Britain to her colonies, be long continued in and supported, to the carrying on that horrible and wicked traffic of slavery, must at last mark out the whole of the British constitution with ruin and destruction; and that the most generous and tenacious people in the world for liberty, may also at last be reduced to slaves. And an Ethiopian may venture to assert, that so long as slavery is continued in any part of the British dominions, that more than one-half of the legislature are the virtual supporters and encouragers of a traffic which ought to be abolished, as it cannot be carried on but by some of the most abandoned and profligate men upon earth.

However, the partizans of such a class of men are generally too many and numerous, whose viciated principles from time to time have led the whole nation into debt, error and disgrace and by their magnetic influence there is a general support given to despotism, oppression and cruelty. For many have acquired great riches by some insidious traffic or illegal gain; and as these become often leading men in governments, vast multitudes by sea and land pursue the same course, and support the same measures; like adventurers in the lottery, each grasping for the highest prize; or as much enamoured with any infamous way of getting riches, as the Spaniards were with the Peruvian vessels of gold. And when ambitious and wicked men are bent upon avarice and covetousness, it leads them on to commit terrible cruelties, and their hearts become hardened in wickedness; so that even their enormous crimes sink in their own estimation, and soften into trivial matters. The housebreakers and highwaymen, petty depredators, think nothing of any mischief or cruelty that they can do, so as they can gain their end and come off safe; but their villainy and crimes appear to other men as they ought to do, and if they can be detected, and taken hold of, they will meet with such punishment as they justly deserve for their crimes. But it is otherwise with the Colonians,[37] the great depredators, pirates, kidnappers, robbers, oppressors and enslavers of men. The laws as reaching from Great-Britain to the West-Indies, do not detect them, but protect the opulent slave-holders; though their opulence and protection by any law, or any government whatsoever, cannot make them less criminal than violators of the common rights and liberties of men. They do not take away a man's property, like other robbers; but they take a man himself, and subject him to their service and bondage, which is a greater robbery, and a greater crime, than taking away any property from men whatsoever. And, therefore, with respect to them, there is very much wanted for regulating the natural rights of mankind, and very much wrong in the present forms of government, as well as much abuse of that which is right.

The Spaniards began their settlements in the West Indies and America, by depredations of rapine, injustice, treachery and murder; and they have continued in the barbarous practice of devastation, cruelty, and oppression ever since: and their principles and maxims in planting colonies have been adopted, in some measure, by every other nation in Europe. This guiltful method of colonization must undoubtedly and imperceptibly have hardened men's hearts, and led them on from one degree of barbarity and cruelty to another: for when they had destroyed, wasted and desolated the native inhabitants, and when many of their own people, enriched with plunder, had retired, or returned home to enjoy their ill-gotten wealth, other resources for men to labour and cultivate the ground, and such other laborious employments were wanted. Vast territories and large possessions, without getting inhabitants to labour for them, were of no use. A general part of what remained of the wretched fugitives, who had the best native right to those possessions, were obliged to make their escape to places more remote, and such as could not, were obliged to submit to the hard labour and bondage of their invaders; but as they had not been used to such harsh treatment and laborious employment as they were then subjected to, they were soon wasted away and became few. Their proud invaders found the advantage of having their labour done for nothing, and it became their general practice to pick up the unfortunate strangers that fell in their way, when they thought they could make use of them in their service. That base traffic of kid-napping and stealing men was begun by the Portuguese on the coast of Africa, and as they found the benefit of it for their own wicked purposes, they soon went on to commit greater depredations. The Spaniards followed their infamous example, and the African slave-trade was thought most advantageous for them, to enable themselves to live in ease and affluence by the cruel subjection and slavery of others. The French and English, and some other nations in Europe, as they founded settlements and colonies in the West Indies, or in America, went on in the same manner, and joined hand in hand with the Portuguese and Spaniards, to rob and pillage Africa, as well as to waste and desolate the inhabitants of the western continent. But the European depredators and pirates have not only robbed and pillaged the people of Africa themselves; but, by their instigation, they have infested the inhabitants with some of the vilest combinations of fraudulent and treacherous villains, even among their own people; and have set up their forts and factories as a reservoir of public and abandoned thieves, and as a den of desperadoes, where they may ensnare, entrap and catch men. So that Africa has been robbed of its inhabitants; its free-born sons and daughters have been stole, and kid-napped, and violently taken away, and carried into captivity and cruel bondage. And it may be said, in respect to that diabolical traffic which is still carried on by the European depredators, that Africa has suffered as much and more than any other quarter of the globe. O merciful God! when will the wickedness of man have an end?

The Royal African Company (as it is called, ought rather to be reversed as unworthy of the name) was incorporated 14th Charles II, and impowered to trade from Salle in South Barbary to the Cape of Good Hope, and to erect forts and factories on the western coast of Africa for that purpose. But this trade was laid open by an act of parliament, Anno 1697,[38] and every private merchant permitted to trade thither, upon paying the sum of ten pounds towards maintaining the forts and garrisons. This Company, for securing their commerce, erected several factories on the coast; the most remarkable are these, viz. on the North part of Guinea, James Fort, upon an island in the River Gambia, Sierra Leona, and Sherbro; and on the South part of Guinea, viz. on the Gold Coast, Dick's Cove, Succunda, Commenda, Cape Coast Castle, Fort Royal, Queen Anne's Point, Charles Fort, Annamabo, Winebah, Shidoe, Acra, &c. In all these places it is their grand business to traffic in the human species; and dreadful and shocking as it is to think, it has even been established by royal authority, and is still supported and carried on under a Christian government; and this must evidently appear thereby, that the learned, the civilized, and even the enlightened nations are become as truly barbarous and brutish as the unlearned.

To give any just conception of the barbarous traffic carried on at those factories, it would be out of my power to describe the miserable situation of the poor exiled Africans, which by the craft of wicked men daily become their prey, though I have seen enough of their misery as well as read; no description can give an adequate idea of the horror of their feelings, and the dreadful calamities they undergo. The treacherous, perfidious and cruel methods made use of in procuring them, are horrible and shocking. Bringing them to the ships and factories, and subjecting them to brutal examinations stripped naked and markings, is barbarous and base. Stowing them in the holds of the ships like goods of burden, with closeness and stench, is deplorable; and, what makes addition to this deplorable situation, they are often treated in the most barbarous and inhuman manner by the unfeeling monsters of Captains. And when they arrive at the destined port in the colonies, they are again stripped naked for the brutal examination of their purchasers to view them, which, to many, must add shame and grief to their other woe, as may be evidently seen with sorrow, melancholy and despair marked upon their countenances. Here again another scene of grief and lamentation arises;—friends and near relations must be parted never to meet again, nor knowing to whence they go. Here daughters are clinging to their mothers, and mothers to their daughters, bedewing each others naked breasts with tears; here fathers, mothers, and children, locked in each others arms, are begging never to be separated; here the husband will be pleading for his wife, and the wife praying for her children, and entreating, enough to melt the most obdurate heart, not to be torn from them, and taken away from her husband; and some will be still weeping for their native shore, and their dear relations and friends, and other endearing connections which they have left behind, and have been barbarously tore away from, and all are bemoaning themselves with grief and lamentation at the prospect of their wretched fate. And when sold and delivered up to their inhuman purchasers, a more heart-piercing scene cannot well take place. The last embrace of the beloved husband and wife may be seen, taking their dear offspring in their arms, and with the most parental fondness, bathing their cheeks with a final parting endearment. But on this occasion they are not permitted to continue long, they are soon torn away by their unfeeling masters, entirely destitute of a hope of ever seeing each other again and no consolation is afforded to them in this sorrowful and truly pitiable situation. Should any of them still linger, and cling together a little longer, and not part as readily as their owners would have them, the flogger is called on, and they are soon drove away with the bloody commiseration of the cutting fangs of the whip lashing their naked bodies. This last exercise of the bloody whip, with many other cruel punishments, generally becomes an appendage of their miserable fate, until their wretched lives be wore out with hunger, nakedness, hard labour, dejection and despair. Alas! alas! poor unhappy mortal! to experience such treatment from men that take upon themselves the sacred name of Christians!

In such a vast extended, hideous and predominant slavery, as the Europeans carry on in their Colonies, some indeed may fall into better hands, and meet with some commiseration and better treatment than others, and a few may become free, and get themselves liberated from that cruel and galling yoke of bondage; but what are these to the whole, even hundreds of thousands, held and perpetrated in all the prevalent and intolerable calamities of that state of bondage and exile. The emancipation of a few, while ever that evil and predominant business of slavery is continued, cannot make that horrible traffic one bit the less criminal. For, according to the methods of procuring slaves in Africa, there must be great robberies and murders committed before any emancipation can take place, and before any lenitive favours can be shewn to any of them, even by the generous and humane. This must evidence that the whole of that base traffic is an enormous evil and wicked thing, which cries aloud for redress, and that an immediate end and stop should be put to it (82-97).

In this advanced aera, when the kings of Europe are become more conspicuous for their manly virtues, than any before them have been, it is to be hoped that they will not any longer suffer themselves to be imposed upon, and be beguiled, and brought into guilt and shame, by any instigations of the cunning craftiness and evil policy of the avaricious, and the vile profligate enslavers of men. And as their wisdom and understanding is great, and exalted as their high dignity, it is also to be hoped that they will exert themselves, in the cause of righteousness and justice, and be like the wisest and the greatest monarchs of old, to hearken to the counsel of the wise men that know the times, and to the righteous laws of God, and to deliver the oppressed, and to put an end to the iniquitous commerce and slavery of men. And as we hear tell of the kings of Europe having almost abolished, the infernal invention of the bloody tribunal of the inquisition, and the Emperor and others making some grand reformations for the happiness and good of their subjects;[39] it is to be hoped also that these exalted and liberal principles will lead them on to greater improvements in civilization and felicitation, and next to abolish that other diabolical invention of the bloody and cruel African slave-trade, and the West-Indian slavery.

But whereas the people of Great-Britain having now acquired a greater share in that iniquitous commerce than all the rest together, they are the first that ought to set an example, lest they have to repent for their wickedness when it becomes too late; lest some impending calamity should speedily burst forth against them, and lest a just retribution for their enormous crimes, and a continuance in committing similar deeds of barbarity and injustice should involve them in ruin. For we may be assured that God will certainly avenge himself of such heinous transgressors of his law, and of all those planters and merchants, and of all others, who are the authors of the Africans graves, severities, and cruel punishments, and no plea of any absolute necessity can possibly excuse them. And as the inhabitants of Great-Britain, and the inhabitants of the colonies, seem almost equally guilty of the oppression, there is great reason for both to dread the severe vengeance of Almighty God upon them, and upon all such notorious workers of wickedness; for it is evident that the legislature of Great-Britain patronises and encourages them, and shares in the infamous profits of the slavery of the Africans. It is therefore necessary that the inhabitants of the British nation should seriously consider these things for their own good and safety, as well as for our benefit and deliverance, and that they may be sensible of their own error and danger, lest they provoke the vengeance of the Almighty against them. For what wickedness was there ever risen up so monstrous, and more likely to bring a heavy rod of destruction upon a nation, than the deeds committed by the West-Indian slavery, and the African slave trade. And even in that part of it carried on by the Liverpool and Bristol merchants, the many shocking and inhuman instances of their barbarity and cruelty are such that every one that heareth thereof has reason to tremble and cry out, *Should not the land tremble for this, and every one mourn that dwelleth therein?*[40]

The vast carnage and murders committed by the British instigators of slavery, is attended with a very shocking, peculiar, and almost unheard of conception, according to the notion of the perpetrators of it; they either consider them as their own property, that they may do with as they please, in life or death; or that the taking away the life of a black man is of no more account than taking away the life of a beast. A very melancholy instance of this happened about the year 1780, as recorded in the courts of law; a master of a vessel bound to the Western Colonies, selected 132 of the most sickly of the black slaves, and ordered them to be thrown overboard into the sea, in order to recover their value from the insurers, as he had perceived that he was too late to get a good market for them in the West-Indies. On the trial, by the counsel for the owners of the vessel against the underwriters, their argument was that the slaves were to be considered the same as horses; and their plea for throwing them into the sea was nothing better than that it might be more necessary to throw them overboard to lighten their vessel than goods of greater value, or something to that effect. These poor creatures, it seems, were tied two and two together when they were thrown into the sea, lest some of them might swim a little for the last gasp of air, and, with the animation of their approaching exit, breath[e] their souls away to the gracious Father of spirits. Some of the last parcel, when they saw the fate of their companions, made their escape from tying by jumping overboard, and one was saved by means of a rope from some in the ship. The owners of the vessel, I suppose, (inhuman connivers of robbery, slavery, murder and fraud) were rather a little defeated in this, by bringing their villainy to light in a court of law; but the inhuman monster of a captain was kept out of the way of justice from getting hold of him.[41] Though such perpetrators of murder and fraud should have been sought after from the British Dan in the East-Indies, to her Beershebah in the West[42] (109-112).

And as we look for our help and sure deliverance to come from God Most High, should it not come in an apparent way from Great-Britain, whom we consider as the Queen of nations, let her not think to escape more than others, if she continues to carry on oppression and injustice, and such pre-eminent wickedness against us: for we are only seeking that justice may be done to us, and what every righteous nation ought to do; and if it be not done, it will be adding iniquity to iniquity against themselves. But let us not suppose that the inhabitants of the British nation will adhere to the ways of the profligate: *For such is the way of an adulterous woman; she eateth, and wipeth her mouth; and saith, I have done no wickedness.* But rather let us suppose, *That whereas iniquity hath abounded, may righteousness much more abound.*[43] For the wickedness that you have done is great, and wherever your traffic and colonies have been extended it is shameful; and the great injustice and cruelty done to the poor Africans crieth to heaven against you; and therefore that it may be forgiven unto you, it cries aloud for universal reformation and national repentance. But let it not suffice that a gracious call from the throne is inviting you, *To a religious observance of God's holy laws, as fearing, lest God's wrath and indignation, should be provoked against you*; but in your zeal for God's holy law, because of the shameful transgression thereof, every man [and] every woman hath reason to mourn apart, and every one that dwelleth in the land ought to mourn and sigh for all the abominations done therein, and for the great wickedness carried on thereby.

And now that blessings may come instead of a curse, and that many beneficent purposes of good might speedily arise and flow from it, and be more readily promoted; I would hereby presume to offer the following considerations, as some outlines of a general reformation which ought to be established and carried on. And first, I would propose, that there ought to be days of mourning and fasting appointed, to make enquiry into that great and preeminent evil for many years past carried on against the Heathen nations, and the horrible iniquity of making merchandize of us, and cruelly enslaving the poor Africans; and that you might seek grace and repentance, and find mercy and forgiveness before God Omnipotent; and that he may give you wisdom and understanding to devise what ought to be done.

Secondly, I would propose that a total abolition of slavery should be made and proclaimed; and that an universal emancipation of slaves should begin from the date thereof, and be carried on in the following manner: That a proclamation should be caused to be made, setting forth the anti-Christian unlawfulness of the slavery and commerce of the human species; and that it should be sent to all the courts and nations in Europe, to require their advice and assistance, and as they may find it unlawful to carry it on, let them whosoever will join to prohibit it. And if such a proclamation be found advisable to the British legislature, let them publish it, and cause it to be published, throughout all the British empire, to hinder and prohibit all men under their government to traffic either in buying or selling men; and, to prevent it, a penalty might be made against it of one thousand pounds, for any man either to buy or sell another man. And that it should require all slave-holders, upon the immediate information thereof, to mitigate the labour of their slaves to that of a lawful servitude, without tortures or oppression; and that they should not hinder, but cause and procure some suitable means of instruction for them in the knowledge of the Christian religion. And agreeable to the late *royal Proclamation, for the Encouragement of Piety and Virtue, and for the preventing and punishing of Vice, Profaneness and Immorality*;[44] that by no means, under any pretence whatsoever, either for themselves or their masters, the slaves under their subjection should not be suffered to work on the Sabbath days, unless it be such works as necessity and mercy may require. But that those days, as well as some other hours selected for the purpose, should be appropriated for the time of their instruction; and that if any of their owners should not provide such suitable instructors for them, that those slaves should be taken away from them and given to others who would maintain and instruct them for their labour. And that it should be made known to the slaves, that those who had been above seven years in the islands or elsewhere, if they had obtained any competent degree of knowledge of the Christian religion, and the laws of civilization, and had behaved themselves honestly and decently, that they should immediately become free; and that their owners should give them reasonable wages and maintenance for their labour, and not cause them to go away unless they could find some suitable employment elsewhere. And accordingly, from the date of their arrival to seven years, as they arrive at some suitable progress in knowledge, and behaved themselves honestly, that they should be getting free in the course of that time, and at the end of seven years to let every honest man and woman become free; for in the course of that time, they would have sufficiently paid their owners by their labour, both for their first purpose, and for the expences attending their education. By being thus instructed in the course of seven years, they would become tractable and obedient, useful labourers, dutiful servants and good subjects; and Christian men might have the honor and happiness to see many of them vieing with themselves to praise the God of their salvation. And it might be another necessary duty for Christians, in the course of that time, to make enquiry concerning some of their friends and relations in Africa; and if they found any intelligent persons amongst them, to give them as good education as they could, and find out a way of recourse to their friends; that as soon as they had made any progress in useful learning and the knowledge of the Christian religion, they might be sent back to Africa, to be made useful there as soon, and as many of them as could be made fit for instructing others. The rest would become useful residents in the colonies; where there might be employment enough given to all free people, with suitable wages according to their usefulness, in the improvement of land; and the more encouragement that could be given to agriculture, and every other branch of useful industry, would thereby encrease the number of the inhabitants; without which any country, however blessed by nature, must continue poor.

And, thirdly, I would propose, that a fleet of some ships of war should be immediately sent to the coast of Africa, and particularly where the slave trade is carried on, with faithful men to direct that none should be brought from the coast of Africa without their own consent and the approbation of their friends, and to intercept all merchant ships that were bringing them away, until such a scrutiny was made, whatever nation they belonged to. And, I would suppose, if Great-Britain was to do any thing of this kind, that it would meet with the general approbation and assistance of other Christian nations; but whether it did or not, it could be very lawfully done at all the British forts and settlements on the coast of Africa; and particular remonstrances could be given to all the rest, to warn them of the consequences of such an evil and enormous wicked traffic as is now carried on. The Dutch have some crocodile settlers at the Cape,[45] that should be called to a particular account for their murders and inhuman barbarities. But all the present governors of the British forts and factories should be dismissed, and faithful and good men appointed in their room; and those forts and factories, which at present are a den of thieves, might be turned into shepherd's tents, and have good shepherds sent to call the flocks to feed beside them. Then would doors of hospitality in abundance be opened in Africa to supply the weary travellers, and that immense abundance which they are enriched with, might be diffused afar; but the character of the inhabitants on the west coast of Africa, and the rich produce of their country, have been too long misrepresented by avaricious plunderers and merchants who deal in slaves; and if that country was not annually ravished and laid waste, there might be a very considerable and profitable trade carried on with the Africans.[46] And, should the noble Britons, who have often supported their own liberties with their lives and fortunes, extend their philanthropy to abolish the slavery and oppression of the Africans, they might have settlements and many kingdoms united in a friendly alliance with themselves, which might be made greatly to their own advantage, as well as they might have the happiness of being useful to promoting the prosperity and felicity of others, who have been cruelly injured and wrongfully dealt with. Were the Africans to be dealt with in a friendly manner, and kind instruction to be administered unto them, as by degrees they became to love learning, there would be nothing in their power, but what they would wish to render their service in return for the means of improving their understanding; and the present British factories, and other settlements, might be enlarged to a very great extent. And as Great-Britain has been remarkable for ages past, for encouraging arts and sciences, and may now be put in competition with any nation in the known world, if they would take compassion on the inhabitants of the coast of Guinea, and to make use of such means as would be needful to enlighten their minds in the knowledge of Christianity, their virtue, in this respect, would have its own reward. And as the Africans became refined and established in light and knowledge, they would imitate their noble British friends, to improve their lands, and make use of that industry as the nature of their country might require, and to supply those that would trade with them, with such productions as the nature of their climate would produce; and, in every respect, the fair Britons would have the preference with them to a very great extent; and, in another respect, they would become a kind of first ornament to Great-Britain for her tender and compassionate care of such a set of distressed poor ignorant people. And were the noble Britons, and their august Sovereign, to cause protection and encouragement to be given to those Africans, they might expect in a short time, if need required it, to receive from thence great supplies of men in a lawful way, either for industry or defence; and of other things in abundance, from so great a source, where every thing is luxurious and plenty, if not laid waste by barbarity and gross ignorance. Due encouragement being given to so great, so just, and such a noble undertaking, would soon bring more revenue in a righteous way to the British nation, than ten times its share in all the profits that slavery can produce;[47] and such a laudable example would inspire every generous and enterprizing mind to imitate so great and worthy a nation, for establishing religion, justice, and equity to the Africans, and, in doing this, would be held in the highest esteem by all men, and be admired by all the world.

These three preceding considerations may suffice at present to shew, that some plan might be adopted in such a manner as effectually to relieve the grievances and oppression of the Africans, and to bring great honour and blessings to that nation, and to all men whosoever would endeavour to promote so great good to mankind; and it might render more conspicuous advantages to the noble Britons, as the first doers of it, and greater honour than the finding of America was at first to those that made the discovery: Though several difficulties may seem to arise at first, and the good to be sought after may appear to be remote and unknown, as it was to explore the unknown regions of the Western Ocean; should it be sought after, like the intrepid Columbus, if they do not find kingdoms of wealth by the way, they may be certain of finding treasures of happiness and of peace in the end. But should there be any yet alive deserving the infamy and character of all the harsh things which I have ascribed to the insidious carriers on of the slavery and commerce of the human species, they will certainly object to any thing of this kind being proposed, or ever thought of, as doing so great a good to the base Black Negroes whom they make their prey. To such I must say again, that it would be but a just commutation for what cannot be fully restored, in order to make restoration, as far as could be, for the injuries already done to them. And some may say, that if they have wages to pay to the labourers for manufacturing the West-India productions, that they would not be able to sell them at such a price as would suit the European market, unless all the different nations agreed to raise the price of their commodities in proportion. Whatever bad neighbours men may have to deal with, let the upright shew themselves to be honest men, and that difficulty, which some may fear, would be but small, as there can be no reason for men to do wrong because others do so; but as to what is consumed in Great-Britain, they could raise the price in proportion, and it would be better to sip the West-India sweetness by paying a little more money for it (if it should be found needful) than to drink the blood of iniquity at a cheaper rate. I know several ladies in England who refuse to drink sugar in their tea, because of the cruel injuries done to the Black People employed in the culture of it at the West-Indies. But should it cost the West-Indians more money to have their manufactories carried by the labour of freemen than with slaves, it would be attended with greater blessings and advantages to them in the end. What the wages should be for the labour of freemen, is a question not so easily determined; yet I should think, that it always should be something more than merely victuals and cloaths; and if a man works by the day, he should have the three hundredth part of what might be estimated as sufficient to keep him in necessary cloaths and provisions for a year, and, added to that, such wages of reward as their usefulness might require. Something of this kind should be observed in free countries, and then the price of provisions would be kept at such a rate as the industrious poor could live, without being oppressed and screwed down to work for nothing, but only barely to live. And were every civilized nation, where they boast of liberty, so ordered by its government, that some general and useful employment were provided for every industrious man and woman, in such a manner that none should stand still and be idle, and have to say that they could not get employment, so long as there are barren lands at home and abroad sufficient to employ thousands and millions of people more than there are. This, in a great measure, would prevent thieves and robbers, and the labour of many would soon enrich a nation. But those employed by the general community should only have their maintenance either given or estimated in money, and half the wages of others, which would make them seek out for something else whenever they could, and half a loaf would be better than no bread. The men that were employed in this manner, would form an useful militia, and the women would be kept from a state of misery and want, and from following a life of dissolute wickedness. Liberty and freedom, where people may starve for want, can do them but little good. We want many rules of civilization in Africa; but, in many respects, we may boast of some more essential liberties than any of the civilized nations in Europe enjoy; for the poorest amongst us are never in distress for want, unless some general and universal calamity happen to us. But if any nation or society of men were to observe the laws of God, and to keep his commandments, and walk in the way of righteousness, they would not need to fear the heat in sultry hot climates, nor the freezing inclemency of the cold, and the storms and hurricanes would not hurt them at all; they might soon see blessings and plenty in abundance showered down upon their mountains and vallies; and if his beneficence was sought after, who martials out the drops of the dew, and bids the winds to blow, and to carry the clouds on their wings to drop down their moisture and fatness on what spot soever he pleaseth, and who causeth the genial rays of the sun to warm and cherish the productions of the earth in every place according to that temperature which he sees meet; then might the temperate climes of Great-Britain be seen to vie with the rich land of Canaan of old, which is now, because of the wickedness of its inhabitants, in comparison of what it was, as only a barren desart.

Particular thanks is due to every one of that humane society of worthy and respectful gentlemen, whose liberality hath supported many of the Black poor about London.[48] *Those that honor their Maker have mercy on the poor; and many blessings are upon the head of the just; may the fear of the Lord prolong their days, and cause their memory to be blessed, and may their number be encreased to fill their expectation with gladness*; for they have not only commiserated the poor in general, *but even those which are accounted as beasts, and imputed as vile in the sight of others.*[49] The part that the British government has taken, to co-operate with them, has certainly a flattering and laudable appearance of doing some good; and the fitting out ships to supply a company of Black People with clothes and provisions, and to carry them to settle at Sierra Leona, in the West coast of Africa, as a free colony to Great-Britain, in a peaceable alliance with the inhabitants, has every appearance of honour, and the approbation of friends. According to the plan, humanity hath made its appearance in a more honorable way of colonization, than any Christian nation have ever done before, and may be productive of much good, if they continue to encourage and support them. But after all, there is some doubt whether their own flattering expectation in the manner as set forth to them, and the hope of their friends may not be defeated and rendered abortive; and there is some reason to fear, that they never will be settled as intended, in any permanent and peaceable way at Sierra Leona.[50]

This prospect of settling a free colony to Great-Britain in a peaceable alliance with the inhabitants of Africa at Sierra Leona, has neither altogether met with the credulous approbation of the Africans here, nor yet been sought after with any prudent and right plan by the promoters of it. Had a treaty of agreement been first made with the inhabitants of Africa, and the terms and nature of such a settlement fixed upon, and its situation and boundary pointed out; then might the Africans, and others here, have embarked with a good prospect of enjoying happiness and prosperity themselves, and have gone with a hope of being able to render their services, in return, of some advantage to their friends and benefactors of Great-Britain. But as this was not done, and as they were to be hurried away at all events, come of them after what would; and yet, after all, to be delayed in the ships before they were set out from the coast, until many of them have perished with cold, and other disorders, and several of the most intelligent among them are dead, and others that, in all probability, would have been most useful for them were hindered from going, by means of some disagreeable jealousy of those who were appointed as governors, the great prospect of doing good seems all to be blown away.[51] And so it appeared to some of those who are now gone, and at last, hap hazard, were obliged to go; who endeavoured in vain to get away by plunging into the water, that they might, if possible wade ashore, as dreading the prospect of their wretched fate, and as beholding their perilous situation, having every prospect of difficulty and surrounding danger.

What with the death of some of the original promoters and proposers of this charitable undertaking, and the death and deprivation of others that were to share the benefit of it, and by the adverse motives of those employed to be the conductors thereof, we think it will be more than what can be well expected, if we ever hear of any good in proportion to so great, well-designed, laudable and expensive charity. Many more of the Black People still in this country would have, with great gladness, embraced the opportunity, longing to reach their native land; but as the old saying is, A burnt child dreads the fire, some of these unfortunate sons and daughters of Africa have been severally unlawfully dragged away from their native abodes, under various pretences, by the insidious treachery of others, and have been brought into the hands of barbarous robbers and pirates, and, like sheep to the market, have been sold into captivity and slavery, and thereby have been deprived of their natural liberty and property, and every connection that they held dear and valuable, and subjected to the cruel service of the hard-hearted brutes called planters. But some of them, by various services either to the public or to individuals, as more particularly in the course of [the] last war, have gotten their liberty again in this free country. They are thankful for the respite, but afraid of being ensnared again; for the European seafaring people in general, who trade to foreign parts, have such a prejudice against Black People, that they use them more like asses than men, so that a Black Man is scarcely ever safe among them. Much assiduity was made use of to perswade the Black People in general to embrace the opportunity of going with this company of transports; but the wiser sort declined from all thoughts of it, unless they could hear of some better plan taking place for their security and safety. For as it seemed prudent and obvious to many of them taking heed to that sacred enquiry, *Doth a fountain send forth at the same place sweet water and bitter*?[52] They were afraid that their doom would be to drink of the bitter water. For can it be readily conceived that government would establish a free colony for them nearly on the spot, while it supports its forts and garrisons, to ensnare, merchandize, and to carry others into captivity and slavery.

Above fifty years ago, P. Gordon, in his Geography, though he was no advocate against slavery, complains of the barbarities committed against the Heathen nations, and the base usage of the negro slaves subjected to bondage as brutes, and deprived of religion as men. His remark on the religion of the American islands, says: "As for the negroe slaves, their lot has hitherto been, and still is, to serve such Christian masters, who sufficiently declare what zeal they have for their conversion, by unkindly using a serious divine some time ago, for only proposing to endeavour the same."[53] This was above half a century ago, and their unchristian barbarity is still continued. Even in the little time that I was in Grenada, I saw a slave receive twenty-four lashes of a whip for being seen at a church on a Sunday, instead of going to work in the fields; and those whom they put the greatest confidence in, are often served in the same manner. The noble proposals offered for instructing the heathen nations and people in his Geography, has been attended to with great supineness and indifference. The author wishes, that "sincere endeavours might be made to extend the limits of our Saviour's kingdom, with those of our own dominions; and to spread the true religion as far as the British sails have done for traffic." And he adds, "Let our planters duly consider, that to extirpate natives, is rather a supplanting than planting a new colony; and that it is far more honourable to overcome paganism in one, than to destroy a thousand pagans. Each convert is a conquest."[54]

To put an end to the nakedness of slavery and merchandizing of men, and to prevent murder, extirpation and dissolution, is what every righteous nation ought to seek after; and to endeavour to diffuse knowledge and instruction to all the heathen nations wherever they can, is the grand duty of all Christian men. But while the horrible traffic of slavery is admitted and practiced, there can be but little hope of any good proposals meeting with success anywhere; for the abandoned carriers of it on have spread the poison of their iniquity wherever they come, at home and abroad. Were the iniquitous laws in support of it, and the whole of that oppression and injustice abolished, and the righteous laws of Christianity, equity, justice and humanity established in the room thereof, multitudes of nations would flock to the standard of truth, and instead of revolting away, they would count it their greatest happiness to be under the protection and jurisdiction of a righteous government. And in that respect, *in the multitude of the people is the King's honour; but in the want of people, is the destruction of the Prince.*[55]

We would wish to have the grandeur and fame of the British empire to extend far and wide; and the glory and honor of God to be promoted by it, and the interest of Christianity set forth among all the nations wherever its influence and power can extend; but not to be supported by the insidious pirates, depredators, murderers and slave-holders. And as it might diffuse knowledge and instruction to others, that it might receive a tribute of reward from all its territories, forts and garrisons, without being oppressive to any. But contrary to this the wickedness of many of the White People who keep slaves, and contrary to all the laws and duties of Christianity which the Scriptures teach, they have in general endeavoured to keep the Black People in total ignorance as much as they can, which must be a great dishonor to any Christian government, and injurious to the safety and happiness of rulers.

But in order to diffuse any knowledge of Christianity to the unlearned Heathens, those who undertake to do any thing therein ought to be wise and honest men. Their own learning, though the more the better, is not so much required as that they should be men of the same mind and principles of the apostle Paul; men that would hate covetousness, and who would hazard their lives for the cause and gospel of our Lord and Saviour Jesus Christ. "I think it needless to express how commendable such a design would be in itself, and how desirable the promotion thereof should be to all who stile themselves Christians, of what party or profession soever they are."[56] Rational methods may be taken to have the Scriptures translated into many foreign languages; "and a competent number of young students of theology might be educated at home in these foreign languages, to afford a constant supply of able men, who might yearly go abroad, and be sufficiently qualified at their first arrival to undertake the great work for which they were sent."[57] But as a hindrance to this, the many Anti-christian errors which are gone abroad into the world, and all the popish superstition and nonsense, and the various assimilations unto it, with the false philosophy which abounds among Christians, seems to threaten with an universal deluge; but God hath promised to fill the world with a knowledge of himself, and he hath set up his bow, in the rational heavens, as well as in the clouds, as a token that he will stop the proud ways of error and delusion, that hitherto they may come, and no farther. The holy arch of truth is to be seen in the azure paths of the pious and wise, and conspicuously painted in crimson over the martyrs tombs. These, with the golden altars of truth, built up by the reformed churches, and many pious, good and righteous men, are bulwarks that will ever stand against all the sorts of error. Teaching would be exceeding necessary to the pagan nations and ignorant people in every place and situation; but they do not need any unscriptural forms and ceremonies to be taught unto them; they can devise superstitions enough among themselves, and church government too, if ever they need any.

And hence we would agree in this one thing with that erroneous philosopher, who has lately wrote *An Apology for Negro Slavery*, "But if the slave is only to be made acquainted with the form, without the substance; if he is only to be decked out with the external trappings of religion; if he is only to be taught the uncheering principles of gloomy superstition; or, if he is only to be inspired with the intemperate frenzy of enthusiastic fanaticism, it were better that he remained in that dark state, where he could not see good from ill."[58] But these words *intemperate, frenzy, enthusiastic*, and *fanaticism* may be variously applied, and often wrongfully; but, perhaps never better, or more fitly, than to be ascribed as the genuine character of this author's brutish philosophy; and he may subscribe it, and the meaning of these words, with as much affinity to himself, as he bears a relation to a *Hume*, or to his friend *Tobin.*[59] The poor negroes in the West-Indies, have suffered enough by such religion as the philosophers of the North produce; Protestants, as they are called, are the most barbarous slave-holders, and there are none can equal the Scotch floggers and negroe-drivers, and the barbarous Dutch cruelties. Perhaps as the church of Rome begins to sink in its power, its followers may encrease in virtue and humanity; so that many, who are the professed adherents thereof, would even blush and abhor the very mention of the cruelty and bloody deeds that their ancestors have committed; and we find slavery itself more tolerable among them, than it is in the Protestant countries.

But I shall add another observation, which I am sorry to find among Christians, and I think it is a great deficiency among the clergy in general, when covetous and profligate men are admitted among them, who either do not know, or dare not speak the truth, but neglect their duty much, or do it with such supineness, that it becomes good for nothing. Sometimes an old woman selling matches, will preach a better, and a more orthodox sermon, than some of the clergy, who are only decked out (as Mr. Turnbul [sic] calls it) with the external trappings of religion. Much of the great wickedness of others lieth at their door, and these words of the Prophet are applicable to them: *And first, saith the Lord, I will recompence their iniquity, and their sin double; because they have defiled my land, they have filled mine inheritance with the carcases of their detestable and abominable things.*[60] Such are the errors of men. Church, signifies an assembly of people; but a building of wood, brick or stone, where the people meet together, is generally called so; and should the people be frightened away by the many abominable dead carcases which they meet with, they should follow the multitudes to the fields, to the vallies, to the mountains, to the islands, to the rivers, and to the ships, and compel them to come in, that the house of the Lord may be filled. But when we find some of the covetous connivers with slave-holders, in the West-

Indies, so ignorant as to dispute whether a Pagan can be baptized without giving him a Christian name, we cannot expect much from them, or think that they will follow after much good. No name, whether Christian or Pagan, has any thing to do with baptism; if the requisite qualities of knowledge and faith be found in a man, he may be baptized let his name be what it will. And Christianity does not require that we should be deprived of our own personal name, or the name of our ancestors; but it may very fitly add another name unto us, Christian, or one anointed. And it may as well be answered so to that question in the English liturgy, *What is your name?*—A Christian.[61]

> "*A Christian is the highest stile of man!*
> *And is there, who the blessed cross wipes off*
> *As a foul blot, from his dishonor'd brow?*
> *If angels tremble, 'tis at such a sight:*
> *The wretch they quit disponding of their charge,*
> *More struck with grief or wonder who can tell*?"[62]

And let me now hope that you will pardon me in all that I have been thus telling you, O ye inhabitants of Great-Britain! to whom I owe the greatest respect; to your king! to yourselves! and to your government! And tho' many things which I have written may seem harsh, it cannot be otherwise evaded when such horrible iniquity is transacted: and tho' to some what I have said may appear as the rattling leaves of autumn, that may soon be blown away and whirled in a vortex where few can hear and know: I must yet say, although it is not for me to determine the manner, that the voice of our complaint implies a vengeance, because of the great iniquity that you have done, and because of the cruel injustice done unto us Africans; and it ought to sound in your ears as the rolling waves around your circum-ambient shores; and if it is not hearkened unto, it may yet arise with a louder voice, as the rolling thunder, and it may encrease in the force of its volubility, not only to shake the leaves of the most stout in heart, but to rend the mountains before them, and to cleave in pieces the rocks under them, and to go on with fury to smite the stoutest oaks in the forest; and even to make that which is strong, and wherein you think that your strength lieth, to become as stubble, and as the fibres of rotten wood, that will do you no good, and your trust in it will become a snare of infatuation to you!

FINIS. (128-148)[63]

NOTES

1. At the end of Cugoano's table of contents, omitted here, a note reads:

> Since these Thoughts and Sentiments have been read by some, I find a general Approbation has been given, and that the things pointed out thereby might be more effectually taken into consideration, I was requested by some friends to add this information concerning myself:—When I was kidnapped and brought away from Africa, I was then about

13 years of age, in the year of the Christian aera 1770; and being about nine or ten months in the slave-gang at Grenada, and about one year at different places in the West-Indies, with Alexander Campbell, Esq; who brought me to England in the end of the year 1772, I was advised by some good people to get myself baptized, that I might not be carried away and sold again.—I was called *Stewart* by my master, but in order that I might embrace this ordinance, I was called *John Stewart,* and I went several times to Dr. Skinner [presumably the clergyman Thomas Skinner who voted in the 1774 Westminster election and who lived in Mary-le-bone street, a few blocks from St James's], who instructed me, and I was baptized by him, and registered at St. James's Church in the year 1773 [the parish register entry for 20 August 1773 reads: "John Stuart—a Black, aged 16 Years"]. Some of my fellow-servants, who assisted me in this, got themselves turned away for it; I have only put my African name to the title of the book.—When I was brought away from Africa, my father and relations were then chief men in the kingdom of Agimaque and Assinee; but what they may be now, or whether dead or alive, I know not. I wish to go back as soon as I can hear any proper security and safe conveyance can be found; and I wait to hear how it fares with the Black People sent to Sierra Leona. But it is my highest wish and earnest prayer to God, that some encouragement could be given to send able school masters, and intelligent ministers, who would be faithful and able to teach the Christian religion. This would be doing great good to the Africans, and be a kind restitution for the great injuries that they have suffered. But still I fear no good can be done near any of the European settlements, while such a horrible and infernal traffic of slavery is carried on by them. Wherever the foot of man can go, at the forts and garrisons it would seem to be wrote with these words—

O earth! O sea! cover not thou the blood of the poor negro slaves.

2. Isaiah 32:8. I have not attempted to trace every possible allusion in Cugoano's pseudobiblical diction.

3. Job 30:25.

4. Cugoano refers to such recent laws as those in Vermont (1777) and Pennsylvania (1780) banning slavery or legislating the gradual emancipation of slaves. Unfortunately, by the end of 1787, slavery was protected by the *Constitution* of the new United States.

5. Inquisition: the institution within the Roman Catholic Church established in the Middle Ages to identify and prosecute heretics. The Inquisition was still operating in Spain and Portugal in the eighteenth century.

6. Matthew 19:19; 7:12.

7. Chain: the great chain of being, the idea that all created things are arranged in an order of descending complexity, from the fully human to inert matter. Some of the defenders of slavery contended that Africans were placed between the human and the monkey on the chain.

8. As he often does, Cugoano places within quotation marks imagined statements. Conversely, he often fails to identify by punctuation statements directly quoted from other sources.

9. Factory: a European trading post on the coast of Africa.

10. All of the places Cugoano mentions in this sentence were located on the Gold Coast of Guinea, in present-day Ghana.

11. Eat: a common alternative spelling of *ate.*

12. The Lord of Hosts.

13. Stouter ones: stronger ones.

14. Alexander Campbell.

15. [Cugoano's note.] The justly celebrated Dr. [Edward] Young [1683-1765], in recommending this divine book of heavenly wisdom to the giddy and thoughtless world, in his Night Thoughts, has the following elegant lines:

Perhaps thou'dst laugh but at thine own expence,
This counsel strange should I presume to give;
Retire and read thy Bible to be gay;
There truths abound of sov'reign aid to peace.
Ah, do not prize it less because inspired.
Read and revere the sacred page; a page,
Where triumphs immortality; a page,
Which not the whole creation could produce;
Which not the conflagration shall destroy;
In nature's ruin not one letter's lost,
'Tis printed in the mind of gods for ever,
Angels and men assent to what I sing!

[Quoted from Young's *The Complaint; or, Night-Thoughts on Life, Death, and Immortality* (London, 1742-1746). Typically for him, Cugoano misquotes and transposes lines from various parts of the poem: the first five lines, slightly misquoted, are from book 8:769-773; the next four are from book 7:1360-1363; the last three are from book 7:1365, 1364, and 1368.]

16. James Tobin (d. 1817), a West Indian planter from the island of Nevis. His *Cursory Remarks upon the Reverend Mr. Ramsay's Essay on the Treatment and Conversion of African Slaves in the Sugar Colonies. By a Friend to the West India Colonies, and Their Inhabitants* (London, 1785) is an attack on James Ramsay (1733-1789), *An Essay on the Treatment and Conversion of African Slaves in the British Sugar Colonies* (London, 1784). In *An Essay on the Slavery and Commerce of the Human Species, Particularly the African* (London, 1786), Thomas Clarkson (1760-1846) calls Tobin "the Cursory Remarker." Equiano also responded to Tobin: see the selection from his work in this anthology, as well as his review in *The Public Advertiser* (28 January 1788) of Tobin's *Cursory Remarks*, reprinted in *Olaudah Equiano's The Interesting Narrative and other Writings*, ed. Vincent Carretta (New York: Penguin USA, 1995).

17. Demetrius: see Acts 19:23-41.

18. [Cugoano's note.] The worthy and judicious author of "An Essay on the Treatment and Conversion of the African Slaves in the British Sugar Colonies."

[Cugoano quotes Tobin, *Cursory Remarks*, 5.]

19. *Cursory Remarks*, 22. Images of the natural order inverted by the pursuit of Folly—the world turned upside down—are common in popular visual prints and chapbooks during the eighteenth century.

20. Rather than quoting a particular source, Cugoano is apparently paraphrasing an accusation frequently found in writings by defenders of the slave trade.

21. See the selection by James Albert Ukawsaw Gronniosaw in this anthology.

22. See the selection by John Marrant in this anthology.

23. [Cugoano's note.] It may be true, that some of the slaves transported from Africa, may have committed crimes in their own country, that require some slavery as a punishment; but, according to the laws of equity and justice, they ought to become free, as soon as their labour has paid for their purchase in the West-Indies or elsewhere.

24. Gewgaws: trinkets.

25. AEthiopian: African.

26. Again, an apparently imagined quotation. Like most abolitionists, Cugoano embraces the theologically traditional belief in the monogenetic development of the human race from a single source: Adam and Eve. Some proponents of slavery argued that humans developed polygenetically, maintaining that Africans and Europeans descended from separate pairs of original parents.

27. Bond-servant: a person obligated by contract to work without wages, usually for a specified period.

28. Year of Jubilee: every fiftieth year was a year of rest for the Israelites, when slaves were freed, land left untilled, and alienated property returned to the former owners. See Leviticus 25: 8-17.

29. In a long section that follows this excerpt, Cugoano relies, without acknowledgment, on William Robertson (1721-1793), *The History of America* (2d ed., London, 1777), for his account of the Spanish conquest of the New World. Nicolas de Ovando (1460-1511), who became Governor of Hispaniola in 1501 and was the principal political rival of Christopher Columbus (1451-1506), introduced the extensive importation of African slaves to the Americas. The treachery of Hernando Cortés (1485-1547) enabled him to kill Montezuma II (1466-1520) and destroy the Mexican empire. Francisco Pizarro (ca. 1478-1541) barbarously deceived and assassinated Atahualpa (d. 1533), the Inca emperor, eradicating the Inca civilization in modern-day Peru.

In his recounting of the fall of Atahualpa, Cugoano includes an incident of a talking book: "And he [Atahualpa] desired to know where Valverde had learned things so extraordinary. In this book, replied the fanatic Monk, reaching out his breviary. The Inca opened it eagerly, and turning over the leaves, lifted it to his ear: This, says he, is silent; it tells me nothing; and threw it with disdain to the ground." The incident is quoted quite directly from Robertson, 2:175. Robertson paraphrases and elaborates an event reported in Nathaniel Crouch (1632?-1725?), *The English Empire in America* (London, 1685; 7th ed. 1739): "Friar Vincent answered, 'That his Book told it him' (giving him his Bible). Atabaliba looked in it, and said, It told him no such thing (throwing it on the Ground)" (19).

30. Robertson 2:166, with minor changes.

31. I have not been able to find a precise source in the published *Prophecies* of either Isaac Newton (1642-1727) or Thomas Newton (1704-1782).

32. Compare Revelation 18:2-3:

> 2. . . . Babylon the great is fallen, is fallen, and is become the habitation of devils, and the hold of every foul spirit, and a cage of every unclean and hateful bird.
> 3. For all nations have drunk of the wine of the wrath of her fornication, and the kings of the earth have committed fornication with her, and the merchants of the earth are waxed rich through the abundance of her delicacies.

33. Mahometan: to call the Islamic nations "Mahometan" wrongfully implies that they worship the human prophet rather than the God Allah.

34. William Bollan (d. 1776), *Britannia Libera; or, a Defence of the Free State of Man in England, against the Claim of any Man there as a Slave. Inscribed and Submitted to the Jurisconsulti, and the Free People of England* (London, 1772), 40.

35. Compare Isaiah 3:15.

36. Deuteronomy 15:6.

37. Colonians: those living in the British colonies.

38. Laid open: the Royal African Company was unable to protect its granted monopoly of the slave trade along the length of the western coast of Africa, so the trade was officially opened to those who were already illegally engaged in it.

39. The emperor is Joseph II (1741-1790) of Austria: *The Annual Register for 1782* (London, 1783) reported on "26th [June]. Slavery is entirely abolished in Austrian Poland, and joy is seen in every peasant's countenance, for that he can now keep the fruit of his labour, unoppressed by a tyrannical lord" (211). The "slavery" found in Eastern Europe was serfdom, a system of forced labor in which the serfs were bound by birth to the land and thereby to the owner of the land. It was not the chattel slavery found in the Americas, under which the slave was the personal property of the master. In practice, however, the most severe forms of serfdom were very like American plantation slavery. The "others" Cugoano refers to include Frederick II "the Great" (1712-1786) of Prussia, and Catherine II "the Great" (1729-1796) of Russia. Frederick abolished serfdom in East Prussia and newly an-

nexed West Prussia in 1773 and published his *Essay on the Forms of Government and Duties of Sovereigns* in 1777, calling on rulers to keep the best interests of their peasants in mind. Catherine's visionary reform program of 1767, the *Great Instruction*, though never enacted, was published in an English translation in 1768.

40. Amos 8: 8.

41. Cugoano refers to the *Zong* case of 1783, which was brought to Sharp's attention by Olaudah Equiano. See the Equiano selection in this anthology, note 234.

42. Because Dan and Beersheba were, respectively, the most northern and southern cities of the Holy Land, the phrase "from Dan to Beersheba" meant from one end of a political realm to another.

43. Proverbs 30:20.

44. *By the King, a Proclamation, for the Encouragement of Piety and Virtue, and for Preventing and Punishing of Vice* . . . (London, 1 June 1787).

45. Cape of Good Hope, South Africa.

46. Daniel Defoe (1660-1731) and Malachy Postlethwayt (1707-1767) were among the many eighteenth-century economic theorists who anticipated Cugoano's commercial argument against the slave trade, though elsewhere in their writings they supported slavery.

47. [Cugoano's note.] A gentleman of my acquaintance told me that, if ever he hears tell of any thing of this kind taking place, he has a plan in contemplation, which would, in some equitable manner, produce from one million to fifteen millions sterling to the British government annually, as it might be required; of which a due proportion of that revenue would be paid by the Africans; and that it would prevent all smuggling and illicit traffic; in a great measure, prevent running into debt, long imprisonment, and all unlawful bankruptcies; effectually prevent all dishonesty and swindling, and almost put an end to all robbery, fraud and theft.

48. The Committee for the Relief of the Black Poor. See the Equiano selection in this anthology.

49. Adapted from Job 18: 3.

50. See the Equiano selection, Chapter 12.

51. Cugoano no doubt refers to Olaudah Equiano here.

52. James 3:11.

53. Patrick Gordon (fl. 1700), *Geography Anatomized; or, a Compleat Geographical Grammar* . . . . *To Which Is Added, the Present State of the European Plantations in the East and West Indies, with a* . . . *Proposal for the Propagation of the Blessed Gospel in all Pagan Countries* (London, 1693; 20th ed., with revised title, 1754). Cugoano's quotations from Gordon are passages that first appear in the second edition, 1699. Given the facts that Cugoano refers to "above fifty years ago," and that the passages are not in the 1754 edition, he probably quotes from the fourteenth edition, 1735, 400-401.

54. Patrick, *Geography*, 416.

55. Proverbs 14:28.

56. Patrick, *Geography*, 415.

57. Patrick, *Geography*, 414.

58. Gordon Turnbull, *An Apology for Negro Slavery; or, The West-India Planters Vindicated from the Charge of Inhumanity* (London, 1786), 42-43. Turnbull identifies himself in the second edition, 1786. Equiano's review in *The Public Advertiser* (5 February 1788) of Turnbull's *Apology* is reprinted in the Penguin edition of *Olaudah Equiano's The Interesting Narrative and Other Writings.* Turnbull had earlier published *Letters to a Young Planter; or, Observations on the Management of a Sugar-Plantation. To Which Is Added, The Planter's Kalendar. Written on the Island of Grenada, by an Old Planter* (London, 1785).

59. Cugoano refers to the notorious comment on race by David Hume (1711-1776) quoted in part by Edward Long (1735-1813): see the Francis Williams selection in this anthology, note 1.

60. Jeremiah 16:18, a fitting final biblical quotation for a work that is itself something of a jeremiad.

61. The question and answer begin the Anglican "catechism, that is to say, an instruction to be learned of every person, before he be brought to be confirmed by the bishop," found in *The Book of Common Prayer.* The catechumen normally responds to the question with his or her name.

62. Young, *Night Thoughts* 4:788-793.

63. *Thoughts and Sentiments* was reprinted in London in 1787, and a French translation was published in Paris in 1788. The numbers in parentheses following the selections in this anthology refer to the page numbers of the 1787 edition used as my copy text, almost half of which is reproduced here. In 1791 Cugoano published what is essentially an abbreviated version of his 1787 book: *Thoughts and Sentiments on the Evil of Slavery; or, the Nature of Servitude as Admitted by the Law of God, Compared to the Modern Slavery of the Africans in the West-Indies; in an Answer to the Advocates for Slavery and Oppression Addressed to the Sons of Africa, By a Native.* He there gives his full name as Quobna Ottobah Cugoano. In 1789 Cugoano was a subscriber to Equiano's *Narrative.*

Five manuscript letters (1786-1791) from Cugoano (using a variant spelling of his baptismal name, John Stuart) to the Prince of Wales, Edmund Burke, George III, and Granville Sharp survive and are reproduced in Paul Edwards's introduction to his facsimile reprint of the 1787 *Thoughts and Sentiments* (London: Dawsons of Pall Mall, 1969), xix-xxiii. All seek patronage and/or support for the opposition to the slave trade from correspondents who, aside from the King, had either been or would become subscribers to Sancho's (Burke) or Equiano's (the Prince of Wales, Sharp) works. With a letter sent on 28 July 1786, Cugoano, along with a man named Green, had gained Sharp's aid in rescuing a slave, Harry Demane, from being forcibly returned to the West Indies by his master. Cugoano's undated letter to Burke is addressed from the home of his employer, Richard Cosway, the painter and friend of Sancho, who subscribed to the works of Equiano (1789) and Cugoano (1791). For letters Cugoano and Equiano co-signed and published in the press, see Vincent Carretta, ed., *Olaudah Equiano's The Interesting Narrative and Other Writings* (New York: Penguin, 1995), appendix E.

Olaudah Equiano

(ca. 1745-31 March 1797)

~

THE INTERESTING NARRATIVE OF THE LIFE OF OLAUDAH EQUIANO, *OR* GUSTAVUS VASSA, *THE AFRICAN.* WRITTEN BY HIMSELF. NINTH EDITION ENLARGED. *London:* PRINTED FOR, AND SOLD BY THE AUTHOR. 1794.[1]

TO THE READER.[2]

AN invidious falsehood having appeared in the Oracle of the 25th,[3] and the Star of the 27th of April 1792,[4] with a view to hurt my character,[5] and to discredit and prevent the sale of my Narrative, asserting, that I was born in the Danish island of Santa Cruz, in the West Indies,[6] it is necessary that, in this edition, I should take notice thereof, and it is only needful of me to appeal to those numerous and respectable persons of character who knew me when I first arrived in England, and could speak no language but that of Africa.[7]

Under this appeal, I now offer this edition of my Narrative to the candid[8] reader, and to the friends of humanity, hoping it may still be the means, in its measure, of showing the enormous cruelties practiced on my sable brethren, and strengthening the generous emulation now prevailing in this country, to put a speedy end to a traffic both cruel and unjust.

Edinburgh, June 1792.[9]

TO the Lords Spiritual and Temporal, and the Commons of the Parliament of Great Britain.[10]

My Lords and Gentlemen,

PERMIT me with the greatest deference and respect, to lay at your feet the following genuine Narrative; the chief design of which is to excite in your august assemblies a sense of compassion for the miseries which the Slave Trade has entailed on my unfortunate countrymen. By the horrors of that trade I was first torn away from all the tender connexions that were dear to my heart; but these, through the mysterious ways of Providence, I ought to regard as infinitely more than compensated by the introduction I have thence obtained to the knowledge of

Olaudah Equiano;

or

GUSTAVUS VASSA,

the African.

the Christian religion, and of a nation which, by its liberal sentiments, its humanity, the glorious freedom of its government, and its proficiency in arts and sciences, has exalted the dignity of human nature.

I am sensible I ought to entreat your pardon for addressing to you a work so wholly devoid of literary merit; but, as the production of an unlettered African, who is actuated by the hope of becoming an instrument towards the relief of his suffering countrymen. I trust that *such a man*, pleading in *such a cause*, will be acquitted of boldness and presumption.[11]

May the god of Heaven inspire your hearts with peculiar benevolence on that important day when the question of Abolition is to be discussed, when thousands, in consequence of your determination, are to look for Happiness or Misery!

I am,

My LORDS and GENTLEMEN,

Your most obedient,

And devoted humble servant,

OLAUDAH EQUIANO,

OR GUSTAVUS VASSA.

March 1789.[12]

CHAPTER I

I BELIEVE it is difficult for those who publish their own memoirs to escape the imputation of vanity; nor is this the only disadvantage under which they labour; it is also their misfortune, that whatever is uncommon is rarely, if ever, believed; and what is obvious we are apt to turn from with disgust, and to charge the writer with impertinence. People generally think those memoirs only worthy to be read or remembered which abound in great or striking events; those, in short, which in a high degree excite either admiration or pity: all others they consign to contempt and oblivion. It is, therefore, I confess, not a little hazardous, in a private and obscure individual, and a stranger too, thus to solicit the indulgent attention of the public; especially when I own I offer here the history of neither a saint, a hero, nor a tyrant.[13] I believe there are a few events in my life which have not happened to many; it is true the incidents of it are numerous; and, did I consider myself an European, I might say my sufferings were great; but, when I compare my lot with that of most of my countrymen,[14] I regard myself as a *particular favourite of Heaven*, and acknowledge the mercies of Providence in every occurrence of my life.[15] If, then, the following narrative does not appear sufficiently interesting to engage general attention, let my motive be some excuse for its publication. I am not so foolishly vain as to expect from it either immortality or literary reputation. If it affords any satisfaction to my numerous friends, at whose request it has been written, or in the smallest degree promotes the interest of humanity, the ends for which it was undertaken will be fully attained, and every wish of my heart gratified. Let it therefore be remembered that, in wishing to avoid censure, I do not aspire to praise.

That part of Africa, known by the name of Guinea, to which the trade for slaves is carried on, extends along the coast above 3400 miles, from Senegal to Angola, and includes a variety of kingdoms. Of these the most considerable is the kingdom of Benin, both as to extent and wealth, the richness and cultivation of the soil, the power of its king, and the number and warlike disposition of the inhabitants. It is situated nearly under the line[16] and extends along the coast about 170 miles, but runs back into the interior part of Africa to a distance hitherto I believe unexplored by any traveller; and seems only terminated at length by the empire of Abyssinia,[17] near 1500 miles from its beginning. This kingdom is divided into many provinces or districts: in one of the most remote and fertile of which [, called Eboe,][18] I was born, in the year 1745, in a charming fruitful vale, named Essaka.[19] The distance of this province from the capital of Benin and the sea coast must be very considerable; for I had never heard of white men or Europeans, nor of the sea; and our subjection to the king of Benin was little more than nominal; for every transaction of the government, as far as my slender observation extended, was conducted by the chiefs or elders of the place. The manners and government of a people who have little commerce with other countries are generally very simple; and the history of what passes in one family or village may serve as a specimen of the whole nation. My father was one of those elders or chiefs I have spoken of, and was styled Embrenché; a term, as I remember, importing the highest distinction, and signifying in our language a mark of grandeur. This mark is conferred on the person entitled to it, by cutting the skin across at the top of the forehead, and drawing it down to the eye-brows; and, while it is in this situation, applying a warm hand, and rubbing it until it shrinks up into a thick *weal* across the lower part of the forehead. Most of the judges and senators were thus marked; my father had long borne it: I had seen it conferred on one of my brothers, and I was also *destined* to receive it by my parents. Those Embrenché, or chief men, decided disputes and punished crimes; for which purpose they always assembled together. The proceedings were generally short; and in most cases the law of retaliation prevailed. I remember a man was brought before my father, and the other judges, for kidnapping a boy; and, although he was the son of a chief or senator, he was condemned to make recompense by a man or woman slave. Adultery, however, was sometimes punished with slavery or death; a punishment which I believe is inflicted on it throughout most of the nations of Africa:[20] so sacred among them is the honour of the marriage bed, and so jealous are they of the fidelity of their wives. Of this I recollect an instance.—A woman was convicted before the judges of adultery, and delivered over, as the custom was, to her husband to be punished. Accordingly he determined to put her to death: but it being found, just before her execution, that she had an infant at her breast; and no woman being prevailed on to perform the part of a nurse, she was spared on account of the child. The men, however, do not preserve the same constancy to their wives, which they expect from them; for they indulge in a plurality, though seldom in more than two. Their mode of marriage is thus:—both parties are usually betrothed when young by their parents (though I have known the males to betroth themselves). On this occasion a feast is prepared, and the bride and bridegroom stand up in the midst of all their friends, who are assembled for the purpose, while he declares she is thenceforth to be looked upon as his wife, and that no other person is to pay any addresses to her. This is also immediately proclaimed in the vicinity, on which the bride retires from the assembly. Some time after, she is brought home to her husband, and then another feast is made, to which the relations of both parties are invited: her parents then deliver her to the bridegroom, accompanied with a number of blessings, and at the same time they tie round her waist a cotton string of the thickness of a goose-quill, which none but married women are permitted to wear: she is now considered as completely his wife; and at this time the dowry is given to the new married pair, which generally consists of portions of land, slaves, and cattle, household goods, and implements of husbandry. These are offered by the friends of both parties; besides which the parents of the bridegroom present gifts to those of the bride, whose property she is looked upon before marriage; but after it she is esteemed the sole property of her husband. The ceremony being now ended, the festival begins, which is celebrated with bonfires, and loud acclamations of joy, accompanied with music and dancing.

We are almost a nation of dancers, musicians, and poets. Thus every great event, such as a triumphant return from battle, or other cause of public rejoicing, is celebrated in public dances, which are accompanied with songs and music suited to the occasion. The assembly is separated into four divisions, which dance either apart or in succession, and each with a character peculiar to itself. The first division contains the married men, who in their dances frequently exhibit feats of arms, and the representation of a battle. To these succeed the married women, who dance in the second division. The young men occupy the third; and the maidens the fourth. Each represents some interesting scene of real life, such as a great achievement, domestic employment, a pathetic story, or some rural sport; and as the subject is generally founded on some recent event, it is therefore ever new. This gives our dances a spirit and variety which I have scarcely seen elsewhere.[21] We have many musical instruments, particularly drums of different kinds, a piece of music which resembles a guitar,[22] and another much like a stickado.[23] These last are chiefly used by betrothed virgins, who play on them on all grand festivals.

As our manners are simple, our luxuries are few. The dress of both sexes is nearly the same. It generally consists of a long piece of calico, or muslin,[24] wrapped loosely round the body, somewhat in the form of a Highland plaid.[25] This is usually dyed blue, which is our favourite colour. It is extracted from a berry, and is brighter and richer than any I have seen in Europe. Besides this, our women of distinction wear golden ornaments, which they dispose with some profusion on their arms and legs. When our women are not employed with the men in tillage, their usual occupation is spinning and weaving cotton, which they afterwards dye, and make into garments. They also manufacture earthen vessels, of which we have many kinds. Among the rest [are] tobacco pipes, made after the same fashion, and used in the same manner, as those in Turkey.[26]

Our manner of living is entirely plain; for as yet the natives are unacquainted with those refinements in cookery which debauch the taste:[27] bullocks, goats, and poultry supply the greatest part of their food. These constitute likewise the principal wealth of the country, and the chief articles of its commerce. The flesh is usually stewed in a pan. To make it savory, we sometimes use also pepper, and other spices, and we have salt made of wood ashes. Our vegetables are mostly plantains,[28] eadas,[29] yams, beans, and Indian corn.[30] The head of the family usually eats alone; his wives and slaves have also their separate tables. Before we taste food, we always wash our hands: indeed our cleanliness on all occasions is extreme; but on this it is an indispensable ceremony. After washing, libation is made, by pouring out a small portion of the drink on the floor, and tossing a small quantity of the food in a certain place,[31] for the spirits of departed relations, which the natives suppose to preside over their conduct, and guard them from evil. They are totally unacquainted with strong or spiritous liquours; and their principal beverage is palm wine. This is got from a tree of that name, by tapping it at the top, and fastening a large gourd to it; and sometimes one tree will yield three or four gallons in a night. When just drawn it is of a most delicious sweetness; but in a few days it acquires a tartish and more spirituous flavour: though I never saw any one intoxicated by it. The same tree also produces nuts and oil. Our principal luxury is in perfumes; one sort of these is an odoriferous wood of delicious fragrance: the other a kind of earth; a small portion of which thrown into the fire diffuses a most powerful odour.[32] We beat this wood into powder, and mix it with palm-oil; with which both men and women perfume themselves.

In our buildings we study convenience rather than ornament. Each master of a family has a large square piece of ground, surrounded with a moat or fence, or enclosed with a wall made of red earth tempered, which, when dry, is as hard as brick. Within this are his houses to accommodate his family and slaves; which, if numerous, frequently present the appearance of a village. In the middle stands the principal building, appropriated to the sole use of the master, and consisting of two apartments; in one of which he sits in the day with his family, the other is left apart for the reception of his friends. He has besides these a distinct apartment in which he sleeps, together with his male children. On each side are the apartments of his wives, who have also their separate day and night houses. The habitations of the slaves and their families are distributed throughout the rest of the enclosure. These houses never exceed one story in height; they are always built of wood, or stakes driven into the ground, crossed with wattles, and neatly plastered within, and without. The roof is thatched with reeds. Our dayhouses are left open at the sides; but those in which we sleep are always covered, and plastered in the inside, with a composition mixed with cow-dung, to keep off the different insects which annoy us during the night. The walls and floors also of these are generally covered with mats. Our beds consist of a platform, raised three or four feet from the ground, on which are laid skins, and different parts of a spungy tree called plaintain. Our covering is calico or muslin, the same as our dress. The usual seats are a few logs of wood; but we have benches, which are generally perfumed, to accommodate strangers; these compose the greater part of our household furniture. Houses so constructed and furnished require but little skill to erect them. Every man is a sufficient architect for the purpose. The whole neighbourhood afford their unanimous assistance in building them, and, in return, receive and expect no other recompense than a feast.

As we live in a country where nature is prodigal of her favours, our wants are few and easily supplied; of course we have few manufactures.[33] They consist for the most part of calicoes, earthen ware, ornaments, and instruments of war and husbandry. But these make no part of our commerce, the principal articles of which, as I have observed, are provisions. In such a state money is of little use; however we have some small pieces of coin, if I may call them such. They are made something like an anchor; but I do not remember either their value or denomination. We have also markets, at which I have been frequently with my mother. These are sometimes visited by stout,[34] mahogany-coloured men from the south west of us: we call them *Oye-Eboe*, which term signifies red men living at a distance. They generally bring us fire-arms, gun-powder, hats, beads, and dried fish. The last we esteemed a great rarity, as our waters were only brooks and springs. These articles they barter with us for odoriferous woods and earth, and our salt of wood-ashes. They always carry slaves through our land; but the strictest account is exacted of their manner of procuring them before they are suffered to pass. Sometimes indeed we sold slaves to them, but they were only prisoners of war, or such among us as had been convicted of kidnapping, or adultery, and some other crimes which we esteemed heinous. This practice of kidnapping induces me to think, that, notwithstanding all our strictness, their principal business among us was to trepan[35] our people. I remember too they carried great sacks along with them, which, not long after, I had an opportunity of fatally seeing applied to that infamous purpose.

Our land is uncommonly rich and fruitful, and produces all kinds of vegetables in great abundance. We have plenty of Indian corn, and vast quantities of cotton and tobacco. Our pine apples grow without culture; they are about the size of the largest sugar-loaf, and finely flavoured. We have also spices of different kinds, particularly pepper; and a variety of delicious fruits which I have never seen in Europe; together with gums of various kinds, and honey in abundance. All our industry is exerted to improve those blessings of nature. Agriculture is our chief employment; and every one, even the children and women, are engaged in it. Thus we are all habituated to labour from our earliest years. Every one contributes something to the common stock; and as we are unacquainted with idleness, we have no beggars. The benefits of such a mode of living are obvious. The West-India planters prefer the slaves of Benin or Eboe to those of any other part of Guinea, for their hardiness, intelligence, integrity, and zeal.[36] Those benefits are felt by us in the general healthiness of the people, and in their vigour and activity; I might have added too in their comeliness. Deformity is indeed unknown amongst us, I mean that of shape. Numbers of the natives of Eboe now in London might be brought in support of this assertion; for, in regard to complexion, ideas of beauty are wholly relative.[37] I remember while in Africa to have seen three negro children, who were tawny, and another quite white, who were universally regarded by myself and the natives in general, as far as related to their complexions, as deformed. Our women too were, in my eyes at least, uncommonly graceful, alert, and modest to a degree of bashfulness; nor do I remember to have ever heard of an instance of incontinence amongst them before marriage. They are also remarkably cheerful. Indeed cheerfulness and affability are two of the leading characteristics of our nation.

Our tillage is exercised in a large plain or common, some hours walk from our dwellings, and all the neighbours resort thither in a body. They use no beasts of husbandry; and their only instruments are hoes, axes, shovels, and beaks, or pointed iron to dig with. Sometimes we are visited by locusts, which come in large clouds, so as to darken the air, and destroy our harvest. This however happens rarely, but when it does, a famine is produced by it. I remember an instance or two wherein this happened. This common is oftimes the theatre of war; and therefore when our people go out to till their land, they not only go in a body, but generally take their arms with them, for fear of a surprise; and when they apprehend an invasion they guard the avenues to their dwellings, by driving sticks into the ground, which are so sharp at one end as to pierce the foot, and are generally dipt in poison. From what I can recollect of these battles, they appear to have been irruptions of one little state or district on the other, to obtain prisoners or booty. Perhaps they were incited to this by those traders who brought the European goods I mentioned amongst us. Such mode of obtaining slaves in Africa is common; and I believe more are procured this way, and by kidnapping, than any other.[38] When a trader wants slaves, he applies to a chief for them, and tempts him with his wares. It is not extraordinary, if on this occasion he yields to the temptation with as little firmness, and accepts the price of his fellow creature's liberty with as little reluctance, as the enlightened merchant. Accordingly, he falls on his neighbours, and a desperate battle ensues. If he prevails, and takes prisoners, he gratifies his avarice by selling them; but, if his party be vanquished, and he falls into the hands of the enemy, he is put to death: for, as he has been known to foment their quarrels, it is thought dangerous to let him survive, and no ransom can save him, though all other prisoners may be redeemed.[39] We have fire-arms, bows and arrows, broad two-edged swords and javelins; we have shields also, which cover a man from head to foot. All are taught the use of the weapons. Even our women are warriors, and march boldly out to fight along with the men. Our whole district is a kind of militia: on a certain signal given, such as the firing of a gun at night, they all rise in arms and rush upon their enemy. It is perhaps something remarkable, that when our people march to the field, a red flag or banner is borne before them. I was once a witness to a battle in our common. We had been all at work in it one day as usual when our people were suddenly attacked. I climbed a tree at some distance, from which I beheld the fight. There were many women as well as men on both sides; among others my mother was there and armed with a broad sword. After fighting for a considerable time with great fury, and many had been killed, our people obtained the victory, and took their enemy's Chief prisoner. He was carried off in great triumph, and, though he offered a large ransom for his life, he was put to death. A virgin of note among our enemies had been slain in the battle, and her arm was exposed in our market-place, where our trophies were always exhibited. The spoils were divided according to the merit of the warriors. Those prisoners which were not sold or redeemed we kept as slaves: but how different was their condition from that of the slaves in the West-Indies! With us they do no more work than other members of the community, even their master. Their food, cloathing, and lodging were nearly the same as theirs, except that they were not permitted to eat with those who were free born and there was scarce any other difference between them, than a superior degree of importance which the head of a family possesses in our state, and that authority which, as such, he exercises over every part of his household. Some of these slaves have even slaves under them, as their own property, and for their own use.

As to religion, the natives believe that there is one Creator of all things, and that he lives in the sun, and is girded round with a belt, that he may never eat or drink; but, according to some, he smokes a pipe, which is our own favourite luxury. They believe he governs events, especially our deaths or captivity; but, as for the doctrine of eternity, I do not remember to have ever heard of it: some however believe in the transmigration of souls in a certain degree. Those spirits, which are not transmigrated, such as our dear friends or relations, they believe always attend them, and guard them from the bad spirits of their foes. For this reason, they always, before eating, as I have observed, put some small portion of the meat, and pour some of their drink, on the ground for them; and they often make oblations[40] of the blood of beasts or fowls at their graves. I was very fond of my mother, and almost constantly with her. When she went to make these oblations at her mother's tomb, which was a kind of small solitary thatched house, I sometimes attended her. There she made her libations, and spent most of the night in cries and lamentations. I have been often extremely terrified on these occasions. The loneliness of the place, the darkness of the night, and the ceremony of libation, naturally awful and gloomy, were heightened by my mother's lamentations; and these, concurring with the doleful cries of birds, by which these places were frequented, gave an inexpressible terror to the scene.

We compute the year from the day on which the sun crosses the line, and, on its setting that evening, there is a general shout throughout the land; at least I can speak from my own knowledge throughout our vicinity. The people at the same time make a great noise with rattles, not unlike the basket rattles used by children here, though much larger, and hold up their hands to heaven for a blessing. It is then the greatest offerings are made; and those children whom our wise men foretell will be fortunate are then presented to different people. I remember many used to come to see me, and I was carried about to others for that purpose. They have many offerings, particularly at full moons; generally two at harvest, before the fruits are taken out of the ground: and, when any young animals are killed, sometimes they offer up part of them as a sacrifice. These offerings, when made by one of the heads of a family, serve for the whole. I remember we often had them at my father's and my uncle's, and their families have been present. Some of our offerings are eaten with bitter herbs. We had a saying among us to any one of a cross temper, "That if they were to be eaten, they should be eaten with bitter herbs."

We practised circumcision like the Jews, and made offerings and feasts on that occasion in the same manner as they did. Like them also, our children were named from some event, some circumstance, or fancied foreboding at the time of their birth. I was named *Olaudah*, which, in our language, signifies vicissitude, or fortunate also; one favoured, and having a loud voice and well spoken.[41] I remember we never polluted the name of the object of our adoration; on the contrary, it was always mentioned with the greatest reverence; and we were totally unacquainted with swearing, and all those terms of abuse and reproach which find the way so readily and copiously into the languages of more civilized people. The only expressions of that kind I remember were "May you rot, or may you swell, or may a beast take you."

I have before remarked, that the natives of this part of Africa are extremely cleanly. This necessary habit of decency was with us a part of religion, and therefore we had many purifications and washings; indeed almost as many, and used on the same occasions, if my recollection does not fail me, as the Jews. Those that touched the dead at any time were obliged to wash and purify themselves before they could enter a dwelling-house. Every woman too, at certain times,[42] was forbidden to come into a dwelling-house, or touch any person, or any thing we ate. I was so fond of my mother I could not keep from her, or avoid touching her at some of those periods, in consequence of which I was obliged to be kept out with her, in a little house made for that purpose, till offering was made, and then we were purified.

Though we had no places of public worship, we had priests and magicians, or wise men. I do not remember whether they had different offices, or whether they were united in the same persons but they were held in great reverence by the people. They calculated our time, and foretold events, as their name imported, for we called them Ah-affoe-way-cah, which signifies calculators, or yearly men, our year being called Ah-affoe. They wore their beards; and, when they died, they were succeeded by their sons. Most of their implements and things of value were interred along with them. Pipes and tobacco were also put into the grave with the corpse, which was always perfumed and ornamented; and animals were offered in sacrifice to them. None accompanied their funerals but those of the same profession or tribe. These buried them after sunset, and always returned from the grave by a different way from that which they went.

These magicians were also our doctors or physicians. They practised bleeding by cupping, and were very successful in healing wounds and expelling poisons. They had likewise some extraordinary method of discovering jealousy, theft, and poisoning; the success of which no doubt they derived from their unbounded influence over the credulity and superstition of the people. I do not remember what those methods were, except that as to poisoning. I recollect an instance or two, which I hope it will not be deemed impertinent here to insert, as it may serve as a kind of specimen of the rest, and is still used by the negroes in the West Indies. A young woman had been poisoned, but it was not known by whom; the doctors ordered the corpse to be taken up by some persons, and carried to the grave. As soon as the bearers had raised it on their shoulders, they seemed seized with some[43] sudden impulse, and ran to and fro', unable to stop themselves. At last, after having passed through a number of thorns and prickly bushes unhurt, the corpse fell from them close to a house, and defaced it in the fall: and the owner being taken up, he immediately confessed the poisoning.[44]

The natives are extremely cautious about poison. When they buy any eatable the seller kisses it all round before the buyer, to shew him it is not poisoned; and the same is done when any meat or drink is presented, particularly to a stranger. We have serpents of different kinds, some of which are esteemed ominous when they appear in our houses, and these we never molest. I remember two of those ominous snakes, each of which was as thick as the calf of a man's leg, and in colour resembling a dolphin in the water, crept at different times into my mother's night-house, where I always lay with her, and coiled themselves into folds, and each time they crowed like a cock. I was desired by some of our wise men to touch these, that I might be interested in the good omens, which I did, for they were quite harmless, and would tamely suffer themselves to be handled; and then they were put into a large open earthen pan, and set on one side of the high-way. Some of our snakes, however, were poisonous: one of them crossed the road one day when I was standing on it, and passed between my feet, without offering to touch me, to the great surprise of many who saw it; and these incidents were accounted by the wise men, and likewise by my mother and the rest of the people, as remarkable omens in my favour.

Such is the imperfect sketch my memory has furnished me with of the manners and customs of a people among whom I first drew my breath. And here I cannot forbear suggesting what has long struck me very forcibly, namely, the strong analogy which even by this sketch, imperfect as it is, appears to prevail in the manners and customs of my countrymen, and those of the Jews, before they reached the Land of Promise, and particularly the patriarchs, while they were yet in that pastoral state which is described in Genesis—an analogy, which alone would induce me to think that the one people had sprung from the other.[45] Indeed this is the opinion of Dr. Gill, who, in his commentary on Genesis, very ably deduces the pedigree of the Africans from Afer and Afra, the descendants of Abraham by Keturah his wife and concubine, (for both these titles are applied to her).[46] It is also conformable to the sentiments of Dr. John Clarke, formerly Dean of Sarum, in his Truth of the Christian Religion: both these authors concur in ascribing to us this original.[47] The reasonings of these gentlemen are still further confirmed by the Scripture Chronology of the Rev. Arthur Bedford;[48] and if any further corroboration were required, this resemblance in so many respects is a strong evidence in support of the opinion. Like the Israelites in their primitive state, our government was conducted by our chiefs, our judges, our wise men, and elders; and the head of a family with us enjoyed a similar authority over his household with that which is ascribed to Abraham and the other patriarchs. The law of retaliation[49] obtained almost universally with us as with them: and even their religion appeared to have shed upon us a ray of its glory, though broken and spent in its passage, or eclipsed by the cloud with which time, tradition, and ignorance might have enveloped it: for we had our circumcision (a rule I believe peculiar to that people): we had also our sacrifices and burnt-offerings, our washings and purifications, on the same occasions as they had.

As to the difference of colour between the Eboan Africans and the modern Jews, I shall not presume to account for it. It is a subject which has engaged the pens of men of both genius and learning, and is far above my strength. The most able and Reverend Mr. T. Clarkson, however, in his much-admired Essay on the Slavery and Commerce of the Human Species, has ascertained the cause, in a manner that at once solves every objection on that account, and, on my mind at least, has produced the fullest conviction. I shall therefore refer to that performance for the theory,[50] contenting myself with extracting a fact as related by Dr. Mitchel.[51] "The Spaniards, who have inhabited America, under the torrid zone, for any time, are become as dark coloured as our native Indians of Virginia, *of which I myself have been a witness.* There is also another instance[52] of a Portuguese settlement at Mitomba, a river in Sierra Leona, where the inhabitants are bred from a mixture of the first Portuguese discoverers with the natives, and are now become, in their complexion, and in the woolly quality of their hair, *perfect negroes*, retaining however a smattering of the Portuguese language."

These instances, and a great many more which might be adduced, while they shew how the complexions of the same persons vary in different climates, it is hoped may tend also to remove the prejudice that some conceive against the natives of Africa on account of their colour. Surely the minds of the Spaniards did not change with their complexions! Are there not causes enough to which the apparent inferiority of an African may be ascribed, without limiting the goodness of God, and supposing he forbore to stamp understanding on certainly his own image, because "carved in ebony?" Might it not naturally be ascribed to their situation? When they come among Europeans, they are ignorant of their language, religion, manners, and customs. Are any pains taken to teach them these? Are they treated as men? Does not slavery itself depress the mind, and extinguish all its fire, and every noble sentiment? But, above all, what advantages do not a refined people possess over those who are rude and uncultivated? Let the polished and haughty European recollect that *his* ancestors were once, like the Africans, uncivilized, and even barbarous. Did Nature make *them* inferior to their sons? and should *they too* have been made slaves? Every rational mind answers, No. Let such reflections as these melt the pride of their superiority into sympathy for the wants and miseries of their sable brethren, and compel them to acknowledge, that understanding is not confined to feature or colour. If, when they look round the world, they feel exultation, let it be tempered with benevolence to others, and gratitude to God, "who hath made of one blood all nations of men for to dwell on all the face of the earth;[53] and whose wisdom is not our wisdom, neither are our ways his ways."

CHAPTER II

I HOPE the reader will not think I have trespassed on his patience in introducing myself to him with some account of the manners and customs of my country. They had been implanted in me with great care, and made an impression on my mind, which time could not erase, and which all the adversity and variety of fortune I have since experienced served only to rivet and record: for, whether the love of one's country be real or imaginary, or a lesson of reason, or an instinct of nature, I still look back with pleasure on the first scenes of my life, though that pleasure has been for the most part mingled with sorrow.

I have already acquainted the reader with the time and place of my birth. My father, besides many slaves, had a numerous family, of which seven lived to grow up, including myself and a sister, who was the only daughter. As I was the youngest of the sons, I became, of course, the greatest favourite with my mother, and was always with her; and she used to take particular pains to form my mind. I was trained up from my earliest years in the arts of agriculture and war:[54] my daily exercise was shooting and throwing javelins; and my mother adorned me with emblems, after the manner of our greatest warriors. In this way I grew up till I was turned the age of eleven, when an end was put to my happiness in the following manner:—Generally, when the grown people in the neighbourhood were gone far in the fields to labour, the children assembled together in some of the neighbours' premises to play; and commonly some of us used to get up a tree to look out for any assailant, or kidnapper, that might come upon us; for they sometimes took those opportunities of our parents' absence, to attack and carry off as many as they could seize. One day, as I was watching at the top of a tree in our yard, I saw one of those people come into the yard of our next neighbour but one, to kidnap, there being many stout young people in it. Immediately, on this, I gave the alarm of the rogue, and he was surrounded by the stoutest of them, who entangled him with cords, so that he could not escape till some of the grown people came and secured him. But, alas! ere long it was my fate to be thus attacked, and to be carried off, when none of the grown people were nigh. One day, when all our people were gone out to their works as usual, and only I and my dear sister were left to mind the house, two men and a woman got over our walls, and in a moment seized us both; and, without giving us time to cry out, or make resistance, they stopped our mouths, tied our hands, and ran off with us into the nearest wood: and continued[55] to carry us as far as they could, till night came on, when we reached a small house, where the robbers halted for refreshment, and spent the night. We were then unbound, but were unable to take any food; and, being quite overpowered by fatigue and grief, our only relief was some sleep, which allayed our misfortune for a short time. The next morning we left the house, and continued travelling all the day. For a long time we had kept the woods, but at last we came into a road which I believed I knew. I had now some hopes of being delivered;[56] for we had advanced but a little way before I discovered some people at a distance, on which I began to cry out for their assistance; but my cries had no other effect than to make them tie me faster, and stop my mouth, and then they put me into a large sack. They also stopped my sister's mouth, and tied her hands; and in this manner we proceeded till we were out of the sight of these people.— When we went to rest the following night they offered us some victuals; but we refused them; and the only comfort we had was in being in one another's arms all that night, and bathing each other with our tears. But, alas! we were soon deprived of even the smallest comfort of weeping together. The next day proved a day of greater sorrow than I had yet experienced; for my sister and I were then separated, while we lay clasped in each other's arms. It was in vain that we besought them not to part us: she was torn from me, and immediately carried away, while I was left in a state of distraction not to be described. I cried and grieved continually; and for several days I did not eat any thing but what they forced into my mouth. At length, after many days travelling, during which I had often changed masters, I got into the hands of a chieftain, in a very pleasant country. This man had two wives and some children, and they all used me extremely well, and did all they could to comfort me; particularly the first wife, who was something like my mother. Although I was a great many days journey from my father's house, yet these people spoke exactly the same language with us. This first master of mine, as I may call him, was a smith,[57] and my principal employment was working his bellows, which were the same kind as I had seen in my vicinity. They were in some respects not unlike the stoves here in gentlemen's kitchens; and were covered over with leather; and in the middle of that leather a stick was fixed, and a person stood up, and worked it, in the same manner as is done to pump water out of a cask with a hand-pump. I believe it was gold he worked, for it was of a lovely bright yellow colour, and was worn by the women on their wrists and ancles. I was there I suppose about a month, and they at last used to trust me some little distance from the house. This liberty I used in embracing every opportunity to inquire the way to my own home: and I also sometimes, for the same purpose, went with the maidens, in the cool of the evenings, to bring pitchers of water from the springs for the use of the house. I had also remarked where the sun rose in the morning, and set in the evening, as I had travelled along; and I had observed that my father's house was towards the rising of the sun. I therefore determined to seize the first opportunity of making my escape, and to shape my course for that quarter; for I was quite oppressed and weighed down by grief after my mother and friends; and my love of liberty, ever great, was strengthened by the mortifying circumstance of not daring to eat with the free-born children, although I was mostly their companion.—While I was projecting my escape one day, an unlucky event happened, which quite disconcerted my plan, and put an end to my hopes. I used to be sometimes employed in assisting an elderly woman slave to cook and take care of the poultry; and one morning, while I was feeding some chickens, I happened to toss a small pebble at one of them, which hit it on the middle, and directly killed it. The old slave, having soon after missed the chicken, inquired after it; and on my relating the accident (for I told her the truth, because my mother would never suffer me to tell a lie) she flew into a violent passion, threatened that I should suffer for it; and, my master being out, she immediately went and told her mistress what I had done. This alarmed me very much, and I expected an instant correction,[58] which to me was uncommonly dreadful; for I had seldom been beaten at home. I therefore resolved to fly; and accordingly I ran into a thicket that was hard by, and hid myself in the bushes. Soon afterwards my mistress and the slave returned, and, not seeing me, they searched all the house, but, not finding me, and I not making answer when they called to me, they thought I had run away, and the whole neighbourhood was raised in the pursuit of me. In that part of the country (as well as ours) the houses and villages were skirted with woods, or shrubberies, and the bushes were so thick, that a man could readily conceal himself in them, so as to elude the strictest search. The neighbours continued the whole day looking for me, and several times many of them came within a few yards of the place where I lay hid. I expected every moment, when I heard a rustling among the trees, to be found out, and punished by my master; but they never discovered me, though they were often so near that I even heard their conjectures as they were looking about for me; and I now learned from them, that any attempt to return home would be hopeless. Most of them supposed I had fled towards home; but the distance was so great, and the way so intricate, that they thought I could never reach it, and that I should be lost in the woods. When I heard this I was seized with a violent panic, and abandoned myself to despair. Night too began to approach, and aggravated all my fears. I had before entertained hopes of getting home, and I had determined when it should be dark to make the attempt; but I was now convinced it was fruitless, and I began to consider that, if possibly I could escape all other animals, I could not those of the human kind; and that, not knowing the way, I must perish in the woods.—Thus was I like the hunted deer:

> Ev'ry leaf and ev'ry whisp'ring breath
> Convey'd a foe, and ev'ry foe a death.[59]

I heard frequent rustlings among the leaves; and, being pretty sure they were snakes, I expected every instant to be stung by them.—This increased my anguish, and the horror of my situation became now quite insupportable. I at length quitted the thicket, very faint and hungry, for I had not eaten or drank any thing all the day, and crept to my master's kitchen, from whence I set out at first, and which was an open shed, and laid myself down in the ashes, with an anxious wish for death to relieve me from all my pains. I was scarcely awake in the morning when the old woman slave, who was the first up, came to light the fire, and saw me in the fire-place. She was very much surprised to see me, and could scarcely believe her own eyes. She now promised to intercede for me, and went for her master, who soon after came, and, having slightly reprimanded me, ordered me to be taken care of, and not ill-treated.

Soon after this my master's only daughter and child by his first wife sickened and died, which affected him so much that for some time he was almost frantic, and really would have killed himself had he not been watched and prevented. However, in a small time afterwards he recovered, and I was again sold. I was now carried to the left of the sun's rising, through many dreary wastes and dismal woods, amidst the hideous roarings of wild beasts.—The people I was sold to used to carry me very often, when I was tired, either on their shoulders or on their backs. I saw many convenient well-built sheds along the roads, at proper distances, to accommodate the merchants and travellers, who lay in those buildings along with their wives, who often accompany them; and they always go well armed.

From the time I left my own nation I always found somebody that understood me till I came to the sea coast. The languages of different nations did not totally differ, nor were they so copious as those of the Europeans, particularly the English.[60] They were therefore easily learned; and, while I was journeying thus through Africa, I acquired two or three different tongues. In this manner I had been travelling for a considerable time, when one evening, to my great surprise, whom should I see brought to the house where I was but my dear sister. As soon as she saw me she gave a loud shriek, and ran into my arms.—I was quite overpowered; neither of us could speak, but, for a considerable time, clung to each other in mutual embraces, unable to do any thing but weep. Our meeting affected all who saw us; and indeed I must acknowledge, in honour of those sable destroyers of human rights, that I never met with any ill treatment, or saw any offered to their slaves, except tying them, when necessary, to keep them from running away. When these people knew we were brother and sister they indulged us to be together; and the man, to whom I supposed we belonged, lay with us, he in the middle, while she and I held one another by the hands across his breast all night; and thus for a while we forgot our misfortunes in the joy of being together: but even this small comfort was soon to have an end; for scarcely had the fatal morning appeared, when she was again torn from me for ever! I was now more miserable, if possible, than before. The small relief which her presence gave me from pain was gone, and the wretchedness of my situation was redoubled by my anxiety after her fate, and my apprehensions lest her sufferings should be greater than mine, when I could not be with her to alleviate them. Yes, thou dear partner of all my childish sports! thou sharer of my joys and sorrows! happy should I have ever esteemed myself to encounter every misery for you, and to procure your freedom by the sacrifice of my own. Though you were early forced from my arms, your image has been always rivetted in my heart, from which neither *time nor fortune* have been able to remove it: so that, while the thoughts of your sufferings have damped my prosperity, they have mingled with adversity, and increased its bitterness.—To that heaven which protects the weak from the strong, I commit the care of your innocence and virtues, if they have not already received their full reward; and if your youth and delicacy have not long since fallen victims to the violence of the African trader, the pestilential stench of a Guinea ship, the seasoning in the European colonies, or the lash and lust of a brutal and unrelenting overseer.[61]

I did not long remain after my sister. I was again sold, and carried through a number of places, till, after travelling a considerable time, I came to a town called Tinmah, in the most beautiful country I had yet seen in Africa. It was extremely rich, and there were many rivulets which flowed through it; and supplied a large pond in the center of the town, where the people washed. Here I first saw and tasted cocoa nuts, which I thought superior to any nuts I had ever tasted before; and the trees, which were loaded, were also interspersed amongst the houses, which had commodious shades adjoining, and were in the same manner as ours, the insides being neatly plastered and whitewashed. Here I also saw and tasted for the first time sugar-cane.[62] Their money consisted of little white shells, the size of the finger nail: they are known in this country by the name of *core*.[63] I was sold here for one hundred and seventy-two of them by a merchant who lived and brought me there.[64] I had been about two or three days at his house, when a wealthy widow, a neighbour of his, came there one evening, and brought with her an only son, a young gentleman about my own age and size. Here they saw me; and, having taken a fancy to me, I was bought of the merchant, and went home with them. Her house and premises were situated close to one of those rivulets I have mentioned, and were the finest I ever saw in Africa: they were very extensive, and she had a number of slaves to attend her. The next day I was washed and perfumed, and when meal-time came, I was led into the presence of my mistress, and ate and drank before her with her son. This filled me with astonishment: and I could scarce help expressing my surprise that the young gentleman should suffer me,[65] who was bound,[66] to eat with him who was free; and not only so, but that he would not at any time either eat or drink till I had taken first, because I was the eldest, which was agreeable to our custom. Indeed every thing here, and all their treatment of me, made me forget that I was a slave. The language of these people resembled ours so nearly, that we understood each other perfectly. They had also the very same customs as we. There were likewise slaves daily to attend us, while my young master and I, with other boys, sported with our darts and bows and arrows, as I had been used to do at home. In this resemblance to my former happy state I passed about two months, and I now began to think I was to be adopted into the family, and was beginning to be reconciled to my situation, and to forget by degrees my misfortunes, when all at once the delusion vanished; for, without the least previous knowledge, one morning early, while my dear master and companion was still asleep, I was awakened out of my reverie to fresh sorrow, and hurried away even among the uncircumcised.[67]

Thus, at the very moment I dreamed of the greatest happiness, I found myself most miserable: and it seemed as if fortune wished to give me this taste of joy only to render the reverse more poignant.[68] The change I now experienced was as painful as it was sudden and unexpected. It was a change indeed from a state of bliss to a scene which is inexpressible by me, as it discovered[69] to me an element I had never before beheld, and till then had no idea of, and wherein such instances of hardship and cruelty continually occurred as I can never reflect on but with horror.

All the nations and people I had hitherto passed through resembled our own in their manners, customs and language: but I came at length to a country, the inhabitants of which differed from us in all those particulars. I was very much struck with this difference, especially when I came among a people who did not circumcise, and eat[70] without washing their hands. They cooked also in iron pots, and had European cutlasses and cross bows, which were unknown to us, and fought with their fists among themselves. Their women were not so modest as ours, for they eat, and drank, and slept, with their men.[71] But, above all, I was amazed to see no sacrifices or offerings among them. In some of those places the people ornamented themselves with scars, and likewise filed their teeth very sharp. They wanted sometimes to ornament me in the same manner, but I would not suffer them; hoping that I might some time be among a people who did not thus disfigure themselves, as I thought they did. At last, I came to the banks of a large river, which was covered with canoes, in which the people appeared to live with their household utensils and provisions of all kinds. I was beyond measure astonished at this, as I had never before seen any water larger than a pond or a rivulet; and my surprise was mingled with no small fear when I was put into one of these canoes, and we began to paddle and move along the river. We continued going on thus till night; and when we came to land, and made fires on the banks, each family by themselves, some dragged their canoes on shore, others staid and cooked in theirs, and laid in them all night. Those on the land had mats, of which they made tents, some in the shape of little houses: In these we slept; and after the morning meal we embarked again, and proceeded as before. I was often very much astonished to see some of the women, as well as the men, jump into the water, dive to the bottom, come up again, and swim about. Thus I continued to travel, sometimes by land, sometimes by water, through different countries, and various nations, till, at the end of six or seven months after I had been kidnapped, I arrived at the sea coast. It would be tedious and uninteresting to relate all the incidents which befel me during this journey, and which I have not yet forgotten; of the various hands I passed through, and the manners and customs of all the different people among whom I lived: I shall therefore only observe, that, in all the places where I was, the soil was exceedingly rich; the pomkins, eadas, plantains, yams, &c. &c. were in great abundance, and of incredible size.[72] There were also vast quantities of different gums, though not used for any purpose; and every where a great deal of tobacco. The cotton even grew quite wild; and there was plenty of red wood. I saw no mechanics[73] whatever in all the way, except such as I have mentioned. The chief employment in all these countries was agriculture, and both the males and females, as with us, were brought up to it, and trained in the arts of war.

The first object which saluted my eyes when I arrived on the coast was the sea, and a slave-ship, which was then riding at anchor, and waiting for its cargo. These filled me with astonishment, which was soon converted into terror, which I am yet at a loss to describe, nor the then feelings of my mind. When I was carried on board I was immediately handled, and tossed up, to see if I were sound,[74] by some of the crew; and I was now persuaded that I had gotten into a world of bad spirits, and that they were going to kill me. Their complexions too differing so much from ours, their long hair, and the language they spoke, which was very different from any I had ever heard, united to confirm me in this belief. Indeed, such were the horrors of my views and fears at the moment, that, if ten thousand worlds had been my own, I would have freely parted with them all to have exchanged my condition with that of the meanest slave in my own country. When I looked round the ship too, and saw a large furnace of copper boiling, and a multitude of black people of every description chained together, every one of their countenances expressing dejection and sorrow, I no longer doubted of my fate, and, quite overpowered with horror and anguish, I fell motionless on the deck and fainted. When I recovered a little, I found some black people about me, who I believed were some of those who brought me on board, and had been receiving their pay; they talked to me in order to cheer me, but all in vain. I asked them if we were not to be eaten by those white men with horrible looks, red faces, and long hair? They told me I was not; and one of the crew brought me a small portion of spirituous liquor in a wine glass; but, being afraid of him, I would not take it out of his hand. One of the blacks therefore took it from him and gave it to me, and I took a little down my palate, which, instead of reviving me, as they thought it would, threw me into the greatest consternation at the strange feeling it produced, having never tasted any such liquor before. Soon after this, the blacks who brought me on board went off, and left me abandoned to despair. I now saw myself deprived of all chance of returning to my native country, or even the least glimpse of hope of gaining the shore, which I now considered as friendly: and I even wished for my former slavery in preference to my present situation, which was filled with horrors of every kind, still heightened by my ignorance of what I was to undergo. I was not long suffered to indulge my grief; I was soon put down under the decks, and there I received such a salutation in my nostrils as I had never experienced in my life; so that with the loathsomeness of the stench, and crying together, I became so sick and low that I was not able to eat, nor had I the least desire to taste any thing. I now wished for the last friend, Death, to relieve me; but soon, to my grief, two of the white men offered me eatables; and, on my refusing to eat, one of them held me fast by the hands, and laid me across, I think, the windlass,[75] and tied my feet, while the other flogged me severely. I had never experienced any thing of this kind before; and although, not being used to the water, I naturally feared that element the first time I saw it; yet, nevertheless, could I have got over the nettings,[76] I would have jumped over the side, but I could not; and, besides, the crew used to watch us very closely who were not chained down to the decks, lest we should leap into the water; and I have seen some of these poor African prisoners most severely cut for attempting to do so, and hourly whipped for not eating. This indeed was often the case with myself. In a little time after, amongst the poor chained men, I found some of my own nation, which in a small degree gave ease to my mind. I inquired of these what was to be done with us? they gave me to understand we were to be carried to these white people's country to work for them. I then was a little revived, and thought, if it were no worse than working, my situation was not so desperate: but still I feared I should be put to death, the white people looked and acted, as I thought, in so savage a manner; for I had never seen among any people such instances of brutal cruelty; and this not only shewn towards us blacks, but also to some of the whites themselves.[77] One white man in particular I saw, when we were permitted to be on deck, flogged so unmercifully with a large rope near the foremast,[78] that he died in consequence of it; and they tossed him over the side as they would have done a brute. This made me fear these people the more; and I expected nothing less than to be treated in the same manner. I could not help expressing my fears and apprehensions to some of my countrymen: I asked them if these people had no country, but lived in this hollow place the ship? they told me they did not, but came from a distant one. "Then," said I, "how comes it in all our country we never heard of them?" They told me, because they lived so very far off. I then asked where were their women? had they any like themselves! I was told they had: "And why," said I, "do we not see them?" they answered, because they were left behind. I asked how the vessel could go? they told me they could not tell; but that there were cloths put upon the masts by the help of the ropes I saw, and then the vessel went on; and the white men had some spell or magic they put in the water when they liked in order to stop the vessel.[79] I was exceedingly amazed at this account, and really thought they were spirits. I therefore wished much to be from amongst them, for I expected they would sacrifice me: but my wishes were vain; for we were so quartered that it was impossible for any of us to make our escape. While we staid on the coast I was mostly on deck; and one day, to my great astonishment, I saw one of these vessels coming in with the sails up. As soon as the whites saw it, they gave a great shout, at which we were amazed; and the more so as the vessel appeared larger by approaching nearer. At last she came to an anchor in my sight, and when the anchor was let go, I and my countrymen who saw it were lost in astonishment to observe the vessel stop; and were now convinced it was done by magic. Soon after this the other ship got her boats[80] out, and they came on board of us, and the people of both ships seemed very glad to see each other. Several of the strangers also shook hands with us black people, and made motions with their hands, signifying, I suppose, we were to go to their country; but we did not understand them. At last, when the ship we were in had got in all her cargo, they made ready with many fearful noises, and we were all put under deck, so that we could not see how they managed the vessel. But this disappointment was the least of my sorrow. The stench of the hold while we were on the coast was so intolerably loathsome, that it was dangerous to remain there for any time, and some of us had been permitted to stay on the deck for the fresh air; but now that the whole ship's cargo were confined together, it became absolutely pestilential. The closeness of the place, and the heat of the climate, added to the number in the ship, which was so crowded that each had scarcely room to turn himself, almost suffocated us. This produced copious perspirations, so that the air soon became unfit for respiration, from a variety of loathsome smells, and brought on a sickness among the slaves, of which many died, thus falling victims to the improvident avarice, as I may call it, of their purchasers. This wretched situation was again aggravated by the galling of the chains, now become insupportable; and the filth of the necessary tubs, into which the children often fell, and were almost suffocated.[81] The shrieks of the women, and the groans of the dying, rendered the whole a scene of horror almost inconceiveable. Happily perhaps for myself I was soon reduced so low here that it was thought necessary to keep me almost always on deck; and from my extreme youth I was not put in fetters. In this situation I expected every hour to share the fate of my companions, some of whom were almost daily brought upon deck at the point of death, which I began to hope would soon put an end to my miseries. Often did I think many of the inhabitants of the deep much more happy than myself; I envied them the freedom they enjoyed, and as often wished I could change my condition for theirs. Every circumstance I met with served only to render my state more painful, and heighten my apprehensions, and my opinion of the cruelty of the whites. One day they had taken a number of fishes; and when they had killed and satisfied themselves with as many as they thought fit, to our astonishment who were on the deck, rather than give any of them to us to eat, as we expected, they tossed the remaining fish into the sea again, although we begged and prayed for some as well as we could, but in vain; and some of my countrymen, being pressed by hunger, took an opportunity, when they thought no one saw them, of trying to get a little privately; but they were discovered, and the attempt procured them some very severe floggings.

One day, when we had a smooth sea, and moderate wind, two of my wearied countrymen, who were chained together (I was near them at the time), preferring death to such a life of misery, somehow made through the nettings, and jumped into the sea: immediately another quite dejected fellow, who, on account of his illness, was suffered to be out of irons, also followed their example; and I believe many more would very soon have done the same, if they had not been prevented by the ship's crew, who were instantly alarmed. Those of us that were the most active were, in a moment, put down under the deck; and there was such a noise and confusion amongst the people of the ship as I never heard before, to stop her, and get the boat out to go after the slaves. However, two of the wretches were drowned, but they got the other, and afterwards flogged him unmercifully, for thus attempting to prefer death to slavery. In this manner we continued to undergo more hardships than I can now relate; hardships which are inseparable from this accursed trade.—Many a time we were near suffocation, from the want of fresh air, which we were often without for whole days together. This, and the stench of the necessary tubs, carried off many. During our passage I first saw flying fishes, which surprised me very much: they used frequently to fly across the ship, and many of them fell on the deck. I also now first saw the use of the quadrant.[82] I had often with astonishment seen the mariners make observations with it, and I could not think what it meant. They at last took notice of my surprise; and one of them, willing to increase it, as well as to gratify my curiosity, made me one day look through it. The clouds appeared to me to be land, which disappeared as they passed along. This heightened my wonder: and I was now more persuaded than ever that I was in another world, and that every thing about me was magic. At last we came in sight of the island of Barbadoes, at which the whites on board gave a great shout, and made many signs of joy to us. We did not know what to think of this; but as the vessel drew nearer we plainly saw the harbour, and other ships of different kinds and sizes: and we soon anchored amongst them off Bridge Town. Many merchants and planters now came on board, though it was in the evening. They put us in separate parcels,[83] and examined us attentively. They also made us jump,[84] and pointed to the land, signifying we were to go there. We thought by this we should be eaten by these ugly men, as they appeared to us; and, when soon after we were all put down under the deck again, there was much dread and trembling among us, and nothing but bitter cries to be heard all the night from these apprehensions, insomuch that at last the white people got some old slaves from the land to pacify us. They told us we were not to be eaten, but to work, and were soon to go on land, where we should see many of our country people. This report eased us much; and sure enough, soon after we were landed, there came to us Africans of all languages. We were conducted immediately to the merchant's yard, where we were all pent up together like so many sheep in a fold, without regard to sex or age. As every object was new to me, every thing I saw filled me with surprise. What struck me first was, that the houses were built with bricks, in stories, and in every other respect different from those in I have seen in Africa: but I was still more astonished on seeing people on horseback. I did not know what this could mean; and indeed I thought these people were full of nothing but magical arts. While I was in this astonishment, one of my fellow prisoners spoke to a countryman of his about the horses, who said they were the same kind they had in their country. I understood them, though they were from a distant part of Africa, and I thought it odd I had not seen any horses there; but afterwards, when I came to converse with different Africans, I found they had many horses amongst them, and much larger than those I then saw. We were not many days in the merchant's custody before we were sold after their usual manner, which is this:—On a signal given, (as the beat of a drum), the buyers rush at once into the yard where the slaves are confined, and make choice of that parcel they like best.[85] The noise and clamour with which this is attended, and the eagerness visible in the countenances of the buyers, serve not a little to increase the apprehensions of the terrified Africans, who may well be supposed to consider them as the ministers of that destruction to which they think themselves devoted.[86] In this manner, without scruple, are relations and friends separated, most of them never to see each other again. I remember in the vessel in which I was brought over, in the men's apartment, there were several brothers, who, in the sale, were sold in different lots; and it was very moving on this occasion to see and hear their cries at parting. O, ye nominal Christians! might not an African ask you, learned you this from your God? who says unto you, Do unto all men as you would men should do unto you?

Is it not enough that we are torn from our country and friends to toil for your luxury and lust of gain? Must every tender feeling be likewise sacrificed to your avarice? Are the dearest friends and relations, now rendered more dear by their separation from their kindred, still to be parted from each other, and thus prevented from cheering the gloom of slavery with the small comfort of being together and mingling their sufferings and sorrows? Why are parents to lose their children, brothers their sisters, or husbands their wives? Surely this is a new refinement in cruelty, which, while it has no advantage to atone for it, thus aggravates distress, and adds fresh horrors even to the wretchedness of slavery.

CHAPTER III

I NOW totally lost the small remains of comfort I had enjoyed in conversing with my countrymen; the women too, who used to wash and take care of me, were all gone different ways, and I never saw one of them afterwards.

I stayed in this island for a few days; I believe it could not be above a fortnight; when I and some few more slaves, that were not saleable among the rest, from very much fretting, were shipped off in a sloop for North America.[87] On the passage we were better treated than when we were coming from Africa, and we had plenty of rice and fat pork. We were landed up a river a good way from the sea, about Virginia county, where we saw few or none of our native Africans, and not one soul who could talk to me. I was a few weeks weeding grass, and gathering stones in a plantation; and at last all my companions were distributed different ways, and only myself was left. I was now exceedingly miserable, and thought myself worse off than any of the rest of my companions; for they could talk to each other, but I had no person to speak to that I could understand. In this state I was constantly grieving and pining, and wishing for death, rather than any thing else. While I was in this plantation, the gentleman, to whom I supposed the estate belonged, being unwell, I was one day sent for to his dwelling house to fan him: when I came into the room where he was, I was very much affrighted at some things I saw, and the more so as I had seen a black woman slave as I came through the house, who was cooking the dinner, and the poor creature was cruelly loaded with various kinds of iron machines; she had one particularly on her head, which locked her mouth so fast that she could scarcely speak; and could not eat nor drink. I was much astonished and shocked at this contrivance, which I afterwards learned was called the iron muzzle. Soon after I had a fan put into my hand, to fan the gentleman while he slept; and so I did indeed with great fear. While he was fast asleep I indulged myself a great deal in looking about the room, which to me appeared very fine and curious. The first object that engaged my attention was a watch which hung on the chimney, and was going. I was quite surprised at the noise it made, and was afraid it would tell the gentleman any thing I might do amiss: and when I immediately after observed a picture hanging in the room, which appeared constantly to look at me, I was still more affrighted, having never seen such things as these before. At one time I thought it was something relative to magic; and not seeing it move, I thought it might be some way the whites had to keep their great men when they died, and offer them libations as we used to do our friendly spirits. In this state of anxiety I remained till my master awoke, when I was dismissed out of the room, to my no small satisfaction and relief, for I thought that these people were all made of wonders. In this place I was called Jacob; but on board the African snow[88] I was called Michael. I had been some time in this miserable, forlorn, and much dejected state, without having any one to talk to, which made my life a burden, when the kind and unknown hand of the Creator (who in very deed leads the blind in a way they know not) now began to appear, to my comfort; for one day the captain of a merchant ship, called the Industrious Bee, came on some business to my master's house. This gentleman, whose name was Michael Henry Pascal, was a lieutenant in the royal navy,[89] but now commanded this trading ship, which was somewhere in the confines of the county many miles off. While he was at my master's house it happened that he saw me, and liked me so well that he made a purchase of me. I think I have often heard him say he gave thirty or forty pounds sterling for me; but I do not now remember which.[90] However, he meant me for a present to some of his friends in England; and I was sent accordingly from the house of my then master (one Mr. Campbell) to the place where the ship lay; I was conducted on horseback by an elderly black man (a mode of travelling which appeared very odd to me). When I arrived I was carried on board a fine large ship, loaded with tobacco, &c. and just ready to sail for England. I now thought my condition much mended; I had sails to lie on, and plenty of good victuals to eat; and every body on board used me very kindly, quite contrary to what I had seen of any white people before; I therefore began to think that they were not all of the same disposition. A few days after I was on board we sailed for England. I was still at a loss to conjecture my destiny. By this time, however, I could smatter a little imperfect English; and I wanted to know as well as I could where we were going. Some of the people of the ship used to tell me they were going to carry me back to my own country, and this made me very happy.[91] I was quite rejoiced at the idea of going back; and thought if I should get home what wonders I should have to tell. But I was reserved for another fate, and was soon undeceived when we came within sight of the English coast. While I was on board this ship, my captain and master named me *Gustavus Vasa.*[92] I at that time began to understand him a little, and refused to be called so, and told him as well as I could that I would be called Jacob; but he said I should not, and still called me Gustavus; and when I refused to answer to my new name, which at first I did, it gained me many a cuff; so at length I submitted, and by which I have been known ever since.[93] The ship had a very long passage; and on that account we had very short allowance of provisions. Towards the last we had only one pound and a half of bread per week, and about the same quantity of meat, and one quart of water a day. We spoke with only one vessel the whole time we were at sea, and but once we caught a few fishes. In our extremities the captain and people told me in jest they would kill and eat me, but I thought them in earnest, and was depressed beyond measure, expecting every moment to be my last. While I was in this situation one evening they caught, with a good deal of trouble, a large shark, and got it on board. This gladdened my poor heart exceedingly, as I thought it would serve the people to eat instead of their eating me; but very soon, to my astonishment, they cut off a small part of the tail, and tossed the rest over the side.[94] This renewed my consternation; and I did not know what to think of these white people; I very much feared they would kill and eat me. There was on board the ship a young lad who had never been at sea before, about four or five years older than myself: his name was Richard Baker.[95] He was a native of America,[96] had received an excellent education, and was of a most amiable temper. Soon after I went on board he shewed me a great deal of partiality and attention, and in return I grew extremely fond of him. We at length became inseparable; and for the space of two years, he was of very great use to me, and was my constant companion and instructor. Although this dear youth had many slaves of his own, yet he and I have gone through many sufferings together on shipboard; and we have many nights lain in each other's bosoms when we were in great distress. Thus such a friendship was cemented between us as we cherished till his death, which, to my very great sorrow, happened in the year 1759, when he was up the Archipelago,[97] on board his majesty's ship the Preston: an event which I have never ceased to regret, as I lost at once a kind interpreter, an agreeable companion, and a faithful friend; who, at the age of fifteen, discovered[98] a mind superior to prejudice; and who was not ashamed to notice, to associate with, and to be the friend and instructor of one who was ignorant, a stranger, of a different complexion, and a slave! My master had lodged in his mother's house in America: he respected him very much, and made him always eat with him in the cabin. He used often to tell him jocularly that he would kill and eat me. Sometimes he would say to me—the black people were not good to eat, and would ask me if we did not eat people in my country. I said, No: then he said he would kill Dick (as he always called him) first, and afterwards me. Though this hearing relieved my mind a little as to myself, I was alarmed for Dick, and whenever he was called I used to be very much afraid he was to be killed; and I would peep and watch to see if they were going to kill him: nor was I free from this consternation till we made the land. One night we lost a man overboard; and the cries and noise were so great and confused, in stopping the ship, that I, who did not know what was the matter, began, as usual, to be very much afraid, and to think they were going to make an offering with me, and perform some magic; which I still believed they dealt in. As the waves were very high, I thought the Ruler of the seas was angry, and I expected to be offered up to appease him. This filled my mind with agony, and I could not any more that night close my eyes again to rest. However, when day-light appeared, I was a little eased in my mind; but still every time I was called I used to think it was to be killed. Some time after this we saw some very large fish, which I afterwards found were called grampusses.[99] They looked to me extremely terrible, and made their appearance just at dusk, and were so near as to blow the water on the ship's deck. I believed them to be the rulers of the sea; and, as the white people did not make any offerings at any time, I thought they were angry with them; and, at last, what confirmed my belief was, the wind just then died away, and a calm ensued, and in consequence of it the ship stopped going. I supposed that the fish had performed this, and I hid myself in the fore-part of the ship, through fear of being offered up to appease them, every minute peeping and quaking; but my good friend Dick came shortly towards me, and I took an opportunity to ask him, as well as I could, what these fish were? not being able to talk much English, I could but just make him understand my question; and not at all, when I asked him if any offerings were to be made to them? However, he told me these fish would swallow any body; which sufficiently alarmed me. Here he was called away by the captain, who was leaning over the quarter-deck[100] railing and looking at the fish; and most of the people were busied in getting a barrel of pitch to light, for them to play with.[101] The captain now called me to him, having learned some of my apprehensions from Dick; and having diverted himself and others for some time with my fears, which appeared ludicrous enough in my crying and trembling, he dismissed me. The barrel of pitch was now lighted and put over the side into the water: by this time it was just dark, and the fish went after it; and, to my great joy, I saw them no more.

However, all my alarms began to subside when we got sight of land; and at last the ship arrived at Falmouth, after a passage of thirteen weeks.[102] Every heart on board seemed gladdened on our reaching the shore, and none more than mine. The captain immediately went on shore, and sent on board some fresh provisions, which we wanted very much: we made good use of them, and our famine was soon turned into feasting, almost without ending. It was about the beginning of the spring 1757 when I arrived in England, and I was near twelve years of age at that time.[103] I was very much struck with the buildings and the pavement of the streets in Falmouth; and, indeed, any object I saw filled me with new surprise. One morning, when I got upon deck, I saw it covered all over with the snow that fell over-night: as I had never seen any thing of the kind before, I thought it was salt; so I immediately ran down to the mate, and desired him, as well as I could, to come and see how somebody in the night had thrown salt all over the deck. He, knowing what it was, desired me to bring some of it down to him: accordingly I took up a handful of it, which I found very cold indeed; and when I brought it to him he desired me to taste it. I did so, and I was surprised beyond measure. I then asked him what it was? he told me it was snow: but I could not in any wise understand him. He asked me if we had no such thing in my country? and I told him, No. I then asked him the use of it, and who made it; he told me a great man in the heavens, called God: but here again I was to all intents and purposes at a loss to understand him; and the more so, when a little after I saw the air filled with it, in a heavy shower, which fell down on the same day. After this I went to church; and having never been at such a place before, I was again amazed at seeing and hearing the service. I asked all I could about it; and they gave me to understand it was worshipping God, who made us and all things. I was still at a great loss, and soon got into an endless field of inquiries, as well as I was able to speak and ask about things. However, my little friend Dick used to be my best interpreter; for I could make free with him, and he always instructed me with pleasure: and from what I could understand by him of this God, and in seeing these white people did not sell one another, as we did, I was much pleased; and in this I thought they were much happier than we Africans. I was astonished at the wisdom of the white people in all things I saw; but was amazed at their not sacrificing, or making any offerings, and eating with unwashed hands, and touching the dead. I likewise could not help remarking the particular slenderness of their women, which I did not at first like; and I thought they were not so modest and shamefaced as the African women.

I had often seen my master and Dick employed in reading; and I had a great curiosity to talk to the books, as I thought they did; and so to learn how all things had a beginning: for that purpose I have often taken up a book, and have talked to it, and then put my ears to it, when alone, in hopes it would answer me; and I have been very much concerned when I found it remained silent.[104]

My master lodged at the house of a gentleman in Falmouth, who had a fine little daughter about six or seven years of age, and she grew prodigiously fond of me; insomuch that we used to eat together, and had servants to wait on us. I was so much caressed by this family that it often reminded me of the treatment I had received from my little noble African master. After I had been here a few days, I was sent on board of the ship; but the child cried so much after me that nothing could pacify her till I was sent for again. It is ludicrous enough, that I began to fear I should be betrothed to this young lady; and when my master asked me if I would stay there with her behind him, as he was going away with the ship, which had taken in the tobacco again? I cried immediately, and said I would not leave him. At last, by stealth, one night I was sent on board the ship again; and in a little time we sailed for Guernsey, where she was in part owned by a merchant, one Nicholas Doberry.[105] As I was now amongst a people who had not their faces scarred, like some of the African nations where I had been, I was very glad I did not let them ornament me in that manner when I was with them. When we arrived at Guernsey, my master placed me to board and lodge with one of his mates, who had a wife and family there; and some months afterwards he went to England, and left me in the care of this mate, together with my friend Dick. This mate had a little daughter aged about five or six years, with whom I used to be much delighted. I had often observed, that when her mother washed her face it looked very rosy; but when she washed mine it did not look so; I therefore tried oftentimes myself if I could not by washing make my face of the same colour as my little play-mate (Mary), but it was all in vain; and I now began to be mortified at the difference in our complexions. This woman behaved to me with great kindness and attention; and taught me every thing in the same manner as she did her own child, and indeed in every respect treated me as such. I remained here till the summer of the year 1757, when my master, being appointed first lieutenant of his Majesty's ship the Roebuck,[106] sent for Dick and me, and his old mate: on this we all left Guernsey, and set out for England in a sloop bound for London. As we were coming up towards the Nore,[107] where the Roebuck lay, a man of war's boat[108] came along-side to press our people; on which each man ran to hide himself.[109] I was very much frightened at this, though I did not know what it meant, or what to think or do. However, I went and hid myself also under a hencoop. Immediately the press-gang came on board with their swords drawn, and searched all about, pulled the people out by force, and put them into the boat. At last I was found out also; the man that found me held me up by the heels while they all made their sport of me, I roaring and crying out all the time most lustily; but at last the mate, who was my conductor, seeing this, came to my assistance, and did all he could to pacify me; but all to very little purpose, till I had seen the boat go off. Soon afterwards we came to the Nore, where the Roebuck lay; and, to our great joy, my master came on board to us, and brought us to the ship. I was amazed indeed to see the quantity of men and the guns. However my surprise began to diminish, as my knowledge increased; and I ceased to feel those apprehensions and alarms which had taken such strong possession of me when I first came among the Europeans, and for some time after. I began now to pass to an opposite extreme; I was so far from being afraid of any thing new which I saw, that, after I had been some time in this ship, I even began to long for an engagement.[110] My griefs too, which in young minds are not perpetual, were now wearing away; and I soon enjoyed myself pretty well, and felt tolerably easy in my present situation. There was a number of boys on board, which still made it more agreeable; for we were always together, and a great part of our time was spent in play. I remained in this ship a considerable time, during which we made several cruises, and visited a variety of places: among others we were twice in Holland, and brought over several persons of distinction from it, whose names I do not now remember. On the passage, one day, for the diversion of those gentlemen, all the boys were called on the quarter-deck, and were paired proportionably, and then made to fight; after which the gentleman gave the combatants from five to nine shillings each. This was the first time I ever fought with a white boy; and I never knew what it was to have a bloody nose before. This made me fight most desperately; I suppose considerably more than an hour; and at last, both of us being weary, we were parted. I had a great deal of this kind of sport afterwards, in which the captain and the ship's company used very much to encourage me. Sometime afterwards the ship went to Leith, in Scotland, from thence to the Orkneys, where I was surprised in seeing scarcely any night; and from thence we sailed with a great fleet, full of soldiers, for England. All this time we had never come to an engagement, though we were frequently cruising off the coast of France; during which we chased many vessels, and took in all seventeen prizes.[111] I had been learning many of the manoeuvres of the ship during our cruise; and I was several times made to fire the guns.

[Equiano recounts his involvement in the successful British military campaign against the French at the siege of Louisbourgh, Canada. He returns to London.]

CHAPTER IV

It was now between three and four years since I first came to England, a great part of which I had spent at sea; so that I became inured to that service, and began to consider myself as happily situated; for my master treated me always extremely well; and my attachment and gratitude to him were very great. From the various scenes I had beheld on ship-board, I soon grew a stranger to terror of every kind, and was, in that respect at least, almost an Englishman. I have often reflected with surprise that I never felt half the alarm at any of the numerous dangers I have been in, that I was filled with at the first sight of the Europeans, and at every act of theirs, even the most trifling, when I first came among them, and for some time afterwards. That fear, however, which was the effect of my ignorance, wore away as I began to know them. I could now speak English tolerably well, and I perfectly understood every thing that was said. I now not only felt myself quite easy with these new countrymen, but relished their society and manners. I no longer looked upon them as spirits, but as men superior to us; and therefore I had the stronger desire to resemble them; to imbibe their spirit, and imitate their manners; I therefore embraced every occasion of improvement; and every new thing that I observed I treasured up in my memory. I had long wished to be able to read and write; and for this purpose I took every opportunity to gain instruction, but had made as yet very little progress. However, when I went to London with my master, I had soon an opportunity of improving myself, which I gladly embraced. Shortly after my arrival, he sent me to wait upon the Miss Guerins,[112] who had treated me with much kindness when I was there before; and they sent me to school.

While I was attending these ladies, their servants told me I could not go to heaven, unless I was baptized. This made me very uneasy; for I had now some faint idea of a future state: accordingly I communicated my anxiety to the eldest Miss Guerin, with whom I was become a favourite, and pressed her to have me baptized; when, to my great joy, she told me I should. She had formerly asked my master to let me be baptized, but he had refused; however, she now insisted on it; and he, being under some obligation to her brother, complied with her request; so I was baptized at St. Margaret's church, Westminster, in February 1759, by my present name.[113] The clergyman, at the same time, gave me a book, called a guide to the Indians, written by the Bishop of Sodor and Man.[114] On this occasion, Miss Guerin and her brother did me the honour to stand as godfather and godmother, and afterwards gave me a treat. I used to attend these ladies about the town, in which service I was extremely happy; as I had thus very many opportunities of seeing London, which I desired of all things. I was sometimes, however, with my master at his rendezvous-house, which was at the foot of Westminster bridge.[115] Here I used to enjoy myself in playing about the bridge stairs, and often in the watermen's wherries with other boys.[116] On one of these occasions there was another boy with me in a wherry, and we went out into the current of the river; while there, two more stout boys came to us in another wherry, and, abusing us for taking the boat, desired me to get into the other wherry-boat. Accordingly I went to get out of the wherry I was in; but just as I had got one of my feet into the other boat, the boys shoved it off, so that I fell into the Thames and, not being able to swim, I should unavoidably have been drowned, but for the assistance of some watermen,[117] who providentially came to my relief.

[Equiano takes part in the successful British military assault on Belle-Isle, off the coast of France, and serves under Pascal on the *Aetna.*]

Our ship having arrived at Portsmouth, we went into the harbour, and remained there till the end of November, when we heard great talk about peace; and, to our very great joy, in the beginning of December we had orders to go up to London with our ship, to be paid off.[118] We received this news with loud huzzas, and every other demonstration of gladness; and nothing but mirth was to be seen through every part of the ship. I too was not without my share of the general joy on this occasion. I thought now of nothing but being freed, and working for myself, and thereby getting money to enable me to get a good education; for I always had a great desire to be able at least to read and write; and while I was on ship-board I had endeavoured to improve myself in both. While I was in the Aetna particularly, the captain's clerk taught me to write, and gave me a smattering of arithmetic as far as the rule of three.[119] There was also one Daniel Queen, about forty years of age, a man very well educated, who messed[120] with me on board this ship, and he likewise dressed and attended the captain. Fortunately this man soon became very much attached to me, and took very great pains to instruct me in many things. He taught me to shave and dress hair a little, and also to read in the Bible, explaining many passages to me, which I did not comprehend. I was wonderfully surprised to see the laws and rules of my country written almost exactly here; a circumstance which I believe tended to impress our manners and customs more deeply on my memory. I used to tell him of this resemblance; and many a time we had sat up the whole night together at this employment. In short he was like a father to me; and some even used to call me after his name; they also styled me the black Christian. Indeed I almost loved him with the affection of a son. Many things I have denied myself that he might have them; and when I used to play at marbles, or any other game, and won a few halfpence, or got any little money, which I did sometimes, for shaving any one, I used to buy him a little sugar or tobacco, as far as my stock of money would go. He used to say, that he and I never should part; and that when our ship was paid off, as I was as free as himself or any other man on board, he would instruct me in his business, by which I might gain a good livelihood. This gave me new life and spirits, and my heart burned within me, while I thought the time long till I obtained my freedom: for though my master had not promised it to me, yet besides the assurances I had received that he had no right to detain me, he always treated me with the greatest kindness, and reposed in me an unbounded confidence; he even paid attention to my morals; and would never suffer me to deceive him, or tell lies, of which he used to tell me the consequences; and that if I did so, God would not love me; so that from all this tenderness, I had never once supposed, in all my dreams of freedom, that he would think of detaining me any longer than I wished.

In pursuance of our orders we sailed from Portsmouth for the Thames, and arrived at Deptford the 10th of December; where we cast anchor just as it was high water. The ship was up about half an hour, when my master ordered the barge to be manned; and all in an instant, without having before given me the least reason to suspect any thing of the matter, he forced me into the barge, saying, I was going to leave him, but he would take care I should not. I was so struck with the unexpectedness of this proceeding, that for some time I could not make a reply, only I made an offer to go for my books and chest of clothes, but he swore I should not move out of his sight; and if I did he would cut my throat, at the same time taking his hanger.[121] I began, however, to collect myself: and, plucking up courage, I told him I was free, and he could not by law serve me so. But this only enraged him the more; and he continued to swear, and said he would soon let me know whether he would or not, and at that instant sprung himself into the barge from the ship, to the astonishment and sorrow of all on board. The tide, rather unluckily for me, had just turned downward, so that we quickly fell down the river along with it, till we came among some outward-bound West-Indiamen;[122] for he was resolved to put me on board the first vessel he could get to receive me. The boat's crew, who pulled against their will, became quite faint at different times, and would have gone ashore; but he would not let them. Some of them strove then to cheer me, and told me he could not sell me, and that they would stand by me, which revived me a little, and encouraged my hopes; for as they pulled along he asked some vessels to receive me, and they would not. But, just as we had got a little below Gravesend, we came alongside of a ship which was going away the next tide for the West Indies; her name was the Charming Sally, Capt. James Doran; and my master went on board and agreed with him for me; and in a little time I was sent for into the cabin. When I came there, Captain Doran asked me if I knew him. I answered that I did not; "Then," said he "you are now my slave." I told him my master could not sell me to him, nor to any one else. "Why," said he, "did not your master buy you?" I confessed he did. But I have served him, said I, many years, and he has taken all my wages and prize-money,[123] for I only got one sixpence during the war; besides this I have been baptized; and by the laws of the land no man has a right to sell me: and I added, that I had heard a lawyer, and others at different times, tell my master so. They both then said that those people who told me so were not my friends: but I replied—It was very extraordinary that other people did not know the law as well as they.[124] Upon this Captain Doran said I talked too much English; and if I did not behave myself well, and be quiet, he had a method on board to make me. I was too well convinced of his power over me to doubt what he said: and my former sufferings in the slave-ship presenting themselves to my mind, the recollection of them made me shudder. However, before I retired, I told them that as I could not get any right among men here, I hoped I should hereafter in Heaven; and I immediately left the cabin, filled with resentment and sorrow. The only coat I had with me my master took away with him, and said, "If your prize-money had been 10,000£. I had a right to it all, and would have taken it." I had about nine guineas, which during my long sea-faring life, I had scraped together from trifling perquisites and little ventures; and I hid it that instant, lest my master should take that from me likewise, still hoping that by some means or other I should make my escape to the shore, and indeed some of my old shipmates told me not to despair, for they would get me back again; and that, as soon as they could get their pay, they would immediately come to Portsmouth to me, where this ship was going: but, alas! all my hopes were baffled, and the hour of my deliverance was yet far off. My master, having soon concluded his bargain with the captain, came out of the cabin, and he and his people got into the boat, and put off; I followed them with aching eyes as long as I could, and when they were out of sight I threw myself on the deck, with a heart ready to burst with sorrow and anguish.[125]

CHAPTER V

THUS, at the moment I expected all my toils to end, was I plunged, as I supposed, in a new slavery: in comparison of which all my service hitherto had been perfect freedom; and whose horrors, always present to my mind, now rushed on it with tenfold aggravation. I wept very bitterly for some time: and began to think that I must have done something to displease the Lord, that he thus punished me so severely. This filled me with painful reflections on my past conduct; I recollected that on the morning of our arrival at Deptford I had rashly sworn that as soon as we reached London I would spend the day in rambling and sport. My conscience smote me for this unguarded expression: I felt that the Lord was able to disappoint me in all things, and immediately considered my present situation as a judgment of Heaven on account of my presumption in swearing: I therefore, with contrition of heart, acknowledged my transgression to God, and poured out my soul before him with unfeigned repentance, and with earnest supplications I besought him not to abandon me in my distress, nor cast me from his mercy for ever. In a little time my grief, spent with its own violence, began to subside; and after the first confusion of my thoughts was over, I reflected with more calmness on my present condition: I considered that trials and disappointments are sometimes for our good, and I thought God might perhaps have permitted this in order to teach me wisdom and resignation; for he had hitherto shadowed me with the wings of his mercy, and by his invisible but powerful hand brought me the way I knew not. These reflections gave me a little comfort, and I rose at last from the deck with dejection and sorrow in my countenance, yet mixed with some faint hope that the *Lord would appear* for my deliverance.

Soon afterwards, as my new master was going ashore, he called me to him, and told me to behave myself well, and do the business of the ship the same as any of the rest of the boys, and that I should fare the better for it; but I made him no answer. I was then asked if I could swim, and I said, No. However I was made to go under the deck, and was well watched. The next tide the ship got under way, and soon after arrived at the Mother Bank, Portsmouth; where she waited a few days for some of the West India convoy. While I was here I tried every means I could devise among the people of the ship to get me a boat from the shore, as there was none suffered to come along side of the ship; and their own, whenever it was used, was hoisted in again immediately. A sailor on board took a guinea[126] from me on pretence of getting me a boat; and promised me, time after time, that it was hourly to come off. When he had the watch upon deck I watched also; and looked long enough, but all in vain; I could never see either the boat or my guinea again. And what I thought was still the worst of all, the fellow gave information, as I afterwards found, all the while to the mates of my intention to go off, if I could in any way do it; but, rogue-like, he never told them he had got a guinea from me to procure my escape. However, after we had sailed, and his trick was made known to the ship's crew, I had some satisfaction in seeing him detested and despised by them all for his behaviour to me. I was still in hopes that my old shipmates would not forget their promise to come for me to Portsmouth; and they did at last, but not till the day before we sailed, some of them did come there, and sent me off some oranges, and other tokens of their regard. They also sent me word they would come off to me themselves the next day or the day after; and a lady also, who lived in Gosport, wrote to me that she would come and take me out of the ship at the same time. This lady had been once very intimate with my former master; I used to sell and take care of a great deal of property for her in different ships; and in return she always shewed great friendship for me; and used to tell my master that she would take me away to live with her: but unfortunately for me, a disagreement soon afterwards took place between them; and she was succeeded in my master's good graces by another lady, who appeared sole mistress of the Aetna, and mostly lodged on board. I was not so great a favourite with this lady as with the former; she had conceived a pique against me on some occasion when she was on board, and she did not fail to instigate my master to treat me in the manner he did.[127]

However the next morning, the 30th of December, the wind being brisk and easterly, the Aeolus frigate,[128] which was to escort the convoy, made a signal for sailing. All the ships then got up their anchors; and, before any of my friends had an opportunity to come off to my relief, to my inexpressible anguish, our ship had got under way. What tumultuous emotions agitated my soul when the convoy got under sail, and I, a prisoner on board, now without hope! I kept my swimming eyes upon the land in a state of unutterable grief; not knowing what to do, and despairing how to help myself. While my mind was in this situation, the fleet sailed on, and in one day's time I lost sight of the wished-for land. In the first expressions of my grief I reproached my fate, and wished I had never been born. I was ready to curse the tide that bore us, the gale that wafted my prison, and even the ship that conducted us; and I called on death to relieve me from the horrors I felt and dreaded, that I might be in that place

> Where slaves are free, and men oppress no more,
> Fool that I was, inur'd so long to pain,
> To trust to hope, or dream of joy again.

~

Now dragg'd once more beyond the western main,
To groan beneath some dastard planter's chain;
Where my poor countrymen in bondage wait
The long enfranchisement of a ling'ring fate:
Hard ling'ring fate! while, ere the dawn of day,
Rous'd by the lash, they go their cheerless way;
And as their souls with shame and anguish burn,
Salute with groans unwelcome morn's return,
And, chiding ev'ry hour the slow-pac'd sun,
Pursue their toils till all his race is run.
No eye to mark their suff'rings with a tear;
No friend to comfort, and no hope to cheer:
Then, like the dull unpity'd brutes, repair
To stalls as wretched, and as coarse a fare;
Thank heaven one day of mis'ry was o'er,
Then sink to sleep, and wish to wake no more.[129]

The turbulence of my emotions, however, naturally gave way to calmer thoughts, and I soon perceived what fate had decreed no mortal on earth could prevent. The convoy sailed on without any accident, with a pleasant gale and smooth sea, for six weeks, till February, when one morning the Aeolus ran down a brig, one of the convoy, and she instantly went down and was ingulfed in the dark recesses of the ocean. The convoy was immediately thrown into great confusion till it was daylight; and the Aeolus was illuminated with lights to prevent any farther mischief. On the 13th of February 1763, from the mast-head, we descried our destined island Montserrat; and soon after I beheld those

Regions of sorrow, doleful shades, where peace
And rest can rarely dwell. Hope never comes
That comes to all, but torture without end
Still urges.[130]

At the sight of this land of bondage, a fresh horror ran through all my frame, and chilled me to the heart. My former slavery now rose in dreadful review to my mind, and displayed nothing but misery, stripes, and chains; and, in the first paroxysm of my grief, I called upon God's thunder, and his avenging power, to direct the stroke of death to me, rather than permit me to become a slave, and to be sold from lord to lord.

In this state of my mind our ship came to an anchor, and soon after discharged her cargo. I now knew what it was to work hard; I was made to help to unload and load the ship. And, to comfort me in my distress in that time, two of the sailors robbed me of all my money, and ran away from the ship. I had been so long used to an European climate that at first I felt the scorching West-India sun very painful, while the dashing surf would toss the boat and the people in it frequently above high-water mark. Sometimes our limbs were broken with this, or even attended with instant death, and I was day by day mangled and torn.

About the middle of May, when the ship was got ready to sail for England, I all the time believing that Fate's blackest clouds were gathering over my head, and expecting their bursting would mix me with the dead, captain Doran sent for me ashore one morning, and I was told by the messenger that my fate was then determined. With trembling steps and fluttering heart I came to the captain, and found with him one Mr. Robert King, a quaker and the first merchant in the place.[131] The captain then told me my former master had sent me there to be sold; but that he had desired him to get me the best master he could, as he told him I was a very deserving boy, which Captain Doran said he found to be true, and if he were to stay in the West Indies he would be glad to keep me himself; but he could not venture to take me to London, for he was very sure that when I came there I would leave him. I at that instant burst out a crying, and begged much of him to take me to England with him, but all to no purpose. He told me he had got me the very best master in the whole island, with whom I should be as happy as if I were in England, and for that reason he chose to let him have me, though he could sell me to his own brother-in-law for a great deal more money than what he got from this gentleman. Mr. King, my new master, then made a reply, and said the reason he had bought me was on account of my good character; and, as he had not the least doubt of my good behaviour, I should be very well off with him. He also told me he did not live in the West Indies, but at Philadelphia, where he was going soon; and, as I understood something of the rules of arithmetic, when we got there he would put me to school, and fit me for a clerk. This conversation relieved my mind a little, and I left those gentlemen considerably more at ease in myself than when I came to them; and I was very thankful to Captain Doran, and even to my old master, for the character they had given me; a character which I afterwards found of infinite service to me. I went on board again, and took my leave of all my shipmates; and the next day the ship sailed. When she weighed anchor I went to the waterside and looked at her with a very wishful and aching heart, and followed her with my eyes until she was totally out of sight. I was so bowed down with grief that I could not hold up my head for many months; and if my new master had not been kind to me, I believe I should have died under it at last. And indeed I soon found that he fully deserved the good character which Captain Doran had given me of him; for he possessed a most amiable disposition and temper, and was very charitable and humane. If any of his slaves behaved amiss, he did not beat or use them ill, but parted with them. This made them afraid of disobliging him; and as he treated his slaves better than any other man on the island, so he was better and more faithfully served by them in return. By this kind treatment I did at last endeavour to compose myself; and with fortitude, though moneyless, determined to face whatever fate had decreed for me. Mr. King soon asked me what I could do; and at the same time said he did not mean to treat me as a common slave. I told him I knew something of seamanship, and could shave and dress hair pretty well; and I could refine wines,[132] which I had learned on shipboard, where I had often done it; and that I could write, and understood arithmetic tolerably well as far as the Rule of Three. He then asked me if I knew any thing of gauging; and, on my answering that I did not, he said one of his clerks should teach me to gauge.[133]

Mr. King dealt in all manner of merchandize, and kept from one to six clerks. He loaded many vessels in a year; particularly to Philadelphia, where he was born, and was connected with a great merchantile house in that city. He had besides many vessels and droggers[134] of different sizes, which used to go about the island and other places to collect rum, sugar, and other goods. I understood pulling and managing those boats very well; and this hard work, which was the first that he set me to, in the sugar seasons, used to be my constant employment. I have rowed the boat, and slaved at the oars, from one hour to sixteen in the twenty-four; during which I had fifteen pence sterling per day to live on, though sometimes only ten pence. However, this was considerably more than was allowed to other slaves that used to work often with me, and belonged to other gentlemen on the island: these poor souls had never more than nine-pence a day, and seldom more than six-pence, from their masters or owners, though they earned them three or four pisterines[135] a day: for it is a common practice in the West Indies, for men to purchase slaves, though they have not plantations themselves, in order to let them out to planters and merchants, at so much a-piece by the day, and they give what allowance they choose out of this produce of their daily work to their slaves for subsistence; this allowance is often very scanty. My master often gave the owners of those slaves two and a half of these pieces per day, and found the poor fellows in victuals himself, because he thought their owners did not feed them well enough according to the work they did. The slaves used to like this very well, and as they knew my master to be a man of feeling,[136] they were always glad to work for him in preference to any other gentleman; some of whom, after they had been paid for these poor people's labours, would not give them their allowance out of it. Many times have I seen these unfortunate wretches beaten for asking for their pay; and often severely flogged by their owners if they did not bring them their daily or weekly money exactly to the time; though the poor creatures were obliged to wait on the gentlemen they had worked for, sometimes more than half the day, before they could get their pay; and this generally on Sundays, when they wanted the time for themselves. In particular, I knew a countryman of mine, who once did not bring the weekly money directly that it was earned; and though he brought it the same day to his master, yet he was staked to the ground for his pretended negligence, and was just going to receive a hundred lashes, but for a gentleman who begged him off fifty. This poor man was very industrious, and by his frugality had saved so much money, by working on shipboard, that he had got a white man to buy him a boat, unknown to his master. Some time after he had this little estate, the governor wanted a boat to bring his sugar from different parts of the island; and, knowing this to be a negro-man's boat, he seized upon it for himself, and would not pay the owner a farthing.[137] The man on this went to his master, and complained to him of this act of the governor; but the only satisfaction he received was to be damned very heartily by his master, who asked him how dared any of his negroes to have a boat. If the justly-merited ruin of the governor's fortune could be any gratification to the poor man he had thus robbed, he was not without consolation. Extortion and rapine are poor providers; and some time after this, the governor died in the King's Bench, in England, as I was told, in great poverty.[138] The last war favoured this poor negro-man,[139] and he found some means to escape from his Christian master;[140] he came to England, where I saw him afterwards several times. Such treatment as this often drives these miserable wretches to despair, and they run away from their masters at the hazard of their lives. Many of them in this place, unable to get their pay when they have earned it, and fearing to be flogged as usual, if they return home without it, run away where they can for shelter, and a reward is often offered to bring them in dead or alive. My master used sometimes in these cases, to agree with their owners, and to settle with them himself; and thereby he saved many of them a flogging.

Once, for a few days, I was let out to fit a vessel, and I had no victuals allowed me by either party; at last I told my master of this treatment, and he took me away from him. In many of the estates, on the different islands where I used to be sent for rum or sugar, they would not deliver it to me, or to any other negro; he was therefore obliged to send a white man along with me to those places; and then he used to pay him from six to ten pisterines a day. From being thus employed, during the time I served Mr. King, in going about the different estates on the island, I had all the opportunity I could wish for, to see the dreadful usage of the poor men; usage that reconciled me to my situation, and made me bless God for the hands into which I had fallen.

I had the good fortune to please my master in every department in which he employed me; and there was scarcely any part of his business, or household affairs, in which I was not occasionally engaged. I often supplied the place of a clerk, in receiving and delivering cargoes to the ships, in tending stores, and delivering goods; and, besides this, I used to shave and dress my master when convenient, and take care of his horse; and when it was necessary, which was very often, I worked likewise on board of different vessels of his. By these means I became very useful to my master, and saved him, as he used to acknowledge, above a hundred pounds a year. Nor did he scruple to say I was of more advantage to him than any of his clerks; though their usual wages in the West Indies are from sixty to a hundred pounds current a year.

I have sometimes heard it asserted, that a negro cannot earn his master the first cost;[141] but nothing can be further from the truth. I suppose nine tenths of the mechanics throughout the West Indies are negro slaves; and I well know the coopers among them earn two dollars a day;[142] the carpenters the same, and oftentimes more; also the masons, smiths, and fishermen, &c. and I have known many slaves whose masters would not take a thousand pounds current for them.[143] But surely this assertion refutes itself; for, if it be true, why do the planters and merchants pay such a price for slaves? And, above all, why do those, who make this assertion, exclaim the most loudly against the abolition of the slave trade? So much are we blinded, and to such inconsistent arguments are they driven by mistaken interest! I grant, indeed, that slaves are sometimes, by half-feeding, half-cloathing, over-working, and stripes,[144] reduced so low, that they are turned out as unfit for service, and left to perish in the woods, or expire on a dunghill.

My master was several times offered by different gentlemen one hundred guineas for me; but he always told them he would not sell me, to my great joy: and I used to double my diligence and care for fear of getting into the hands of those men who did not allow a valuable slave the common support of life. Many of them used to find fault with my master for feeding his slaves so well as he did; although I often went hungry, and an Englishman might think my fare very indifferent; but he used to tell them he always would do it, because the slaves thereby looked better and did more work.

While I was thus employed by my master, I was often a witness to cruelties of every kind, which were exercised on my unhappy fellow slaves. I used frequently to have different cargoes of new negroes in my care for sale; and it was almost a constant practice with our clerks, and other whites, to commit violent depredations on the chastity of the female slaves; and these I was, though with reluctance, obliged to submit to at all times, being unable to help them. When we have had some of these slaves on board my master's vessels to carry them to other islands, or to America, I have known our mates to commit these acts most shamefully, to the disgrace, not of Christians only, but of men. I have even known them gratify their brutal passion with females not ten years old; and these abominations some of them practised to such scandalous excess, that one of our captains discharged the mate and others on that account. And yet in Montserrat I have seen a negro-man staked to the ground, and cut most shockingly,[145] and then his ears cut off bit by bit, because he had been connected with a white woman who was a common prostitute: as if it were no crime in the whites to rob an innocent African girl of her virtue; but most heinous in a black man only to gratify a passion of nature, where the temptation was offered by one of a different colour, though the most abandoned woman of her species.

One Mr. Drummond told me that he had sold 41,000 negroes, and that he once cut off a negro-man's leg for running away.—I asked him, if the man had died in the operation? How he, as a Christian, could answer for the horrid act before God? And he told me, answering was a thing of another world; but what he thought and did were policy. I told him that the Christian doctrine taught us to do unto others as we would that others should do unto us. He then said that his scheme had the desired effect—it cured that man and some others of running away.

Another negro man was half hanged, and then burnt, for attempting to poison a cruel overseer. Thus by repeated cruelties are the wretched first urged to despair, and then murdered, because they still retain so much of human nature about them as to wish to put an end to their misery, and retaliate on their tyrants! These overseers are indeed for the most part persons of the worst character of any denomination of men in the West Indies. Unfortunately, many humane gentlemen, by not residing on their estates, are obliged to leave the management of them in the hands of these human butchers, who cut and mangle the slaves in a shocking manner on the most trifling occasions, and altogether treat them in every respect like brutes. They pay no regard to the situation of pregnant women, nor the least attention to the lodging of the field-negroes. Their huts, which ought to be well covered, and the place dry where they take their little repose, are often open sheds, built in damp places; so that, when the poor creatures return tired from the toils of the field, they contract many disorders, from being exposed to the damp air in this uncomfortable state, while they are heated, and their pores are open. This neglect certainly conspires with many others to cause a decrease in the births as well as in the lives of the grown negroes. I can quote many instances of gentlemen who reside on their estates in the West Indies, and then the scene is quite changed; the negroes are treated with lenity and proper care, by which their lives are prolonged, and their masters are profited. To the honour of humanity, I knew several gentlemen who managed their estates in this manner; and they found that benevolence was their true interest. And, among many I could mention in several of the islands, I knew one in Montserrat[146] whose slaves looked remarkably well, and never needed any fresh supplies of negroes; and there are many other estates, especially in Barbadoes, which, from such judicious treatment, need no fresh stock of negroes at any time. I have the honour of knowing a most worthy and humane gentleman, who is a native of Barbadoes, and has estates there.[147] This gentleman has written a treatise on the usage of his own slaves. He allows them two hours for refreshment at mid day; and many other indulgencies and comforts, particularly in their lying;[148] and, besides this, he raises more provisions on his estate than they can destroy; so that by these attentions he saves the lives of his negroes, and keeps them healthy, and as happy as the condition of slavery can admit. I myself, as shall appear in the sequel, managed an estate, where, by those attentions, the negroes were uncommonly cheerful and healthy, and did more work by half than by the common mode of treatment they usually do. "For want, therefore, of such care and attention to the poor negroes, and otherwise oppressed as they are, it is no wonder that the decrease should require 20,000 new negroes annually to fill up the vacant places of the dead.

"Even in Barbadoes, notwithstanding those humane exceptions which I have mentioned, and others I am acquainted with, which justly make it quoted as a place where slaves meet with the best treatment, and need fewest recruits of any in the West Indies, yet this island requires 1000 negroes annually to keep up the original stock, which is only 80,000. So that the whole term of a negro's life may be said to be there but sixteen years![149] and yet the climate here is in every respect the same as that from which they are taken, except in being more wholesome."[150] Do the British colonies decrease in this manner? And yet what a prodigious difference is there between an English and West India climate.

While I was in Montserrat, I knew a negro man, named Emanuel Sankey, who endeavoured to escape from his miserable bondage, by concealing himself on board of a London ship: but fate did not favour the poor oppressed man; for being discovered when the vessel was under sail, he was delivered up again to his master. This *Christian master* immediately pinned the wretch down to the ground at each wrist and ankle, and then took some sticks of sealing-wax, and lighted them, and dropped it all over his back.[151] There was another master who was noted for cruelty, and I believe he had not a slave but what had been cut, and had pieces fairly taken out of the flesh: and after they had been punished thus, he used to make them get into a long wooden box or case he had for that purpose, in which he shut them up during pleasure.[152] It was just about the height and breadth of a man; and the poor wretches had no room when in the case to move.

It was very common in several of the islands, particularly in St. Kitt's, for the slaves to be branded with the initial letters of their master's name, and a load of heavy iron hooks hung about their necks. Indeed, on the most trifling occasions they were loaded with chains, and often other instruments of torture were added. The iron muzzle, thumb-screws, &c. are so well known, as not to need a description, and were sometimes applied for the slightest faults. I have seen a negro beaten till some of his bones were broken, for only letting a pot boil over. It is not uncommon, after a flogging, to make slaves go on their knees, and thank their owners, and pray, or rather say, God bless them. I have often asked many of the men slaves (who used to go several miles to their wives, and late in the night, after having been wearied with a hard day's labour) why they went so far for wives, and why they did not take them of their own master's negro women, and particularly those who lived together as household slaves? Their answers have ever been—"Because when the master or mistress choose to punish the women, they make the husbands flog their own wives, and that they could not bear to do." Is it surprising that usage like this should drive the poor creatures to despair, and make them seek a refuge in death from those evils which render their lives intolerable—while,

> With shudd'ring horror pale, and eyes aghast,
> They view their lamentable lot, and find
> No rest![153]

This they frequently do. A negro man on board a vessel of my master's, while I belonged to her, having been put in irons for some trifling misdemeanor, and kept in that state for some days, being weary of life, took an opportunity of jumping overboard into the sea; however, he was picked up without being drowned. Another, whose life was also a burden to him, resolved to starve himself to death, and refused to eat any victuals: this procured him a severe flogging; and he also, on the first occasion which offered, jumped overboard at Charles Town,[154] but was saved.

Nor is there any greater regard shewn to the little property than there is to the persons and lives of the negroes. I have already related an instance or two of particular oppression out of many which I have witnessed; but the following is frequent in all the islands. The wretched field slaves, after toiling all the day for an unfeeling owner, who gives them but little victuals, steal sometimes a few moments from rest or refreshment to gather some small portion of grass, according as their time will admit. This they commonly tie up in a parcel; either a bit's worth (six-pence)[155] or half a bit's worth; and bring it to town, or to the market, to sell. Nothing is more common than for the white people on this occasion to take the grass from them without paying for it; and not only so, but too often also to my knowledge, our clerks, and many others, at the same time, have committed acts of violence on the poor, wretched, and helpless females, whom I have seen for hours stand crying to no purpose, and get no redress or pay of any kind. Is not this one common and crying sin, enough to bring down God's judgment on the islands? He tells us, the oppressor and the oppressed are both in his hands; and if these are not the poor, the broken-hearted, the blind, the captive, the bruised, which our Saviour speaks of, who are they? One of these depredators once, in St. Eustatia, came on board of our vessel, and bought some fowls and pigs of me; and a whole day after his departure with the things, he returned again and wanted his money back: I refused to give it, and, not seeing my captain on board, he began the common pranks with me; and swore he would even break open my chest and take my money. I therefore expected, as my captain was absent, that he would be as good as his word; and he was just proceeding to strike me, when fortunately a British seaman on board, whose heart had not been debauched by a West India climate, interposed and prevented him. But had the cruel man struck me, I certainly should have defended myself at the hazard of my life; for what is life to a man thus oppressed? He went away, however, swearing; and threatened that whenever he caught me on shore he would shoot me, and pay for me afterwards.

The small account in which the life of a negro is held in the West Indies is so universally known, that it might seem impertinent to quote the following extract, if some people had not been hardy enough of late to assert that negroes are on the same footing in that respect as Europeans. By the 329th Act, page 125, of the Assembly of Barbadoes, it is enacted, "That if any negro, or other slave, under punishment by his master, or his order, for running away, or any other crime or misdemeanor towards his said master, unfortunately shall suffer in life or member, no person whatsoever shall be liable to a fine; but if any man shall out of *wantonness, or only of bloody-mindedness, or cruel intention, wilfully kill a negro, or other slave, of his own, he shall pay into the public treasury fifteen pounds sterling*."[156] And it is the same in most, if not all, of the West India islands. Is not this one of the many acts of the islands which call loudly for redress? And do not the assembly which enacted it, deserve the appellation of savages and brutes rather than of Christians and men? It is an act at once unmerciful, unjust, and unwise; which for cruelty would disgrace an assembly of those who are called barbarians; and for its injustice and *insanity* would shock the morality and common sense of a Samaide or a Hottentot.[157]

Shocking as this and many other acts of the bloody West India code at first view appear, how is the iniquity of it heightened when we consider to whom it may be extended. Mr. James Tobin, a zealous labourer in the vineyard of slavery, gives an account[158] of a French planter, of his acquaintance, in the island of Martinico, who shewed him many Mulattoes working in the fields like beasts of burden; and he told Mr. Tobin, these were all the produce of his own loins! And I myself have known similar instances. Pray, reader, are these sons and daughters of the French planter less his children by being begotten on black women! And what must be the virtue of those legislators, and the feelings of those fathers, who estimate the lives of their sons, however begotten, at no more than fifteen pounds, though they should be murdered, as the act says, *out of wantonness and bloody-mindedness*? But is not the slave trade entirely at war with the heart of man? And surely that which is begun, by breaking down the barriers of virtue, involves in its continuance destruction to every principle, and buries all sentiments in ruin!

I have often seen slaves, particularly those who were meagre, in different islands, put into scales and weighed, and then sold from three-pence to six-pence, or nine-pence a pound. My master, however, whose humanity was shocked at this mode, used to sell such by the lump. And at or after a sale, even those negroes born in the islands, it is not uncommon to see taken from their wives, wives taken from their husbands, and children from their parents, and sent off to other islands, and wherever else their merciless lords choose; and probably never more during life see each other! Oftentimes my heart has bled at these partings; when the friends of the departed have been at the water-side, and with sighs and tears have kept their eyes fixed on the vessel till it went out of sight.

A poor Creole negro I knew well, who, after having often been thus transported from island to island, at last resided in Montserrat. This man used to tell me many melancholy tales of himself. Generally, after he had done working for his master, he used to employ his few leisure moments to go a fishing. When he had caught any fish, his master would frequently take them from him without paying him; and at other times some other white people would serve him in the same manner. One day he said to me, very movingly, "Sometimes when a white man take away my fish, I go to my master, and he get me my right; and when my master, by strength, take away my fishes, what me must do? I can't go to any body to be righted"; then, said the poor man, looking up above, "I must look up to God Mighty in the top for right." This artless tale moved me much, and I could not help feeling the just cause Moses had in redressing his brother against the Egyptian.[159] I exhorted the man to look up still to the God in the top, since there was no redress below. Though I little thought then that I myself should more than once experience such imposition, and need the same exhortation hereafter, in my own transactions in the islands; and that even this poor man and I should some time after suffer together in the same manner, as shall be related hereafter.

Nor was such usage as this confined to particular places or individuals; for, in all the different islands in which I have been (and I have visited no less than fifteen) the treatment of the slaves was nearly the same; so nearly indeed, that the history of an island, or even a plantation, with a few such exceptions as I have mentioned, might serve for a history of the whole. Such a tendency has the slave-trade to debauch men's minds, and harden them to every feeling of humanity! For I will not suppose that the dealers in slaves are born worse than other men—No! it is the fatality of this mistaken avarice, that it corrupts the milk of human kindness, and turns it into gall. And, had the pursuits of those men been different, they might have been as generous, as tender-hearted, and just, as they are unfeeling, rapacious, and cruel. Surely this traffic cannot be good, which spreads like a pestilence, and taints what it touches! Which violates that first natural right of mankind, equality and independency, and gives one man a dominion over his fellows which God could never intend! For it raises the owner to a state as far above man as it depresses the slave below it; and, with all the presumption of human pride, sets a distinction between them, immeasurable in extent, and endless in duration! Yet how mistaken is the avarice even of the planters. Are slaves more useful by being thus humbled to the condition of brutes, than they would be if suffered to enjoy the privileges of men? The freedom which diffuses health and prosperity throughout Britain answers you—No. When you make men slaves, you deprive them of half their virtue, you set them, in your own conduct, an example of fraud, rapine, and cruelty, and compel them to live with you in a state of war; and yet you complain that they are not honest or faithful! You stupify them with stripes, and think it necessary to keep them in a state of ignorance; and yet you assert that they are incapable of learning; that their minds are such a barren soil or moor, that culture would be lost on them; and that they came from a climate, where nature (though prodigal of her bounties in a degree unknown to yourselves) has left man alone scant and unfinished, and incapable of enjoying the treasures she has poured out for him! An assertion at once impious and absurd.[160] Why do you use those instruments of torture? Are they fit to be applied by one rational being to another? And are ye not struck with shame and mortification, to see the partakers of your nature reduced so low? But, above all, are there no dangers attending this mode of treatment? Are you not hourly in dread of an insurrection? Nor would it be surprising; for when

> ... No peace is given
> To us enslav'd, but custody severe;
> And stripes and arbitrary punishment
> Inflicted—What peace can we return?
> But to our power, hostility and hate;
> Untam'd reluctance, and revenge, tho' slow,
> Yet ever plotting how the conqueror least
> May reap his conquest, and may least rejoice
> In doing what we most in suff'ring feel.[161]

But, by changing your conduct, and treating your slaves as men, every cause of fear would be banished. They would be faithful, honest, intelligent and vigorous; and peace, prosperity, and happiness would attend you.

CHAPTER VI

IN the preceding chapter I have set before the reader a few of those many instances of oppression, extortion and cruelty, to which I have been a witness in the West Indies; but, were I to enumerate them all, the catalogue would be tedious and disgusting. The punishments of the slaves, on every trifling occasion, are so frequent, and so well known, together with the different instruments with which they are tortured, that it cannot any longer afford novelty to recite them; and they are too shocking to yield delight either to the writer or the reader. I shall therefore hereafter only mention such as incidentally befel myself in the course of my adventures.

In the variety of departments in which I was employed by my master, I had an opportunity of seeing many curious scenes in different islands; but, above all, I was struck with a celebrated curiosity called Brimstone-Hill, which is a high and steep mountain, some few miles from the town of Plymouth, in Montserrat.[162] I had often heard of some wonders that were to be seen on this hill, and I went once with some white and black people to visit it. When we arrived at the top, I saw under different cliffs great flakes of brimstone, occasioned by the steams of various little ponds, which were then boiling naturally in the earth. Some of these ponds were as white as milk, some quite blue, and many others of different colours. I had taken some potatoes with me, and I put them into different ponds, and in a few minutes they were well boiled. I tasted some of them, but they were very sulphurous; and the silver shoe-buckles, and all the other things we had among us of that metal, were, in a little time, turned as black as lead.

Whilst I was in the island, one night I felt a strange sensation, viz. I was told that the house where I lived was haunted by spirits. And once, at midnight, as I was sleeping on a large chest, I felt the whole building shake in an uncommon and astonishing manner; so much so, that it shook me off the chest where I then lay; I was exceedingly frightened, and thought it was the visitation of the spirits. It threw me into such a tremor as is not to be described. I instantly covered my head all over as I lay, and did not know what to think or do; and in this consternation, a gentleman, who lay in the next room just by me came out, and I was glad to hear him, and made a sham cough, and he asked me, if I felt the earthquake. I told him I was shook off the chest where I lay, but did not know what occasioned it; and he told me it was an earthquake, and shook him out of his bed. At hearing this I became easy in my mind.

At another time a circumstance of this kind happened, when I was on board of a vessel in Montserrat-road, at midnight, as we were asleep, and it shook the vessel in the most unaccountable manner imaginable, and to me it seemed as when a vessel or a boat runs on gravel, as near as I can describe it. Many things on board were moved out of their places, but happily no damage was done.

About the end of the year 1763, kind Providence seemed to be rather more favourable to me. One of my master's vessels, a Bermudas sloop, about sixty tons burthen, was commanded by one Captain Thomas Farmer, an Englishman, a very alert and active man, who gained my master a great deal of money by his good management in carrying passengers from one island to another; but very often his sailors used to get drunk, and run away with the vessel's boat, which hindered him in his business very much. This man had taken a liking to me; and had many different times begged of my master to let me go a trip with him as a sailor: but he would tell him he could not spare me, though the vessel sometimes could not go for want of hands, for sailors were generally very scarce in the island. However, at last, from necessity, or force, my master was prevailed on, though very reluctantly, to let me go with this captain; but he gave him great charge to take care that I did not run away; for, if I did, he would make him pay for me. This being the case, the captain had for some time a sharp eye upon me whenever the vessel anchored: and as soon as she returned I was sent for on shore again. Thus was I slaving, as it were for life, sometimes at one thing, and sometimes at another; so that the captain and I were nearly the most useful men in my master's employment. I also became so useful to the captain on ship board, that many times, when he used to ask for me to go with him, though it should be but twenty-four hours, to some of the islands near us, my master would answer he could not spare me; at which the captain would swear, and would not go the trip, and tell my master that I was better to him on board than any three white men he had; for they used to behave ill in many respects, particularly in getting drunk, and then they frequently got the boat stove,[163] so as to hinder the vessel from coming back so soon as she might have done. This my master knew very well; and, at last, by the captain's constant entreaties, after I had been several times with him, one day, to my great joy, told me the captain would not let him rest, and asked whether I would go aboard as a sailor, or stay on shore and mind the stores, for he could not bear any longer to be plagued in this manner. I was very happy at this proposal, for I immediately thought I might in time stand a chance by being on board to get a little money, or possibly make my escape if I should be used ill: I also expected to get better food, and in greater abundance; for I had oftentimes felt much hunger, though my master treated his slaves, as I have observed, uncommonly well; I therefore, without hesitation, answered him, that I would go and be a sailor if he pleased. Accordingly I was ordered on board directly. Nevertheless, between the vessel and the shore, when she was in port, I had little or no rest, as my master always wished to have me along with him. Indeed he was a very pleasant gentleman, and but for my expectations on shipboard I should not have thought of leaving him. But the captain liked me also very much, and I was entirely his right-hand man. I did all I could to deserve his favour, and in return I received better treatment from him than any other I believe ever met with in the West-Indies in my situation.

After I had been sailing for some time with this captain, I at length endeavoured to try my luck and commence merchant. I had but a very small capital to begin with; for one single half bit, which is equal to three pence in England, made up my whole stock. However I trusted to the Lord to be with me; and at one of our trips to *St. Eustatia*, a Dutch island, I bought a glass tumbler with my half bit, and when I came to Montserrat I sold it for a bit, or sixpence. Luckily we made several successive trips to St. Eustatia (which was a general mart for the West Indies, about twenty leagues from Montserrat), and in our next, finding my tumbler so profitable, with this one bit I bought two tumblers more; and when I came back I sold them for two bits, equal to a shilling sterling. When we went again, I bought with these two bits four more of these glasses, which I sold for four bits on our return to Montserrat; and in our next voyage to St. Eustatia, I bought two glasses with one bit, and with the other three I bought a jug of Geneva,[164] nearly about three pints in measure. When we came to Montserrat I sold the gin for eight bits, and the tumblers for two, so that my capital now amounted in all to a dollar, well husbanded and acquired in the space of a month or six weeks, when I blessed the Lord that I was so rich. As we sailed to different islands, I laid this money out in various things occasionally, and it used to turn out to very good account, especially when we went to Guadaloupe, Grenada, and the rest of the French islands. Thus was I going all about the islands upwards of four years, and ever trading as I went, during which I experienced many instances of ill usage, and have seen many injuries done to other negroes in our dealings with whites; and, amidst our recreations, when we have been dancing and merry-making, they, without cause, have molested and insulted us. Indeed I was more than once obliged to look up to God on high, as I had advised the poor fisherman some time before. And I had not been long trading for myself in the manner I have related above, when I experienced the like trial in company with him as follows: This man being used to the water, was upon an emergency put on board of us by his master to work as another hand, on a voyage to Santa Cruz; and at our sailing he had brought his little all for a venture, which consisted of six bits worth of limes and oranges in a bag; I had also my whole stock; which was about twelve bits' worth of the same kind of goods, separate in two bags; for we had heard these fruits sold well in that island. When we came there, in some little convenient time, he and I went ashore with our fruits to sell them; but we had scarcely landed, when we were met by two white men, who presently[165] took our three bags from us. We could not at first guess what they meant to do, and for some time we thought they were jesting with us; but they too soon let us know otherwise; for they took our ventures immediately to a house hard by adjoining the fort, while we followed all the way begging of them to give us our fruits, but in vain. They not only refused to return them, but swore at us, and threatened if we did not immediately depart, they would flog us well. We told them these three bags were all we were worth in the world; and that we brought them with us to sell when we came from Montserrat, and shewed them the vessel. But this was rather against us, as they now saw we were strangers as well as slaves. They still therefore swore, and desired us to be gone; and even took sticks to beat us; while we, seeing they meant what they said, went off in the greatest confusion and despair. Thus, in the very minute of gaining more by three times than I ever did by any venture in my life before, was I deprived of every farthing I was worth. An insupportable misfortune! but how to help ourselves we knew not. In our consternation we went to the commanding officer of the fort, and told him how we had been served by some of his people; but we obtained not the least redress: he answered our complaints only by a volley of imprecations against us, and immediately took a horse-whip, in order to chastise us, so that we were obliged to turn out much faster than we came in. I now, in the agony of distress and indignation, wished that the ire of God, in his forked lightning, might transfix these cruel oppressors among the dead. Still, however, we persevered;

went back again to the house, and begged and besought them again and again for our fruits, till at last some other people that were in the house asked if we would be contented if they kept one bag, and gave us the other two. We, seeing no remedy whatever, consented to this; and they, observing one bag to have both kinds of fruit in it, which belonged to my companion, kept that; and the other two, which were mine, they gave us back. As soon as I got them, I ran as fast as I could and got the first negro man I could to help me off; my companion, however, stayed a little longer to plead; he told them the bag they had was his, and likewise all that he was worth in the world; but this was of no avail, and he was obliged to return without it. The poor old man, wringing his hands, cried bitterly for his loss; and, indeed, he then did look up to God on high, which so moved me with pity for him, that I gave him nearly one third of my fruits. We then proceeded to the market to sell them; and Providence was more favourable to us than we could have expected, for we sold our fruits uncommonly well; I got for mine about thirty-seven bits. Such a surprising reverse of fortune in so short a space of time seemed like a dream to me, and proved no small encouragement for me to trust the Lord in any situation. My captain afterwards frequently used to take my part, and get me my right when I have been plundered or used ill by these tender Christian depredators; among whom I have shuddered to observe the unceasing blasphemous execrations which are wantonly thrown out by persons of all ages and conditions; not only without occasion, but even as if they were indulgencies and pleasures.

At one of our trips to St. Kitt's, I had eleven bits of my own; and my friendly captain lent me five bits more, with which I bought a Bible. I was very glad to get this book, which I scarcely could meet with any where. I think there was none sold in Montserrat;[166] and, much to my grief, from being forced out of the Aetna in the manner I have related, my Bible, and the Guide to the Indians, the two books I loved above all others, were left behind.

While I was in this place, St. Kitt's, a very curious imposition on human nature took place:—A white man wanted to marry in the church a free black woman that had land and slaves at Montserrat: but the clergyman told him it was against the law of the place to marry a white and a black in the church. The man then asked to be married on the water, to which the parson consented, and the two lovers went in one boat, and the parson and clerk in another, and thus the ceremony was performed. After this the loving pair came on board our vessel, and my captain treated them extremely well, and brought them safe to Montserrat.

The reader cannot but judge of the irksomeness of this situation to a mind like mine, in being daily exposed to new hardships and impositions, after having seen many better days, and been, as it were, in a state of freedom and plenty; added to which, every part of the world in which I had hitherto been in seemed to me a paradise in comparison of the West-Indies. My mind was therefore hourly replete with inventions and thoughts of being freed, and, if possible, by honest and honourable means; for I always remembered the old adage, and I trust that it has ever been my ruling principle, "that Honesty is the best policy"; and likewise that other golden precept—"To do unto all men as I would they should do unto me." However, as I was from early years a predestinarian,[167] I thought whatever fate had determined must ever come to pass; and therefore, if ever it were my lot to be freed, nothing could prevent me, although I should at present see no means or hope to obtain my freedom; on the other hand, if it were my fate not to be freed, I never should be so, and all my endeavours for that purpose would be fruitless. In the midst of these thoughts I therefore looked up with prayers anxiously to God for my liberty; and at the same time used every honest means, and did all that was possible on my part to obtain it. In process of time I became master of a few pounds, and in a fair way of making more, which my friendly captain knew very well: this occasioned him sometimes to take liberties with me; but whenever he treated me waspishly, I used plainly to tell him my mind, and that I would die before I would be imposed upon as other negroes were, and that to me life had lost its relish when liberty was gone. This I said, although I foresaw my then well-being or future hopes of freedom (humanly speaking) depended on this man. However, as he could not bear the thoughts of my not sailing with him, he always became mild on my threats: I therefore continued with him; and, from my great attention to his orders and his business, I gained him credit, and, through his kindness to me, I at last procured my liberty. While I thus went on, filled with the thoughts of freedom, and resisting oppression as well as I was able, my life hung daily in suspense, particularly in the surfs I have formerly mentioned, as I could not swim. These are extremely violent throughout the West-Indies, and I was ever exposed to their howling rage and devouring fury in all the islands. I have seen them strike and toss a boat right up on end, and maim several on board. Once in the island of Grenada, when I and about eight others were pulling a large boat with two puncheons[168] of water in it, a surf struck us, and drove the boat and all in it about half a stone's throw among some trees, and above the high-water mark. We were obliged to get all the assistance we could from the nearest estate to mend the boat, and launch it into the water again. At Montserrat one night, in pressing hard to get off the shore on board, the punt[169] was overset with us four times; the first time I was very near being drowned; however, the jacket I had on kept me above water a little space of time, while I called on a man near me who was a good swimmer, and told him I could not swim; he then made haste to me, and, just as I was sinking, he caught hold of me and brought me to sounding,[170] and then he went and brought the punt also. As soon as we turned the water out of her, lest we should be used ill for being absent, we attempted again three times more, and as often the horrid surfs served us as at first; but at last, the fifth time we attempted, we gained our point, at the imminent hazard of our lives. One day also, at Old Road, in Montserrat, our captain and three men besides myself, were going in a large canoe in quest of rum and sugar, when a single surf tossed the canoe an amazing distance from the water, and some of us near a stone's throw from each other; most of us were very much bruised; so that I and many more often said, and really thought, that there was not such another place under the heavens as this. I longed, therefore, much to leave it, and daily wished to see my master's promise performed of going to Philadelphia.

While we lay in this place, a very cruel thing happened on board of our sloop, which filled me with horror; though I found afterwards such practices were frequent. There was a very clever and decent free young mulatto-man who sailed a long time with us; he had a free woman for his wife, by whom he had a child; and she was then living on shore, and all very happy. Our captain and mate, and other people on board, and several elsewhere, even the natives of Bermudas, then with us, all knew this young man from a child that he was always free, and no one had ever claimed him as their property: however, as might too often overcomes right in these parts, it happened that a Bermudas captain, whose vessel lay there for a few days in the road, came on board of us, and seeing the mulatto-man, whose name was Joseph Clipson, he told him he was not free, and that he had orders from his master to bring him to Bermudas. The poor man could not believe the captain to be in earnest; but he was very soon undeceived, his men laying violent hands on him; and although he shewed a certificate of his being born free in St. Kitt's, and most people on board knew that he served his time[171] to boat building and always passed for a free man, yet he was forcibly taken out of our vessel. He then asked to be carried ashore, before the secretary or magistrates, and these infernal invaders of human rights promised him he should; but, instead of that, they carried him on board of the other vessel; and the next day, without giving the poor man any hearing on shore, or suffering him even to see his wife or child, he was carried away, and probably doomed never more in this world to see them again. Nor was this the only instance of this kind of barbarity I was a witness to. I have since often seen in Jamaica, and other islands, free men, whom I have known in America, thus villainously trepanned and held in bondage. I have heard of two similar practices even in Philadelphia: and were it not for the benevolence of the quakers in that city, many of the sable race, who now breathe the air of liberty, would, I believe, be groaning under some planter's chains. These things opened my mind to a new scene of horror, to which I had been before a stranger. Hitherto I had thought only slavery dreadful; but the state of a free negro appeared to me now equally so at least, and in some respects even worse, for they live in constant alarm for their liberty, which is but nominal, for they are universally insulted and plundered without the possibility of redress; for such is the equity of the West Indian laws, that no free negro's evidence will be admitted in their courts of justice. In this situation, is it surprising that slaves, when mildly treated, should prefer even the misery of slavery to such a mockery of freedom? I was now completely disgusted with the West Indies, and thought I never should be entirely free till I had left them.

> With thoughts like these my anxious boding mind
> Recall'd those pleasing scenes I left behind;
> Scenes where fair Liberty, in bright array
> Makes darkness bright, and e'en illumines day;
> Where no complexion, wealth, or station can
> Protect the wretch who makes a slave of man.[172]

I determined to make every exertion to obtain my freedom, and to return to Old England. For this purpose, I thought a knowledge of navigation might be of use to me; for, though I did not intend to run away unless I should be ill used, yet, in such a case, if I understood navigation, I might attempt my escape in our sloop, which was one of the swiftest sailing vessels in the West Indies, and I could be at no loss for hands to join me: and, if I should make this attempt, I had intended to have gone for England; but this, as I said, was only to be in the event of my meeting with any ill usage. I therefore employed the mate of our vessel to teach me navigation, for which I agreed to give him twenty four dollars, and actually paid him part of the money down; though, when the captain, some time after, came to know that the mate was to have such a sum for teaching me, he rebuked him, and said it was a shame for him to take any money from me. However, my progress in this useful art was much retarded by the constancy of our work. Had I wished to run away, I did not want opportunities, which frequently presented themselves; and particularly at one time, soon after this. When we were at the island of Guadaloupe there was a large fleet of merchantmen bound for Old France; and, seamen then being very scarce, they gave from fifteen to twenty pounds a man for the run. Our mate, and all the white sailors, left our vessel on this account, and went on board of the French ships. They would have had me also gone with them, for they regarded me, and swore to protect me, if I would go; and, as the fleet was to sail the next day, I really believe I could have got safe to Europe at that time. However, as my master was kind, I would not attempt to leave him; still remembering the old maxim, that "honesty is the best policy," I suffered them to go without me. Indeed my captain was much afraid of my leaving him and the vessel at that time, as I had so fair an opportunity: but I thank God, this fidelity of mine turned out much to my advantage hereafter, when I did not in the least think of it; and made me so much in favour with the captain, that he used now and then to teach me some parts of navigation himself. But some of our passengers, and others, seeing this, found much fault with him for it, saying, it was a very dangerous thing to let a negro know navigation; thus I was hindered again in my pursuits. About the latter end of the year 1764, my master bought a larger sloop, called the Prudence, about seventy or eighty tons, of which my captain had the command. I went with him into this vessel, and we took a load of new slaves for Georgia and Charles Town. My master now left me entirely to the captain, though he still wished me to be with him; but I, who always much wished to lose sight of the West Indies, was not a little rejoiced at the thoughts of seeing any other country. Therefore, relying on the goodness of my captain, I got ready all the little venture I could; and, when the vessel was ready, we sailed to my great joy. When we got to our destined places, Georgia and Charles Town, I expected I should have an opportunity of selling my little property to advantage; but here, particularly in Charles Town, I met with buyers, white men, who imposed on me as in other places. Notwithstanding, I was resolved to have fortitude: thinking no lot or trial too hard when kind Heaven is the rewarder.

We soon got loaded again, and returned to Montserrat; and there, among the rest of the islands, I sold my goods well; and in this manner I continued trading during the year 1764; meeting with various scenes of imposition, as usual. After this, my master fitted out his vessel for Philadelphia, in the year 1765; and during the time of loading her, and getting ready for the voyage, I worked with double alacrity, from the hope of getting money enough by these voyages to buy my freedom, if it should please God; and also to see the city of Philadelphia, which I had heard a great deal about for some years past; besides which, I had always longed to prove[173] my master's promise the first day I came to him. In the midst of these elevated ideas, and while I was about getting my little merchandise in readiness, one Sunday my master sent for me to his house. When I came there I found him and the captain together; and, on my going in, I was struck with astonishment at his telling me he heard that I meant to run away from him when I got to Philadelphia: "And therefore," said he "I must sell you again: you cost me a great deal of money, no less than forty pounds sterling; and it will not do to lose so much. You are a valuable fellow," continued he, "and I can get any day for you one hundred guineas, from many gentlemen in this island." And then he told me of Captain Doran's brother-in-law, a severe master, who ever wanted to buy me to make me his overseer. My captain also said, he could get much more than a hundred guineas for me in Carolina. This I knew to be a fact: for the gentleman that wanted to buy me, came off several times on board of us, and spoke to me to live with him, and said he would use me well. When I asked what work he would put me to, he said, as I was a sailor, he would make me a captain of one of his rice vessels. But I refused; and fearing, at the same time, by a sudden turn I saw in the captain's temper, he might mean to sell me, I told the gentleman I would not live with him on any condition, and that I certainly would run away with his vessel: but he said he did not fear that, as he would catch me again: and then he told me how cruelly he would serve me if I should do so. My captain, however, gave him to understand that I knew something of navigation: so he thought better of it; and, to my great joy, he went away. I now told my master, I did not say I would run away in Philadelphia, neither did I mean it, as he did not use me ill, nor yet the captain: for if they did, I certainly would have made some attempts before now; but as I thought that if it were God's will I ever should be freed it would be so; and, on the contrary, if it was not his will it would not happen; so I hoped, if ever I were freed, whilst I was used well, it should be by honest means; but as I could not help myself, he must do as he please! I could only hope and trust in the God of heaven; and at that instant my mind was big with inventions, and full of schemes to escape. I then appealed to the captain, whether ever he saw any sign of my making the least attempt to run away; and asked him if I did not always come on board according to the time for which he gave me liberty; and, more particularly, when all our men left us at Guadaloupe, and went on board the French fleet, and advised me to go with them, whether I might not, and that he could not have got me again. To my no small surprise, and very great joy, the captain confirmed every syllable I said, and even more; for he said he had tried different times to see if I would make any attempt of this kind, both at St. Eustatia and in America, and he never found that I made the smallest; but, on the contrary, I always came on board according to his orders; and he did really believe, if ever I meant to run away, that, as I could never have had a better opportunity, I would have done it the night the mate and all the people left our vessel at Guadaloupe. The captain then informed my master, who had been thus imposed on by our mate (though I did not know who was my enemy), the reason the mate had for imposing this lie upon him; which was, because I had acquainted the captain with the provisions the mate had given away, or taken out of the vessel. This speech of the captain was like life to the dead to me, and instantly my soul glorified God; and still more so on hearing my master immediately say that I was a sensible fellow, and he never did intend to use me as a common slave; and that, but for the entreaties of the captain, and his character of me, he would not have let me go from the stores about as I had done; that also, in so doing, he thought by carrying one little thing or other to different places to sell I might make money. That he also intended to encourage me in this, by crediting me with half a puncheon of rum and half a hogshead of sugar at a time; so that, from being careful, I might have money enough, in some time, to purchase my freedom: and, when that was the case, I might depend upon it he would let me have it for forty pounds sterling money, which was only the same price he gave for me. This soon gladdened my poor heart beyond measure; though indeed it was no more than the idea I had formed in my mind of my master long before; and I immediately made him this reply: "Sir, I always had that very thought of you, indeed I had, and that made me so diligent in serving you." He then gave me a large piece of silver coin, such as I had never seen or had before, and told me to get ready for the voyage, and he would credit me with a tierce[174] of sugar and another of rum; he also said that he had two amiable sisters in Philadelphia, from whom I might get some necessary things. Upon this my noble captain desired me to go aboard; and, knowing the African mettle, he charged me not to say any thing of this matter to any body; and he promised that the lying mate should not go with him any more. This was a change indeed; in the same hour to feel the most exquisite pain, and in the turn of a moment, the fullest joy. It caused in me such sensations as I was only able to express in my looks; my heart was so overpowered with gratitude that I could have kissed both of their feet. When I left the room, I immediately went, or rather flew, to the vessel, which being loaded, my master, as good as his word, trusted me with a tierce of rum and another of sugar, when we sailed, and arrived safe at the elegant town of Philadelphia. I soon sold my goods here pretty well; and in this charming town I found every thing plentiful and cheap.

While I was in this place a very extraordinary occurrence befel me. I had been told one evening of a *wise* woman,[175] a Mrs. Davis, who revealed secrets, foretold events, &c. I put little faith in this story at first, as I could not conceive that any mortal could foresee the future disposals of Providence, nor did I believe in any other revelation than that of the holy Scriptures; however, I was greatly astonished at seeing this woman in a dream that night, though a person I never before beheld in my life; this made such an impression on me, that I could not get the idea the next day out of my mind, and I then became as anxious to see her as I was before indifferent; accordingly, in the evening, after we left off working, I enquired where she lived, and being directed to her, to my inexpressible surprise, beheld the very woman in the very same dress she appeared to me to wear in the vision. She immediately told me I had dreamed of her the preceding night; related to me many things that had happened with a correctness that astonished me; and finally told me I should not be long a slave. This was the more agreeable news, as I believed it the more readily from her having so faithfully related the past incidents of my life. She said I should be twice in very great danger of my life within eighteen months, which, if I escaped, I should afterwards go on well; so, giving me her blessing, we parted. After staying here some time till our vessel was loaded and I had bought in my little traffic, we sailed from this agreeable spot for Montserrat, once more to encounter the raging surfs.

We arrived safe at Montserrat, where we discharged our cargo, and I sold my things well. Soon after that we took slaves on board for St. Eustatia, and from thence to Georgia. I had always exerted myself, and did double work, in order to make our voyage as short as possible; and from thus overworking myself while we were at Georgia I caught a fever and ague.[176] I was very ill for eleven days, and near dying; eternity was now exceedingly impressed on my mind, and I feared very much that awful event. I prayed the Lord therefore to spare me; and I made a promise in my mind to God, that I would be good if ever I should recover. At length, from having an eminent doctor to attend me, I was restored again to health: and soon after we got the vessel loaded, and set off for Montserrat. During the passage, as I was perfectly restored, and had much business of the vessel to mind, all my endeavours to keep up my integrity, and perform my promise to God, began to fail; and in spite of all I could do, as we drew nearer and nearer to the islands, my resolutions more and more declined, as if the very air of that country or climate seemed fatal to piety. When we were safe arrived at Montserrat, and I had got ashore, I forgot my former resolutions.—Alas! how prone is the heart to leave that God it wishes to love! And how strongly do the things of this world strike the senses and captivate the soul!—After our vessel was discharged, we soon got her ready, and took in, as usual, some of the poor oppressed natives of Africa, and other negroes; we then set off again for Georgia and Charles-town. We arrived at Georgia, and, having landed part of our cargo, proceeded to Charles-town with the remainder. While we were there I saw the town illuminated; the guns were fired, and bonfires and other demonstrations of joy shewn, on account of the repeal of the stamp-act.[177] Here I disposed of some goods on my own account; the white men buying them with smooth promises and fair words, giving me, however, but very indifferent payment. There was one gentleman particularly who bought a puncheon of rum of me, which gave me a great deal of trouble; and although I used the interest of my friendly captain, I could not obtain any thing for it; for, being a negro man, I could not oblige him to pay me. This vexed me much, not knowing how to act; and I lost some time in seeking after this Christian; and though, when the sabbath came (which the negroes usually make their holiday) I was inclined to go to public worship, but, instead of that, I was obliged to hire some black men to help me to pull a boat across the water to go in quest of this gentleman. When I found him, after much entreaty, both from myself and my worthy captain, he at last paid me in dollars, some of them, however, were copper, and of consequence of no value; but he took advantage of my being a negro man, and obliged me to put up with those or none, although I objected to them. Immediately after, as I was trying to pass them in the market amongst other white men, I was abused for offering to pass bad coin; and though I shewed them the man I had got them from, I was within one minute of being tied up and flogged without either judge or jury; however, by the help of a good pair of heels, I ran off and so escaped the bastinadoes[178] I should have received. I got on board as fast as I could, but still continued in fear of them until we sailed, which, I thank God, we did, not long after; and I have never been amongst them since.

We soon came to Georgia, where we were to complete our lading: and here worse fate than ever attended me: for one Sunday night, as I was with some negroes, in their master's yard, in the town of Savannah, it happened that their master, one Doctor Perkins, who was a very severe and cruel man, came in drunk; and not liking to see any strange negroes in his yard, he, and a ruffian of a white man he had in his service, beset me in an instant, and both of them struck me with the first weapons they could get hold of. I cried out as long as I could for help and mercy; but though I gave a good account of myself, and he knew my captain, who lodged hard by him, it was to no purpose. They beat and mangled me in a shameful manner, leaving me nearly dead. I lost so much blood from the wounds I received, that I lay quite motionless, and was so benumbed that I could not feel any thing for many hours. Early in the morning they took me away to the jail. As I did not return to the ship all night, my captain not knowing where I was, and being uneasy that I did not then make my appearance, he made inquiry after me; and, having found where I was, immediately came to me. As soon as the good man saw me so cut and mangled, he could not forbear weeping; he soon got me out of jail to his lodgings, and immediately sent for the best doctors in the place, who at first declared it as their opinion that I could not recover. My captain, on this, went to all the lawyers in the town for their advice, but they told him they could do nothing for me as I was a negro. He then went to Dr. Perkins, the hero who had vanquished me, and menaced him, swearing he would be revenged of him, and challenged him to fight. But cowardice is ever the companion of cruelty—and the Doctor refused. However, by the skilfulness of one Doctor Brady of that place, I began at last to amend; but, although I was so sore and bad, with the wounds I had all over me, that I could not rest in any posture, yet I was in more pain on account of the captain's uneasiness about me than I otherwise should have been. The worthy man nursed and watched me all the hours of the night and I was, through his attention, and that of the doctor, able to get out of bed in about sixteen or eighteen days. All this time I was very much wanted on board, as I used frequently to go up and down the river for rafts, and other parts of our cargo, and stow them, when the mate was sick or absent. In about four weeks I was able to go on duty; and in a fortnight after, having got in all our lading, our vessel set sail for Montserrat; and in less than three weeks we arrived there safe, towards the end of the year. This ended my adventures in 1765; for I did not leave Montserrat again till the beginning of the following year.

CHAPTER VII

EVERY day now brought me nearer my freedom, and I was impatient till we proceeded again to sea, that I might have an opportunity of getting a sum large enough to purchase it. I was not long ungratified; for in the beginning of the year 1766, my master bought another sloop, named the Nancy, the largest I had ever seen. She was partly laden, and was to proceed to Philadelphia. Our captain had his choice of three, and I was well pleased he chose this, which was the largest, for, from his having a large vessel, I had more room, and could carry a larger quantity of goods with me. Accordingly, when we had delivered our old vessel, the Prudence, and completed the lading of the Nancy, having made near three hundred per cent. by four barrels of pork I brought from Charlestown, I laid in as large a cargo as I could, trusting to God's Providence to prosper my undertaking. With these views I sailed for Philadelphia. On our passage, when we drew near the land, I was for the first time surprised at the sight of some whales, having never seen any such large sea monsters before; and, as we sailed by the land, one morning I saw a puppy whale close by the vessel; it was about the length of a wherry boat, and it followed us all the day until we got within the Capes. We arrived safe and in good time at Philadelphia, and I sold my goods there chiefly to the Quakers. They always appeared to be a very honest discreet sort of people, and never attempted to impose on me; I therefore liked them, and ever after chose to deal with them in preference to any others.

One Sunday morning, while I was here, as I was going to church, I chanced to pass a meeting house. The doors being open, and the house full of people, it excited my curiosity to go in. When I entered the house, to my great surprise, I saw a very tall woman standing in the midst of them, speaking in an audible voice something which I could not understand. Having never seen any thing of this kind before, I stood and stared about me for some time, wondering at this odd scene. As soon as it was over, I took an opportunity to make enquiry about the place and people, when I was informed they were called Quakers. I particularly asked what that woman I saw in the midst of them had said, but none of them were pleased to satisfy me;[179] so I quitted them, and soon after, as I was returning, I came to a church crowded with people; the church-yard was full likewise, and a number of people were even mounted on ladders, looking in at the windows. I thought this a strange sight, as I had never seen churches, either in England or the West Indies, crowded in this manner before. I therefore made bold to ask some people the meaning of all this, and they told me the Rev. George Whitfield was preaching.[180] I had often heard of this gentleman, and had wished to see and hear him; but I had never before had an opportunity. I now therefore resolved to gratify myself with the sight, and pressed in amidst the multitude. When I got into the church I saw this pious man exhorting the people with the greatest fervour and earnestness, and sweating as much as ever I did while in slavery on Montserrat beach. I was very much struck and impressed with this; I thought it strange I had never seen divines exert themselves in this manner before, and was no longer at a loss to account for the thin congregations they preached to.[181]

When we had discharged our cargo here, and were loaded again, we left this fruitful land once more, and set sail for Montserrat. My traffic had hitherto succeeded so well with me, that I thought, by selling my goods when we arrived at Montserrat, I should have enough to purchase my freedom. But as soon as our vessel arrived there, my master came on board, and gave orders for us to go to St. Eustatia, and discharge our cargo there, and from thence to proceed to Georgia. I was much disappointed at this; but thinking, as usual, it was of no use to murmur at the decrees of fate, I submitted without repining, and we went to St. Eustatia. After we had discharged our cargo there, we took in a live cargo, (as we call a cargo of slaves.) Here I sold my goods tolerably well; but not being able to lay out all my money in this small island to as much advantage as in many other places, I laid out only part, and the remainder I brought away with me neat. We sailed from hence for Georgia, and I was glad when we got there, though I had not much reason to like the place from my last adventure in Savannah; but I longed to get back to Montserrat and procure my freedom, which I expected to be able to purchase when I returned. As soon as we had arrived here I waited on my careful doctor, Mr. Brady, to whom I made the most grateful acknowledgments in my power for his former kindness and attention during my illness.

[Equiano and his captain are disappointed in their expectations of profiting at the death of a silversmith, who had promised to leave the captain his property. For helping him care for the silversmith while he is dying, the captain promises Equiano £10 from his anticipated inheritance. The property turns out to be worthless.]

We set sail once more for Montserrat, and arrived there safe, but much out of humour with our friend the silversmith. When we had unladen the vessel, and I had sold my venture, finding myself master of about forty-seven pounds—I consulted my true friend, the captain, how I should proceed in offering my master the money for my freedom. He told me to come on a certain morning, when he and my master would be at breakfast together. Accordingly, on that morning, I went, and met the captain there, as he had appointed. When I went in I made my obeisance to my master, and with my money in my hand, and many fears in my heart, I prayed him to be as good as his offer to me, when he was pleased to promise me my freedom as soon as I could purchase it. This speech seemed to confound him; he began to recoil; and my heart that instant sunk within me. "What!" said he, "give you your freedom? Why, where did you get the money; Have you got forty pounds sterling?" "Yes, sir," I answered. "How did you get it"; replied he; I told him,

"Very honestly." The captain then said he knew I got the money very honestly, and with much industry, and that I was particularly careful. On which my master replied, I got money much faster than he did; and said he would not have made me the promise he did if he had thought I should have got money so soon. "Come, come," said my worthy captain, clapping my master on the back, "Come, Robert, (which was his name), I think you must let him have his freedom;—you have laid your money out very well; you have received good interest for it all this time, and here is now the principal at last. I know Gustavus has earned you more than an hundred a-year, and he will still save you money, as he will not leave you: Come, Robert, take the money." My master then said, he would not be worse than his promise; and, taking the money, told me to go to the Secretary at the Register Office, and get my manumission[182] drawn up. These words of my master were like a voice from heaven to me; in an instant all my trepidation was turned into unutterable bliss; and I most reverently bowed myself with gratitude, unable to express my feelings, but by the overflowing of my eyes, and a heart replete with thanks to God; while my true and worthy friend the captain congratulated us both with a peculiar degree of heartfelt pleasure. As soon as the first transports of my joy were over, and I had expressed my thanks to these my worthy friends in the best manner I was able, I rose with a heart full of affection and reverence, and left the room in order to obey my master's joyful mandate of going to the Register Office. As I was leaving the house, I called to mind the words of the Psalmist, in the 126th Psalm, and like him, "I glorified God in my heart, in whom I trusted." These words had been impressed on my mind from the very day I was forced from Deptford to the present hour, and I now saw them, as I thought, fulfilled and verified. My imagination was all rapture as I flew to the Register Office: and, in this respect, like the apostle Peter,[183] (whose deliverance from prison was so sudden and extraordinary, that he thought he was in a vision), I could scarcely believe I was awake. Heavens! who could do justice to my feelings at this moment? Not conquering heroes themselves, in the midst of a triumph—Not the tender mother who has just regained her long-lost infant, and presses it to her heart—Not the weary hungry mariner, at the sight of the desired friendly port—Not the lover, when he once more embraces his beloved mistress, after she had been ravished from his arms!—All within my breast was tumult, wildness, and delirium! My feet scarcely touched the ground, for they were winged with joy, and, like Elijah, as he rose to Heaven, they "were with lightning sped as I went on."[184] Every one I met I told of my happiness, and blazed about the virtue of my amiable master and captain.

When I got to the office and acquainted the Register with my errand, he congratulated me on the occasion, and told me he would draw up my manumission for half price, which was a guinea. I thanked him for his kindness; and having received it, and paid him, I hastened to my master to get him to sign it, that I might fully be released. Accordingly he signed the manumission that day; so that, before night, I who had been a slave in the morning, trembling at the will of another, now became my own master, and compleatly free. I thought this was the happiest day I had ever experienced; and my joy was still heightened by the blessings and prayers of the sable race, particularly the aged, to whom my heart had ever been attached with reverence.

As the form of my manumission has something peculiar in it, and expresses the absolute power and dominion one man claims over his fellow, I shall beg leave to present it before my readers at full length:

Montserrat. — To all men unto whom these presents shall come: I Robert King, of the parish of St. Anthony, in the said island, merchant, send greeting: Know ye, that I the aforesaid Robert King, for, and in consideration of the sum of seventy pounds current money of the said island,[185] to me in hand paid, and to the intent that a negro man slave, named Gustavus Vasa, shall and may become free, have manumitted, emancipated, enfranchised, and set free, and by these presents do manumit, emancipate, enfranchise, and set free, the aforesaid negro man-slave, named Gustavus Vasa, for ever; hereby giving, granting, and releasing unto him, the said Gustavus Vasa, all right, title, dominion, sovereignty, and property, which, as lord and master over the aforesaid Gustavus Vasa, I have had, or which I now have, or by any means whatsoever I may or can hereafter possibly have over him the aforesaid Negro, for ever. In witness whereof, I the abovesaid Robert King, have unto these presents set my hand and seal, this tenth day of July, in the year of our Lord one thousand seven hundred and sixty-six.

ROBERT KING

Signed, sealed, and delivered in the presence of Terry Legay.

Montserrat,
Registered the within manumission, at full length, this eleventh day of July, 1766, in liber D.[186] TERRY LEGAY, Register.

In short, the fair as well as black people immediately styled me by a new appellation, to me the most desirable in the world, which was freeman, and at the dances I gave, my Georgia superfine blue cloathes made no indifferent appearance, as I thought. Some of the sable females, who formerly stood aloof, now began to relax, and appear less coy, but my heart was still fixed on London, where I hoped to be ere long. So that my worthy captain, and his owner my late master, finding that the bent of my mind was towards London, said to me, "We hope you won't leave us, but that you will still be with the vessels." Here gratitude bowed me down; and none but the generous mind can judge of my feelings, struggling between inclination and duty. However, notwithstanding my wish to be in London, I obediently answered my benefactors that I would go in the vessel, and not leave them; and from that day I was entered on board as an able-bodied sailor, at thirty-six shillings per month, besides what perquisites I could make. My intention was to make a voyage or two, entirely to please these my honoured patrons; but I determined that the year following, if it pleased God, I would see Old England once more, and surprise my old master, Capt. Pascal, who was hourly in my mind; for I still loved him, notwithstanding his usage of me, and I pleased myself with thinking of what he would say when he saw what the Lord had done for me in so short a time, instead of being, as he might perhaps suppose, under the cruel yoke of some planter. With these kind of reveries I often used to entertain myself, and shorten the time till my return: and now, being as in my original free African state, I embarked on board the Nancy, after having got all things ready for our voyage. In this state of serenity we sailed for St. Eustatia; and having smooth seas and pleasant weather, we soon arrived there: after taking our cargo on board, we proceeded to Savannah in Georgia, in August 1766.

[Equiano conducts trade in Georgia and is again cheated and abused by Whites.]

We set sail for Montserrat. The Captain and mate had been both complaining of sickness when we sailed, and as we proceeded on our voyage they grew worse. This was about November, and we had not been long at sea before we began to meet with strong northerly gales and rough seas; and in about seven or eight days all the bullocks were near being drowned, and four or five of them died. Our vessel, which had not been tight at first, was much less so now: and, though we were but nine in the whole, including five sailors and myself, yet we were obliged to attend to the pump, every half or three quarters of an hour. The captain and mate came on deck as often as they were able, which was now but seldom; for they declined so fast, that they were not well enough to make observations above four or five times the whole passage. The whole care of the vessel rested therefore upon me; and I was obliged to direct her by mere dint of reason,[187] not being able to work a traverse.[188] The Captain was now very sorry he had not taught me navigation, and protested, if ever he should get well again, he would not fail to do so: but in about seventeen days his illness increased so much, that he was obliged to keep his bed, continuing sensible, however, till the last, constantly having the owner's interest at heart; for this just and benevolent man ever appeared much concerned about the welfare of what he was intrusted with. When this dear friend found the symptoms of death approaching, he called me by my name; and, when I came to him, he asked (with almost his last breath) if he had ever done me any harm? "God forbid I should think so," I replied, "I should then be the most ungrateful of wretches to the best of benefactors." While I was thus expressing my affection and sorrow by his bed-side, he expired without saying another word, and the day following we committed his body to the deep. Every man on board loved him, and regretted his death; but I was exceedingly affected at it, and found that I did not know, till he was gone, the strength of my regard for him. Indeed I had every reason in the world to be attached to him; for, besides that he was in general mild, affable, generous, faithful, benevolent, and just, he was to me a friend and father; and had it pleased Providence that he had died but five months before, I verily believe I should not have obtained my freedom when I did; and it is not improbable that I might not have been able to get it at any rate afterwards.

The captain being dead, the mate came on the deck, and made such observations as he was able,[189] but to no purpose. In the course of a few days more, the few bullocks that remained were found dead; but the turkeys I had, though on the deck, and exposed to so much wet and bad weather, did well, and I afterwards gained near three hundred per cent. on the sale of them; so that in the event it proved a happy circumstance for me that I had not bought the bullocks I intended, for they must have perished with the rest; I could not help looking upon this, otherwise trifling circumstance, as a particular providence of God, and was thankful accordingly. The care of the vessel took up all my time, and engaged my attention entirely. As we were now out of the variable winds, I thought I should not be much puzzled to hit the islands. I was persuaded I steered right for Antigua, which I wished to reach, as the nearest to us; and in the course of nine or ten days we made that island, to our great joy; and the day after we came safe to Montserrat.

Many were surprised when they heard of my conducting the sloop into the port, and I now obtained a new appellation, and was called captain. This elated me not a little, and it was quite flattering to my vanity to be thus styled by as high a title as any sable freeman in this place possessed. When the death of the captain became known, he was much regretted by all who knew him; for he was a man universally respected. At the same time the sable captain lost no fame; for the success I had met with increased the affection of my friends in no small measure; and I was offered, by a gentleman of the place, the command of his sloop to go amongst the islands, but I refused.

CHAPTER VIII

AS I had now, by the death of my captain, lost my great benefactor and friend, I had little inducement to remain longer in the West Indies, except my gratitude to Mr. King, which I thought I had pretty well discharged in bringing back his vessel safe, and delivering his cargo to his satisfaction. I began to think of leaving this part of the world, of which I had been long tired, and of returning to England, where my heart had always been; but Mr. King still pressed me very much to stay with his vessel; and he had done so much for me, that I found myself unable to refuse his requests, and consented to go another voyage to Georgia, as the mate from his ill state of health, was quite useless in the vessel. Accordingly, a new captain was appointed, whose name was William Phillips, an old acquaintance of mine; and, having refitted our vessel, and taken several slaves on board, we set sail for St. Eustatia, where we staid but a few days; and on the 30th of January, 1767, we steered for Georgia. Our new captain boasted strangely of his skill in navigating and conducting a vessel; and, in consequence of this, he steered a new course, several points more to the westward than we ever did before; this appeared to me very extraordinary.

On the 4th of February, which was soon after we had got into our new course, I dreamt the ship was wrecked amidst the surfs and rocks, and that I was the means of saving every one on board; and on the night following I dreamed the very same dream. These dreams, however, made no impression on my mind; and the next evening, it being my watch below, I was pumping the vessel a little after eight o'clock, just before I went off the deck, as is the custom, and being weary with the duty of the day, and tired at the pump (for we made a good deal of water),[190] I began to express my impatience, and I uttered with an oath, "Damn the vessel's bottom out." But my conscience instantly smote me for the expression. When I left the deck I went to bed, and had scarcely fallen asleep when I dreamed the same dream again about the ship that I had dreamt the two preceding nights. At twelve o'clock the watch was changed; and, as I had always the charge of the captain's watch, I then went upon deck. At half after one in the morning, the man at the helm saw something under the lee-beam that the sea washed against,[191] and he immediately called to me that there was a grampus, and desired me to look at it. Accordingly I stood up and observed it for some time; but when I saw the sea wash up against it again and again, I said it was not a fish but a rock. Being soon certain of this, I went down to the captain, and, with some confusion, told him the danger we were in, and desired him to come upon deck immediately. He said it was very well, and I went up again. As soon as I was upon deck, the wind, which had been pretty high, having abated a little, the vessel began to be carried sideways towards the rock, by means of the current. Still the captain did not appear. I therefore went to him again and told him the vessel was then near a large rock, and desired he would come up with all speed. He said he would, and I returned on the deck. When I was upon the deck again I saw we were not above a pistol shot from the rock, and I heard the noise of the breakers all around us.[192] I was exceedingly alarmed at this; and the captain not having yet come on the deck, I lost all patience; and, growing quite enraged, I ran down to him again, and asked him, why he did not come up, and what he could mean by all this? "The breakers," said I, "are around us, and the vessel is almost on the rock." With that he came on the deck with me, and we tried to put the vessel about, and get her out of the current, but all to no purpose, the wind being very small. We then called all hands up immediately; and after a little we got up one end of a cable, and fastened it to the anchor. By this time the surf foamed round us, and made a dreadful noise on the breakers, and the very moment we let the anchor go, the vessel struck against the rocks. One swell now succeeded another, as it were one wave calling on its fellow. The roaring of the billows increased, and, with one single heave of the swells, the sloop was pierced and transfixed among the rocks! In a moment a scene of horror presented itself to my mind, such as I never had conceived or experienced before. All my sins stared me in the face; and especially I thought that God had hurled his direful vengeance on my guilty head for cursing the vessel on which my life depended. My spirits at this forsook me, and I expected every moment to go to the bottom: I determined if I should still be saved, that I would never swear again. And in the midst of my distress, while the dreadful surfs were dashing with unremitting fury among the rocks, I remembered the Lord, though fearful that I was undeserving of forgiveness, and I thought that as he had often delivered he might yet deliver; and, calling to mind the many mercies he had shewn me in times past, they gave me some small hope that he might still help me. I then began to think how we might be saved; and, I believe no mind was ever like mine so replete with inventions and confused with schemes, though how to escape death I knew not. The captain immediately ordered the hatches to be nailed down on the slaves in the hold, where there were above twenty, all of whom must unavoidably have perished if he had been obeyed. When he desired the men to nail down the hatches I thought that my sin was the cause of this, and that God would charge me with these people's blood. This thought rushed upon my mind that instant with such violence, that it quite overpowered me, and I fainted. I recovered just as the people were about to nail down the hatches; perceiving which, I desired them to stop. The captain then said it must be done; I asked him why? He said, that every one would endeavour to get into the boat, which was but small, and thereby we should be drowned; for it would not have carried above ten at the most. I could no longer restrain my emotion, and I told him he deserved drowning for not knowing how to navigate the vessel; and I believe the people would have tossed him overboard if I had given them the least hint of it. However, the hatches were not nailed down; and, as none of us could leave the vessel then on account of the darkness, and as we knew not where to go, and were convinced besides that the boat could not survive the surfs, and besides being broken, we all said we would remain on the dry part of the vessel, and trust to God till day-light appeared, when we should know better what to do.

I then advised to get the boat prepared against morning, and some of us began to set about it; but some abandoned all care of the ship, and themselves, and fell to drinking. Our boat had a piece out of her bottom near two feet long, and we had no materials to mend her; however, necessity being the mother of invention, I took some pump leather and nailed it to the broken part, and plastered it over with tallow-grease. And, thus prepared, with the utmost anxiety of mind, we watched for day-light, and thought every minute an hour, till it appeared. At last it saluted our longing eyes, and kind Providence accompanied its approach with what was no small comfort to us; for the dreadful swell began to subside; and the next thing that we discovered to raise our drooping spirits, was a small key, or desolate island, about five or six miles off; but a barrier soon presented itself; for there was not water enough for our boat to go over the reefs, and this threw us again into a sad consternation; but there was no alternative, we were therefore obliged to put but few things in the boat at once; and, what was still worse, all of us were frequently under the necessity of getting out to drag and lift it over the reefs. This cost us much labour and fatigue; and, what was yet more distressing, we could not avoid having our legs cut and torn very much with the rocks. There were only four people that would work with me at the oars; and they consisted of three black men and a Dutch creole sailor;[193] and, though we went with the boat five times that day, we had no others to assist us. But, had we not worked in this manner, I really believe the people could not have been saved; for not one of the white men did any thing to preserve their lives; and indeed they soon got so drunk that they were not able, but lay about the deck like swine, so that we were at last obliged to lift them into the boat, and carry them on shore by force. This want[194] of assistance made our labour intolerably severe; insomuch that, by putting on shore so often that day, the skin was partly stript off my hands.

However, we continued all the day to toil and strain our exertions, till we had brought all on board safe to the shore; so that out of thirty-two people we lost not one.

My dream now returned upon my mind with all its force; it was fulfilled in every part; for our danger was the same I had dreamt of; and I could not help looking on myself as the principal instrument in effecting our deliverance: for, owing to some of our people getting drunk, the rest of us were obliged to double our exertions; and it was fortunate we did, for in a very little time longer the patch of leather on the boat would have been worn out, and she would have been no longer fit for service. Situated as we were, who could think that men should be so careless of the danger they were in? for, if the wind had but raised the swell as it was when the vessel struck, we must have bid a final farewell to all hopes of deliverance; and though I warned the people who were drinking, and entreated them to embrace the moment of deliverance, nevertheless they persisted, as if not possessed of the least spark of reason. I could not help thinking, that if any of these people had been lost, God would charge me with their lives, which, perhaps, was one cause of my labouring so hard for their preservation, and indeed every one of them afterwards seemed so sensible of the service I had rendered them, that while we were on the key, I was a kind of chieftain amongst them. I brought some limes, oranges, and lemons ashore; and, finding it to be a good soil where we were, I planted several of them as a token to any one that might be cast away hereafter. This key, as we afterwards found, was one of the Bahama islands, which consist of a cluster of large islands, with smaller ones or keys, as they are called, interspersed among them. It was about a mile in circumference, with a white sandy beach running in a regular order along it. On that part of it where we first attempted to land, there stood some very large birds, called flamingoes: these, from the reflection of the sun, appeared to us, at a little distance, as large as men; and, when they walked backwards and forwards, we could not conceive what they were: our captain swore they were cannibals. This created a great panic among us; and we held a consultation how to act. The captain wanted to go to a key that was within sight, but a great way off; but I was against it, as in so doing we should not be able to save all the people; "And therefore," said I, "let us go on shore here, and perhaps these cannibals may take to the water." Accordingly, we steered towards them; and when we approached them, to our very great joy and no less wonder, they walked off one after the other very deliberately; and at last they took flight, and relieved us entirely from our fears. About the key there were turtles and several sorts of fish in such abundance that we caught them without bait, which was a great relief to us after the salt provisions on board.[195] There was also a large rock on the beach, about ten feet high, which was in the form of a punch-bowl at the top; this we could not help thinking Providence had ordained to supply us with rain-water; and it was something singular, that, if we did not take the water when it rained, in some little time after it would turn as salt as sea-water.

Our first care, after refreshment, was, to make ourselves tents to lodge in, which we did as well as we could with some sails we had brought from the ship. We then began to think how we might get from this place, which was quite uninhabited; and we determined to repair our boat, which was very much shattered, and to put to sea in quest of a ship, or some inhabited island. It took us up, however, eleven days before we could get the boat ready for sea, in the manner we wanted it, with a sail and other necessaries. When we had got all things prepared, the captain wanted me to stay on shore, while he went to sea in quest of a vessel to take all the people off the key; but this I refused; and the captain and myself, with five more, set off in the boat towards New Providence.[196]

[With the help of the crew of a wrecker, a vessel that looked for wrecks whose contents could be claimed for salvage, Equiano saves his men and reaches New Providence.]

We stayed in New Providence about seventeen or eighteen days; during which time I met with many friends, who gave me encouragement to stay there with them, but I declined it; though, had not my heart been fixed on England, I should have stayed, as I liked the place extremely, and there were some free black people here who were very happy, and we passed our time pleasantly together, with the melodious sound of the catguts under the lime and lemon trees.[197] At length Capt. Phillips hired a sloop to carry him and some of the slaves that he could not sell here, to Georgia; and I agreed to go with him in this vessel, meaning now to take my farewell of that place. When the vessel was ready, we all embarked; and I took my leave of New Providence, not without regret. We sailed about four o'clock in the morning, with a fair wind, for Georgia; and, about eleven o'clock the same morning, a sudden and short gale sprung up and blew away most of our sails; and, as we were still among the keys, in a very few minutes it dashed the sloop against the rocks. Luckily for us the water was deep; and the sea was not so angry, but that, after having for some time laboured hard, and being many in number, we were saved through God's mercy: and, by using our greatest exertions, we got the vessel off. The next day we returned to [New] Providence, where we soon got her again refitted. Some of the people swore that we had spells set upon us, by somebody in Montserrat; and others said that we had witches and wizzards amongst the poor helpless slaves; and that we never should arrive safe at Georgia. But these things did not deter me; I said, "Let us again face the winds and seas, and swear not, but trust to God, and he will deliver us." We therefore once more set sail; and with hard labour, in seven days time, arrived safe at Georgia.

After our arrival we went up to the town of Savannah; and the same evening I went to a friend's house to lodge, whose name was Mosa, a black man. We were very happy at meeting each other; and, after supper, we had a light till between nine and ten o'clock at night. About that time the watch or patrole came by, and, discerning a light in the house, they knocked at the door; we opened it, and they came in and sat down, and drank some punch with us; they also begged some limes of me, as they understood I had some, which I readily gave them. A little after this, they told me I must go to the watch-house with them; this surprised me a good deal after our kindness to them, and I asked them, Why so? They said that all negroes, who had a light in their houses after nine o'clock were to be taken into custody, and either pay some dollars, or be flogged. Some of these people knew that I was a free man; but, as the man of the house was not free, and had his master to protect him, they did not take the same liberty with him they did with me. I told them that I was a free man, and just arrived from [New] Providence; that we were not making any noise, and that I was not a stranger in that place, but was very well known there: "Besides," said I, "what will you do with me?"—"That you shall see," replied they; "but you must go to the watch-house with us." Now, whether they meant to get money from me or not, I was at a loss to know; but I thought immediately of the oranges and limes at Santa Cruz: and seeing that nothing would pacify them, I went with them to the watch-house, where I remained during the night. Early the next morning these imposing ruffians flogged a negro man and woman that they had in the watch-house, and then they told me that I must be flogged too; I asked why? and if there was no law for free men? and told them if there was I would have it put in force against them. But this only exasperated them the more, and they instantly swore they would serve me as Doctor Perkins had done; and were going to lay violent hands on me; when one of them, more humane than the rest, said, that as I was a free man they could not justify stripping me by law. I then immediately sent for Dr. Brady, who was known to be a honest and worthy man; and on his coming to my assistance, they let me go.

This was not the only disagreeable incident I met with while I was in this place; for, one day, while I was a little way out of the town of Savannah, I was beset by two white men, who meant to play their usual tricks with me in the way of kidnapping. As soon as these men accosted me, one of them said to the other, "This is the very fellow we are looking for, that you lost": and the other swore immediately that I was the identical person. On this they made up to me, and were about to handle me; but I told them to be still and keep off, for I had seen those tricks played upon other free blacks, and they must not think to serve me so. At this they paused a little, and one said to the other—it will not do; and the other answered that I talked too good English. I replied, I believed I did; and I had also with me a revengeful stick equal to the occasion; and my mind was likewise good. Happily, however, it was not used; and, after we had talked together a little in this manner, the rogues left me.

I stayed in Savannah some time, anxiously trying to get to Montserrat once more to see Mr. King, my old master, and then to take a final farewell of the American quarter of the globe. At last I met with a sloop called the Speedwell, Captain John Bunton, which belonged to Grenada, and was bound to Martinico, a French island, with a cargo of rice; and I shipped myself on board of her.

Before I left Georgia, a black woman who had a child lying dead, being very tenacious of the church burial service, and not able to get any white person to perform it, applied to me for that purpose. I told her I was no parson; and, besides, that the service over the dead did not affect the soul. This however did not satisfy her; she still urged me very hard; I therefore complied with her entreaties, and at last consented to act the parson for the first time in my life. As she was much respected, there was a great company both of white and black people at the grave. I then accordingly assumed my new vocation, and performed the funeral ceremony to the satisfaction of all present; after which I bade adieu to Georgia, and sailed for Martinico.[198]

CHAPTER IX

I THUS took a final leave of Georgia; for the treatment I had received in it disgusted me very much against the place; and when I left it and sailed for Martinico, I determined never more to revisit it. My new captain conducted his vessel safer than my former one; and, after an agreeable voyage, we got safe to our intended port. While I was on this island I went about a good deal, and found it very pleasant: in particular, I admired the town of St. Pierre, which is the principal one in the island, and built more like an European town than any I had seen in the West Indies. In general also, slaves were better treated, had more holidays, and looked better than those in the English islands.[199] After we had done our business here, I wanted my discharge, which was necessary; for it was then the month of May, and I wished much to be at Montserrat to bid farewell to Mr. King, and all my other friends there, in time to sail for Old England in the July fleet.[200] But, alas! I had put a great stumbling block in my own way, by which I was near losing my passage that season to England. I had lent my captain some money, which I now wanted, to enable me to prosecute my intentions. This I told him; but when I applied for it, though I urged the necessity of my occasion, I met with so much shuffling from him,[201] that I began at last to be afraid of losing my money, as I could not recover it by law; for I have already mentioned, that throughout the West Indies no black man's testimony is admitted, on any occasion, against any white person whatever, and therefore my own oath would have been of no use. I was obliged therefore, to remain with him till he might be disposed to return it to me. Thus we sailed from Martinico for the Grenades.[202] I frequently pressing the captain for my money, to no purpose; and, to render my condition worse, when we got there, the captain and his owners quarrelled; so that my situation became daily more irksome: for besides that we on board had little or no victuals allowed us, and I could not get my money nor wages, as I could then have gotten my passage free to Montserrat had I been able to accept it. The worst of all was, that it was growing late in July, and the ships in the islands must sail by the 26th of that month. At last, however, with a great many entreaties, I got my money from the captain, and took the first vessel I could meet with for St. Eustatia. From thence I went in another to Basseterre in St. Kitt's, where I arrived on the 19th of July. On the 22d, having met with a vessel bound to Montserrat, I wanted to go in her; but the captain and others would not take me on board until I should advertise myself, and give notice of my going off the island.[203] I told them of my haste to be in Montserrat; and that the time then would not admit of advertising, it being late in the evening, and the vessel about to sail; but he insisted it was necessary, and otherwise he said he would not take me. This reduced me to great perplexity; for if I should be compelled to submit to this degrading necessity, which every black freeman is under, of advertising himself like a slave, when he leaves an island, and which I thought a gross imposition upon any freedom, I feared I should miss that opportunity of going to Montserrat, and then I could not get to England that year. The vessel was just going off, and no time could be lost; I immediately therefore set about with a heavy heart, to try who I could get to befriend me in complying with the demands of the captain. Luckily I found, in a few minutes, some gentlemen of Montserrat whom I knew; and having told them my situation, I requested their friendly assistance in helping me off the island. Some of them, on this, went with me to the captain, and satisfied him of my freedom; and, to my very great joy, he desired me to go on board. We then set sail, and the next day, the 23d, I arrived at the wished-for place, after an absence of six months, in which I had more than once experienced the delivering hand of Providence, when all human means of escaping destruction seemed hopeless. I saw my friends with a gladness of heart, which was increased by my absence, and the dangers I had escaped; and I was received with great friendship by them all, but particularly by Mr. King, to whom I related the fate of his sloop, the Nancy, and the causes of her being wrecked. I now learned, with extreme sorrow, that his house was washed away during my absence, by the bursting of a pond at the top of a mountain that was opposite the town of Plymouth. It swept [a] great part of the town away, and Mr. King lost a great deal of property from the inundation, and nearly his life. When I told him I intended to go to London that season, and that I had come to visit him before my departure, the good man expressed a great deal of affection for me, and sorrow that I should leave him, and warmly advised me to stay there; insisting, as I was much respected by all the gentlemen in the place, that I might do very well, and in a short time have land and slaves of my own. I thanked him for this instance of his friendship; but, as I wished very much to be in London, I declined remaining any longer there, and begged he would excuse me. I then requested he would be kind enough to give me a certificate of my behaviour while in his service, which he very readily complied with, and gave me the following:

Montserrat, 26th of July, 1767.

The bearer hereof, Gustavus Vasa, was my slave for upwards of three years, during which he has always behaved himself well, and discharged his duty with honesty and assiduity.

ROBERT KING.

To all whom this may concern.

Having obtained this, I parted from my kind master, after many sincere professions of gratitude and regard, and prepared for my departure for London. I immediately agreed to go with one Capt. John Hamer, for seven guineas (the passage to London), on board a ship called the Andromache; and on the 24th and 25th, I had free dances, as they are called, with some of my friends and countrymen, previous to my setting off: after which I took leave of all my friends, and on the 26th I embarked for London, exceedingly glad to see myself once more on board of a ship, and still more so, in steering the course I had long wished for. With a light heart I bade Montserrat farewell, and never had my feet on it since; and with it I bade adieu to the sound of the cruel whip, and all other dreadful instruments of torture! adieu to the offensive sight of the violated chastity of the sable females, which has too often accosted my eyes! adieu to oppressions (although to me less severe than to most of my countrymen!) and adieu to the angry howling dashing surfs! I wished for a grateful and thankful heart to praise the Lord God on high for all his mercies! in this extacy I steered the ship all night.

We had a most prosperous voyage, and, at the end of seven weeks, arrived at Cherry-garden stairs.[204] Thus were my longing eyes once more gratified with a sight of London, after having been absent from it above four years. I immediately received my wages, and I never had earned seven guineas so quick in my life before; I had thirty-seven guineas in all, when I got cleared of the ship. I now entered upon a scene quite new to me, but full of hope. In this situation my first thoughts were to look out for some of my former friends, and amongst the first of those were the Miss Guerins. As soon as I had regaled myself I went in quest of those kind ladies, whom I was very impatient to see; and, with some difficulty and perseverance, I found them at May's-hill, Greenwich. They were most agreeably surprised to see me, and I was quite overjoyed at meeting with them. I told them my history, at which they expressed great wonder, and freely acknowledged it did their cousin, Capt. Pascal, no honour. He then visited there frequently; and I met him, four or five days after, in Greenwich-park. When he saw me, he appeared a good deal surprised, and asked me how I came back? I answered, "In a ship." To which he replied dryly, "I suppose you did not walk back to London on the water." As I saw, by his manner, that he did not seem to be sorry for his behaviour to me, and that I had not much reason to expect any favour from him, I told him that he had used me very ill, after I had been such a faithful servant to him for so many years; on which, without saying any more, he turned about and went away. A few days after this I met Capt. Pascal at Miss Guerin's house, and asked him for my prize-money. He said there was none due to me; for if my prize-money had been 1,000£ he had a right to it all. I told him I was informed otherwise, on which he bade me defiance, and, in a bantering tone, desired me to commence a law-suit against him for it: "There are lawyers enough," said he, "that will take the cause in hand, and you had better try it." I told him then that I would try it, which enraged him very much; however, out of regard to the ladies, I remained still, and never made any farther demand of my right. Some time afterwards, these friendly ladies asked me what I meant to do with myself, and how they could assist me. I thanked them, and said, if they pleased, I would be their servant; but if not I had thirty-seven guineas, which would support me for some time, and I would be much obliged to them to recommend me to some person who would teach me a business whereby I might earn my living. They answered me very politely, that they were sorry it did not suit them to take me as their servant, and asked me what business I should like to learn? I said, hair-dressing. They then promised to assist me in this; and soon after, they recommended me to a gentleman, whom I had known before, one Capt. O'Hara, who treated me with much kindness, and procured me a master,[205] a hair-dresser, in Coventry-court, Haymarket, with whom he placed me. I was with this man from September till the February following. In that time we had a neighbour in the same court, who taught the French-horn. He used to blow it so well that I was charmed with it, and agreed with him to teach me to blow it. Accordingly he took me in hand, and began to instruct me, and I soon learned all the three parts.[206] I took great delight in blowing on this instrument, the evenings being long; and besides that I was fond of it, I did not like to be idle, and it filled up my vacant hours innocently. At this time also I agreed with the Rev. Mr. Gregory, who lived in the same court, where he kept an academy and an evening school, to improve me in arithmetic. This he did as far as Barter and Aligation; so that all the time I was here I was entirely employed.[207] In February 1768, I hired myself to Dr. Charles Irving, in Pall-mall, so celebrated for his successful experiments in making sea-water fresh; and here I had plenty of hair-dressing to improve my hand. This gentleman was an excellent master; he was exceedingly kind and good-tempered; and allowed me in the evenings to attend my schools, which I esteemed a great blessing; therefore I thank God and him for it, and used all diligence to improve the opportunity. This diligence and attention recommended me to the notice and care of my three preceptors, who, on their parts, bestowed a great deal of pains in my instruction, and besides were all very kind to me. My wages, however, which were by two-thirds less than ever I had in my life (for I had only 12£. per ann.) I soon found would not be sufficient to defray this extraordinary expence of masters, and my own necessary expences; my old thirty-seven guineas had by this time worn all away to one. I thought it best, therefore, to try the sea again in quest of more money, as I had been bred to it, and had hitherto found the profession of it successful. I had also a very great desire to see Turkey, and I now determined to gratify it. Accordingly, in the month of May, 1768, I told the Doctor of my wish to go to sea again, to which he made no opposition; and we parted on friendly terms. The same day I went into the city in quest of a master.[208] I was extremely fortunate in my enquiry; for I soon heard of a gentleman who had a ship going to Italy and Turkey, and he wanted a man who could dress hair well. I was overjoyed at this, and went immediately on board of his ship, as I had been directed, which I found to be fitted up with great taste, and I already foreboded no small pleasure in sailing in her. Not finding the gentleman on board, I was directed to his lodgings, where I met with him the next day, and gave him a specimen of my dressing. He liked it so well that he hired me immediately, so that I was perfectly happy, for the ship, master, and voyage, were entirely to my mind. The ship was called the Delawar, and my master's name was John Jolly, a neat, smart, good-humoured man, just such a one as I wished to serve. We sailed from England in July following, and our voyage was extremely pleasant. We went to Villa Franca, Nice, and Leghorn; and in all these places I was charmed with the richness and beauty of the countries, and struck with the elegant buildings with which they abound. We had always in them plenty of extraordinary good wines and rich fruits, which I was very fond of; and I had frequent occasions of gratifying both my taste and curiosity; for my captain always lodged on shore in those places, which afforded me opportunities to see the country around. I also learned navigation of the mate, which I was very fond of. When we left Italy, we had delightful sailing among the Archipelago islands, and from thence to Smyrna in Turkey. This is a very ancient city; the houses are built of stone, and most of them have graves adjoining to them; so that they sometimes present the appearance of church-yards. Provisions are very plentiful in this city, and good wine less than a penny a pint. The grapes, pomegranates, and many other fruits, were also the richest and largest I ever saw or tasted. The natives are well-looking and strong made, and treated me always with great civility. In general I believe they are fond of black people;[209] and several of them gave me pressing invitations to stay amongst them, although they keep the Franks, or Christians,[210] separate, and do not suffer them to dwell immediately amongst them. I was astonished in not seeing women in any of their shops, and very rarely any in the streets; and whenever I did they were covered with a veil from head to foot, so that I could not see their faces, except when any of them, out of curiosity, uncovered them to look at me, which they sometimes did. I was surprised to see how the Greeks are, in some measure, kept under by the Turks, as the negroes are in the West-Indies by the white people. The less refined Greeks, as I have already hinted, dance here in the same manner as we do in our nation.

On the whole, during our stay here, which was about five months, I liked the place and the Turks extremely well. I could not help observing one remarkable circumstance there; the tails of the sheep are flat, and so very large, that I have known the tail even of a lamb to weigh from eleven to thirteen pounds. The fat of them is very white and rich, and is excellent in puddings, for which it is much used. Our ship being at length richly loaded with silk and other articles, we sailed for England.

In May 1769, soon after our return from Turkey, our ship made a delightful voyage to Oporto, in Portugal, where we arrived at the time of the carnival. On our arrival, there were sent on board of us thirty-six articles to be observed, with very heavy penalties if we should break any of them; and none of us even dared to go on board any other vessel, or on shore, till the Inquisition had sent on board and searched for every thing illegal, especially bibles.[211] All we had were produced, and certain other things were sent on shore till the ships were going away; and any person, in whose custody a bible was found concealed, was to be imprisoned and flogged, and sent into slavery for ten years. I saw here many magnificent sights, particularly the garden of Eden,[212] where many of the clergy and laity went in procession in their several orders with the host, and sung Te Deum.[213] I had a great curiosity to go into some of their churches, but could not gain admittance without using the necessary sprinkling of holy water at my entrance. From curiosity, and a wish to be holy, I therefore complied with this ceremony, but its virtues were lost upon me, for I found myself nothing the better for it. This place abounds with plenty of all kinds of provisions. The town is well built and pretty, and commands a fine prospect. Our ship having taken in a load of wine, and other commodities, we sailed for London, and arrived there in July following.

Our next voyage was to the Mediterranean. The ship was again got ready, and we sailed in September for Genoa. This is one of the finest cities I ever saw; some of the edifices were of beautiful marble, and made a most noble appearance; and many had very curious fountains before them. The churches were rich and magnificent, and curiously adorned both in the inside and out. But all this grandeur was, in my eyes, disgraced by the galley-slaves, whose condition, both there and in other parts of Italy, is truly piteous and wretched.[214] After we had staid there some weeks, during which we bought many different things we wanted, and got them very cheap, we sailed to Naples, a charming city, and remarkably clean. The bay is the most beautiful I ever saw; the moles for shipping are excellent. I thought it extraordinary to see grand operas acted here on Sunday nights, and even attended by their Majesties.[215] I too, like these great ones, went to those sights, and vainly served God in the day while I thus served mammon effectually at night.[216] While we remained here, there happened an eruption of Mount Vesuvius, of which I had a perfect view. It was extremely awful; and we were so near that the ashes from it used to be thick on our deck. After we had transacted our business at Naples, we sailed with a fair wind once more for Smyrna, where we arrived in December. A seraskier, or officer, took a liking to me here, and wanted me to stay, and offered me two wives; however I refused the temptation, thinking one was as much as some could manage, and more than others would venture on. The merchants here travel in caravans or large companies. I have seen many caravans from India, with some hundreds of camels, laden with different goods. The people of these caravans are quite brown. Among other articles, they brought with them a great quantity of locusts, which are a kind of pulse, sweet and pleasant to the palate, and in shape resembling French beans, but longer.[217] Each kind of goods is sold in a street by itself, and I always found the Turks very honest in their dealings. They let no Christians into their mosques, or churches, for which I was very sorry; as I was always fond of going to see the different modes of worship of the people wherever I went. The plague broke out while we were in Smyrna, and we stopped taking goods into the ship till it was over. She was then richly laden, and we sailed in about March 1770 for England. One day in our passage we met with an accident which was near burning the ship. A black cook, in melting some fat, overset the pan into the fire under the deck, which immediately began to blaze, and the flame went up very high under the foretop. With the fright, the poor cook became almost white, and altogether speechless. Happily, however, we got the fire out without doing much mischief. After various delays in this passage, which was tedious, we arrived in Standgate-creek in July;[218] and at the latter end of the year, some new event occurred, so that my noble captain, the ship, and I, all separated.

In April 1771, I shipped myself as a steward with Capt. William Robertson, of the ship Grenada Planter, once more to try my fortune in the West-Indies; and we sailed from London for Madeira, Barbadoes, and the Grenadas. When we were at this last place, having some goods to sell, I met once more with my former kind of West-India customers.

A white man, an islander, bought some goods of me to the amount of some pounds, and made me many fair promises as usual, but without any intention of paying me. He had likewise bought goods from some more of our people, whom he intended to serve in the same manner; but he still amused us with promises. However, when our ship was loaded and near sailing, this honest buyer discovered[219] no intention or sign of paying for any thing he had bought of us; but, on the contrary, when I asked him for my money, he threatened me and another black man he had bought goods of, so that we found we were like to get more blows than payment. On this we went to complain to one Mr. M'Intosh, a justice of the peace; we told his worship of the man's villainous tricks, and begged that he would be kind enough to see us redressed: but being negroes, although free, we could not get any remedy; and our ship being then just upon the point of sailing, we knew not how to help ourselves, though we thought it hard to lose our property in this manner. Luckily for us, however, this man was also indebted to three white sailors, who could not get a farthing from him; they therefore readily joined us, and we all went together in search of him. When we found where he was, we took him out of a house and threatened him with vengeance; on which, finding he was likely to be handled roughly, the rogue offered each of us some small allowance, but nothing near our demands. This exasperated us much; and some were for cutting his ears off; but he begged hard for mercy, which was at last granted him, after we had entirely stripped him. We then let him go, for which he thanked us, glad to get off so easily, and ran into the bushes, after having wished us a good voyage. We then repaired on board, and shortly after set sail for England. I cannot help remarking here a very narrow escape we had from being blown up, owing to a piece of negligence of mine. Just as our ship was under sail, I went down under the cabin to do some business, and had a lighted candle in my hand, which, in my hurry, without thinking, I held in a barrel of gunpowder. It remained in the powder until it was near catching fire, when fortunately I observed it, and snatched it out in time and providentially no harm happened; but I was so overcome with terror, that I immediately fainted at the deliverance.

In twenty-eight days time we arrived in England, and I got clear of this ship. But, being still of a roving disposition, and desirous of seeing as many different parts of the world as I could, I shipped myself soon after, in the same year, as steward on board of a fine large ship, called the Jamaica, Captain David Watt; and we sailed from England in December 1771, for Nevis and Jamaica. I found Jamaica to be a very fine, large island, well peopled, and the most considerable of the West-India islands. There were a vast number of negroes here,[220] whom I found, as usual, exceedingly imposed upon by the white people, and the slaves punished as in the other islands. There are negroes whose business it is to flog slaves; they go about to different people for employment, and the usual pay is from one to four bits. I saw many cruel punishments inflicted on the slaves in the short time I staid here. In particular I was present when a poor fellow was tied up and kept hanging by the wrists at some distance from the ground, and then some half hundred weights were fixed to his ancles, in which posture he was flogged most unmercifully. There were also, as I heard, two different masters noted for cruelty on the island, who had staked up two negroes naked, and in two hours the vermin stung them to death. I heard a gentleman, I well knew, tell my captain, that he passed sentence on a negro man to be burnt alive for attempting to poison an overseer. I pass over numerous instances, in order to relieve the reader by a milder scene of roguery. Before I had been long on the island, one Mr. Smith, at Port Morant, bought goods of me to the amount of twenty-five pounds sterling; but when I demanded payment from him, he was each time going to beat me, and threatened that he would put me in gaol. One time he would say I was going to set his house on fire; at another he would swear I was going to run away with his slaves. I was astonished at this usage from a person who was in the situation of a gentleman,[221] but I had no alternative, and was therefore obliged to submit. When I came to Kingston, I was surprised to see the number of Africans, who were assembled together on Sundays; particularly at a large commodious place called Spring Path. Here each different nation of Africa meet and dance, after the manner of their own country. They still retain most of their native customs: they bury their dead, and put victuals, pipes, and tobacco, and other things in the grave with the corpse, in the same manner as in Africa. Our ship having got her loading, we sailed for London, where we arrived in the August following. On my return to London, I waited on my old and good master, Dr. Irving, who made me an offer of his service again. Being now tired of the sea, I gladly accepted it. I was very happy in living with this gentleman once more; during which time we were daily employed in reducing old Neptune's dominions by purifying the briny element, and making it fresh.[222] Thus I went on till May 1773, when I was roused by the sound of fame to seek new adventures, and to find, towards the North Pole, what our Creator never intended we should, a passage to India. An expedition was now fitting out to explore a north-east passage, conducted by the Honourable Constantine John Phipps, late[223] Lord Mulgrave, in his Majesty's sloop of war the Race Horse. My master being anxious for the reputation of this adventure, we therefore prepared every thing for our voyage, and I attended him on board the Race Horse, the 24th day of May 1773.

[The expedition fails to find a Northeast Passage.]

CHAPTER X

OUR voyage to the North Pole being ended,[224] I returned to London with Dr. Irving, with whom I continued for some time, during which I began seriously to reflect on the dangers I had escaped, particularly those of my last voyage, which made a lasting impression on my mind, and, by the grace of God, proved afterwards a mercy to me: it caused me to reflect deeply on my eternal state, and to seek the Lord with full purpose of heart ere it be too late. I rejoiced greatly; and heartily thanked the Lord for directing me to London, where I was determined to work out my own salvation, and, in so doing, procure a title to heaven; being the result of a mind blinded by ignorance and sin.

In process of time I left my master, Doctor Irving, the purifier of waters. I lodged in Coventry-court, Haymarket, where I was continually oppressed and much concerned about the salvation of my soul, and was determined (in my own strength) to be a first-rate Christian.[225] I used every means for this purpose; and, not being able to find any person amongst those with whom I was then acquainted that acquiesced with me in point of religion, or, in scripture language, that would shew me any good, I was much dejected, and knew not where to seek relief; however, I first frequented the neighbouring churches, St. James's, and others, two or three times a day, for many weeks: still I came away dissatisfied: something was wanting that I could not obtain, and I really found more heart-felt relief in reading my bible at home than in attending the church; and, being resolved to be saved, I pursued other methods. First I went among the people called Quakers, whose meeting at times was held in silence, and I remained as much in the dark as ever. I then searched into the Roman Catholic principles, but was not in the least edified. I, at length, had recourse to the Jews, which availed me nothing, as the fear of eternity daily harassed my mind and I knew not where to seek shelter from the wrath to come.[226] However, this was my conclusion, at all events, to read the Four Evangelists,[227] and whatever sect or party I found adhering thereto, such I would join. Thus I went on heavily without any guide to direct me the way that leadeth to eternal life. I asked different people questions about the manner of going to heaven, and was told different ways. Here I was much staggered, and could not find any at that time more righteous than myself, or indeed so much inclined to devotion. I thought we should not all be saved (this is agreeable to the holy scriptures), nor would all be damned. I found none among the circle of my acquaintance that kept holy the Ten Commandments. So righteous was I in my own eyes, that I was convinced I excelled many of them in that point, by keeping eight out of ten; and finding those, who in general termed themselves Christians, not so honest or so good in their morals as the Turks.[228] I really thought the Turks were in a safer way of salvation than my neighbours; so that between hopes and fears I went on, and the chief comforts I enjoyed were in the musical French-horn, which I then practised, and also dressing of hair. Such was my situation some months, experiencing the dishonesty of many people here. I determined at last to set out for Turkey, and there to end my days. It was now early in the spring 1774. I sought for a master, and found a Captain John Hughes, commander of a ship called Anglicania, fitting out in the river Thames, and bound to Smyrna in Turkey. I shipped myself with him as a steward; at the same time I recommended to him a very clever black man, John Annis, as a cook. This man was on board the ship near two months doing his duty; he had formerly lived many years with Mr. William Kirkpatrick, a gentleman of the island of St. Kitt's, from whom he parted by consent, though he afterwards tried many schemes to inveigle the poor man. He had applied to many captains, who traded to St. Kitt's, to trepan him; and when all their attempts and schemes of kidnapping proved abortive, Mr. Kirkpatrick came to our ship at Union-stairs,[229] on Easter Monday, April the 4th, with two wherry-boats and six men, having learned that the man was on board; and tied, and forcibly took him away from the ship, in the presence of the crew and the chief mate, who had detained him after he had information to come away. I believe this was a combined piece of business;[230] but, be that as it may, it certainly reflected great disgrace on the mate, and captain also, who, although they had desired the oppressed man to stay on board, yet notwithstanding this vile act on the man who had served him, he did not in the least assist to recover him, or pay me a farthing of his wages, which was about five pounds. I proved the only friend he had, who attempted to regain him his liberty, if possible, having known the want of liberty myself. I sent, as soon as I could, to Gravesend, and got knowledge of the ship in which he was; but unluckily she had sailed the first tide after he was put on board. My intention was then immediately to apprehend Mr. Kirkpatrick, who was about setting off for Scotland; and having obtained a *habeas corpus* for him,[231] and got a tipstaff[232] to go with me to St. Paul's Church yard, where he lived; he, suspecting something of this kind, set a watch to look out. My being known to them obliged me to use the following deception: I whitened my face, that they might not know me, and this had the desired effect. He did not go out of his house that night, and next morning I contrived a well-plotted stratagem, notwithstanding he had a gentleman in his house to personate him. My direction to the tipstaff had the desired effect; he got admittance into the house, and conducted him to a judge, according to the writ. When he came there, his plea was, that he had not the body in custody, on which he was admitted to bail. I proceeded immediately to that well-known philanthropist, Granville Sharp, Esq. who received me with the utmost kindness, and gave me every instruction that was needful on the occasion.[233] I left him in full hopes that I should gain the unhappy man his liberty, with the warmest sense of gratitude towards Mr. Sharp for his kindness. But, alas! my attorney proved unfaithful; he took my money, lost me many months employ, and did not the least good in the cause; and when the poor man arrived at St. Kitt's, he was, according to custom, staked to the ground with four pins through a cord, two on his wrists, and two on his ancles, was cut and flogged most unmercifully, and afterwards loaded cruelly with irons about his neck. I had two very moving letters from him while he was in this situation; and I made attempts to go after him at a great hazard, but was sadly disappointed: I also was told of it by some very respectable families, now in London, who saw him in St. Kitt's, in the same state, in which he remained till kind death released him out of the hands of his tyrants.[234] During this disagreeable business, I was under strong convictions of sin, and thought that my state was worse than any man's; my mind was unaccountably disturbed; I often wished for death, though, at the same time, convinced I was altogether unprepared for that awful summons:

suffering much by villains in the late cause, and being much concerned about the state of my soul, these things (but particularly the latter) brought me very low; so that I became a burden to myself, and viewed all things around me as emptiness and vanity, which could give no satisfaction to a troubled conscience. I was again determined to go to Turkey, and resolved, at that time, never more to return to England. I engaged as steward on board a Turkeyman (the Wester Hall, Capt. Lina), but was prevented by means of my late captain, Mr. Hughes, and others. All this appeared to be against me, and the only comfort I then experienced was in reading the Holy Scriptures, where I saw that "there is no new thing under the sun," Eccles. i. 9. and what was appointed for me I must submit to. Thus I continued to travel in much heaviness, and frequently murmured against the Almighty, particularly in his providential dealings; and, awful to think! I began to blaspheme, and wished often to be any thing but a human being. In these severe conflicts the Lord answered me by awful "visions of the night, when deep sleep falleth upon men, in slumberings upon the bed," Job xxxiii. 15. He was pleased, in much mercy, to give me to see, and in some measure understand, the great and awful scene of the Judgment-day, that "no unclean person, no unholy thing, can enter into the kingdom of God," Eph[esians]. v. 5. I would then, if it had been possible, have changed my nature with the meanest worm on the earth, and was ready to say to the mountains and rocks, "fall on me," Rev[elation]. vi. 16. but all in vain. I then, in the greatest agony, requested the divine Creator, that he would grant me a small space of time to repent of my follies and vile iniquities, which I felt were grievous. The Lord, in his manifold mercies, was pleased to grant my request, and being yet in a state of time, the sense of God's mercies was so great on my mind when I awoke, that my strength entirely failed me for many minutes, and I was exceedingly weak. This was the first spiritual mercy I ever was sensible of, and being on praying ground, as soon as I recovered a little strength, and got out of bed and dressed myself I invoked heaven from my inmost soul, and fervently begged that God would never again permit me to blaspheme his most holy name. The Lord, who is long-suffering, and full of compassion to such poor rebels as we are, condescended to hear and answer. I felt that I was altogether unholy, and saw clearly what a bad use I had made of the faculties I was endowed with: they were given me to glorify God with; I thought, therefore, I had better want them here, and enter into life eternal, than abuse them and be cast into hell fire. I prayed to be directed, if there were any holier persons than those with whom I was acquainted, that the Lord would point them out to me. I appealed to the searcher of hearts, whether I did not wish to love him more, and serve him better. Notwithstanding all this, the reader may easily discern, if a believer, that I was still in nature's darkness. At length I hated the house in which I lodged, because God's most holy name was blasphemed in it; then I saw the word of God verified, viz. "Before they call, I will answer; and while they are yet speaking, I will hear."[235]

I had a great desire to read the Bible the whole day at home; but not having a convenient place for retirement, I left the house in the day, rather than stay amongst the wicked ones; and that day, as I was walking, it pleased God to direct me to a house where there was an old sea-faring man, who experienced much of the love of God shed abroad in his heart. He began to discourse with me; and, as I desired to love the Lord, his conversation rejoiced me greatly; and indeed I had never heard before the love of Christ to believers set forth in such a manner, and in so clear a point of view. Here I had more questions to put to the man than his time would permit him to answer: and in that memorable hour there came in a Dissenting Minister;[236] he joined our discourse, and asked me some few questions; among others, where I heard the gospel preached? I knew not what he meant by hearing the gospel; I told him I had read the gospel: and he asked me where I went to church, or whether I went at all, or not? To which I replied, "I attended St. James's, St. Martin's, and St. Ann's, Soho."—"So," said he, "you are a churchman?" I answered, I was.[237] He then invited me to a love feast at his chapel that evening.[238] I accepted the offer, and thanked him; and soon after he went away. I had some further discourse with the old christian, added to some profitable reading, which made me exceedingly happy. When I left him he reminded me of coming to the feast; I assured him I would be there. Thus we parted, and I weighed over the heavenly conversation that had passed between these two men, which cheered my then heavy and drooping spirit more than any thing I had met with for many months. However, I thought the time long in going to my supposed banquet. I also wished much for the company of these friendly men; their company pleased me much; and I thought the gentleman very kind in asking me, a stranger, to a feast; but how singular did it appear to me, to have it in a chapel! When the wished for hour came I went, and happily the old man was there, who kindly seated me, as he belonged to the place. I was much astonished to see the place filled with people, and no signs of eating and drinking. There were many ministers in the company. At last they began by giving out hymns, and between the singing, the ministers engaged in prayer: in short, I knew not what to make of this sight, having never seen any thing of the kind in my life before now. Some of the guests began to speak their experience, agreeable to what I read in the Scriptures: much was said by every speaker of the providence of God, and his unspeakable mercies to each of them. This I knew in a great measure, and could most heartily join them. But when they spoke of a future state, they seemed to be altogether certain of their calling and election of God;[239] and that no one could ever separate them from the love of Christ, or pluck them out of his hands. This filled me with utter consternation, intermingled with admiration. I was so amazed as not to know what to think of the company; my heart was attracted, and my affections were enlarged; I wished to be as happy as them, and was persuaded in my mind that they were different from the world "that lieth in wickedness," 1 John v. 19. Their language and singing, &c. did well harmonize; I was entirely overcome, and wished to live and die thus. Lastly, some persons produced some neat baskets full of buns, which they distributed about; and each person communicated with his neighbour, and sipped water out of different mugs, which they handed about to all who were present. This kind of Christian fellowship I had never seen, nor ever thought of seeing on earth; it fully reminded me of what I had read in the Holy

Scriptures of the primitive Christians,[240] who loved each other and broke bread, in partaking of it, even from house to house. This entertainment (which lasted about four hours) ended in singing and prayer. It was the first soul-feast I ever was present at. These last twenty-four hours produced me things, spiritual and temporal, sleeping and waking, judgment and mercy, that I could not but admire the goodness of God, in directing the blind, blasphemous sinner in the path that he knew not of, even among the just; and instead of judgment he has shewed mercy, and will hear and answer the prayers and supplications of every returning prodigal;

O! to grace how great a debtor
Daily I'm constrain'd to be.[241]

After this I was resolved to win heaven, if possible; and if I perished, I thought it should be at the feet of Jesus, in praying to him for salvation. After having been an eye-witness to some of the happiness which attended those who feared God, I knew not how, with any propriety, to return to my lodgings, where the name of God was continually profaned, at which I felt the greatest horror; I paused in my mind for some time, not knowing what to do; whether to hire a bed elsewhere, or go home again. At last, fearing an evil report might arise, I went home, with a farewell to card-playing and vain-jesting, &c. I saw that time was very short, eternity long, and very near; and I viewed those persons alone blessed, who were found ready at midnight-call, or when the Judge of all, both quick[242] and dead, cometh.

The next day I took courage, and went to Holborn, to see my new and worthy acquaintance, the old man, Mr. C—; he, with his wife, a gracious woman, were at work at silk-weaving; they seemed mutually happy, and both quite glad to see me, and I more to see them. I sat down, and we conversed much about soul matters, &c. Their discourse was amazingly delightful, edifying, and pleasant. I knew not at last how to leave this agreeable pair, till time summoned me away. As I was departing, they lent me a little book, entitled "The Conversion of an Indian."[243] It was in questions and answers. The poor man came over the sea to London, to enquire after the Christian's God, who (through rich mercy) he found, and had not his journey in vain. The above book was of great use to me, and at that time was a means of strengthening my faith; however, in parting, they both invited me to call on them when I pleased. This delighted me, and I took care to make all the improvement from it I could: and so far I thanked God for such company and desires. I prayed that the many evils I felt within might be done away, and that I might be weaned from my former carnal acquaintances. This was quickly heard and answered, and I was soon connected with those whom the Scripture calls the excellent of the earth. I heard the gospel preached, and the thoughts of my heart and actions were laid open by the preachers, and the way of salvation by Christ alone was evidently set forth. Thus I went on happily for near two months; and I once heard, during this period, a reverend gentleman, Mr. Green, speak of a man who had departed this life in full assurance of his going to glory. I was much astonished at the assertion; and did very deliberately inquire how he could get at this knowledge. I was answered fully, agreeably to what I read in the oracles of truth; and was told also, that if I did not experience the new birth, and the pardon of my sins, thro' the blood of Christ, before I died, I could not enter the kingdom of heaven. I knew not what to think of this report, as I thought I kept eight commandments out of ten; then my worthy interpreter told me I did not do it, nor could I; and he added, that no man ever did or could keep the commandments, without offending in one point. I thought this sounded very strange, and puzzled me much for many weeks; for I thought it a hard saying. I then asked my friend Mr. L—d, who was clerk in a chapel, why the commandments of God were given, if we could not be saved by them? To which he replied, "The law is a school-master to bring us to Christ," who alone could, and did keep the commandments, and fulfilled all their requirements for his elect people, even those to whom he had given a living faith, and the sins of those chosen vessels *were already* atoned for and forgiven them whilst living;[244] and if I did not experience the same before my exit, the Lord would say at that great day to me, "Go, ye cursed," &c. &c. for God would appear faithful in his judgments to the wicked, as he would be faithful in shewing mercy to those who were ordained to it before the world was; therefore Christ Jesus seemed to be all in all to that man's soul. I was much wounded at this discourse, and brought into such a dilemma as I never expected. I asked him, if *he* was to die that moment, whether he was sure to enter the kingdom of God; and added, "Do you *know* that your sins are forgiven you?" he answered in the affirmative. Then confusion, anger, and discontent seized me, and I staggered much at this sort of doctrine; it brought me to a stand, not knowing which to believe, whether salvation by works, or by faith only in Christ. I requested him to tell me how I might know when my sins were forgiven me. He assured me he could not, and that none but God alone could do this. I told him it was very mysterious; but he said it was really matter of fact, and quoted many portions of Scripture immediately to the point, to which I could make no reply. He then desired me to pray to God to shew me these things. I answered that I prayed to God every day. He said, "I perceive you are a churchman." I answered, I was. He then entreated me to beg of God, to shew me what I was, and the true state of my soul. I thought the prayer very short and odd; so we parted for that time. I weighed all these things over, and could not help thinking how it was possible for a man to know his sins were forgiven him in this life. I wished that God would reveal this self-same thing to me. In a short time after this, I went to Westminster chapel; the late Rev. Dr. Peckwell preached from Lam[entations]. iii 39.[245] It was a wonderful sermon; he clearly shewed that a living man had no cause to complain for the punishments of his sins; he evidently justified the Lord in all his dealings with the sons of men; he also shewed the justice of God in the eternal punishment of the wicked and impenitent. The discourse seemed to me like a two-edged sword cutting all ways; it afforded me much joy, intermingled with many fears about my soul; and when it was ended, he gave it out that he intended, the ensuing week, to examine all those who meant to attend the Lord's table. Now I thought much of my good works, and, at the same time, was doubtful of my being a proper object to receive the sacrament: I was full of meditation till the day of examining. However, I went to the chapel, and, though much distressed, I addressed the reverend gentleman, thinking, if I was not right, he would endeavour to convince me of it. When I conversed with him, the first thing he asked me was, What I knew of Christ? I told him I believed in him, and had been baptized in his name. "Then," said he, "when were you brought to the knowledge of God; and how were you convinced of sin?" I knew not what he meant by these questions; I told him I kept eight commandments out of ten; but that I sometimes swore on board of ship, and sometimes when on shore, and broke the sabbath. He then asked me if I could read; I answered, "Yes."—"Then," said he, "do you read in the Bible, he that offends in one point is guilty of all?"[246] I said, "Yes." Then he assured me, that one sin unattoned for was as sufficient to damn a soul, as one leak was to sink a ship. Here I was struck with awe; for the minister exhorted me much, and reminded me of the shortness of time, and the length of eternity, and that no unregenerate soul, or any thing unclean, could enter the kingdom of Heaven.

He did not admit me as a communicant;[247] but recommended me to read the scriptures, and hear the word preached; not to neglect fervent prayer to God, who has promised to hear the supplications of those who seek him in godly sincerity; so I took my leave of him, with many thanks, and resolved to follow his advice, so far as the Lord would condescend to enable me. During this time I was out of employ, nor was likely to get a situation suitable for me, which obliged me to go once more to sea. I engaged as steward of a ship called the Hope, Captain Richard Strange, bound from London to Cadiz in Spain. In a short time after I was on board, I heard the name of God much blasphemed, and I feared greatly lest I should catch the horrible infection. I thought if I sinned again, after having life and death set evidently before me, I should certainly go to hell. My mind was uncommonly chagrined, and I murmured much at God's providential dealings with me, and was discontented with the commandments, that I could not be saved by what I had done; I hated all things, and wished I had never been born; confusion seized me, and I wished to be annihilated. One day I was standing on the very edge of the stern of the ship, thinking to drown myself; but this scripture was instantaneously impressed on my mind, "That no murderer hath eternal life abiding in him," I John iii. 15. Then I paused, and thought myself the unhappiest man living. Again, I was convinced that the Lord was better to me than I deserved, and I was better off in the world than many. After this I began to fear death; I fretted, mourned, and prayed, till I became a burden to others, but more so to myself. At length I concluded to beg my bread on shore, rather than go again to sea amongst a people who feared not God, and I entreated the captain three different times to discharge me; he would not, but each time gave me greater encouragement to continue with him, and all on board shewed me very great civility: notwithstanding all this, I was unwilling to embark again. At last some of my religious friends advised me, by saying it was my lawful calling, consequently it was my duty to obey, and that God was not confined to place, &c. particularly Mr. G. Smith,[248] the governor of Tothill-fields, Bridewell, who pitied my case, and read the eleventh chapter of the Hebrews to me, with exhortations. He prayed for me, and I believe that he prevailed on my behalf, as my burden was then greatly removed, and I found a heartfelt resignation to the will of God. The good man gave me a pocket Bible, and Alleine's Alarm to the Unconverted.[249] We parted, and the next day I went on board again. We sailed for Spain, and I found favour with the captain. It was the fourth of the month of September when we sailed from London, and we had a delightful voyage to Cadiz, where we arrived the twenty-third of the same month. The place is strong, commands a fine prospect, and is very rich. The Spanish galleons frequent that port, and some arrived whilst we were there. I had many opportunities of reading the Scriptures. I wrestled hard with God in fervent prayers, who had declared in his word that he would hear the groanings and deep sighs of the poor in spirit. I found this verified to my utter astonishment and comfort in the following manner: On the morning of the 6th of October (I pray you to attend) all that day, I thought I should see or hear something supernatural. I had a secret impulse on my mind of something that was to take place, which drove me continually for that time to a throne of grace. It pleased God to enable me to wrestle with him, as Jacob did: I prayed that if sudden death were to happen, and I perished, it might be at Christ's feet.

In the evening of the same day, as I was reading and meditating on the fourth chapter of the Acts, twelfth verse,[250] under the solemn apprehensions of eternity, and reflecting on my past actions, I began to think I had lived a moral life, and that I had a proper ground to believe I had an interest in the divine favour; but still meditating on the subject, not knowing whether salvation was to be had partly for our own good deeds, or solely as the sovereign gift of God:—in this deep consternation the Lord was pleased to break in upon my soul with his bright beams of heavenly light; and in an instant, as it were, removing the veil, and letting light into a dark place, Isa[iah]. xxv. 7.[251] I saw clearly, with the eye of faith, the crucified Saviour bleeding on the cross on Mount Calvary: the Scriptures became an unsealed book, I saw myself a condemned criminal under the law, which came with its full force to my conscience, and when "the commandment came sin revived, and I died."[252] I saw the Lord Jesus Christ in his humiliation, loaded and bearing my reproach, sin, and shame. I then clearly perceived, that by the deed of the law no flesh living could be justified. I was then convinced, that by the first Adam sin came, and by the second Adam (the Lord Jesus Christ) all that are saved must be made alive. It was given me at that time to know what it was to be born again, John iii. 5.[253] I saw the eighth chapter to the Romans, and the doctrines of God's decrees verified, agreeable to his eternal, everlasting and unchangeable purposes. The word of God was sweet to my taste, yea sweeter than honey and the honey comb. Christ was revealed to my soul as the chiefest among ten thousand. These heavenly moments were really as life to the dead, and what John calls an earnest of the Spirit.[254] This was indeed unspeakable, and, I firmly believe, undeniable by many. Now every leading providential circumstance that happened to me, from the day I was taken from my parents to that hour, was then, in my view, as if it had but just then occurred. I was sensible of the invisible hand of God, which guided and protected me, when in truth I knew it not: still the Lord pursued me although I slighted and disregarded it; this mercy melted me down. When I considered my poor wretched state, I wept, seeing what a great debtor I was to sovereign free grace.[255] Now the Ethiopian was willing to be saved by Jesus Christ,[256] the sinner's only surety, and also to rely on none other person or thing for salvation. Self was obnoxious, and good works he had none; for it is God that worketh in us both to will and to do. Oh! the amazing things of that hour can never be told—it was joy in the Holy Ghost! I felt an astonishing change; the burden of sin, the gaping jaws of hell, and the fears of death, that weighed me down before, now lost their horror; indeed I thought death would now be the best earthly friend I ever had. Such were my grief and joy, as, I believe, are seldom experienced. I was bathed in tears, and said, What am I, that God should thus look on me, the vilest of sinners? I felt a deep concern for my mother and friends, which occasioned me to pray with fresh ardour; and, in the abyss of thought, I viewed the unconverted people of the world in a very awful state, being without God and without hope.

It pleased God to pour out on me the spirit of prayer and the grace of supplication, so that in loud acclamations I was enabled to praise and glorify his most holy name. When I got out of the cabin, and told some of the people what the Lord had done for me, alas! who could understand me or believe my report! None but to whom the arm of the Lord was revealed. I became a barbarian to them in talking of the love of Christ: his name was to me as ointment poured forth; indeed it was sweet to my soul, but to them a rock of offence. I thought my case singular, and every hour a day until I came to London, for I much longed to be with some to whom I could tell of the wonders of God's love towards me, and join in prayer to him whom my soul loved and thirsted after. I had uncommon commotions within, such as few can tell aught[257] about. Now the Bible was my only companion and comfort; I prized it much, with many thanks to God that I could read it for myself, and was not left to be tossed about or led by man's devices and notions. The worth of a soul cannot be told.—May the Lord give the reader an understanding in this. Whenever I looked in the Bible I saw things new, and many texts were immediately applied to me with great comfort; for I knew that to me was the word of salvation sent. Sure I was that the Spirit which indited the word opened my heart to receive the truth of it as it is in Jesus—that the same Spirit enabled me to act with faith upon the promises which were precious to me, and enabled me to believe to the salvation of my soul. By free grace I was persuaded that I had a part and lot in the first resurrection,[258] and was enlightened with the "light of the living," Job xxxiii. 30. I wished for a man of God, with whom I might converse; my soul was like the chariots of Aminadab, Canticles vi. 12. These, among others, were the precious promises that were so powerfully applied to me: "All things whatsoever ye shall ask in prayer, believing, ye shall receive," Matt[hew]. xxi. 22. "Peace I leave with you, my peace I give unto you," John xiv. 27. I saw the blessed Redeemer to be the fountain of life, and the well of salvation. I experienced him to be all in all; he had brought me by a way that I knew not, and he had made crooked paths straight. Then in his name I set up his Ebenezer,[259] saying, Hitherto He hath helped me: and could say to the sinners about me, Behold what a Saviour I have! Thus I was, by the teaching of that all glorious Deity, the great One in Three, and Three in One, confirmed in the truths of the Bible; those oracles of everlasting truth, on which every soul living must stand or fall eternally, agreeably to Acts iv. 12. "Neither is there salvation in any other, for there is no other name under heaven given among men whereby we must be saved, but only Jesus Christ." May God give the reader a right understanding in these facts! "To him that believeth, all things are possible, but to them that are unbelieving, nothing is pure," Titus i. 15.

During this period we remained at Cadiz until our ship got laden. We sailed about the 4th of November; and, having a good passage, we arrived in London the month following, to my comfort, with heart-felt gratitude to God, for his rich and unspeakable mercies.

On my return, I had but one text which puzzled me, or that the devil endeavoured to buffet me with, viz. Rom[ans]. xi. 6.[260] and as I had heard of the Rev. Mr. Romaine, and his great knowledge in the Scriptures, I wished much to hear him preach. One day I went to Blackfriars church, and, to my great satisfaction and surprise, he preached from that very text. He very clearly shewed the difference between human works and free election, which is according to God's sovereign will and pleasure.[261] These glad tidings set me entirely at liberty, and I went out of the church rejoicing, seeing my spots[262] were those of God's children. I went to Westminster chapel,[263] and saw some of my old friends, who were glad when they perceived the wonderful change that the Lord had wrought in me, particularly Mr. G. Smith, my worthy acquaintance, who was a man of a choice spirit, and had great zeal for the Lord's service. I enjoyed his correspondence till he died in the year 1784. I was again examined in that same chapel, and was received into church-fellowship amongst them: I rejoiced in spirit, making melody in my heart to the God of all my mercies. Now my whole wish was to be dissolved, and to be with Christ—but, alas! I must wait my appointed time.

[Equiano's "Miscellaneous Verses" on his religious conversion.]

CHAPTER XI

[Equiano travels to the Mediterranean.]

Having taken at this place some fine wines, fruits, and money, we proceeded to Cadiz, where we took about two tons more of money, &c. and then sailed for England in the month of June. When we were about the north latitude 42, we had contrary winds for several days, and the ship did not make in that time above six or seven miles straight course. This made the captain exceedingly fretful and peevish; and I was very sorry to hear God's most holy name often blasphemed by him. One day, as he was in that impious mood, a young gentleman on board, who was a passenger, reproved him, and said, he acted wrong, for we ought to be thankful to God for all things, as we were not in want of any thing on board; and though the wind was contrary for us, yet it was fair for some others, who perhaps stood in more need of it than we. I immediately seconded this young gentleman with some boldness, and said we had not the least cause to murmur, for that the Lord was better to us than we deserved, and that he had done all things well. I expected that the captain would be very angry with me for speaking, but he replied not a word. However, before that time, or hour, on the following day, being the 21st of June, much to our great joy and astonishment, we saw the providential hand of our benign Creator, whose ways with his blind creatures are past finding out. The preceding night I dreamed that I saw a boat immediately off the starboard main shrouds; and exactly at half past one o'clock the following day at noon, while I was below, just as we had dined in the cabin, the man at the helm cried out, A boat! which brought my dream that instant into my mind. I was the first man that jumped on the deck; and looking from the shrouds onward, according to my dream, I descried a little boat at some distance; but, as the waves were high, it was as much as we could do sometimes to discern her; we, however, stopped the ship's way, and the boat which was extremely small, came alongside with eleven miserable men, whom we took on board immediately. To all human appearance, these people must have perished in the course of an hour, or less; the boat being small, it barely contained them. When we took them up they were half drowned, and had no victuals, compass, water, or any other necessary whatsoever, and had only one bit of an oar to stir with, and that right before the wind; so that they were obliged to trust entirely to the mercy of the waves. As soon as we got them all on board, they bowed themselves on their knees, and, with hands and voices lifted up to heaven, thanked God for their deliverance; and I trust that my prayers were not wanting amongst them at the same time. This mercy of the Lord quite melted me, and I recollected his words, which I saw thus verified, in the 107th Psalm, "O give thanks unto the Lord, for he is good, for his mercy endureth for ever. Hungry and thirsty, their souls fainted in them. They cried unto the Lord in their trouble, and he delivered them out of their distresses. And he led them forth by the right way, that they might go to a city of habitation. O that men would praise the Lord for his goodness, and for his wonderful works to the children of men. For he satisfieth the longing soul, and filleth the hungry soul with goodness."

"Such as sit in darkness and in the shadow of death:"

"Then they cried unto the Lord in their trouble, and he saved them out of their distresses. They that go down to the sea in ships; that do business in great waters; these see the works of the Lord, and his wonders in the deep. Whoso is wise and will observe these things, even they shall understand the loving kindness of the Lord."[264]

The poor distressed captain said, "that the Lord is good; for, seeing that I am not fit to die, he therefore gave me a space of time to repent." I was very glad to hear this expression, and took an opportunity, when convenient, of talking to him on the providence of God. They told us they were Portuguese, and were in a brig loaded with corn,[265] which shifted that morning at five o clock, owing to which the vessel sunk that instant with two of the crew; and how these eleven got into the boat (which was lashed to the deck) not one of them could tell. We provided them with every necessary, and brought them all safe to London: and I hope the Lord gave them repentance unto eternal life.

At our arrival, I was happy once more amongst my friends and brethren till November, when my old friend, the celebrated Dr. Irving, bought a remarkable fine sloop, about 150 tons. He had a mind for a new adventure, in cultivating a plantation at Jamaica and the Musquito Shore; he asked me to go with him, and said that he would trust me with his estate in preference to any one. By the advice, therefore, of my friends, I accepted of the offer, knowing that the harvest was fully ripe in those parts, and I hoped to be an instrument, under God, of bringing some poor sinner to my well-beloved master, Jesus Christ. Before I embarked, I found with the Doctor four Musquito Indians, who were chiefs in their own country, and were brought here by some English traders for some selfish ends.[266] One of them was the Musquito king's son, a youth of about eighteen years of age; and whilst he was here he was baptized by the name of George. They were going back at the government's expence, after having been in England about twelve months, during which they learned to speak pretty good English. When I came to talk to them, about eight days before we sailed, I was very much mortified in finding that they had not frequented any churches since they were here, and were baptized,[267] nor was any attention paid to their morals. I was very sorry for this mock Christianity, and had just an opportunity to take some of them once to church before we sailed. We embarked in the month of November 1775, on board of the sloop Morning Star, Captain David Miller, and sailed for Jamaica. In our passage I took all the pains that I could to instruct the Indian prince in the doctrines of Christianity, of which he was entirely ignorant; and, to my great joy, he was quite attentive, and received with gladness the truths that the Lord enabled me to set forth to him. I taught him in the compass of eleven days all the letters, and he could put even two or three of them together, and spell them. I had Fox's Martyrology with cuts,[268] and he used to be very fond of looking into it, and would ask many questions about the papal cruelties he saw depicted there, which I explained to him. I made such progress with this youth, especially in religion, that when I used to go to bed at different hours of the night, if he was in his bed, he would get up on purpose to go to prayer with me, without any other clothes than his shirt; and before he would eat any of his meals amongst the gentlemen in the cabin, he would first come to me to pray, as he called it. I was well pleased at this, and took great delight in him, and used much supplication to God for his conversion. I was in full hope of seeing daily every appearance of that change which I could wish; not knowing the devices of Satan, who had many of his emissaries to sow his tares[269] as fast as I sowed the good seed, and pull down as fast as I built up. Thus we went on nearly four-fifths of our passage, when Satan at last got the upper hand. Some of his messengers, seeing this poor heathen much advanced in piety, began to ask him whether I had converted him to Christianity, laughed and made their jest at him, for which I rebuked them as much as I could; but this treatment caused the prince to halt between two opinions. Some of the true sons of Belial,[270] who did not believe that there was any hereafter, told him never to fear the devil, for there was none existing; and if ever he came to the prince, they desired he might be sent to them. Thus they teazed the poor innocent youth, so that he would not learn his book any more! He would not drink nor carouse with these ungodly actors, nor would he be with me even at prayers. This grieved me very much. I endeavoured to persuade him as well as I could, but he would not come; and entreated him very much to tell me his reasons for acting thus. At last he asked me, "How comes it that all the white men on board, who can read and write, observe the sun, and know all things, yet swear, lie, and get drunk, only excepting yourself?" I answered him, the reason was, that they did not fear God; and that if any one of them died so, they could not go to, or be happy with God. He replied, that if a certain person went to hell, he would go to hell too! I was sorry to hear this; and, as he sometimes had the tooth-ach, and also some other persons in the ship at the same time, I asked him if their tooth-ach made his easy? he said, No. Then I told him, if he and these people went to hell together, their pains would not make his any lighter. This had great weight with him, it depressed his spirits much; and he became ever after, during the passage, fond of being alone. When we came into the latitude of Martinico, and near making the land, one morning we had a brisk gale of wind, and, carrying too much sail, the mainmast went over the side. Many people were then all about the deck, and the yards, masts, and rigging, came tumbling all about us, yet there was not one of us in the least hurt, although some were within a hair's breadth of being killed; and, particularly, I saw two men, who, by the providential hand of God, were most miraculously preserved from being smashed to pieces. On the fifth of January we made Antigua and Montserrat, and ran along the rest of the islands: and on the fourteenth we arrived at Jamaica. One Sunday, while we were there, I took the Musquito, prince George, to church, where he saw the sacrament administered. When we came out we saw all kinds of people, almost from the church door for the space of half a mile down to the water-side, buying and selling all kinds of commodities: and these acts afforded me great matter of exhortation to this youth, who was much astonished. Our vessel being ready to sail for the Musquito shore, I went with the Doctor on board a Guineaman,[271] to purchase some slaves to carry with us, and cultivate a plantation; and I chose them all of my own countrymen, some of whom came from Lybia.[272] On the 12th of February we sailed from Jamaica, and on the eighteenth arrived at the Musquito shore, at a place called Dupeupy. All our Indian guests now, after I had admonished them, and a few cases of liquor given them by the Doctor, took an affectionate leave of us, and went ashore, where they were met by the Musquito king, and we never saw one of them afterwards. We then sailed to the southward of the shore, to a place called Cape Gracias a Dios, where there was a large lagoon or lake, which received the emptying of two or three very fine large rivers, and abounded much in fish and land tortoise. Some of the native Indians came on board of us here; and we used them well, and told them we were come to dwell amongst them, which they seemed pleased at. So the Doctor and I, with some others, went with them ashore; and they took us to different places to view the land, in order to choose a place to make a plantation of. We fixed on a spot near a river's bank, in a rich soil; and, having got our necessaries out of the sloop, we began to clear away the woods, and plant different kinds of vegetables, which had a quick growth. While we were employed in this manner, our vessel went northward to Black River to trade.[273] While she was there, a Spanish guarda costa[274] met with and took her. This proved very hurtful, and a great embarrassment to us. However, we went on with the culture of the land. We used to make fires every night all around us, to keep off wild beasts, which, as soon as it was dark, set up a most hideous roaring. Our habitation being far up in the woods, we frequently saw different kinds of animals; but none of them ever hurt us, except poisonous snakes, the bite of which the Doctor used to cure by giving to the patient, as soon as possible, about half a tumbler of strong rum, with a good deal of Cayenne pepper in it. In this manner he cured two natives, and one of his own slaves. The Indians were exceedingly fond of the Doctor, and they had good reason for it; for I believe they never had such an useful man amongst them. They came from all quarters to our dwelling; and some *woolwow*, or flat-headed Indians,[275] who lived fifty or sixty miles above our river, and this side of the South Sea,[276] brought us a good deal of silver in exchange for our goods. The principal articles we could get from our neighbouring Indians were turtle oil, and shells, little silk grass, and some provisions; but they would not work at any thing for us, except fishing; and a few times they assisted to cut some trees down, in order to build us houses; which they did exactly like the Africans, by the joint labour of men, women, and children. I do not recollect any of them to have had more than two wives. These always accompanied their husbands when they came to our dwelling, and then they generally carried whatever they brought to us, and always squatted down behind their husbands. Whenever we gave them any thing to eat, the men and their wives ate separate. I never saw the least sign of incontinence amongst them. The women are ornamented with beads, and fond of painting themselves; the men also paint, even to excess, both their faces and shirts; their favourite colour is red. The women generally cultivate the ground, and the men are all fishermen and canoe-makers. Upon the whole, I never met any nation that were so simple in their manners as these people, or had so little ornament in their houses. Neither had they, as I ever could learn, one word expressive of an oath. The worst word I ever heard amongst them when they were quarreling, was one that they had got from the English, which was, "you rascal." I never saw any mode of worship among them; but in this they were not worse than their European brethren or neighbours, for I am sorry to say that there was not one white person in our dwelling, nor any where else, that I saw in different places I was at on the shore, that was better or more pious than those unenlightened Indians; but they either worked or slept on Sundays; and, to my sorrow, working was too much Sunday's employment with ourselves; so much so, that in some length of time we really did not know one day from another. This mode of living laid the foundation of my decamping at last. The natives are well made and warlike; and they particularly boast of having never been conquered by the Spaniards. They are great drinkers of strong liquors when they can get them. We used to distill rum from pine-apples, which were very plentiful here; and then we could not get them away from our place. Yet they seemed to be singular, in point of honesty, above any other nation I was ever amongst. The country being hot, we lived under an open shed, where we had all kinds of goods, without a door or a lock to any one article; yet we slept in safety, and never lost any thing, or were disturbed. This surprised us a good deal; and the Doctor, myself, and others, used to say, if we were to lie in that manner in Europe we should have our throats cut the first night. The Indian governor goes once in a certain time all about the province or district, and has a number of men with him as attendants and assistants. He settles all the differences among the people, like the judges here, and is treated with very great respect. He took care to give us timely notice before he came to our habitation, by sending his stick as a token, for rum, sugar, and gunpowder, which we did not refuse sending; and at the same time we made the utmost preparation to receive his honour and his train. When he came with his tribe, and all our neighbouring chieftains, we expected to find him a grave reverend judge, solid and sagacious; but, instead of that, before he and his gang came in sight, we heard them very clamorous; and they even had plundered some of our good neighbouring Indians, having intoxicated themselves with our liquor. When they arrived we did not know what to make of our new guests, and would gladly have dispensed with the honour of their company. However, having no alternative, we feasted them plentifully all the day till the evening; when the Governor, getting quite drunk, grew very unruly, and struck one of our most friendly chiefs, who was our nearest neighbour, and also took his gold-laced hat from him. At this a great commotion took place; and the Doctor interfered to make peace, as we could all understand one another, but to no purpose; and at last they became so outrageous, that the Doctor, fearing he might get into trouble, left the house, and made the best of his way to the nearest wood, leaving me to do as well as I could among them. I was so enraged with the governor, that I could have wished to have seen him tied fast to a tree, and flogged for his behaviour; but I had not people enough to cope with his party. I therefore thought of a stratagem to appease the riot. Recollecting a passage I had read in the life of Columbus, when he was amongst the Indians in Jamaica,[277] where, on some occasion, he frightened them, by telling them of certain events in the heavens, I had recourse to the same expedient, and it succeeded beyond my most sanguine expectations. When I had formed my determination, I went in the midst of them, and taking hold of the governor, I pointed up to the heavens. I menaced him and the rest: I told them God lived there, and that he was angry with them, and they must not quarrel so; that they were all brothers, and if they did not leave off, and go away quietly, I would take the book (pointing to the bible), read, and *tell* God to make them dead. This was something like magic. The clamour immediately ceased, and I gave them some rum and a few other things; after which they went away peaceably; and the Governor afterwards gave our neighbour, who was called Captain Plasmyah, his hat again. When the Doctor returned, he was exceedingly glad at my success in thus getting rid of our troublesome guests. The Musquito people within our vicinity, out of respect to the Doctor, myself, and his people, made entertainments of the grand kind, called in their tongue *tourrie* or *drykbot.* The English of this expression is, a feast of drinking about, of which it seems a corruption of language. The drink consisted of pine-apples roasted, and casades[278] chewed or beaten in mortars; which, after lying some time, ferments, and becomes so strong as to intoxicate, when drank in any quantity. We had timely notice given to us of the entertainment. A white family, within five miles of us, told us how the drink was made; I and two others went before the time to the village, where the mirth was appointed to be held, and there we saw the whole art of making the drink and also the kind of animals that were to be eaten there. I cannot say the sight of either the drink or the meat were enticing to me. They had some thousands of pine apples roasting, which they squeezed, dirt and all, into a canoe they had there for the purpose. The casade drink was in beef barrels and other vessels, and looked exactly like hog-wash. Men, women, and children were thus employed in roasting the pine-apples, and squeezing them with their hands. For food they had many land torpins or tortoises, some dried turtle, and three large alligators alive, and tied fast to the trees. I asked the people what they were going to do with these alligators? and I was told they were to be eaten. I was much surprised at this, and went home not a little disgusted at the preparations. When the day of the feast was come, we took some rum with us, and went to the appointed place, where we found a great assemblage of these people, who received us very kindly. The mirth had begun before we came; and they were dancing with music: and the musical instruments were nearly the same as those of any other sable people; but, as I thought, much less melodious than any other nation I ever knew. They had many curious gestures in dancing, and a variety of motions and postures of their bodies, which to me were in no wise attracting. The males danced by themselves, and the females also by themselves, as with us. The Doctor shewed his people the example, by immediately joining the women's party, though not by their choice. On perceiving the women disgusted, he joined the males. At night there were great illuminations, by setting fire to many pine-trees, while the drykbot went round merrily by calabashes or gourds: but the liquor might more justly be called eating than drinking. One Owden, the oldest father in the vicinity, was drest in a strange and terrifying form. Around his body were skins adorned with different kinds of feathers, and he had on his head a very large and high head-piece, in the form of a grenadier's cap, with prickles like a porcupine; and he made a certain noise which resembled the cry of an alligator. Our people skipped amongst them out of complaisance, though some could not drink of their tourrie; but our rum met with customers enough, and was soon gone. The alligators were killed, and some of them roasted. Their manner of roasting is by digging a hole in the earth, and filling it with wood, which they burn to coal, and then they lay sticks across, on which they set the meat. I had a raw piece of the alligator in my hand: it was very rich: I thought it looked like fresh salmon, and it had a most fragrant smell, but I could not eat any of it. This merry-making at last ended without the least discord in any person in the company, although it was made up of different nations and complexions.

The rainy season came on here about the latter end of May, which continued till August very heavily; so that the rivers were overflowed, and our provisions then in the ground were washed away. I thought this was in some measure a judgment upon us for working on Sundays, and it hurt my mind very much. I often wished to leave this place and sail for Europe; for our mode of procedure, and living in this heathenish form was very irksome to me. The word of God saith, "What does it avail a man if he gain the whole world, and lose his own soul?"[279] This was much and heavily impressed on my mind; and, though I did not know how to speak to the Doctor for my discharge, it was disagreeable for me to stay any longer. But about the middle of June I took courage enough to ask him for it. He was very unwilling at first to grant me my request; but I gave him so many reasons for it, that at last he consented to my going, and gave me the following certificate of my behaviour:

> The bearer, Gustavus Vassa, has served me several years with strict honesty, sobriety, and fidelity. I can, therefore, with justice recommend him for these qualifications; and indeed in every respect I consider him as an excellent servant. I do hereby certify that he always behaved well, and that he is perfectly trustworthy.
>
> CHARLES IRVING.
> *Musquito shore, June* 15, 1776

Though I was much attached to the Doctor, I was happy when he consented to my going. I got every thing ready for my departure, and hired some Indians, with a large canoe, to carry me off. All my poor countrymen, the slaves, when they heard of my leaving them, were very sorry, as I had always treated them with care and affection, and did every thing I could to comfort the poor creatures, and render their condition easy. Having taken leave of my old friends and companions, on the 18th of June, accompanied by the Doctor, I left that spot of the world, and went southward above twenty miles along the river. There I found a sloop, the captain of which told me he was going to Jamaica. Having agreed for my passage with him and one of the owners, who was also on board, named Hughes, the Doctor and I parted, not without shedding tears on both sides. The vessel then sailed along the river till night, when she stopped in a lagoon within the same river. During the night a schooner, belonging to the same owners came in, and, as she was in want of hands, Hughes, the owner of the sloop, asked me to go in the schooner as a sailor, and said he would give me wages. I thanked him; but I said I wanted to go to Jamaica. He then immediately changed his tone, and swore, and abused me very much, and asked how I came to be freed! I told him, and said that I came into that vicinity with Dr. Irving, whom he had seen that day. This account was of no use; he still swore exceedingly at me, and cursed the master for a fool that sold me my freedom, and the Doctor for another in letting me go from him.

Then he desired me to go in the schooner, or else I should not go out of the sloop as a free man. I said this was very hard, and begged to be put on shore again; but he swore that I should not. I said I had been twice amongst the Turks, yet had never seen any such usage with them, and much less could I have expected any thing of this kind among the Christians. This incensed him exceedingly; and, with a volley of oaths and imprecations, he replied, "Christians! Damn you, you are one of St. Paul's men;[280] but by G —, except you have St. Paul's or St. Peter's faith, and walk upon the water to the shore, you shall not go out of the vessel!" which I now found was going amongst the Spaniards towards Carthagena, where he swore he would sell me.[281] I simply asked him what right he had to sell me? But, without another word, he made some of his people tie ropes round each of my ancles, and also to each wrist, and another rope round my body, and hoisted me up without letting my feet touch or rest upon any thing. Thus I hung, without any crime committed, and without judge or jury, merely because I was a freeman, and could not by the law get any redress from a white person in those parts of the world. I was in great pain from my situation, and cried and begged very hard for some mercy, but all in vain. My tyrant in a rage brought a musquet out of the cabin, and loaded it before me and the crew, and swore that he would shoot me if I cried any more. I had now no alternative; I therefore remained silent, seeing not one white man on board who said a word on my behalf. I hung in that manner from between ten and eleven o'clock at night till about one in the morning; when, finding my cruel abuser fast asleep, I begged some of his slaves to slacken the rope that was round my body, that my feet might rest on something. This they did at the risk of being cruelly used by their master, who beat some of them severely at first for not tying me when he commanded them. Whilst I remained in this condition, till between five and six o'clock next morning, I trusted & prayed to God to forgive this blasphemer, who cared not what he did, but when he got up out of his sleep in the morning was of the very same temper and disposition as when he left me at night. When they got up the anchor, and the vessel was getting under way, I once more cried and begged to be released; and now being fortunately in the way of their hoisting the sails, they loosed me. When I was let down, I spoke to one Mr. Cox, a carpenter, whom I knew on board, on the impropriety of this conduct. He also knew the Doctor, and the good opinion he ever had of me. This man then went to the captain, and told him not to carry me away in that manner; that I was the Doctor's steward, who regarded me very highly, and would resent this usage when he should come to know it. On which he desired a young man to put me ashore in a small canoe I brought with me. This sound gladdened my heart and I got hastily into the canoe, and set off whilst my tyrant was down in the cabin; but he soon spied me out, when I was not above thirty or forty yards from the vessel, and, running upon the deck with a loaded musquet in his hand, he presented it at me, and swore heavily and dreadfully, that he would shoot me that instant, if I did not come back on board. As I knew the wretch would have done as he said, without hesitation, I put back to the vessel again; but, as the good Lord would have it, just as I was alongside he was abusing the captain for letting me go from the vessel; which the captain returned, and both of them soon got into a very great heat. The young man that was with me, now got out of the canoe; the vessel was sailing on fast with a smooth sea; and I then thought it was neck or nothing,[282] so at that instant I set off again for my life, in the canoe, towards the shore; and fortunately the confusion was so great amongst them on board, that I got out of the reach of the musquet shot, unnoticed, while the vessel sailed on with a fair wind a different way; so that they could not overtake me without tacking:[283] but, even before that could be done, I should have been on shore, which I soon reached, with many thanks to God for this unexpected deliverance. I then went and told the other owner, who lived near that shore (with whom I had agreed for my passage) of the usage I had met with. He was very much astonished, and appeared very sorry for it. After treating me with kindness, he gave me some refreshment, and three heads of roasted Indian corn, for a voyage of about eighteen miles south, to look for another vessel. He then directed me to an Indian chief of a district, who was also the Musquito admiral, and had once been at our dwelling; after which I set off with the canoe across a large lagoon alone (for I could not get any one to assist me) though I was much jaded,[284] and had pains in my bowels, by means of the rope I had hung by the night before. I was therefore at different times unable to manage the canoe, for the paddling was very laborious. However, a little before dark, I got to my destined place, where some of the Indians knew me, and received me kindly. I asked for the admiral; and they conducted me to his dwelling. He was glad to see me, and refreshed me with such things as the place afforded; and I had a hammock to sleep in. They acted towards me more like Christians than those whites I was amongst the last night, though they had been baptized. I told the admiral I wanted to go to the next port to get a vessel to carry me to Jamaica; and requested him to send the canoe back which I then had, for which I was to pay him. He agreed with me, and sent five able Indians with a large canoe to carry me and my things to my intended place, about fifty miles; and we set off the next morning. When we got out of the lagoon and went along shore, the sea was so high that the canoe was oftentimes very near being filled with water. We were obliged to go ashore, and drag her across different necks of land; we were also two nights in the swamps, which swarmed with musquito flies, and they proved troublesome to us. This tiresome journey of land and water ended, however, on the third day, to my great joy; and I got on board of a sloop commanded by one captain Jenning. She was then partly loaded, and he told me he was expecting daily to sail for Jamaica; and having agreed with me to work my passage, I went to work accordingly. I was not many days on board before we sailed; but, to my sorrow and disappointment, though used to such tricks, we went to the southward along the Musquito shore, instead of steering for Jamaica. I was compelled to assist in cutting a great deal of mahogany wood on the shore as we coasted along it, and load the vessel with it, before she sailed. This fretted me much; but, as I did not know how to help myself among these deceivers, I thought patience was the only remedy I had left, and even that was forced. There was much hard work and little victuals on board, except by good luck we happened to catch turtles. On this coast there was also a particular kind of fish called manatee, which is most excellent eating, and the flesh is more like beef than fish; the scales are as large as a shilling, and the skin thicker than I ever saw that of any other fish.[285] Within the brackish waters along shore there were likewise vast numbers of alligators, which made the fish scarce. I was on board this sloop sixteen days, during which, in our coasting, we came to another place, where there was a smaller sloop called the Indian Queen, commanded by one John Baker. He also was an Englishman, and had been a long time along the shore trading for turtle shells and silver, and had got a good quantity of each on board. He wanted some hands very much; and, understanding I was a freeman, and wanted to go to Jamaica, he told me if he could get one or two men more, that he would sail immediately for that Island; he also pretended to show me some marks of attention and respect, and promised to give me forty five shillings sterling a month if I would go with him. I thought this much better than cutting wood for nothing. I therefore told the other captain that I wanted to go to Jamaica in the other vessel; but he would not listen to me: and, seeing me resolved to go in a day or two, he got the vessel under sail, intending to carry me away against my will. This treatment mortified me extremely. I immediately, according to an agreement I had made with the captain of the Indian Queen, called for her boat, which was lying near us, and it came along-side; and by the means of a north pole shipmate which I met with in the sloop I was in, I got my things into the boat, and went on board of the Indian Queen, July the 10th. A few days after I was there, we got all things ready and sailed; but again, to my great mortification, this vessel still went to the south, nearly as far as Carthagena, trading along the coast, instead of going to Jamaica, as the captain had promised me: and, what was worst of all, he was a very cruel and bloody-minded man, and was a horrid blasphemer. Among others, he had a white pilot, one Stoker, whom he beat often as severely as he did some negroes he had on board. One night in particular, after he had beaten this man most cruelly, he put him into the boat, and made two negroes row him to a desolate key, or small island; and he loaded two pistols; and swore bitterly that he would shoot the negroes if they brought Stoker on board again. There was not the least doubt but that he would do as he said, and the two poor fellows were obliged to obey the cruel mandate; but, when the captain was asleep, the two negroes took a blanket, at the risque of their lives, and carried it to the unfortunate Stoker, which I believe was the means of saving his life from the annoyance of insects. A great deal of entreaty was used with the captain the next day, before he would consent to let Stoker come on board; and when the poor man was brought on board he was very ill, from his situation during the night, and he remained so till he was drowned a little time after. As we sailed southward we came to many uninhabited islands, which were overgrown with fine large cocoa-nut trees. As I was very much in want of provisions, I brought a boat load of the nuts on board, which lasted me and others for several weeks, and afforded us many a delicious repast in our scarcity. One day, before this, I could not help observing the providential hand of God, that ever supplies all our wants, though in the ways and manner we know not. I had been a whole day without food, and made signals for boats to come off, but in vain. I therefore earnestly prayed to God for relief in my need; and at the close of the evening I went off the deck. Just as I laid down I heard a noise on the deck; and, not knowing what it meant, I went directly on the deck again, when what should I see but a fine large fish, about seven or eight pounds, which had jumped aboard! I took it, and admired, with thanks, the good hand of God; and what I considered as not less extraordinary, the captain, who was very avaricious, did not attempt to take it from me, there being only him and I on board; for the rest were all gone ashore trading. Sometimes the people did not come off for some days: this used to fret the captain, and then he would vent his fury on me by beating me, or making me feel in other cruel ways. One day especially, in this wild, wicked, and mad career, after striking me several times with different things, and once across my mouth, even with a red burning stick out of the fire, he got a barrel of gunpowder on the deck, and swore that he would blow up the vessel. I was then at my wit's end, and earnestly prayed to God to direct me. The head was out of the barrel; and the captain took a lighted stick out of the fire to blow himself and me up, because there was a vessel then in sight coming in, which he supposed was a Spanish Guarda Costa, and he was afraid of falling into their hands. Seeing this, I got an axe, unnoticed by him, and placed myself between him and the powder, having resolved in myself, as soon as he attempted to put the fire in the barrel, to chop him down that instant. I was more than an hour in this situation; during which he struck me often, still keeping the fire in his hand for this wicked purpose. I really should have thought myself justifiable in any other part of the world if I had killed him, and prayed to God, who gave me a mind which rested solely on himself. I prayed for resignation, that his will might be done: and the following two portions of his holy word, which occurred to my mind, buoyed up my hope, and kept me from taking the life of this wicked man. "He hath determined the times before appointed, and set bounds to our habitations," Acts xvii. 26. And, "Who is there among you that feareth the Lord, that obeyeth the voice of his servant, that walketh in darkness and hath no light? let him trust in the name of the Lord, and stay upon his God," Isaiah l. 10. And this, by the grace of God, I was enabled to do. I found him a present help in the time of need, and the captain's fury began to subside as the night approached: but I found,

> That he who cannot stem his anger's tide
> Doth a wild horse without a bridle ride.[286]

The next morning we discovered that the vessel which had caused such a fury in the captain was an English sloop. They soon came to an anchor where we were, and, to my no small surprise, I learned that Dr. Irving was on board of her on his way from the Musquito shore to Jamaica. I was for going immediately to see this old master and friend, but the captain would not suffer me to leave the vessel. I then informed the Doctor, by letter, how I was treated, and begged that he would take me out of the sloop: but he informed me that it was not in his power, as he was a passenger himself; but he sent me some rum and sugar for my own use. I now learned that after I had left the estate which I managed for this gentleman on the Musquito shore, during which the slaves were well fed and comfortable, a white overseer had supplied my place: this man, through inhumanity and ill-judged avarice, beat and cut the poor slaves most unmercifully; and the consequence was, that every one got into a large Puriogua canoe, and endeavoured to escape; but, not knowing where to go, or how to manage the canoe, they were all drowned; in consequence of which the Doctor's plantation was left uncultivated, and he was now returning to Jamaica to purchase more slaves and stock it again.

On the 14th of October, the Indian Queen arrived at Kingston in Jamaica. When we were unloaded I demanded my wages, which amounted to eight pounds five shillings sterling; but Captain Baker refused to give me one farthing, although it was the hardest earned money I ever worked for in my life. I found out Dr. Irving upon this, and acquainted him of the captain's knavery. He did all he could to help me to get my money; and we went to every magistrate in Kingston (and there were nine), but they all refused to do any thing for me, and said my oath could not be admitted against a white man. Nor was this all; for Baker threatened that he would beat me severely if he could catch me, for attempting to demand my money; and this he would have done; but that I got, by means of Dr. Irving, under the protection of Capt. Douglas, of the Squirrel man of war.[287] I thought this exceedingly hard usage; though indeed I found it to be too much the practice there to pay free negro men for their labour in this manner.

One day I went with a free negro tailor, named Joe Diamond, to one Mr. Cochran, who was indebted to him some trifling sum; and the man, not being able to get his money, began to murmur. The other immediately took a horse-whip to pay him with it; but by the help of a good pair of heels, the tailor got off. Such oppressions as these made me seek for a vessel to get off the island as fast as I could: and, by the mercy of God, I found a ship in November bound for England, when I embarked with a convoy, after having taken a last farewell of Dr. Irving. When I left Jamaica he was employed in refining sugars; and offered me a place, but I refused. And some months after my arrival in England I learned, with much sorrow, that this my amiable friend was dead, owing to his having eaten some poisoned fish.

We had many very heavy gales of wind in our passage; in the course of which no material incident occurred, except that an American privateer,[288] falling in with the fleet, was captured and set fire to by his Majesty's ship the Squirrel.

On January the seventh, 1777, we arrived at Plymouth. I was happy once more to tread upon English ground; and, after passing some little time at Plymouth and Exeter among some pious friends, whom I was happy to see, I went to London, with a heart replete with thanks to God for all past mercies.

CHAPTER XII

SUCH were the various scenes to which I was a witness, and the fortune I experienced until the year 1777. Since that period, my life has been more uniform, and the incidents of it fewer than in any other equal number of years preceding; I therefore hasten to the conclusion of a narrative, which I fear the reader may think already sufficiently tedious.

I had suffered so many impositions in my commercial transactions in different parts of the world, that I became heartily disgusted with the seafaring life, and was determined not to return to it, at least for some time. I therefore once more engaged in service shortly after my return, and continued for the most part in this situation until 1784.[289]

Soon after my arrival in London, I saw a remarkable circumstance relative to African complexion, which I thought so extraordinary that I shall beg leave just to mention it: A white negro woman, that I had formerly seen in London and other parts, had married a white man, by whom she had three boys, and they were every one mulattoes, and yet they had fine light hair. In 1779, I served Governor Macnamara,[290] who had been a considerable time on the coast of Africa. In the time of my service I used to ask frequently other servants to join me in family prayer; but this only excited their mockery. However, the Governor, understanding that I was of a religious turn, wished to know what religion I was of; I told him I was a protestant of the church of England, agreeable to the thirty-nine articles of that church;[291] and that whomsoever I found to preach according to that doctrine, those I would hear. A few days after this, we had some more discourse on the same subject; when he said he would, if I chose, as he thought I might be of service in converting my countrymen to the Gospel-faith, get me sent out as a missionary to Africa. I at first refused going, and told him how I had been served on a like occasion by some white people the last voyage I went to Jamaica, when I attempted, (if it were the will of God) to be the means of converting the Indian prince; and said I supposed they would serve me worse than Alexander the coppersmith did St. Paul,[292] if I should attempt to go amongst them in Africa. He told me not to fear, for he would apply to the Bishop of London to get me ordained.[293] On these terms I consented to the Governor's proposal to go to Africa, in hope of doing good, if possible, amongst my countrymen; so, in order to have me sent out properly, we immediately wrote the following letters to the late Bishop of London:

To The Right Reverend Father in God, ROBERT, *Lord Bishop of London.*

THE MEMORIAL OF GUSTAVUS VASSA,[294]
SHEWETH,

THAT your memorialist is a native of Africa, and has a knowledge of the manners and customs of the inhabitants of that country.

That your memorialist has resided in different parts of Europe for twenty-two years last past, and embraced the Christian faith in the year 1759.

That your memorialist is desirous of returning to Africa as a missionary, if encouraged by your Lordship, in hopes of being able to prevail upon his countrymen to become Christians; and your memorialist is the more induced to undertake the same, from the success that has attended the like undertakings when encouraged by the Portuguese through their different settlements on the coast of Africa, and also by the Dutch; both governments encouraged the blacks, who by their education are qualified to undertake the same, and are found more proper than European clergymen, unacquainted with the language and customs of the country.

Your memorialist's only motive for soliciting the office of a missionary is, that he may be a means, under God, of reforming his countrymen and persuading them to embrace the Christian religion. Therefore your memorialist humbly prays your Lordship's encouragement and support in the undertaking.

GUSTAVUS VASSA.
At Mr. Guthrie's, Tailor,
No. 17, Hedge-lane.

MY LORD, I have resided near seven years on the coast of Africa, for most part of the time as commanding officer. From the knowledge I have of the country and its inhabitants, I am inclined to think that the within plan will be attended with great success, if countenanced by your Lordship. I beg further to represent to your Lordship, that the like attempts, when encouraged by other governments, have met with uncommon success; and at this very time I know a very respectable character, a black priest, at Cape Coast Castle.[295] I know the within-named Gustavus Vassa, and believe him a moral good man. I have the honour to be,

My Lord,
Your Lordship's
Humble and obedient Servant,
Grove, 11th March, 1779.
MATT. MACNAMARA.

This letter was also accompanied by the following from Dr. Wallace, who had resided in Africa for many years, and whose sentiments on the subject of the African mission were the same with Governor Macnamara's:

MY LORD, *March* 13, 1779.

I have resided near five years in Senegambia, on the coast of Africa, and have had the honour of filling very considerable employments in that province. I do approve of the within plan, and think the undertaking very laudable and proper, and that it deserves your Lordship's protection and encouragement, in which case it must be attended with the intended success. I am, my Lord,

Your Lordship's
humble and obedient Servant,
THOMAS WALLACE.

With these letters I waited on the Bishop, by the Governor's desire, and presented them to his Lordship. He received me with much condescension and politeness; but, from some certain scruples of delicacy, and saying the Bishops were not of opinion in sending a new missionary to Africa, he declined to ordain me.

My sole motive for thus dwelling on this transaction, or inserting these papers, is the opinion which gentlemen of sense and education, who are acquainted with Africa, entertain of the probability of converting the inhabitants of it to the faith of Jesus Christ, if the attempt were countenanced by the legislature.

Shortly after this I left the Governor, and served a nobleman in the Dorsetshire militia, with whom I was encamped at Coxheath for some time;[296] but the operations there were too minute and uninteresting to make a detail of.

In the year 1783, I visited eight counties in Wales, from motives of curiosity. While I was in that part of the country, I was led to go down into a coal-pit in Shropshire, but my curiosity nearly cost me my life; for while I was in the pit the coals fell in, and buried one poor man, who was not far from me: upon this I got out as fast as I could, thinking the surface of the earth the safest part of it.

In the spring of 1784, I thought of visiting old ocean again. In consequence of this I embarked as steward on board a fine new ship called the London, commanded by Martin Hopkins, and sailed for New York. I admired this city very much; it is large and well-built, and abounds with provisions of all kinds. [While we lay here, a circumstance happened which I thought extremely singular:—One day a malefactor was to be executed on a gallows; but with condition that if any woman, having nothing on but her shift, married the man under the gallows, his life was to be saved. This extraordinary privilege was claimed; a woman presented herself; and the marriage ceremony was performed.][297]

Our ship having got laden, we returned to London in January 1785. When she was again ready for another voyage, the captain being an agreeable man, I sailed with him from hence in the spring, March 1785, for Philadelphia. On the 5th of April we took our departure from the land's end, with a pleasant gale; and, about nine o'clock that night the moon shone bright, and the sea was smooth, while our ship was going free by the wind at the rate of about four or five miles an hour.—At this time another ship was going nearly as fast as we on the opposite point, meeting us right in the teeth, yet none on board observed either ship until we struck each other forcibly head and head, to the astonishment and consternation of both crews. She did us much damage, but I believe we did her more; for when we passed by each other, which we did very quickly, they called to us to bring to, and hoist out our boats, but we had enough to do to mind ourselves; and in about eight minutes we saw no more of her. We refitted as well as we could the next day, and proceeded on our voyage, and in May arrived at Philadelphia.

I was very glad to see this favourite old town once more; and my pleasure was much increased in seeing the worthy Quakers, freeing and easing the burthens of many of my oppressed African brethren. It rejoiced my heart when one of these friendly people took me to see a free-school they had erected for every denomination of black people, whose minds are cultivated here, and forwarded to virtue; and thus they are made useful members of the community. Does not the success of this practice say loudly to the planters, in the language of scripture—"Go ye, and do likewise?"[298]

[With his fellow Africans, Equiano presents an address of thanks to the Quakers in London. Equiano recalls the details of a Quaker wedding he had attended in London.]

We returned to London in August, and our ship not going immediately to sea, I shipped as a steward in an American ship called the Harmony, Captain John Willett, and left London in March 1786, bound to Philadelphia. Eleven days after sailing, we carried our foremast away.[299] We had a nine weeks passage, which caused our trip not to succeed well, the market for our goods proving bad; and, to make it worse, my commander began to play me the like tricks as others too often practise on free negroes in the West Indies. But, I thank God, I found many friends here who in some measure prevented him. On my return to London in August, I was very agreeably surprised to find, that the benevolence of government adopted the plan of some philanthropic individuals, to send the Africans from hence to their native quarter, and that some vessels were then engaged to carry them to Sierra Leona; an act which redounded to the honour of all concerned in its promotion, and filled me with prayers and much rejoicing.[300] There was then in the city a select committee of gentlemen for the black poor, to some of whom I had the honour of being known; and as soon as they heard of my arrival, they sent for me to the committee. When I came there, they informed me of the intention of government; and, as they seemed to think me qualified to superintend part of the undertaking, they asked me to go with the black poor to Africa.[301] I pointed out to them many objections to my going; and particularly I expressed some difficulties on the account of the slave-dealers, as I would certainly oppose their traffic in the human species by every means in my power. However, these objections were overruled by the gentlemen of the committee, who prevailed on me to consent to go; and recommended me to the honourable Commissioners of his Majesty's Navy, as a proper person to act as commissary for government in the intended expedition; and they accordingly appointed me, in November 1786, to that office, and gave me sufficient power to act for the government in the capacity of commissary; having received my warrant and the following order:

By the principal Officers and Commissioners of his Majesty's Navy.

WHEREAS you are directed, by our warrant of the 4th of last month, to receive into your charge, from Mr. Joseph Irwin,[302] the surplus provisions remaining of what was provided for the voyage, as well as the provisions for the support of the black poor, after the landing at Sierra Leona, with the clothing, tools, and all other articles provided at government's expence; and as the provisions were laid in at the rate of two months for the voyage, and for four months after the landing, but the number embarked being so much less than we expected, whereby there may be a considerable surplus of provisions, clothing, &c. these are, in addition to former orders, to direct and require you to appropriate or dispose of such surplus to the best advantage you can for the benefit of government, keeping and rendering to us a faithful account of what you do therein. And for your guidance in preventing any white persons going, who are not intended to have the indulgence of being carried thither, we send you herewith a list of those recommended by the committee for the black poor, as proper persons to be permitted to embark, and acquaint you that you are not to suffer any others to go who do not produce a certificate from the committee for the black poor, of their having their permission for it. For which this shall be your warrant. Dated at the Navy Office, January 16, 1787.

To Mr. Gustavus Vassa, Commissary of Provisions and Stores for the Black Poor to Sierra Leona.

J. HINSLOW.
GEO. MARSH.[303]
W. PALMER.

I proceeded immediately to the executing of my duty on board the vessels destined for the voyage, where I continued till the March following.

During my continuance in the employment of government I was struck with the flagrant abuses committed by the agent, and endeavoured to remedy them, but without effect. One instance, among many which I could produce, may serve as a specimen. Government had ordered to be provided all necessaries (slops,[304] as they are called, included) for 750 persons; however, not being able to muster more than 426,[305] I was ordered to send the superfluous slops, &c. to the king's stores at Portsmouth;[306] but, when I demanded them for that purpose from the agent, it appeared they had never been bought, though paid for by government. But that was not all, government were not the only objects of peculation;[307] these poor people suffered infinitely more; their accommodations were most wretched; many of them wanted beds, and many more clothing and other necessaries. For the truth of this, and much more, I do not seek credit from my own assertion. I appeal to the testimony of Capt. Thompson, of the Nautilus,[308] who convoyed us, to whom I applied in February 1787 for a remedy, when I had remonstrated to the agent in vain, and even brought him to be a witness of the injustice and oppression I had complained of.[309] I appeal also to a letter written by these wretched people, so early as the beginning of the preceding January, and published in the Morning Herald, on the fourth of that month, signed by twenty of their chiefs.[310]

I could not silently suffer government to be thus cheated, and my countrymen plundered and oppressed, and even left destitute of the necessaries for almost their existence. I therefore informed the Commissioners of the Navy of the agent's proceeding; but my dismission was soon after procured by the means of Samuel Hoare, banker[311] in the city; and he moreover, empowered the same agent to receive on board, at the government expence, a number of persons as passengers, contrary to the orders I received. By this I suffered a considerable loss in my property: however, the Commissioners were satisfied with my conduct, and wrote to Capt. Thompson, expressing their approbation of it.

Thus provided, they proceeded on their voyage; and at last, worn out by treatment, perhaps, not the most mild, and wasted by sickness, brought on by want of medicine, clothes, bedding, &c. they reached Sierra Leona just at the commencement of the rains.[312] At that season of the year it is impossible to cultivate the lands; their provisions therefore were exhausted before they could derive any benefit from agriculture; and it is not surprising that many, especially the Lascars,[313] whose constitutions are very tender, and who had been cooped up in ships from October to June, and accommodated in the manner I have mentioned, should be so wasted by their confinement as not long to survive it.

Thus ended my part of the long-talked of expedition to Sierra Leona; an expedition, which, however unfortunate in the event, was humane and politic in its design, nor was its failure owing to government; every thing was done on their part; but there was evidently sufficient mismanagement attending the conduct and execution of it to defeat its success.[314]

I should not have been so ample in my account of this transaction, had not the share I bore in it been made the subject of partial animadversion, and even my dismission from my employment thought worthy of being made, by Hoare and others, matter of public triumph. The motive which might influence any person to descend to a petty contest with an obscure African, and to seek gratification by his depression, perhaps it is not proper here to enquire into or relate, even if its detection were necessary to my vindication;[315] but I thank Heaven it is not. I wish to stand by my own integrity, and not to shelter myself under the impropriety of another; and I trust the behaviour of the Commissioners of the Navy to me entitles me to make this assertion; for after I had been dismissed, March 24,[316] I drew up a memorial thus;

To The Right Honourable the Lords Commissioners of his Majesty's Treasury.
The Memorial and Petition of GUSTAVUS VASSA, *a black man, late Commissary to the Black Poor, going to* AFRICA.

HUMBLY SHEWETH,

THAT your Lordships' memorialist was, by the Honourable the Commissioners of his Majesty's Navy, on the 4th of December last, appointed to the above employment by warrant from that board;

That he accordingly proceeded to the execution of his duty on board of the Vernon, being one of the ships appointed to proceed to Africa with the above poor;

That your memorialist, to his great grief and astonishment, received a letter of dismission, from the Honourable Commissioners of the Navy, by your Lordships' orders:

That, conscious of having acted with the most perfect fidelity and the greatest assiduity in discharging the trust reposed in him, he is altogether at a loss to conceive the reasons of your Lordships' having altered the favourable opinion you were pleased to conceive of him, sensible that your Lordships would not proceed to so severe a measure without some apparent good cause; he therefore has every reason to believe that his conduct has been grossly misrepresented to your Lordships, and he is the more confirmed in his opinion, because, by opposing measures of others concerned in the same expedition, which tended to defeat your Lordships' humane intentions, and to put the government to a very considerable additional expence, he created a number of enemies, whose misrepresentations, he has too much reason to believe, laid the foundation of his dismission. Unsupported by friends, and unaided by the advantages of a liberal education, he can only hope for redress from the justice of his cause, in addition to the mortification of having been removed from his employment, and the advantage which he reasonably might have expected to have derived therefrom. He has had the misfortune to have sunk a considerable part of his little property in fitting himself out, and in other expences arising out of his situation, an account of which he here annexes. Your memorialist will not trouble your Lordships with a vindication of any part of his conduct, because he knows not of what crimes he is accused; he, however, earnestly entreats that you will be pleased to direct an enquiry into his behaviour during the time he acted in the public service; and, if it be found that his dismission arose from false representations, he is confident that in your Lordships' justice he shall find redress.

Your petitioner therefore humbly prays that your Lordships will take his case into consideration, and that you will be pleased to order payment of the above referred to account, amounting to 32£.4s. and also the wages intended, which is most humbly submitted. *London, May* 12, 1787.

The above petition was delivered into the hands of their Lordships, who were kind enough, in the space of some few months afterwards, without hearing, to order me 50£. sterling—that is 18£. wages for the time (upwards of four months) I acted a faithful part in their service.—Certainly the sum is more than a free negro would have had in the western colonies!!!

From that period to the present time my life has passed in an even tenor, and [a] great part of my study and attention has been to assist in the cause of my much injured countrymen.

March the 21st, 1788, I had the honour of presenting the Queen with a petition on behalf of my African brethren, which was received most graciously by her Majesty;[317]

[Equiano petitions the queen to support the abolition of the slave trade.]

The negro consolidated act, made by the assembly of Jamaica last year, and the new act of amendment now in agitation there, contain a proof of the existence of those charges that have been made against the planters relative to the treatment of their slaves.[318]

I hope to have the satisfaction of seeing the renovation of liberty and justice, resting on the British government, to vindicate the honour of our common nature. These are concerns which do not perhaps belong to any particular office: but, to speak more seriously to every man of sentiment, actions like these are the just and sure foundation of future fame; a reversion,[319] though remote, is coveted by some noble minds as a substantial good. It is upon these grounds that I hope and expect the attention of gentlemen in power. These are designs consonant to the elevation of their rank, and the dignity of their stations; they are ends suitable to the nature of a free and generous government; and, connected with views of empire and dominion, suited to the benevolence and solid merit of the legislature.

It is a pursuit of substantial greatness.—May the time come—at least the speculation to me is pleasing—when the sable people shall gratefully commemorate the auspicious aera of extensive freedom: then shall those persons[320] particularly be named with praise and honour, who generously proposed and stood forth in the cause of humanity, liberty, and good policy; and brought to the ear of the legislature designs worthy of royal patronage and adoption. May Heaven make the British senators the dispersers of light, liberty and science, to the uttermost parts of the earth: then will be glory to God on the highest, on earth peace, and goodwill to men.—Glory, honour, peace, &c. to every soul of man that worketh good; to the Britons first, (because to them the Gospel is preached), and also to the nations. "Those that honour their Maker have mercy on the poor."[321] "It is righteousness exalteth a nation; but sin is a reproach to any people:[322] destruction shall be to the workers of iniquity,[323] and the wicked shall fall by their own wickedness."[324] May the blessings of the Lord be upon the heads of all those who commiserated the cases of the oppressed negroes, and the fear of God prolong their days; and may their expectations be filled with gladness! "The liberal devise liberal things, and by liberal things shall stand," Isaiah xxxii. 8. They can say with pious Job, "Did not I weep for him that was in trouble; Was not my soul grieved for the poor?" Job xxx. 25.

As the inhuman traffic of slavery is now taken into[325] the consideration of the British legislature, I doubt not, if a system of commerce was established in Africa, the demand for manufactures would most rapidly augment, as the native inhabitants would[326] insensibly adopt the British fashions, manners, customs, &c. In proportion to the civilization, so will be the consumption of British manufactures.

The wear and tear of a continent, nearly twice as large as Europe, and rich in vegetable and mineral productions, is much easier conceived than calculated.

A case in point.—It cost the Aborigines of Britain little or nothing in clothing, &c. The difference between their forefathers and the present generation, in point of consumption, is literally infinite. The supposition is most obvious. It will be equally immense in Africa.—The same cause, viz. civilization, will ever have the same effect.

It is trading upon safe grounds. A commercial intercourse with Africa opens an inexhaustible source of wealth to the manufacturing interests of Great Britain,[327] and to all which the slave-trade is an objection.

If I am not misinformed, the manufacturing interest is equal, if not superior, to the landed interest, as to the value, for reasons which will soon appear. The abolition of slavery, so diabolical, will give a most rapid extension of manufactures, which is totally and diametrically opposite to what some interested people assert.

The manufacturers of this country must and will, in the nature and reason of things, have a full and constant employ, by supplying the African markets.

Population, the bowels and surface of Africa, abound in valuable and useful returns; the hidden treasures of centuries will be brought to light and into circulation. Industry, enterprize, and mining, will have their full scope, proportionably as they civilize. In a word, it lays open an endless field of commerce to the British manufacturers and merchant adventurers. The manufacturing interest and the general interests are synonimous. The abolition of slavery would be in reality an universal good.

Tortures, murder, and every other imaginable barbarity and iniquity are practised upon the poor slaves with impunity. I hope the slave-trade will be abolished. I pray it may be an event at hand. The great body of manufacturers, uniting in the cause, will considerably facilitate and expedite it; and, as I have already stated, it is most substantially their interest and advantage, and as such the nation's at large, (except those persons concerned in the manufacturing neck-yokes, collars, chains, hand-cuffs, leg-bolts, drags, thumb-screws, iron-muzzles, and coffins; cats,[328] scourges, and other instruments of torture used in the slave trade). In a short time one sentiment alone will prevail, from motives of interest as well as justice and humanity. Europe contains one hundred and twenty millions of inhabitants. Query.—How many millions doth Africa contain? Supposing the Africans, collectively and individually, to expend 5£. a head in raiment and furniture yearly when civilized, &c. an immensity beyond the reach of imagination!

This I conceive to be a theory founded upon facts, and therefore an infallible one. If the blacks were permitted to remain in their own country, they would double themselves every fifteen years. In proportion to such increase will be the demand for manufactures. Cotton and indigo grow spontaneously in most parts of Africa; a consideration this of no small consequence to the manufacturing towns of Great Britain. It opens a most immense, glorious, and happy prospect—the clothing, &c. of a continent ten thousand miles in circumference, and immensely rich in productions of every denomination in return for manufactures.

[329]Since the first publication of my Narrative, I have been in a great variety of scenes in many parts of Great Britain, Ireland, and Scotland, an account of which might well be added here;[330] but as this would swell the volume too much, I shall only observe in general, that in May 1791, I sailed from Liverpool to Dublin where I was very kindly received, and from thence to Cork, and then travelled over many counties in Ireland. I was every where exceedingly well treated, by persons of all ranks. I found the people extremely hospitable, particularly in Belfast, where I took my passage on board of a vessel for Clyde, on the 29th of January, and arrived at Greenock on the 30th. Soon after I returned to London, where I found persons of note from Holland and Germany, who requested me to go there; and I was glad to hear that an edition of my Narrative had been printed in both places, also in New York. I remained in London till I heard the debate in the house of Commons on the Slave Trade, April the 2d and 3d. I then went to Soham in Cambridgeshire, and was married on the 7th of April to Miss Cullen, daughter of James and Ann Cullen, late of Ely.[331]

I have only therefore to request the reader's indulgence, and conclude. I am far from the vanity of thinking there is any merit in this Narrative; I hope censure will be suspended, when it is considered that it was written by one who was as unwilling as unable to adorn the plainness of truth by the colouring of imagination.

My life and fortune have been extremely chequered, and my adventures various. Even those I have related are considerably abridged. If any incident in this little work should appear uninteresting and trifling to most readers, I can only say, as my excuse for mentioning it, that almost every event of my life made an impression on my mind, and influenced my conduct. I early accustomed myself to look at the hand of God in the minutest occurrence, and to learn from it a lesson of morality and religion; and in this light every circumstance I have related was to me of importance. After all, what makes any event important, unless by it's observation we become better and wiser, and learn "to do justly, to love mercy, and to walk humbly before God!"[332] To those who are possessed of this spirit, there is scarcely any book or incident so trifling that does not afford some profit, while to others the experience of ages seems of no use; and even to pour out to them the treasures of wisdom is throwing the jewels of instruction away.[333]

THE END.

NOTES

1. Equiano published nine editions of *The Interesting Narrative*: 1 and 2 in 1789 (London); 3 in 1790 (London); 4 in 1791 (Dublin); 5 in 1792 (Edinburgh); 6 and 7 in 1793 (London); 8 (Norwich) and 9 (London) in 1794. During 1789 *The Interesting Narrative* was reviewed favorably in *The General Magazine and Impartial Review* and *The Monthly Review*, ambivalently by Mary Wollstonecraft (1759-1797) in *The Analytical Review*, and negatively in *The Gentleman's Magazine.*

2. This letter appears in editions 5-9.

3. The attack in *The Oracle* reads:

> It was well observed by Chubb, that there is no absurdity, however gross, but popular credulity has a throat wide enough to swallow it. It is a fact that the Public may depend on, that *Gustavus Vasa*, who has publicly asserted that he was kidnapped in Africa, never was upon that Continent, but was born and bred up in the Danish Island of Santa Cruz, in the West Indies. *Ex hoc uno disce omnes* [this one fact tells all]. What, we will ask any man of plain understanding, must that cause be, which can lean for support on falsehoods as audaciously propagated as they are easily detected?
>
> Modern Patriotism, which wantons so much in sentiment, is *really* founded rather in private interested views, than in a regard for the Public Weal. The conduct of the friends to the Abolition is a proof of the justice of this remark. It is a fact, of which, perhaps, the People are not apprized, but which it well becomes them to know, that WILBERFORCE and the THORNTONS are concerned in settling the Island of Bulam in Sugar Plantations; of course their interests clash with those of the present Planters and hence their clamour against the Slave Trade.
>
> "Old Cato is as great a Rogue as You."

["Chubb" probably refers to Thomas Chubb (1679-1747), whose assessment of human credulity can be found in *A Discourse on Miracles, Considered as Evidence to Prove the Divine Original of a Revelation* (London, 1741): "Man is a creature not only *capable* of being imposed upon by *others*, but likewise of imposing upon *himself*. . . . As men are thus *capable* of misleading themselves, so *sometimes*, and under *some circumstances*, the delusion is *catching*" (72-73).

The writer in *The Oracle* refers to William Wilberforce (1759-1833), leader in the House of Commons of the movement to abolish the slave trade, along with Henry Thornton (1760-1815), chairman of the Sierra Leone Company court of directors, and William Thornton (1761-1828), a slave-owning West Indian Quaker who moved to the United States and who supported his friend Henry Smeathman's proposal for resettling Afro-Britons in Sierra Leone. None of them participated in the short-lived scheme of the Bulama Island Association to set up an agricultural colony off the coast of Western Africa, which the West Indian planters rightly saw as a potential commercial threat to their own interests.

The Old Cato quotation is from Alexander Pope (1688-1744), *The Epistle to Bathurst* (London, 1733), 68.]

4. The attack in *The Star* reads: "The Negroe, called GUSTAVUS VASA, who has published an history of his life, and gives so admirable an account of the laws, religion, and natural productions of the interior parts of Africa; and in which he relates his having been kidnapped in his infancy, is neither more nor less, than a native of the Danish island of Santa Cruz" [present-day St. Croix in the United States Virgin Islands]. Both newspaper attacks appeared while Equiano was in Scotland, preparing and promoting the fifth edition of his book.

5. [Equiano's note]

> —"Speak of me as I am,
> Nothing extenuate, nor set down aught
> In malice." [William Shakespeare, *Othello* 5.2.342.]

6. [Equiano's note]

> I may now justly say,
> "There is a lust in man no charm can tame,
> Of loudly publishing his [our] neighbour's shame;
> On eagles wings immortal scandals fly,
> But [While] virtuous actions are but born and die."*

[Equiano's verse quotation is taken, with minor changes indicated in brackets, from Stephen Harvey's translation of Juvenal, *Satire* 9, first published in 1697.]

**London.* The Country Chronicle and Weekly Advertiser for Essex, Herts, Kent, Surry, Middlesex, &c. Tuesday, February 19th, 1788.—Postscript.

"We are sorry the want of room prevents us from giving place to the favors of GUSTAVUS VASSA on the Slave Trade. The zeal of this worthy African, in favour of his brethren, would do honour to any colour or to any cause."

7. [Equiano's note] My friend Mrs. Baynes, formerly Miss Guerin, at Southhampton, and many others of her friends.
John Hill, Esq. Custom-house, Dublin.
Admiral Affleck.
Admiral George Balfour, Portsmouth.
Captain Gallia, Greenock.
Mrs. Shaw, James-street, Covent-Garden, London.

8. Candid: fair-minded.

9. "*Edinburgh, June* 1792" in editions 8 and 9; edition 6 reads, "*London, Dec.* 30, 1792"; edition 7 reads, "*London, August* 1793."

10. In editions 1 and 2, this address, followed by the "List of Subscribers," is placed immediately after the title page.

11. Equiano's description of himself as humble and unpretentious is quite conventional for writers of autobiographies during the period. A writer of a spiritual autobiography, such as Equiano's, would be especially aware of the danger of sounding too proud. By "unlettered" he means lacking formal education, particularly in the classical

languages of Greek and Latin. Two kinds of *countrymen* appear in this letter: those he addresses are his political countrymen, whose culture and values he has embraced and to whom he appeals as a British subject with the right to petition the members of Parliament; those he refers to in the letter itself are his fellow native Africans, his countrymen by birth.

12. *March* 1789: edition 1 reads, "Union-Street, Mary-le-bone, March 24, 1789"; edition 2 reads, "No. 10, Union-Street, Mary-le-bone, Dec. 24, 1789"; editions 3 and 4 read, "No. 4, Taylor's Buildings, St. Martin's-Lane, October 30, 1790"; edition 5 reads, "June 1792"; edition 6 reads, "December 1792"; editions 7 and 8 read, "March 1789."

13. The "history of neither a saint, a hero, nor a tyrant" was increasingly seen in the seventeenth and eighteenth centuries as the proper subject for autobiography, biography, and the novel. In his *Rambler* 60 (13 October 1750), Samuel Johnson (1709-1784) tells us why: "Our passions are therefore more strongly moved, in proportion as we can more readily adopt the pains or pleasures proposed to our minds, by recognising them as once our own, or considering them as naturally incident to our state of life. It is not easy for the most artful writer to give us an interest in happiness or misery, which we think ourselves never likely to feel, and with which we have never yet been made acquainted. Histories of the downfall of kingdoms, and revolutions of empires, are read with great tranquillity; the imperial tragedy pleases common auditors only by its pomp of ornament, and grandeur of ideas; and the man whose faculties have been engrossed by business, and whose heart never fluttered but at the rise or fall of stocks, wonders how the attention can be seized, or the affections agitated by a tale of love."

14. Countrymen: used here to mean those born in the same geographical area, in the widest sense, Africa.

15. Providence is God as the designer, caretaker, and superintendent of the world and its inhabitants, especially humankind. As the derivation of the term from the Latin *provideo* (to look forward) implies, events in God's creation happen by plan, not chance. And because God is benevolent, all events, no matter how apparently evil, are part of the grand design whose outline has been revealed to humans in the Bible. Equiano's references here to being "a particular favourite" and elsewhere to particular providences convey his belief that God has invested the events of his individual life with significance not as easily recognized in the lives of most humans.

16. That is, nearly on the equator.

17. Abyssinia: the ancient name for modern Ethiopia.

18. The passage in brackets appears only in the 1st edition of 1789.

19. [Equiano's note, editions 8 and 9] See the Observations on a Guinea Voyage, in a series of letters, addressed to the Rev. T. Clarkson, by Jas. Field, Stanfield, in 1788, page 21—"I never saw a happier race of people than those of the kingdom of Benin, seated in ease and plenty, the Slave Trade, and its unavoidable bad effects excepted; every thing bore the appearance of friendship, tranquillity, and primitive independence."

[Equiano quotes from letter 4 of Stanfield (d. 1824), *Observations on a Voyage to the Coast of Africa, in a Series of Letters to Thomas Clarkson, by James Field Stanfield, Formerly a Mariner in the African Trade.* The immediate context of Stanfield's observation is probably also relevant here: he is responding to the assertions made by proponents of the slave trade that West Indian slavery was a material improvement in the living conditions of Africans. The manuscript of Stanfield's *Observations* was approved for publication by the Society for Effecting the Abolition of the Slave Trade, which ordered three thousand copies printed for distribution.

Equiano's homeland was that of the present Ibo people of modern Nigeria.]

20. [Equiano's note, all editions] See Benezet's Account of Guinea throughout.

[Anthony Benezet (1713-1784), *Some Historical Account of Guinea, Its Situation, Produce, and the General Disposition of Its Inhabitants. With an Inquiry into the Rise and Progress of the Slave Trade, Its Nature, and Lamentable Effects* (London, 1788). Much of Equiano's description of Africa, as he indicates, parallels that found in Benezet, which in turn is largely an acknowledged digest of previous accounts by European travelers.

Benezet's writings against the slave trade were republished and distributed throughout Britain after his death by the Society for Effecting the Abolition of the Slave Trade.

Equiano's emphasis on the sanctity of marriage and the consequent severe punishment for adultery contrasts sharply with the common proslavery assertions of African sexual promiscuity, which, the apologists for slavery claimed, accounted for the low birthrate among slaves that required the constant resupply provided by the slave trade. For example, James Grainger (1721?-1766), *An Essay on the More Common West-India Diseases* (London, 1764): "Black women are not so prolific as the white inhabitants, because they are less chaste" (14).]

21. [Equiano's note, all editions] When I was in Smyrna [under the dominion of Turkey] I have frequently seen the Greeks dance after this manner.

22. The ancestor of the modern banjo.

23. Stickado: xylophone.

24. Calico, or muslin: types of cotton cloth.

25. Highland: Scottish.

26. [Equiano's note, all editions] The bowl is earthen, curiously figured, to which a long reed is fixed as a tube. This tube is sometimes so long as to be borne by one, and frequently, out of grandeur, by two boys.

27. Such "refinements" were usually associated with the French during the period.

28. Plantain: a type of banana that must be cooked before eaten.

29. Eadas: from a West African word for an edible tuberous plant.

30. Indian corn: what is commonly known in North America as corn and in Europe as maize. Distinguished from Guinea corn, or millet.

31. In only the first edition, the passage "by pouring . . . certain place" reads "by pouring out a small portion of the food, in a certain place."

32. [Equiano's note, all editions] When I was in Smyrna I saw the same kind of earth, and brought some of it with me to England; it resembles musk in strength, but is more delicious in scent, and is not unlike the smell of a rose.

33. Equiano's description would probably have reminded his readers of a well-known passage from Michel Adanson (1727-1806), *A Voyage to Senegal, the Isle of Goree, and the River Gambia* (London, 1759): "Which way soever I turned my eyes on this pleasant spot, I beheld a perfect image of pure nature: an agreeable solitude, bounded on every side by a charming landskip; the rural situation of cottages in the midst of trees; the ease and indolence of the Negroes, reclined under the shade of their spreading foliage; the simplicity of their dress and manners; the whole revived in my mind, the idea of our first parents, and I seemed to contemplate the world in its primeval state" (54).

Adanson's passage reappears frequently in the anti-slave-trade works of the period, including Benezet's *Account* and Thomas Day (1748-1789) and John Bicknell, *The Dying Negro* (London, 1773), a poem Equiano quotes later in his *Narrative*. Adanson's comment was so popular because it could be used as eyewitness evidence to refute the proslavers' argument that they were saving Africans from the hardships of their homeland by removing them to the West Indies.

34. Stout: strong, powerful.

35. Trepan: to ensnare, to trick.

36. Contemporaneous accounts disagree. For example, James Grainger (1721?-1766), in *The Sugar-Cane: A Poem* (London, 1764), 2:75, notes, "teeth-fil'd Ibbos or *Ebboes*, as they are more commonly called, are a numerous nation. Many of them have their teeth filed, and blackened in an extraordinary manner. They make good slaves when bought young; but are, in general, foul feeders, many of them greedily devouring the raw guts of fowls: They also feed on dead mules and horses; whose carcases, therefore, should be buried deep, that the Negroes may not come at them. But the surest way is to burn them; otherwise they will be apt, privily, to kill those useful animals, in order to feast on them." In *An Essay on the More Common West-India Diseases. . . . To which Are Added, Some Hints on the Management . . . of*

Negroes (London, 1764), he remarks, "In the Ibbo country, the women chiefly work; they, therefore, are to be preferred to the men of the same country at a negroe sale" (7).

Bryan Edwards (1743-1800) says:

> All the Negroes imported from these vast and unexplored regions [the Bight of Benin] . . . are called in the West Indies *Eboes*; and in general they appear to be the lowest and most wretched of all the nations of Africa. In complexion they are much yellower than the Gold Coast and Whidah Negroes; but it is a sickly hue, and their eyes appear as if suffused with bile, even when they are in perfect health. I cannot help observing too, that the conformation of the face, in a great majority of them, very much resembles that of the baboon. . . .
>
> The great objection to the Eboe as slaves, is their constitutional timidity, and despondency of mind; which are so great as to occasion them very frequently to seek, in a voluntary death, a refuge from their own melancholy reflections. They require therefore the gentlest and mildest treatment to reconcile them to their situation; but if their confidence be once obtained, they manifest as great fidelity, affection, and gratitude, as can reasonably be expected from men in a state of slavery. The females of this nation are better labourers than the men, probably from having been more hardly treated in Africa.
>
> The depression of spirits which these people seem to be under, on their first arrival in the West Indies, gives them an air of softness and submission, which forms a striking contrast to the frank and fearless temper of the Koromantyn Negroes. Nevertheless, the Eboes are in fact more truly savage than any nation of the Gold Coast; inasmuch as many tribes among them . . . have been, without doubt, accustomed to the shocking practice of feeding on human flesh. . . .
>
> Of the religious opinions and modes of worship of the Eboes, we know but little; except that . . . they pay adoration to certain reptiles, of which the guana (a species of lizard) is in the highest estimation. They universally practice circumcision. (*The History, Civil and Commercial, of the british Colonies in the West Indies. In Two Volumes* [London, 1793], 2:69-71).

37. The relativity of the significance of skin color was often remarked by Equiano's contemporaries; for example, Adanson notes in *A Voyage*, "It came into my head, that my colour, so opposite to the blackness of the Africans, was the first thing that struck the children: those poor little creatures were then in the same case as our own infants, the first time they see a Negroe" (74).

38. [Equiano's note, all editions] See Benezet's account of Africa throughout.

[Equiano seems to be referring to what is essentially an earlier version of *Some Historical Account of Guinea*: *A Short Account of that Part of Africa, Inhabited by the Negroes. With Respect to the Fertility of the Country; the Good Disposition of Many of the Natives, and the Manner by which the SLAVE TRADE Is Carried on. Extracted from Divers Authors, in Order to Shew the Iniquity of that Trade, and the Falsity of the ARGUMENTS usually Advanced in its Vindication. With Quotations from Several Persons of Note, viz. GEORGE WALLIS, FRANCIS HUTCHESON, and JAMES FOSTER. . . . The Second Edition, with Large Additions and Amendments* (Philadelphia, 1762).]

39. Compare Willem Bosman's observation, quoted in Benezet's *Account* (155): "If the person who occasioned the beginning of the war be taken, they will not easily admit him to ransom, though his weight in gold be offered, for fear he should in future form some new design against their repose."

40. Oblation: an offering.

41. Of the name Olaudah, Paul Edwards remarks, in his introduction to the facsimile reprint of the first edition of the *Narrative* (London: Dawsons of Pall Mall, 1969), "The second element of the name may be either *ude*, 'fame' . . . or *uda*, 'resonant, resounding. . . .' The latter seems more likely, though I have been told that a name composed of *ola*, 'orna-

ment,' and *ude*, having the sense of 'ornament of fame,' might signify 'fortunate.' But I know of no occurrence of any such name in modern times" (lxxiv).

42. Certain times: during menstruation.

43. [Equiano's note, all editions 1-9] See also Lieut. Matthew's Voyage, p. 123.

[The reference is to *A Voyage to the River Sierra-Leone, on the Coast of Africa; Containing an Account of the Trade and Productions of the Country, and of the Civil and Religious Customs and Manners of the People; in a Series of Letters to a Friend in England. By John Matthews, Lieutenant in the Royal Navy; During his Residence in that Country in the Years 1785, 1786, and 1787* (London, 1788). Matthews describes a very similar custom in Africa. Matthews was one of the principal witnesses for the slavery interest at the hearings held in Parliament on the slave trade.]

44. [Equiano's note, all editions] An instance of this kind happened at Montserrat, in the West Indies, in the year 1763. I then belonged to the ship Charming Sally, Capt. Doran.—The chief mate, Mr. Mansfield, and some of the crew being one day on shore, were present at the burying of a poisoned negro girl. Though they had often heard of the circumstance of the running in such cases, and had even seen it, they imagined it to be a trick of the corpse bearers. The mate therefore desired two of the sailors to take up the coffin, and carry it to the grave. The sailors, who were all of the same opinion, readily obeyed; but they had scarcely raised it to their shoulders before they began to run furiously about, quite unable to direct themselves, till at last, without intention, they came to the hut of him who had poisoned the girl. The coffin then immediately fell from their shoulders against the hut, and damaged part of the wall. The owner of the hut was taken into custody on this, and confessed the poisoning.—I give this story as it was related by the mate and crew on their return to the ship. The credit which is due to it I leave with the reader.

[Slave owners in general were quite anxious about their vulnerability to being poisoned by their domestic slaves. For example, in 1740, slaves in New York City were accused of conspiring to poison their masters; and *The London Chronicle* (8 April 1789) carried stories of slaves in Jamaica and London accused of "the horrid practice of administering poison."]

45. [Equiano's note, editions 6-9] See 1 Chron. 1. 33. Also John Brown's [A] Dictionary of the [Holy] Bible [Edinburgh, 1788] on the same verse.

[Equiano's linking of Africans with Jews reflects the widespread belief among both supporters and opponents of the slave trade that, in the words of John Gill (1697-1771), cited below in the *Narrative*, "all *Africa* and a considerable part of *Asia* were possessed by the four sons of *Ham* and their posterity" (73). The point of contention between the two sides was over the issue of whether these descendants of Ham were, like him, cursed for his having mocked Noah. If so, they were doomed to be "most wicked and miserable, and few of them have hitherto enjoyed the light of the gospel" (Brown [1722-1787], *Dictionary*, 2:573). Since Brown's *Dictionary* is arranged topically and does not annotate particular verses, Equiano is probably thinking here (and again in chapter 11, when he cites Brown) of Matthew Henry (1662-1714), *An Exposition of the Old Testament, in Four Volumes* (London, 1710), 8th ed. (Edinburgh, 1772), which he bought in London on 2 May 1777.

Equiano certainly knew the discussions of the subject found in Granville Sharp (1735-1813), *The Just Limitation of Slavery* (London, 1776), Thomas Clarkson (1760-1846), *Essay on the Slavery and Commerce of the Human Species* (London, 1786), and Ottobah Cugoano (1757?-1791+), *Thoughts and Sentiments on the Evil and Wicked Traffic of the Slavery and Commerce of the Human Species* (London, 1787).]

46. John Gill, *An Exposition of the Old Testament, in which Are Recorded the Original of Mankind, of the Several Nations of the World, and of the Jewish Nation in Particular . . . .* (London, 1788), 158.

47. *The Truth of the Christian Religion. In Six Books. By Hugo Grotius. Corrected and Illustrated with Notes by Mr. Le Clerc. To which Is Added, a Seventh Book, Concerning this*

Question, What Christian Church We Ought to Join Ourselves to? By the Said Mr. Le Clerc. Ninth Edition. Done into English by John Clarke. (London, 1786).

48. Confirmed . . . Bedford: editions 1 and 2 read: "confirmed by the scripture chronology." See Arthur Bedford (1668-1745), *The Scripture Chronology Demonstrated by Astronomical Calculations, and also by the Year of Jubilee, and the Sabbatical Year among the Jews; or, An Account of Time from the Creation of the World . . . .* (London, 1730), 229.

49. Law of retaliation: *lex talionis*, the law of an eye for an eye and a tooth for a tooth.

50. [Equiano's note, all editions] Page 178 to 216.

51. [Equiano's note, all editions] Philos. Trans. No. 476. Sect. 4. cited by the Rev. Mr. Clarkson, p. 205.

[Clarkson quotes the concluding sentence of John Mitchel, "Causes of the Different Colours of Persons in Different Climates," a paper read at meetings of the Royal Society from 3 May to 14 June 1744. Mitchel's paper is found in *The Philosophical Transactions (From the Year 1743 to the Year 1750) Abridged and Disposed under General Heads. . . . By John Martyn* [1699-1768] (London, 1756), 10: 926-949.

Mitchel's larger conclusions may be relevant to Equiano's position on color:

> From what has been said about the cause of the colour of black and white people, we may justly conclude, that they might very naturally be both descended from one and the same parents, as we are otherwise better assured from Scripture, that they are . . . for the different colours of people have been demonstrated to be only the necessary effects and natural consequences of their respective climes, and ways of life . . . that they are the most suitable for the preservation of health, and the ease and convenience of mankind in these climes, and ways of living: so that the black colour of the negroes of *Africa*, instead of being a curse denounced on them, on account of their forefather *Ham*, as some have idly imagined, is rather a blessing, rendering their lives, in that intemperate region, more tolerable, and less painful: whereas, on the other hand, the white people, who look on themselves as the primitive race of man, from a certain superiority of worth, either supposed or assumed, seem to have the least pretention to it of any, either from history or philosophy; for they seem to have degenerated more from the primitive and original complexion, in *Noah* and his sons, than even the *Indians* and negroes; and that to the worst extreme, the most delicate, tender, and sickly (10:947).
>
> [W]e do not affirm, that either Blacks or Whites were originally descended from one another, but that both were descended from people of an intermediate tawny colour; whose posterity became more and more tawny, i.e., black, in the southern regions, and less so, or white, in the northern climes: whilst those who remained in the middle regions, where the first men resided, continued of their primitive tawny complexions; which we see confirmed by matter of fact, in all the different people in the world (10:948).]

52. [Equiano's note, all editions] Same page.

[Clarkson quotes from a *Treatise upon the Trade from Great Britain to Africa, by an African Merchant* (London, 1772), which is a proslavery tract.]

53. [Equiano's note, all editions] Acts xvii. 26.

54. Arts . . . exercise: editions 1-4 read "art of war; my daily exercise."

55. Mouths . . . continued: editions 1-7 read "mouths, and ran off with us into the nearest wood. Here they tied our hands, and continued."

56. Equiano's use of *deliverance* here to mean only physical salvation, as opposed to its later meaning in the *Narrative* of spiritual salvation, parallels the dual use of the term in spiritual biographies, including fictional ones, like *Robinson Crusoe* (1719), by Daniel Defoe (1660-1731). During the stage of his life before being exposed to Christianity, Equiano fails to yet recognize that, from a theological perspective, release from the slavery of sin is far more important than release from bodily bondage.

57. Smith: blacksmith.

58. Reads "flogging" in editions 1-8.

59. Adapted or misremembered from Sir John Denham (1615-1669), *Cooper's Hill* (1642): "Now ev'ry leaf, and ev'ry moving breath/Presents a foe, and ev'ry foe a death" (lines 287-288).

60. The use of language was considered a uniquely human achievement, separating humans from animals; hence, the more civilized the people, the more developed, or copious, the language was thought to be.

61. Equiano refers to the four stages of the African slave trade: the original capture by other Africans and transportation to the coast, during which many died from hunger, thirst, and exhaustion; the Middle Passage across the Atlantic, when disease and despair posed the most lethal threats; the seasoning, or period between arrival in the West Indies and full-time employment on the plantations, when the Africans were gradually introduced to the life of forced labor and suddenly introduced to a new and therefore deadly disease environment; and the final stage of enslavement.

62. Equiano may be subtly reminding his readers of the common abolitionist argument that sugar could be profitably cultivated in Africa by free native labor.

63. The phrase "they are known . . . *core*" was added in the fifth and subsequent editions.

Core: cowry, a shell used as currency in West Africa.

64. Equiano must mean 172 pounds of cowry shells because the price of a slave in the eighteenth century ranged between 100 and 300 pounds of shells.

65. Suffer me: allow me.

66. Bound: enslaved.

67. Uncircumcised: like the Jews, Equiano uses this contemptuous label to distinguish other races from his own; at the same time, it reminds his readers of the Jewish-African relationship he sees.

68. Equiano refers to fortune here because, as a pagan, he still saw life as a matter of chance, rather than as a working out of Providential design and order.

69. Discovered: revealed.

70. Eat: a variant spelling of *ate.*

71. Equiano may be making the point that these Africans, the ones who have direct contact with the Europeans, are consequently the most morally corrupted. In *Thoughts upon Slavery* (London, 1774), John Wesley (1703-1791) says that "the Negroes who inhabit the coast of *Africa* . . . are represented by them who have no motive to flatter them, as remarkably sensible, . . . as industrious, . . . As fair, just, and honest in all their dealings, unless where Whitemen have taught them otherwise, . . . And as far more mild, friendly and kind to Strangers, than any of our Forefathers were" (16).

72. Pomkins: pumpkins.

73. Mechanics: skilled craftsmen or artisans.

74. Sound: healthy.

75. Windlass: a winch, or crank, used to wind a heavy rope or chain to lift a weight.

76. Nettings: "a sort of fence, formed of an assemblage of ropes, fastened across each other" (William Falconer [1732-1769], *An Universal Dictionary of the Marine* [London, 1769; reprint, London, 1784], hereafter cited in the notes as Falconer). These nettings were placed along the sides of the ship to form a caged enclosure to prevent the slaves from jumping overboard to try to escape or commit suicide.

77. The abolitionists frequently argued that the slave trade brutalized the enslavers as well as the enslaved. The tyrannical captain became almost a stock figure in the literature. The apologists for slavery argued that the trade served as a nursery for seamen. Evidence supports the abolitionists' claims that the trade was even more lethal, on an average percentage basis, for the crews than for the slaves. The Privy Council in 1789 estimated that the average mortality rate for slaves during the Middle Passage was 12.5 percent. Modern esti-

mates of the mortality rate of 15 percent for slaves mean that of the approximately 10 million Africans taken to the Americas between 1600 and 1900, about 1.5 million died at sea. More than twice that number of African slaves died during the same period either while still in Africa or on their way to the Orient. The mortality rate of the much smaller number of marine slavers is estimated at about 20 percent. For both slaves and enslavers, the death rate varied with length of voyage, time, and age.

78. Foremast: the term *ship* was "particularly applied to a vessel furnished with three masts, each of which is composed of a lower mast, top mast, and top-gallant mast, with the usual machinery thereto belonging. The mast . . . placed at the middle of the ship's length, is called the main-mast, . . . that which is placed in the fore-part, the fore-mast, . . . and that which is towards the stern [the rear] is termed the mizen-mast" (Falconer).

79. Spell or magic: the anchor.

80. Boat: "a small open vessel, conducted on the water by rowing or sailing" (Falconer).

81. Necessary tubs: latrines.

82. Quadrant: "an instrument used to take the altitude of the sun or stars at sea, in order to determine the latitude of the place; or the sun's azimuth, so as to ascertain the magnetical variation" (Falconer).

83. Parcels: groups.

84. Made us jump: as a sign of health and strength.

85. Equiano refers to what was known as the *scramble*, described from the perspective of an observer by Alexander Falconbridge (d. 1792) in *An Account of the Slave Trade on the Coast of Africa* (London, 1788):

> On a day appointed, the negroes were landed, and placed altogether in a large yard, belonging to the merchants to whom the ship was consigned. As soon as the hour agreed on arrived, the doors of the yard were suddenly thrown open, and in rushed a considerable number of purchasers, with all the ferocity of brutes. Some instantly seized such of the negroes as they could conveniently lay hold of with their hands. Others, being prepared with several handkerchiefs tied together, encircled with these as many as they were able. While others, by means of a rope, effected the same purpose. It is scarcely possible to describe the confusion of which this mode of selling is productive. It likewise causes much animosity among the purchasers, who, not unfrequently upon these occasions, fall out and quarrel with each other. The poor astonished negroes were so much terrified by these proceedings, that several of them, through fear, climbed over the walls of the court yard, and ran wild about the town; but were soon hunted down and retaken. (34)

Falconbridge's *Account* was written at the behest of the Society for Effecting the Abolition of the Slave Trade, which printed and distributed six thousand copies.

86. Devoted: doomed.

87. Sloop: "a small vessel furnished with one mast" (Falconer).

88. Snow: "generally the largest of all two-masted vessels employed by Europeans, and the most convenient for navigation" (Falconer).

89. Pascal (d. 1787?): appointed lieutenant, 9 December 1745; commander, 21 August 1759; post-captain, 20 June 1765.

90. This would have been a rather high price for a young, untrained boy, though in times of war, as at this point in Equiano's life, the price was somewhat inflated because of the disruption of the supply of slaves from Africa. Compare Granville Sharp's comment in *A Representation of the Injustice and Dangerous Tendency of Tolerating Slavery; or of Admitting the Least Claim of Private Property in the Persons of Men, in England* . . . (London, 1769): "a stout young Negro, who can read and write, and is approved of in domestic service, is sold for no more than thirty pounds in England; whereas it is certain, that such a one might be sold, at least, for the same sum in the West Indies; and sometimes, perhaps, for near double the money" (43-44).

91. At this point in his life, Equiano is, of course, being deceived by those who tell him he is returning to his country, but they are also being ironically prophetic because once he experiences life in England he always sees it, rather than North America or the West Indies, as his home.

92. Pascal probably renamed Equiano to hide his status as a slave: "Some British officers went so far as to carry their own slaves to sea in the King's ships, but this was best done under disguise, for naval opinion in general and the Admiralty's in particular inclined to regard a man-of-war as a little piece of British territory in which slavery was improper" (N.A.M. Rodger, *The Wooden World: An Anatomy of the Georgian Navy* [London: Fontana Press, 1990], 160).

By being renamed *Gustavus Vassa*, Equiano becomes the namesake of Gustavus I, or Gustavus Vassa (1496-1560), the noble Swede who led his people to freedom from Danish rule in 1521-1523 and went on to become a very successful king of liberated Sweden. But a British audience also associated the name with eighteenth-century arguments over political freedom in Britain because the government of Sir Robert Walpole had used the Licensing Act of 1737 to block the planned performance in 1738 of Henry Brooke's transparently anti-Walpole play, *Gustavus Vasa, The Deliverer of his Country*. Although published in 1739, the play was not staged in England until 1805, when it was performed at Covent Garden. (Retitled *The Patriot*, the play was performed in 1742 in Dublin.) Republication of *Gustavus Vasa* in 1761, 1778, 1796, and 1797 kept the play and its discourse of political slavery before the British public, and in the nineteenth century William Wordsworth considered using Vasa as the subject of an epic poem. *The Poetical Works of John Scott* (London, 1782) includes the suggestion that scenes from the play be used as subjects for paintings.

Slaves were often given ironically inappropriate names of powerful historical figures like Caesar and Pompey to emphasize their subjugation to their masters' wills. Equiano probably expected his readers to recognize the parallel between the Swedish freedom-fighter and the modern leader of his people's struggle against the slave trade, as well as the irony of his initial resistance to his new name.

93. And by which name I have been known ever since: only the first edition reads "and was obliged to bear the present name, by which I have been known ever since."

94. The English generally tended to consider sharks to be inedible. Sharks frequently followed slave ships, drawn to them by the bodies of dead slaves thrown overboard in the course of the Middle Passage. Considered one of the greatest terrors of the sea, the shark was often brutally treated when caught, and what Equiano witnesses is probably a case of gratuitous cruelty. Returning the finless shark to the ocean dooms it to a lingering and painful death.

95. Baker had been with Pascal at least since 20 June 1755, when his name appeared with Pascal's on the muster book of the *Roebuck* (PRO ADM 36/6472).

96. America: though a native of North America, he was a British subject, since the United States of America did not officially exist until 1783.

97. Archipelago: the islands of Greece. Baker died at sea on 21 February 1759 (PRO ADM 36/6367).

98. Discovered: revealed.

99. Grampus: a whale, porpoise, or dolphin; the name often used to refer to the killer whale.

100. Quarter-deck: "the Quarter of a ship [is] . . . that part of a ship's side which lies towards the stern [rear]. Although the lines by which the quarter and bow [front] of a ship, with respect to her length, are only imaginary, . . . if we were to divide the ship's sides into five equal portions, the names of each space would be readily enough expressed. Thus the first, from the stern, would be the quarter; the second, abaft [behind] the midships; the third, the midships; the fourth before the midships; and the fifth, the bow" (Falconer).

101. Compare "seamen have a custom when they meet a *whale*, to fling him out an empty *tub* by way of amusement, to divert him from laying violent hands upon the ship" (Jonathan Swift [1667-1745], preface to *A Tale of a Tub* [London, 1704]).

102. As Equiano says earlier, this was an exceptionally long voyage, almost twice the normal time of about seven weeks.

103. Equiano is mistaken. According to the *Roebuck*'s muster book, he appeared on the ship on 1 January 1756 (PRO ADM 36/6472). Equiano must either have been born before 1745 or been younger than he says he was when he was kidnapped: if he had been eleven years old when he was kidnapped, more than a year seems to have passed, though he now tells us he "was near twelve years of age." He has told us that six or seven months passed between his being kidnapped and his arrival on the coast of Africa; his trip to Barbados must have taken about two months; he was in Barbados for almost two weeks; his voyage to Virginia should have taken about a week; he was in Virginia for perhaps a month; and the passage to England took thirteen weeks. At least thirteen months have passed. He may have exaggerated his own age because the younger he was when he left Africa, the less credible his memory of his homeland would be.

Equiano's memory fails him at other times: he misremembers the dates of his first seeing George Whitefield and the celebration in Charleston of the repeal of the Stamp Act later in his *Narrative*; several of the revisions he makes after the first edition readjust the time scheme of his story.

104. Other Black and White writers had used the motif of the talking book. See the selections from Gronniosaw, Marrant, and Cugoano in this anthology.

Yet another version of the story appears in *The Life, History, and Unparaleled Sufferings of John Jea, The African Preacher. Compiled and Written by Himself* (Portsea, 1812?): "My master's sons also endeavoured to convince me, by their reading in the behalf of their father; but I could not comprehend their dark sayings, for it surprised me much, how they could take that blessed book into their hands, and to be so superstitious as to want to make me believe that the book did talk with them; so that every opportunity when they were out of the way, I took the book, and held it up to my ears, to try whether the book would talk with me or not, but it proved to be all in vain, for I could not hear it speak one word" (33).

105. Probably either Nicholas Dobree or his son Nicholas, born about 1727, in St. Peter Port, Guernsey.

106. Pascal, a lieutenant since 9 December 1745, became the first lieutenant on the *Roebuck* on 13 July 1756; the muster book identifies Baker as his servant and "Gust. Vasa" as the captain's servant (PRO ADM 36/6472).

107. The Nore: an area near the mouth of the Thames where naval military fleets assembled during this period.

108. Man of war: "ships of war are properly equipped with artillery, ammunition, and all the necessary martial weapons and instruments for attack or defence. They are distinguished from each other by their several ranks or classes" (Falconer). Because the next few pages of Equiano's *Narrative* are full of naval terminology, a general note from Falconer on the different classes, or rates, of men of war and the significance of the *Royal George* may be helpful:

> Rates [are] the orders or classes into which the ships of war are divided, according to their force and magnitude. . . .
>
> The British fleet is accordingly distributed into six rates, exclusive of the inferior vessels that usually attend on naval armaments; as sloops of war, armed ships, bomb-ketches, fire-ships and . . . schooners commanded by lieutenants.
>
> Ships of the first rate mount 100 cannon. . . . They are manned by 850 men. . . . Ships of the second rate carry 90 guns upon three decks. . . . Ships of the third rate carry from 64 to 80 cannon. . . . Ships of the fourth rate mount from 60 to 50 guns, upon two decks, and the quarter deck. . . . All vessels of war, under the fourth rate, are usually comprehended under the general names of frigates, and never appear in the line of battle[,]. . . . a general name given to the arrangement or order in which a fleet of ships of war are disposed to engage an enemy. . . .

> Nothing more evidently manifests the great improvement of the marine art, and the degree of perfection to which it has arrived in England, than the facility of managing our first rates; which were formerly esteemed incapable of government, unless in the most favourable weather of the summer. In testimony of this observation we may, with great propriety, produce the example of the Royal George, which, during the whole course of the late war [the Seven Years' War], was known to be as easily navigated, and as capable of service, as any of the inferior ships of the *line*, and that frequently in the most tempestuous seasons of the year."

The *Royal George* was still newsworthy because it had sunk while being repaired in 1782, drowning eight hundred people, and attempts were made throughout the 1780s to salvage parts of the ship.

The *Roebuck* was a fifth rate 40 (that is, with forty guns).

109. The Royal Navy had the authority to forcibly draft experienced seamen into service by boarding incoming merchant vessels or sending press-gangs ashore to impress, or press, those they wanted. Since Britain was fighting France in the Seven Years' War of 1756-1763 (called in North America the French and Indian War), the first truly worldwide war, the navy's press-gangs were very active.

At the end of this chapter, Equiano becomes a member of a press-gang led by Pascal. In 1760, Pascal faced the possibility of legal prosecution for having pressed men he mistakenly thought had deserted from the navy. In a letter to the Admiralty Board dated 5 May 1760, Francis Holburne (1704-1771), the King's Harbourmaster at Plymouth, supported Pascal, and the Board approved his recommendation that His Majesty's Solicitor be ordered to defend Pascal, should he be prosecuted.

110. An engagement: reads "a battle" only in the first edition. Falconer defines *engagement* as follows: "in a naval sense, implies a particular or general battle at sea; or an action of hostility between single ships, or *detachments*, or *squadrons* of ships of war."

111. Prize: "a vessel taken from the enemy by a ship of war, privateer, or armed merchantman" (Falconer). The captain and crew divided the value of the prizes (vessel and contents), the prize-money, among themselves.

112. Elizabeth Martha (b. 1721), Maynard Peter (1726-1760), and Mary (b. 1728) were the children of Maynard and Elizabeth Guerin. On 1 May 1774, Mary became the second wife of Arthur Baynes, surgeon-general to the garrison at Gibraltar. He died at the age of sixty-five in Southampton on 25 March 1789 (PRO PROB 11/1182). While he served on the *Roebuck*, Pascal's wages were paid on 24 March 1757 to "Maynard Guerin Atty," who obviously acted as Pascal's authorized agent, the same role Guerin was playing for the members of several army regiments at the time of his death on 6 May 1760. Guerin's two sisters were his only heirs (PRO PROB 11/856).

113. The entry in the parish register for 9 February reads "Gustavus Vassa a Black born in Carolina 12 years old." During the eighteenth century, the term "Carolina" comprised both North and South Carolina.

114. Thomas Wilson (1663-1755), *An Essay towards an Instruction for the Indians; Explaining the Most Essential Doctrines of Christianity. Which May Be of Use to Such Christians, as Have not well Considered the Meaning of the Religion they Profess; or, Who Profess to Know GOD, but in Works Do Deny Him. in Several Short and Plain Dialogues . . . .* (London, 1740).

115. Rendezvous-house: a place, usually an inn near the Thames, where the commanding officer of a press-gang lodged his gang, received volunteers, gathered information, and which he used as the base of operations for impressing seamen from local taverns.

116. Wherry: "a light sharp boat, used in a river or harbour for carrying passengers from place to place" (Falconer).

117. Waterman: one who manages a boat or ferry.

118. Although the war was effectively over, the Treaty of Paris, which recognized most of Britain's great territorial gains at the expense of the French, was not signed until 10 February 1763.

119. Captain's clerk: Patrick Hill (PRO ADM 32/5).

Rule of three: the rule for calculating the fourth proportional number from three given numbers: the fourth is to the third as the second is to the first.

120. Daniel Queen: listed in the *Aetna*'s pay book as Daniel Quin, able seaman.

Mess: "a particular company of officers or crew of a ship, who eat, drink, and associate together" (Falconer).

121. Hanger: a short, curved broadsword that hangs from the belt.

122. West-Indiamen: ships that carried trade to the West Indies.

123. Prize-money: in wartime, crews shared the value of the prizes — the captured ships and their cargoes.

124. This incident in Equiano's life predates by almost a decade the Mansfield Decision discussed in the introduction.

125. With . . . burst: edition 1 reads "while my heart was ready to burst."

Pascal's apparently unaccountable behavior towards Equiano may be explained by some information not found in the *Narrative.* "Gustavus Vassan" [sic] had been promoted from the status of servant to the naval rating, or status, of able seaman on 29 September 1762 (PRO ADM 32/5), thus making it much harder for Pascal to hide his condition as a slave when Pascal, along with other British officers, was permitted to enter the service of Britain's ally, Portugal, in an attempt to upgrade the Potuguese navy. The status of able seaman was the most skilled, most prestigious, and best paid of the ratings of sailors below the rank of officers by either commission or warrant. But since the ratings were determined by the commanding officer and since, as his owner, Pascal would pocket Vassa's earnings, Pascal's promotion of Vassa may have been at least as much a self-service as a recognition of Vassa's seamanship.

126. Guinea: twenty-one shillings; a pound was worth twenty shillings.

127. [Equiano's note, all editions] Thus was I sacrificed to the envy and resentment of this woman, for knowing that the lady whom she had succeeded in my master's good graces designed to take me into her service; which, had I once got on shore, she would not have been able to prevent. She felt her pride alarmed at the superiority of her rival in being attended by a black servant; it was not the less to prevent this than to be revenged on me, that she caused the captain to treat me thus cruelly.

[As Equiano implies, having a black servant was a common eighteenth-century mark of conspicuous consumption.]

128. *Aeolus* frigate: a fifth rate 32.

129. [Equiano's note, all editions] "The dying Negro," a poem originally published in 1773. Perhaps it may not be deemed impertinent here to add, that this elegant and pathetic [emotionally moving] little poem was occasioned, as appears by the advertisement prefixed to it, by the following incident: "A black who a few days before, had run away from his master, and got himself christened, with intent to marry a white woman, his fellow servant, being taken, and sent on board a ship in the Thames, took an opportunity of shooting himself through the head."

[Equiano conflates and misquotes lines from the first three editions of Thomas Day and John Bicknell, *The Dying Negro, a Poetical Epistle, from a Black, Who Shot Himself on Board a Vessel in the River Thames, to his Intended Wife* (London, 1773).]

130. Milton, *Paradise Lost,* 1:65-68. The second line of Milton's text reads "And rest can never dwell."

131. Quaker: during the eighteenth century, the Society of Friends, or Quakers, put increasing pressure on its members to renounce slavery, eventually threatening slave dealers or owners with expulsion. The need to repeat the threat suggests that King was not the only Quaker to ignore the strictures of the Society. He was probably the same Robert King

involved in a legal action on 13 April 1769 against Walter Tullideph "for Slaves and other live Stock and Plantation" in Montserrat (PRO PC 2/113).

132. To refine wine: to purify or clarify it.

133. Gauging: determining the capacity of vessels.

134. Droggers: coasting vessels used in the West Indies.

135. [Equiano's note, all editions] These pisterines are of the value of a shilling. [The following phrase, "a day," was added in the eighth and ninth eds.]

136. Man of feeling: someone who could empathize with others.

137. Farthing: a fourth of a penny, the smallest English coin.

138. King's Bench: King's Bench Prison for debtors. Checking the Prison Commitment Books and the Inquest Reports on deaths in the King's Bench has not led to a certain identification of the Montserrat official to whom Equiano refers, but the fact that he relies on hearsay information, combined with some coincidences, suggests that he may be mistakenly thinking of Michael White, confirmed in 1764 as Deputy Lieutenant Governor of Montserrat. Although White's will shows that he died a wealthy man (PR PROB 11/1128), *The Gentleman's Magazine* for February 1785 (and consequently published some time after February) says simply that on 15 February died "Hon[orable] Michael White, Lieut. Gov. of Montserrat." Another Michael White was committed to the King's Bench Prison on 18 April and not discharged until 29 November 1785 (PRO PRIS 5/1). Writing several years after the facts and perhaps under the influence of wishful thinking, Equiano may have confused the two Michael Whites.

139. The last war: the American Revolution. He may have taken advantage of the disruption caused by the capture of Montserrat in 1782 by the French.

140. Christian master: one of many times in his *Narrative* Equiano uses *Christian* ironically, or even sarcastically, to stress the frequent incongruity between the profession of Christianity and the practice, particularly among slave owners.

141. The first cost: the price the master paid for him.

142. Coopers: barrel-makers.

143. Thousand pounds current: a thousand pounds in local, or soft, currency; equal to about 571 pounds sterling, or hard currency, at the contemporaneous rate of exchange.

144. Stripes: floggings.

145. Cut most shockingly: castrated.

146. [Equiano's note, all editions] Mr. Dubury, and many others in Montserrat.

147. [Equiano's note, all editions] Sir Philip Gibbes, Bart. [Baronet] Barbadoes. [The following was added to the note in the ninth ed.] See his *Instructions for the Treatment of Negroes, inscribed to the Society for propagating the Gospel in foreign Parts*, 1786. (Sold by Shepperson and Reynolds, London) p. 32, 33.

> "If negroes decrease in number, the decrease must be ever imputed to a want of care, or a want of judgment in the treatment of them.—All animals, rational and irrational, are known to increase in all countries where ease and plenty prevail, and where want and oppression are not felt. This is universally acknowledged: so that where the decrease happens, the design of Providence to increase and multiply is unwisely, as well as impiously, frustrated by the want of care and humanity, or the want of judgment and attention. The people of Barbadoes need not extend their inquiries to distant countries. At St. Vincents they may learn, that a vessel from Africa bound to Barbadoes, I believe, since the commencement of the present century, was stranded on that island. Such of the people as saved themselves from shipwreck settled at St. Vincents. Under all these difficulties which men must suffer from such a misfortune, in an almost uninhabited island (for St. Vincents at that time had very few native Indians) these Africans made a settlement, and have increased to a very considerable number.—Here is a proof, that the negroes will increase even in this climate, when they do not live and labour under circumstances that obstruct population."

[Equiano is not quoting from the 1786 edition, which has only thirty pages, but from the "Second Edition, with Additions" of 1788. Gibbes (1731-1815) was one of Equiano's original subscribers.]

148. Lying: being given time for rest and recovery while, and immediately after, giving birth.

149. [Equiano's note.] Benezet's Account of Guinea, p. 16. [Equiano's information comes from pp. 72-80, which in turn, Benezet acknowledges, is derived from William Burke (1729-1798) and Edmund Burke (1729-1797), *An Account of the European Settlements in America*, 2nd ed. (London, 1758).]

150. Compare Burke, *An Account*: "notwithstanding that the climate is in every respect, except that of being more wholesome, exactly resembling the climate from whence they come" (2:124).

151. The reference to sealing wax echoes an oft-repeated account first found in Sir Hans Sloane (1660-1753), *A Voyage to the Islands Madera, Barbados, Nieves, St. Christophers and Jamaica* . . . . (London, 1707).

152. During pleasure: as long as the master pleased.

153. Milton, *Paradise Lost* 2:616-618. Milton's second line reads, "View'd first their lamentable lot, and found."

154. Charles Town: Charleston, South Carolina.

155. Either a bit's worth (six-pence): reads, in the first edition only, "either a bit, worth six pence."

156. This act, passed 8 August 1688, is frequently mentioned by the opponents of the slave trade. For example, Benezet refers to it in his *Account of Guinea* (1788), 70. In contrast to the treatment of Black slaves, an act passed 3 October 1688 in Barbados declared that poor White apprentices, upon proven mistreatment, would be set free from their master or mistress. As the first major British settlement in the West Indies (1627), Barbados established precedents followed by the other colonies regarding the status and treatment of slaves.

157. Equiano is probably trying to sound unbiased by using examples from the geographical and racial extremes of humankind, commonly thought to be neither Negroes nor Caucasians. On the "Samiade," compare Oliver Goldsmith (1728-1774), *An History of the Earth, and Animated Nature* (London, 1774): "The first distinct race of men is found round the polar regions. The Laplanders, the Esquimaux Indians, the Samoeid Tartars, the inhabitants of Nova Zembla, the Borandians, the Greenlanders, and the natives of Kamskatka, may be considered as one peculiar race of people, all greatly resembling each other in their stature, their complexion, their customs, and their ignorance. . . . These nations not only resemble each other in their deformity, their dwarfishness, the colour of their hair and eyes, but they have all, in a great measure, the same inclinations, and the same manners, being all equally rude, superstitious, and stupid" (2:214).

For the Hottentots, compare "An Account of the Cape of Good Hope; by Mr. John Maxwel. Philosophical Transaction No. 310, p. 2423," in *Memoirs of the Royal Society; or, a New Abridgment of the Philosophical Transactions. . . . By Mr. [Benjamin] Baddam*, 3d ed. (London, 1745): "The *Hottentots* . . . are a race of men distinct both from *Negroes* and *European Whites*; for their hair is woolly, short and frizzled; their noses flat, and lips thick; but their skin is naturally as white as ours. . . . Mr. *Maxwel* takes them to be the most lazy, and ignorant part of mankind" (60, 61).

Equiano might better have followed the advice Benezet offers in his *Account of Guinea* (1788): "But nothing shews more clearly how unsafe it is to form a judgment of distant people from the accounts given of them by travellers, who have taken but a transient view of things, than the case of the Hottentots, . . . those several nations of Negroes who inhabit the most southern part of Africa: *these people* are represented by several authors, who appear to have very much copied their relations one from the other, as so savage and barbarous as to have little of human, but the shape: but these accounts are strongly contradicted by others, particularly Peter Kolben [1675-1726], who has given a circumstantial relation of the disposition and manners of those people. He was a man of learning, sent from the court of Prussia solely to make astronomical observations there; and having no interest in the slavery of the Negroes, had not the same inducement as most other relators had, to misrepresent the natives of Africa" (85).

158. [Equiano's note in editions 3-9.] In his "Cursory Remarks."

[The passage to which Equiano refers is a footnote on page 38 of James Tobin, *Cursory Remarks upon the Reverend Mr. Ramsay's Essay* (London, 1785). James Ramsay (1733-1789) had published *An Essay on the Treatment and Conversion of African Slaves in the Sugar Colonies* in 1784. Equiano had earlier defended his friend Ramsay, a subscriber to the *Narrative*, and attacked Tobin's writings, in *The Public Advertiser*, 28 January 1788.

In a manuscript volume in the Rhodes House Library, Oxford, Ramsay mentions Equiano twice:

> Gustavus Vasa, is a well known instance of what improvement a Negroe is capable. He was kidnapped when about 11 years old perhaps above 1000 miles in land. He continued a slave for many years till he by his industry bought out his own freedom. He has learned to read and write; and in vindication of the rights of his colour has not been afraid to contend in Argument with men of high rank [Thomas Townshend, Lord Sidney (1733-1800), for example], and acuteness of parts. But the extent of his abilities appeared very clearly, when Government resolved to return the Negroes lately to Africa. Those to whom the management of the expedition was committed, dreaded so much his influence over his countrymen, that they contrived to procure an order for his being sent ashore. In particular, his knowledge of the Scriptures is truly surprising, and shows that he could study and really understand them.
>
> A letter addressed "To Civis," who had published a newspaper article defending slavery, begins, "Sir, After taking a competent time to frame your answer concerning the inferiority of the Negroe race you have in your letter of Aug. 19th [in *The Morning Chronicle and London Advertiser*] thought proper to group all your adversaries together, that you might level them at a single volley. But Benezet Junior, Humanitas, Christian and Goodenough [all pseudonyms of writers against the slave trade who published responses to "Civis" in *The Morning Chronicle*], not being sufficiently numerous to entitle you to a triumph, Mr. Ramsay and Mr. [John] Newton [(1725-1807), author of the anti-slave-trade *Thoughts upon the African Slave Trade*, 1788] are added and poor Gustavus Vasa is made in shape of a pig to bring up the rear.... [In his letter of 19 August "Civis" says, "If I were even to allow some share of merit to Gustavus Vasa, Ignatius Sancho, &c. it would not prove equality more, than a pig having been taught to fetch a card, letters, &c. would show it not to be a pig, but some other animal."] I think it is not quite fair to attack persons who give their names to the public, in a mask; while you yourself wish to fight in Masquerade, I have no desire to make the discovery.... You are hurt at being proposed to be pitted against Gustavus Vasa. [In his letter to "Civis," printed 11 July 1788, "Christian" writes, "Now I am far from thinking Civis one of the lowest of the white race; I dare say he is a very respectable person. Yet, from any thing that has appeared under his name, I should not fear to have a black correspondent of yours, Gustavus Vasa, pitted against him, and the publick left to determine which of the two has the best claim to humanity."] As a Christian you must allow that the knowledge of Revelation is the most sublime science, that can adorn human nature. Now with out wishing to imitate your sneering manner or to express the least contempt for your abilities, of which I sincerely entertain an high opinion I propose that the point of inferiority may be determined, by your favorite Mr. Gibbons [Edward Gibbon, (1737-1794), author of *The Decline and Fall of the Roman Empire*, vol. 1, 1776, widely considered a mocker of Christianity] from your or Vasa's most sensible account of your religion." (MSS BRIT EMP. S.2)

Ramsay's manuscript letter is a draft of the letter printed in the 11 September 1788 issue of *The Morning Chronicle* under the pseudonym "George Fox," the name of the founder (1624-1691) of the Society of Friends, or Quakers.]

159. Exodus 7:1-25.

160. [Equiano's footnote in editions 8 and 9.] See the Observations on a Guinea Voyage, in a series of letters to the Rev. T. Clarkson, by James Field, Stanfield, in 1788, p. 21, 22.—"The subjects of the king of Benin, at Gatoe, where I was, had their markets regular and well stocked; they teemed with luxuries unknown to the Europeans."

161. Adapted from Beelzebub's speech in Milton, *Paradise Lost*, 2:332-340. According to Matthew 12:24, Beelzebub is "the prince of the devils."

162. Equiano seems to confuse Brimstone Hill, the location of the defending fortress on St. Christopher's (St. Kitt's) island, with one of the dormant volcanoes on Montserrat, many miles to the south.

163. Stove: past participle of *stave*: to put a hole in.

164. Geneva: gin.

165. Presently: soon.

166. Presumably to keep the knowledge of Christianity from the slaves. There was much dispute during the period over whether Christianity, with its doctrine of the equality of souls, posed a revolutionary threat to the institution of slavery, or whether its promise of an afterlife that could compensate for the sufferings endured in the present served to support the institution.

167. Predestinarian: one who believes that external forces, not one's own choices, determine the events and direction of one's life. If Equiano refers to his African childhood beliefs, they were quite compatible with the side of Methodism associated with George Whitefield, who emphasized a Calvinistic faith in election, or predestination, whereby God has chosen some few people to be saved and the rest to be eternally damned. John Wesley, Whitefield's cofounder of Methodism, was relatively Arminian in his faith, stressing the role of free will in the attainment of salvation through Christ available to all true believers.

168. Puncheons: large casks for holding liquids.

169. Punt: an open boat with squared ends and a flat bottom, propelled in shallow water by a pole.

170. Sounding: where he could touch bottom.

171. Served his time: been apprenticed for a specified period.

172. I have not been able to identify the source of these lines. Perhaps Equiano is the author.

173. To prove: to test.

174. Tierce: 42 gallons.

175. *Wise*: "skilled in hidden arts," Samuel Johnson (1709-1784), *A Dictionary of the English Language* (London, 1755).

176. Ague: a recurrent chill.

177. Repeal of the Stamp Act: Although Equiano sets this event in 1765, the Stamp Act was repealed by Parliament in London on 18 March 1766, and news of the repeal reached America a few weeks later.

178. Bastinadoes: beating with a cudgel or stick.

179. Unlike members of the Church of England or Roman Catholics, Quakers believed that the Bible's teachings were supplemented by individual divine inspiration, the "inner light" available to both men and women, that could be shared in public meetings. These particular messages from God were not always comprehensible by others. Equiano's anecdote anticipates the more famous episode recorded by James Boswell in 1763 in his *Life of Johnson* (London, 1791): "Next day, Sunday, July 31, I told him I had been that morning at a meeting of the people called Quakers, where I had heard a woman preach. JOHNSON. 'Sir, a woman's preaching is like a dog's walking on his hinder legs. It is not done well; but

you are surprized to find it done at all.'" The egalitarian Quakers did not recognize an authority standing between the believer and God, and thus did not have a class of clergy (minister, preacher, or priest) separate from a congregation. As Equiano later discovered, when no member of a meeting was prompted to speak, public worship was conducted silently, a frequent occurrence.

180. Since George Whitefield (1714-1770) was in Great Britain between 7 July 1765 and 16 September 1768, Equiano could not have heard the famous Methodist preacher in Philadelphia in either 1766 or 1767. He probably heard the evangelist in Savannah, Georgia, in February 1765: the 14 and 21 February issues of *The Georgia Gazette*, a weekly newspaper, report that the minister was in town while the sloop *Prudence*, on which Equiano served under Thomas Farmer, was in port.

181. Whitefield was both praised and condemned for the fervor with which he preached, especially to the poor, who were often ignored by more restrained and less evangelical Anglican ministers. William Hogarth satirizes his style of preaching in the print *Credulity, Superstition, and Fanaticism. A Medley* (London, 1762).

182. Manumission: emancipation from slavery or bondage.

183. [Equiano's note, all editions] Acts xii. 9.

184. Elijah is carried to heaven in 2 Kings 2:1-18.

185. Local currency was normally inflated in relation to pounds sterling.

186. Liber D: book, or register, D. The use of authenticating documentation, including correspondence, became a hallmark of eighteenth-century autobiographical and biographical writings, both fictional and nonfictional. The technique is epitomized in James Boswell's *Life of Johnson* (1791).

187. By mere dint of reason: "by my former experience" in the first edition only.

188. Traverse: "in navigation, implies a compound course, or an assembly of various courses, lying at different angles with the meridian. . . . The true course and distance resulting from this diversity of courses is discovered by collecting the difference of latitude and departure of each course, and reducing the whole into one departure and one difference of latitude, according to the known rules of trigonometry" (Falconer). Equiano may be saying that he does not know how to use a traverse-board, "a thin piece of board, marked with all the points of the compass, and having eight holes bored in each, and eight small pegs hanging from the center of the board. It is used to determine the different courses run by a ship during the period of the watch; and to ascertain the distance of each course" (Falconer).

189. Observation: "the art of measuring the altitude of the sun or a star, in order to determine the latitude, or the sun's azimuth" (Falconer).

190. Made . . . water: leaked.

191. Helm: "a long and flat piece of timber, or an assemblage of several pieces, suspended along the hind part of a ship's stern-post, where it turns upon hinges to the right or left, serving to direct the course of the vessel, as the tail of a fish guides the body. The helm is usually composed of three parts . . . the rudder, the tiller, and the wheel, except in small vessels, where the wheel is unnecessary" (Falconer).

Lee-beam: *lee* is "an epithet used by seamen to distinguish that part of the hemisphere to which the wind is directed, from the other part whence it arises: which latter is accordingly called *to windward*" (Falconer).

192. Breakers: "a name given by sailors to those billows [large rolling waves] that break violently over rocks lying under the surface of the sea. They are distinguished both by their appearance and sound, as they cover that part of the sea with a perpetual foam, and produce a hoarse and terrible roaring, very different from what the waves usually have in a deeper bottom. When a ship is unhappily driven amongst breakers, it is hardly possible to save her, as every billow that heaves her upwards serves to dash her down with additional force, when it breaks over the rocks or sand beneath it" (Falconer).

193. Dutch Creole: a person of Dutch descent born in the western hemisphere.

194. Want: lack.

195. Before refrigeration became possible, the only way to preserve meat was by heavily salting it.

196. New Providence: the capital of the Bahamas.

197. Catguts: used to make the strings of musical instruments.

198. Martinico: modern-day Martinique.

199. There was much contemporaneous debate about whether slaves were relatively worse off in the British West Indies than in the French, where their treatment was regulated, at least in theory but not always in practice, since 1685 by the *Code Noir*. Underlying the debate was the dispute over whether slavery was best regulated by the metropolitan European government in Paris or London or by the local Caribbean colonial governments.

200. That is, before the hurricane season suspended maritime travel.

201. Shuffling: shifty or deceitful behavior.

202. Grenades: the Grenadines.

203. Advertise myself: in case anyone had a claim on him as a fugitive slave.

204. Cherry Garden Stairs: a landing place on the south bank of the Thames, about four miles below Westminster Palace.

205. Master: not an owner but an employer who will teach him the skill of hair-dressing.

206. Three parts of the French horn: "The tones of the *French Horn* are soft, rich, and mellow" *The Musical Dictionary* (London, 1835).

207. According to the ledgers for Poor Rates and Cleansing Rates, Francis Grigory and John Grigory lived in different houses in Coventry-court, Haymarket, in 1767. The former may be the Francis Gregory, who received his B.A. from Christ Church, Oxford, in 1742; the latter may be the John Gregory who received his B.A. from St. Mary Hall, Oxford, in 1727. Francis had lived in Coventry-court since at least 1764 and is probably the man Equiano refers to; John does not appear in the ledgers until 1767.

Barter: in arithmetic, "The computation of the quantity or value of one commodity, to be given for a known quantity and value of another; the 'rule' or method of computing this" (*Oxford English Dictionary*).

Alligation: "The arithmetical rule that teaches to adjust the price of compounds, formed of several ingredients of different values" (Johnson, *Dictionary*).

208. Master: of a ship, that is.

209. Equiano's comments on the Turks may be seen as unintentionally ironic. Although he does not say much about slavery in the Middle East, Islamic slave traders had taken as many as four million slaves from Africa before the European transatlantic slave trade began and perhaps an additional three million in the nineteenth century after most of the European trade ended.

210. Franks, or Christians: since the time of the Crusades, when many of the European invaders originated from what is now France, the Turks used the terms *Frank* and *Christian* interchangeably. The infidel Christians were segregated from the Muslim population to avoid religious corruption of the latter by the former.

211. Inquisition: the institution within the Roman Catholic Church established to identify and prosecute heretics.

Among the major disagreements between the Roman Catholic Church and the Protestant denominations are those over the relationship between the Bible and divine truth and the way to salvation. For most Protestants, including Anglicans, the Bible is sufficient for salvation, containing all that a believer needs to know, and accessible to the individual believer; Roman Catholic doctrine maintains that the Bible is necessary but not sufficient, needing to be supplemented by the teachings of the Church Fathers who wrote after the composition of the Bible, which is best mediated to lay-people through the Church, that is, by those properly trained to read it. Some Protestant sects, notably the Quakers, while rejecting the doctrine of mediation by a Church, held that the Bible must be supplemented by postbiblical personal revelations and visitations by the Holy Spirit. Roman Catholics and

Protestants also disagree about which books of the Bible are canonical. Hence, the importation of Bibles, particularly Protestant ones, was perceived in Roman Catholic countries as spreading heresy and undermining the authority of the Church.

212. Garden of Eden: I have found no reference to a garden with this name in Oporto in contemporaneous travelers' accounts.

213. The host: the consecrated bread or wafer of Holy Communion. Te Deum: Te Deum laudamus—We praise Thee, God—the first words of a Latin hymn, used on special occasions of rejoicing and thanks, such as celebrations of victory.

214. Galley: "a kind of low flat-built vessel, furnished with one deck, and navigated with sails and oars, particularly in the Mediterranean" (Falconer). The galley-slaves, who included convicts and non-Christian prisoners of war, were often noted by contemporaneous travelers to southern France and Italy. See, for example, letter 14 in Tobias Smollett (1721-1771), *Travels through France and Italy* (London, 1766).

215. Ferdinand IV and Maria Carolina.

216. Mammon: the demonic god of worldliness and materialism.

217. Locusts: locust-tree beans.

Pulse: edible seeds of pod-bearing plants.

218. Standgate-creek: Stangate Stairs is a landing place on the south bank of the Thames, opposite Westminster Palace.

219. Discovered: revealed.

220. Were: "was" in editions 1-5.

Throughout the British West Indies, of which Jamaica was by far the most populous (with about 300,000 people; Barbados had 100,000), more than 90 percent of the total population of 500,000 were of African descent on the eve of the American Revolution. By comparison, at midcentury, of the approximately 2 million people in the North American colonies that would become the United States, overall about 20 percent were of African descent, but within those Colonies the rate ranged from 2 percent in Massachusetts to 60 percent in South Carolina. Blacks composed 44 percent of the population of Virginia, 20 percent of Georgia, and 2.4 percent of Pennsylvania. In England, with 6.5 million people in 1771, the 14,000-20,000 Blacks made up less than 0.2 percent of the total population and were concentrated in the slave-trading ports of Bristol, Liverpool, and especially London.

221. Situation of a gentleman: Equiano plays upon the difference between birth and behavior in definitions of a *gentleman*. By Johnson's first definition, a *gentleman* is "a man of birth; a man of extraction, though not noble"; by his second, "a man raised above the vulgar by his character or post" (*Dictionary*). Here, as elsewhere in his *Narrative*, Equiano implies that though a man may have the status of a gentleman (Johnson's first definition), he can fail to behave like one (Johnson's second definition).

222. Neptune: Roman god of the sea.

223. Late: "since" in editions 1-5 because Phipps (1744-1792) succeeded his father, Constantine Phipps, as second Baron Mulgrave of Ireland in 1775, two years "since" the voyage (he received an English peerage as Lord Mulgrave 16 June 1790). By the time of the publication of the sixth edition of the *Narrative* in 1793, he had become "late," having died 10 October 1792. Mulgrave was one of Equiano's original subscribers.

Horatio Nelson (1758-1805), later Viscount Nelson, the hero of the naval Battle of Trafalgar, in which he died, was a member of this Arctic expedition.

224. The expedition is most fully described in *A Voyage towards the North Pole Undertaken by His Majesty's Command 1773. By Constantine John Phipps* (London, 1774), an account on which Equiano relies for some of his own details and phrasing, though Equiano includes information not found in Phipps. The *Racehorse* and the *Carcass* were structurally reinforced bomb-vessels.

In the surviving musters for this voyage of the *Racehorse* (PRO ADM/36/7490), which cover the period 24 May to 31 October 1773, Charles Irving, surgeon, is listed as having come aboard on 26 April. The name Vassa does not appear; however, there is a Gustavus

Weston on the musters. He joined the expedition on 17 May and is identified as being an able seaman, aged 28, born in South Carolina. Given that the spelling on the muster lists of foreign names was often at best approximate, and that the personal and professional data match those found on earlier musters, in Equiano's own estimate of his birthdate, and his place of birth given at his baptism, Gustavus Weston is very probably Olaudah Equiano. Because the muster and pay books for the *Racehorse* are lacking for the period between October 1773 and January 1775, I have been unable to determine precisely when Gustavus Weston was discharged from the ship, but he was certainly gone by the latter date.

225. Given the Methodist belief (consistent with the Thirty-nine Articles that constitute the doctrine of the Church of England) in the necessity of divine grace for salvation, Equiano's attempt to achieve salvation on his own is doomed to failure, and his dissatisfaction with his present condition is inevitable.

226. Presumably, what Equiano means is that Judaism availed him nothing because it has a much less fully developed concept of an afterlife than is found in the Christian faiths.

227. The first four books of the New Testament: Matthew, Mark, Luke, and John.

228. Turks: since the Turks were conventionally seen as brutal infidels, comparing hypocritical or false Christians unfavorably to them was a common rhetorical ploy used by satirists. For an example, see Hogarth's *Credulity*, where the smiling Turk is clearly a more sane and positive figure than the lunatic Methodists he (and we) observe.

229. Union-stairs: a landing place on the North bank of the Thames, about three and a half miles downriver from Westminster Palace.

230. Combined piece of business: the mate, captain, and Kirkpatrick conspired against Annis.

231. Habeas corpus: "you shall have the body," a legal writ used to release someone from illegal restraint.

232. Tipstaff: constable or bailiff, so called because, as a sign of his office, he carried a staff with a metal tip.

233. Granville Sharp (1735-1813), who subscribed for two copies of the *Narrative*: this may have been Equiano's first of several encounters with the great abolitionist, who had brought the Somerset case before Mansfield in 1772. Sharp later told his niece, Jemima Sharp, that Equiano had been recommended to him by General James Edward Oglethorpe (1696-1785), the philanthropic founder of Georgia, originally a slave-free colony (Sharp papers at Hardwicke Court, Gloustershire). Equiano's personal opinion of Sharp is expressed in what he wrote on the flyleaf of one of his books:

Gustavus V.
His Book.
Given to him
By that Truly Pious,
And Benevolent man
Mr. Granville Sharp.
April the 13th 1779.
London.

On 19 March 1783, Sharp recorded in his journal that "Gustavus Vassa, a negro, called on me, with an account of 130 negroes being thrown alive into the sea" (Prince Hoare [1755-1834], *Memoirs of Granville Sharp* [London, 1820], 236). Equiano brought Sharp the report in *The Morning Chronicle and London Advertiser* (18 March 1783) of the case of the slaveship *Zong*, whose captain, falsely asserting a lack of water, threw 132 sick Africans into the sea so that the owner of the cargo could make a claim for the insurance money on them.

234. The *London Chronicle* (27 April 1774) gives a different account of the Annis affair, which was newsworthy in part because Kirkpatrick's behavior was clearly illegal in light of the well-known Mansfield decision in the Somerset case of 1772:

A few days ago a Merchant, who had kept a Black Servant some years, having some words with him they parted by consent; and the Black had his Master's leave to go; he accordingly went, and entered himself as a Cook on board a West India ship; the Master hearing where he was, went with two Gentlemen and two Watermen and took the poor Fellow by violence, tying his hands and legs, and carried him on board a ship bound to St. Kitt's, on which he was put in chains to be carried into slavery; but several Gentlemen seeing the transaction, employed an Attorney to serve the Merchant with a habeas corpus to produce the body: the habeas was returned that the body was not to be found, though it is said the ship did not sail through the Downs for St. Kitt's till some days after the habeas was served; therefore the Gentlemen have ordered the Attorney to proceed against the Master; and also on the Captain's return to proceed against him for violently and by force taking a man out of the kingdom.

235. Isaiah 65:24.

236. Dissenting minister: either a Protestant who was not a member of the Church of England, or one of the Methodist lay preachers who, beginning in 1760, took out licenses as dissenting preachers.

237. Because Equiano names Anglican churches in Westminster, the dissenting minister identifies him as a Church of England man.

238. Love feast: religious gatherings intended to commemorate Christ's Last Supper and Christian fellowship. As Equiano soon discovers, the soul, not the body, was fed.

239. Calling and election of God: the Calvinistic belief that divine grace, or salvation, was freely given by God, not earned by humans through their actions or good works. Those who are to be saved have been predestined by God; thus, faith is sufficient, and good works may be a sign of salvation but not a cause.

240. Primitive Christians: those living in the early days of the faith, before the establishment of Churches and the rise of doctrinal disputes.

241. Quoted from Robert Robinson (1735-1790), "Come Thou fount of every blessing," no. 417 in *The Methodist Hymn Book* (1933 ed.).

242. Quick: alive.

243. Except for the London setting, this sounds like another reference to an edition of Thomas Wilson's *An Essay towards an Instruction for the Indians*, a copy of which Equiano had been given when he was baptized and which he subsequently lost.

244. [Equiano's note, lacking in editions 1-5.] Romans, chapter viii. verses 1, 2, 3.

245. Editions 1-7 read "Rev. Mr. P——."

Henry Peckwell (1747-1787), Calvinistic divine and writer, who frequently preached at the Chapel, in the New Way, Westminster.

Lamentations 3:39: "Wherefore doth a living man complain, a man for the punishment of his sins?"

246. James 2:10.

247. Communicant: a person entitled to receive the sacrament of Communion.

248. "Mr. G.S." in editions 1-7.

George Smith (d. 1784) was praised by prison reformers, including John Howard (1726?-1790), for his management of the Tothill-fields, or Westminster, Bridewell (a bridewell was a house of correction in which prisoners were forced to work). In his *State of the Gaols in London, Westminster, and Borough of Southwark. . . .* (London, 1776), William Smith says of George Smith, "The present keeper is a sober, careful, pious man; reads prayers and exhorts the prisoners every day, and sometimes oftener; by such a conduct he tames the fierce and abandoned savage, and makes those hardened wretches preserve a decent deportment, which is a very rare thing in most of the other gaols, where they appear like so many disorderly fiends, cloathed with wickedness, and steeled with daring effrontery" (26).

249. Joseph Alleine (1634-1668), *An Alarme to Unconverted Sinners* (1673), frequently reprinted in the eighteenth century.

250. "Neither is there salvation in any other: for there is none other name under heaven given among men, whereby we must be saved."

251. "Isa. xxv. 7." added in editions 8 and 9.

252. Romans 7:9.

253. "Jesus answered, 'Verily, verily, I say unto thee, Except a man be born of water and *of* the Spirit, he cannot enter into the kingdom of God.'"

254. [Equiano's note, all editions] John xvi. 13, 14, &.

255. Free grace: the phrase is somewhat redundant because *grace* means God's love and protection freely given to the sinner.

256. Equiano alludes to Acts of the Apostles 8:26-39, where the Ethiopian eunuch accepts Christ as his Saviour and is baptized by Philip. *Ethiopian* was a term used to describe any Black African.

257. [Equiano's note, all editions] Acts xxii. 17.

258. A part and lot in: editions 1-5 read "a part in." The first resurrection was that of Jesus.

259. Set up his Ebenezer: Ebenezer was the name of the stone Samuel set up to commemorate God's role in his victory at Mizpeh over the unbelievers (1 Samuel 7:12). Equiano is, of course, using the term figuratively.

260. "And if by grace, then *is it* no more of works: otherwise grace is no more grace. But if *it be* of works, then is it no more grace: otherwise work is no more work."

261. In *A Seasonable Antidote against Popery. In a Dialogue upon Justification* (London, 1757), William Romaine (1714-1795) gives us the gist of what Equiano probably heard him preach:

> And hereby the Believer is entitled to immortal Happiness, on Account of what Christ hath done for him, the Comfort of which he enjoys by what the Holy Spirit hath wrought in him, viz. a believing Apprehension and Conviction that he has an Interest in the Righteousness of the God-Man. This is I think the true Gospel of Jesus Christ, which is evidently no Covenant of Faith and Repentance, but a Revelation of Grace and Mercy, and in which we have the free Promises of eternal Life, but not annexed to the Performance of Faith and Repentance, as Works of Man, or the terms or Conditions of the Covenant, but to Jesus Christ, and to the perfect Obedience, and full Satisfaction he hath made for Sin: For the Gift of God is eternal Life through Jesus Christ our Lord. (6-7)
>
> This justifying Faith is the Gift of the Holy Spirit. He gives us Evidence of our being justified, by bearing his Testimony with our Spirits, that we are the Children of God, and these Fruits do not justify us, but prove us to be justified, as the Fruits upon a Tree don't make it alive, but prove it to be alive. (33-34)

262. Spots: sins.

263. Not the Anglican St. Margaret's of Westminster, in which he had been baptized, but the New Way Chapel, where he had earlier heard Peckwell preach.

264. Equiano is selectively quoting from the psalm.

265. Corn: a general word for cereal grains, but not maize.

266. Musquito Indians: a corruption of *Miskito*, a people living on the Caribbean coast of Central America who, although their king was nominally under the authority of the Jamaican governor, were in effect military allies of Britain against Spain and rebellious slaves. According to Thomas Jefferys (d. 1771), in *The West India Atlas* (London, 1794), "The Mosquitoes were divided into four principal tribes, under the protection of the English: their chiefs have the commissions of Captain, General, Admiral, &c. which were given them with some presents by the Governor of Jamaica, whom they did regard as the King of the World. The implacable hatred they bear to the Spaniards, by whom their ancestors were driven from the fertile plains they enjoyed near Lake Nicaragua, goes almost as far back as the discovery of America, and their friendship for the English is as old as the expeditions of the Buccaniers against their common enemy" (11).

267. And were baptized: editions 1-4 read "to be baptized." The revision, though grammatically clumsy, is more consistent with the sense of the rest of the sentence: to baptize the Indians without teaching them Christian theology and morality was indeed to practice mock-religion.

268. John Fox (1517-1587), *The Acts and Monuments of the Church, or Book of Martyrs,* an anti-Roman Catholic work often reprinted in the eighteenth century in abridged editions with "cuts," or woodcut illustrations.

269. Tares: weed seeds.

270. Belial: a demonic personification mentioned in 2 Corinthians 6:15.

271. Guinea-man: a ship coming from the coast of Guinea with a cargo of slaves.

272. [Equiano's note.] See John Brown's Scripture Dictionary, 1 Chron. i-33. Also Purver's Bible, with Notes on Gen. xxv. 4. [Neither the phrase "some of whom came from Lybia" nor the note appear in editions 1-4. Anthony Purver (1702-1777), *A New and Literal Translation of All the Books of the Old and New Testament; with Notes Explanatory. . . .* (London, 1764): "Alexander Polyhistor & Cleodemus Malchus, who both wrote the History of the Barbarians in Greek, say that Apher, one Abraham's Offspring, led an Army against Libya, and getting the Victory, settled there; from whom his Posterity were called Africans" (1:47)].

273. Black River: called Rio Tinto by the Spaniards.

274. Guarda costa: a ship of the Spanish Colonial coast guard.

275. Woolwow or flat-headed Indians: Ulua Indians, who flattened the heads of their infants by binding them. In Jefferys's *West-India Atlas,* the "Woolvas" are located to the south of the "Moskito King's Party," in present-day Nicaragua.

276. South Sea: the Pacific Ocean.

277. Editions 1-8 read "Columbus, when he was amongst the Indians in Mexico or Peru." On his fourth voyage, to frighten the Indians of Jamaica into supplying his men with provisions, Columbus used his knowledge of an impending lunar eclipse to convince them that his God could punish them with a famine if they continued to refuse his requests.

278. Casades: cassava.

279. Matthew 16:26.

280. Perhaps a reference to Paul's Epistle to the Galatians 3:28: "There is neither Jew nor Greek, there is neither bond nor free, there is neither male nor female: for ye are all one in Christ Jesus." Or perhaps to Paul's epistle to Philemon, in which he returns a slave, Onesimus, to his master, telling the latter to receive him "not now as a servant, but above a servant, a brother beloved, specially to me, but how much more unto thee, both in the flesh, and in the Lord?" (Philemon 16).

On a less spiritual level, the con artists found around St. Paul's in London were called "St. Paul's men."

281. Carthagena: in Spanish New Granada, now Columbia.

282. Neck or nothing: all or nothing, a desperate attempt.

283. Tacking: changing course.

284. Jaded: wearied.

285. Manatee: the sea cow, an aquatic mammal.

286. Adapted from Colley Cibber's play *Love's Last Shift* 2.7.

287. Captain Stair Douglass of the *Squirrel,* a sixth rate 20.

288. Privateer: "a vessel, armed and equipped by particular merchants, and furnished with a military commission by the admiralty, or the officers who superintend the marine department of a country, to cruise against the enemy, and take, sink, or burn their shipping, or otherwise annoy them as opportunity offers. These vessels are generally governed on the same plan with his majesty's ships, although they are guilty of many scandalous depredations, which are very rarely practised by the latter" (Falconer).

289. Engaged in service: worked as a servant.

290. Matthias Macnamara was appointed Lieutenant Governor at James Island in 1774 and Governor of Senegambia in late 1775. In August 1778, after he lost two civil suits brought against him by a subordinate, the Council of Trade removed him as Governor.

291. Thirty-nine Articles: the articles of faith, published in 1563, that constitute the Creed of the Church of England.

292. Alexander the coppersmith did St. Paul: a reference to Paul's Second Epistle to Timothy 4:14-15:

> 14. Alexander the coppersmith did me much evil: the Lord reward him according to his works:
>
> 15. Of whom be thou ware also; for he hath greatly withstood our words.

293. Bishop of London: Robert Lowth (1710-1787).

294. Memorial: a written petition and/or statement of facts.

295. Philip Quaque (1741-17 October 1816), the Black Anglican minister at Cape Coast Castle, discussed in the introduction to this anthology.

296. A nobleman in the Dorsetshire militia: probably George Pitt (1721-1803), Baron Rivers, Colonel of the Dorset militia from 1757 and an original subscriber for two copies of Equiano's *Narrative.*

297. The bracketed passage appears only in editions 1-4 and was probably inadvertently dropped by the printer in later editions.

298. Luke 10:37.

299. Carried our foremast away: the foremast broke off and went overboard.

300. For the plan, see *Plan of a Settlement to Be Made near Sierra Leona, on the Grain Coast of Africa. Intended more particularly for the Service and Happy Establishment of Blacks and People of Colour, to Be Shipped as Freemen under the Direction of the Committee for Relieving the Black Poor, and under the Protection of the British Government. By Henry Smeathman, Esq. Who Resided in that Country near Four Years* (London, 1786).

Smeathman (d. 1786) had spent time in Africa conducting research for a treatise on termites and while there had married into the families of the local African rulers, King Tom and Cleveland, whose father was English. His concern for the presence and plight of Blacks under British rule was prompted by Britain's defeat in the American Revolution: "And whereas many black persons, and people of Colour, Refugees from America, disbanded from his Majesty's Service by sea or land, or otherwise distinguished objects of British humanity, are at this time in the greatest distress, they are invited to avail themselves of the advantages of the plan proposed" (16-17). The charitable impulse was complemented by the desire to abolish the slave trade and to demonstrate that Africa could generate wealth without being forced to export its human resources. In February 1786, Smeathman brought his proposal for a multiracial settlement in Africa to the Committee for the Relief of the Black Poor, headed by Jonas Hanway (1712-1786), a group of London businessmen who raised more than £1,000 to provide relief, health care, clothing, and jobs to needy Blacks. The Committee approved a version of the plan in May and quickly received a promise from the Treasury of up to £14 per person to support transporting the settlers of the projected self-governing village of Granville Town (named in honor of Sharp, the philanthropist and abolitionist), in the Province of Freedom to be established on land bought from local African authorities. The political constitution of the projected community was outlined in Sharp's *A Short Sketch of Temporary Regulations (until Better Shall Be Proposed), for the Intended Settlement on the Grain Coast of Africa, near Sierra Leone* (London, 1786).

A letter from the government to the Committee for the Black Poor reveals a sense of urgency:

> I am commanded by the Lords Commissioners of His Majesty's Treasury to acquaint you that they have taken Measures for the Civil Officers apprehending such Blacks as they may meet with committing any Act of Vagrancy who have received the Bounty of the public on Condition of their going to Serra Leona [*sic*], with an Intention to have them sent from

Time to Time on Board the Ships prepared to convey them to the place of their Destination and the better to enable My Lords to carry their Intentions into Execution, I am directed to desire You will send them a List of the Names of such as have received the said Bounty, and who are not now on board the Ships, and to request that You will favour them with any Observations that may occur to You or any other Plan that You are of Opinion may more effectually carry the Intentions of this Board respecting the sending the Blacks to Serra Leona into Execution with as little delay as possible. (PRO T 27/38, dated 4 December 1786)

The Morning Herald (2 January 1787) reported that the authorities acted promptly: "The Mayor has given orders to the City Marshals, the Marshalmen, and Constables, to take up all the blacks they find begging about the streets, and to bring them before him, or some other Magistrate, that they may be sent home, or to the new colony that is going to be established in Africa; near twenty are already taken up, and lodged in the two Compters" [the Poultry and Wood Street city prisons for debtors].

301. Equiano was the only person of African descent to be involved in the organization of the project. His full title was "Commissary on the part of Government," making him the intended official representative of the British government in the anticipated negotiations with local African authorities about the acquisition of land for the settlement. He was thus the only Afro-Briton in the century to serve at so high a level of administrative power. He was appointed to the position by the Navy Board, headed by Sir Charles Middleton, the very close friend of Equiano's friend, James Ramsay.

302. Only the first edition reads "Mr. Irving." Upon Smeathman's sudden death on 1 July 1786, his clerk and friend, Joseph Irwin (d. 1787), who had never been to Africa, was the freed slaves' own choice to succeed Smeathman as Agent Conductor of the resettlement project.

303. Marsh was Clerk of the Acts of the Navy.

304. Slops: ready-made clothes.

305. Copies of Equiano's muster lists for the *Atlantic*, *Belisarius*, and *Vernon* transport ships are in PRO T 1/643 (no. 487). The settlers were not exclusively Black and included mixed-race couples. His lists total 459 people: 344 Blacks (290 men, 43 women, 11 children) and 115 Whites (31 men, 75 women, 9 children). The muster numbers continued to rise and fall because people who left, were expelled, or died before and during the passage were often replaced by others.

306. The king's stores: the royal naval storehouses.

307. Peculation: embezzlement.

308. Thompson: Thomas Boulden Thompson. One of the reasons for Equiano's dismissal was Thompson's letter of 21 March 1787 complaining to the Navy Board "of the conduct of Mr Gustavus Vasa, which has been, since he held the situation of Commissary, turbulent and discontented, taking every means to actuate the minds of the Blacks to discord: and I am convinced that unless some means are taken to quell his spirit of sedition, it will be fatal to the peace of the settlement and dangerous to those intrusted with the guiding it." Thompson also complains of Irwin's conduct (PRO T 1/643). Sharp, too, expresses disapproval of Equiano's behavior in a letter of July 1787 to Sharp's brother (Prince Hoare, *Memoirs of Granville Sharp* [London, 1820], 313). The comments by Thompson and Sharp are similar in content to those printed in the 29 December 1786 issue of *The Morning Herald*. *Nautilus*: a 16-gun sloop.

309. [Equiano's note, only in edition 9] He then told the agent before me, he was informed by Mr. Steele, M.P. that the said expedition had cost 33,000£ and he desired that the things might be had.

[Thomas Steele (1753-1823) was joint secretary to the Treasury Board, 1783-1791, member of Parliament, and one of Equiano's original subscribers. The government expended £15,679 13 s. 4 d. on the Black Poor (PRO T 29/60, 29 July 1789).]

310. Equiano seems to refer to the following item in the 2-5 January issue of *the Morning Herald*: "Six of the leaders of these poor deceived people, Captains of hundreds and Captains of fifties [the divisions of the intended settlers], came up last week from the Belisarius and Atlantic, at Gravesend, and waited upon Lord George Gordon, to pray the continuance of his protection, and to stop their sailing, till the meeting of parliament, that the public might know their unhappy situation. Their poverty is made the pretence for their transportation, and the inferior orders of them decoyed on board the ships, are already subjected to a treatment and controul, little short of the discipline of Guinea-men."

Lord George Gordon (1751-1793) gained notoriety in 1780 for his role in the anti-Roman Catholic Gordon riots, but because of his opposition to the transportation of convicts he was seen in the last years of his life as a champion of social underdogs. Guinea-men were ships engaged in the slave trade.

311. [Equiano's note, only in edition 9] Witness Thomas Steele, Esq. M.P. of the Treasury, and Sir Charles Middleton, Bart. &. I should publicly have exposed him, (even in writing falsely of me last March) were it not out of respect to the worthy Quakers and others.

[Sir Charles Middleton (1726-1813), Baronet, later Lord Barham, and from 1778-1790 Comptroller of the Navy; rear admiral of the white (24 September 1787), rear admiral of the red (21 October 1790), vice admiral of the white (1 February 1793), vice admiral of the red (12 April 1794), admiral of the blue (1 June 1795). An active opponent of the African slave trade, Middleton had appointed Equiano Commissary, and he was one of the original subscribers to *The Interesting Narrative.* Middleton had been Ramsay's commanding officer in 1755, when Ramsay served in the Royal Navy as assistant surgeon, and acted as the clergyman Ramsay's patron, presenting him in 1781 to the livings of Teston and Nettlestead, Kent. Ramsay died in Middleton's London home 20 July 1789.

Samuel Hoare (1751-1825): one of the Quaker members of the Committee for the Black Poor, succeeding Jonas Hanway on the latter's death on 5 September 1786 as chairman; treasurer of the Society for Effecting the Abolition of the Slave Trade; and a partner in the banking-house of Barnet, Hill, Barnet, and Hoare in Lombard Street: a very powerful enemy. Equiano had already named Hoare as an opponent in a letter to *The Public Advertiser*, 14 July 1787.

Equiano was dismissed while the vessels were at Plymouth, awaiting their final embarkation for Africa.]

312. The 411 passengers still aboard when the vessels left Plymouth on 9 April 1787 arrived on the African coast on 9 May.

313. Lascars: East Indian sailors, usually classified in the period as Blacks. Approximately fifty such sailors, stranded in Britain by ships of the East India Company, sought resettlement in Africa.

314. The government's role largely ended with the payment of transportation costs. The Province of Freedom was conceived as a self-governing free settlement, not as a British colony. It was "unfortunate in the event" in that the settlers who had not died of disease had been dispersed in December 1789, when a local African chieftain, King Jimmy, destroyed the town in misdirected retaliation following the abduction of some of his people by a U.S. slave ship.

315. [Equiano's note, keyed in editions 1-4 to "triumph" in the sentence above.] See the Public Advertiser, July 14, 1787.

[Equiano's letter to *The Public Advertiser* reads:

> An extract of a letter from on board one of the ships with the Blacks, bound to Africa, having appeared on the 2nd and 3rd inst. in the public papers, wherein injurious reflexions, prejudicial to the character of Vasa, the Black Commissary, were contained, he thinks it necessary to vindicate his character from these misrepresentations, informing the public, that the principal crime which caused his dismission, was an information he laid before the Navy Board, accusing the Agent of unfaithfulness in his office, in not providing such nec-

essaries as were contracted for the people, and were absolutely necessary for their existence, which necessaries could not be obtained from the Agents. The same representation was made by Mr. Vasa to Mr. Hoare, which induced the latter, who had before appeared to be Vasa's friend, to go to the Secretary of the Treasury, and procure his dismission. The above Gentleman impowered the Agent to take many passengers in, contrary to the orders given to the Commissary.]

316. After his dismissal, Equiano was soon attacked by "X" in *The Public Advertiser* (11 April 1787):

> The Public will naturally suspend their belief as to the improbable tales propagated concerning the Blacks, especially as the cloven hoof of the author of those reports is perfectly manifest. That one of the persons employed in conducting those poor people is discharged, is certainly true, his own misconduct having given too good reason for his dismission. The Blacks have never refused to proceed on the voyage, but the ships have been delayed at Plymouth by an accidental damage which one of them received in a gale of wind. To sum up all, should the expedition prove unsuccessful, it can only be owing to the over-care of the committee, who, to avoid the most distant idea of compulsion, did not even subject the Blacks to *any* government, except such as they might chuse for themselves. And among such ill-informed people, this delicacy may have fatal consequences.

Three days later, the same newspaper carried another anonymous attack:

> The expedition of the Blacks to Sierra leone is not in the least retarded by the dismission of V— the Black who was appointed to superintend the Blacks.
>
> The assertions made by that man that the Blacks were to be treated as badly as West-India negroes, and that he was discharged to make room for the appointment of a man who would exercise tyranny to those unfortunate men, shew him to be capable of advancing falsehoods as deeply black as his jetty face. The true reason for his being discharged, was gross misbehaviour, which had not only rendered him disagreeable to the officers and crew, but had likewise drawn on him the dislike of those over whom he had been appointed. . . .
>
> Let us hear no more of those *black* reports which have been so industriously propagated; for if they are continued, it is rather more than probable that most of the *dark* transactions of a *Black* will be brought to *light.*

317. [Equiano's note.] At the request of some of my most particular friends I take the liberty of inserting it here.

[Her Majesty was Queen Charlotte (1744-1818), royal consort of King George III. Benezet, through the American-born painter Benjamin West (1738-1820), had petitioned her on the same subject in 1783.]

318. *The Consolidated Slave Act of Jamaica*, passed 2 March 1792, replacing the *Act* of 1788, actually diminished some of the penalties against the brutality of slave owners prescribed by the earlier law. In a letter of 9 April 1792, Edmund Burke accurately characterized the *Act* to Henry Dundas (1742-1811) as "arrant trifling."

319. Reversion: a legal term meaning the return to the grantor, or to his or her estate if the grantor has died, of a granted estate after the grant has expired.

320. [Equiano's note, all editions] Granville Sharp, Esq; The Rev. Thomas Clarkson; the Rev. James Ramsey [sic]; our approved friends, men of virtue, are an honour to their country, ornamental to human nature, happy in themselves, and benefactors to mankind!

[Clarkson (1760-1846), author of *An Essay on the Slavery and Commerce of the Human Species, Particularly the African* (London, 1786) and the two-volume *History of the Abolition of the African Slave-Trade* (London, 1808), was a subscriber to the *Narrative* and also a friend of Equiano. To help Equiano promote the sale of his book, on 9 July 1789 he wrote to the Reverend Mr. Jones of Trinity College, Cambridge:

> Dear Sir
>
> I take the Liberty of introducing to your Notice Gustavus Vassa, the Bearer, a very honest, ingenious, and industrious African, who wishes to visit Cambridge. He takes with him a few Histories containing his own Life written by himself, of which he means to dispose to defray his Journey. Would you be so good as to recommend the Sale of a few and you will confer a favour on your already obliged and obedient Servant
>
> Thomas Clarkson. (Cambridgeshire County Record Office: Vassa 132/B 1-17).]

321. Proverbs 14:31.
322. Proverbs 14:34.
323. Proverbs 10:29.
324. Proverbs 11:5.
325. Is now taken into: editions 1-5 read "is to be taken into." Although it would take nineteen years to complete, the parliamentary struggle to end the slave trade began in May 1788, when the issue of abolition was brought forward in the House of Commons.
326. Would: editions 1-8 read "will."

Equiano's call for the replacement of the slave trade had been anticipated by earlier writers, including Benezet and Malachy Postlethwayt (1707-1767), the latter in *Britain's Commercial Interest Explained and Improved* (London, 1757). The philanthropically inspired Province of Freedom had been intended as well to reap economic benefits for Britain, and in 1790, before he learned that Granville Town had been destroyed, Sharp published anonymously *Free English Territory in Africa*, proposing the creation of the St. George's Bay Company for trade. Commercial interests played an even greater part in the design of the settlement established by the Sierra Leone Company, incorporated by Parliament in 1791 to build Freetown on the physical and economic remains of the Province of Freedom. Along with the survivors of Granville Town, more than a thousand Afro-Britons, resettled from Nova Scotia, established Freetown in February 1792. Henry Thornton (1760-1815), future Chairman of the Sierra Leone Company Court of Directors, and John Clarkson (1764-1828), brother of Thomas and future recruiting Agent for the Company as well as Governor of the colony, were both among Equiano's original subscribers.

327. [Equiano's note, only in edition 9] In the ship Trusty, lately for the new settlement of Sierra Leona, in Africa, were 1300 pairs of shoes (an article hitherto scarcely known to be exported to that country) with several others equally new, as articles of export.—Thus will it not become the interest as well as the duty of every artificer, mechanic, and tradesman, publicly to enter their protest against this traffic of the human species? What a striking—what a beautiful contrast is here presented to view, when compared with the cargo of a slave-ship! Every feeling heart indeed sensibly participates of the joy, and with a degree of rapture reads barrels of *flour* instead of *gunpowder—biscuits and bread* instead of *horsebeans—implements of husbandry* instead of *guns* for destruction, rapine, and murder—and various articles of *usefulness* are the pleasing substitutes for the *torturing thumb-screw* and the *galling chain*, &.
328. Drags: weights attached to the leg to impede movement.

Cats: cat of nine tails, "A scourge composed of nine strings of whip-cord, each string having nine knots" (Francis Grose, *A Dictionary of Buckish Slang, University Wit, and Pickpocket Eloquence* [London, 1811]).

329. This paragraph is lacking in editions 1-4.
330. [Equiano's note, lacking in editions 1-5.] Viz. Some curious adventures beneath the earth, in a river in Manchester,—and a most astonishing one under the Peak of Derbyshire—and in Sept. 1792, I went 90 fathoms down St. Anthony's Colliery, at Newcastle, under the river Tyne, some hundreds of yards on Durham side.

331. [Equiano's note, lacking in editions 1-4.] See Gentleman's Magazine for April 1792, Literary and Biographical Magazine and British Review for May 1792, and the Edinburgh Historical Register or Monthly Intelligencer for April 1792.

[*The Gentleman's Magazine*, 62:384, reads, "At Soham, co. Cambridge, Gustavus Vassa, the African, well known in England as the champion and advocate for procuring a suppression of the slave-trade, to Miss Cullen, daughter of Mr. C. of Ely, in same county."

The Soham Register for Marriages, No. 220, reads, "Gustavus Vassa (an African) of the Parish of St. Martin in the Fields in the Co. of Middlesex Bachelor, and Susanah [sic] Cullen of this Parish Spnr [spinster] were Married in this Church by License from Drs [Doctors] Commons this seventh Day of April in the Year One Thousand seven Hundred and ninety two By me Charles Hill Curate." The marriage was witnessed by Francis Bland and Thomas Cullen.

Gustavus and Susanna Vassa had two daughters: Ann Mary (or Maria), born 16 October 1793 and baptized 30 January 1794; and Joanna, born 11 April and baptized 29 April 1795. Ann Mary (or Maria) died 21 July 1797, and Susanna was buried 21 February 1796, aged 34. Joanna inherited on her twenty-first birthday in 1816 Vassa's estate, worth £950, equivalent to about £80,000 or $120,000 in 1996.]

332. Micah 6:8.

333. Equiano died 31 March 1797. His death is recorded in the April 1797 issue of *The Gentleman's Magazine*, 67:356, in the "Obituary of remarkable Persons": "In London, Mr. Gustavus Vasa, the African, well known to the publick by the interesting narrative of his life, supposed to be written by himself."

Granville Sharp wrote to his niece Jemima on 22 February 1811 that he had seen Equiano, "a sober honest man," in his last moments: "I went to see him when he lay upon his death bed, and had lost his voice so that he could only whisper" (Granville Sharp Papers, Gloustershire Record Office).

Benjamin Banneker

(9 November 1731-9 October 1806)

~

COPY OF A LETTER FROM BENJAMIN BANNEKER TO THE SECRETARY OF STATE, WITH HIS ANSWER. (Philadelphia: Printed and Sold by Daniel Lawrence, 1792).

Maryland, Baltimore County, August 19, 1791.

SIR,

I am fully sensible of the greatness of that freedom which I take with you on the present occasion, a liberty which seemed to me scarcely allowable, when I reflected on that distinguished and dignified station in which you stand, and the almost general prejudice and prepossession, which is so prevalent in the world against those of my complexion.

I suppose it is a truth too well attested to you, to need a proof here, that we are a race of beings that have long labored under the abuse and censure of the world; that we have long been looked upon with an eye of contempt; and that we have long been considered rather as brutish than human, and scarcely capable of mental endowments.

Sir, I hope I may safely admit, in consequence of that report which has reached me, that you are a man far less inflexible in sentiments of this nature, than many others; that you are measurably friendly and well disposed towards us; and that you are willing and ready to lend your aid and assistance to our relief from those many distresses and numerous calamities to which we are reduced.

Now Sir, if this is founded in truth, I apprehend you will embrace every opportunity to eradicate that train of absurd and false ideas and opinions which so generally prevails with respect to us; and that your sentiments are concurrent with mine, which are, that one universal Father has given being to us all; and that he hath not only made us all of one flesh, but that he hath also, without partiality, afforded us all the same sensations and endowed us all with the same faculties; and that however variable we may be in society or religion, however diversified in situation or color, we are all of the same family, and stand in the same relation to him.

Sir, if these are sentiments of which you are fully persuaded, I hope you cannot but acknowledge that it is the indispensable duty of those who maintain for themselves the rights of human nature, and who possess the obligations of

Christianity, to extend their power and influence to the relief of every part of the human race from whatever burden or oppression they may unjustly labor under; and this, I apprehend, a full conviction of the truth and obligation of these principles should lead all to.

Sir, I have long been convinced that if your love for yourselves, and for those inestimable laws which preserved to you the rights of human nature, was founded on sincerity, you could not but be solicitous that every individual, of whatever rank or distinction, might with you equally enjoy the blessings thereof; neither could you rest satisfied short of the most active effusion of your exertions, in order to their promotion from any state of degradation, to which the unjustifiable cruelty and barbarism of men may have reduced them.

Sir, I freely and cheerfully acknowledge that I am of the African race, and in that color which is natural to them of the deepest dye; and it is under a sense of the most profound gratitude to the Supreme Ruler of the Universe that I now confess to you that I am not under that state of tyrannical thraldom and inhuman captivity to which many of my brethren are doomed, but that I have abundantly tasted of the fruition of those blessings, which proceed from that free and unequalled liberty with which you are favored; and which, I hope, you will willingly allow you have mercifully received from the immediate hand of that Being from whom proceedeth every good and perfect gift.

Sir, suffer me to recall to your mind that time in which the arms and tyranny of the British crown were exerted, with every powerful effort, in order to reduce you to a state of servitude: look back, I entreat you, on the variety of dangers to which you were exposed; reflect on that time in which every human aid appeared unavailable, and in which every hope and fortitude wore the aspect of inability to the conflict, and you cannot but be led to a serious and grateful sense of your miraculous and providential preservation; you cannot but acknowledge, that the present freedom and tranquillity which you enjoy you have mercifully received, and that it is the peculiar blessing of Heaven.

This, Sir, was a time when you clearly saw into the injustice of a state of slavery, and in which you had just apprehensions of the horrors of its condition. It was now that your abhorrence thereof was so excited, that you publicly held forth this true and invaluable doctrine, which is worthy to be recorded and remembered in all succeeding ages: "We hold these truths to be self-evident, that all men are created equal; that they are endowed by their Creator with certain inalienable rights, and that among these are, life, liberty, and the pursuit of happiness."[1]

Here was a time, in which your tender feelings for yourselves had engaged you thus to declare you were then impressed with proper ideas of the great violation of liberty, and the free possession of those blessings to which you were entitled by nature; but, Sir, how pitiable is it to reflect, that although you were so fully convinced of the benevolence of the Father of Mankind, and of his equal and impartial distribution of these rights and privileges which he hath conferred upon them, that you should at the same time counteract his mercies, in detaining by fraud and violence so numerous a part of my brethren under groaning captivity and cruel oppression, that you should at the same time be found guilty of that most criminal act, which you professedly detested in others, with respect to yourselves.

I suppose that your knowledge of the situation of my brethren is too extensive to need a recital here; neither shall I presume to prescribe methods by which they may be relieved, otherwise than by recommending to you and all others, to wean yourselves from those narrow prejudices which you have imbibed with respect to them, and as Job proposed to his friends, "put your soul in their souls' stead";[2] thus shall your hearts be enlarged with kindness and benevolence towards them; and thus shall you need neither the direction of myself or others, in what manner to proceed herein.

And now, Sir, although my sympathy and affection for my brethren hath caused my enlargement thus far, I ardently hope that your candor and generosity will plead with you in my behalf, when I make known to you, that it was not originally my design; but having taken up my pen in order to direct to you, as a present, a copy of an Almanac which I have calculated for the succeeding year, I was unexpectedly and unavoidably led thereto.

This calculation is the production of my arduous study, in this my advanced stage of life; for having long had unbounded desires to become acquainted with the secrets of nature, I have had to gratify my curiosity herein, through my own assiduous application to Astronomical Study, in which I need not recount to you the many difficulties and disadvantages, which I have had to encounter.

And although I had almost declined to make my calculation for the ensuing year, in consequence of that time which I had allotted therefor, being taken up at the Federal Territory, by the request of Mr. Andrew Ellicott;[3] yet finding myself under several engagements to Printers of this state, to whom I had communicated my design, on my return to my place of residence, I industriously applied myself thereto, which I hope I have accomplished with correctness and accuracy; a copy of which I have taken the liberty to direct to you, and which I humbly request you will favorably receive; and although you may have the opportunity of perusing it after its publication, yet I choose to send it to you in manuscript previous thereto, that thereby you might not only have an earlier inspection, but that you might also view it in my own hand writing.

And now, Sir, I shall conclude, and subscribe myself, with the most profound respect,

Your most obedient humble servant,
BENJAMIN BANNEKER

To Mr. BENJAMIN BANNEKER.

Philadelphia, August 30, 1791.

SIR,

I THANK you, sincerely, for your letter of the 19th instant,[4] and for the Almanac it contained. Nobody wishes more than I do, to see such proofs as you exhibit, that nature has given to our black brethren talents equal to those of the other colors of men; and that the appearance of the want of them is owing merely to the degraded condition of their existence, both in Africa and America. I can add with truth, that nobody wishes more ardently to see a good system commenced for raising the condition, both of their body and mind, to what it ought to be, as far as the imbecility of their present existence, and other circumstances, which cannot be neglected, will admit.

I have taken the liberty of sending your Almanac to Monsieur de Condozett,[5] Secretary of the Academy of Sciences at Paris, and Member of the Philanthropic Society, because I considered it as a document to which your whole color had a right for their justification, against the doubts which have been entertained of them.

I am with great esteem, Sir,
Your most obedient
Humble Servant,
THOMAS JEFFERSON.

The following Account, taken from BANNEKER'S Almanac, is inserted here, for the Information of the Public.[6]

Baltimore, August 20, 1791.

BENJAMIN BANNEKER, a free Black, is about 59 years of age: he was born in Baltimore county; his father an African, and his mother the offspring of African parents.[7] His father and mother having obtained their freedom, were able to send him to an obscure school, where he learned, when a boy, reading, writing, and arithmetic, as far as double position; and to leave him, at their deaths, a few acres of land, upon which he has supported himself ever since, by means of economy and constant labor, and preserved a fair reputation. To struggle incessantly against want, is no ways favorable to improvement: what he had learned, however, he did not forget; for as some hours of leisure will occur in the most toilsome life, he availed himself of these, not to read and acquire knowledge from writings of genius and discovery, for of such he had none, but to digest and apply, as occasions presented, the few principles of the few rules of mathematics he had been taught at school. This kind of mental exercise formed his chief amusement, and soon gave him a facility in calculation that was often serviceable to his neighbours, and at length attracted the attention of the Messrs. Ellicott, a family remarkable for their ingenuity and turn to the useful mechanics. It is about three years since Mr. George Ellicott lent him Mayer's Tables, Ferguson's Astronomy, Leadbeater's Lunar Tables,[8] and some Astronomic Instruments, but without accompanying them with either hint or instruction, that might further his studies, or lead him to apply them to any useful result. These books and instruments, the first of the kind he had ever seen, opened a new world to Benjamin, and from thenceforward he employed his leisure in Astronomical Researches.

He now took up the idea of the calculations for an Almanac, and actually completed an entire set for the last year, upon his original stock of Arithmetic. Encouraged by his first attempt, he entered upon his calculation for 1792 which, as well as the former, he began and finished without the least information or assistance from any person, or other books than those I have mentioned; so that whatever merit is attached to his present performance, is exclusively and peculiarly his own.

I have been the more careful to investigate those particulars, and to ascertain their reality, as they form an interesting fact in the History of Man; and as you may want them to gratify curiosity, I have no objection to your selecting them for your account of Benjamin.

NOTES

1. Banneker quotes the beginning of the Declaration of Independence (1776), which Thomas Jefferson (1743-1826), a lifelong slave owner, drafted. Banneker may not have known of Jefferson's negative comments on Blacks in general and the works of Sancho and Wheatley in particular in *Notes on the State of Virginia* (London, 1787).

2. Compare Job 16:4: "I also could speak as ye *do*: if your soul were in my soul's stead, I could heap up words against you, and shake my head at you."

3. Andrew Ellicott (1754-1820), mathematician, surveyor, and publisher of *The United States Almanack* series since at least 1782. His father and uncles, all renowned for their mechanical skills, founded Ellicott City, Maryland, in 1775. Between 1791 and 1793, he supervised the survey of the lands ceded by Maryland and Virginia that would become the District of Columbia.

4. Instant: of the current month.

5. Marquis de Condorcet, Marie Jean Antoine Nicolas Caritat (1743-1794).

6. Written by James McHenry (1753-1816), a member of the Maryland Senate.

7. Born free in Maryland, Banneker was the grandson of an Englishwoman, Molly Welsh, who had been convicted in England of stealing a pail of milk and transported to Maryland around 1683 to be sold as an indentured servant for seven years. After regaining her freedom, she had saved enough money by 1692 to buy a small farm and two African slaves. She eventually freed them, marrying the one, Banaky, who said he had been a prince in Africa. Although intermarriage between White women and slaves had been illegal in Maryland since 1664, intermarriage beween free Blacks and Whites was not proscribed by law in the colony before 1717. In 1730 the eldest daughter of Molly and Banaky, Mary, married Robert, a former slave who took her surname rather than that of his previous owner. The spelling of their surname soon became fixed as Banneker.

Their son, Benjamin, received some formal schooling, but for the most part was self-educated through reading and observation. He soon earned a reputation for having genius as a mathematician and engineer. He was a clockmaker and astronomer before being appointed, at the suggestion of Jefferson, to the commission that surveyed the future District of Columbia. Banneker's greatest fame was achieved with the annual publication of his almanacs during the 1790s.

8. The books Ellicott lent Banneker in 1788 included [Tobias Mayer (1723-1762)] *Tabulae Motuum Solis et Lunae Novae et Correctae. Auctore Tobia Mayer: Quibus Accedit Methodus Longitudinum Promota, Eodem Auctore. Editae Jussu Praefectorum Rei Longitudinariae* [edited and translated by the Rev. Nevil Maskelyne (1732-1811)] (London, 1770); James Ferguson (1710-1770), *Astronomy Explained Upon Sir Isaac Newton's Principles, and Made Easy for Those Who Have not Studied Mathematics* (London, 1756), and Ferguson, *An Easy Introduction to Astronomy, For Young Gentlemen and Ladies: Describing the Figure, Motions and Dimensions of the Earth; the Different Seasons, Gravity and Light; the Solar Systems, the Transit of Venus, and its Use in Astronomy; the Moon's Motions and Phases; the Eclipses of the Sun and Moon; the Cause of the Ebbing and Flowing of the Tides, &c.*, 4th ed. (London, 1779); Charles Leadbetter (fl. 1728), *A Compleat System of Astronomy. In Two Volumes, Containing the Description and Use of the Sector, the Laws of Spheric Geometry; the Projection of the Sphere Orthographically and Stereographically upon the Planes of the Meridian, Ecliptic and Horizon; the Doctrine of the Sphere, and the Eclipses of the Sun and Moon for Thirty-seven Years. Together with all the Precepts of Calculation. Also New Tables of the Motions of the Planets, Fix'd Stars, and the First Satellite of Jupiter; of Right and Oblique Ascensions, and of Logistical Logarithms. To the Whole Are Prefix'd Astronomical Definitions for the benefit of Young Students*, 2d. ed. (London, 1742).

George Liele

(ca. 1751-1825)

"AN ACCOUNT of several Baptist Churches, consisting chiefly of NEGRO SLAVES: particularly of one at *Kingston*, in JAMAICA; and another at *Savannah* in GEORGIA."

From *THE BAPTIST ANNUAL REGISTER, FOR 1790, 1791, 1792, AND PART OF 1793*. By JOHN RIPPON, D.D. SOLD BY Messrs. DILLY, BUTTON, AND THOMAS, LONDON; BROWN, JAMES, AND COTTLE, BRISTOL; OGLE, EDINBURGH; ALLEIN, DUBLIN; AND MAY BE HAD OF THE BAPTIST MINISTERS IN NEW YORK, PHILADELPHIA, BOSTON, RICHMOND, SAVANNAH, AND CHARLESTON, IN AMERICA [1793].

A LETTER from the late Rev. Mr. Joseph Cook of the Euhaw, upper Indian Land, South Carolina, bearing date Sept. 15, 1790, says, "A poor negro, commonly called, among his own friends, Brother George, has been so highly favoured of God, as to plant the first Baptist Church in Savannah, and another in Jamaica." This account produced an earnest desire to know the circumstances of both these societies. Hence letters were written to the Rev. Mr. Cook, at the Euhaw; to Mr. Jonathan Clarke, at Savannah; to Mr. Wesley's people at Kingston; with a view to obtain information, in which particular regard was had to the *character* of this poor but successful minister of Christ. Satisfactory accounts have been received from each of these quarters, and a letter from brother George himself, containing an answer to more than fifty questions proposed in a letter to him: We presume to give an epitome of the whole to our friends, hoping they will have the goodness to let a plain unlettered people convey their ideas in their own simple way.

Brother George's words are distinguished by inverted commas, and what is not so marked, is either matter compressed or information received from such persons to whom application has been made for it.

GEORGE LIELE, called also George *Sharp* because his owner's name was *Sharp*,[1] in a letter dated Kingston, Dec. 18, 1791, says, "I was born in Virginia, my father's name was Liele, and my mother's name Nancy; I cannot ascertain much of them, as I went to several parts of America when young, and at length resided in

New Georgia; but was informed both by white and black people, that my father was the only black person who knew the Lord in a spiritual way in that country: I also had a natural fear of God from my youth, and was often checked in conscience with thoughts of death, which barred me from many sins and bad company. I knew no other way at that time to hope for salvation but only in the performance of my good works." *About two years before the late war*,[2] "the Rev. Mr. Matthew Moore,[3] one Sabbath afternoon, as I stood with curiosity to hear him, he unfolded all my dark views, opened my best behaviour and good works to me, which I thought I was to be saved by, and I was convinced that I was not in the way to heaven, but in the way to hell. This state I laboured under for the space of five or six months. The more I heard or read, the more I saw that I was condemned as a sinner before God; till at length I was brought to perceive that my life hung by a slender thread, and if it was the will of God to cut me off at that time, I was sure I should be found in hell, as sure as God was in heaven. I saw my condemnation in my own heart, and I found no way wherein I could escape the damnation of hell, only through the merits of my dying Lord and Saviour Jesus Christ; which caused me to make intercession with Christ, for the salvation of my poor immortal soul; and I full well recollect, I requested of my Lord and Master to give me a work, I did not care how mean it was, only to try and see how good I would do it." When he became acquainted with the method of salvation by our Lord Jesus Christ, he soon found relief, particularly at a time when he was earnestly engaged in prayer; yea, he says, "I felt such love and joy as my tongue was not able to express. After this I declared before the congregation of believers the work which God had done for my soul, and the same minister, the Rev. Matthew Moore, baptized me, and I continued in this church about four years, till the [e]vacuation of Savannah by the British."[4] When Mr. Liele was called by grace himself, he was desirous of promoting the felicity of others. One who was an eye-witness of it, says, *That he began to discover his love to other negroes, on the same plantation with himself, by reading hymns among them, encouraging them to sing, and sometimes by explaining the most striking parts of them.* His own account is this, "Desiring to prove the sense I had of my obligations to God, I endeavoured to instruct the people of my own colour in the word of God: the white brethren seeing my endeavours, and that the word of the Lord seemed to be blessed, gave me a call at a quarterly meeting to preach before the congregation." Afterwards Mr. Moore took the sense of the church concerning brother Liele's abilities, when it appeared to be their unanimous opinion, "that he was possessed of ministerial gifts," and, according to the custom which obtains in some of the American churches, he was licensed as a probationer.[5] He now exercised at different plantations, especially on those Lord's Day evenings when there was no service performed in the church to which he belonged; and preached "about three years at Brunton land, and at Yamacraw,"[6] which last place is about half a mile from Savannah. Mr. Henry Sharp, his master, being a deacon of the church which called George Liele to the work of the ministry, some years before his death gave him his freedom, only he continued in the family till his master's exit. Mr. Sharp in the time of the war was an officer, and was at last killed in the king's service, by a ball which shot off his hand.[7] The author of this account handled the bloody glove, which he wore when he received the fatal wound. Some persons were at this time dissatisfied with George's liberation, and threw him into prison, but by producing the proper papers he was released; his particular friend in this business was colonel Kirkland. "At the [e]vacuation of the country I was partly obliged to come to Jamaica, as an indented servant,[8] for money I owed him, he promising to be my friend in this country. I was landed at Kingston, and by the colonel's recommendation to general Campbell, the governor of the Island,[9] I was employed by him two years, and on his leaving the island, he gave me a written certificate from under his own hand of my good behaviour. As soon as I had settled Col. Kirkland's demand on me, I had a certificate of my freedom from the vestry and governor, according to the act of this Island, both for myself and family. Governor Campbell left the Island. I began, about September 1784, to preach in Kingston, in a small private house, to a good smart congregation, and I formed the church with four brethren from America besides myself, and the preaching took very good effect with the poorer sort, especially the slaves. The people at first persecuted us both at meetings and baptisms, but, God be praised, they seldom interrupt us now. We have applied to the HONOURABLE HOUSE OF ASSEMBLY, with a petition of our distresses, being poor people, desiring to worship Almighty God according to the tenets of the Bible, and they have granted us liberty, and given us their sanction. Thanks be to God we have liberty to worship him as we please in Kingston. You ask about those who 'in a judgment of charity,' have been converted to Christ. I think they are about four hundred and fifty. I have baptized four hundred in Jamaica. At Kingston I baptize in the sea, at Spanish Town in the river, and at convenient places in the country. We have nigh THREE HUNDRED AND FIFTY MEMBERS; a few white people among them, one white brother of the first battalion of royals, from England, baptized by Rev. Thomas Davis. Several members have been dismissed to other churches, and twelve have died. I have sent enclosed an account of the conversion and death of some. A few of Mr. Wesley's people, after immersion,[10] join us and continue with us. We have, together with well wishers and followers, in different parts of the country, about fifteen hundred people. We receive none into the church without a few lines from their owners of their good behaviour towards them and religion. The creoles of the country,[11] after they are converted and baptized, as God enables them, prove very faithful. I have deacons and elders, a few; and teachers of small congregations in the town and country, where convenience suits them to come together; and I am pastor. I preach twice on the Lord's Day, in the forenoon and afternoon, and twice in the week, and have not been absent six Sabbath Days since I formed the church in this country. I receive nothing for my services; I preach, baptize, administer the Lord's Supper, and travel from one place to another to publish the gospel, and to settle church affairs, all freely. I have one of the chosen men, whom I baptized, a deacon of the church, and a native of this country, who keeps the regulations of church matters; and I promoted a FREE SCHOOL for the instruction of the children, both free and slaves, and he is the schoolmaster.

"I cannot justly tell what is my age, as I have no account of the time of my birth, but I suppose I am about forty years old. I have a wife and four children. My wife was baptized by me in Savannah, at Brunton land, and I have every satisfaction in life from her. She is much the same age as myself. My eldest son is nineteen years, my next son seventeen, the third fourteen, and the last child, a girl of eleven years; they are all members of the church. My occupation is a farmer, but as the seasons, in this part of the country, are uncertain, I also keep a team of horses, and waggons for the carrying goods from one place to another, which I attend to myself, with the assistance of my sons; and by this way of life have gained the good will of the public, who recommend me to business, and to some very principal work for government.

"I have a few books, some good old authors and sermons, and one large bible that was given me by a gentleman: a good many of our members can read, and all are desirous to learn; they will be very thankful for a few books to read on Sundays and other days.

"The last accounts I had from Savannah were, that the Gospel had taken very great effect both there and in South Carolina. Brother Andrew Bryan,[12] a black minister at Savannah, has TWO HUNDRED MEMBERS, in full fellowship, and had certificates from their owners of ONE HUNDRED MORE, who had given in their experiences and were ready to be baptized. Also I received accounts from Nova Scotia of a black Baptist preacher, Brother David George,[13] who was a member of the church at Savannah; he had the permission of the governor to preach in three provinces;[14] his members in full communion were then SIXTY, white and black, the Gospel spreading. Brother Amos is at Providence,[15] he writes me that the Gospel has taken good effect, and is spreading greatly; he has about THREE HUNDRED MEMBERS. Brother Jessy Gaulfing,[16] another black minister, preaches near Augusta, in South Carolina, at a place where I used to preach; he was a member of the church at Savannah, and has SIXTY MEMBERS; and a great work is going on there.

"I agree to election, redemption, the fall of Adam, regeneration, and perseverance, knowing the promise is to all who endure, in grace, faith, and good works, to the end, shall be saved.

"There is no Baptist church in this country but ours. We have purchased a piece of land, at the east end of Kingston, containing three acres, for the sum of 155£.[17] currency, and on it have begun a meeting-house fifty-seven feet in length by thirty-seven in breadth. We have raised the brick wall eight feet high from the foundation, and intend to have a gallery. Several gentlemen, members of the house of assembly, and other gentlemen, have subscribed towards the building about 40£. The chief part of our congregation are SLAVES, and their owners allow them, in common, but three or four bits per week[18] for allowance to feed themselves; and out of so small a sum we cannot expect any thing that can be of service from them; if we did it would soon bring a scandal upon religion; and the FREE PEOPLE in our society are but poor, but they are all willing, both free and slaves, to do what they can. As for my part, I am too much entangled with the affairs of the world to go on, as I would, with my design, in supporting the cause: this has, I acknowledge, been a great hindrance to the Gospel in one way; but as I have endeavoured to set a good example of industry before the inhabitants of the land, it has given general satisfaction another way.—And, Rev. Sir, we think the Lord has put it in the power of the Baptist societies in England to help and assist us in completing this building, which we look upon will be the greatest undertaking ever was in this country for the bringing of souls from darkness into the light of the Gospel.—And as the Lord has put it into your heart to enquire after us, we place all our confidence in you, to make our circumstances known to the several Baptist churches in England; and we look upon you as our father, friend, and brother.

"Within the brick wall we have a shelter, in which we worship, until our building can be accomplished.

"Your — letter was read to the church two or three times, and did create a great deal of love and warmness throughout the whole congregation, who shouted for joy and comfort, to think that the Lord had been so gracious as to satisfy us in this country with the very same religion with — our beloved brethren in the old country, according to the scriptures; and that such a worthy — of London, should write in so loving a manner to such poor worms as we are. And I beg leave to say, That the whole congregation sang out that they would, through the assistance of God, remember you in their prayers. They altogether give their Christian love to you, and all the worthy professors of Jesus Christ in your church at London, and beg the prayers of your congregation, and the prayers of the churches in general, wherever it pleases you to make known our circumstances. I remain with the utmost love—Rev. Sir, your unworthy fellow-labourer, servant, and brother in Christ.

GEORGE LIELE.

P.S. We have chosen twelve trustees, all of whom are members of our church, whose names are specified in the title; the title proved and recorded in the secretary's office of this island.

I would have answered your letter much sooner, but am encumbered with business: the whole island under arms;[19] several of our members and a deacon were obliged to be on duty; and I being trumpeter to the troop of horse in Kingston, am frequently called upon. And also by order of government I was employed in carrying all the cannon that could be found lying about this part of the country. This occasioned my long delay, which I beg you will excuse." (332-337)[20]

To the Rev. Mr. JOHN RIPPON.[21]
Kingston in Jamaica, Nov. 26, 1791.

REVEREND SIR,

THE perusal of your letter of the 15th July last, gave me much pleasure—to find that you had interested yourself to serve the glorious cause Mr. Liele is engaged in.

He has been for a considerable time past very zealous in the ministry, but his congregation being chiefly slaves, they had it not in their power to support him, therefore he has been obliged to do it from his own industry; this has taken a considerable part of his time and much of his attention from his labours in the ministry: however, I am led to believe that it has been of essential service to the cause of GOD, for his industry has set a good example to his flock, and has put it out of the power of enemies of religion to say, that he has been eating the bread of idleness, or lived upon the poor slaves. The idea that too much prevails here amongst the masters of slaves is, that if their minds are considerably enlightened by religion or otherwise, that it would be attended with the most dangerous consequences; and this has been the only cause why the Methodist ministers and Mr. Liele have not made a greater progress in the ministry amongst the slaves. Alas! how much is it to be lamented, that a full QUARTER OF A MILLION of poor souls should so long remain in a state of nature; and that masters should be so blind to their own interest as not to know the difference between obedience inforced by the lash of the whip and that which flows from religious principles. Although I much admire the *general doctrine* preached in the Methodist church, yet I by no means approve of their discipline set up by Mr. Wesley, that reverend man of God. I very early saw into the impropriety of admitting slaves into their societies *without permission of their owners*, and told them the consequences that would attend it: but they rejected my advice; and it has not only prevented the increase of their church, but has raised them many enemies. Mr. Liele has very wisely acted a different part. He has, I believe, admitted no slaves into society but those who had obtained permission from their owners, by which he has made many friends; and I think the almighty is now opening a way for another church in the capital, where the Methodists could not gain any ground: a short time will determine it, of which I shall advise you.—I really have not time to enter so fully on this subject as I wish, being very much engaged in my own temporal affairs, and at present having no clerk.—The love I bear to the cause of *God*, and the desire I have of being any ways instrumental to the establishing of it in this land of darkness, has led me to write this: but before I conclude, I have some very interesting particulars to lay before you.—Mr. Liele has by the aid of his congregation and the assistance of some few people, raised the walls of a church ready to receive the roof, but has not the means to lay it on and finish it; nor do I see any prospect of its going further, without he receives the aids of some religious institution from home. One hundred and fifty pounds, I think, would complete it; and if this sum could be raised, it would greatly serve the cause of *GOD*, and might be the means of bringing many hundred souls, who are now in a state of darkness, to the knowledge of our great Redeemer. If this could be raised, the sooner the better. Our family contributed towards the purchase of the Methodist chapel; nor shall our mite be wanting to forward this work if it meets with any encouragement from home.—I am a stranger to you, but you may know my character from Daniel Shea, Esq; and John Parker, Esq; merchants in your city; or from Mr. Samuel Yockney,[22] tea-dealer, in Bedford Row.

Perhaps you may expect me to say something of Mr. Liele's character. He is a very industrious man—decent and humble in his manners, and, I think, a good man. This is my opinion of him. I love all Christians of every denomination, and remain, with respect and sincere regard,

Reverend Sir,
Your friend and servant,
STEPHEN COOKE. (338-339)

NOTES

1. Henry Sharp, a Baptist deacon in Burke County, Georgia.
2. That is, about 1773.
3. [Note in original.] Mr. Moore was an ordained Baptist minister, of the county of Burke, in Georgia; he died, it seems, some time since. EDITOR. [Moore was the pastor of the Buckhead Creek Baptist Church.]
4. Savannah was evacuated in June 1782.
5. Liele became the first Afro-Briton licensed and ordained to serve as a Baptist preacher-missionary in America.
6. In December 1777, Pastor George Liele formed a Black Baptist congregation at Yamacraw.
7. Sharp was a Loyalist militia officer during the American Revolution.
8. Indented servant: an indentured servant was one bound to serve someone for a specified length of time stipulated in a written contract that had indented edges.
9. Major General Campbell, governor of Jamaica 1782-1790.
10. "Mr. Wesley's people, after immersion" refers to former Methodists, followers of John Wesley (1703-1791), who have undergone baptism as adults, according to Baptist belief and practice.
11. "Creoles of the country," in this context, refers to people of African descent born in Jamaica.
12. Liele had converted Andrew Bryan (1737-1812), a slave belonging to Jonathan Bryan, Esq.
13. See the selection by David George in this anthology.
14. Three provinces: Liele is mistaken; David George was licensed to preach in only two provinces.
15. Providence: New Providence in the Bahamas.
16. Jesse Gaulphin, or Galfin, is mentioned as well in David George's account in this anthology.
17. [Note in original.] 140£. currency is 100£. sterling.
18. [Note in original.] A bit is seven-pence halfpenny currency, or about five-pence halfpenny sterling.
19. Under arms: probably in response to the recent series of slave revolts in the neighboring island colonies of Haiti and Dominica, as well as to the hostilities with Revolutionary France.
20. Additional information on Liele is given by John Clark in John Clark, Walter Dendy, and James M. Phillippo, *The Voice of Jubilee: A Narrative of the Baptist Mission, Jamaica, from its Commencement* (London: John Snow, 1865):

> During the early part of his ministry, Mr. Liele suffered much opposition, and was often treated with contumely and insult. On one occasion, when the church was about to cele-

brate the Lord's Supper, a gentleman (so called) rode into the chapel, and, urging his horse through the midst of the people to the very front of the pulpit, exclaimed in terms of insolence and profanity, "Come, old Liele, give my horse the Sacrament!" Mr. Liele coolly replied, "No, sir, you are not fit yourself to receive it." After maintaining his position for some time the intruder rode out. On another ordinary Sabbath, three young gentlemen walked into the chapel during service, and, going up to the table where the bread and wine had been placed, one of them took the bread, and, breaking it, gave it to his companion, who, with a horrid oath, swore that it was good ship-bread, and presented it to the third, who refused to take it. It must not be withheld that the two former were in a few days removed into the presence of that God with whose Institution they had so profanely trifled. One died in a state of awful madness from brain-fever; the other went out of the harbour in a boat, which was upset, and he was never seen again.

Mr. Liele was charged with preaching sedition [1794] for which he was thrown into prison, loaded with irons, and his feet fastened in the stocks. Not even his wife or children were permitted to see him. At length he was tried for his life; but no evil could be proved against him, and he was honourably acquitted. He was also thrown into gaol for a balance due to the builder of his chapel. He refused to take the benefit of the Insolvent Debtors' Act, and remained in prison [1797-1801] until he had fully paid all that was due. (31-32)

21. Rippon (1751-1836) edited *The Baptist Annual Register* from 1790 until 1802.

22. Probably the same Samuel Yockney who was one of Equiano's original subscribers.

David George

(1743?-ca. 1810)

~

"An Account of the Life of Mr. DAVID GEORGE, from Sierra Leone in Africa; given by himself in a Conversation with Brother RIPPON of London, and Brother [Samuel] PEARCE [1766-1799] of Birmingham."

From *THE BAPTIST ANNUAL REGISTER, FOR 1790, 1791, 1792, AND PART OF 1793* (London, 1793).

I was born in Essex county, Virginia,[1] about 50 or 60 miles from Williamsburg, on Nottaway[2] river, of parents who were brought from Africa, but who had not the fear of God before their eyes. The first work I did was fetching water, and carding[3] of cotton; afterwards I was sent into the field to work about the Indian corn and tobacco, till I was about 19 years old. My father's name was John, and my mother's Judith. I had four brothers, and four sisters, who, with myself, were all born in slavery: our master's name was Chapel[4]—a very bad man to the Negroes. My oldest sister was called Patty; I have seen her several times so whipped that her back has been all corruption, as though it would rot. My brother Dick ran away, but they caught him, and brought him home; and as they were going to tie him up, he broke away again, and they hunted him with horses and dogs, till they took him; then they hung him up to a cherry-tree in the yard, by his two hands, quite naked, except his breeches, with his feet about half a yard from the ground. They tied his legs close together, and put a pole between them, at one end of which one of the owner's sons sat, to keep him down, and another son at the other. After he had received 500 lashes, or more, they washed his back with salt water, and whipped it in, as well as rubbed it with a rag; and then directly sent him to work in pulling off the suckers of tobacco. I also have been whipped many a time on my naked skin, and sometimes till the blood has run down over my waistband; but the greatest grief I then had was to see them whip my mother, and to hear her, on her knees, begging for mercy. She was master's cook, and if they only thought she might do any thing better than she did, instead of speaking to her as to a servant, they would strip her directly, and cut away.[5] I believe she was on her death-bed when I got off, but I have never heard since. Master's rough and cruel usage was the reason of my running-away. Before this time I used to drink, but not steal; did not fear hell; was without knowledge; though I went sometimes to Nottaway, the

English church,[6] about eight or nine miles off. I left the plantation about midnight, walked all night, got into Brunswick county,[7] then over Roanoak river, and soon met with some White travelling people, who helped me on to Pedee[8] river. When I had been at work there two or three weeks, a hue and cry found me out, and the master said to me, there are 30 guineas offered for you, but I will have no hand in it: I would advise you to make your way towards Savannah river. I hearkened to him, but was several weeks going. I worked there, I suppose, as long as two years, with John Green, a white man, before they came after me again. Then I ran away up among the Creek Indians. As I travelled from Savannah river, I came to Okemulgee[9] river, near which the Indians observed my track. They can tell the Black people's feet from their own, because they are hollow in the midst of their feet, and the Black's feet are flatter than theirs. They followed my track down to the river, where I was making a long raft to cross over with. One of these Indians was a king,[10] called Blue Salt;[11] he could talk a little broken English. He took and carried me about 17 or 18 miles into the woods to his camp, where they had bear meat, deer meat, turkies, and wild potatoes. I was his prize, and lived with him from the Christmas month till April, when he went into his town, Augusta, in the Creek nation. I made fences, dug the ground, planted corn, and worked hard; but the people were kind to me. S.C.[12] my master's son, came there for me, from Virginia, I suppose 800 miles, and paid king Blue Salt for me in rum, linnen, and a gun; but before he could take me out of the Creek nation, I escaped and went to the Nautchee Indians,[13] and got to live with their king, Jack, who employed me a few weeks. S.C. was waiting this while in hopes to have me. Mr. Gaulfin,[14] who lived on Savannah river, at Silver Bluff,[15] and who was afterwards my master, traded in these parts among the Indians in deer skins. He had a manager here, whose name was John Miller. Mr. Miller knew king Jack, and agreed with him and S.C. as to the price Mr. Gaulfin was to pay for me. So I came away from king Jack, who gave me into the hands of John Miller. Now I mended deer skins, and kept their horses together, that they might not wander too far and be lost. I used also once a year to go down with the horses, carrying deer skins, to Mr. Gaulfin's, at Silver Bluff. The distance, I think, was 400 miles, over five or six rivers, which we crossed in leather boats. After three years, when I came down, I told Mr. Gaulfin, that I wished to live with him at Silver Bluff. He told me I should: so he took me to wait upon him, and was very kind to me. I was with him about four years, I think, before I was married.[16] Here I lived a bad life, and had no serious thoughts about my soul; but after my wife was delivered of our first child, a man of my own colour, named Cyrus, who came from Charlestown, South Carolina, to Silver Bluff, told me one day in the woods, That if I lived so, I should never see the face of God in glory (Whether he himself was a converted man or not, I do not know). This was the first thing that disturbed me, and gave me much concern. I thought then that I must be saved by prayer. I used to say the Lord's prayer, that it might make me better, but I feared that I grew worse; and I continued worse and worse, as long as I thought I would do some thing to make me better; till at last there seemed as if there was no possibility of relief, and that I must go to hell. I saw myself a mass of sin. I could not read, and had no scriptures. I did not think of Adam and Eve's sin, but *I* was sin. I felt my *own* plague; and I was so overcome that I could not wait upon my master. I told him *I was ill.* I felt myself at the disposal of Sovereign mercy. At last in prayer to God I began to think that he would deliver me, but I did not know how. Soon after I saw that I could not be saved by any of my own doings, but that it must be by God's mercy—that my sins had crucified Christ; and now the Lord took away my distress. I was sure that the Lord took it away, because I had such pleasure and joy in my soul, that no man could give me. Soon after I heard brother George Liele preach, who, as you both know, is at Kingston in Jamaica.[17] I knew him ever since he was a boy. I am older than he; I am about fifty. His sermon was suitable, on *Come unto me all ye that labour, and are heavy laden, and I will give you rest.*[18] When it was ended, I went to him and told him I was so; That I was weary and heavy laden, and that the grace of God had given me rest. Indeed his whole discourse seemed for me. Afterwards brother Palmer,[19] who was pastor at some distance from Silver Bluff, came and preached to a large congregation at a mill of Mr. Gaulfin's;[20] he was a very powerful preacher; and as he was returning home Lord's-day evening, I went with him two or three miles, and told him how it was with me. About this time more of my fellow-creatures began to seek the Lord. Afterwards Brother Palmer came again and wished us to beg Master to let him preach to us; and he had leave, and came frequently. There were eight of us now who had found the great blessing and mercy from the Lord, and my wife was one of them, and brother Jesse Gaulfin that you mention in the History of us poor slaves, was another.[21] Brother Palmer appointed a Saturday evening to hear what the Lord had done for us, and the next day he baptized us in the Mill-stream. Some time afterwards, when Brother George Liele came again, and preached in a corn field, I had a great desire to pray with the people myself, but I was ashamed, and went to a swamp and poured out my heart before the Lord. I then came back to Brother George Liele, and told him my case. He said, "In the intervals of service you should engage in prayer with the friends." At another time, when he was preaching, I felt the same desire, and after he had done, I began in prayer—it gave me great relief, and I went home with a desire for nothing else but to talk to the brothers and sisters about the Lord. Brother Palmer formed us into a church, and gave us the Lord's supper at Silver Bluff.[22] Then I began to exhort in the church, and learned to sing hymns. The first I learned out of book was a hymn by that great writing man, Watts, which begins with "Thus saith the wisdom of the Lord."[23] Afterwards the church advised with Brother Palmer about my speaking to them, and keeping them together; I refused, and felt I was unfit for all that, but Brother Palmer said this word to me, "Take care that you don't offend the Lord." Then I thought that he knew best, and I agreed I would do as well as I could. So I was appointed to the office of an Elder and received instruction from Brother Palmer how to conduct myself. I proceeded in this way till the American war was coming on, when the Ministers were not allowed to come amongst us lest they should furnish us with too much knowledge. The Black people all around attended with us, and as Brother Palmer must not come, I had the whole management, and used to preach among them myself. Then I got a spelling book and began to read. As Master was a great man, he kept a White school-master to teach the White children to read. I used to go to the little children to teach me a, b, c. They would give me a lesson, which I tried to learn, and then I would go to them again, and ask them if I was right? The reading so ran in my mind, that I think I learned in my sleep as really as when I was awake; and I can now read the Bible, so that what I have in my heart, I can see again in the Scriptures. I continued preaching at Silver Bluff, till the church, constituted with eight, encreased to thirty or more, and till the British came to the city [of] Savannah and took it.[24] My Master was an Antiloyalist; and being afraid, he now retired from home and left the Slaves behind. My wife and I, and the two children we then had,[25] and fifty or more of my Master's people, went to Ebenezer, about twenty miles [up river] from Savannah, where the King's forces were. The General[26] sent us over the big Ogeechee river to Savages' Plantation, where the White people, who were Loyalists, reported that I was planning to carry the Black people back to their slavery; and I was thrown into prison, and laid there about a month, when Colonel Brown,[27] belonging to the British, took me out. I staid some time in Savannah, and at Yamacraw[28] a little distance from it, preaching with brother George Liele. He and I worked together also a month or two: he used to plow, and I to weed Indian-corn. I and my family went into Savannah, at the beginning of the siege.[29] A [cannon] ball came through the roof of the stable where we lived, and much shattered it, which made us remove to Yamacraw, where we sheltered ourselves under the floor of a house on the ground. Not long after the siege was raised, I caught the small pox, in the fall of the year, and thought I should have died, nor could I do any more than just walk in the spring. My wife used to wash for General Clinton,[30] and out of the little she got maintained us. I was then about a mile from Savannah, when the Americans were coming towards it a second time. I wished my wife to escape, and to take care of herself and of the children,[31] and let me die there. She went: I had about two quarts of Indian corn, which I boiled; I ate a little, and a dog came in and devoured the rest; but it pleased God [that] some people who came along the road gave me a little rice: I grew better, and as the troops did not come so near as was expected, I went into Savannah, where I met my family, and tarried there about two years, in a hut belonging to Lawyer Gibbons, where I kept a butcher's stall. My wife had a brother, who was half an Indian by his mother's side, and half a Negro. He sent us a steer, which I sold, and had now in all 13 dollars, and about three guineas besides, with which I designed to pay our passage, and set off for Charlestown;[32] but the British light horse came in,[33] and took it all away. However as it was a good time for the sale of meat, I borrowed money from some of the Black people to buy hogs, and soon re-paid them, and agreed for a passage to Charlestown, where Major P. the British commander,[34] was very kind to me. When the British were going to evacuate Charlestown,[35] they advised me to go to Halifax, in Nova Scotia, and gave the few Black people, and it may be as many as 500 White people, their passage for nothing.[36] We were 22 days on the passage, and used very ill on board. When we came off Halifax, I got leave to go ashore. On shewing my papers to General Patterson, he sent orders, by a Serjeant, for my wife and children to follow me. This was before Christmas, and we staid there till June; but as no way was open for me to preach to my own color, I got leave to go to Shelburne (150 miles, or more, I suppose, by sea), in the suit[37] of General Patterson, leaving my wife and children for a while behind. Numbers of my own color were here, but I found the White people were against me. I began to sing the first night, in the woods, at a camp, for there were no houses then built; they were just clearing and preparing to erect a town. The Black people came far and near, it was so new to them: I kept on so every night in the week, and appointed a meeting for the first Lord's-day, in a valley between two hills, close by the river; and a great number of White and Black people came, and I was so overjoyed with having an opportunity once more of preaching the word of God, that after I had given out the hymn, I could not speak for tears. In the afternoon we met again, in the same place, and I had great liberty from the Lord. We had a meeting now every evening, and those poor creatures who had never heard the gospel before, listened to me very attentively: but the White people, the justices, and all, were in an uproar, and said that I might go out into the woods, for I should not stay there. I ought to except one White man, who knew me at Savannah, and who said I should have his lot to live upon as long as I would, and build a house if I pleased. I then cut down poles, stripped bark, and made a smart hut, and the people came flocking to the preaching every evening for a month, as though they had come for their supper. Then Governor Parr came from Halifax,[38] brought my wife and children, gave me six months provisions for my family, and a quarter of an acre of land to cultivate for our subsistence. It was a spot where there was plenty of water, and which I had before severely wished for, as I knew it would be convenient for baptizing at any time. The weather being severe, and the ground covered with snow, we raised a platform of poles for the hearers to stand upon, but there was nothing over their heads. Continuing to attend, they desired to have a Meeting house built. We had then a day of hearing what the Lord had done, and I and my wife heard their experiences, and I received four of my own color; brother Sampson [Colbert], brother John, sister Offee, and sister Dinah;[39] these all wear well, at Sierra Leone, except brother Sampson, an excellent man, who died on his voyage to that place. The first time I baptized here was a little before Christmas, in the creek which ran through my lot. I preached to a great number of people on the occasion, who behaved very well. I now formed the church with us six, and administered the Lord's supper in the Meeting-house before it was finished. They went on with the building, and we appointed a time every other week to hear experiences. A few months after I baptized nine more, and the congregation very much increased. The worldly Blacks, as well as the members of the church, assisted in cutting timber in the woods, and in getting shingles; and we used to give a few coppers to buy nails. We were increasing all the winter, and baptized almost every month, and administered the Lord's supper first of all once in two months; but the frame of the Meeting [house] was not all up, nor had we covered it with shingles till about the middle of the summer, and then it had no pulpit, seats, nor flooring.

About this time, Mr. William Taylor and his wife [Ann], two [White] Baptists, who came from London to Shelburn, heard of me. She came to my house when I was so poor that I had no money to buy any potatoes for feed, and was so good as to give my children somewhat, and me money enough to buy a bushel of potatoes; which one produced thirty-five bushels. The church was now grown to about fifty members. At this time a White person, William Holmes, who, with Deborah his wife, had been converted by reading the scriptures, and lived at Jones's Harbour, about twenty miles down the river, came up for me, and would have me go with him in his schooner to his house, and then to a town they called Liverpool, inhabited by White people. Many have been baptized there by Mr. Chippenham,[40] of Annapolis, in Nova Scotia. Mr. Jesse Dexter preached to them, but was not their pastor. It is a mixed communion church. I preached there; the Christians were all alive and we had a little heaven together. We then returned to brother Holmes's, and he and his wife came up with me to Shelburn, and gave their experiences to the church on Thursday, and were baptized on Lord's-day. Their relations who lived in the town were very angry, raised a mob, and endeavoured to hinder their being baptized. Mrs. Holmes's sister especially laid hold of her hair to keep her from going down into the water; but the justices commanded peace, and said that she should be baptized as she herself desired it. Then they were all quiet. Soon after this the persecution increased, and became so great, that it did not seem possible to preach, and I thought I must leave Shelburn. Several of the Black people had houses upon my lot; but forty or fifty disbanded soldiers were [un]employed, who came with the tackle of ships, and turned my dwelling house, and every one of their houses, quite over; and the Meeting house they would have burned down, had not the ring-leader of the mob himself prevented it. But I continued preaching in it till they came one night, and stood before the pulpit, and swore how they would treat me if I preached again. But I stayed and preached, and the next day they came and beat me with sticks, and drove me into a swamp. I returned in the evening, and took my wife and children over the river to Birch town,[41] where some Black people were settled, and there seemed a greater prospect of doing good than at Shelburn. I preached at Birch Town from the fall till about the middle of December, and was frequently hearing experiences, and baptized about twenty there. Those who desired to hear the word of God, invited me from house to house, and so I preached. A little before Christmas, as my own color persecuted me there, I set off with my family, to return to Shelburn; and coming down the river the boat was frozen, but we took whip-saws[42] and cut away the ice till we came to Shelburn. In my absence the Meeting house was occupied by a sort of tavern-keeper, who said, "The old Negro wanted to make a heaven of this place, but I'll make a hell of it." Then I preached in it as before, and as my house was pulled down, lived in it also. The people began to attend again, and in the summer there was a considerable revival of religion. Now I went down about twenty miles to a place called Ragged Island, among some White people, who desired to hear the word. One White sister[43] was converted there while I was preaching concerning the disciples, who left all and followed Christ. She came up afterwards, gave her experience to our church, and was baptized, and two Black sisters with her. Then her other sister gave in her experience; and joined us without Baptism, to which she would have submitted, had not her family cruelly hindered her; but she was the only one in our society who was not baptized.

By this time [ca.1791] the Christians at St. John's,[44] about 200 miles from Shelburn, over the bay of Fundy, in New Brunswick, had heard of me, and wished me to visit them. Part of the first Saturday I was there was spent in hearing the experiences of the Black people; four were approved, some of whom had been converted in Virginia: a fortnight after I baptized them in the river, on the Lord's-day. Numerous spectators, White and Black, were present, who behaved very well. But on Monday many of the inhabitants made a disturbance, declaring that nobody should preach there again without a licence from the Governor.[45] He lived at Frederick town, about a hundred miles from thence up St. John's river. I went off in the packet[46] to him, Colonel Allen,[47] who knew me in Charlestown, lived but a few miles from the Governor, and introduced me to him; upon which his secretary gave me a licence.[48] I returned then to St. John's, and preached again, and left brother Peter Richards to exhort among them. He afterwards died on the passage, just going into Sierra Leone, and we buried him there. When I got back to Shelburn, I sent brother Sampson Colbert, one of my Elders, to St. John's, to stay there. He was a loving brother, and the Lord had endowed him with great gifts.—When the experiences of nine or ten had been related there, they sent for me to come and baptize them. I went by water to Halifax, and walked from thence to Haughton[49] about 80 miles from Annapolis, and not far from New Brunswick. There is a large church at Haughton, I think the largest in Nova Scotia. They are all Baptists; Mr. Scott is their minister. We spent one Sabbath together, and all day long was a day to be remembered. When I was landing at St. John's, some of the people who intended to be baptized were so full of joy that they ran out from waiting at table on their masters, with the knives and forks in their hands, to meet me at the water side. This second time of my being at St. John's I staid preaching about a fortnight, and baptized ten people. Our going down into the water seemed to be a pleasing sight to the whole town, White people and Black. I had now to go to Frederick Town again, from whence I obtained the licence before; for one of our brethren had been there, and heard the experiences of three of the people, and they sent to me, intreating that I would not return until I had been and baptized them. Two brethren took me to Frederick Town in a boat. I baptized on the Lord's-day, about 12 o'clock: a great number of people attended. The Governor said he was sorry he could not come down to see it; but he had a great deal of company that day, which also hindered one of his servants from being baptized. I came back to St. John's, and home to Shelburn. Then I was sent for to Preston, and left brother Hector Peters, one of my Elders, with them. In returning to Shelburn, with about 30 passengers, we were blown off into the sea, and lost our course. I had no blanket to cover me, and got frost-bitten in both my legs up to my knees, and was so ill when I came towards land, that I could not walk. The church met me at the river side, and carried me home. Afterwards, when I could walk a little, I wanted to speak of the Lord's goodness, and the brethren made a wooden sledge, and drew me to [the] Meeting [house]. In the spring of the year I could walk again, but have never been strong since.

The next fall, Agent (afterwards Governor) Clarkson came to Halifax, about settling the new colony at Sierra Leone.[50] The White people in Nova Scotia were very unwilling that we should go, though they had been very cruel to us, and treated many of us as bad as though we had been slaves.[51] They attempted to persuade us that if we went away we should be made slaves again. The brethren and sisters all round at St. John's, Halifax, and other places, Mr. Wesley's people and all,[52] consulted what was best to do, and sent in their names to me, to give to Mr. Clarkson, and I was to tell him that they were willing to go. I carried him their names, and he appointed to meet us at Birch Town the next day. We gathered together there, in the Meeting-house of brother Moses,[53] a blind man, one of Mr. Wesley's preachers. Then the Governor read the proclamation, which contained what was offered, in case we had a mind willingly to go, and the greatest part of us were pleased and agreed to go. We appointed a day over at Shelburn, when the names were to be given to the Governor. Almost all the Baptists went, except a few of the sisters whose husbands were inclined to go back to New York; and sister Lizze, a Quebec Indian, and brother Lewis, her husband, who was an half Indian, both of whom were converted under my ministry, and had been baptized by me. There are a few scattered Baptists yet at Shelburn, St. John's, Jones's Harbour,[54] and Ragged Island,[55] beside the congregations at the places I mentioned before. The meeting-house lot, and all our land at Shelburn, it may be half an acre, was sold to merchant Black for about 7£.

We departed and called at Liverpool, a place I mentioned before. I preached a farewel sermon there; I longed to do it. Before I left the town, Major Collins, who with his wife used to hear me at this place, was very kind to me, and gave me some salted herrings, which were very acceptable all the way to Sierra Leone. We sailed from Liverpool to Halifax, where we tarried three or four weeks, and I preached from house to house, and [gave] my farewel sermon in Mr. Marchington's Methodist Meeting-house.[56] There is also a Mr. William Black,[57] at Halifax, a smart preacher, one of Mr. Wesley's, who baptizes those Christians who desire it by immersion.[58]

Our passage from Halifax to Sierra Leone was seven weeks, in which we had very stormy weather. Several persons died on the voyage, of a catching fever, among whom were three of my Elders, Sampson Colwell [Colbert], a loving man, Peter Richards, and John Williams.

There was great joy to see the land. The high mountain, at some distance from Free-town, where we now live, appeared like a cloud to us.[59] I preached the first Lord's day,[60] it was a blessed time, under a sail, and so I did for several weeks after. We then erected a hovel for a Meeting-house, which is made of posts put into the ground, and poles over our heads, which are covered with grass. While I was preaching under the sails, sisters Patty Webb and Lucy Lawrence were converted, and they, with old sister Peggy, brother Bill Taylor, and brother Sampson

Haywood, three who were awakened before they came this voyage, have since been baptized in the river.

On the voyage from Halifax to Sierra Leone, I asked the Governor if I might not hereafter go to England? and some time after we arrived there, I told him I wished to see the Baptist brethren who live in his country. He was a very kind man to me and to every body; he is very free and good natured, and used to come to hear me preach, and would sometimes sit down at our private meetings; and he liked that I should call my last child by his name. And I sent to Mr. Henry Thornton,[61] O what a blessed man is that! he is brother, father, every thing. He ordered me five guineas, and I had leave to come over. When I came away from Sierra Leone, I preached a farewel sermon to the church, and encouraged them to look to the Lord, and submit to one another, and regard what is said to them by my three Elders, brethren Hector Peters, and John Colbert, who are two exhorters, and brother John Ramsey.

~

A FEW, from NUMEROUS, TESTIMONIALS to the CHARACTER of Mr. DAVID GEORGE.

Shelburn, Nova Scotia, Oct. 22, 1790.

I HAVE known the bearer, Mr. David George, above five years in this settlement, and know that he hath conducted himself like a good christian; and he is a very industrious good citizen.

GEO. WHITE, *Justice of Peace.*

~

THESE are to certify, that David George, a Baptist preacher, is an inhabitant of the town of Shelburn, and province of Nova Scotia; That he bears a good character, is charitable, sober, honest, and industrious, and is entitled to the attention of all well-disposed people. Witness my hand this second day of December, 1791.

STEPHEN SKINNER, *Agent for the District of Shelburn.*

~

Ship York, Sierra Leone, 10*th Dec.* 1792.

My Dear Friends,

I BEG leave to recommend to your brotherly love and Christian kindness, the bearer of this letter, Mr. David George, as a sincere Christian, and an humble, diligent, and faithful minister of the word of God, which has ever been blessed from his lips, as it has always been exemplified in his conversation. He is connected with Christians of the Baptist profession, but his heart embraces, with ingenuous love, all who love God and our Saviour Jesus Christ. His intention, in visiting England, is to see and converse with Christians of all denominations, and particularly to acquaint himself with the Baptist ministers; hoping by these means to increase in Christian knowledge, and to be still better qualified for administering the word of God. I earnestly request you, for Christ's sake, to shew him all kind offices, particularly to introduce him to the most humble, pious, experienced Christians of your acquaintance; not much among those who move in the circle of fashionable christianity. I remain, your affectionate Friend and servant,

MELVILL HORNE.[62]

~

To REV. JOHN NEWTON,
REV. RICH. CECIL,
REV. HENRY FOSTER,
REV. MR. SCOTT.

GOVERNOR Clarkson, in the most unreserved manner, assured me that he esteemed David George as his brother, and that he believes him to be the best man, without exception, in the colony at Sierra Leone.

EDITOR. (473-484)

~

From *The Baptist Annual Register, for 1794, 1795, 1796-1797* (1798).

"Extracts of letters from Mr. David George, the Negro Minister, at *Free Town*, SIERRA LEONE, dated from Sept. 13 to Oct. 10 1793."

After we had been in the Downs four days,[63] we sailed; but the wind soon came a-head, and drove us almost back to our former station, where we continued a fortnight. We then were bound for Plymouth,[64] but running foul of another vessel, our bowsprit was carried away; after this we sprung a leak, and we put into Plymouth, and got repaired again. The day after we put to sea we were chased by two cutters,[65] from early in the morning till about twelve o'clock, when one left us, but the other began to fire at us: we hove too but when they came up and spoke with us they were satisfied. We now stood on our passage. Our topmast was carried away before we came to Bulam,[66] and there we were on a rock until the tide rose and got us off. Before we arrived at Sierra Leone, our topmast was carried away again, but we got safe there on the 7th of August last, about five in the afternoon; and I found my wife, all my children, and my congregation well. The vessel was hourly expected, but it was thought I would not return so soon. I was well received by Mr. Downe, our Governor;[67] and when the people of the colony heard that I was come, they rejoiced much, and at my landing they came down so thick that I could scarcely get along. Some of them took me by the hand and led me through. I have great reason to thank Almighty God for his goodness who carried me over the seas, and returned me safe home again. I was hearty all the homeward bound passage. On Lord's day, the 11th, I preached in my congregation from Thomas's words, John xx. 28. *My Lord and my God.* The Spirit of the Lord seemed to give me utterance, and the meeting was joyful. It is a very healthful time with us for this part of the year. There are not many ill. We are now building on our Town Lots, and some on their Farms; and the people begin to be seasoned to the country. They are getting into a good way, especially those that are on their lands; and I am in great hope we shall all do well in a few years. I am very glad to tell you that the work of God revives here among our people, and I hope it will begin among the NATIVES OF AFRICA. I had the pleasure of baptizing one person the first of September, and four more on Saturday the 6th of October. My Elders, Sir, and all the congregation, thank you for your goodness to me while I was in London, and we all humbly give thanks to the Gentlemen, and every one of the brothers in your congregation, and in others, for the charity they have shewn our church, in the blessed gift of a meeting-house, which the Lord has put it into your hearts to make us a present of: and also for the kind offer, that if the Lord should encline any one of us to come home,[68] to get instruction in the ministry, you would keep him a year and teach him. Thank the dear Friend that considered us in this;[69] we take it as a great favour, and leave it to the Lord, hoping that he may make some one of us fit to carry on his great work, and be useful; but a direct answer to this we hope to send in a short time. I want to hear from you, and all the brothers, and all the ministers. I want to know how religion flourishes in London.

Please to tell these few words to all my friends in Christ, and, after a while, if the brothers want me to come again, you must let me know, and I'll try and come.

The church in Sierra Leone, together with me, cease not in our prayers to make mention of you all; all the brothers, and the sisters, and all my acquaintance in London. Hoping that you will not forget me and them at a throne of grace.

Please to forward the letters to Brother Geard of Hitchin, and Brother [Samuel] Pearce of Birmingham: and give my heart love to Brother [Abraham] Booth and Brother Thomas,[70] and to the Brother a good way out, where the Gentlemen were so kind to me.[71] (94-96)

~

"Letters from two Negro Brethren, viz. the Pastor [David George] and Elder [John Cuthbert] of the Baptist Church in Sierra Leone."

SIERRA LEONE. *Freetown*, Nov. 12, 1794 (Extract).

Dear Brother Rippon, I am sorry to inform you, that on Sunday, the 28th of Sept. about eight o'clock in the morning, there came into our harbour, under English colours, a French fleet consisting of seven sail: one ship of fifty guns, two frigates, two brigs, and two ships of twenty guns. We thought they were our friends until they came up abreast of the town. But without sending in any message, they poured a broad-side upon the town. At the first fire the governor ordered the colours to be struck,[72] but it prevailed nothing. They kept up a constant fire for the space of an hour and a half. The people had not time to take with them so much as their clothes, but Whites and Blacks were obliged to run back into the mountains. The French landed and plundered our houses of all that we had; broke and destroyed every thing. They burned all the Company's stores, and every house that the Company had in the colony; the church in which Mr. Horne used to preach, and all the buildings; destroyed the cannon, killed all the cattle, hogs, goats, sheep and fowls. They burned but six of the *settlers houses*; yet they have left us in a bad condition. In all the firing they killed but one child, about seven years old, and wounded four more. One man and one woman had their legs shot off; she is since dead with her wound; the others are like to do well. In all this I see the hand of God. It was his mercy that there were not a greater number of the people killed, for thinking that our friends were coming, all went to see the fleet, and were at water side in multitudes when they fired on the town. As they took away all the clothes from everybody, whites and blacks, so they stripped me among the rest, of all my clothes; they did not leave me a second shirt to my back. My wife and children were almost naked. Sir, will you be pleased to lay it before our Brothers, and before all the Baptist churches in London. I would be very glad if they will consider me in my condition, and will send me some old clothes; if it be ever so coarse I will be thankful. My family is well, and so is my congregation; and we all, with one heart pray that God would sanctify his hand to us. We beg the earnest prayers of all Christ's people, in particular our Baptist brothers and sisters in London. I remain your Brother in God.

DAVID GEORGE. (215-216)

~

Extracts of letters from David George to John Rippon and Samuel Pearce, dated June 30th and July 2, 1795.

On the 26th,[73] the vessel arrived with clothes from our christian friends afar off. What shall we say? Is not God for us! He heard the cry of the poor, and gave his people in London an heart to think of us—of his poor people in Africa. O that we may all ever praise the Lord for his goodness. The clothing was welcome to the congregation, and is distributed throughout the whole society; every one had some. We know not how to be thankful enough for the goodness of christians in London; but with one heart we join to thank them. And we wish that you, our brother in God, would give our hearty thanks to every one of the congregation[74] who remembered us, as they are well known to you. Next Lord's-day, July the 5th, we hope to spend as a day of prayer and THANKSGIVING to the Lord, for his kindness to us in causing us to be remembered by Christians in a far country.[75]

I did intend, as I wrote you in April last, to go as soon as I could to preach the gospel among the natives, and to take Thomas London, a member of our church, with me as an interpreter,[76] but the natives are now at war with one another, though they are at peace with us.

I am well, and my family; and my congregation in general are very hearty. The rains are just begun with us, and the colony is in a thriving condition since the French left us.

Since I came from England I have had the pleasure of baptizing three brothers and seven sisters; one of the brothers is an African born. I am ready to do what little good I can for Christ. I hope the Lord will spread the glad tidings of the gospel throughout Africa, in his own due time.

Let our humble and hearty thanks be known to all the Baptist churches for the favors they have done us, in providing for a place of worship where we may serve the Lord. We hope that the house will be built in his name; but we do not think proper to go about it immediately, nor does our Governor. (255-256)

~

"EXTRACT of a LETTER from Mr. DAVID GEORGE, concerning the Negro Church, and the two missionaries, Messrs. Grigg and Rodway.[77]"

Free Town, Africa, 19th April, 1796.

My dear Brother,

I RECEIVED your very kind letter, with the trunk, which Mr. Etheridge has been pleased to send—for which I, in the name of my brethren and sisters, return him our most grateful acknowledgements—May the Lord reward him an hundred-fold. The names of those who received the garments your people were so kind as to send, I will transmit to you in my next; they have afforded us a most comfortable supply of those clothes we stood most in need of—may the Lord bless your congregation for their kindness to us. We have received all the linen, and divided it agreeable to your directions. My brothers and sisters with me, are also at a loss how to express our gratitude to our heavenly Father for his goodness, in inclining the heart of Samuel Whitbread, Esq. to take notice of us. Shirts and shifts we stood much in need of—our *wants* in that article are now in a great measure supplied. We intend to write to him a letter of thanks,[78] if in our power, before the ship sails—if not, you may expect it with the next, which will sail, in about three weeks hence.

These things, with the hymn and tune books, we received from brothers Rodway and Grigg, who appear to be two most excellent young men, and well qualified for being Missionaries—Mr. Rodway has been rather poorly since his arrival here, but Mr. Grigg has kept his health amazing well—has been for some time at Port Logo—has made considerable progress in the language, and is much respected, and greatly beloved by all the people there; at present he is come down to *Free Town*, and intends staying till the rains are over.

I gave the book to governor Dawes, which you was pleased to send, he kindly received it, and returns you many thanks for it. He still thinks, and we agree with him, that it will be most prudent to defer *building our meeting [house]*, till once peace shall have taken place, (which we pray God, may be soon). We have preserved the writings of it you sent,[79] and intend, when the time shall come, to build it on the same spot, on which the present meeting [house] stands.

The two missionaries have preached frequently with us, much to our satisfaction, and I trust to our edification likewise—they have not had opportunity for examining yet into our experiences, being so much taken up with their own business, in which they seem to engage with becoming spirit—they have been no expence to any of us.

We have appointed the afternoon of the first Tuesday of the month, to be kept as a meeting of prayer for the success of the Gospel in all the churches, and *for its spread throughout the whole earth*. We have had a day of fasting and prayer lately, on account of the missionaries, Messrs. Rodway and Grigg—they were both present—this was *a most delightful season*—I trust the Divine Presence was in the midst of us.

We return you ten thousand thanks for your good advices—May the Lord enable us to act, and to walk in the way we ought—We have constant remembrance of you and of our dear brothers and sisters with you at the throne of grace—May the work of the Lord prosper among you.—We beg your prayers for us—yea we trust we have them—O that the Almighty would be pleased to pour out more and more of his Spirit—may the wilderness every where soon become as a fruitful field—may men be blessed in our Jesus, and all the ends of the earth speedily call him blessed.

We have had two deaths, since I last wrote to you, Euphemea Demps,[80] whom I baptized about ten years ago in America, and one of my own children, Jane George, aged 12 years, they both died very comfortably. I have collected many of their dying sayings; Mr. Clarke, the chaplain, would have inserted them, but has not time at present—his love to you, and all your people—he preaches commonly once a week in our meeting [house]—we meet at an earlier hour than usual on the Lord's day, and go all of us to his place of worship to hear him—he intends writing to you by the first opportunity. The young men who came out as catechists with him are doing well, much beloved by all—they keep their school in our meeting-house, and frequently attend with us.

We have had no additions of members since I wrote to you last—Mr. Macaulay's compliments to you—Governor Dawes is coming home[81]—My wife is but poorly at present. All the rest of my family, with myself, are well; for which we desire to bless God.

I remain your affectionate brother,
DAVID GEORGE[82] (409-410)

NOTES

1. Actually Sussex County, around 1743.

2. Nottaway: Nottoway.

3. Carding: combing out fibers with a card, or wire-toothed brush, to ready them for being spun.

4. Chapel: probably James Chappell (d. 1769).

5. Cut away: with whips.

6. Nottaway, the English church: Nottoway, an Anglican (Church of England) church.

7. Brunswick County then included present-day Greensville County.

8. Pedee: Pee Dee.

9. Okemulgee: Okmulgee.

10. King: chief.

11. Blue Salt: perhaps of the Lower Creek Oktchunalgi (Salt) clan. Blue Salt was one of the Lower Creek chiefs who negotiated with the British in 1768 over the disputed ownership of land.

12. Probably Samuel Chappell (ca. 1722-1765).

13. Nautchee: Natchez.

14. George Galphin had emigrated from Ulster in the 1730s and was so well connected with the local Indians that he became the American Indian agent, keeping the normally pro-British tribes neutral during the American Revolution. In addition to his two legitimate children, he had offspring with Indian and mulatto women, all of whom he acknowledged in his will, leaving them freedom, land, and slaves.

15. Silver Bluff: in South Carolina, southeast of Augusta, Georgia.

16. Around 1770 he married Phillis, who may have been part-Indian.

17. [Rippon's note.] See an account of him in the *Register*, p. 332. [See the selection by George Liele in this anthology.]

18. Matthew 11:28.

19. Reverend Wait Palmer (1722-1795), a White Baptist evangelist from Connecticut who preached throughout the South.

20. Given White fear of slave insurrections, it was quite unusual for slaves to be granted such an opportunity to congregate.

21. [Rippon's note.] The account to which he refers is in p. 336 of the *Register*. [See the selection by George Liele. As was the common practice, Jesse Gaulfin the slave was known by the surname of his master.]

22. Formed sometime before December 1777, and almost certainly between 1773 and 1775, the Silver Bluff Baptist Church was probably the first exclusively Afro-British and subsequently the first exclusively African-American church.

23. The three volumes of *Hymns and Spiritual Songs* by Isaac Watts (1674-1748) were frequently published in Great Britain and North America during the eighteenth century. The first line of Watts's hymn reads, "Thus saith the mercy of the Lord."

24. Lieutenant Colonel Archibald Campbell captured Savannah on 29 December 1779 (the British held the city until June 1782). The British took Augusta on 29 January 1779. Silver Bluff, twelve miles from Augusta, lay in the path of the British troops advancing from Savannah. Galphin's trading post, converted into Fort Galphin, fell to the British, who renamed it Fort Dreadnought and held it until May 1781, by which time Galphin was dead.

25. Jesse and David.

26. British General Augustine Prevost had approached Savannah from British Florida.

27. Probably Colonel Thomas Brown.

28. Yamacraw: now a section of greater Savannah.

29. The unsuccessful American campaign against the British in Savannah was led by General Benjamin Lincoln in October 1779, in conjunction with a French naval assault

commanded by Admiral d'Estaing. Savannah's population comprised a few hundred Indians, fewer than two thousands Whites, and about five thousand Blacks, most serving as laborers working on the city's fortifications and consequently absolutely essential to the British victory against the numerically superior enemy. Many of the Blacks were still slaves, belonging to Loyalists, and when Savannah was evacuated in June 1782, they maintained that status when taken to British East Florida and Jamaica.

Like the other refugee Blacks, George carried "freedom papers," his signed on 1 January 1780 by the town adjutant, Edward Cooper, enabling "the Bearer to pass and repass about his lawful Business unmolested." An earlier permit, signed by John Wright on 11 December 1779, identified George as a "Free Negro Man" and "a good Subject to King George."

30. General Henry Clinton (1730-1795), commander in chief of the British forces, was in New York until early 1780.

31. Jesse, David, and Ginny.

32. Charlestown: Charleston, South Carolina, which fell to Clinton on 12 May 1780. At the end of May, Clinton returned to New York, leaving General Charles Cornwallis (1738-1805) in command.

33. Light horse: cavalry.

34. Major P.: Major General James Paterson, who had been chosen by General Clinton to be military commandant of Charleston after its fall to the British. He was subsequently ordered to command the military district of Halifax, Nova Scotia. George and five hundred other refugees left with Patterson on 19 November 1782, reaching Halifax in December and Shelburne on 25 June 1783. George's family joined him there a month later.

35. Sir Guy Carleton (1724-1808), Clinton's successor as commander in chief, evacuated Charleston in late 1782.

36. Of the 30,000-35,000 Loyalists who sought refuge in Nova Scotia, more than 3,000 were free Blacks.

37. Shelburne: formerly Port Roseway, recently renamed in honor of William Petty (1737-1805), first Marquis of Lansdowne and second Earl of Shelburne, for his role as prime minister from July 1782 to February 1783 in ending the war in America. Suit: suite.

38. Lieutenant Colonel John Parr (1725-1791), Governor since 9 October 1782.

39. Thus, David George became the first Black Baptist minister of the first Black Baptist church in present-day Canada.

40. Chippenham: Rev. Thomas Handley Chipman (1756-1830).

41. A census conducted in 1784 lists the members of George's family and their ages: David, forty; his wife Phillis, twenty-five; Jesse, ten; David, seven; Marry [*sic*], three; and Jane, one.

42. Whip-saw: a narrow two-person crosscut saw.

43. Elizabeth, wife of Jonathan Locke II.

44. Saint John, New Brunswick.

45. Governor: the brother of Sir Guy, Thomas Carleton had become the first Lieutenant Governor of New Brunswick in 1784.

Under the New Brunswick *Act for Preserving the Church of England* (1786), dissenting ministers had to take oaths of allegiance and obtain a license before they could evangelize outside of the church in which they had been elected pastor.

46. Packet: a regularly scheduled passenger boat.

47. Colonel Isaac Allen, now a supreme court judge.

48. [Rippon's note.] Secretary's Office, Frederick-town,
17th July, 1792.

I do hereby certify, that David George, a free Negro man, has permission from his Excellency the Lieutenant Governor, to instruct the Black people in the knowledge, and exhort them to the practice of, the Christian religion.

Jon. Odell, Secretary.

49. Haughton: Horton, present-day Wolfville, Nova Scotia.

50. Royal Navy Lieutenant John Clarkson (1765-1828), Agent for the Sierra Leone Company, and brother of Thomas Clarkson (1760-1846), the abolitionist. The Sierra Leone Company, with Henry Thornton (1760-1815) as Chairman of its Court of Directors, had been incorporated by Parliament in 1791 with the purpose of establishing a commercial settlement on the ruins of Granville Town, destroyed by a local African ruler at the end of 1789. When Thomas Peters (ca.1738- 25 June 1792), a former slave who sought refuge in Nova Scotia, came to London to seek official redress for the complaints of the Afro-Britons in North America, the directors of the Sierra Leone Company offered him and his people the opportunity for resettlement in their newly established Freetown in Sierra Leone. The Treasury agreed to pay for the transportation of the settlers, and the Company sent Clarkson, whose brother was one of its directors, as their recruiting Agent to Nova Scotia. With 1,190 Afro-British settlers on fifteen ships, Clarkson sailed on 15 January 1792, and they arrived at Sierra Leone between 28 February and 9 March 1793 (the transports had been separated at sea by storms).

Clarkson's conduct so impressed the Company that the directors appointed him Governor of Sierra Leone. In the soon developing tensions between the Company and the settlers, which led to a confrontation between Clarkson and Peters on 8 April 1792, strikes by some of the settlers over the issues of governance and the company's attempt to collect quitrents on the settlers' lands, and an abortive rebellion in 1800, George always remained loyal to Clarkson and the Company, even at the expense of his influence in the colony. Parliament granted the Company a charter in 1800, and in 1808 control of the settlement was transferred from the Company to the British government, and Sierra Leone became a crown colony.

51. [Rippon's note.] This Governor Clarkson also has confirmed to the EDITOR.

[The Loyalist Blacks in Nova Scotia had been given generally smaller plots of land and those less arable than the plots given to Loyalist Whites. Consequently, many of the Blacks were compelled to work for the richer Whites at lower wages than the poorer Whites received. Hence the Blacks were both wanted and resented by the local Whites.]

52. The Methodist followers of John Wesley (1703-1791).

53. Moses Wilkinson, also mentioned in the selection by Boston King in this anthology.

54. Jones's Harbour: near present-day Harding Point.

55. Ragged Island: present-day Lockeport.

56. Philip Marchinton (1736-1808), a wealthy merchant, owned the meetinghouse. Although the Methodist congregation had recently excommunicated Marchinton for some now unknown infraction, he retained possession of the building.

57. William Black (1760-1834), a Wesleyan Methodist.

58. [Rippon's note.] Baptism by immersion, in an occasional way, not only obtains in Mr. Wesley's connexions, as above, but also in some of the West India islands, as well as in Kentucky, and other parts of North America; and it is said to be done, even under the permission of Dr. Coke himself.

EDITOR.

[William Black, the American Methodist evangelist, and Thomas Coke (1747-1814), chosen by John Wesley as Superintendent of overseas Methodist missions, are also mentioned in the selection by Boston King in this anthology.]

59. Sierra Leone gained its name, meaning lion mountain, because Spanish explorers thought that its dominant peak resembled a reclining lion.

60. George thus became the founder of the first Baptist church in Africa.

61. Henry Thornton: Chairman, Sierra Leone Company Court of Directors.

62. [Rippon's note.] Rev. Mr. Melvill Horne was curate to Mr. Fletcher of Medley, and is now the much-loved officiating clergyman at Sierra Leone.

EDITOR.

63. The Downs: the English Channel off the southeast coast of Kent in England, where ships often rested at anchor before setting out to sea.

64. Plymouth: on the southern coast of England.

65. Cutters: single-masted vessels.

66. Bulom Shore, on the African coast, just north of Sierra Leone.

67. Downe, our Governor: the Governor was William Dawes (d. 1836).

68. [Rippon's note.] By *home* he means England. When the brethren, Rippon and Pearce, were collecting from him the account of his life, which appears in the preceding volume, page 473, they both observed, that in speaking of this country he generally called it *home*; and being asked why he did so, he replied, "Almost all our people, in different parts call it so."

69. [Rippon's note.] He probably means Dr. Ryland. EDITOR.

[The Rev. Dr. John Ryland was pastor of Broadway Baptist Church in Bristol, principal of the only Baptist seminary in England, the Bristol Baptist Academy, and a leader in the Baptist Missionary Society, organized in 1792.]

70. Perhaps Joshua Thomas (1719-1797), pastor of Leominster Baptist Church, 1754-1797.

71. [Rippon's note.] He means Mr. [Matthew] Walker, Minister at Saffron Walden, Messrs Searles the Bankers in that town, and Mr. B. Cleaver of Newport, near Walden.

72. Zachary Macaulay (1768-1838), acting Governor in Dawes's absence in England, raised the flag of truce.

73. Rippon inserts here "(he does not say of what month,)."

74. [Rippon's note.] Several benevolent individuals also, belonging to the churches in Wild-street and Goodman's-field, have, this September, forwarded an handsome contribution.

75. Rippon inserts here the observation "ASTONISHING GRATITUDE."

76. [Rippon's note.] Thomas London is a native African.

77. Before becoming missionaries to Africa, Jacob Grigg had been a member of the Baptist church in Launceston, Cornwall, and James Rodway had been a member of the Baptist church in Hillsley, Gloucestershire. They left England on 2 November 1795, arriving at Sierra Leone on 1 December 1795.

78. [Rippon's note.] When Esquire Whitbread heard of Mr. Rippon's endeavour to procure a quantity of clothes for the christian negroes, at Sierra Leone, who had lately been plundered by some of the French; he sent Mr. R[ippon] a twenty pound bank note, "towards furnishing the wardrobe" of these distressed creatures; wishing it to be laid out for shirts and shifts [chemises]—it was accordingly done. The *letter of thanks* for this generosity, mentioned above, was duly written at Sierra Leone, signed with the name of each man and woman, who shared in the distributions. The sight of this letter would surely have given the benevolent Whitbread great pleasure, but it came to the hands of Mr. R[ippon] a few hours after Mr. Whitbread died.

[Whitbread (1726-1796), the wealthy brewer, had contributed money for the relief of the original settlers of Granville Town in 1788, and was a member of the St. George's Company, which evolved into the Sierra Leone Company.]

79. George refers to the deed of trust Rippon had sent earlier.

80. In the list of settlers who enrolled in Birchtown in 1791, Euphemea is recorded as a member of the family of John Demps, perhaps his wife.

81. [Rippon's note.] The Governor is safely arrived in England, and speaks respectfully of Messrs. Rodway and Grigg.

[Zachary Macaulay (1768-1838) had come to Sierra Leone in January 1793 as a member of the council and to assist Dawes, whom he succeeded as Governor. He was acting Governor in 1794, while Dawes was recuperating in England.]

82. George died in Africa around 1810, succeeded as pastor to his congregation by Hector Peters, who, after the abolition of the slave trade in 1807, had returned to the settlement from further into the interior of Africa, where he had been a dealer in slaves.

Boston King

(1760?-1802)

~

"Memoirs of the Life of BOSTON KING, a Black Preacher. Written by Himself, during his Residence at Kingswood-School." *The Methodist Magazine For MARCH*, 1798 [London, 1798].

IT is by no means an agreeable task to write an account of my Life, yet my gratitude to Almighty God, who considered my affliction, and looked upon me in my low estate, who delivered me from the hand of the oppressor, and established my goings, impels me to acknowledge his goodness: And the importunity of many respectable friends, whom I highly esteem, have induced me to set down, as they occurred to my memory, a few of the most striking incidents I have met with in my pilgrimage. I am well aware of my inability for such an undertaking, having only a slight acquaintance with the language in which I write, and being obliged to snatch a few hours, now and then, from pursuits, which to me, are more profitable. However, such as it is, I present it to the Friends of Religion and Humanity, hoping that it will be of some use to mankind.

I was born in the Province of South Carolina, 28 miles from Charles-Town.[1] My father was stolen away from Africa when he was young. I have reason to believe that he lived in the fear and love of GOD. He attended to that true Light that lighteth every man that cometh into the world. He lost no opportunity of hearing the Gospel, and never omitted praying with his family every night. He likewise read to them, and to as many as were inclined to hear. On the Lord's-Day he rose very early, and met his family: After which he worked in the field till about three in the afternoon, and then went into the woods and read till sun-set: The slaves being obliged to work on the Lord's-Day to procure such things as were not allowed by their masters. He was beloved by his master, and had the charge of the Plantation as a driver for many years.[2] In his old age he was employed as a mill-cutter.[3] Those who knew him, say, that they never heard him swear an oath, but on the contrary, he reproved all who spoke improper words in his hearing. To the utmost of his power he endeavoured to make his family happy, and his death was a very great loss to us all. My mother was employed chiefly in attending upon those that were sick, having some knowledge of the virtue of herbs,[4] which she learned from the Indians. She likewise had the care of making the people's clothes, and on these accounts was indulged with many privileges which the rest of the slaves were not.

When I was six years old I waited in the house upon my master. In my 9th year I was put to mind the cattle. Here I learnt from my comrades the horrible sin of Swearing and Cursing. When 12 years old, it pleased GOD to alarm me by a remarkable dream. At mid-day, when the cattle went under the shade of the trees, I dreamt that the world was on fire, and that I saw the supreme Judge descend on his great white Throne! I saw millions of millions of souls; some of whom ascended up to heaven; while others were rejected, and fell into the greatest confusion and despair. This dream made such an impression upon my mind, that I refrained from swearing and bad company, and from that time acknowledged that there was a GOD; but how to serve GOD I knew not. Being obliged to travel in different parts of America with race-horses, I suffered many hardships. Happening one time to lose a boot belonging to the Groom, he would not suffer me to have any shoes all that Winter, which was a great punishment to me. When 16 years old, I was bound apprentice to a trade. After being in the shop about two years, I had the charge of my master's tools, which being very good, were often used by the men, if I happened to be out of the way: When this was the case, or any of them were lost, or misplaced, my master beat me severely, striking me upon the head, or any other part without mercy. One time in the holy-days, my master and the men being from home, and the care of the house devolving upon me and the younger apprentices, the house was broke open, and robbed of many valuable articles, thro' the negligence of the apprentice who had then the charge of it. When I came home in the evening, and saw what had happened, my consternation was inconceivable, as all we had in the world could not make good the loss. The week following, when the master came to town, I was beat in a most unmerciful manner, so that I was not able to do any thing for a fortnight. About eight months after, we were employed in building a store-house, and nails were very dear at that time, it being in the American war, so that the work-men had their nails weighed out to them; on this account they made the younger apprentices watch the nails while they were at dinner. It being my lot one day to take care of them, which I did till an apprentice returned to his work, and then I went to dine. In the mean time he took away all the nails belonging to one of the journeymen, and he being of a very violent temper, accused me to the master with stealing of them. For this offence I was beat and tortured most cruelly, and was laid up three weeks before I was able to do any work. My proprietor, hearing of the bad usage I received, came to town, and severely reprimanded my master for beating me in such a manner, threatening him, that if he ever heard the like again, he would take me away and put me to another master to finish my time, and make him pay for it.[5] This had a good effect, and he behaved much better to me, the two succeeding years, and I began to acquire a proper knowledge of my trade. My master being apprehensive that Charles-Town was in danger on account of the war, removed into the country, about 38 miles off. Here we built a large house for Mr. Waters, during which time the English took Charles-Town. Having obtained leave one day to see my parents, who lived about 12 miles off, and it being late before I could go, I was obliged to borrow one of Mr. Waters's horses; but a servant of my master's, took the horse from me to go a little journey, and stayed two or three days longer than he ought. This involved me in the greatest perplexity, and I expected the severest punishment, because the gentleman to whom the horse belonged was a very bad man, and knew not how to shew mercy. To escape his cruelty, I determined to go to Charles-Town, and throw myself into the hands of the English.[6] They received me readily, and I began to feel the happiness of liberty, of which I knew nothing before, altho' I was much grieved at first, to be obliged to leave my friends, and reside among strangers. In this situation I was seized with the small-pox, and suffered great hardships; for all the Blacks affected with that disease, were ordered to be carried a mile from the camp, lest the soldiers should be infected, and disabled from marching. This was a grievous circumstance to me and many others. We lay sometimes a whole day without any thing to eat or drink; but Providence sent a man, who belonged to the York volunteers whom I was acquainted with, to my relief. He brought me such things as I stood in need of; and by the blessing of the Lord I began to recover.

By this time, the English left the place; but as I was unable to march with the army, I expected to be taken by the enemy. However when they came, and understood that we were ill of the small-pox, they precipitately left us for fear of the infection. Two days after, the waggons were sent to convey us to the English Army, and we were put into a little cottage, (being 25 in number) about a quarter of a mile from the Hospital.

Being recovered, I marched with the army to Chamblem.[7] When we came to the head-quarters, our regiment was 35 miles off. I stayed at the head-quarters three weeks, during which time our regiment had an engagement with the Americans, and the man who relieved me when I was ill of the small-pox, was wounded in the battle, and brought to the hospital.[8] As soon as I heard of his misfortune, I went to see him, and tarried with him in the hospital six weeks, till he recovered; rejoicing that it was in my power to return him the kindness he had shewed me. From thence I went to a place about 35 miles off, where we stayed two months: at the expiration of which, an express came to the Colonel to decamp in fifteen minutes. When these orders arrived I was at a distance from the camp, catching some fish for the captain that I waited upon; upon returning to the camp, to my great astonishment, I found all the English were gone, and had left only a few militia. I felt my mind greatly alarmed, but Captain Lewes, who commanded the militia, said, "You need not be uneasy, for you will see your regiment before 7 o'clock to-night." This satisfied me for the present, and in two hours we set off. As we were on the march, the Captain asked, "How will you like me to be your master?" I answered, that I was Captain Grey's servant. "Yes," said he; "but I expect that they are all taken prisoners before now; and I have been long enough in the English service, and am determined to leave them."[9] These words roused my indignation, and I spoke some sharp words to him. But he calmly replied, "If you do not behave well, I will put you in irons, and give you a dozen stripes every morning." I now perceived that my case was desperate, and that I had nothing to trust to, but to wait the first opportunity for making my escape. The next morning, I was sent with a little boy over the river to an island to fetch the Captain some horses. When we came to the Island we found about fifty of the English horses, that Captain Lewes had stolen from them at different times while they were at Rockmount.[10] Upon our return to the Captain with the horses we were sent for, he immediately set off by himself. I stayed till about 10 o'clock, and then resolved to go to the English army. After travelling 24 miles, I came to a farmer's house, where I tarried all night, and was well used. Early in the morning I continued my journey until I came to the ferry, and found all the boats were on the other side of the river: After anxiously waiting some hours, Major Dial crossed the river, and asked me many questions concerning the regiment to which I belonged. I gave him satisfactory answers, and he ordered the boat to put me over. Being arrived at the headquarters, I informed my Captain that Mr. Lewes had deserted. I also told him of the horses which Lewes had conveyed to the Island. Three weeks after, our Lighthorse[11] went to the Island and burnt his house; they likewise brought back forty of the horses, but he escaped. I tarried with Captain Grey about a year, and then left him, and came to Nelson's-ferry. Here I entered into the service of the commanding officer of that place. But our situation was very precarious, and we expected to be made prisoners every day; for the Americans had 1600 men, not far off; whereas our whole number amounted only to 250: But there were 1200 English about 30 miles off; only we knew not how to inform them of our danger, as the Americans were in possession of the country. Our commander at length determined to send me with a letter, promising me great rewards, if I was successful in the business. I refused going on horse-back, and set off on foot about 3 o'clock in the afternoon; I expected every moment to fall in with the enemy, whom I well knew would shew me no mercy. I went on without interruption, till I got within six miles of my journey's end, and then was alarmed with a great noise a little before me. But I stepped out of the road, and fell flat upon my face till they were gone by. I then arose, and praised the Name of the Lord for his great mercy, and again pursued my journey, till I came to Mums-corner tavern. I knocked at the door, but they blew out the candle. I knocked again, and intreated the master to open the door. At last he came with a frightful countenance, and said, "I thought it was the Americans; for they were here about an hour ago, and I thought they were returned again." I asked, How many were there? he answered, "about one hundred." I desired him to saddle his horse for me, which he did, and went with me himself. When we had gone about two miles, we were stopped by the picket-guard, till the Captain came out with 30 men: As soon as he knew that I had brought an express from Nelson's-ferry, he received me with great kindness, and expressed his approbation of my courage and conduct in this dangerous business. Next morning, Colonel Small gave me three shillings, and many fine promises, which were all that I ever received for this service from him. However he sent 600 men to relieve the troops at Nelson's-ferry.[12]

Soon after I went to Charles-Town, and entered on board a man of war.[13] As we were going to Chesepeak-bay, we were at the taking of a rich prize.[14] We stayed in the bay two days, and then sailed for New-York,[15] where I went on shore. Here I endeavoured to follow my trade, but for want of tools was obliged to relinquish it, and enter into service.[16] But the wages were so low that I was not able to keep myself in clothes, so that I was under the necessity of leaving my master and going to another. I stayed with him four months, but he never paid me, and I was obliged to leave him also, and work about the town until I was married.[17] A year after I was taken very ill, but the Lord raised me up again in about five weeks. I then went out in a pilot-boat. We were at sea eight days, and had only provisions for five, so that we were in danger of starving. On the 9th day we were taken by an American whale-boat. I went on board them with a chearful countenance, and asked for bread and water, and made very free with them. They carried me to Brunswick,[18] and used me well. Notwithstanding which, my mind was sorely distressed at the thought of being again reduced to slavery, and separated from my wife and family; and at the same time it was exceeding difficult to escape from my bondage, because the river at Amboy was above a mile over, and likewise another to cross at Staten-Island. I called to remembrance the many great deliverances the Lord had wrought for me, and besought him to save me this once, and I would serve him all the days of my life. While my mind was thus exercised, I went into the jail to see a lad whom I was acquainted with at New-York. He had been taken prisoner, and attempted to make his escape, but was caught 12 miles off: They tied him to the tail of a horse, and in this manner brought him back to Brunswick. When I saw him, his feet were fastened in the stocks, and at night both his hands. This was a terrifying sight to me, as I expected to meet with the same kind of treatment, if taken in the act of attempting to regain my liberty. I was thankful that I was not confined in a jail, and my master used me as well as I could expect; and indeed the slaves about Baltimore, Philadelphia, and New-York, have as good victuals as many of the English; for they have meat once a day, and milk for breakfast and supper; and what is better than all, many of the masters send their slaves to school at night, that they may learn to read the Scriptures. This is a privilege indeed. But alas, all these enjoyments could not satisfy me without liberty! Sometimes I thought, if it was the will of GOD that I should be a slave, I was ready to resign myself to his will; but at other times I could not find the least desire to content myself in slavery.

Being permitted to walk about when my work was done, I used to go to the ferry, and observed, that when it was low water the people waded across the river; tho' at the same time I saw there were guards posted at the place to prevent the escape of prisoners and slaves. As I was at prayer one Sunday evening, I thought the Lord heard me, and would mercifully deliver me. Therefore putting my confidence in him, about one o'clock in the morning I went down to the river side, and found the guards were either asleep or in the tavern. I instantly entered into the river, but when I was a little distance from the opposite shore, I heard the sentinels disputing among themselves: One said, "I am sure I saw a man cross the river." Another replied, "There is no such thing." It seems they were afraid to fire at me, or make an alarm, lest they should be punished for their negligence. When I got a little distance from the shore, I fell down upon my knees, and thanked GOD for this deliverance. I travelled till about five in the morning, and then concealed myself till seven o'clock at night, when I proceeded forward, thro' bushes and marshes, near the road, for fear of being discovered. When I came to the river, opposite Staten-Island, I found a boat; and altho' it was very near a whale-boat, yet I ventured into it, and cutting the rope, got safe over. The commanding officer, when informed of my case, gave me a passport, and I proceeded to New-York.

When I arrived at New-York, my friends rejoiced to see me once more restored to liberty, and joined me in praising the Lord for his mercy and goodness. But not withstanding this great deliverance, and the promises I had made to serve GOD, yet my good resolutions soon vanished away like the morning dew: The love of this world extinguished my good desires, and stole away my heart from GOD, so that I rested in a mere form of religion for near three years. About which time, (in 1783,) the horrors and devastation of war happily terminated,[19] and peace was restored between America and Great Britain, which diffused universal joy among all parties, except us, who had escaped from slavery, and taken refuge in the English army; for a report prevailed at New-York, that all the slaves, in number 2000, were to be delivered up to their masters, altho' some of them had been three or four years among the English. This dreadful rumour filled us all with inexpressible anguish and terror, especially when we saw our old masters coming from Virginia, North-Carolina, and other parts, and seizing upon their slaves in the streets of New-York, or even dragging them out of their beds. Many of the slaves had very cruel masters, so that the thoughts of returning home with them embittered life to us. For some days we lost our appetite for food, and sleep departed from our eyes. The English had compassion upon us in the day of distress, and issued out a Proclamation, importing, That all slaves should be free, who had taken refuge in the British lines, and claimed the sanction and privileges of the Proclamations respecting the security and protection of Negroes. In consequence of this, each of us received a certificate from the commanding officer at New-York, which dispelled all our fears, and filled us with joy and gratitude.[20] Soon after, ships were fitted out, and furnished with every necessary for conveying us to Nova Scotia.[21] We arrived at Burch Town in the month of August, where we all safely landed.[22] Every family had a lot of land, and we exerted all our strength in order to build comfortable huts before the cold weather set in.

That Winter, the work of religion began to revive among us, and many were convinced of the sinfulness of sin, and turned from the error of their ways. It pleased the Lord to awaken my wife under the preaching of Mr. Wilkinson;[23] she was struck to the ground, and cried out for mercy: she continued in great distress for near two hours, when they sent for me. At first I was much displeased, and refused to go; but presently my mind relented, and I went to the house, and was struck with astonishment at the sight of her agony. In about six days after, the Lord spoke peace to her soul: she was filled with divine consolation, and walked in the light of GOD's countenance about nine months. But being unacquainted with the corruptions of her own heart, she again gave place to bad tempers, and fell into great darkness and distress. Indeed, I never saw any person, either before or since, so overwhelmed with anguish of spirit on account of backsliding, as she was. The trouble of her soul brought afflictions upon her body, which confined her to bed a year and a half.

However, the Lord was pleased to sanctify her afflictions, and to deliver her from all her fears. He brought her out of the horrible pit, and set her soul at perfect liberty. The joy and happiness which she now experienced, were too great to be concealed, and she was able to testify of the goodness and loving-kindness of the Lord, with such liveliness and power, that many were convinced by her testimony, and sincerely sought the Lord. As she was the first person at Burch Town that experienced deliverance from evil tempers, and exhorted and urged others to seek and enjoy the same blessing, she was not a little opposed by some of our Black brethren. But these trials she endured with the meekness and patience becoming a christian; and when Mr. FREEBORN GARRETTSON came to Burch Town to regulate the society and form them into classes,[24] he encouraged her to hold fast her confidence, and cleave to the Lord with her whole heart.

Soon after my wife's conversion, the Lord strove powerfully with me. I felt myself a miserable wretched sinner, so that I could not rest night or day. I went to Mr. BROWN, one evening, and told him my case. He received me with great kindness and affection, and intreated me to seek the Lord with all my heart. The more he spoke to me, the more my distress increased; and when he went to prayer, I found myself burdened with a load of guilt too heavy for me to bear. On my return home, I had to pass thro' a little wood, where I intended to fall down on my knees and pray for mercy; but every time I attempted, I was so terrified, that I thought my hair stood upright, and that the earth moved beneath my feet. I hastened home in great fear and horror, and yet hoped that the Lord would bless me as well as my neighbours: for the work of the Lord prospered greatly among us, so that sometimes in our class-meetings, six or seven persons found peace, before we were dismissed.

Notwithstanding I was a witness of the great change which many experienced, yet I suffered the enemy, through unbelief, to gain such advantage over me, that instead of rejoicing with them, and laying hold of the same blessing, I was tempted to envy their happiness, and sunk deeper into darkness and misery. I thought I was not worthy to be among the people of GOD, nor even to dwell in my own house; but was fit only to reside among the beasts of the forest. This drove me out into the woods, when the snow lay upon the ground three or four feet deep, with a blanket, and a fire-brand in my hand. I cut the boughs of the spruce tree and kindled a fire. In this lonely situation I frequently intreated the Lord for mercy. Sometimes I thought that I felt a change wrought in my mind, so that I could rejoice in the Lord; but I soon fell again thro' unbelief into distracting doubts and fears, and evil-reasonings. The devil persuaded me that I was the most miserable creature upon the face of the earth, and that I was predestinated to be damned before the foundation of the world. My anguish was so great, that when night appeared, I dreaded it as much as the grave.

I laboured one year under these distressing temptations, when it pleased GOD to give me another offer of mercy. In 1784, I and sixteen persons worked for

Mrs. ROBINSON; all of them were devoted to GOD, except myself and two others. The divine presence was with these men, and every night and morning they kept a prayer-meeting, and read some portion of Scripture. On the 5th of January, as one of them was reading the Parable of the Sower,[25] the word came with power to my heart. I stood up and desired him to explain the parable; and while he was shewing me the meaning of it, I was deeply convinced that I was one of the stony-ground hearers. When I considered how many offers of mercy I had abused from day to day, and how many convictions I had trifled away, I was astonished that the Lord had borne with me so long. I was at the same time truly thankful that he gave me a desire to return to him, and resolved by the grace of GOD to set out afresh for the kingdom of Heaven.

As my convictions increased, so did my desires after the Lord; and in order to keep them alive, I resolved to make a covenant with him in the most solemn manner I was able. For this purpose I went into the garden at midnight, and kneeled down upon the snow, lifting up my hands, eyes, and heart to Heaven; and intreated the Lord, who had called me by his Holy Spirit out of ignorance and wickedness, that he would increase and strengthen my awakenings and desires, and impress my heart with the importance of eternal things; and that I might never find rest or peace again, till I found peace with him, and received a sense of his pardoning love. The Lord mercifully looked down upon me, and gave me such a sight of my fallen state, that I plainly saw, without an interest in Christ, and an application of his attoning blood to my conscience, I should be lost to all eternity. This led me to a diligent use of all the means of Grace, and to forsake and renounce every thing that I knew to be sinful.

The more convictions increased, and the more I felt the wickedness of my own heart; yet the Lord helped me to strive against evil, so that temptations instead of prevailing against me, drove me nearer to him. The first Sunday in March, as I was going to the preaching, and was engaged in prayer and meditation, I thought I heard a voice saying to me, "Peace be unto thee!" I stopped, and looked round about, to see if any one was near me. But finding myself alone, I went forward a little way, when the same words were again powerfully applied to my heart, which removed the burden of misery from it; and while I sat under the sermon, I was more abundantly blessed. Yet in the afternoon, doubts and fears again arose in my mind. Next morning I resolved like Jacob, not to let the Lord go till he blessed me indeed.[26] As soon as my wife went out, I locked the door, and determined not to rise from my knees until the Lord fully revealed his pardoning love. I continued in prayer about half an hour, when the Lord again spoke to my heart, "Peace be unto thee." All my doubts and fears vanished away: I saw, by faith, heaven opened to my view; and Christ and his holy angels rejoicing over me. I was now enabled to believe in the name of Jesus, and my Soul was dissolved into love. Every thing appeared to me in a different light to what they did before; and I loved every living creature upon the face of the earth. I could truly say, I was now become a new creature. All tormenting and slavish fear, and all the guilt and weight of sin were done away. I was so exceedingly blessed, that I could no longer conceal my happiness, but went to my brethren and told them what the Lord had done for my soul.

I continued to rejoice in the sense of the favour and love of God for about six weeks, and then the enemy assaulted me again; he poured in a flood of temptations and evil-reasonings; and suggested, that I was deceiving myself: The temptation alarmed and dejected me, and my mind was discomposed. Then the enemy pursued his advantage, and insulted me with his cruel upbraidings, insinuating,—"What is become of all your joy, that you spoke of a few days ago? You see, there is nothing in it." But blessed be the Lord, he did not suffer the enemy to rejoice long over me; for while I heard Mr. GARRETTSON preaching from John ix. 25, "One thing I know, that whereas I was blind, now I see"; the words were so suitable to my experience, that I was encouraged to exercise fresh faith upon the Lord; and he removed every doubt and fear; and re-established me in his peace and favour. I then could say with the Psalmist, "the fear of the Lord is the beginning of wisdom,"[27] for I had him always before my eyes, and in some measure walked in the light, as he is in the light. I found his ways were ways of pleasantness, and all his paths were peace.

Soon after, I found a great concern for the salvation of others; and was constrained to visit my poor ungodly neighbours, and exhort them to fear the Lord, and seek him while he might be found. Those that were under convictions, I prayed with them, and pointed them to the Saviour, that they might obtain the same mercy he had bestowed upon me. In the year 1785, I began to exhort both in families and prayer-meetings, and the Lord graciously afforded me his assisting presence.

The Goodness and Mercy of GOD supported me in the various trials and exercises which I went through; nevertheless I found great reluctance to officiate as an exhorter among the people, and had many doubts and fears respecting my call to that duty, because I was conscious of my great ignorance and insufficiency for a work of such importance, and was often overwhelmed with grief and sorrow: But the Lord relieved me by impressing upon my mind these words, "I will send, by whom I will send." In the year 1787, I found my mind drawn out to commiserate my poor brethren in Africa; and especially when I considered that we who had the happiness of being brought up in a christian land, where the Gospel is preached, were notwithstanding our great privileges, involved in gross darkness and wickedness; I thought, what a wretched condition then must those poor creatures be in, who never heard the Name of GOD or of CHRIST; nor had any instruction afforded them with respect to a future judgment. As I had not the least prospect at that time of ever seeing Africa, I contented myself with pitying and praying for the poor benighted inhabitants of that country which gave birth to my forefathers. I laboured in Burchtown and Shelwin two years, and the word was blessed to the conversion of many, most of whom continued stedfast in the good way to the heavenly kingdom.

About this time the country was visited with a dreadful famine, which not only prevailed at Burchtown, but likewise at Chebucto,[28] Annapolis, Digby, and other places. Many of the poor people were compelled to sell their best gowns for five pounds of flour, in order to support life. When they had parted with all their clothes, even to their blankets, several of them fell down dead in the streets, thro' hunger. Some killed and eat their dogs and cats; and poverty and distress prevailed on every side; so that to my great grief I was obliged to leave Burchtown, because I could get no employment. I travelled from place to place, to procure the necessaries of life, but in vain. At last I came to Shelwin on the 20th of January. After walking from one street to the other, I met with Capt. Selex, and he engaged me to make him a chest. I rejoiced at the offer, and returning home, set about it immediately. I worked all night, and by eight o'clock next morning finished the chest, which I carried to the Captain's house, thro' the snow which was three feet deep. But to my great disappointment he rejected it. However he gave me directions to make another. On my way home, being pinched with hunger and cold, I fell down several times, thro' weakness, and expected to die upon the spot. But even in this situation, I found my mind resigned to the divine will, and rejoiced in the midst of tribulation; for the Lord delivered me from all murmurings and discontent, altho' I had but one pint of Indian meal left for the support of myself and wife. Having finished another chest, I took it to my employer the next day; but being afraid he would serve me as he had done before, I took a saw along with me in order to sell it. On the way, I prayed that the Lord would give me a prosperous journey, and was answered to the joy of my heart, for Capt. Selex paid me for the chest in Indian-corn; and the other chest I sold for 2s. 6d. and the saw for 3s. 9d. altho' it cost me a guinea; yet I was exceeding thankful to procure a reprieve from the dreadful anguish of perishing by famine. Oh what a wonderful deliverance did GOD work for me that day! And he taught me to live by faith, and to put my trust in him, more than I ever had done before.

While I was admiring the goodness of GOD, and praising him for the help he afforded me in the day of trouble, a gentleman sent for me, and engaged me to make three flat-bottomed boats for the salmon-fishery, at 1£. each. The gentleman advanced two baskets of Indian-corn, and found nails and tar for the boats. I was enabled to finish the work by the time appointed, and he paid me honestly. Thus did the kind hand of Providence interpose in my preservation; which appeared still greater, upon viewing the wretched circumstances of many of my black brethren at that time, who were obliged to sell themselves to the merchants, some for two or three years; and others for five or six years. The circumstances of the white inhabitants were likewise very distressing, owing to their great imprudence in building large houses, and striving to excel one another in this piece of vanity. When their money was almost expended, they began to build small fishing vessels; but alas, it was too late to repair their error. Had they been wise enough at first to turn their attention to the fishery, instead of fine houses, the place would soon have been in a flourishing condition; whereas it was reduced in a short time to a heap of ruins, and its inhabitants were compelled to flee to other parts of the continent for sustenance.

Next Winter, the same gentleman employed me to build him some more boats. When they were finished he engaged me to go with him to Chebucto, to build a house, to which place he intended to remove his family. He agreed to give me 2£. per month, and a barrel of mackrel, and another of herrings, for my next Winter's provision. I was glad to embrace this offer, altho' it gave me much pain to leave the people of GOD. On the 20th of April I left my wife and friends, and sailed for Chebucto. When we arrived at that place, my employer had not all the men necessary for the fishing voyage; he therefore solicited me to go with him; to which I objected, that I was engaged to build a house for him. He answered, that he could purchase a house for less money than build one; and that if I would go with him to Bayshallow, I should greatly oblige him; to which I at length consented. During our stay at Chebucto, perceiving that the people were exceeding ignorant of religious duties, and given up to all manner of wickedness, I endeavoured to exhort them to flee from the wrath to come, and to turn unto the Lord Jesus. My feeble labours were attended with a blessing to several of them, and they began to seek the Lord in sincerity and truth, altho' we met with some persecution from the baser sort.

On the 2d of June we sailed for Bayshallow; but in the Gulph of St. Lawrence we met with a great storm, and expected every moment would be our last. In about 24 hours the tempest abated, and was succeeded by a great fog, in which we lost the company of one of our vessels, which had all our provisions on board for the fishing season. July 18, we arrived at the River Pisguar, and made all necessary preparations for taking the salmon; but were greatly alarmed on account of the absence of the vessel belonging to us; but on the 29th, to our great joy, she arrived safe; which was four days before the salmon made their appearance. We now entered upon our business with alacrity, and Providence favoured us with good success.

My employer, unhappy for himself as well as others, was as horrible a swearer as I ever met with. Sometimes he would stamp and rage at the men, when they did not please him, in so dreadful a manner, that I was stupified like a drunken man, and knew not what I was doing. My soul was exceedingly grieved at his ungodly language; I repented that I ever entered into his service, and was even tempted to murmur against the good Providence of GOD. But the case of righteous Lot, whose soul was vexed day by day with the ungodly deeds of the people of Sodom, occurred to my mind;[29] and I was resolved to reprove my master when a proper opportunity offered. I said to him, "Dear sir, don't you know that the Lord hath declared, that he will not hold them guiltless who take his Name in vain? And that all profane swearers shall have their portion in the lake that burneth with fire and brimstone?" He bore the reproof with patience, and scarce ever gave me an unkind word; notwithstanding which, he persisted in his impiety, and the men, encouraged by his example, imitated him to the utmost of their ability. Being much grieved with their sinful deeds, I retired into the woods for meditation and prayer. One day when I was alone, and recollecting the patient sufferings of the servants of GOD for the Truth's sake, I was ashamed of myself, on account of the displeasure I felt at my ship-mates, because they would not be persuaded by me to forsake their sins. I saw my folly in imagining that it was in my power to turn them from their evil ways. The Lord shewed me, that this was his prerogative; and that my duty consisted in intreating them, and bearing patiently their insults, as GOD for Christ's sake had borne with me. And he gave me a resolution to reprove in a right spirit, all that swore in my presence.

Next day my master began to curse and swear in his usual manner. When I saw him a little calm, I intreated him not to come into the boat any more, but give me orders how to proceed; assuring him, that I would do every thing according to his pleasure to the utmost of my power; but that if he persisted in his horrible language, I should not be able to discharge my duty. From that time he troubled me no more, and I found myself very comfortable, having no one to disturb me. On the 11th of August we sailed for home; and my master thanked me for my fidelity and diligence, and said, "I believe if you had not been with me, I should not have made half a voyage this season." On the 16th we arrived at Chebucto, and unloaded the vessels. When this business was finished, we prepared for the herring-fishery in Pope's Harbour, at which place we arrived on the 27th of August, and began to set the nets and watch for the herrings. One day as we were attending our net at the mouth of the harbour, we dropped one of the oars, and could not recover it; and having a strong west wind, it drove us out to sea. Our alarm was very great, but the kind hand of Providence interposed and saved us; for when we were driven about two miles from our station, the people on shore saw our danger, and immediately sent two boats to our assistance, which came up with us about sun-set, and brought us safe into the harbour.

October 24th, we left Pope's Harbour, and came to Halifax, where we were paid off, each man receiving 15£. for his wages; and my master gave me two barrels of fish agreeable to his promise. When I returned home, I was enabled to clothe my wife and myself; and my Winter's store consisted of one barrel of flour, three bushels of corn, nine gallons of treacle,[30] 20 bushels of potatoes which my wife had set in my absence, and the two barrels of fish; so that this was the best Winter I ever saw in Burchtown.

In 1791, I removed to Prestent,[31] where I had the care of the [Wesleyan] Society by the appointment of Mr. William Black,[32] almost three years. We were in all 34 persons, 24 of whom professed faith in Christ. Sometimes I had a tolerable congregation. But alas, I preached a whole year in that place without seeing any fruit of my labours. On the 24th of Jan. 1792, after preaching in the morning I was greatly distressed, and said to the Lord, "How long shall I be with these people before thy work prospers among them! O Lord GOD! if thou hast called me to preach to my Black Brethren, answer me this day from heaven by converting one sinner, that I may know that thou hast sent me." In the afternoon I preached from James ii. 19. "Thou believest that there is one GOD; thou doest well. The devils also believe, and tremble." Towards the conclusion of the meeting, the divine presence seemed to descend upon the congregation: Some fell flat upon the ground, as if they were dead; and others cried out aloud for mercy. After prayer, I dismissed the public congregation; but many went away with great reluctance. While the Society was meeting, Miss F— knocked at the door, and said, "This people is the people of GOD; and their GOD shall be my GOD." She then desired to be admitted among us, that she might declare what the Lord had done for her soul. We opened the door, and she said, "Blessed be the Name of the Lord for ever, for I know he hath pardoned my sins for the sake of his Son Jesus Christ. My mind has been so greatly distressed for these three weeks, that I could scarcely sleep; and particularly the last night I did not close mine eyes; but while I was under the preaching all my grief vanished away, and such light broke in upon my soul, that I was enabled to believe unto salvation. O praise the Lord with me, all ye that love his Name; for he hath done great things for my soul." All the Society were melted into tears of joy, when they heard her declarations: and she immediately entered into connexion with us, and many others in a few weeks after. From this time the work of the Lord prospered among us in a wonderful manner. I blessed GOD for answering my petition, and was greatly encouraged to persevere in my labours.

The Blacks attended the preaching regularly; but when any of the White inhabitants were present, I was greatly embarrassed, because I had no learning and I knew that they had. But one day Mr. Ferguson, and several other gentlemen came to hear me; the Lord graciously assisted me, and gave me much liberty in speaking the Truth in my simple manner. The gentlemen afterwards told our Preachers, that they liked my discourse very well; and the Preachers encouraged me to use the talents which the Lord had entrusted me with.

I continued to labour among the people at Prestent with great satisfaction, and the Society increased both in number and love, till the beginning of the year 1792, when an opportunity was afforded us of removing from Nova Scotia to Sierra Leone.[33] The advantages held out to the Blacks were considered by them as valuable. Every married man was promised 30 acres of land, and every male child under 15 years of age, was entitled to five acres. We were likewise to have a free passage to Africa, and upon our arrival, to be furnished with provisions till we could clear a sufficient portion of land necessary for our subsistence. The Company likewise engaged to furnish us with all necessaries, and to take in return the produce of the new plantations. Their intention being, as far as possible in their power, to put a stop to the abominable slave-trade. With respect to myself, I was just got into a comfortable way, being employed by a gentleman, who gave me two shillings per day, with victuals and lodging; so that I was enabled to clothe myself and family, and provide other necessaries of life: But recollecting the concern I had felt in years past, for the conversion of the Africans, I resolved to embrace the opportunity of visiting that country; and therefore went to one of the Agents employed in this business, and acquainted him with my intention. The gentleman informed Mr. Clarkson, that I was under no necessity of leaving Nova Scotia, because I was comfortably provided for: But when I told them, that it was not for the sake of the advantages I hoped to reap in Africa, which induced me to undertake the voyage, but from a desire that had long possessed my mind, of contributing to the best of my poor ability, in spreading the knowledge of Christianity in that country. Upon which they approved of my intention, and encouraged me to persevere in it. The Preachers likewise gave us the Rules of the Society, and many other little books which they judged might be useful to us: they also exhorted us to cleave to the Lord with our whole heart, and treated us with the tenderness and affection of parents to their children. After praying with us, we parted with tears, as we never expected to meet again in this world.

January 16, we sailed for Africa;[34] and on the 22d, we met with a dreadful storm which continued sixteen days. Some of the men who had been engaged in a sea-faring life for 30 or 40 years, declared, that they never saw such a storm before. Our fleet, consisting of 15 ships, were dispersed, and only five of us kept together. We lost one man, who was washed overboard; he left a wife and four children; but what most affected me was, that he died as he had lived, without any appearance of religion. I was upon deck at the same time that he met with this misfortune, but the Lord wonderfully preserved me. After the storm abated, we had a very pleasant passage. But the situation of my wife greatly distressed me. She was exceeding ill most of the voyage; sometimes, for half a day together, she was not able to speak a word. I expected to see her die before we could reach land, and had an unaccountable aversion to bury her in the sea. In the simplicity of my heart, I intreated the Lord to spare her, at least till we reached the shore, that I might give her a decent burial, which was the last kind office I could perform for her. The Lord looked upon my sincerity, and restored her to perfect health.

March 6, we arrived safe at Sierra Leone; and on the 27th, my wife caught a putrid fever.[35] For several days she lost her senses, and was as helpless as an infant. When I enquired into the state of her mind, she could give me no satisfactory answer, which greatly heightened my distress. On Friday, while we were at prayer with her, the Lord mercifully manifested his love and power to her soul; she suddenly rose up, and said, "I am well: I only wait for the coming of the Lord. Glory be to his Name, I am prepared to meet him, and that will be in a short time." On Sunday, while several of our friends were with her, she lay still; but as soon as they began singing this hymn, "Lo! he comes, with clouds descending, Once for favour'd sinners slain," &c.[36] She joined with us, till we came to the last verse, when she began to rejoice aloud, and expired in a rapture of love. She had lived in the fear of GOD, and walked in the light of his countenance for above eight years.[37]

About two months after the death of my wife, I was likewise taken ill of the putrid fever.[38] It was an universal complaint, and the people died so fast, that it was difficult to procure a burial for them. This affliction continued among us for three months, when it pleased the Lord to remove the plague from the place. It was a happy circumstance, that before the rainy season commenced, most of us had built little huts to dwell in; but as we had no house sufficient to hold the congregation, we preached under a large tree when the weather would permit. The people regularly attended the means of Grace, and the work of the Lord prospered. When the rains were over, we erected a small chapel, and went on our way comfortably. I worked for the Company, for 3s. per day, and preached in my turn. I likewise found my mind drawn out to pity the native inhabitants, and preached to them several times, but laboured under great inconveniencies to make them understand the Word of GOD, as I could only visit them on the Lord's-Day. I therefore went to the Governor,[39] and solicited him to give me employment in the

Company's Plantation on Bullam Shore, in order that I might have frequent opportunities of conversing with the Africans. He kindly approved of my intention, and sent me to the Plantation to get ship-timber in company with several others. The gentleman who superintended the Plantation, treated me with the utmost kindness, and allowed six men to help me to build a house for myself, which we finished in 12 days. When a sufficient quantity of timber was procured, and other business for the Company in this place compleated, I was sent to the African town to teach the children to read, but found it difficult to procure scholars, as the parents shewed no great inclination to send their children. I therefore said to them, on the Lord's-Day after preaching, "It is a good thing that GOD has made the White People, and that he has inclined their hearts to bring us into this country, to teach you his ways, and to tell you that he gave his Son to die for you; and if you will obey his commandments he will make you happy in this world, and in that which is to come; where you will live with him in heaven;—and all pain and wretchedness will be at an end;—and you shall enjoy peace without interruption, joy without bitterness, and happiness to all eternity. The Almighty not only invites you to come unto him, but also points out the way whereby you may find his favour, viz. turn from your wicked ways, cease to do evil, and learn to do well. He now affords you a means which you never had before; he gives you his Word to be a light to your feet, and a lantern to your paths; and he likewise gives you an opportunity of having your children instructed in the Christian Religion. But if you neglect to send them, you must be answerable to GOD for it."

The poor Africans appeared attentive to the exhortation, altho' I laboured under the disadvantage of using an interpreter. My scholars soon increased from four to twenty; fifteen of whom continued with me five months. I taught them the Alphabet, and to spell words of two syllables; and likewise the Lord's-Prayer. And I found them as apt to learn as any children I have known. But with regard to the old people, I am doubtful whether they will ever abandon the evil habits in which they were educated, unless the Lord visits them in some extraordinary manner.

In the year 1793, the gentlemen belonging to the Company told me, that if I would consent to go to England with the Governor, he would procure me two or three years schooling, that I might be better qualified to teach the natives. When this proposal was first mentioned to me, it seemed like an idle tale; but upon further conversation on the subject, difficulties were removed, and I consented. On the 26th of March 1794, we embarked for England, and arrived at Plymouth, after a pleasant voyage, on the 16th of May. On the 1st of June we got into the Thames, and soon after, Mrs. Paul, whom I was acquainted with in America, came to Wapping, and invited me to the New Chapel in the City-Road, where I was kindly received.

When I first arrived in England, I considered my great ignorance and inability, and that I was among a wise and judicious people, who were greatly my superiors in knowledge and understanding; these reflections had such an effect upon me, that I formed a resolution never to attempt to preach while I stayed in the country; but the kind importunity of the Preachers and others removed my objections, and I found it profitable to my own soul, to be exercised in inviting sinners to Christ; particularly one Sunday, while I was preaching at Snowsfields-Chapel, the Lord blessed me abundantly, and I found a more cordial love to the White People than I had ever experienced before. In the former part of my life I had suffered greatly from the cruelty and injustice of the Whites, which induced me to look upon them, in general, as our enemies: And even after the Lord had manifested his forgiving mercy to me, I still felt at times an uneasy distrust and shyness towards them; but on that day the Lord removed all my prejudices; for which I bless his holy Name.

In the month of August 1794, I went to Bristol; and from thence Dr. Coke took me with him to Kingswood-School,[40] where I continued to the present time, and have endeavoured to acquire all the knowledge I possibly could, in order to be useful in that sphere which the blessed hand of Providence may conduct me into, if my life is spared. I have great cause to be thankful that I came to England, for I am now fully convinced, that many of the White People, instead of being enemies and oppressors of us poor Blacks, are our friends, and deliverers from slavery, as far as their ability and circumstances will admit. I have met with the most affectionate treatment from the Methodists of London, Bristol, and other places which I have had an opportunity of visiting. And I must confess, that I did not believe there were upon the face of the earth a people so friendly and humane as I have proved them to be. I beg leave to acknowledge the obligations I am under to Dr. Coke, Mr. Bradford, and all the Preachers and people; and I pray GOD to reward them a thousand fold for all the favours they have shewn to me in a strange land.

BOSTON KING.
Kingswood-School, June 4, 1796.

☞ About the latter end of September, 1796, Boston King embarked for Sierra Leone; where he arrived safe, and resumed the employment of a school-master in that Colony; the number of scholars under his care are about forty; and we hope to hear that they will not only learn the English Language, but also attain some knowledge of the way of salvation thro' faith in the Lord Jesus Christ.[41]

NOTES

1. Richard Waring owned the plantation on which King was born around 1760.

2. Driver: overseer of other slaves.

3. As King's context suggests, cutting in the mill was less arduous work than field-cutting.

4. Virtue: power.

5. The "master," to whom he is apprenticed, is King's employer, not Richard Waring, his owner, who is referred to here as his "proprietor."

6. Charleston had been under British control since 12 May 1780, when General Henry Clinton, commander in chief of the British forces in North America, accepted the surrender of General Benjamin Lincoln, commander of the city's garrison, after a siege that had

begun on 1 April. In 1779 Clinton had issued the Philipsburg Proclamation, offering freedom of employment to any slave deserting an enemy owner and forbidding the sale or restitution to a prior owner of any such former slave. Thus, the British forces gained manpower while weakening the economy of the enemy.

7. Chamblem: the British base was at Camden, where Lord Cornwallis had his headquarters.

8. The engagement occurred on 16 August 1780, when Cornwallis defeated General Horatio Gates.

9. Captain Lewes commands the local Loyalist American militia; Grey is a Captain in the regular British (English) army. The British had recruited four local militia regiments, who proved to be of dubious quality. Lewes may have been a member of the Rocky Mount Militia Regiment, under the command of Matthew Floyd, many of whose troops defected to the enemy.

10. Rockmount: Rocky Mount.

11. Light-horse: cavalry.

12. The British abandoned their post at Nelson's Ferry on the Santee River in mid-May 1781.

13. When the British left Charleston in December 1782, they took with them 5,327 people of African descent, both slaves belonging to Loyalist masters and now-emancipated refugees from Rebel owners. The majority of these Blacks were taken to British East Florida and Jamaica, but many went to New York and Nova Scotia and a few to England.

14. A great prize: A captured enemy ship was called a "prize."

15. New York remained under British control from September 1776 until late November 1783 and was the headquarters of the successive commanders in chief of the British military forces.

16. Service: domestic, not military, service.

17. King's wife, Violet, was twelve years his senior and had been owned by Colonel Young of Wilmington, North Carolina. According to the "Book of Negroes," compiled at the order of the British commander-in-chief, Sir Guy Carleton, to register some 3,000 Blacks (1,336 men, 914 women, 750 children) willing to emigrate from New York to other parts of the British empire, Boston King was a "Stout [sturdy] fellow," twenty-three years old, and Violet King a "Stout wench" of thirty-five years (PRO 30/55/100, ff. 70-71. Of those registered, 460 were former slaves from South Carolina.

18. [New] Brunswick: in New Jersey.

19. Although the Peace of Paris officially ending the war was not signed until 3 September 1783, major hostilities on land had effectively ended with George Washington's victory over Lord Cornwallis in the battle of Yorktown on 19 October 1781.

20. The cause of their fear was article 7 of the provisional peace treaty signed in Paris on 30 November 1782, which obliged the British to withdraw their military forces "with all convenient Speed, and without causing any *Destruction*, or carrying away any *Negroes* or other *Property* of the American Inhabitants." King could have learned of the treaty's provisions in the New York *Royal Gazette* on 26 March 1783. Article 7 was not altered in the final Treaty. The British insisted that article 7 did not apply to those Blacks who had sought refuge behind British lines before the treaty was signed. The "Book of Negroes" was compiled to defend the British government against possible property claims by American slave owners. Of the approximately 500,000 slaves in North America at the beginning of the civil war now known as the American Revolution, perhaps as many as 100,000 ended up behind the British lines, many of whom remained slaves of Loyalist owners.

21. Boston and Violet King were among the 409 passengers who sailed on 31 July 1783 from New York to Shelburne (formerly Port Roseway) aboard the military transport *L'Abondance*, commanded by Lieutenant Philips.

22. Birchtown was named after Brigadier General Samuel Birch, British commander of New York City, whose initials appeared on the certificates of transport (G.B.C., for Gen-

eral Birch's Certificate) for Blacks, in effect giving them freedom papers. Birchtown, home to the new free Blacks, was a suburb of Shelburne, where White Loyalists lived with their Black slaves and servants.

23. Moses Wilkinson, a "Blind & lame" former slave who had fled to the British from his owner, Miles Wilkinson, in "Nancy Mun" (Nansemond County), Virginia ("Book of Negroes," ff. 90-91). He was thirty-six in 1783 and still alive in 1811.

24. Freeborn Garretson (1752-1827), an American Methodist missionary sent to Nova Scotia by the Baltimore conference of Methodists, had manumitted his own slaves immediately upon his conversion in 1775.

25. See Matthew 13:3-9.

26. See Genesis 32:24-29.

27. Psalm 111:10.

28. Chedabucto (present-day Guysborough, renamed in honor of Carleton).

29. See Genesis 19:1-26.

30. Treacle: molasses.

31. Preston.

32. The son of a Yorkshire immigrant family, Black had first come to Nova Scotia in 1783 as a twenty-three-year-old Methodist evangelist.

33. Lieutenant John Clarkson (1764-1828), brother of Thomas Clarkson the abolitionist, came to Halifax as the agent of the Sierra Leone Company seeking volunteers for resettlement. King was a lifelong admirer of Clarkson, as his manuscript letters to Clarkson from Sierra Leone, included as items 32 (1 June 1797) and 33 (16 January 1798) in *"Our Children Free and Happy": Letters from Black Settlers in Africa in the* 1790s, ed. Christopher Fyfe (Edinburgh: Edinburgh University Press, 1991), demonstrate. On the Company and Clarkson's mission, see the David George selection in this anthology.

34. Fifteen vessels with 1,190 free Blacks left Halifax, Nova Scotia.

35. Putrid fever: malaria.

36. Written by the Anglican John Cennick (1718-1755).

37. Violet was one of the 112 settlers who died by 11 April.

38. In July alone, 800 of the settlers contracted malaria.

39. Governor Richard Dawes appointed King a schoolteacher and missionary on 3 August 1793 at an annual salary of £60. By 1793, King had remarried.

40. Thomas Coke (1747-1814) had been ordained by John Wesley and appointed by him in 1784 Superintendent of overseas Methodist missions. Kingswood-School was a Methodist secondary school near Bristol opened by John Wesley in 1748.

41. King succeeded James Jones as the Granville Town teacher, but he soon left that position to continue his ministry one hundred miles south of Freetown, among the Sherbro people, where he died in 1802.

Venture Smith

(1729?-19 September 1805)

A NARRATIVE OF THE LIFE AND ADVENTURES OF VENTURE, A NATIVE OF AFRICA: But resident above sixty years in the United States of America. *RELATED BY HIMSELF. New-London*: PRINTED BY C. HOLT, AT THE BEE-OFFICE. 1798.

PREFACE.

THE following account of the life of VENTURE, is a relation of simple facts, in which nothing is added in substance to what he related himself. Many other interesting and curious passages of his life might have been inserted; but on account of the bulk to which they must necessarily have swelled this narrative, they were omitted. If any should suspect the truth of what is here related, they are referred to people now living who are acquainted with most of the facts mentioned in the narrative.

The reader is here presented with an account, not of a renowned politician or warrior, but of an untutored African slave, brought into this Christian country at eight years of age, wholly destitute of an education but what he received in common with other domesticated animals, enjoying no advantages that could lead him to suppose himself superior to the beasts, his fellow servants. And if he shall derive no other advantage from perusing this narrative, he may experience those sensations of shame and indignation that will prove him to be not wholly destitute of every noble and generous feeling.

The subject of the following pages, had he received only a common education, might have been a man of high respectability and usefulness; and had his education been suited to his genius, he might have been an ornament and an honor to human nature. It may, perhaps, not be unpleasing to see the efforts of a great mind wholly uncultivated, enfeebled and depressed by slavery, and struggling under every disadvantage.—The reader may here see a Franklin and a Washington[1] in a state of nature, or rather in a state of slavery. Destitute as he is of all education, and broken by hardships and infirmities of age, he still exhibits striking traces of native ingenuity and good sense.

This narrative exhibits a pattern of honesty, prudence and industry, to people of his own colour; and perhaps some white people would not find themselves degraded by imitating such an example.

The following account is published in compliance with the earnest desire of the subject of it, and likewise a number of respectable persons who are acquainted with him.

CHAPTER I

Containing an account of his life, from his birth to the time of his leaving his native country.

I WAS born at Dukandarra,[2] in Guinea, about the year 1729. My father's name was Saungm Furro, Prince of the Tribe of Dukandarra. My father had three wives. Polygamy was not uncommon in that country, especially among the rich, as every man was allowed to keep as many wives as he could maintain. By his first wife he had three children. The eldest of them was myself, named by my father, Broteer. The other two were named Cundazo and Soozaduka. My father had two children by his second wife, and one by his third. I descended from a very large, tall and stout[3] race of beings, much larger than the generality of people in other parts of the globe, being commonly considerable above six feet in height, and every way well proportioned.

The first thing worthy of notice which I remember was, a contention between my father and mother, on account of my father's marrying his third wife without the consent of his first and eldest, which was contrary to the custom generally observed among my countrymen. In consequence of this rupture, my mother left her husband and country, and travelled away with her three children to the eastward. I was then five years old. She took not the least sustenance along with her, to support either herself or children. I was able to travel along by her side; the other two of her offspring she carried one on her back, and the other being a sucking child, in her arms. When we became hungry, my mother used to set us down on the ground, and gather some of the fruits which grew spontaneously in that climate. These served us for food on the way. At night we all lay down together in the most secure place we could find, and reposed ourselves until morning. Though there were many noxious animals there, yet so kind was our Almighty protector, that none of them were ever permitted to hurt or molest us. Thus we went on our journey until the second day after our departure from Dukandarra, when we came to the entrance of a great desert.[4] During our travel in that we were often affrighted with the doleful howlings and yellings of wolves, lions, and other animals. After five days travel we came to the end of this desert, and immediately entered into a beautiful and extensive interval country. Here my mother was pleased to stop and seek a refuge for me. She left me at the house of a very rich farmer. I was then, as I should judge, not less than one hundred and forty miles from my native place, separated from all my relations and acquaintance. At this place my mother took her farewell of me, and set out for her own country. My new guardian, as I shall call the man with whom I was left, put me into the business of tending sheep, immediately after I was left with him. The flock which I kept with the assistance of a boy, consisted of about forty. We drove them every morning between two and three miles to pasture, into the wide and delightful plains. When night drew on, we drove them home and secured them in the cote.[5] In this round I continued during my stay there. One incident which befel me when I was driving my flock from pasture, was so dreadful to me in that age, and is to this time so fresh in my memory, that I cannot help noticing it in this place. Two large dogs sallied out of a certain house and set upon me. One of them took me by the arm, and the other by the thigh, and before their master could come and relieve me, they lacerated my flesh to such a degree that the scars are very visible to the present day. My master was immediately sent for. He came and carried me home, as I was unable to go myself on account of my wounds. Nothing remarkable happened afterwards until my father sent for me to return home.

Before I dismiss this country, I must just inform my reader what I remember concerning this place. A large river runs through this country in a westerly course. The land for a great way on each side is flat and level, hedged in by a considerable rise of the country at a great distance from it. It scarce ever rains there, yet the land is fertile; great dews fall in the night which refresh the soil. About the latter end of June or first of July, the river begins to rise, and gradually increases until it has inundated the country for a great distance, to the height of seven or eight feet. This brings on a slime which enriches the land surprisingly. When the river has subsided, the natives begin to sow and plant, and the vegetation is exceeding rapid. Near this rich river my guardian's land lay. He possessed, I cannot exactly tell how much, yet this I am certain of respecting it, that he owned an immense tract. He possessed likewise a great many cattle and goats. During my stay with him I was kindly used, and with as much tenderness, for what I saw, as his only son, although I was an entire stranger to him, remote from friends and relations. The principal occupations of the inhabitants there, were the cultivation of the soil and the care of their flocks. They were a people pretty similar in every respect to that of mine, except in their persons, which were not so tall and stout. They appeared to be very kind and friendly. I will now return to my departure from that place.

My father sent a man and horse after me. After settling with my guardian for keeping me, he took me away and went for home. It was then about one year since my mother brought me here. Nothing remarkable occurred to us on our journey until we arrived safe home.

I found then that the difference between my parents had been made up previous to their sending for me. On my return, I was received both by my father and mother with great joy and affection, and was once more restored to my paternal dwelling in peace and happiness. I was then about six years old.

Not more than six weeks had passed after my return, before a message was brought by an inhabitant of the place where I lived the preceding year to my father, that that place had been invaded by a numerous army, from a nation not far distant, furnished with musical instruments, and all kinds of arms then in use; that they were instigated by some white nation who equipped and sent them to subdue and possess the country; that his nation had made no preparation for war, having been for a long time in profound peace that they could not defend themselves against such a formidable train of invaders, and must therefore necessarily evacuate their lands to the fierce enemy, and fly to the protection of some chief; and that if he would permit them they should come under his rule and protection when they had to retreat from their own possessions. He was a kind and merciful prince, and therefore consented to these proposals.

He had scarcely returned to his nation with the message, before the whole of his people were obliged to retreat from their country, and come to my father's dominions.

He gave them every privilege and all the protection his government could afford. But they had not been there longer than four days before news came to them that the invaders had laid waste their country, and were coming speedily to destroy them in my father's territories. This affrighted them, and therefore they immediately pushed off to the southward, into the unknown countries there, and were never more heard of.

Two days after their retreat, the report turned out to be but too true. A detachment from the enemy came to my father and informed him, that the whole army was encamped not far out of his dominions, and would invade the territory and deprive his people of their liberties and rights, if he did not comply with the following terms. These were to pay them a large sum of money, three hundred fat cattle, and a great number of goats, sheep, asses, &c.

My father told the messenger he would comply rather than that his subjects should be deprived of their rights and privileges, which he was not then in circumstances to defend from so sudden an invasion. Upon turning out those articles, the enemy pledged their faith and honor that they would not attack him. On these he relied and therefore thought it unnecessary to be on his guard against the enemy. But their pledges of faith and honor proved no better than those of other unprincipled hostile nations; for a few days after a certain relation of the king came and informed him, that the enemy who sent terms of accommodation to him and received tribute to their satisfaction, yet meditated an attack upon his subjects by surprise, and that probably they would commence their attack in less than one day, and concluded with advising him, as he was not prepared for war, to order a speedy retreat of his family and subjects. He complied with this advice.

The same night which was fixed upon to retreat, my father and his family set off about break of day. The king and his two younger wives went in one company, and my mother and her children in another. We left our dwellings in succession, and my father's company went on first. We directed our course for a large shrub plain, some distance off, where we intended to conceal ourselves from the approaching enemy, until we could refresh and rest ourselves a little. But we presently found that our retreat was not secure. For having struck up a little fire for the purpose of cooking victuals, the enemy who happened to be encamped a little distance off, had sent out a scouting party who discovered us by the smoke of the fire, just as we were extinguishing it, and about to eat. As soon as we had finished eating, my father discovered the party, and immediately began to discharge arrows at them. This was what I first saw, and it alarmed both me and the women, who being unable to make any resistance, immediately betook ourselves to the tall thick reeds not far off, and left the old king to fight alone. For some time I beheld him from the reeds defending himself with great courage and firmness, till at last he was obliged to surrender himself into their hands.

They then came to us in the reeds, and the very first salute I had from them was a violent blow on the head with the fore part of a gun, and at the same time a grasp round the neck. I then had a rope put about my neck, as had all the women in the thicket with me, and we were immediately led to my father, who was likewise pinioned and haltered for leading. In this condition we were all led to the camp. The women and myself being pretty submissive, had tolerable treatment from the enemy, while my father was closely interrogated respecting his money which they knew he must have. But as he gave them no account of it, he was instantly cut and pounded on his body with great inhumanity, that he might be induced by the torture he suffered to make the discovery. All this availed not in the least to make him give up his money, but he despised all the tortures which they inflicted, until the continued exercise and increase of torment, obliged him to sink and expire. He thus died without informing his enemies of the place where his money lay. I saw him while he was thus tortured to death. The shocking scene is to this day fresh in my mind, and I have often been overcome while thinking on it. He was a man of remarkable stature. I should judge as much as six feet and six or seven inches high, two feet across his shoulders, and every way well proportioned. He was a man of remarkable strength and resolution, affable, kind and gentle, ruling with equity and moderation.

The army of the enemy was large, I should suppose consisting of about six thousand men. Their leader was called Baukurre. After destroying the old prince, they decamped and immediately marched towards the sea, lying to the west, taking with them myself and the women prisoners.

In the march a scouting party was detached from the main army. To the leader of this party I was made waiter, having to carry his gun, &c.—As we were a scouting we came across a herd of fat cattle, consisting of about thirty in number. These we set upon, and immediately wrested from their keepers, and afterwards converted them into food for the army. The enemy had remarkable success in destroying the country wherever they went. For as far as they had penetrated they laid the habitations waste and captured the people. The distance they had now brought me was about four hundred miles. All the march I had very hard tasks imposed on me, which I must perform on pain of punishment. I was obliged to carry on my head a large flat stone used for grinding our corn, weighing as I should suppose, as much as 25 pounds; besides victuals, mat and cooking utensils. Though I was pretty large and stout of my age, yet these burthens were very grievous to me, being only about six years and an half old.

We were then come to a place called Malagasco.—When we entered the place we could not see the least appearance of either houses or inhabitants, but upon stricter search found that instead of houses above ground they had dens in the sides of hillocks, contiguous to ponds and streams of water. In these we perceived they had all hid themselves, as I suppose they usually did upon such occasions. In order to compel them to surrender, the enemy contrived to smoke them out with faggots. These they put to the entrance of the caves and set them on fire. While they were engaged in this business, to their great surprise some of them were desperately wounded with arrows which fell from above on them. This mystery they soon found out. They perceived that the enemy discharged these arrows through holes on the top of the dens directly into the air.—Their weight brought them back, point downwards on their enemies heads, whilst they were smoking the inhabitants out. The points of their arrows were poisoned, but their enemy had an antidote for it, which they instantly applied to the wounded part. The smoke at last obliged the people to give themselves up. They came out of their caves, first spatting[6] the palms of their hands together, and immediately after extended their arms, crossed at their wrists, ready to be bound and pinioned. I should judge that the dens above mentioned were extended about eight feet horizontally into the earth, six feet in height and as many wide. They were arched overhead and lined with earth, which was of the clay kind, and made the surface of their walls firm and smooth.

The invaders then pinioned the prisoners of all ages and sexes indiscriminately, took their flocks and all their effects, and moved on their way towards the sea. On the march the prisoners were treated with clemency, on account of their being submissive and humble. Having come to the next tribe, the enemy laid siege and immediately took men, women, children, flocks, and all their valuable effects. They then went on to the next district which was contiguous to the sea, called in Africa, Anamaboo.[7] The enemies provisions were then almost spent, as well as their strength. The inhabitants knowing what conduct they had pursued, and what were their present intentions, improved the favorable opportunity, attacked them, and took enemy, prisoners, flocks and all their effects. I was then taken a second time. All of us were then put into the castle,[8] and kept for market. On a certain time I and other prisoners were put on board a canoe, under our master, and rowed away to a vessel belonging to Rhode-Island, commanded by capt. Collingwood, and the mate Thomas Mumford. While we were going to the vessel, our master told us all to appear to the best possible advantage for sale. I was bought on board by one Robertson Mumford, steward of said vessel, for four gallons of rum, and a piece of calico, and called VENTURE, on account of his having purchased me with his own private venture.[9] Thus I came by my name. All the slaves that were bought for that vessel's cargo, were two hundred and sixty.

CHAPTER II

Containing an account of his life, from the time of his leaving Africa, to that of his becoming free.

AFTER all the business was ended on the coast of Africa, the ship sailed from thence to Barbadoes. After an ordinary passage, except great mortality by the small pox, which broke out on board, we arrived at the island of Barbadoes: but when we reached it, there were found, out of the two hundred and sixty that sailed from Africa, not more than two hundred alive. These were all sold, except myself and three more, to the planters there.

The vessel then sailed for Rhode-Island, and arrived there after a comfortable passage. Here my master sent me to live with one of his sisters, until he could carry me to Fisher's Island, the place of his residence. I had then completed my eighth year. After staying with his sister some time I was taken to my master's place to live.

When we arrived at Narraganset, my master went ashore in order to return a part of the way by land, and gave me the charge of the keys of his trunks on board the vessel, and charged me not to deliver them up to anybody, not even to his father without his orders. To his directions I promised faithfully to conform. When I arrived with my master's articles at his house, my master's father asked me for his son's keys, as he wanted to see what his trunks contained. I told him that my master intrusted me with the care of them until he should return, and that I had given him my word to be faithful to the trust, and could not therefore give him or any other person the keys without my master's directions. He insisted that I should deliver to him the keys, threatening to punish me if I did not. But I let him know that he should not have them let him say what he would. He then laid aside trying to get them. But notwithstanding he appeared to give up trying to obtain them from me, yet I mistrusted that he would take some time when I was off my guard, either in the daytime or at night to get them, therefore I slung them round my neck, and in the daytime concealed them in my bosom, and at night I always lay with them under me, that no person might take them from me without being apprized of it. Thus I kept the keys from everybody until my master came home. When he returned he asked where VENTURE was. As I was then within hearing, I came, and said, here sir, at your service. He asked me for his keys, and I immediately took them off my neck and reached them out to him. He took them, stroked my hair, and commended me, saying in presence of his father that his young VENTURE was so faithful that he never would have been able to have taken the keys from him but by violence; that he should not fear to trust him with his whole fortune, for that he had been in his native place so habituated to keeping his word, that he would sacrifice even his life to maintain it.

The first of the time of living at my master's own place, I was pretty much employed in the house at carding wool and other household business. In this situation I continued for some years, after which my master put me to work out of doors. After many proofs of my faithfulness and honesty, my master began to put great confidence in me. My behavior to him had as yet been submissive and obedient. I then began to have hard tasks imposed on me. Some of these were to pound four bushels of ears of corn every night in a barrel for the poultry, or be rigorously punished. At other seasons of the year I had to card wool until a very late hour. These tasks I had to perform when I was about nine years old. Some time after I had another difficulty and oppression which was greater than any I had ever experienced since I came into this country. This was to serve two masters. James Mumford, my master's son, when his father had gone from home in the morning, and given me a stint[10] to perform that day, would order me to do *this* and *that* business different from what my master directed me. One day in particular, the authority which my master's son had set up, had like to have produced melancholy effects. For my master having set me off my business to perform that day and then left me to perform it, his son came up to me in the course of the day, big with authority, and commanded me very arrogantly to quit my present business and go directly about what he should order me. I replied to him that my master had given me so much to perform that day, and that I must therefore faithfully complete it in that time. He then broke out into a great rage, snatched a pitchfork and went to lay me over the head therewith; but I as soon got another and defended myself with it, or otherwise he might have murdered me in his outrage. He immediately called some people who were within hearing at work for him, and ordered them to take his hair rope and come and bind me with it. They all tried to bind me but in vain, tho' there were three assistants in number. My upstart master then desisted, put his pocket handkerchief before his eyes and went home with a design to tell his mother of the struggle with young VENTURE. He told her that their young VENTURE had become so stubborn that he could not controul him, and asked her what he should do with him. In the mean time I recovered my temper, voluntarily caused myself to be bound by the same men who tried in vain before, and carried before my young master, that he might do what he pleased with me. He took me to a gallows made for the purpose of hanging cattle on, and suspended me on it. Afterwards he ordered one of his hands to go to the peach orchard and cut him three dozen of whips to punish me with. These were brought to him, and that was all that was done with them, as I was released and went to work after hanging on the gallows about an hour.

After I had lived with my master thirteen years, being then about twenty two years old, I married Meg, a slave of his who was about my age. My master owned a certain Irishman,[11] named Heddy, who about that time formed a plan of secretly leaving his master. After he had long had this plan in meditation he suggested it to me. At first I cast a deaf ear to it, and rebuked Heddy for harboring in his mind such a rash undertaking. But after he had persuaded and much enchanted me with the prospect of gaining my freedom by such a method, I at length agreed to accompany him. Heddy next inveigled two of his fellow servants to accompany us. The place to which we designed to go was the Mississippi. Our next business was to lay in a sufficient store of provisions for our voyage. We privately collected out of our master's store, six great old cheeses, two firkins[12] of butter, and one whole batch of new bread. When we had gathered all our own clothes and some more, we took them all about midnight, and went to the water side. We stole our master's boat, embarked, and then directed our course for the Mississippi river.

We mutually confederated not to betray or desert one another on pain of death. We first steered our course for Montauk Point, the east end of Long-Island.

After our arrival there we landed, and Heddy and I made an incursion into the island after fresh water, while our two comrades were left at a little distance from the boat employed at cooking. When Heddy and I had sought some time for water, he returned to our companions, and I continued on looking for my object. When Heddy had performed his business with our companions who were engaged in cooking, he went directly to the boat, stole all the clothes in it, and then travelled away for East-Hampton, as I was informed. I returned to my fellows not long after. They informed me that our clothes were stolen, but could not determine who was the thief, yet they suspected Heddy as he was missing. After reproving my two comrades for not taking care of our things which were in the boat, I advertised[13] Heddy and sent two men in search of him. They pursued and overtook him at Southampton and returned him to the boat. I then thought it might afford some chance for my freedom, or at least a palliation for my running away, to return Heddy immediately to his master, and inform him that I was induced to go away by Heddy's address.[14] Accordingly I set off with him and the rest of my companions for our master's, and arrived there without any difficulty. I informed my master that Heddy was the ringleader of our revolt, and that he had used us ill. He immediately put Heddy into custody, and myself and companions were well received and went to work as usual.

Not a long time passed after that, before Heddy was sent by my master to New-London gaol. At the close of that year I was sold to a Thomas Stanton, and had to be separated from my wife and one daughter, who was about one month old. He resided at Stonington-point. To this place I brought with me from my late master's, two johannes,[15] three old Spanish dollars, and two thousand of coppers, besides five pounds of my wife's money. This money I got by cleaning gentlemen's shoes and drawing boots, by catching musk-rats and minks, raising potatoes and carrots, &c. and by fishing in the night, and at odd spells.

All this money, amounting to near twenty-one pounds York currency,[16] my master's brother, Robert Stanton, hired of me, for which he gave me his note. About one year and a half after that time, my master purchased my wife and her child, for seven hundred pounds old tenor.[17] One time my master sent me two miles after a barrel of molasses, and ordered me to carry it on my shoulders. I made out to carry it all the way to my master's house. When I lived with Captain George Mumford, only to try my strength, I took up on my knees a tierce[18] of salt containing seven bushels, and carried it two or three rods.[19] Of this fact there are several eye witnesses now living.

Towards the close of the time that I resided with this master, I had a falling out with my mistress. This happened one time when my master was gone to Long-Island a gunning. At first the quarrel began between my wife and her mistress. I was then at work in the barn, and hearing a racket in the house, induced me to run there and see what had broken out. When I entered the house, I found my mistress in a violent passion with my wife, for what she informed me was a mere trifle; such a small affair that I forbear to put my mistress to the shame of having it known. I earnestly requested my wife to beg pardon of her mistress for the sake of peace, even if she had given no just occasion for offence. But whilst I was thus saying my mistress turned the blows which she was repeating on my wife to me. She took down her horsewhip, and while she was glutting her fury with it, I reached out my great black hand, raised it up and received the blows of the whip on it which were designed for my head. Then I immediately committed the whip to the devouring fire.

When my master returned from the island, his wife told him of the affair, but for the present he seemed to take no notice of it, and mentioned not a word about it to me. Some days after his return, in the morning as I was putting on a log in the fire-place, not suspecting harm from any one, I received a most violent stroke on the crown of my head with a club two feet long and as large round as a chair-post. This blow very badly wounded my head, and the scar of it remains to this day. The first blow made me have my wits about me you may suppose, for as soon as he went to renew it, I snatched the club out of his hands and dragged him out of the door. He then sent for his brother to come and assist him, but I presently left my master, took the club he wounded me with, carried it to a neighboring Justice of the Peace, and complained of my master. He finally advised me to return to my master, and live contented with him till he abused me again, and then complain. I consented to do accordingly. But before I set out for my master's, up he come, and his brother Robert after me. The Justice improved this convenient opportunity to caution my master. He asked him for what he treated his slave thus hastily and unjustly, and told him what would be the consequence if he continued the same treatment towards me. After the Justice had ended his discourse with my master, he and his brother set out with me for home, one before and the other behind me. When they had come to a bye place, they both dismounted their respective horses and fell to beating me with great violence. I became enraged at this and immediately turned them both under me, laid one of them across the other, and stamped both with my feet what I would.

This occasioned my master's brother to advise him to put me off. A short time after this I was taken by a constable and two men. They carried me to a blacksmith's shop and had me hand-cuffed. When I returned home my mistress enquired much of her waiters whether VENTURE was hand-cuffed. When she was informed that I was, she appeared to be very contented and was much transported with the news. In the midst of this content and joy, I presented myself before my mistress, shewed her my hand-cuffs, and gave her thanks for my gold rings. For this my master commanded a negro of his to fetch him a large ox chain. This my master locked on my legs with two padlocks. I continued to wear the chain peaceably for two or three days, when my master asked me with contemptuous hard names whether I had not better be freed from my chains and go to work. I answered him, No. Well then, said he, I will send you to the West-Indies or banish you, for I am resolved not to keep you. I answered him I crossed the waters to come here, and I am willing to cross them to return.

For a day or two after this not any one said much to me, until one Hempsted Miner, of Stonington, asked me if I would live with him. I answered him that I would. He then requested me to make myself discontented and to appear as unreconciled to my master as I could before that he bargained with him for me; and that in return he would give me a good chance to gain my freedom when I came to live with him. I did as he requested me. Not long after Hempsted Miner purchased me of my master for fifty-six pounds lawful. He took the chain and padlocks from off me immediately after.

It may here be remembered, that I related a few pages back, that I hired out a sum of money to Mr. Robert Stanton, and took his note for it. In the fray between my master Stanton and myself, he broke open my chest containing his brother's note to me, and destroyed it. Immediately after my present master bought me, he determined to sell me at Hartford. As soon as I became apprized of it, I bethought myself that I would secure a certain sum of money which lay by me, safer than to hire it out to a Stanton. Accordingly I buried it in the earth, a little distance from Thomas Stanton's, in the road over which he passed daily. A short time after my master carried me to Hartford, and first proposed to sell me to one William Hooker of that place. Hooker asked whether I would go to the German Flats with him. I answered, No. He said I should, if not by fair means I should by foul. If you will go by no other measures, I will tie you down in my sleigh. I replied to him, that if he carried me in that manner, no person would purchase me, for it would be thought that he had a murderer for sale. After this he tried no more, and said he would not have me as a gift.

My master next offered me to Daniel Edwards, Esq., of Hartford, for sale. But not purchasing me, my master pawned me to him for ten pounds, and returned to Stonington. After some trial of my honesty, Mr. Edwards placed considerable trust and confidence in me. He put me to serve as his cup-bearer and waiter.[20] When there was company at his house, he would send me into his cellar and other parts of his house to fetch wine and other articles occasionally for them. When I had been with him some time, he asked me why my master wished to part with such an honest negro, and why he did not keep me himself. I replied that I could not give him the reason, unless it was to convert me into cash, and speculate with me as with other commodities. I hope that he can never justly say it was on account of my ill conduct that he did not keep me himself. Mr. Edwards told me that he should be very willing to keep me himself, and that he would never let me go from him to live, if it was not unreasonable and inconvenient for me to be parted from my wife and children; therefore he would furnish me with a horse to return to Stonington, if I had a mind for it. As Miner did not appear to redeem me I went, and called at my old master Stanton's first to see my wife, who was then owned by him. As my old master appeared much ruffled at my being there, I left my wife before I had spent any considerable time with her, and went to Colonel O. Smith's. Miner had not as yet wholly settled with Stanton for me, and had before my return from Hartford given Col. Smith a bill of sale of me. These men once met to determine which of them should hold me, and upon my expressing a desire to be owned by Col. Smith, and upon my master's settling the remainder of the money which was due to Stanton for me, it was agreed that I should live with Col. Smith.

This was the third time of my being sold, and I was then thirty-one years old. As I never had an opportunity of redeeming myself[21] whilst I was owned by Miner, though he promised to give me a chance, I was then very ambitious of obtaining it. I asked my master one time if he would consent to have me purchase my freedom. He replied that he would. I was then very happy, knowing that I was at that time able to pay part of the purchase money, by means of the money which I some time since buried. This I took out of the earth and tendered to my master, having previously engaged a free negro man to take his security for it, as I was the property of my master, and therefore could not safely take his obligation myself. What was wanting in redeeming myself, my master agreed to wait on me for, until I could procure it for him. I still continued to work for Col. Smith. There was continually some interest accruing on my master's note to my friend the free negro man above named, which I received, and with some besides which I got by fishing, I laid out in land adjoining my old master Stanton's. By cultivating this land with the greatest diligence and economy, at times when my master did not require my labor, in two years I laid up ten pounds. This my friend tendered my master for myself, and received his note for it.

Being encouraged by the success which I had met in redeeming myself, I again solicited my master for a further chance of completing it. The chance for which I solicited him was that of going out to work the ensuing winter. He agreed to this on condition that I would give him one quarter of my earnings. On these terms I worked the following winter, and earned four pounds sixteen shillings, one quarter of which went to my master for the privilege, and the rest was paid him on my own account. This added to the other payments made up forty four pounds, eight shillings, which I had paid on my own account. I was then about thirty five years old.

The next summer I again desired he would give me a chance of going out to work. But he refused and answered that he must have my labor this summer, as he did not have it the past winter. I replied that I considered it as hard that I could not have a chance to work out when the season became advantageous, and that I must only be permitted to hire myself out in the poorest season of the year. He asked me after this what I would give him for the privilege per month. I replied that I would leave it wholly with his own generosity to determine what I should return him a month. Well then, said he, if so two pounds a month. I answered him that if that was the least he would take I would be contented.

Accordingly I hired myself out at Fisher's Island, and earned twenty pounds; thirteen pounds six shillings of which my master drew for the privilege, and the remainder I paid him for my freedom. This made fifty-one pounds two shillings which I paid him. In October following I went and wrought six months at Long Island. In that six month's time I cut and corded four hundred cords of wood,[22] besides threshing out seventy-five bushels of grain, and received of my wages down only twenty pounds, which left remaining a larger sum. Whilst I was out that time, I took up on my wages only one pair of shoes. At night I lay on the hearth, with one coverlet over and another under me. I returned to my master and gave him what I received of my six months' labor. This left only thirteen pounds eighteen shillings to make up the full sum for my redemption. My master liberated me, saying that I might pay what was behind if I could ever make it convenient, otherwise it would be well. The amount of the money which I had paid my master towards redeeming my time, was seventy-one pounds two shillings. The reason of my master for asking such an unreasonable price, was he said, to secure himself in case I should ever come to want. Being thirty-six years old, I left Col. Smith once for all. I had already been sold three different times, made considerable money with seemingly nothing to derive it from, been cheated out of a large sum of money, lost much by misfortunes, and paid an enormous sum for my freedom.

CHAPTER III

Containing an account of his life, from the time of his purchasing his freedom to the present day.

MY wife and children were yet in bondage to Mr. Thomas Stanton. About this time I lost a chest containing besides clothing, about thirty-eight pounds in paper money. It was burnt by accident. A short time after I sold all my possessions at Stonington, consisting of a pretty piece of land and one dwelling house thereon, and went to reside at Long-Island. For the first four years of my residence there, I spent my time in working for various people on that and at the neighboring islands. In the space of six months I cut and corded upwards of four hundred cords of wood. Many other singular and wonderful labors I performed in cutting wood there, which would not be inferior to those just recited, but for brevity sake I must omit them. In the aforementioned four years what wood I cut at Long-Island amounted to several thousand cords, and the money which I earned thereby amounted to two hundred and seven pounds ten shillings. This money I laid up carefully by me. Perhaps some may enquire what maintained me all the time I was laying up money. I would inform them that I bought nothing which I did not absolutely want.[23] All fine clothes I despised in comparison with my interest, and never kept but just what clothes were comfortable for common days, and perhaps I would have a garment or two which I did not have on at all times, but as for superfluous finery I never thought it to be compared with a decent homespun dress, a good supply of money and prudence. Expensive gatherings of my mates I commonly shunned, and all kinds of luxuries I was perfectly a stranger to; and during the time I was employed in cutting the aforementioned quantity of wood, I never was at the expence of six-pence worth of spirits. Being after this labour forty years of age, I worked at various places, and in particular on Ram-Island, where I purchased Solomon and Cuff, two sons of mine, for two hundred dollars each.

It will here be remembered how much money I earned by cutting wood in four years. Besides this I had considerable money, amounting in all to near three hundred pounds. When I had purchased my two sons, I had then left more than one hundred pounds. After this I purchased a negro man, for no other reason than to oblige him, and gave for him sixty pounds. But in a short time after he run away from me, and I thereby lost all that I gave for him, except twenty pounds which he paid me previous to his absconding.[24] The rest of my money I laid out in land, in addition to a farm which I owned before, and a dwelling house thereon. Forty four years had then completed their revolution since my entrance into this existence of servitude and misfortune. Solomon my eldest son, being then in his seventeenth year, and all my hope and dependence for help, I hired him out to one Charles Church, of Rhode-Island, for one year, on consideration of his giving him twelve pounds and an opportunity of acquiring some learning. In the course of the year, Church fitted out a vessel for a whaling voyage, and being in want of hands to man her, he induced my son to go, with the promise of giving him, on his return, a pair of silver buckles, besides his wages. As soon as I heard of his going to sea, I immediately set out to go and prevent it if possible.—But on my arrival at Church's, to my great grief, I could only see the vessel my son was in almost out of sight going to sea. My son died of the scurvy in this voyage, and Church has never yet paid me the least of his wages. In my son, besides the loss of his life, I lost equal to seventy-five pounds.

My other son being but a youth, still lived with me. About this time I chartered a sloop of about thirty tons burthen,[25] and hired men to assist me in navigating her. I employed her mostly in the wood trade to Rhode-Island, and made clear of all expenses above one hundred dollars with her in better than one year. I had then become something forehanded,[26] and being in my forty-fourth year, I purchased my wife Meg, and thereby prevented having another child to buy, as she was then pregnant. I gave forty pounds for her.

During my residence at Long-Island, I raised one year with another, ten cart loads of water-melons, and lost a great many every year besides by the thievishness of the sailors. What I made by the water-melons I sold there, amounted to nearly five hundred dollars. Various other methods I pursued in order to enable me to redeem my family. In the night time I fished with setnets and pots for eels and lobsters, and shortly after went [on] a whaling voyage in the service of Col. Smith. After being out seven months, the vessel returned, laden with four hundred barrels of oil. About this time, I become possessed of another dwelling-house, and my temporal affairs were in a pretty prosperous condition. This and my industry was what alone saved me from being expelled [from] that part of the island in which I resided, as an act was passed by the select-men of the place, that all negroes residing there should be expelled.

Next after my wife, I purchased a negro man for four hundred dollars. But he having an inclination to return to his old master, I therefore let him go. Shortly after I purchased another negro man for twenty-five pounds, whom I parted with shortly after.

Being about forty-six years old, I bought my oldest child Hannah of Ray Mumford, for forty-four pounds, and she still resided with him. I had already redeemed from slavery myself, my wife and three children, besides three negro men.

About the forty-seventh year of my life, I disposed of all my property at Long-Island, and came from thence into East-Haddam. I hired myself out at first to Timothy Chapman, for five weeks, the earnings of which time I put up carefully by me. After this I wrought for Abel Bingham about six weeks. I then put my money together and purchased of said Bingham ten acres of land, lying at Haddam neck, where I now reside.—On this land I labored with great diligence for two years, and shortly after purchased six acres more of land contiguous to my other. One year from that time I purchased seventy acres more of the same man, and paid for it mostly with the produce of my other land. Soon after I bought this last lot of land, I set up a comfortable dwelling house on my farm, and built it from the produce thereof. Shortly after I had much trouble and expence with my daughter Hannah, whose name has before been mentioned in this account. She was married soon after I redeemed her, to one Isaac, a free negro, and shortly after her marriage fell sick of a mortal disease; her husband a dissolute and abandoned wretch, paid but little attention to her in her illness. I therefore thought it best to bring her to my house and nurse her there. I procured her all the aid mortals could afford, but notwithstanding this she fell a prey to her disease, after a lingering and painful endurance of it.

The physician's bills for attending her during her illness amounted to forty pounds. Having reached my fifty-fourth year, I hired two negro men, one named William Jacklin, and the other Mingo. Mingo lived with me one year, and having received his wages, run in debt to me eight dollars, for which he gave me his note. Presently after he tried to run away from me without troubling himself to pay up his note. I procured a warrant, took him, and requested him to go to Justice Throop's of his own accord, but he refusing, I took him on my shoulders, and carried him there, distant about two miles. The justice asking me if I had my prisoner's note with me, and replying that I had not, he told me that I must return with him and get it. Accordingly I carried Mingo back on my shoulders, but before we arrived at my dwelling, he complained of being hurt, and asked me if this was not a hard way of treating our fellow creatures. I answered him that it would be hard thus to treat our honest fellow creatures. He then told me that if I would let him off my shoulders, he had a pair of silver shoe-buckles, one shirt and a pocket handkerchief, which he would turn out to me. I agreed, and let him return home with me on foot; but the very following night, he slipped from me, stole my horse and has never paid me even his note. The other negro man, Jacklin, being a comb-maker by trade, he requested me to set him up, and promised to reward me well with his labor. Accordingly I bought him a set of tools for making combs, and procured him stock. He worked at my house about one year, and then run away from me with all his combs, and owed me for all his board.

Since my residence at Haddam neck, I have owned of boats canoes, and sail vessels, not less than twenty. These I mostly employed in the fishing and trafficking[27] business, and in these occupations I have been cheated out of considerable money by people whom I traded with taking advantage of my ignorance of numbers.

About twelve years ago, I hired a whale-boat and four black men, and proceeded to Long-Island after a load of round clams. Having arrived there, I first purchased of James Webb, son of Orange Webb, six hundred and sixty clams, and afterwards, with the help of my men, finished loading my boat. The same evening, however, this Webb stole my boat, and went in her to Connecticut river, and sold her cargo for his own benefit. I thereupon pursued him, and at length, after an additional expence of nine crowns, recovered the boat; but for the proceeds of her cargo I never could obtain any compensation.

Four years after, I met with another loss, far superior to this in value, and I think by no less wicked means. Being going to New-London with a grand-child, I took passage in an Indian's boat, and went there with him. On our return, the Indian took on board two hogsheads[28] of molasses, one of which belonged to Capt. Elisha Hart, of Saybrook, to be delivered on his wharf. When we arrived there, and while I was gone, at the request of the Indian, to inform Captain Hart of his arrival, and receive the freight for him, one hogshead of the molasses had been lost overboard by the people in attempting to land it on the wharf. Although I was absent at the time, and had no concern whatever in the business, as was known to a number of respectable witnesses, I was nevertheless prosecuted by this conscientious gentleman, (the Indian not being able to pay for it) and obliged to pay upwards of ten pounds lawful money, with all the costs of court. I applied to several gentlemen for counsel in this affair, and they advised me, as my adversary was rich, and threatened to carry the matter from court to court till it would cost me more than the first damages would be, to pay the sum and submit to the injury; which I accordingly did, and he has often since insultingly taunted me with my unmerited misfortune. Such a proceeding as this, committed on a defenceless stranger, almost worn out in the hard service of the world, without any foundation in reason or justice, whatever it may be called in a christian land, would in my native country have been branded as a crime equal to highway robbery. But Captain Hart was a *white gentleman*, and I a *poor African*, therefore it was *all right, and good enough for the black dog.*

I am now sixty nine years old. Though once strait and tall, measuring without shoes six feet one inch and an half, and every way well proportioned, I am now bowed down with age and hardship. My strength which was once equal if not superior to any man whom I have ever seen, is now enfeebled so that life is a burden, and it is with fatigue that I can walk a couple of miles, stooping over my staff. Other griefs are still behind, on account of which some aged people, at least, will pity me. My eye-sight has gradually failed, till I am almost blind, and whenever I go abroad one of my grand-children must direct my way; besides for many years I have been much pained and troubled with an ulcer on one of my legs. But amidst all my griefs and pains, I have many consolations; Meg, the wife of my youth, whom I married for love, and bought with my money, is still alive. My freedom is a privilege which nothing else can equal. Notwithstanding all the losses I have suffered by fire, by the injustice of knaves, by the cruelty and oppression of false hearted friends, and the perfidy of my own countrymen whom I have assisted and redeemed from bondage, I am now possessed of more than one hundred acres of land, and three habitable dwelling houses. It gives me joy to think that I *have* and that I *deserve* so good a character, especially for *truth* and *integrity*. While I am now looking to the grave as my home, my joy for this world would be full—IF my children, Cuff for whom I paid two hundred dollars when a boy, and Solomon who was born soon after I purchased his mother—If Cuff and Solomon—O! that they had walked in the way of their father. But a father's lips are closed in silence and in grief!—Vanity of vanities, all is vanity![29]

FINIS.

CERTIFICATES

STONINGTON, *November* 3, 1798.

THESE certify, that VENTURE, a free negro man, aged about 69 years, and was, as we have ever understood, a native of Africa, and formerly a slave to Mr. James Mumford, of Fisher's-Island, in the state of New York; who sold him to Mr. Thomas Stanton, 2d, of Stonington, in the state of Connecticut, and said Stanton sold said VENTURE to Col. Oliver Smith, of the aforesaid place. That said VENTURE hath sustained the character of a faithful servant, and that of a temperate, honest and industrious man, and being ever intent on obtaining his freedom, he was indulged by his masters after the ordinary labour on the days of his servitude, to improve the nights in fishing and other employments to his own emolument, in which time he procured so much money as to purchase his freedom from his late master Col. Smith; after which he took upon himself the name of VENTURE SMITH, and has since his freedom purchased a negro woman, called Meg, to whom he was previously married, and also his children who were slaves, and said VENTURE has since removed himself and family to the town of East-Haddam, in this state, where he hath purchased lands on which he hath built a house, and there taken up his abode.[30]

NATHANIEL MINOR, Esq.
ELIJAH PALMER, Esq.
Capt. AMOS PALMER,
ACORS SHEFFIELD,
EDWARD SMITH.

NOTES

1. Benjamin Franklin (1706-1790) and George Washington (1732-1799).
2. Dukandarra: perhaps a reference to Tenkodogo, capital of the State of Tenkodogo, one of the Mossi States in what is now Upper Volta.
3. Stout: strongly built.

4. Desert: an uninhabited and uncultivated wilderness, not necessarily dry.
5. Cote: sheepfold.
6. Spatting: clapping.
7. Anamaboo: on the coast of present-day Ghana.
8. The castle: probably Cape Coast Castle, the principal British factory.
9. Venture: an investment with an equally great chance of gain or loss.
10. Stint: task.
11. Owned an Irishman: presumably an indentured servant, obligated to serve his master for a specific number of years.
12. Firkins: small casks.
13. Advertised: issued a wanted notice for.
14. Address: persuasive discourse.
15. Johannes: the name by which a Portuguese gold coin, worth about 36 shillings sterling, was known in the British American colonies.
16. York currency: paper money issued by colonial New York.
17. Old tenor: paper money issued by the colonies of Massachusetts and Rhode Island before 1741, when new tenor, or a new issue of currency, replaced it. After 1741, 27 shillings of old tenor money was legally equivalent to 6 shillings, 9 pence of the new tenor.
18. Tierce: a cask that could hold about forty-two gallons.
19. Rods: a rod is a measurement of length equal to 5.5 yards or 16.5 feet.
20. Cup-bearer and waiter: positions of "trust and confidence" because of the opportunities they gave a slave to poison his master.
21. Redeeming myself: buying my freedom.
22. Cords of wood: although there were local variations in the amount, a cord of wood was usually a measure of cut wood stacked eight feet long, four feet across, and four feet high.
23. Want: lack, need.
24. Apparently Smith bought the man under the same terms that Col. Smith had purchased Venture Smith, with the agreement that the slave could redeem himself.
25. Thirty tons burthen: able to carry a cargo, or burden, of thirty tons.
26. Forehanded: wealthy.
27. Trafficking: transporting.
28. Hogsheads: casks capable of holding sixty-three gallons.
29. Ecclesiates 1:2-5:

"Vanity of vanities, saith the Preacher, vanity of vanities; all *is* vanity!

What profit hath a man of all his labour which he hath taken under the sun?

One generation passeth away, and *another* generation cometh: but the earth abideth for ever.

The sun also riseth, and the sun goeth down, and hasteth to his place where he arose."

30. What little is known of Smith beyond the information he gives here is found in the 1897 edition of the *Narrative* (New London, Connecticut), "Revised and Republished with Traditions by H.M. Selden. Haddam, Connecticut." The traditions mainly concern Smith's strength and size, which clearly had attained the status of local legend after his death: he was said to weigh over 300 pounds and measure 6 feet around his waist (32). We also learn that of the "four strong men" who bore his coffin to its burial in the cemetery of the First Congregational Church in East Haddam, "the two in front were white, proving the respect he had won, while two of his own race assisted in the rear" (36). The inscription on his "brown-stone slab" read:

SACRED TO THE MEMORY OF
VENTURE SMITH,
AFRICAN.
Though the son of a King, he was kidnapped

and sold as a slave, but by his industry
he acquired money to purchase
his freedom.
WHO DIED SEPT. 19, 1805,
IN YE 77TH YEAR OF HIS AGE.

The stone on the adjoining grave read:

SACRED TO THE MEMORY OF
MARGET SMITH,
RELICT [widow] OF VENTURE SMITH,
WHO DIED
DEC. THE 17TH, A.D. 1809,
IN THE 79TH YEAR OF HER AGE.

At last, Vincent Carretta's anthology makes readily available a key but all-too-often unheard voice from the eighteenth century. Major literary figures are juxtaposed alongside barely known writers, and all are made accessible by a lucid introduction and precise notes. *Unchained Voices* will prove a truly valuable student source-book."

—Roy Porter, Wellcome Institute for the History of Medicine

"*Unchained Voices* is wide and deep, careful and sensitive. No comparable text does so much so well. Bringing together the most important work of sixteen transatlantic writers illuminates a critical half-century as nothing has done before. The annotation, especially for Equiano, is extraordinary in range and helpfulness."

—John Sekora, North Carolina Central University

"The most thoughtfully constructed and the most thoroughly annotated anthology of eighteenth-century African American and Anglo African literature I know of, Carretta's volume meets a genuine and long-standing need."

—William L. Andrews, University of North Carolina–Chapel Hill

"These eighteenth-century black authors possess a strength, resilience, and humanity, a spirit that transcends self-pity, from which we today, in the world that they in part have bequeathed us, have much to learn. Meticulously edited and generously annotated, Carretta's anthology is an invaluable addition to the growing number of editions and critical inquiries in the field of black Atlantic studies."

—Adam S. Potkay, College of William and Mary

VINCENT CARRETTA, professor of English literature at the University of Maryland, is the author of several books on eighteenth-century literature and, most recently, the editor of Olaudah Equiano's *The Interesting Narrative and Other Writings.*

Front cover illustration of Francis Williams courtesy of
the Board of Trustees of the Victoria & Albert Museum, London.

Cover design by Rebecca Lloyd Lemna

THE UNIVERSITY PRESS OF KENTUCKY

Lexington, Kentucky